GREAT VICTORIAN LIVES

Limerick County Library
30012 00544199 2

THE TIMES

GREAT VICTORIAN LIVES

AN ERA IN OBITUARIES

GENERAL EDITOR: IAN BRUNSKILL

EDITED BY PROFESSOR ANDREW SANDERS

TIMES BOOKS

Published in 2007 by Times Books

HarperCollins Publishers
77–85 Fulham Palace Road
London w6 8JB

www.harpercollins.co.uk
Visit the book lover's website

1

ISBN 13 978-0-00-725973-1
ISBN 10 0-00-725973-5

British Library Cataloguing in Publication Data

A catalogue record for this book is available from the British Library.

Research by Maria Cleminson
Design by Mark Thomson

Typeset in FF Nexus by
Rowland Phototypesetting Ltd, Bury St Edmunds, Suffolk

Printed and bound in Great Britain by
Clays Ltd, St Ives plc

CONTENTS

INTRODUCTION

Ian Brunskill
Obituaries Editor of *The Times*

By the middle of the 19th century, when the obituaries collected here began to appear, *The Times* was well on the way to becoming a British institution, secure in its values, confident of its position and proud of the influence it exercised in the world. That confidence and influence had been hard won. The London press, when *The Times* was founded (as the *Daily Universal Register*) in 1785, was notable as much for its venality as for anything else. In the rough and tumble of political life, newspapers and journals were there to fight a corner or settle a score. Precisely which corner or score was not always important, if the price was right.

The Times had dragged itself on to higher ground. Thomas Barnes, Editor from 1817 to his death in 1841, began to build the paper into a significant independent force in British politics. His successor, John Thadeus Delane, whose obituary is reprinted here, consolidated the work; at the height of his 36-year editorship, the paper's prestige was considerable, its power much feared – and its support could not be bought.

In 1854 Delane gave a ringing summation of the paper's understanding of its role. Attacked in Parliament by the Leader of the Opposition, he replied the next morning in a leading article: 'We hold ourselves responsible, not to Lord Derby or the House of Lords, but to the people of England, for the accuracy and fitness of that which we think proper to publish . . . This journal never was, and we trust never will be, the journal of any Minister, and we place our own independence far above the highest marks of confidence that could be given us by any servant of the Crown.'

That defiant firmness of judgement and independence of thought lent significant weight to the paper's obituary coverage. In an area where the risks of personal bias and *parti-pris* are great, Delane saw that *The Times*'s unique authority gave it a valuable advantage over less high-minded rivals. He determined to make the most of it, expanding the paper's reporting of important deaths to the point where obituaries became an essential and enduring element of *The Times*'s editorial core. Other papers' efforts came nowhere near.

Delane was aware that he lived in an age both fascinated by historical greatness and well stocked with remarkable personalities of its own. He saw that the demise of a prominent national figure would capture the public imagination as nothing else could. It was worth covering in depth and, if necessary, at considerable length. The death of the Duke of Wellington, he told his deputy, 'will be the only topic'.

Readers seemed to agree. Wellington's obituary, all 47,000 words of it, dominated *The Times* over two days in September 1852; such was the demand that it was republished as a pamphlet for separate sale. Similarly, in 1865, when the paper's circulation stood at 65,000, the publication of Palmerston's obituary on 18 October added more than 11,000 copies to the daily sale.

In its early days, the paper's approach to obituary coverage had been haphazard. Notable deaths had been recorded, from the French Revolution onwards, but there was no great consistency of quality or tone. If *The Times* found itself without an obituary of an important person who had died, it was not above plagiarism, or simply reprinting a notice from another publication (as it did with the life of General Lee, included here). All this changed under Delane. There was no attempt to be comprehensive, and nothing like the daily obituary column of modern times, but Delane made sure that *The Times* would rise to the big occasion in matchless style.

In doing so, he was able to call on the remarkable editorial team that he and his predecessor had assembled. Some of these 'Men of *The Times*' were to be found each night at 'the office' in Printing House Square, writing leading articles and editing reports; some wrote to order from Oxford and Cambridge colleges and country rectories; some were critics whose engagement showed the paper's commitment to serious coverage of music, literature, theatre and the visual arts; some were diplomatic specialists, at home in Europe's embassies; some were foreign correspondents in the field. Together with the Editor's own contacts in the corridors of power, and those of the Walter family, hereditary 'chief proprietors' of *The Times*, they made up a formidable intelligence network, and among them were some formidable minds.

A leading role in the paper's obituary coverage was for many years taken by Charles Dod, founder of *Dod's Parliamentary Companion* and, as head of the *Times* gallery staff at Westminster, responsible for setting new standards in the reporting of parliamentary debates. After Dod's death in 1855, much work on obituaries was done by the versatile Scottish man of letters Eneas Dallas; one of the paper's most prolific book reviewers and author of a well-regarded study of poetry, *The Gay Science*, Dallas also volunteered to report from inside Paris when the French capital was under siege. Among the many obituary notices in which Dallas's was the sole or principal hand were those of Dickens, Palmerston, the Austrian Chancellor Prince Metternich, Thackeray, the historian and politician Thomas Babington Macaulay, and Albert, the Prince Consort.

From 1868 much responsibility was taken by Edward Walford, antiquary, biographer and prolific author, a former Editor of the *Gentleman's Magazine* and the compiler of such reference works as *Hardwicke's Titles of Courtesy* and the *Shilling Baronetage and Knightage.* Obituaries of leading statesmen might be furnished by Henry Reeve, a hugely influential figure both at *The Times* and behind the scenes in political life; known by his *Times* colleagues, not entirely affectionately, as *Il Pomposo,* he had risen from humble beginnings to become an intimate of Government ministers and royalty. The Reverend Thomas Mozley – pupil, friend and brother-in-law to John Henry Newman and himself a participant in the Oxford Movement and the upheavals it wrought in the Victorian Church of England – was responsible for the lives of such leading Tractarians as John Keble and Edward Bouverie Pusey. W. H. Russell, the great foreign correspondent whose vivid dispatches from the Crimea brought home to the British public the realities of war, supplied obituaries of military men. Leonard Courtney, a leader writer who had read mathematics at Cambridge, wrote on scientists; Tom Taylor, the paper's art critic, covered painters; Antonio Gallenga, a colourful Italian exile turned foreign correspondent, accounted for several of his compatriots.

It is only thanks to the paper's meticulously kept archive and the published volumes of its official history that we can know now in such detail who did what. None of these authors received a byline. Anonymity was, and would long continue to be, the *Times*'s watchword. The self-effacing Thomas Barnes had his own death marked only by a two-line announcement which made no reference to the fact that he had, for 24 years, been Editor of *The Times.*

The *Times* obituaries were the paper's verdict, not the individual author's, however well-informed or personally distinguished he might be. Delane made sure of this. He was away when Palmerston died, but he instructed his deputy to retrieve the prepared obituary from 'the little basket which hangs over the davenport in my breakfast room' – he had revised it himself at home in Searjants' Inn.

Delane saw to it that most of the important notices were prepared well ahead of time, and regularly updated as required. There are tales – reassuring to a 21st-century obituary editor – of copy being frantically written in the office late at night, or even in the train up to town from Ramsgate, when the paper had for some reason been caught unprepared. On the whole, however, as I hope this collection confirms, the major obituaries published in the 19th-century *Times* were the products of authoritative inside knowledge, and of long and careful thought. Here are the lives of some of the leading figures of the 19th century as they were recorded and judged by one of the defining institutions of the age, a paper that, as a correspondent once remarked approvingly to Delane, contrived somehow or other to be 'always in at the Death!'

INTRODUCTION

Professor Andrew Sanders

Readers of this collection of Victorian obituaries will discover a series of reasoned, and often admirably critical, assessments of public lives. They were all written before the age of Hollywood stardom and the emergence of the cult of celebrity fostered by the popular media. Victorian obituarists and biographers who dealt with public achievements did not see it as their business to probe into the private circumstances of their subjects; nor did they suppose that their readers would be interested in them reporting issues that they probably assumed were little better than backstairs gossip. Theirs was an age when 'A' and 'B' lists of celebrities were still determined by *Burke's Peerage* and the *Almanach de Gotha*, and when very few people outside princely houses were famous for merely being famous. Fashions were both worn and created exclusively by the upper classes, and 'sport' was still largely regarded as the genteel matter of hunting, shooting and fishing. W. G. Grace, a Bristol doctor by profession and a gentleman cricketer by calling, was essentially an admired amateur. The idea that Mrs Grace might somehow be a 'celebrity' merely by association with her husband's sporting prowess would have seemed preposterous. This present selection of thoughtful obituaries offers a sample of the 'innumerable biographies' that Thomas Carlyle thought formed the essence of history. It serves to illuminate a range of cultural, social and political issues of the Victorian century by offering a select view of public life expressed in exclusively Victorian terms.

The first obituary reprinted in this present collection is that of Thomas Arnold, the headmaster of Rugby school and the fosterer of much of the earnestness that shaped Victorian Britain. Two years after his death, a substantial biography of Arnold was published by his former pupil, Arthur Stanley. It was a book that had achieved something of the status of a classic by the end of the century. The problem with Stanley's life of Dr Arnold, and indeed with any piously uncritical Victorian biography, lies now in the fact that Arnold – together with three other 'Eminent Victorians' – had been debunked by that slick master of innuendo, Lytton Strachey. Strachey's *Eminent Victorians* first appeared in 1918 and, in the often cynical and disillusioned post-First World War world, it had an immediate appeal. Strachey knew that a military metaphor for his historical method was appropriate: he described how an 'explorer of the past' had now to 'attack his subject in unexpected places; he will fall upon the flank, or the rear; he will shoot a sudden, revealing searchlight into obscure recesses, hitherto undivined'. The achievements and reputations of Strachey's four 'eminent' Victorians have long since recovered from his tactical assaults, but, since 1918, both the strategies and the 'art' of biography have undergone a radical shift. Twentieth and twenty-first century biographers are generally disinclined either to describe the heroism of earnestness or to overlook moral shortcomings and sexual peccadillos; they also tend to suffer neither fools nor would-be saints gladly.

It is, however, in the pre-Stracheyan context that we must both place and understand Victorian obituaries. Most obituarists, prompted by a sense of the historical significance of biography, readily recognised that the lives of their subjects had a social context. Nineteenth-century Britain had been required to redefine itself and its role models in order to cope with the changes brought about by industrialisation, urbanisation and an increase in literacy. As a 'newspaper of record', *The Times* acknowledged its responsibility in recording the impact of these social readjustments. As the readers of Carlyle's *On Heroes, Hero-Worship, and the Heroic in History* realised, heroism had to be re-examined in the light of the idea of the self-made man; they would also have appreciated that the evolving concept of heroism in Victorian Britain could not remain an exclusively male prerogative. The first generation of Victorian women included professional writers of the first eminence, but it is significant that neither the Brontë sisters nor Charlotte's biographer, Elizabeth Gaskell, were deemed worthy of an obituary notice in *The Times*. In the period after 1865, however, partly as a result of John Delane's resolution to enhance the status of his newspaper, the lives and achievements of professional women, as opposed to the mere social prestige accorded to titled women, were to find their proper place in the *The Times*'s obituary columns.

From what was called 'The Age of Reform' onwards, new avenues of expression for both men and women were slowly broadening out. Some of the obituaries included in the present collection remind us of the opening up of government and its institutions to those who did not form part of the old Establishment: Benjamin Disraeli, born a Jew, not only rose to the highest political office, but he also made determined efforts to open up the House of Commons to those practising Jews who were unable to take the requisite Christian oath of allegiance to sit in the House. The campaigns in the 1880s of the avowed atheist, Charles Bradlaugh, mark a further shift away from the confessional narrowness which had defined the State at the beginning of the century. The issue of women's suffrage (which seems to vex John Stuart Mill's obituarist) was not to be resolved until after the Great War, but it is clear from the enterprise of Harriet Martineau, George Eliot and Elizabeth Garrett Anderson that social, educational and professional liberation for women were seen as the proper precursors to the achievement of full political rights.

It is significant too that a good number of the men and women commemorated in this volume were classic Victorian examples of what Samuel Smiles famously described as 'Self-Help'. Smiles (1812–1904), who wrote a life of George Stephenson in 1857 and who would go on to publish *Lives of the Engineers* in 1867, first issued his bestselling *Self-Help* in 1859. Smiles saw the spirit of self-help as 'the root of all genuine growth in the individual', which constituted 'the true source of national vigour and strength', and his aim was to provide role models for a newly aspirant class of what the Victorians referred to as 'mechanics'. This body of skilled working men was to form a vital part of the emergent lower middle class, who, once enfranchised from 1867 onwards, began to change the political balance of power. What Smiles recognised was that the true gentleman was manifest in all classes as the 'honest, truthful, upright, polite, temperate, courageous, self-respecting and self-helping' citizen. This was in marked contrast to the upper-class definition of gentlemanliness, but Smiles clearly struck a profound note in a society where national wealth substantially came from trade and manufacture rather than from land. Writers and artists as well as men of science, invention and commerce were the new heroes, and this is reflected in *The Times*. Although his obituarist did not know the true extent of Dickens's rise from childhood adversity, the novelist had, by the time of his death, emerged as the quintessential product of Victorian social mobility fostered by the application of an innate genius; *The Times* also recognised the achievement of other notable meritocrats who had risen above the humble circumstances of their birth – men and women such as George Stephenson, Thomas Carlyle, Michael Faraday, David Livingstone, George Eliot and Thomas Cook. Its 19-century obituary columns also honoured the philanthropical energy of men who had either made their money as enterprising manufacturers (Sir Titus Salt) or as City business men (Sir Moses Montefiore).

Victorian society was, however, far from class-less. Britain's traditional ruling class remained entrenched and *The Times* remained duly deferential to those who had been born great. Its obituary of Queen Victoria herself (arguably the most influential woman of her generation) is so substantial and detailed that its very length precludes its inclusion in such a selection as this. The Queen's tastes, antipathies and patronage are nonetheless evident in many of the other obituaries reprinted in this collection. This is equally true of Prince Albert, whose untimely death in 1861 occasioned lengthy and adulatory tributes, which often skirted over the widespread unpopularity Albert had experienced earlier in his life, and whose obituary notice is not included here. To give a full flavour of each person's life and of the period, each obituary has been included here in its entirety, though they vary hugely in length. In order to include as wide and representative a selection as possible in the space available, it has been necessary to omit some fulsome tributes paid to others – from members of the Royal Family, to the upper clergy of the

Church of England, Oxbridge dons, admirals and generals and lawyers and medical men who seem to posterity not to have made such a lasting contribution to the advancement of their professions. One celebrated British army officer, Lord Lucan, is included for the part he played in the *debâcle* of the Charge of the Light Brigade; he also forms part of a loosely linked group of obituary subjects (Delane, Tennyson and Florence Nightingale) who all share a connection with *The Times*'s critical reporting of the Crimean War. It has proved impossible, again due to its length, to include the death notice of the greatest soldier of the century, the Duke of Wellington, who died in 1852. Wellington's career, both as a soldier and as a politician, also substantially fell outside the Victorian age, but his great funeral procession through London was perhaps the most memorable state occasion of the period. One great military figure remembered here, Robert E. Lee, ended his days regarded as an ignominious figure by a good many of his fellow Americans. His rehabilitation as a man of honour and a great strategist may have begun with the kind of posthumous tribute of which *The Times*'s is a fine example.

Four Prime Ministers, all of them accorded very long obituaries in *The Times*, firmly merit inclusion here: Peel, Palmerston, Disraeli and Gladstone all made profound contributions to the history of parliamentary government in the United Kingdom. Each of them also extended Britain's international influence and resolutely established the country as, for the most part, a highly respected European power-broker. The substance of the political careers of all four would probably demand tributes of a similar expansiveness nowadays. So might the lives of a number of foreign heads of state, or heads of government. Abraham Lincoln's assassination, which so appalled his contemporaries on both sides of the Atlantic, did not occasion what could strictly be described as an obituary, but *The Times*'s reporting of the event captures something of its immediate impact and perceived long-term import. Though it is not included here, the shocked telling of the assassination of Tsar Alexander II is comparable, and an account that suggests how alien Russian affairs may have seemed to British readers of *The Times* in 1881. The former Emperor Napoleon III received a surprisingly generous obituary notice, despite the fact that he had so often been dismissed by the British press as a charlatan during his reign, while his arch enemy, Otto von Bismarck, the Chancellor of the new German Empire which he had forged into existence, earns the extraordinarily flattering compliment that he was 'one of the rare men who leave indelible marks on the world's history'. Pope Pius IX's demise in 1878 might well have elicited a similar adulatory comment, but his obituary dwells instead on the Pontiff's manifest disappointments, diplomatic shortcomings and political failures, as much as on the great changes he both wrought and witnessed in the Roman Catholic Church.

When it came to foreign politicians and revolutionaries who spent their lives in exile *The Times* obituarists are far more guarded and ambiguous in their opinions. As the death notice of Lajos Kossuth implies, here was a man past his political peak. Kossuth, with Mazzini and Garibaldi, had been much admired by mid-century British liberals, and his obituary – representative of all three – demonstrates the combination of political inconsistency, frustrated energy and old-age compromise, common enough characteristics in unfulfilled politicians, that appeared to disconcert the three obituarists. It will probably surprise modern readers that both Karl Marx and Friedrich Engels receive such short shrift from their obituarists (the tribute to Marx, who died in London, was actually contributed by the paper's *Paris* correspondent). Both men were long-term residents in England and both were familiar to a tight-knit international community of socialist thinkers but neither, *The Times* seems to suggest, possessed much immediate relevance to an exclusively British political world view. The fact that the major theoretical works of both had, at the time of their deaths, yet to appear in articulate English translations may well have contributed to this feeling of relative indifference.

William Morris, one of the rare contemporary Englishmen to acknowledge Marx's importance – though his overt and conspicuous involvement with socialist politics is given the briefest of mentions – emerges from his *Times* obituary as ambiguous in quite another way. If there are anomalies in Morris's career they lie in the balance of his distinctive achievement as a poet and his work as a craftsman and designer. Morris's marriage is barely alluded to and his wife's long association with Dante Gabriel Rossetti is passed over without mention.

Morris's obituary is representative in this way – in most cases the irregular domestic circumstances of the writers, musicians and painters whose obituaries appear in this collection are left unmentioned. This may be the result of an ignorance of the facts, or a matter of tact, but for the most part we may be left to assume that the private lives of artists were always regarded as challenging conventional views of sexual and marital morality. Only in the case of the once-provocative Oscar Wilde does an obituary see a fall from social grace as salutary; it views him as the kind of artist whose essentially flippant approach to life made him prone to overstep the mark.

In nearly all cases of those Victorians accorded obituaries in *The Times*, the secrets kept behind closed doors, and of their hearts, were left to be revealed not just before the Court of Heaven but by inquisitive, and sometimes prying, post-Victorian biographers.

All obituaries have been taken directly from The Times *and therefore use the original spelling and punctuation throughout.*

THOMAS ARNOLD

Pioneer educator and historian: 'A death more to be mourned as a public loss . . . could scarcely have occurred.'

15 JUNE 1842

WE ANNOUNCED ON Monday the death of the Rev. Thomas Arnold, D. D., head master of Rugby School, which took place at Rugby on Sunday morning last, after a few hours' illness of a disease of the heart. He had been master of Rugby school 15 years. Dr. Arnold had latterly devoted the whole of his time unoccupied by scholastic duties to his lectures on Modern History and to his History of Rome, and was contemplating a retirement, in the course of a few years, to his favourite residence at Fox-how, in Westmoreland. Dr. Arnold had, we believe, attained the age of 52. He was born at Cowes, Isle of Wight, and was the son of the late Mr. William Arnold, collector of Her Majesty's Customs of that port. He was educated at Winchester school, and thence went to Corpus Christi College, Oxford. He was afterwards Fellow of Oriel. Dr. Arnold married a daughter of the late Rev. John Penrose, and has left behind him a numerous family. On Sunday morning Dr. Arnold was seized with pain and oppressed breathing, indicating to his medical attendants some sudden and severe affection, most probably of a spasmodic nature, in the heart. A loss more precious to his family, his friends, his country – a death more to be mourned as a public loss – could scarcely have occurred. Dr. Arnold had a sharp attack of fever some little time since, but appeared to have recovered from it. His father died early in life, and from a similar disease, we believe.

Arnold, born in the same year as Keats and Carlyle, only narrowly made it into the Victorian era. He died, prematurely, just short of his forty-seventh birthday while still in post as headmaster of Rugby School. He was, nevertheless, one of four *Eminent Victorians* selected to have their posthumous reputations sapped by Lytton Strachey in 1918. Arnold had transformed the moral and educational ethos of Rugby, an achievement variously celebrated in the work of two strikingly contrasted ex-pupils: Arthur Penryn Stanley (whose influential *Life and Correspondence of Thomas Arnold D. D.* appeared in 1844) and Thomas Hughes's enduringly popular *Tom Brown's Schooldays by an Old Boy* (1857).

FELIX MENDELSSOHN

Composer: 'He will be lamented wherever his name was known or his art be loved.'

4 NOVEMBER 1847

IT IS WITH no ordinary regret that we have received intelligence of the premature and most unlooked-for death of Dr. Felix Mendelssohn Bartholdy. He expired at Leipsic, on Thursday last, after a short illness, which brought on paralysis of the brain. The triumphant reception which he had met with in London last spring, and the magnificent productions which were then heard under the directing influence of his genius, will never be forgotten by those who witnessed them. Never had the great musician of our time appeared to be more full of life, energy, and creative power. But upon his return to Germany in the beginning of May, these brilliant recollections were damped by the death of a favourite sister, who had just fallen a victim to the same form of cerebral disease. Dr. Mendelssohn retired to Interlachen, in Switzerland, for the summer months, where although he had shaken off the fatigues of the London season, this family affliction seemed to have given him some foreboding of his own impending fate. He returned to his duties at Leipsic, but very few weeks elapsed before his imperishable labours were terminated for ever. He had not yet completed his 39th year, having been born on the 3rd of February, 1809.

We shall leave it to others to tender an appropriate homage to the musical works of this great composer, and to celebrate his memorable achievements in that art of which he was so perfect a master. But the people of this country owe, and will surely pay, no slender and indifferent tribute to his memory, for he loved England as heartily as his own home; and from early youth to the splendid maturity of the last season he has found amongst us several of his warmest friends and many of his proudest distinctions. The genius of Shakspeare awakened in the youth of 17 years the inimitable fancy and grace of the overture to the *Midsummer Night's Dream*, which he afterwards produced at the Conservatoire in Paris and at the Philharmonic Concerts in 1829. The poetry of Oesian and the stern scenery of the Scotch Isles inspired the *Halls of Fingal*. And, above all, the Church music of England and the great oratorios, which are the objects of our traditional veneration, led his mind to those awful conceptions which he realized in *St. Paul* and in *Elijah*. The latter work was first produced by its author at the Birmingham festival of last year, and in the English tongue. Of the thousands who have already been excited or touched by its sublime choruses and its affecting melodies, none could have imagined that those were the last strains of their illustrious author's life, and that the genius which seemed already to have approached so nearly to an heavenly inspiration was about to leave us for ever. Like Mozart, like Raphael, the beauty of youth seemed in Mendelssohn to have exhausted the fullness of life; and his career has terminated in its glory, before it had concluded the abundant labours of a perfect artist's existence.

From early childhood Felix Mendelssohn was already the wonder and the pride of the musical schools of Berlin. At eight years old he was already one of the most accomplished pianoforte players of the age; and his musical science kept pace with his astonishing power of execution and of ear. In boyhood he was profoundly versed in the works of Sebastian Bach, and the severer masters; and throughout his life his mind was keenly alive to all that was great in intellect or beautiful in poetry. Goethe had affectionately greeted his early promise, and never was the promise of a marvellous precocity more amply fulfilled.

A more striking proof of the great general cultivation and refinement of Felix Mendelssohn's mind could hardly be given than in his masterly adaptation of the resources of his art to several of the most sublime and terrible creations of the Greek drama. His music to the *Œdipus Colonus* and the *Antigone* was as nearly akin to the genius of Sophocles as if his imagination had been nurtured in the traditions of classical antiquity. In like manner his sacred oratorios were penetrated with the spirit of the Bible. He was wont to construct and combine these great epics himself from the sacred volume, which was the subject of his constant and devout meditation. In *St. Paul*, it was the nascent energy of the Church of Christ, impersonated in the Apostle of the Gentiles, which inspired his imagination. In the *Elijah*, it was the servant of God labouring in his appointed course, against the perversity of the world, and the infirmities of his own imperfect nature, until he had perfected the work which was given him to do. But in all these productions, whilst the execution is that of a great musician, the conception belongs to the highest range of poetry.

In all the relations of life, Felix Mendelssohn has left few men of lesser genius who can equal him in the humbler graces and the more private virtues. He was affectionate, generous, and true beyond the common virtue of men. In his profession he leaves no equal, but no enemy, almost no rival; his many and early triumphs had never for an instant impaired the simplicity of his character, or the unassuming cordiality of his manners. His conversation was unusually animated, and even brilliant; never more so than when he had shaken off his customary pursuits, to revel in those natural beauties which he passionately enjoyed, to animate his household circle with his pleasantry, or discourse on the subjects which could elevate and excite his mind. To those who had the happiness of living in habitual intercourse with him, this most unhappy loss is one to which all the sympathy of the world can bring but a slight alleviation; but he will be lamented wherever his name was known or his art beloved.

In 1847 the *Musical Times* paid tribute to Mendelssohn as an 'adopted son of England' and as 'probably the first who opened a regular musical inter-communication between Germany and England'. Mendelssohn's commitment to his British audiences had been at its most conspicuous in the spring and summer of 1846. His final and triumphant engagement had taken place on 18 August when he had conducted the first performance of his oratorio *Elijah* at Birmingham, the city which had commissioned the work. Mendelssohn, a pioneer in the revival of interest in the music of Bach, was also celebrated in his own time as the conductor of the Leipzig Gewandhaus Orchestra. He had received an honorary Doctorate from the University of Leipzig in 1835.

* * *

GEORGE STEPHENSON

Inventor and engineer: The 'Father of Railways.'

12 AUGUST 1848

IT IS WITH much concern that we announce the decease of Mr. George Stephenson, the celebrated engineer. He died at his establishment in Derbyshire on Saturday last, aged 67. Few men have obtained, or deserved, a higher reputation. He rose from the humblest life from the elasticity of his native talent overcoming the obstacles of narrow circumstances and even confined education. In his profession he was as happy and ingenious in his discoveries as generous in imparting the benefit of them to the world. In the history of railroad enterprise and movement the name of George Stephenson will live.

This relatively short notice of Stephenson, who had died on 12 August at Tapton House, Chesterfield, is fulsome in its praise but singularly brief in detail about his considerable engineering achievements. His death was ascribed to a cold caught while inspecting the beloved greenhouses which he had erected on his estate in the hope of eclipsing those of Chatsworth. The most adulatory contemporary study of Stephenson's career, Samuel Smiles's *Life of George Stephenson*, was to appear in 1859.

* * *

WILLIAM WORDSWORTH

Poet: 'Few poets have exercised greater influence in his own country.'

23 APRIL 1850

IT IS WITH feelings of much regret that we announce today the death of William Wordsworth. The illustrious poet breathed his last at noon on Tuesday by the side of that beautiful lake in Westmoreland which his residence and his verse had rendered famous. We are not called upon in his case to mourn over the untimely fate of genius snatched away in the first feverish struggles of development, or even in the noonday splendour of its mid career. Full of years, as of honours, the old man had time to accomplish all that he was capable of accomplishing ere he was called away. It may well be, that he had not carried out to completion many of his plans, but it is a natural incident to humanity that execution falls far short of design. What a man could not accomplish in something like half a century of a poetical career under all the favourable conditions of unbroken quiet, moderate but sufficient means, and vigorous health, may fairly be supposed to have been beyond his reach. Therefore, as far as concerns the legacy of song William Wordsworth has bequeathed to his country, we have nothing to regret. Removed by taste and temperament from the busy scenes of the world, his long life was spent in the conception and elaboration of his poetry in the midst of the sylvan solitudes to which he was so fondly attached. His length of days permitted him to act as the guardian of his own fame, – he could bring his maturer judgment to bear upon the first bursts of his youthful inspiration, as well as upon the more measured flow of his maturest compositions. Whatever now stands in the full collection of his works has received the final *imprimatur* from the poet's hand, sitting in judgment upon his own works under the influence of a generation later than his own. It is sufficiently characteristic of the man, that little has been altered, and still less condemned. Open at all times to the influences of external nature, he was singularly indifferent to the judgment of men, or rather so enamoured of his own judgment that he could brook no teacher. Nature was his book, he would admit no interpretation but his own. It was this which constituted the secret of his originality and his strength, at the same time that the abuse of the principle laid him open at times to strictures, the justice of which few persons but the unreasoning fanatics of his school would now be prepared to deny.

But we feel this is not a season for criticism. There is so much in the character, as well as in the works of William Wordsworth, to deserve hearty admiration, that we may indulge in the language most grateful to our feelings without overstepping the decent limits of propriety and plain sincerity. We would point out, in the first place, one of the great excellencies of the departed worthy. His life was as pure and spotless as his song. It is rendering a great service to humanity when a man exalted by intellectual capacities above his fellow-men holds out to them in his own person the example of a blameless life. As long as men are what they are it is well that the fashion of virtue should be set them by men whose rare abilities are objects of envy and emulation even to the most dissolute and unprincipled. If this be true of the statesman, of the warrior, of the man of science, it is so in a tenfold degree of the poet and the man of letters. Their works are in the hands of the young and inexperienced. Their habits of life become insensibly mixed up with their compositions in the minds of their admirers. They spread the moral infection wider than other men, because those brought within their influence are singularly susceptible of contamination. The feelings, the passions, the imagination, which are busy with the compositions of the poet, are quickly interested in the fashion of his life. From 'I would fain write so' to 'I would fain live so' there is but a little step. Under this first head the English nation owes a deep debt of gratitude to William Wordsworth. Neither by the influence of his song, nor by the example of his life, has he corrupted or enervated our youth; by one, as by the other, he has purified and elevated, not soiled and abased, humanity. If we may pass from this more general and important consideration to a more limited sphere of action, we would point out the example of the venerable old man who now lies sleeping by the side of the Westmoreland lake to the attention of all who aim at high literary distinction. To William Wordsworth his art was his all, and sufficed to him as its own rich reward. We do not find him trucking the inspirations of his genius for mere sums of money, nor aiming at political and social distinctions by prostituting the divine gift that was in him. He appears to have felt that in the successful cultivation of his art he was engaged in a laborious, if in a delightful occupation. Could he succeed, he was on the level of the greatest men of his age, although he might not have a single star or riband to hang up against the wall of his rustic cottage, nor a heavy balance at his banker's as evidence of his success. These things are but the evidence of one species of triumph, the poet, the dramatist, the historian, should aim at distinctions of another kind.

If we think the present occasion an unfit one for cold criticism, we may without impropriety devote a few brief sentences to the excellences of the compositions of the Poet of Rydal Mount. There must be something essentially 'English' in his inspirations, for while few poets have exercised greater influence in his own country, on the continent his works are little known even to students who have devoted much time and attention to English literature. In Germany, for example, you will find translations at the chief seats of literary society of the poetry of Scott, Byron, Moore, and Shelley: Southey and Coleridge are less known; the name of Wordsworth scarcely pronounced at all. Of France the same thing may with truth be said. In either country there may be rare instances of students of the highest order, of a Guizot, a Merimée, a Humboldt, a Bunsen, who are well acquainted with the writings of Wordsworth, and share our insular admiration for his beauties, but such exceptions are few indeed. There must, therefore, be some development of 'English' thought in Wordsworth which is the secret of his success amongst ourselves, as of his failure in securing an European reputation. It is certain that some of the great poets whose names we have mentioned have left it upon record that they are indebted for the idea of some of their most beautiful passages to the teaching and example of Wordsworth, and yet the scholars have charmed an audience which the master could not obtain. It is probably the case that in no country of Europe is the love for a country life so strongly developed as in England, and no man who could not linger out a summer day by the river bank or on the hill side is capable of appreciating Wordsworth's poetry. The familiarity with sylvan scenes, and an habitual calm delight under the influence of nature, are indispensable requisites before the tendency of the song can be understood which works by catching a divine inspiration even from the dewy fragrance of the heatherbell and the murmur of the passing brook. It was not in Wordsworth's genius to people the air with phantoms, but to bring the human mind in harmony with the operations of nature, of which he stood forth the poet and the interpreter. We write with the full recollection of many lovely human impersonations of the departed poet present to our minds; but his great aim appears to have been that which we have endeavoured to shadow out as distinctly as our limited space would permit.

Before concluding we would advert to a point which is perhaps more in keeping with the usual subjects of our columns than the humble tribute of admiration we have endeavoured to offer to the illustrious man who has just been called away. Let us hope that the office of Poet Laureate, which was dignified by its two last possessors, may never be conferred upon a person unworthy to succeed them. The title is no longer an honour, but a mere badge of ridicule, which can bring no credit to its wearer. It required the reputation of a Southey or a Wordsworth to carry them through an office so entirely removed from the ideas and habits of our time without injury to their fame. Let whatever emoluments go with the name be commuted into a pension, and let the pension be bestowed upon a deserving literary man without the ridiculous accompaniment of the bays. We know well enough that birthday odes have long since been exploded; but why retain a nickname, not a title, which must be felt as a degradation rather than an honour by its wearer? Having said thus much, we will leave the subject to the better judgment of those whose decision is operative in such matters. Assuredly, William Wordsworth needed no such Court distinctions or decorations. His name will live in English literature, and his funeral song be uttered, amidst the spots which he has so often celebrated, and by the rivers and hills which inspired his verse.

Wordsworth died at midday on 23 April 1850. Readers of this obituary may well have been inclined to agree with the poet himself who in 1801 had remarked to a friend that 'in truth my life has been unusually barren of events'. A version of his great autobiographical poem, *The Prelude: Growth of a Poet's Mind* was not to appear until shortly after his death and full revelations about his time in France during the early stages of the Revolution were only made in the 1920s. In November 1791 Wordsworth had crossed the Channel to France and, on 6 December, had moved from Paris to Orléans where he met Annette Vallon. He and Annette moved to Blois in February 1792. He was alone in Paris when Annette gave birth to his daughter Anne-Caroline on 15 December and he was back in England, without Annette and his daughter, by the end of the month. *The Prelude* memorably describes both the elation and the later disillusion occasioned by the political upheaval in France but it does not mention the liaison with Annette. Wordsworth's eventless and 'blameless' life was therefore more open to question than his *Times* obituarist knew. Despite the claim that 'he might not have a single star or riband to hang up against the wall of his rustic cottage', some of his admirers, including Browning in his poem *The Lost Leader*, regarded the sometime-radical Wordsworth's acceptance of government appointments as a sell-out. He was succeeded as Poet Laureate by Tennyson.

SIR ROBERT PEEL

Politician: 'One of the most sagacious statesmen that England ever produced.'

2 JULY 1850

A GREAT AGE has lost a great man. Sir Robert Peel, whom all parties and all nations associate more than any other statesman with the policy and glory of this empire, is now a name of the past. He has been taken, as it were, from his very seat in the Senate, with nothing to prepare us for his departure, and everything now to remind us of it, with his powers unabated, and his part unfulfilled. Although gradually removed during the last four years from the sphere of party, he had still political friends to be reconciled, a social position to be repaired, motives to be appreciated, and acts to be justified by the tardy and conflicting testimony of results. A devoted band of admirers hoped to see him set right with all the world, while life and strength still remained; and that day of peaceful triumph seemed not very distant. There were others who still saw in Sir Robert Peel the man who had more than once saved his country at the cost of his party, and might again be called to a task which demanded such marvellous powers and so singular a position. The page that recorded his last great effort was scarcely spread before the eyes of the nation when the object of all these hopes and calculations was suddenly withdrawn, and they who speculate or dream over the great game of politics have to readjust their thoughts to the loss of the principal actor.

The highest possible estimate of Sir Robert Peel's services is that which we are invited to take from the mouth of his opponents. If we are to trust them, we are to believe that but for Sir Robert Peel this country would long since have repudiated the exact performance of its pecuniary obligations; that half our fellow subjects would still be excluded by their creed from office and power; and that the means of existence would still be obstructed and enhanced in their way to a teeming and industrious population. Nor can it be denied that this estimate has a very general consent in its favour. If it be asked who bound England to the faithful discharge of the largest debt ever contracted or imagined by man, and who thereby raised her credit and advanced her prosperity to an unexampled standard, one name, and one only, will present itself to the mind of either Englishman or foreigner, and that name is Peel. If, again, it be asked who admitted eight or nine million British subjects to the rights of British citizenship, the answer still is Peel. If, lastly, it be asked who opened the gates of trade, and bade the food of man flow hither from every shore in an uninterrupted stream, it is still Peel who did it. On these three monuments of wisdom and beneficence other names may be written, but the name of Peel is first and foremost. Yet they were no ordinary achievements. It is within the memory of the living generation that every one of these three things was generally thought impossible, and was wholly despaired of even by those who were most clearly convinced of their moral and political obligation. These things, too, were not done on any mean stage, but in the greatest empire of the world, and where the difficulties were in proportion to the work. But how far does the name of Peel justly occupy this honourable position? Was he the author of these three great acts? Others, indeed, originated and proposed, for they were freer to originate, and it is always easy to gain the start of a statesman more or less implicated in existing legislation and encumbered by his supporters. But to confine ourselves to Sir Robert's last and crowning achievement, it must be said that while others advised the repeal of the Corn Laws when it was their interest to do so, he was the first to propose it when everything was to be lost by it – when, in fact, he did lose everything by it. His was the risk, so his must be the renown. His right is now proved, not by what he did, but by what he suffered, and he is the confessed author of free trade, because he has been a martyr to it. We cannot question the conscientious convictions of those who drove Sir Robert from power, but in so doing they testify that but for him the Corn Laws would not have been repealed.

But these acts, great as they were, and insulated as they seem, were only parts of a series, and by no means the most laborious parts. The amelioration of our criminal code, the reform of our police, the introduction of simpler forms and more responsible management into every part of our administrative system, took up large parts of Sir Robert's career, while there was not a subject that could possibly come within his reach that he did not grasp resolutely and well. We have had to differ from him; we do differ from him; but we must admit that no man ever undertook public affairs with a more thorough determination to leave the institutions of his country in an orderly, honest, and efficient state.

But are we wholly to pass over the ambiguities of this honourable career? Must it be left to the future historian to relate that when England lost her greatest living statesman, there were points of his character too tender to be touched, and that all parties agreed to slur over what they could not all praise? Surely not. Truth is as sacred as the grave, and the grief confessed by all may, perhaps, infuse new gravity and candour into a painful discussion. Sir Robert, so it is said, besides many smaller violences to the conscience of his followers, twice signally betrayed them. Twice he broke them up, and we now behold the result in a smitten and divided party. They give us the most undeniable proofs that their indignation is sincere. Suicide is so frequent a form of indignant adjuration that we cannot help respecting such an evidence of wrong. But with the knell of departed greatness sounding in our ear, it is time to view these acts by the light of the future. Posterity will ask, – Were they right or were they wrong? Our own answer shall be without hesitation or reserve. They were among the most needful and salutary acts that ever were given man to do. Grant that Sir Robert compassed them unfairly, and it must at least be admitted that he had a fine taste for glory and prized the gifts of Heaven when he saw them. But is it possible that a man should do such deeds, and a whole life full of them, and yet do them basely? To confess that were indeed a keen satire on man, if not a presumptuous imputation on his Maker. But perhaps there is some semblance of truth in it. Take, then, the long list of earth's worthies from the beginning of story to the present hour, and let us be candid with them. It will not be easy to find many of that canonized throng whose patriotism has not been alloyed with some baseness, who have not won triumphs with subtlety, deceived nations to their good, countermined against fraudful antagonists, or otherwise sinned against their own greatness. But when we have employed towards other men the candour imposed upon us in the case of Sir Robert Peel, we find these imperfections rather a condition of humanity than a fault of the individual. Nearly all great things, even the greatest of them, have been done in this earthly fashion. In the language of purists all government is bad, Courts are corrupt, and policy a word of opprobrium. An abstract philosopher, indeed, can easily be abstractedly good, but when once we have to deal with the human material there is no choice but to condescend.

But a charge so oft repeated, and so fixed upon the man, demands a closer scrutiny. That charge is double-dealing. It is not that Sir Robert was 'a double-minded man,' and, therefore, 'unstable in his ways,' but that he assembled his followers on one understanding and used them for another; or, to take a milder supposition, that he gave way to a different set of impulses when on one side of the House from those which swayed him on the other. Some sort of doubleness is alleged, and some sort must be conceded, though it may not be easily described. Sir Robert was one man by parentage, education, friends, and almost every circumstance of his very early entrance into public life, and another man by the workings of his great intellect, the expansion of his sympathies, and his vast and varied experience. He was early taught to worship George III, and to adore the very shadow of Pitt, for his father published a pamphlet to prove that the National Debt was a positive source of prosperity. From this ultra-Tory household he passed to Harrow, where, as the world knows, he was the contemporary of Byron, of Aberdeen, and other great men, but it was at Oxford that he chiefly acquired confidence and fame. He was the most distinguished son of that University, and its most cherished representative. Thirty years ago Peel was to do everything for the Universities, the Church of England, the aristocracy, and every man and every thing that reposes under those institutions. The only question was, whether he would stand by them – whether he was stanch; for in those days it was the office of a statesman to do what he was bid. It is enough for our present purpose to remind our readers that he first took office under Perceval, continued under Lord Liverpool, Eldon all the time being Lord Chancellor; that as Irish Secretary he was early pressed into the service of the Orange party; and that meanwhile old Sir Robert Peel, himself in Parliament, showed a most amiable vigilance for the integrity of his son's opinions. In fact, never was a rising young statesman blessed with so many fathers and mothers, and godfathers and godmothers. Tories and Orangemen, Oxford and the Church, Perceval and Lord Liverpool, Eldon, and we believe we must add Wellington, with old Sir Robert to hold all together, constituted a political nursery in which it was scarcely possible to go wrong. Unfortunately for his numerous patrons and advisers, Peel had something else in him than a capacity for receiving nursery impressions. He was a great man, and broke through his trammels, but his life was spent in that long and painful struggle. His affections, his friendships, his pledges, and his speeches kept in record against him, held him back, while his far-seeing and active solicitude for his country drew him on. His life was one long contest, for warm pledges are not easily broken, nor, on the other hand, are deep convictions easily belied. But is it impossible for a really honest man to suffer such a struggle? All history and every man's own experience will tell him that it is not impossible. The larger a man's capacity, and the kindlier his nature, the wider also will be his sympathies; and the more likely also will he be to embrace and feel many conflicting considerations. His heart may draw him one way, and his reason another. The influence of a sudden event, the force of some new argument, the excitement of some discussion, the persuasion of some example may ever and anon take possession of the imagination and senses, while the mind within pursues its even tenour, finds out truth at last, and then holds it fast. But the age wherein we live is interested in vindicating the character of its own statesman. Be he double or single, Sir Robert Peel was the type and representative of his generation. We have lived in a period of transition, and Sir Robert has conducted us safely through it. England has changed as well as he.

Sir Robert has died 'in harness.' He never sought repose, and his almost morbid restlessness rendered him incapable of enjoying it. His was a life of effort. The maxim that if anything is worth doing, it is worth doing well, seemed ever present to his mind, so that everything he did or said was somewhat over-laboured. His official powers, as some one said the other day, were Atlantean, and his Ministerial expositions on the same gigantic scale. There was an equal appearance of effort, however, in his most casual remarks, at least when in public, for he would never throw away a chance; and he still trusted to his industry rather than to his powers. But a man whose life is passed in the service of the public, and whose habits are Parliamentary or official, is not to be judged by ordinary rules, for he can scarcely fail to be cold, guarded, and ostentatious. What is a senate but a species of theatre, where a part must be acted, feelings must be expressed, and applause must be won? Undoubtedly the habit of political exhibition told on Sir Robert's manner and style, and even on his mind. His egotism was proverbial, but besides the excessive use of the first person, it occasionally betrayed him into performances at variance both with prudence and taste. His love of applause was closely allied to a still more dangerous appetite for national prosperity, without sufficient regard to its sources and permanence. It was this that seduced him into encouraging, instead of controlling the railway mania. Had the opportunity been allowed, we are inclined to think he would have falsified the common opinion as to his excessive discretion, and astonished mankind with some splendid, if successful, novelties. His style of speaking was admirably adapted for its purpose, for it was luminous and methodical, while his powerful voice and emphatic delivery gave almost too much assistance to his language, for it was apt to be redundant and common-place. He had not that strong simplicity of expression which is almost a tradition of the old Whig school, and is no slight element of its power. We had almost omitted Sir Robert's private character. This is not the place to trumpet private virtues, which never shine better than when they are really private. Suffice it to say that Sir Robert was honoured and beloved in every relation of private life.

Such is the man, the statesman, and the patriot, with his great virtues, and perhaps his little failings, that has fallen at his post. Under Providence he has been our chief guide from the confusions and darkness that hung round the beginning of this century to the comparatively quiet haven in which we are now embayed. Under the lamentable circumstances of his departure, we again revert with renewed satisfaction to the speech which, little as he thought it, was his farewell to the nation. Not the least prominent or least pleasing portion of that speech was its calm, retrospective, and conciliatory character, and, in particular, the manner in which he unconsciously took leave of the man whose policy he stood up to review, and who had entered public life with him, under the same master, forty-one years ago. Having in his introductory sentences declared his cordial concurrence with many parts of the Ministerial policy during their whole period of office, when he came at last to speak of the course recently taken by our diplomacy, he observed, – 'I have so little disposition – and I say it with truth, for the feelings which have actuated me for the last four years remain unabated (hear, hear) – I have so little disposition, I say, for entering into any angry or hostile controversy, that I shall make no reference whatever to many of the topics which were introduced into that most able and most temperate speech, which made us proud of the man who delivered it (loud and general cheering), and in which he vindicated with becoming spirit, and with an ability worthy of his name and place, that course of conduct which he had pursued. (Cheers.)' The man who said this had his heart in the right place, and no reconciliation forced by the agonies, the terrors, or the weakness of a deathbed ever exceeded the feeling of that simple and spontaneous acknowledgment. Sir Robert, it is a comfort to think, has left us with words of peace and candour on his lips, and that same peace and candour, we cannot help believing, will be awarded to his memory by his own political opponents.

In the following brief narrative of the principal facts in the life of the great statesman who has just been snatched from among us, we must disclaim all intention of dealing with his biography in any searching or ambitious spirit. The national loss is so great, the bereavement so sudden, that we cannot sit down calmly either to eulogize or arraign the memory of the deceased. We cannot forget that it was not a week ago we were occupied in recording and commenting upon his last eloquent address to that Assembly which had so often listened with breathless attention to his statesman-like expositions of policy. We freely confess, too, that, however much under ordinary circumstances we feel it our duty to be prepared with such information as is most likely to interest the public, the death of poor Sir Robert Peel was an exceptional case. It was too revolting to prepare the biography of so great a man while he was yet alive – crushed and mangled indeed, and with little hope of recovery – but still alive. We could do little else when the mournful intelligence reached us that Sir Robert Peel was no more than pen a few expressions of sorrow and respect. Even now the following imperfect record of facts, prepared, as it has been, in the course of a few hours, must be accepted as a poor substitute for the biography of that great Englishman whose loss will be felt almost as a private bereavement by every family throughout the British Empire.

Sir Robert Peel was in the 63d year of his age, having been born near Bury, in Lancashire, on the 5th of February, 1788. His father was a manufacturer on a grand scale, and a man of much natural ability, and of almost unequalled opulence. Full of a desire to render his son and probable successor worthy of the influence and the vast wealth which he had to bestow, the first Sir Robert Peel took the utmost pains personally with the early training of the future Prime Minister. He retained his son under his own immediate superintendence until he arrived at a sufficient age to be sent to Harrow. Mr. Robert Peel went to Harrow certainly a ready recipient of scholarship, but by no means an advanced schoolboy. From the outset he was assiduous, docile, and submissive, yet in the prompt and vigorous performance of school duties he lagged for a time behind boys who in everything but experience were infinitely his inferiors. This, however, was only a temporary check at the threshold of a great career. He advanced rapidly and securely, and soon left all competition in the rear; but he wanted the animal energy and buoyancy of spirit which give pre-eminence out of school. Lord Byron, his contemporary at Harrow, was a better declaimer and a more amusing actor, but in sound learning and laborious application to school duties young Peel had no equal. So marked was his superiority in these respects that the unanimous opinion of the little senate to which he then gave laws was, that he could not fail to be a Cabinet Minister at an early age. Masters and scholars shared this sentiment. He had scarcely completed his 16th year when he left Harrow and became a gentleman commoner of Christ Church, Oxford, where he took the degree of A. B., in Michaelmas Term, 1808, with unprecedented distinction. Advisedly it may be said that his success was unprecedented, for the present system of examination being then new, no man before his time ever took the honours of a double first class – first in classics, first in mathematics. It did so happen that Mr. Peel was the first recipient of that much-prized object of youthful ambition.

The year 1809 saw him attain his majority, and saw him also take his seat in the House of Commons as member for the ancient city of Cashel, in the county of Tipperary – a place not then returning the nominee of the popular party in Ireland, but the man who, on account of party interests or other considerations, could find favour in the sight of Mr. Richard Pennefather, who, in the phraseology of that day, 'had the patronage of Cashel.' Whether similarity of opinion in matters political, or a more direct influence, may have led to Mr. Peel's being member for Cashel, one need not at this distance of time too minutely inquire. Whatever may have been the consideration, the 12 voters of Cashel (then the only electors in that city) enjoyed his first services in Parliament, and continued to call him their member till the general election in 1812, when he came in for Chippenham, a Wiltshire borough, where he acquired – probably by means similar to those used at Cashel – the honour of a seat in Parliament. The main difference between the two boroughs consisted in the fact that in the former case he had only 12 constituents, in the latter 135.

The first Sir Robert Peel had long been a member of the House of Commons, and the early efforts of his son in that assembly were regarded with considerable interest, not only on account of his University reputation, but also because he was the son of such a father. He did not, however, begin public life by staking his fame on the results of one elaborate oration; on the contrary, he rose now and then on comparatively unimportant occasions; made a few brief modest remarks, stated a fact or two, explained a difficulty when he happened to understand the matter in hand better than others, and then sat down without taxing too severely the patience or good-nature of all auditory accustomed to great performances. Still in the second year of his Parliamentary course he ventured to make a set speech, when, at the commencement of the session of 1810, he seconded the address in reply to the King's speech. Thenceforward for 19 years a more highflying Tory than Mr. Peel was not to be found within the walls of Parliament. Lord Eldon applauded him as a young and valiant champion of those abuses in the State which were then fondly called 'the institutions of the country,' Lord Sidmouth regarded him as his rightful political heir, and even the Duke of Cumberland patronised Mr. Peel. He further became the favourite *elève* of Mr. Perceval, then First Lord of the Treasury, and entered office as Under-Secretary for the Home Department. Mr. Richard Ryder, uncle of the present Earl of Harrowby, was at that time the principal Secretary. He continued in the Home Department for two years, not often speaking in Parliament, but rather qualifying himself for those prodigious labours in debate, in council, and in office, which it has since been his lot to encounter and perform.

In the month of May, 1812, Mr. Perceval fell by the hand of an assassin, and the composition of the Ministry necessarily underwent a great change. The result, so far as Mr. Peel was concerned, was that he was appointed Chief Secretary to the Lord-Lieutenant of Ireland. This was an office which in those days, and long afterwards, it was the practice of successive Governments to confer upon the most promising of the youthful members of their party. Mr. Peel had only reached his 26th year when, in the month of September, 1812, the duties of that anxious and laborious position were intrusted to his hands. The late Duke of Richmond held the office of Viceroy, and Mr. Vesey Fitzgerald, afterwards Lord Fitzgerald, that of Chancellor of the Exchequer for Ireland. The Legislative Union was then but lately consummated, and the demand for Catholic emancipation had given rise to an agitation of only very recent date. But in proportion to its novelty so was its vigour. Mr. Peel was, therefore, as the representative of the old Tory Protestant school, called upon to encounter a storm of unpopularity such as not even an Irish Secretary has ever been exposed to. No term of reproach was too strong; no amount of obloquy considered disproportioned to the high enormities which the Roman Catholic party charged upon him whom they would never call by any other appellation than 'Orange Peel.' That he bore it all with becoming fortitude, and resented it as often as it was safe to do so, is no more than the subsequent course of his life would lead one to expect. But he sometimes went a little further, and condescended personally to take notice of the offensive violence which marked the course of Irish opposition. The late Mr. O'Connell at various public meetings, and in various forms, through the agency of the press, poured forth upon Mr. Peel a torrent of invective, which went beyond even his extraordinary performances in the science of scolding. At length he received from Mr. Peel a communication in the shape of a hostile message. Sir Charles Saxton, who was Under-Secretary in Ireland, had an interview first with Mr. O'Connell and afterwards with a friend of that gentleman, a Mr. Lidwell. Negotiations went on for three or four days, when Mr. O'Connell was taken into custody and bound over to keep the peace towards all his fellow-subjects in Ireland. Mr. Peel and his friend immediately came to this country, and subsequently proceeded to the continent. Mr. O'Connell followed them to London, but the police were active enough to bring him before the Chief Justice of England, when he entered into recognizances to keep the peace towards all His Majesty's subjects; and so ended one of the few personal squabbles in which Mr. Peel had ever been engaged. For six years he held the office of Chief Secretary to the Lord-Lieutenant, at a time when the government was conducted upon what might be called 'anti-conciliation principles.' The opposite course was commenced by Mr. Peel's immediate successor Mr. Charles Grant, now Lord Glenelg. That a Chief Secretary so circumstanced, struggling to sustain extreme Orangeism in its dying agonies, should have been called upon to encounter great toil and anxiety, is a truth too obvious to need illustration. That in these straits Mr. Peel acquitted himself with infinite address was as readily acknowledged at that time as it has ever been, even in the zenith of his fame. He introduced and defended many Irish measures, including some peace-preservation bills. The establishment of the constabulary force in that country has, however, been amongst the most permanent results of his administration. It is, moreover, one which may be considered as the experimental or preliminary step to the introduction of that system of metropolitan police, which gives security to person and property amidst the congregated millions of the vast cluster of cities, boroughs, and villages which we call London, and which has since been extended to every considerable provincial town. The minor measures of Sir Robert Peel's administration in Ireland possess, at this distance of time, but few features of interest to readers who live in the year 1850. He held office in that country under three successive Viceroys, the Duke of Richmond, Earl Whitworth and Earl Talbot, all of whom have long since passed away from this life, their names and their deeds alike forgotten. But the history of their Chief Secretary happens not to have been composed of such perishable materials, and we now approach one of the most memorable passages of his eventful career. He was Chairman of the great Bullion Committee; but before he engaged in that stupendous task he had resigned the Chief-Secretaryship of Ireland. As a consequence of the report of that committee, he took charge of and introduced the bill for authorizing a return to cash payments which bears his name, and which measure received the sanction of Parliament in the year 1819. That measure brought upon Mr. Peel no slight or temporary odium. The first Sir Robert Peel was then alive, and altogether differed from his son as to the tendency of his measure. It was roundly asserted at the time, and very faintly denied, that it rendered that gentleman a more wealthy man; by something like half a million sterling, than he had previously been. The deceased statesman, however, must in common justice be acquitted of any sinister purpose.

This narrative now reaches the year 1820, when we have to relate the only domestic event in the history of Sir Robert Peel which requires notice. On the 8th of June, at Upper Seymour-street, London, being then in the 33d year of his age, he married Julia, daughter of General Sir John Floyd, who had then attained the age of 25.

Two years afterwards there was a lull in public affairs, which gave somewhat the appearance of tranquillity; Lord Sidmouth was growing old, he thought that his system was successful, and that at length he might find repose. He considered it then consistent with his public duty to consign to younger and stronger hands the seats of the Home Department. He accepted a seat in the Cabinet without office, and continued to give his support to Lord Liverpool, his ancient political chief. In permitting his mantle to fall upon Mr. Peel he thought he was assisting to invest with authority one whose views and policy were as narrow as his own, and whose practice in carrying them out would be not less rigid and uncompromising. But, like many others, he lived long enough to be grievously disappointed by the subsequent career of him whom the Liberal party have since called 'the great Minister of progress,' and whom their opponents have not scrupled to designate by appellations too harsh to be repeated in these hours of sorrow and bereavement. On the 17th January, 1822, Mr. Peel was installed at the head of the Home Department, where he remained undisturbed till the political demise of Lord Liverpool in the spring of 1827. And here for a moment the narrative of his official life may be interrupted in order to remind the reader that he did not always represent in Parliament such insignificant places as Cashel and Chippenham. The most distinguished man that has filled the chair of the House of Commons in the present century was Charles Abbott, afterwards Lord Colchester. In the summer of 1817 this gentleman had completed 16 years of hard service in that most eminent office, and he had represented the University of Oxford for 11 years. His valuable labours having been rewarded with a pension and a peerage, he took his seat, full of years and honours, among the hereditary legislators of the land, and left a vacancy in the representation of his *alma mater*, which Mr. Peel above all living men was deemed the most fitting person to occupy. At that time he was an intense Tory – or as the Irish called him, the Orange Protestant of the deepest dye – one prepared to make any sacrifice for the maintenance of Church and State as established by the Revolution of 1688. Who, therefore, so fit as he to represent the loyalty, learning and orthodoxy of Oxford? To have done so and been the object of Mr. Canning's young ambition, but in 1817 he could not be so ungrateful to Liverpool as to reject its representation even for the early object of his Parliamentary affections. Mr. Peel therefore was returned in the month of June without opposition, for that constituency which many consider the most important in the land – a constituency with which Mr. Peel remained on the best possible terms for an unbroken period of 12 years. The question of the repeal of the penal laws affecting the Roman Catholics, which severed so many political connexions, was, however, destined to separate Mr. Peel from Oxford. In the year 1828 rumours of the coming change were rife, and many expedients were devised to extract from Mr. Secretary Peel his opinions on the Catholic question. But with the impenetrable reserve which ever marked his character he baffled inquiry and left all curiosity at fault. At last the hard necessities of the Government rendered farther concealment impossible, and out came the frightful truth that Mr. Peel was no longer an Orangeman. The ardent friends who had frequently supported his Oxford elections, and the hot partisans who shouted 'Peel and Protestantism' at the Brunswick Clubs, reviled him for his defection in no measured terms. On the 4th of February, 1829, he addressed a letter to the Vice-Chancellor of Oxford, stating in many well turned phrases that the Catholic question must be forthwith adjusted, under advice in which he concurred; and that, therefore, he considered himself bound to resign that trust which the University had during so many years confided to his hands. Mr. Peel's resignation was accepted; but as the avowed purpose of that important step was to give his constituents an opportunity of pronouncing an opinion upon a change of policy, he merely accepted the Chiltern Hundreds with the intention of immediately becoming a candidate for that seat in Parliament which he had just vacated. At this election Mr. Peel was opposed by Sir Robert Inglis, who was elected by 755 to 609. Mr. Peel was therefore obliged to cast himself on the favour of Sir Mannasseh Lopez, who returned him for the borough of Westbury in Wiltshire, which undignified constituency he continued to represent during two years, until at the general election in 1830, he was chosen for Tamworth, in the representation for which borough he has continued for exactly 20 years.

The main features of his official life still remain to be noticed. With the exception of Lord Palmerston no statesman of modern times has spent so many years in the civil service of the Crown as Sir Robert Peel. If no account be taken of the short time he was engaged upon the Bullion Committee in effecting the change in the currency, and in opposing for a few months the Ministries of Mr. Canning and Lord Goderich, it may be stated that from 1810 to 1830 he formed part of the Government, and presided over it as First Minister in 1834–5, as well as from 1841 to 1846 inclusive. During the time that he held the office of Home Secretary under Lord Liverpool he effected many important changes in the administration of domestic affairs, and many legislative improvements of a practical and comprehensive character. But his fame as a member of Parliament was principally sustained at this period of his life by the extensive and admirable alterations which he effected in the criminal law. Romilly and Mackintosh had preceded him in the great work of reforming and humanizing the code of England. For his hand, however, was reserved the introduction of ameliorations which they had long toiled and struggled for in vain. The Ministry through whose influence he was enabled to carry these salutary reforms lost its chief in the person of Lord Liverpool during the early part of the year 1827. When Mr. Canning undertook to form a Government, Mr. Peel, the late Lord Eldon, the Duke of Wellington, and other eminent Tories of that day, threw up office, and are said to have persecuted Mr. Canning with a degree of rancour far outstripping the legitimate bounds of political hostility. At least those were the sentiments expressed by some of the less discreet friends of Mr. Canning. It was certainly the opinion held by the late Lord George Bentinck when he said that 'they hounded to the death my illustrious relative;' and the ardour of his subsequent opposition to Sir Robert Peel evidently derived its intensity from a long cherished sense of the injuries supposed to have been inflicted upon Mr. Canning. In the language of Lord George Bentinck, and in that of many others who had not the excuse of private friendship, there was much of exaggeration, if not of absolute error. It is the opinion of men not ill informed respecting the sentiments of Canning that he considered Peel as his true political successor – as a statesman competent to the task of working out that large and liberal policy which he fondly hoped the Tories might, however tardily, be induced to sanction. At all events, he is believed not to have entertained towards Mr. Peel any personal hostility, and to have stated during his short-lived tenure of office that that gentleman was the only member of his party who had not treated him with ingratitude and unkindness.

In the month of January, 1828, the Wellington Ministry took office and held it till November, 1830. Mr. Peel's reputation suffered during this period very rude shocks. He gave up, as already stated, his anti-Catholic principles, lost the force of 20 years consistency, and under unheard of disadvantages introduced the very measure he had spent so many years in opposing. The debates upon Catholic Emancipation, which preceded the great Reform question, constitute a period in the life of Sir Robert Peel which 20 years ago every one would have considered its chief and prominent feature. There can be no doubt that the course he then adopted demanded greater moral courage than at any previous period of his life he had been called upon to exercise. He believed himself incontestably in the right; he believed, with the Duke of Wellington, that the danger of civil war was imminent, and that such an event was immeasurably a greater evil than surrendering the boasted constitution of 1688. But he was called upon to snap asunder a Parliamentary connexion of 12 years with a great University, in which the most interesting period of his youth had been passed; he was called upon to encounter the reproaches of adherents whom he had often led in well fought contests against the advocates of what was termed 'civil and religious liberty;' he had further to tell the world that the character of public men for consistency, however precious, is not to be directly opposed to the common weal; and to communicate to many the novel as well as unpalatable truth that what they deemed 'principle' must give way to what he called 'expediency.' It is to be expected, however, that posterity will do him the justice to acknowledge that, if he accomplished much, he suffered much in the performance of what he believed to be his highest duties.

When he ceased to be a Minister of the Crown, that general movement throughout Europe which succeeded the deposition of the elder branch of the Bourbons rendered Parliamentary reform as unavoidable as two years previously Catholic emancipation had been. He opposed this change, no doubt with increased knowledge and matured talents, but with impaired influence and few Parliamentary followers. The history of the reform debates will show that Mr. (then Sir Robert) Peel made many admirable speeches which served to raise his reputation, but never for a moment turned the tide of fortune against his adversaries, and in the first session of the first reformed Parliament he found himself at the head of a party that in numbers little exceeded one hundred. As soon as it was practicable he rallied his broken forces; either he or some of his political friends gave them the name of 'Conservatives,' and it required but a short interval of reflection and observation to prove to his sagacious intellect that the period of reaction was at hand. Every engine of party organization was put into vigorous activity, and before the summer of 1834 reached its close he was at the head of a compact, powerful, and well-disciplined Opposition. Such a high impression of their vigour and efficiency had King William IV received, that when, in November, Lord Althorp became a peer, and the Whigs therefore lost their leader in the House of Commons, His Majesty sent to Italy to summon Sir Robert Peel to his councils, with a view to the immediate formation of a Conservative Ministry. Sir Robert accepted this heavy responsibility, though he thought that the King had grievously mistaken the condition of the country and the chances of success which awaited his political friends. A new House of Commons was instantly called, and for nearly three months Sir Robert Peel maintained a gallant struggle against the most formidable opposition that for nearly a century past any Minister has been called upon to encounter. At no time did his command of temper, his almost exhaustless resources of information, his vigorous and comprehensive intellect appear to create such astonishment or draw forth expressions of such unbounded admiration as in the early part of the year 1835. But, after a well-fought contest, he retired once more into opposition till the close of the second Melbourne Administration in 1841. It was in the month of April, 1835, that Lord Melbourne was restored to power, but the continued enjoyment of office did not much promote the political interests of his party, and from various causes the power of the Whigs began to decline. The commencement of a new reign gave them some popularity, but in the new House of Commons, elected in consequence of that event, the Conservative party were evidently gaining strength; still, after the failure of 1834–5, it was no easy task to dislodge an existing Ministry, and at the same time to be prepared with a Cabinet and a party competent to succeed them. Sir Robert Peel, therefore, with characteristic caution, 'bided his time,' conducting the business of Opposition throughout the whole of this period with an ability and success of which history affords few examples. He had accepted the Reform Bill as the established law of England, and as the system upon which the country was thenceforward to be governed. He was willing to carry it out in its true spirit, but he would proceed no further. He marshalled his Opposition upon

the principle of resistance to any further organic changes, and he enlisted the majority of the peers and nearly the whole of the country gentlemen of England in support of the great principle of protection to British industry. The little manoeuvres and small political intrigues of the period are almost forgotten, and the remembrance of them is scarcely worthy of revival. It may, however, be mentioned that in 1839 Ministers, being left in a minority, resigned, and Sir Robert Peel, when sent for by the Queen, demanded that certain ladies in the household of Her Majesty, – the near relatives of eminent Whig politicians, – should be removed from the personal service of the Sovereign. As this was refused, he abandoned for the time any attempt to form a Government, and his opponents remained in office till September, 1841. It was then Sir Robert Peel became First Lord of the Treasury, and the Duke of Wellington, without office, accepted a seat in the Cabinet, taking the management of the House of Lords. His Ministry was formed emphatically on Protectionist principles, but the close of its career was marked by the adoption of free trade doctrines in the widest and most liberal sense. We do not here propose to reopen a question already decided, but to record the fact that Sir Robert Peel's sense of public duty impelled him once more to incur the odium and obloquy which attend a fundamental change of policy, and a repudiation of the political partisans by whose ardent support a Minister may have attained office and authority. It was his sad fate to encounter more than any man ever did of that most painful hostility which such conduct, however necessary, never fails to produce. This great change in our commercial policy, however unavoidable, must be regarded as the proximate cause of Sir Robert Peel's final expulsion from office in the month of July, 1846. His administration, however, had been signalized by several measures of great political importance. Among the earliest and most prominent of these were his financial plans, the striking feature of which was an income-tax; greatly extolled for the exemption it afforded from other burdens pressing more severely on industry, but loudly condemned for its irregular and unequal operation, a vice which has since rendered its contemplated increase impossible.

Of the Ministerial life of Sir Robert Peel little more remains to be related except that which properly belongs rather to the history of the country than to his individual biography. But it would be unjust to the memory of one of the most sagacious statesmen that England ever produced to deny that his latest renunciation of political principles required but two short years to attest the vital necessity of that unqualified surrender. If the corn laws had been in existence at the period when the political system of the Continent was shaken to its centre and dynasties crumbled into dust, a question would have been left in the hands of the democratic party of England, the force of which neither skill nor influence could then have evaded. Instead of broken friendships, shattered reputations for consistency, or diminished rents, the whole realm of England might have borne a fearful share in that storm of wreck and revolution which had its crisis on the 10th of April, 1848.

In the course of his long and eventful life many honours were conferred upon Sir Robert Peel. Wherever he went, and almost at all times, he attracted universal attention, and was always received with the highest consideration. At the close of the year 1836 the University of Glasgow elected him their Lord Rector, and the Conservatives of that city in January, 1837, invited him to a banquet at which 3,000 gentlemen assembled to do honour to their great political chief. But this was only one among many occasions on which he was 'the great guest.' Perhaps the most remarkable of these banquets was that given to him in 1835 at Merchant Tailors' Hall by 300 members of the House of Commons. Many other circumstances might be related to illustrate the high position which Sir Robert Peel occupied in this country. Anecdotes innumerable might be recorded to show the extraordinary influence in Parliament which made him 'the great commoner' of the age; for Sir Robert Peel was not only a skilful and adroit debater, but by many degrees the most able and one of the most eloquent men in either house of Parliament. Nothing could be more stately or imposing than the long array of sounding periods in which he expounded his doctrines, assailed his political adversaries, or vindicated his own policy. But when the whole land laments his loss, when England mourns the untimely fate of one of her noblest sons, the task of critical disquisition upon literary attainments or public oratory possesses little attraction. It may be left for calmer moments, and a more distant time, to investigate with unforgiving justice the sources of his errors, or to estimate the precise value of services which the public is now disposed to regard with no other feelings than those of unmingled gratitude.

The news of Peel's death, three days after being thrown from his horse on Constitution Hill on 29 June 1850, was greeted with a great outpouring of public grief, particularly amongst working class Londoners. To his fellow parliamentarians, however, Peel had emerged as a deeply ambiguous figure, a personally admirable man who had been prepared to betray his party in the interests of what he perceived to be the greater good of the country at large. *The Times* obituary is frank about its disapproval of these betrayals though it is equally fulsome in its praise of Peel's very considerable political achievements. While readily acknowledging his distinctive genius as a Prime Minister it tends to play down the lasting significance of Peel's two periods as Home Secretary (1822–1827 and 1828–1830). In 1826 he had begun the process of radically reforming the criminal justice system and in 1829 had introduced the Metropolitan Police Improvement Bill that established London's police force – hence the popular nicknames 'Bobbies' and 'Peelers' still occasionally attached to the force. In the words of later Prime Minister, Harold Wilson, he was 'undoubtedly the greatest reforming Home Secretary of all time'.

* * *

J. M. W. TURNER, R. A.

Artist: 'Mastering every mode of expression, combining scientific labour with an air of negligent profusion.'

19 DECEMBER 1851

THE FINE ARTS in this country have not produced a more remarkable man than Joseph Mallord William Turner, whose death it was yesterday our duty to record; and although it would here be out of place to revive the discussions occasioned by the peculiarities of Mr. Turner's style in his later years, he has left behind him sufficient proofs of the variety and fertility of his genius to establish an undoubted claim to a prominent rank among the painters of England. His life had been extended to the verge of human existence; for, although he was fond of throwing mystery over his precise age, we believe that he was born in Maiden-lane, Covent-garden, in the year 1775, and was consequently, in his 76th or 77th year. Of humble origin, he enjoyed the advantages of an accurate rather than a liberal education. His first studies, some of which are still in existence, were in architectural design, and few of those who have been astonished or enchanted by the profusion and caprice of form and colour in his mature pictures would have guessed the minute and scientific precision with which he had cultivated the arts of linear drawing and perspective. His early manhood was spent partly on the coast, where he imbibed his inexhaustible attachment for marine scenery and his acquaintance with the wild and varied aspect of the ocean. Somewhat later he repaired to Oxford, where he contributed for several years the drawing to the *University Almanac.* But his genius was rapidly breaking through all obstacles, and even the repugnance of public opinion; for, before he had completed his 30th year he was on the high road to fame. As early as 1790 he exhibited his first work, a watercoloured drawing of the entrance to Lambeth, at the exhibition of the Academy; and in 1793 his first oil painting. In November, 1799, he was elected an associate, and in February, 1802, he attained the rank of a Royal Academician. We shall not here attempt to trace the vast series of his paintings from his earlier productions, such as the 'Wreck,' in Lord Yarborough's collection, the 'Italian Landscape,' in the same gallery, the pendant to Lord Ellesmere's Vanderwelde, or Mr. Munro's 'Venus and Adonis,' in the Titianesque manner, to the more obscure, original, and, as some think, unapproachable productions of his later years, such as the 'Rome,' the 'Venice,' the 'Golden Bough,' the 'Téméraire,' and the 'Tusculum.' But while these great works proceeded rapidly from his palette, his powers of design were no less actively engaged in the exquisite water-coloured drawings that have formed the basis of the modern school of 'illustration.' The 'Liberstudiorum' had been commenced in 1807 in imitation of Claude's 'Liber veritatis,' and was etched, if we are not mistaken, by Turner's own hand. The title page was engraved and altered half-a-dozen times from his singular and even nervous attention to the most trifling details. But this volume was only the precursor of an immense series of drawings and sketches, embracing the topography of this country in the 'River Scenery' and the 'Southern Coast' – the scenery of the Alps, of Italy, and great part of Europe – and the ideal creations of our greatest poets, from Milton to Scott and Rogers, all imbued with the brilliancy of a genius which seemed to address itself more peculiarly to the world at large when it adopted the popular form of engraving. These drawings are now widely diffused in England, and form the basis of several important collections, such as those of Petworth, of Mr. Windus, Mr. Fawkes, and Mr. Munro. So great is the value of them that 120 guineas have not unfrequently been paid for a small sketch in watercolours; and a sketchbook, containing chalk drawings of one of Turner's river tours on the continent, has lately fetched the enormous sum of 600 guineas. The prices of his more finished oil paintings have ranged in the last few years from 700 to 1,200 or 1,400 guineas. All his works may now be said to have acquired triple or quadruple the value originally paid for them. Mr. Turner undoubtedly realized a very large fortune, and great curiosity will be felt to ascertain the posthumous use he has made of it. His personal habits were peculiar, and even penurious, but in all that related to his art he was generous to munificence, and we are not without hope that his last intentions were for the benefit of the nation, and the preservation of his own fame. He was never married, he was not known to have any relations, and his wants were limited to the strictest simplicity. The only ornaments of his house in Queen Anne-street were the pictures by his own hand, which he had constantly refused to part with at any price, among which the 'Rise and Fall of Carthage' and the 'Crossing the Brook' rank among the choicest specimens of his finest manner.

Mr. Turner seldom took much part in society, and only displayed in the closest intimacy the shrewdness of his observation and the playfulness of his wit. Everywhere he kept back much of what was in him, and while the keenest intelligence, mingled with a strong tinge of satire, animated his brisk countenance, it seemed to amuse him to be but half understood. His nearest social ties were those formed in the Royal Academy, of which he was by far the oldest member, and to whose interests he was most warmly attached. He filled at one time the chair of Professor of Perspective, but without conspicuous success, and that science has since been taught in the Academy by means better suited to promote it than a course of lectures. In the composition and execution of his works Mr. Turner was jealously sensitive of all interference or supervision. He loved to deal in the secrets and mysteries of his art, and many of his peculiar effects are produced by means which it would not be easy to discover or to imitate.

We hope that the Society of Arts or the British Gallery will take an early opportunity of commemorating the genius of this great artist, and of reminding the public of the prodigious range of his pencil, by forming a general exhibition of his principal works, if, indeed, they are not permanently gathered in a nobler repository. Such an exhibition will serve far better than any observations of ours to demonstrate that it is not by those deviations from established rules which arrest the most superficial criticism that Mr. Turner's fame or merit are to be estimated. For nearly 60 years Mr. Turner contributed largely to the arts of this country. He lived long enough to see his greatest productions rise to uncontested supremacy, however imperfectly they were understood when they first appeared in the earlier years of this century; and, though in his later works and in advanced age, force and precision of execution have not accompanied his vivacity of conception, public opinion has gradually and steadily advanced to a more just appreciation of his power. He is the Shelley of English painting – the poet and the painter both alike veiling their own creations in the dazzling splendour of the imagery with which they are surrounded, mastering every mode of expression, combining scientific labour with an air of negligent profusion, and producing in the end works in which colour and language are but the vestments of poetry. Of such minds it may be said in the words of Alastor:—

'Nature's most secret steps
'He, like her shadow, has pursued, wheree'er
'The red volcano overcanopies
'The fields of snow and pinnacles of ice
'With burning smoke; or where the starry domes
'Of diamond and of gold expand above
'Numberless and immeasurable halls,
'Frequent with crystal column and clear shrines
'Of pearl, and thrones radiant with chrysolite.

'Nor had that scene of ampler majesty
'Than gems or gold – the varying roof of heaven
'And the green earth – lost in his heart its claims
'To love and wonder ......'

It will devolve on our contemporaries, more exclusively devoted than ourselves to the history of the fine arts to record with greater fullness and precision the works of Mr. Turner's long and active life; but in these hasty recollections we have endeavoured to pay a slight tribute to the memory of a painter who possessed many of the gifts of his art in extraordinary abundance, and who certainly in dying leaves not his like behind. He will be buried, by his own desire, in St. Paul's Cathedral, by the side of Sir Joshua Reynolds.

Turner, who had been born on 23 April 1775, died on 19 December 1851 at his cottage on Cheyne Walk at Chelsea. The fate of the many major paintings remaining unsold in his possession was not known until his will was made public. His estate, amounting to some £140,000, was not finally settled until 1857, the will having been disputed by relatives. Two pictures – *Dido building Carthage* and *Sun rising through Vapour* – were specifically left to the newly founded National Gallery on condition that they should hang next to two pictures by Claude. The other 'finished' paintings in his collection were also left to the nation under the proviso that they should be housed within ten years in a building attached to the National Gallery called 'Turner's Gallery'. He also left money for the establishment of almshouses for 'decayed artists'. These two ambitions were frustrated. Although the National Gallery (and, by succession, the Tate) inherited the paintings, no dedicated 'Turner Gallery' was established until the 'Clore' Gallery, designed by James Stirling, was added to Tate Britain in 1982–1986. *The Times*'s pious hope that 'an early opportunity of commemorating the genius of this great artist' was very belatedly, and only in part, realised when the Turner Prize for visual artists under the age of 50 was initiated in 1984.

ISAMBARD KINGDOM BRUNEL

Engineer: 'born an engineer.'

15 SEPTEMBER 1859

OUR COLUMNS OF Saturday last contained the ordinary record of the death of one of our most eminent engineers, Mr. I. K. Brunel. The loss of a man whose name has now for two generations, from the commencement of this century to the present time, been identified with the progress and the application of mechanical and engineering science, claims the notice due to those who have done the State some service. This country is largely indebted to her many eminent civil engineers for her wealth and strength, and Mr. Brunel will take a high rank among them when the variety and magnitude of his works are considered, and the original genius he displayed in accomplishing them. He was, as it were, born an engineer, about the time his father had completed the block machinery at Portsmouth, then one of the most celebrated and remarkable works of the day, and which remains efficient and useful. Those who recollect him as a boy recollect full well how rapidly, almost intuitively, indeed, he entered into and identified himself with all his father's plans and pursuits. He was very early distinguished for his powers of mental calculation, and not less so for his rapidity and accuracy as a draughtsman. His power in this respect was not confined to professional or mechanical drawings only. He displayed an artist-like feeling for and a love of art, which in later days never deserted him. He enjoyed and promoted it to the last, and the only limits to the delight it afforded him were his engrossing occupations and his failing health.

The bent of his mind when young was clearly seen by his father and by all who knew him. His education was therefore directed to qualify him for that profession in which he afterwards distinguished himself. His father was his first, and, perhaps, his best tutor. When he was about 14 he was sent to Paris, where he was placed under the care of M. Masson, previous to entering the college of Henri Quartre, where he remained two years. He then returned to England, and it may be said that, in fact, he then commenced his professional career under his father, Sir I. Brunel, and in which he rendered him important assistance – devoting himself from that time forward to his profession exclusively and ardently. He displayed even then the resources, not only of a trained and educated mind, but great, original, and inventive power. He possessed the advantage of being able to express or draw clearly and accurately whatever he had matured in his own mind. But not only that; he could work out with his own hands, it he pleased, the models of his own designs, whether

in wood or iron. As a mere workman he would have excelled. Even at this early period steam navigation may be said to have occupied his mind, for he made the model of a boat, and worked it with locomotive contrivances of his own. Everything he did, he did with all his might and strength, and he did it well. The same energy, thoughtfulness, and accuracy, the same thorough conception and mastery of whatever he undertook distinguished him in all minor things, whether working as a tyro in his father's office, or as the engineer of the Great Western Railway Company, or, later, in the conception and design in all its details of the Great Eastern. Soon after his return to England his father was occupied, among other things, with plans for the formation of a tunnel under the Thames. In 1825 this work was commenced, and Brunel took an active part in the work under his father. There are many of his fellow labourers now living who well know the energy and ability he displayed in that great scientific struggle against physical difficulties and obstacles of no ordinary magnitude, and it may be said that at this time the anxiety and fatigue he underwent, and an accident he met with, laid the foundation of future weakness and illness. Upon the stoppage of that undertaking by the irruption of the river in 1828, he became employed on his own account upon various works. Docks at Sunderland and Bristol were constructed by him, and when it was proposed to throw a suspension bridge across the Avon at Clifton, his design and plan was approved by Mr. Telford, then one of the most eminent engineers of the day. This work was never completed. He thus became known, however, in Bristol, and when a railway was in contemplation between London and Bristol, and a company formed, he was appointed their engineer. He had previously been employed, however, as a railway engineer in connexion with the Bristol and Glocestershire and the Merthyr and Cardiff tramways. In these works his mind was first turned to the construction of railways, and when he became engineer of the Great Western Railway Company he recommenced and introduced what is popularly called the broad guage, and the battle of the guages began. This is not the place or the time to say one word upon this controversy. No account of Mr. Brunel's labours, however, would be complete without mentioning so important a circumstance in his life. Considering the Great Western Railway as an engineering work alone, it may challenge a comparison with any other railway in the world for the general perfection of its details, and the speed and ease of travelling upon it. Many of its structures, such as the viaduct at Hanwell, the Maidenhead-bridge, which has the flattest arch of such large dimensions ever attempted in brickwork, the Box-tunnel, which, at the date of its construction, was the longest in the world, and the bridges and tunnels between Bath and Bristol deserve the attention of the professional student. They are all more or less remarkable and original works.

In the South Devon and Cornish railways there are also works of great magnitude and importance. The sea wall of the South Devon Railway, and, above all, the bridge over the Tamar, called the Albert-bridge from the interest taken in it by the Prince Consort, deserve to be specially mentioned, together with the bridge over the Wye at Chepstow, as works which do honour to the genius of the engineer and the country too. It was on the South Devon Railway that he adopted the plan which had been previously tried on the London and Croydon line, – viz., of propelling the carriages by atmospheric pressure. This plan failed, but he entertained a strong opinion that this power would be found hereafter capable of adoption for locomotive purposes. It is impossible, in such a rapid sketch as this of his energetic and professional life, to do more than notice, or rather catalogue, his works. It was in connexion with the interests of the Great Western Railway that he first conceived the idea of building a steamship to run between England and America. The Great Western was built accordingly. The power and tonnage of this vessel was about double that of the largest ship afloat at the time of her construction. Subsequently, as the public know, the Great Britain was designed and built under Mr. Brunel's superintendence. This ship, the result, as regards magnitude, of a few years' experience in iron shipbuilding, was not only more than double the tonnage of the Great Western, and by far the largest ship in existence, but she was more than twice as large as the Great Northern, the largest iron ship which at that time had been attempted. While others hesitated about extending the use of iron in the construction of ships, Mr. Brunel saw that it was the only material in which a very great increase of dimensions could safely be attempted. The very accident which befell the Great Britain upon the rocks in Dundrum Bay showed conclusively the skill he had then attained in the adaptation of iron to the purposes of shipbuilding. The means taken under his immediate direction to protect the vessel from the injury of winds and waves attracted at the time much attention, and they proved successful, for the vessel was again floated, and is still afloat.

While noticing these great efforts to improve the art of shipbuilding, it must not be forgotten that Mr. Brunel, we believe, was the first man of eminence in his profession who perceived the capabilities of the screw as a propeller. He was brave enough to stake a great reputation upon the soundness of the reasoning upon which he had based his conclusions. From his experiments on a small scale in the Archimedes he saw his way clearly to the adoption of that method of propulsion which he afterwards adopted in the Great Britain. And in the report to his directors in which he recommended it, he conveyed his views with so much clearness and conclusiveness that when, with their approbation, he submitted it to the Admiralty he succeeded in persuading them to give it a trial in Her Majesty's navy, under his direction. In the progress of this trial he was much thwarted; but the Rattler, the ship which was at length placed at his disposal, and fitted under his direction with engines and screw by Messrs. Maudslay and Field, gave results which justified his expectations under somewhat adverse circumstances. She was the first screw ship which the British navy possessed, and it must be added, to the credit of Brunel, that though she had originally been built for a paddle ship, her performance with a screw was so satisfactory that numerous screw ships have since been added to the navy. Thus prepared by experience and much personal devotion to the subject of steam navigation by means of large ships, he, in the later part of 1851 and the beginning of 1852, begun to work out the idea he had long entertained – that to make long voyages economically and speedily by steam required that the vessels should be large enough to carry the coal for the entire voyage outwards, and, unless the facilities for obtaining coal were very great at the outport, then for the return voyage also; and that vessels much larger than any then built could be navigated with great advantages from the mere effects of size. Hence originated the Great Eastern. The history of this great work is before the public, and its success in a nautical point of view is admitted, as well as the strength and stability of the construction of the vessel. More than this cursory notice of this last memorial of his skill cannot now be given. All the circumstances attending the construction, the launching, the trial of this great ship are before the public. It would hardly be just, however, to the memory of this distinguished engineer if we were to conclude this notice without an allusion to his private character and worth. Few men were more free from that bane of professional life – professional jealousy. He was always ready to assist others, and to do justice to their merits. It is a remarkable circumstance that in the early part of his career he was brought into frequent conflict with Robert Stephenson, as Stephenson was with him, and that, nevertheless, their mutual regard and respect were never impaired. Brunel was ever ready to give his advice and assistance whenever Stephenson desired it, and the public will recollect how earnestly and cordially during the launch of the Great Eastern Stephenson gave his assistance and lent the weight of his authority to his now deceased friend. Such rivalry and such unbroken friendship as theirs are rare, and are honourable to both.

The death of Mr. Brunel was hastened by the fatigue and mental strain caused by his effort to superintend the completion of the Great Eastern, and in these efforts his last days were spent. But we must not forget to mention that for several years past that Mr. Brunel had been suffering from ill-heath brought on by over exertion. Nevertheless he allowed himself no relaxation from his professional labours, and it was during the period of bodily pain and weakness that his greatest difficulties were surmounted and some of his greatest works achieved. Possessing a mind strong in the consciousness of rectitude, he pursued, in single hearted truthfulness, what he believed to be the course of duty, and in his love of and devotion to his profession he accomplished, both at home and abroad, on the continent and in India, works, the history of which will be the best monument to his memory. With an intellect singularly powerful and acute, for nothing escaped his observation in any branch of science which could be made available in his own pursuits, yet it was accompanied by humility and a kindliness of heart which endeared him to all who knew him and enjoyed his friendship. The very boldness and originality of his works, of which he was never known to boast, while it added to his fame added no little to his anxiety, and not unfrequently encompassed him with difficulty – 'Great was the glory, but greater was the strife,' which told ultimately upon his health and strength, and finally closed his life when he was little more than 53 years of age. We have left unnoticed many of his works, and many that deserve the attention and study of the young engineer. They will find their record in professional works, and in them his works will hereafter be fully described and considered. Mr. Brunel was a member of the Royal Society, having been elected at the early age of 26. In 1857 he was admitted by the University of Oxford to the honorary degree of Doctor of Civil Laws, a distinction of which he was justly proud.

Brunel, who reputedly smoked forty cigars a day, suffered a stroke shortly before the *Great Eastern* made her maiden voyage to New York. He died on 15 September. The obituary, rightly, praises Brunel's huge achievements as a railway engineer and as an innovatory ship designer and it briefly notes his one great failure: the Atmospheric Railway at Dawlish (which only ran for a year). His espousal of the broad gauge for the Great Western Railway, which led to what *The Times* calls 'the battle of the guages [*sic*]', only became a lost cause in 1892 (when the standard gauge was imposed on all British lines). The obituarist's comment on Brunel's 'artist-like feeling for and love of art' was borne out by his contentious design for the Clifton Suspension Bridge and by his own sense of triumph in producing uniformity in the 15-man committee vetting his designs on 'the most ticklish subject – taste'. Largely thanks to the fund-raising efforts of the Institute of Civil Engineers, who considered the Clifton project to be a fitting memorial to the great man, work on the bridge was restarted three years after Brunel's death and completed in 1864. The obituarist also mentions the accident at Dundrum Bay in Ireland which nearly brought about the end of the *Great Britain* (the ship had to be refloated from the rocks on which she had run aground in 1846 by James Bremner, but the cost of salvage in 1847 bankrupted the Great Western Steamship Company). The steady decline in the ship's fortunes finally led to her being abandoned in the Falkland Islands only to be towed back to Bristol for restoration in 1970.

ROBERT STEPHENSON

Engineer: 'His heart was worthy of his head.'

12 OCTOBER 1859

THE DEATH OF STEPHENSON comes with startling rapidity upon that of Brunel. Both men of rare genius, and both occupying a sort of double throne at the head of their profession, they have gone to their rest together, and their rivalry has ceased. Distinguished sons of distinguished fathers, the two men who in these latter years have done most to perfect the art of travel, and in this way to cultivate social intercourse, multiply wealth, and advance civilization, have been struck down at one fell swoop in all the maturity of their power. Mr. Stephenson's health had been delicate for about two years, and he complained of failing strength just before his last journey to Norway. In Norway he became very unwell; his liver was so much affected that he hurried home, and when he arrived at Lowestoft he was so weak that he had to be carried from his yacht to the railway, and thence to his residence in Gloucester-square, where his malady grew so rapidly as to leave from the first but faint hope of his recovery. He had not strength enough to resist the disease, and he gradually sunk until at length he expired yesterday morning. If his loss will be felt severely in his profession, it will be still more poignantly felt in his large circle of friends and acquaintances, for he was as good as he was great, and the man was even more to be admired than the engineer. His benevolence was unbounded, and every year he expended thousands in doing good unseen. His chief care in this way was for the children of old friends who had been kind to him in early life, sending them to the best schools and providing for them with characteristic generosity. His own pupils regarded him with a sort of worship, and the number of men belonging to the Stephenson school who have taken very high rank in their peculiar walk shows how successful he was in his system of training, and how strong was the force of his example. The feeling of his friends and associates was not less warm. A man of the soundest judgment and the strictest probity, with a noble heart and most genial manner, he won the confidence of all who knew him, and perhaps in all London there were not more pleasant social gatherings than those which were to be found in his house in Gloucester-square, he himself being the life of the party. Without a spark of professional jealousy in his own nature, he was liked by all his fellow engineers, if they did not know him sufficiently to bear him affection; and we do not believe that even those who had the most reason to wish him out of the way, such as the promoters of the Suez Canal, which he strenuously opposed, ever bore him any ill will. He has passed away, if not very full of years, yet very full of honours – the creator of public works, a benefactor of his race, the idol of his friends.

He was certainly born under very humble circumstances. George Stephenson, his father, deemed himself a right happy man when, on earnings of 1*l.* a week, he could offer his hand and fortune to the pretty farm servant, Fanny Henderson. He took her to his home at Willington-quay, on the north bank of the Tyne, about six miles below Newcastle, towards the end of 1802, and his biographer tells us that his signature, as it appears in the parish books on the occasion of his marriage, was that of a person who had just learnt to write. On the 16th of December in the following year George Stephenson's only son, Robert, was born; and there on Willington-quay he was familiarized from his earliest years with the steady industry of his parents, for when his father was not busy in shoemaking or cutting out shoe lasts, or cleaning clocks, or making clothes for the pitmen he was occupied with some drawing or model with which he sought to improve himself. Robert's mother very soon died, and his father, whose heart was bound up in the boy, had to take the sole charge of him. George Stephenson felt deeply his own want of education, and in order that his son might not suffer from the same cause, sent him first to a school at Long Benton, and afterwards to the school of a Mr. Bruce, in Newcastle, one of the best seminaries of the district, although the latter was rather expensive for Stephenson. There young Robert remained for three years, and his father not only encouraged him to study for himself but also made him in a measure the instrument of his own better education, by getting the lad to read for him at the library in Newcastle, and bring home the results of his weekly acquirements, as well as frequently a scientific book which father and son studied together. On leaving school, at the age of 15, Robert Stephenson was apprenticed to Mr. Nicholas Wood, at Killingworth, to learn the business of the colliery, where he served for three years, and became familiar with all the departments of underground work. His father was engaged at the same colliery, and the evenings of both were usually devoted to their mutual improvement. Mr. Smiles describes the animated discussions which in this way took place in their humble cottage, these discussions frequently turning on the then comparatively unknown powers of the locomotive engine daily at work on the waggon-way. The son was even more enthusiastic than the father on the subject. Robert would suggest alterations and improvements in all the details of the machine. The father would make every possible objection, defending the existing arrangements, but proud, nevertheless, of his son's suggestions, often warmed by his brilliant anticipations of the triumph of the locomotive, and perhaps anxious to pump him as much as he could. It was probably out of these discussions that there arose in George Stephenson's mind the desire to give his son a still better education. He sent him in the year 1820 to the Edinburgh University, where Hope was lecturing on chymistry, Sir John Leslie on natural philosophy, and Jameson on natural history. Though young Stephenson remained in Edinburgh but six months it is supposed that he did as much work in that time as most students do in a three years' course. It cost his father some 80*l*., but the money was not grudged when the son returned to Killingworth in the summer of 1821, bringing with him the prize for mathematics, which he had gained at the University.

In 1822 Robert Stephenson was apprenticed to his father, who had by this time started his locomotive manufactory at Newcastle; but his health giving way after a couple of years' exertion, he accepted a commission to examine the gold and silver mines of South America. The change of air and scene contributed to the restoration of his health, and, after having founded the Silver Mining Company of Columbia, he returned to England in December, 1827, by way of the United States and Canada, in time to assist his father in the arrangements of the Liverpool and Manchester Railway, by placing himself at the head of the factory at Newcastle. About this time, indeed, he seems to have almost exclusively devoted his attention to the study of the locomotive engine, the working of which he explained jointly with Mr. Locke, in a report replying to that of Messrs. Walker and Rastrick, who advocated stationary engines. How well he succeeded in carrying out the ideas of his father was afterwards seen when he obtained the prize of 500*l*. offered by the directors of the Liverpool and Manchester Railway for the best locomotive. He himself gave the entire credit of the invention to his father and Mr. Booth, although we believe that the 'Rocket,' which was the designation of the prize-winning engine, was entered in the name of Robert Stephenson. Even this locomotive, however, was far from perfect, and was not destined to be the future model. The young engineer saw where the machine was defective, and designed the 'Planet,' which, with its multitubular boiler, with cylinders in the smoke-box, with its cranked axletree, and with its external framework, forms, in spite of some modifications, the type of the locomotive engines employed up to the present day. About the same time he designed for the United States an engine specially adapted to the curves of American railways, and named it the 'Bogie,' after a kind of low waggon used on the quay at Newcastle. To Robert Stephenson we are accordingly indebted for the type of the locomotive engines used in both hemispheres.

The next great work upon which Mr. Stephenson was engaged was the survey and construction of the London and Birmingham Railway, which he undertook in 1833. He had already been employed in the execution of a branch from the Liverpool and Manchester Railway, and in the construction of the Leicester and Swannington line, so that he brought to his new undertaking considerable experience. On being appointed engineer to the company he settled in London, and had the satisfaction of seeing the first sod cut on the 1st of June, 1834, at Chalk Farm. The line was complete in four years, and on the 15th of September, 1838, was opened. The difficulties of this vast undertaking are now all forgotten, but at the time they were so formidable that one poor fellow, who had contracted for the Kilsby tunnel, died of fright at the responsibility which he had assumed. It was ascertained that about 200 yards from the south end of the tunnel there existed, overlaid by a bed of clay 40 feet thick, a hidden quicksand. The danger was so imminent that it was seriously proposed to abandon the tunnel altogether, but Robert Stephenson accepted the responsibility of proceeding, and in the end conquered every difficulty. He worked with amazing energy, walking the whole distance between London and Birmingham more than 20 times in the course of his superintendence. All this time, however, he had not ceased to devote his attention to the manufactory in Newcastle, convinced that good locomotives are the first step to rapid transit; and his assistance was sought by many companies anxious to secure his advice if not more constant service. His evidence before Parliamentary committees was grasped at, and it may be said that in one way or another he has been engaged on all the railways in England, while in conjunction with his father he has directed the execution of more than a third of the various lines in the country. Father and son were consulted as to the Belgium system of railways, and obtained from King Leopold the Cross of the Legion of Honour in 1844. For similar services performed in Norway, which he visited in 1846, Robert Stephenson received the Grand Cross of St. Olof. So also he assisted either in actually making or in laying out the systems of lines in Switzerland, in Germany, in Denmark, in Tuscany, in Canada, in Egypt, and in India. As the champion of locomotive in opposition to stationary engines, he resisted to the uttermost the atmospheric railway system, which was backed with the authority of Brunel, and had at one time a considerable repute, although it is now nearly forgotten. In like manner he had to fight with Mr. Brunel the battle of the gauges, the narrow against the broad gauge, and it is superfluous to say that he was successful here as in all his undertakings. In the sphere of railways he has been since the death of his father the foremost man, the safest guide, the most active worker.

Of his railway doings we have spoken in very general terms, only mentioning the great Kilsby tunnel incidentally. It is, however, in this tunnel and in the bridges which he erected for railway purposes that his genius as an engineer is most strikingly displayed, and by these it is that he will be best remembered, Of his bridges, of course, we refer to the high level one at Newcastle, constructed of wood and iron, to the Victoria-bridge at Berwick, built of stone and brick, to the bridge in wrought and cast iron across the Nile, to the Conway and the Britannia bridges over the Menai Straits, and to the Victoria-bridge over the St. Lawrence. Those who care to examine the matter more closely will find a full account of most of these works in an article on iron bridges contributed by Mr. Stephenson himself to the *Encyclopaedia Britannica.* They are all splendid works, and have made his name famous over the world. The idea of the tubular bridge was an utter novelty, and, as carried out at the Menai Straits, was a grand achievement. Considering the enormous span of a bridge placed across these straits, the immense weight which it has to sustain, and the height to which it must be raised in order that great ships may pass beneath, the undertaking seamed chimerical, and he must have been a man of great daring, as well as of no common experience, who could think of conquering the difficulty. Robert Stephenson, however, fairly faced the difficulty, and threw bridges of 460 feet span from pier to pier across this formidable gulf. It was the first thing of the kind ever attempted, and the success was so triumphant that under Mr. Stephenson's auspices it has been repeated more than once. In the Egyptian railway there are two tubular bridges, one over the Damietta branch of the Nile, and the other over the large canal near Besket-al-Saba; but they have this peculiarity, that the trains run not, as at the Menai Straits, within the tube, but on the outside upon the top. It is with this method of tubular bridging that Stephenson's name is peculiarly identified, and by which he will probably be best known to posterity as distinguished from his father, who has almost the entire credit of the railway system.

It will not be supposed that Mr. Robert Stephenson's labours were confined to the construction and survey of railways. We have reports of his on the London and Liverpool systems of waterworks. In 1847 he was returned as member of Parliament for Whitby, in the Conservative interest. He took a great interest in all scientific investigations and was a member of more than one Scientific Society. As a specimen of his liberality in the cause of science, it may be mentioned that he placed his yacht the Titania – and it is said he had the best manned yacht in the Squadron – at the disposal of Professor Piazzi Smyth, who was sent out with very limited means to Tenerife to make sundry scientific observations, and thus materially assisted the researches of that gentleman. In the same spirit he came forward in 1855, and paid off a debt amounting to 3,100*l.*, which the Newcastle Literary and Philosophical Society had incurred, his motive being, to use his own phrase, gratitude for the benefits which he himself had received from it in early life, and a hope that other young men might find it equally useful. It was like the man to do so, for, as we have already suggested, his heart was worthy of his head, and in one form or another he was always doing good.

Robert Stephenson, the only son of George Stephenson, died at his house in Gloucester Square, north of Hyde Park, on 12 October 1859, just short of a month after Brunel. The achievements of both men were a matter of national pride but Stephenson's relatively humble origins and somewhat basic education rendered him all the more heroic as a prime example of what Samuel Smiles styled 'Self Help'. Smiles approvingly quotes Stephenson's modest claim that the development of the railway locomotive was due to 'not one man, but to the efforts of a nation of mechanical engineers.' Robert Stephenson was buried in Westminster Abbey underneath a monumental brass designed by Sir George Gilbert Scott. A window in the west aisle of the north transept of the Abbey, installed in 1862, commemorates both Stephensons, father and son.

* * *

WILLIAM MAKEPEACE THACKERAY

Novelist and humourist: 'He . . . shrouded an over tender heart in a transparent veil of cynicism.'

24 DECEMBER 1863

MR. THACKERAY was found dead in his bed on Thursday morning. Sudden as the loss of Peel, or of Talfourd, or of Lord Macaulay, whose death saddened the Christmas holydays three years ago, – sudden, also, as other recent deaths of able men who laboured worthily in the world's eye, but whose calling did not bring them so near as that of a foremost novelist to the world's heart, has been this new cause of public grief. For a few days past Mr. Thackeray had been slightly unwell, yet he was about among his friends, and he was out even on Wednesday evening. But when called at about 9 o'clock on Thursday morning he was found dead in his bed, with placid face, having apparently died without suffering pain. Mr. Thackeray's age was but 52, and he seemed a man large, vigorous, cheerful, with yet a quarter of a century of life in him. There were some parts of his character that never felt the touch of his years, and these were tenderly remembered yesterday at many a Christmas fireside. There was to the last in him the sensibility of a child's generous heart that time had not sheathed against light touches of pleasure and pain. His sympathy was prompt and keen, but the same quick feeling made him also over sensitive to the small annoyances that men usually learn to take for granted as but one form of the friction that belongs to movements of all kinds. He was sensitive to his sensitiveness, and did in his writings what thousands of men do in their lives, shrouded an over tender heart in a transparent veil of cynicism. Often he seemed to his readers to be trifling or nervously obtruding himself into his story when he was but shrinking from the fell discovery of his own simple intensity of feeling. In his most polished works, *Vanity Fair, Esmond,* or the *Newcomes* – in which last book the affected cynicism, that, after all, could not strike deeper than into the mere surface of things, is set aside, and more nearly than in any other of his works discharge is made of the whole true mind of William Makepeace Thackeray – in these his masterpieces there is nothing better, nothing more absolutely genuine and perfect in its way than the pure spirit of frolic in some of his comic rhymes. He could play with his 'Pleaseman X,' very much as a happy child plays with a toy; and how freely and delightfully the strength of his wit flowed into the child's pantomime tale of the *Rose and the Ring.* It is not now the time for taking exact measure of the genius of the true writer we have lost. What sort of hold it took upon the English mind and heart his countrymen knew by the sad and gentle words that yesterday connected the sense of his loss in almost every household with the great English festival of lovingkindness. There are men who, appealing to widely spread forms of ignorance or prejudice, have more readers than Mr. Thackeray, and yet the loss of one of these writers on the eve of Christmas would have struck home nowhere beyond the private circle of his friends. Whatever the extent or limit of his genius, Mr. Thackeray found the way to the great generous English heart. And the chief secret of his power was the simple strength of sympathy within him, that he might flinch from expressing fully but that was none the less the very soul of his successful work. Quickly impressible, his mind was raw to a rough touch; but the same quality gave all the force of its truth to his writing, all the lively graces to his style. That part of him which was the mere blind he put up at the inconveniently large window in his breast, degenerated into formula; and there were some who might be pardoned for becoming weary at the repetition of old patterns of sarcasm at the skin-deep vanities of life. But the eye was a dull one that could not look through this muslin work into a mind that so to speak, was always keeping Christmas, although half ashamed to be known at the clubs as guilty of so much indulgence in the luxuries of kindly fellowship, and so continual an enjoyment of the purest side of life. Whatever little feuds may have gathered about Mr. Thackeray's public life lay lightly on the surface of the minds that chanced to be in contest with him. They could be thrown off in a moment, at the first shock of the news that he was dead. In the course of his active career there are few of his literary brethren with whom he has not been brought into contact. At one time he was a fellow-worker with us in this journal. He worked much and variously; many and various also were his friends. To some of the worthiest in the land he was joined in friendship that had endured throughout the lifetime of a generation, and there are very humble rooms in London where there were tears yesterday for him whose left hand did not know what his right hand had done in silent charity. — *Examiner*

Thackeray was found dead on Christmas Eve morning in 1863 at the house he had built for himself at Palace Green in Kensington. The obituary reflects both the admiration and affection in which he was held by his contemporaries, but it makes no mention of his education, his early struggles to make a name for himself in the literary world and, above all, of his difficult private circumstances. In 1836, by which time he had squandered most of his inheritance, he married Isabella Shawe who was to bear him three daughters (two of whom survived into adulthood). In 1840, after an attempted suicide, Isabella was diagnosed as incurably insane and was confined to a private mental asylum. She was not to die until 1894. Charlotte Brontë, who was ignorant of Isabella's condition, had caused some real embarrassment to Thackeray when she dedicated the second edition of *Jane Eyre* to him in January 1848. There was idle speculation concerning a supposed connection between the character of Mr. Rochester and Thackeray himself.

NICHOLAS, CARDINAL WISEMAN

First Archbishop of Westminster: 'the only [English Roman Catholic] who had earned for himself a wide and lasting reputation for ability and learning.'

15 FEBRUARY 1865

WE REGRET TO learn that the long illness of his Eminence Cardinal Wiseman has at length reached a fatal termination. He died yesterday, at the comparatively early age of 62.

Nicholas Wiseman was the son of the late Mr. James Wiseman, merchant, of Waterford and of Seville, in which latter city the late Cardinal was born on the 2nd of August, 1802. The family of Wiseman is one of considerable antiquity, and they appear to have had lands in the county of Essex since the reign of Edward IV. Soon after the Reformation Sir John Wiseman, who had been one of the Auditors of the Exchequer under Henry VIII, and was knighted for his bravery at the Battle of Spurs, acquired by purchase Much Canfield-park in that county. His grandson, William, who married into the noble family of Capel, afterwards Earls of Essex, was created a baronet by King Charles I in 1628, and a younger brother of the second baronet was Lord Bishop of Dromore. The title has continued in a direct line of succession down to the present time and is now represented by Sir William Saltonstall Wiseman, eighth baronet, who is a captain in the Royal Navy. From a younger branch of this family the late Cardinal traditionally claimed descent. His Eminence's mother, whose maiden name was Strange, and whose family, in spite of large confiscations of their property under Oliver Cromwell, is still seated at Aylward's Town Castle, in the county of Kilkenny, lived to see her son elevated to a Cardinal's hat, and died full of years in 1851.

Though born upon Spanish soil, young Nicholas Wiseman, when he was little more than five years old, was sent to England. He arrived at Portsmouth in January, 1808, in the Melpomene frigate, Captain Parker, and was sent, while still very young, to a boarding school at Waterford. In March, 1810, he was transferred thence to the Roman Catholic College of St. Cuthbert, at Ushaw, near Durham, where he remained until 1818. In that year he obtained leave to quit Ushaw for Rome, where he arrived in the December of that year and became one of the first members of the English College, then recently founded at Rome. In the next year he had the honour of preaching before the then Pope, Pius VII, and, having pursued with diligence the usual course of philosophical and theological studies, he maintained a public disputation on theology, and was created a doctor in Divinity July 7, 1824, shortly before the completion of his 22nd year.

In the following Spring he received holy orders, and in 1827 was nominated Professor of Oriental languages in the Roman University, being at that time Vice-Rector of the English College, to the rectorship of which he was promoted in the year 1829. He had already distinguished himself, not merely as a theologian, but also as a scholar, for in 1827 he composed and printed a learned work, entitled *Horoe Syriacæ* chiefly drawn from Oriental manuscripts in the Library of the Vatican.

Dr. Wiseman returned to England in 1835, and in the winter of that year delivered a series of lectures, during the season of Advent, at the Sardinian Chapel in Lincoln's-inn fields. In the Lent of the following year, at the request of the late Bishop Bramston, then Vicar-Apostolic of the London District, he delivered at St. Mary's, Moorfields, another course of lectures, in which he vindicated, at considerable length, the principal doctrines and practices of the Roman Catholic Church, and with such success, that the Roman Catholics of the metropolis presented him with a gold medal, commemorative of their gratitude and of their high regard for his talents and acquirements. These 'Lectures' were speedily followed by a '*Treatise on the Holy Eucharist*,' which occasioned a theological controversy with Dr. Turton, the late Bishop of Ely, and by another work, in two volumes, entitled '*Lectures on the Connexion between Science and Revealed Religion*.' In the Lent of the year 1837, when he happened to be in Rome, he delivered four lectures on the 'Offices and Ceremonies of Holy Week,' which were afterwards given to the world as a separate publication.

In 1840 the late Pope Gregory XVI increased the number of his Vicars Apostolic in England from four to eight, and Dr. Wiseman was appointed coadjutor to the late Bishop Walsh, then Vicar Apostolic of the Midland District, being at the same time elevated to the Presidency of St. Mary's College, Oscott, near Birmingham. While there he took the deepest interest in the theological movement at Oxford which is associated with the names of Dr. Newman and Dr. Pusey, and which has furnished Rome with such an abundant store of recruits. In 1848, on the death of Bishop Griffiths, Dr. Wiseman became Pro-Vicar-Apostolic of the London district, and subsequently was nominated coadjutor to Dr.Walsh, *cum jure successionis* on the translation of that prelate to London. Bishop Walsh survived his translation but a short time, and on his death, in 1849, Bishop Wiseman succeeded him as Vicar Apostolic.

The next stage in Dr. Wiseman's life is that which, as it has been more controverted than any other, so also is that by which his name will be longest remembered. In August, 1850, Bishop Wiseman was summoned to Rome to the 'threshold of the Apostles,' by his Holiness Pope Pius IX, who on the 29th of the following September issued his celebrated 'Apostolical Letter,' re-establishing the Roman Catholic hierarchy in England and Wales, at the same time issuing a 'Brief' elevating

Dr. Wiseman to the 'Archbishopric of Westminster.' In a private consistory, held the following day, the new 'Archbishop' was raised by the Sovereign Pontiff to the dignity of a Cardinal Priest, the ancient church of St. Pudentiana, at Rome, in conformity with the ecclesiastical custom, being selected by him as his title. His Eminence was the seventh Englishman who has been elevated to the hat of a Cardinal since the Reformation, his predecessors in this respect having been Cardinal Pole, Cardinal Allen, Cardinal Howard, Cardinal York, Cardinal Weld and Cardinal Acton.

The name of Cardinal Wiseman was well known in that portion of the literary world which interests itself in controversy, as one of the most frequent and able contributors to the *Dublin Review*, of which he was for some years the joint editor. Among other productions of his pen which appeared in that periodical we may name his *Strictures on the High Church Movement in Oxford*, which were reprinted by the Catholic Institute about 20 years ago for circulation in a cheap form, under the attractive title of *High Church Claims*. His Eminence's *Essays and Contributions to the Dublin Review* were collected and published, with a preface by the author, in 3 volumes 8vo. in 1853. It is also understood that he contributed to the *Penny Cyclopaedia* the article which treats on the 'Catholic Church.' Among the best known of his Eminence's other controversial and miscellaneous publications are his *Fabiola*, a tale of the Early Christians; his *Reminiscences of the Four last Popes; A Letter on Catholic Unity*, addressed to the late Earl of Shrewsbury; *A Letter to the Rev. J. H. Newman, on the Controversy relating to the Oxford Tracts for the Times*; and *A Letter addressed to John Poynder, Esq., upon his Work entitled 'Popery in Alliance with Heathenism.'* To these must be added his *Appeal to the Reason and Good Feeling of the People of England*, respecting the Papal aggression, in which he endeavoured to prove that the matter at issue was merely a question relating to the internal and spiritual organization of the English Roman Catholics and in no sense a temporal measure, or one which involved any practical assault on the freedom of Protestants.

To the London world and to the public at large Cardinal Wiseman's name was rendered most familiar by his frequent appearance upon the platform as a public lecturer upon a wide range of subjects connected with education, history, art and science; and in this capacity his Eminence always found an attentive and eager audience, even among those who were most conscientiously opposed to his spiritual claims and pretensions, and who most thoroughly noted him as 'Archbishop of Westminster.'

The illness of which his Eminence has died has been of long standing, and when he left England for Rome in the Spring of 1860, there were many of his friends who feared that they would see his face no more. But he lived to return to England, and to recover some portion of his former health. It is almost superfluous to add that his Eminence's loss will be severely felt among the English Roman Catholics, both lay and clerical, as he was nearly the only member of their body who had earned for himself a wide and lasting reputation for ability and learning.

> Given the continuing antipathy to Roman Catholicism in England and indeed the furore which had greeted the announcement of Wiseman's appointment to the newly created see of Westminster, this obituary offers a surprisingly sympathetic commentary on his achievement. In the eighteenth century the religious lives of the small body of English Catholics had been regulated by Vicars Apostolic. Plans to create a series of new dioceses to cope with increasing numbers of the faithful were formulated in the late 1840s but had to be shelved due to legal problems in England and to the eviction of Pius IX from his see by the short-lived Roman Republic. On 7 October 1850, however, Wiseman was able to issue a florid pastoral letter 'from out the Flaminian Gate' announcing the new hierarchy and his own elevation to be both Cardinal and Archbishop of Westminster and asserting that 'Catholic England has been restored to its orbit in the ecclesiastical firmament'. Popular, and official, wrath was stirred by the supposed presumption of the Vatican in usurping the title of 'Westminster', the seat of British Government, hence *The Times's* patronising adoption here of apostrophes for Wiseman's dignity and see. On 22 October 1850 an editorial in the same newspaper had greeted the appointment as 'one of the grossest acts of folly and impertinence which the court of Rome has ventured to commit since the crown and people of England threw off its yoke'.

ABRAHAM LINCOLN

American statesman: 'a singular depth of insight.'

15 APRIL 1865

The News of the Assassination in New York (from our Special Southern Correspondent)

IT MAY SAFELY be affirmed that in the history of mankind no civilized capital ever wore the aspect which, upon the receipt of the ghastly tidings of this morning, New York at this hour presents. There was excitement, doubtless, in Paris when Henry I of Navarre fell before Ravaillac's dagger, – in London when Mr. Perceval yielded his life to a maniac's bullet, – in Rome when Cardinal Rossi fell slaughtered in the public streets; but what facilities had Paris, London, or Rome for thrilling in an instant the public heart and brain compared with those which the diffusive penny press and swiftly recurring telegrams of America place at this hour at the disposal of New York? Or was there ever a nation so sensitively plastic to the impress of great national sentiments as the keenly sentient, mercurial, quick witted population which, in wild bewilderment, surges and sways through the thronging streets now under my gaze? Last night the people of this great city went to bed, lulled by their cheerful optimism, reckoning of the rebellion as already a thing of the past, little heeding difficulties, social, financial, and economical, which might well make a statesman stand aghast; believing that Abraham Lincoln and William H. Seward were the chief apostles of the revived American Union, which is described in a work recently published as synonymous with the new Heaven and the new Earth. This morning they woke to the stunning consciousness that in the night the shadow of a great and ghastly crime had passed over the land; that assassination, sudden and unlooked for, executed with remorseless cruelty, but intrepid effrontery, had engraven its hideous tale upon that page which records four years of horrors without parallel, culminating in the abhorred crime which has added to the victims of this war the names of Abraham Lincoln, and, as seems too probable, of William H. Seward. A thousand American cities, linked together by a network of lightning, have this morning awakened to the simultaneous knowledge that he who 12 hours ago was their first citizen, the chief architect of their fabric of a resuscitated Union, the figure-head round which clustered their hopes and pride, is numbered with the dead. Already over hundreds of thousands of square miles is every particular and detail of the rash and bloody deed of last night scrutinized by millions of eager eyes. It is believed that precisely at the same hour two ruffians, manifestly in concert with each other, lifted their hands against the two most valued lives of the Republican party – that upon the night of Good Friday Abraham Lincoln was stricken with his death-wound in his private box at Ford's Theatre; that the small pocket pistol which launched the fatal bullet was found, still smoking, on the floor of the box; that the undaunted assassin, having entered the box from the rear, stretched his hand over Mrs. Lincoln's shoulder until the muzzle of his pistol almost touched the President's head; that the bullet, designedly (as it would seem) propelled by a small charge of powder, did not pass through the head, but lodged in the brain about three inches from its point of entrance; that the ruffian who fired it, rescuing himself without difficulty from Colonel Parker, of General Grant's Staff, who was in the box with Mr. and Mrs. Lincoln, calmly stepped from the private box upon the stage; that, brandishing with melodramatic gesture a naked dagger in his hand, he pronounced the well-known motto of the State of Virginia, '*Sic semper tyrannis,*' in apparent justification of a deed against the atrocity of which all that is noble and manly in that proud old State will recoil with indignant execration; that, turning with unruffled imperturbability, he left the stage and made his exit from the theatre by one of the side scenes with which he seemed familiar, and, mounting a horse which was attached to a tree in the immediate neighbourhood of the theatre, galloped swiftly off into the night, and was lost.

But it was reserved for his accomplice to exhibit still more undaunted nerve, although wherever this tale is read humanity will shudder at the heartless cruelty which could instigate an assassin to force his way to the bedside of a suffering old man already half dead, and to anticipate by a savage act of vindictive butchery the fatal event whereby Mr. Seward's life seemed yesterday but too gravely menaced. It must be remembered that Mr. Seward is 65 years old, and it would appear there are justifiable grounds for the general belief that the sufferer, if ever he arose from his sick bed again, could scarcely have recovered, even without the horrible events of last night, from a fracture of the arm and jawbone, and from the exhaustion which is known to have followed his accident, without a sensible abatement of those singular powers, physical and mental, which have enabled him during these last four years to flood every European Foreign-office with a deluge of despatches such as never issued in like space of time from any single pen. Boldly entering Mr. Seward's residence under the pretext of being the bearer of some important medicine which Dr. Verdi designed for his patient, the assassin, undeterred by three men who attempted to interpose, forced a road to his victim's bedside, and with his knife deeply wounded Dr. Seward's face and throat. Closing with Mr. Frederick Seward (the Assistant-Secretary of State, and eldest son to the sufferer), the ruffian dealt him a blow upon the head which fractured his skull in two places, and has probably terminated Mr. Frederick Seward's earthly career. Almost simultaneously he poniarded a male nurse in attendance upon Mr. Seward, inflicting wounds since pronounced to be mortal. Upon Major Seward (another son, if I am not mistaken, of the Secretary of State) the miscreant inflicted injuries which, though not likely to be fatal, effectually prevented any further interference with his own escape from under a roof which had looked down within a few seconds upon the grim horrors of a fourfold assassination. Mounting his horse outside the door he saved himself, like his associate by swift flight, and up to the present hour both have escaped detection and capture. The public voice seems unanimous in pronouncing the assassin of President Lincoln to be an actor named Wilkes Booth (the brother of the more celebrated Edwin Booth, who has lately won high reputation in this city by his admirable impersonation for 100 nights of *Hamlet*), whose face, it is asserted, was recognized by many spectators acquainted with him. As I write, revelations flashed along the electric wires, indicating the existence of a preconcerted conspiracy, in which Wilkes Booth was a principal, and which was designed to have taken effect on the 4th of March, are placarded at the corners of the street, and devoured by thousands of hungry eyes. The feeling with which the brief record 'Abraham Lincoln expired at 22 minutes past 7 this morning' is read may be conceived by those of your readers who are acquainted with the character and temperament of Americans.

How shall I describe the scene which already New York presents? There is, as I have already said, no city upon earth permeated by nerves of such exquisite sensibility, vibrating at the slightest access of popular fever, carrying spasmodic sensation through a dense mass of human beings, which in any other capital I have ever seen would take hours to learn and understand what is here known, felt, and appreciated in a few passionate seconds. In a hundred instances during the last four years your correspondents have portrayed the fever fits of New York – mass meetings in this Square or that, processions longer than that which welcomed the Prince of Wales, convulsions which shook Wall-street and Broadway like an all pervading ague – but I doubt whether a scene like that of this morning has yet been witnessed. The chronic excitement of this war influences this strange population as cumulative poisons are said to act upon their victims. Instead of a dispersion of electricity through the medium of these popular thunderbursts, the excitement of the mass seems to accumulate and be hoarded; until, upon the occasion of each recurrent explosion, the reserve of delirious passion is greater and greater in volume. There have often before been paroxysms of sanguine intoxication in this city, or of depression, if not of despair, but never before has the thunderbolt fallen from a smiling sky, never has the proud and swelling note of victory been converted in the twinkling of an eye into the wail of a nation. Abraham Lincoln had grown to be regarded, in a higher degree than any soldier or sailor, as the impersonation of the war power of the Union. Creeping into Washington in disguise and with timid irresolution to be inaugurated as chief magistrate upon the 4th of March, 1861, he lived so to conciliate and, within four brief years, to win popular affection that his second inauguration upon the 4th of March, 1865, was the ovation of an almost unanimous people. The estimates of his character and of the calibre of his intellect since he was suddenly tossed to the surface of a great nation have been numerous and contradictory; but the opinion seems to be daily gaining ground that impartial history will assign to him one of the highest places among the statesmen who have hitherto presided over the North in the supreme agony of the nation. There can be quoted against Mr. Lincoln no such extravagant vaunts or unseemly denunciations of others, no such rash predictions or disingenuous colourings, as crowd the despatches of Mr. Seward; on the other hand, there are thousands of Mr. Lincoln's anecdotes and quaint conceits, none of which fail to indicate shrewdness, while many reveal a singular depth of insight into the circumstances under which they were spoken. It was mentioned to me by one of the Southern Peace Commissioners that at the recent conference in Hampton Roads he was deeply impressed by the ascendancy of Mr. Lincoln throughout the interview over Mr. Seward. The flags at half-mast, the festoons of crape hung out by each store in succession, and already creeping along the whole length of Broadway upon either side of the street, the eager closing of shutters and suspension of business in Wall-street, the feverish bewilderment of thousands, who can as yet but half realize the truth, the agitated swaying to and fro of hurrying multitudes in the streets, the frenzied accents of grief and rage, the tolling bells, the deep boom of the minute guns, are fitting expressions of the public grief, for they indicate not only the lamentation that a just, temperate, calm, and well-intentioned statesman has died in the track of duty by the most appalling of deaths, but that in one of the most awful of crises which ever overtook a nation his successor should be Andrew Johnson.

Dreadful as is the fashion of his death, if ever man was *felix opportunitate mortis* that man may be pronounced to be Abraham Lincoln. The difficulties which he has surmounted during his first term of office, stupendous as they have been, are feathers, trifles, air bubbles when compared with those which await his successor during the four coming years. But there can hardly be two opinions that in the interest of the South no event could be more prejudicial, or more deeply to be deprecated, than the foul assassination of last night. There breathes nowhere in the Northern States a partisan so blinded by sectional passion or so exasperated against Secessia as to imagine that the execrable crime of which Washington was last night the scene could be regarded by Jefferson Davis, Robert E. Lee, and the men who share their confidence, otherwise than with unmeasured detestation and poignant regret. This is not the place nor the moment for attempting to expatiate upon the character of Mr. Davis. But having long occupied a position which afforded peculiar facilities for understanding him, I cannot forbear briefly saying that, be his faults what they may, the time is not far distant when history will mete out to Mr. Davis that justice which is at present denied to him not only, as is natural, by Northerners, but also by many of his own ignorant and ungrateful countrymen. Meantime the natural vindictiveness, consequent upon the fearful crime of last night, will be employed to intensify Northern bitterness against Mr. Davis. There is already a disposition to draw a line of demarcation between him and General Lee, which none would resent more than the latter. The advocates of harshness will be fearfully augmented by the crime of last night, against which Mr. Davis, whose leniency throughout this war has amounted to a weakness, and who under terrible provocation has never permitted one act of retaliation, would revolt with unutterable horror. The denunciations of General Grant for his liberal-terms to the Confederates who surrendered to him will be fiercer than ever, especially those which proceed from General Butler, and which are embittered with obvious personal malignity against the General. It has always seemed to me that the surrender of General Lee and the opportunity for generosity so admirably seized by General Grant bridged over the gulf which divides the two sections to a degree which none could have hoped two months ago. But the bullet of a dastardly assassin has in one instant neutralized the effect of the great stride towards conciliation so happily taken by General Grant.

This is not strictly an obituary, but it conveys much of the sense of horror and the awareness of the severity and abruptness of America's loss which was felt on both sides of the Atlantic. Lincoln's assassination is compared to those of Henry IV of France in May 1610, of the British Prime Minister Spencer Perceval in May 1812, and of Count (not Cardinal) Rossi, the Papal Minister of Justice, in November 1849. On 14 April 1865 Lincoln had been shot in the head while attending a performance of the play *Our American Cousin* at Ford's Theater in Washington. He died the next day. After firing the fatal shot, his assassin, John Wilkes Booth, jumped from Lincoln's box, on to the stage (breaking his leg in the process). Witnesses differed as to whether he shouted 'Sic semper tyrannis' or 'The South is avenged'. Booth was shot while resisting arrest on 26 April. Lincoln was buried at Springfield, Illinois, on 4 May 1865.

LORD PALMERSTON

Statesman: 'There was never a statesman who more truly represented England.'

18 OCTOBER 1865

THE FEARS WHICH for months past the state of Lord Palmerston's health has excited have at length been realized. The great statesman is no more. Many who saw him towards the close of last Parliament, broken and bent by a recent attack of illness, shook their heads and whispered to each other that he could never meet another Parliament. That fear has been quickly and fatally verified. The bulletins we have published will have prepared most persons for the sad news which we have to announce to-day, that Lord Palmerston died yesterday morning, at a quarter to 11.

There never was a statesman who more truly represented England than Lord Palmerston. His name is now added to that splendid but very short list of Ministers, from Walpole to Pitt and from Pitt to Peel, who in times of great difficulty have rendered England prosperous at home and famous abroad, and who, while obtaining place from the Court, have derived their chief power from the country. Pitt, properly speaking, belonged to the last century, and there have been but three men in the present century who attained to the same enviable position. The first was Canning, a great spirit, but greater in what he devised than in what he accomplished; for no sooner had he reached the pinnacle of power, and excited the brightest hopes of the nation, than, sick at heart, he fell before the intrigues of rivals, leaving it to others to avenge his death and to prosecute his policy. After Canning, two statesmen from among his colleagues, the one his rival the other his disciple – Peel and Palmerston – gradually rose to the highest offices in the realm, and won, as only great characters win, the most sweet voices of the multitude. They have this in common – both were trained in the Tory camp, both forsook the traditions of Toryism, both have been decried as the most inconsistent statesmen that ever lived. Yet no two men could be more unlike, and the inconsistency of each was so different, that what in the one was a failing in the other was a virtue. Sir Robert Peel gave up his principles; Lord Palmerston merely relinquished his party. Less sociable than Palmerston, and less capable of forming new alliances, Peel clung to the Tories while rejecting their dogmas, and compelled them again and again to follow a course which they had learnt from his own lips to regard as the road to destruction. Free and frank, of a jovial nature, hail fellow with good men and true of every rank and politicians of every shade, Lord Palmerston was less fettered by party ties, and, so the objects dearest to his heart were attained, cared little whether the men with whom he sat on the Treasury benches were styled Whigs or Tories, Liberal-Conservatives, or Conservative-Liberals. His very consistency in this respect has been denounced as a fault. It has been said that he was constant only in the retention of office; that he was fixed only to the Treasury bench; that his one principle was that of the Vicar of Bray. He was a member of every Government since 1807, with the exception of those years in which Sir Robert Peel, and subsequently Lord Derby, held the reins. He began life as a Pittite; gradually he developed into a Canningite; when the Whigs came into power he renewed his youth; when they had fallen into disrepute he expanded into a Conservative-Liberal; afterwards he stood forward as the Tory chief of a Radical Cabinet; and he closed his wonderful career as the head of a Ministry with the motto of 'Rest and be thankful.' In all these changes there may be traced a consistency of purpose which, when the clue to it is perceived, becomes entitled to our highest respect; and this clue is furnished in the fact that, whatever changes come over the domestic or colonial policy of England, her foreign policy is unalterable. That policy is indeed, more or less modified by the circumstances of the time, by the amount of our resources, by the temper of our allies, by the spirit of the nation; but in principle it is always the same. Our domestic reforms are for the most part carried in the face of a formidable Opposition; but our foreign policy is supported by overwhelming majorities, and by a national enthusiasm which nothing can resist. We have never a dispute about the principle; it is a tradition based on the universal sentiment of patriotism, and handed from generation to generation – from Cabinet to Cabinet. The Minister of such a policy may through all changes adhere to the Treasury bench if he can; nothing need remove him from it but his personal relations with its other occupants; and he who, like Lord Palmerston, can preserve his seat there through the vicissitudes of half a century is indeed a great man as well as a great statesman.

Henry John Temple was the third Viscount Palmerston, and was born at Broadlands, near Romsey, on the 20th of October, 1784. Although an Irish Peer, his descent is traced to Saxon earls anterior to the Conquest. In the arms of his family may still be seen the eagle displayed of that Leofric, Earl of Mercia, who is remarkable chiefly for his treatment of his wife, the Lady Godiva. Lord Palmerston, however, bears a nearer resemblance to another and less mythological member of his family, of whom his father was the heir male – Sir William Temple, the friend of William III, the patron of Dean Swift, the author of that triple alliance which bound England, Sweden, and the States-General to prevent France from entering the Netherlands, and, singularly enough, a statesman who, while he remained in public life, was always on the winning side, and had the credit of all the popular acts of the Government after the Restoration. M. Capefigue, in noting this resemblance, has been pleased to observe that the chief point of similarity between the Minister of William III and the Minister of Queen Victoria lies in the utter hatred which both had to everything French, and thinks that on one occasion, as he was dining with Lord Palmerston, he made a terrible home thrust when he recalled the unpleasant fact that Sir William Temple, in bequeathing his property to his grand-daughters, stipulated that they should not marry Frenchmen. It gave M. Capefigue considerable satisfaction that Lord Palmerston could only laugh at the remark; it never entered into his head that the statement is quite unfounded, there being no mention of such a condition in the will of Sir W. Temple. Not from Sir William Temple, however – it was from Sir John Temple, younger brother of the diplomatist, and the same of whom Archbishop Sheldon said, 'He has the curse of the Gospel, for all men speak well of him,' that Lord Palmerston was descended. The first viscount of the name was the grandson of Sir John Temple, and was created a peer in 1722. Little more has to be said of him than this, – that his wife was regarded as a perfect model of conjugal affection, her will being quoted with admiration in the *Annual Register*. The second viscount, the father of our great statesman, was grandson of the first, and, like his grandmother, has been regarded as a pattern of conjugal tenderness. The epitaph which he wrote on the death of his first wife is said to be the most pathetic ever penned; and written at a time when our poetry had reached its lowest ebb, when all was artifice and platitude, phrase and frippery, it must be admitted that the lines have a genuine tenderness which it is almost impossible to find, in other compositions of the period. To his father, indeed, Lord Palmerston owes much of that taste for literature which furnished many a happy illustration to his speeches in Parliament, besides enabling him in his younger days to join with Croker and Peel in assailing the Whigs with literary satire. Of his father's lively humour the late Lord Palmerston himself gave an amusing illustration in one of those anecdotes with which he, of all men, knew best how to parry the questions of political opponents or the entreaties of troublesome deputations. He said that it was his father's habit, in placing wine before his guests, to say, 'Here is claret, gentlemen; here is sherry; but I cannot answer for them, I can only give you the word of my wine merchant for them. Here is port, however, for which I can give my own word, – it is very good – I made it myself.' If he was a bad judge of wine, he was considered a good judge of pictures. He collected in Broadlands a gallery of paintings which, at the beginning of the century, had a high repute, and Sir Joshua Reynolds, in bequeathing to his friends the works of his own easel unsold at the time of his death, gave to the Earl of Upper Ossory the first choice and to Lord Palmerston the second. He enjoyed the gift of his artistic friend ten years, and, dying in 1802, left by his second wife, who did not long survive him, two sons and two daughters. Of these sons, Henry John Temple, the elder, is the subject of the present sketch; the younger was afterwards known as Sir William Temple, the British Envoy at the Court of Naples.

Not much is known regarding the early life of Henry John Temple. He was one of the late flowering plants. Always remarkable for his ability, and generally successful in his undertakings, he rejoiced in a splendid constitution, and had to get rid of a certain excess of animal spirits before his ambition could rise to the level of his powers. There is a long period of some five and forty years – considerably more than the half of a man's life – which Lord Palmerston passed in comparative inactivity, and which is a puzzle to the biographer whose idea of the man is derived from the later glories of his career. To account for this anomaly, it has by some of his eulogists been asserted that he was never at heart a Tory, that he was out of his element in the Ministry of Liverpool and Castlereagh, and that he never truly lived until he escaped from the thraldom of Tory ideas and joined the friends of liberality and progress. This theory is quite unfounded. Lord Palmerston was at the last what he was at the first. There is no real difference between Palmerston Secretary-at-War, Palmerston Foreign Secretary, Palmerston Home Secretary, and Palmerston Prime Minister. The explanation of his backwardness lies wholly on the surface, and is what we have already indicated. He was never what would be called an ambitious man; and, delighting in society, he found in the pleasures of private life what, together with the cares of his particular office, was sufficient in his hot youth, if not fully to occupy his powers, at all events to employ his time. Whatever he had to do he did well, but it is quite evident in his parliamentary history that he never cared to go out of his way for work. As Secretary-at-War for some 20 years, he hardly ever made a speech except on the subject of the army, and then only when he was compelled to do so. As Foreign Secretary for a period little less, he in like manner confined his attention to the business of his own department. At a time when he was the most popular statesman in England, he was content to serve now under his junior, and now under his rival. On the dissolution of the Aberdeen Cabinet he consented to serve even under Lord Derby if certain of his colleagues could be induced to follow the same course. It was not until every possible combination had been tried, and every possible Premier had given up the task in despair, that, as a last resource, Lord Palmerston was asked to form a Government. He at once accepted the position which he had not sought and filled with dignity to himself and advantage to the country an office which, from his never having grasped at it, persons who measure men, not according to their deserts, but according to their demands, regarded as beyond his power.

In the little that is known concerning the early life of Lord Palmerston there is not much that is remarkable. He received his education at Harrow, at Edinburgh, and at Cambridge. He went to Harrow a little after Lord Aberdeen, and about the same time as Sir Robert Peel and Lord Byron. Thence he proceeded to Edinburgh, to enjoy the benefit of Dugald Stewart's instruction; and, by the way, it may be noted as something peculiar that he was one of the very few Tories who followed the example of the young Whigs of that generation in sitting at the feet of the great Whig Professor of Moral Philosophy and Political Economy. It certainly does not appear that he entered with any enthusiasm into the studies which absorbed every inmate of Stewart's family; and one might with some show of reason accept it as a proof of this apathy that his name is not to be found among the members of that Speculative Society which was joined by every man of mark in the University, and which, besides Lord Lansdowne, Henry Brougham, Sydney Smith, Francis Jeffrey, Francis Horner, Walter Scott, and Lord John Russell, included Lord Palmerston's own brother, Sir William Temple. But he himself stated about two years ago in one of his speeches, 'I passed three years of my youth in studying at the University of Edinburgh, and I will frankly own, without disparagement to any other seat of learning at which I had the fortune to reside, that I enjoyed greater advantages in the acquirement of useful knowledge and sound principles during the three years' residence in Edinburgh than I possessed at any other place.' Certainly, the influence of Stewart's training was at a later period apparent in the strong determination expressed by Lord Palmerston to maintain those principles of government of which Huskisson was the exponent. So long as Huskisson remained in the Cabinet he felt certain that these doctrines would be honoured; when Huskisson was ejected from the Duke of Wellington's Ministry on purely personal grounds he too seceded, because he had no guarantee, he said, that these doctrines would have the weight to which they were entitled. We may add that it must have been in Stewart's classroom that a phrase which he often turned to good account in his speeches, and on one memorable occasion with most brilliant effect, first caught his fancy and left upon it an indelible impression – 'The fortuitous concourse of atoms.' Having been inoculated at Edinburgh, where he remained three years, with these liberal views and this inkling of philosophy, he turned southward again to the University which Pitt represented in Parliament, and which was at that time the chief school of thought in England. Almost all his political contemporaries who took a leading position, whether in the Whig or in the Tory ranks, were Cambridge men. If Byron, Coleridge, and Wordsworth are to be classed among our greatest poets, it would appear that in other departments than that of politics Cambridge had, at the beginning of the present century, a pre-eminence over the sister University of Oxford. Lord Palmerston, who had in the meantime succeeded to his title through the death of his father, entered at St. John's College in 1803, and worked in good earnest for academical success at a time when it was not usual for a nobleman to present himself for any but an honorary degree.

The Temples were a family predestined to rule. Within the space of 50 years Macaulay has counted among the sons and grandsons of the Countess Temple alone, and she died in 1752, three First Lords of the Treasury (George Grenville, W. Pitt, and Lord Grenville), three Secretaries of State, two Keepers of the Privy Seal, and four First Lords of the Admiralty. Although Lord Palmerston belonged to a different branch of the Temple family, he too, whose father had been a Lord both of the Admiralty and of the Treasury, looked forward to political life, and, in 1806, immediately on the death of Pitt, offered himself to the University of Cambridge as a candidate to represent it in Parliament. He was opposed, on this occasion, by Lord Henry Petty, who had become Chancellor of the Exchequer in room of the 'heaven-born Minister' and who thus came to the election with a weight of Ministerial influence which his rival found it vain to withstand. That rival, however, was not to be discouraged. He presented himself again as a candidate in 1807, when he failed of success by only two votes; and in 1811 he tried his fortune a third time, in this case attaining the object of his ambition so unmistakably that he continued to represent the University until, in 1831, he gave mortal offence to his constituents by joining the Whigs. In the meantime, however, he found his way into Parliament, at first through the pocket borough of Bletchingley, and then through the borough of Newport, in the Isle of Wight. Nor was he long in Parliament before he enjoyed the sweets of office. The notorious Ministry of 'All the Talents' soon fell to pieces; and, as if in mockery of that splendid coalition, a Ministry succeeded to power headed by a nobleman whose natural incapacity was aided by a natural indolence, and whose indolence was aggravated not only by sickness, but also, to make assurance doubly sure, by continual opiates, under the influence of which he would fall asleep over his papers. Not able to touch animal food, not caring to open his mouth, often found sleeping at his desk, it would be one of the marvels of government that the Duke of Portland contrived to keep a Cabinet together for more than a couple of years, were we not too well acquainted with the truth of Oxenstiern's commonplace regarding the wisdom of rulers. It was in this singular Ministry, whose great achievement was the Walcheren disaster, that Lord Palmerston first entered upon office. He entered on the office which his father had long enjoyed, as a Lord of the Admiralty; and when, on the quarrel of Castlereagh and Canning on the subject of the Walcheren expedition, the Duke of Portland resigned, and Perceval was called upon to form a Government, Lord Palmerston became Secretary at War. A number of writers, in recording this fact, have fallen into the mistake of confounding the Secretary *at* War with the Secretary *for* War, and thence inferring that Lord Palmerston at the early age of five-and-twenty succeeded Lord Castlereagh as War Minister while we were engaged in the gigantic contest with Napoleon. Castlereagh was Colonial Secretary, as such was Secretary for War, and in that double office was succeeded by Lord Liverpool. Palmerston succeeded Sir James Pulteney as Secretary at War, doubtless a very important post, but one which by no means implied a seat in the Cabinet.

For some 20 years, amid all sorts of changes, he held the same appointment. Lord Liverpool succeeded Perceval as Premier – still Palmerston held to the War-office. Canning reigned in the room of Lord Liverpool – still Palmerston was found at the War-office. Lord Goderich assumed the position of Canning – still Palmerston remained at the War-office. The Duke of Wellington displaced Lord Goderich – still Palmerston and the War-office seemed to be inseparable. The secret of this devotion to the one office is partly to be found in the Secretary's want of ambition, but chiefly in his perfect mastery of the business of his office at a time when it was of peculiar importance to his colleagues that it should be well represented in the House of Commons. During the first few years of his appointment he was the financer of the army, while we were engaged in the most costly war on which this country had ever entered, and when it was of the greatest moment that our resources should be turned to the best account. When the war came to an end, the Whigs, who had always been lukewarm in supporting it, joined with the Radicals in their outcry against standing armies and in their demand for retrenchment. As in our time the Manchester school of politicians required that our military establishments should be reduced to their condition in 1835, so, on the conclusion of peace, the refrain of many a debate through many a year of Parliament was that we should reduce our military establishments to their condition in 1792. It was in urging this policy of retrenchment that Joseph Hume first signalized himself; and it must be evident that, to meet the attacks of such an opponent, Lord Palmerston had a still more difficult game to play than when, backed with all the enthusiasm of the nation, he regulated the expenses of an army whose victories continually appealed to the national pride. He fought the battle of the Government with consummate skill, and by the accuracy of his information, the readiness of his wit, and the abundance of his good humour, sorely troubled honest Joseph Hume, who, compelled to take his seat silenced and discomfited, but neither convinced nor discouraged, would return to the charge on the following night, would read out sum upon sum, and would announce the 'tottle of the whole' with all the assurance of a man born with the multiplication table in his head but only to undergo a renewal of the process at the hands of his adroit adversary. If Lord Palmerston was thus successful in parrying the thrusts of his arithmetical opponents, it was in a great measure because he had a good case to defend, and because, being, as Hume termed him, 'the alpha and the omega of the War-office,' he had imbued that department with his own spirit, introducing order where before there had been only confusion, efficiency where there had been only stagnation, and economy where all had been profusion and waste. On one occasion, in reply to the attack of his indefatigable foe, he had the satisfaction of announcing a miracle which so staggered honest Joseph that he refused to believe it. He said that, by a careful supervision of past accounts and calling-up of arrears, he had for the two previous years been able to conduct the enormous business of his office without cost or charge to the country. Poor Hume, who was in those days very unpopular in the House, could not understand it, and insisted that the expenses had been increased; but it was only to see Lord Palmerston get up, and hear him, to the enjoyment of his audience, quote in his airiest style the ancient saying that there are but two things over which the immortal gods have no control – past events and arithmetic. Although Mr. Hume refused what the immortal gods are compelled to accept, the announcement of Lord Palmerston regarding the management of the War-office is by no means incredible to any one acquainted with the financial position of the various public departments during the early years of the present century. The state of our accounts was disgraceful. When Lord Henry Petty was Chancellor of the Exchequer, in 1806, he brought forward a Bill for the better auditing the public accounts, and on that occasion somewhat startled the House of Commons by the assertion that in some of the offices there had been no audit for more than 20 years, that in all the offices the accounts were more or less in arrear and apparently without check, and that, taking altogether, public money had been expended to the amount of 455,000,000*l.* which had never been accounted for, a sum at that time larger than the National Debt. The arrear and confusion, the peculation and the waste which Lord Palmerston found at the War-office were but a part of this extravagant system. He brought his clear head and his vigorous habit to bear upon it, and succeeded in repelling the attacks of Hume not less by the fact that he had of his own accord effected the most important reforms in his department than by that art of fence of which he had the most perfect mastery.

Lord Palmerston in those days, we have said, rarely opened his mouth in the House of Commons, unless to propose the Army Estimates or to answer some question relating to the army. Whatever he did in this way was always remarkable for clearness and brevity, but otherwise his colleagues obtained from him very little assistance in debate. Canning in vain expressed the wish that he could bring 'that three-decker Palmerston into action.' Palmerston held to his post, thought only of the army, and refrained from general discussion so entirely that one of the many names which in his lifetime have been given to him was 'the silent friend.' In his first 20 years of office he probably did not rise to address the House of Commons on any subject beyond his own department more than a dozen times; and, curiously enough, on those rare occasions, it was not to questions of foreign policy, in which as a War Minister it might be supposed that he would be chiefly interested, that his attention was turned. He spoke of the Catholic claims, of the law of copyright, of the game laws, of usury laws, of church extension, of slavery, of electioneering. Only once did he canvass our foreign policy, and that was in the first speech which he delivered in Parliament. The speech was a defence of the celebrated expedition to

Copenhagen – an expedition of which the only defence that could then be offered to the country was that the result had been most successful, while the information on the strength of which it had been projected could not on any account be divulged. It was a good speech, terse, clear, forcible; and we may remark, as something characteristic of Lord Palmerston's first Parliamentary effort, that it was not only devoted to a question of foreign policy, it was also devoted to a defence of official secrecy, and it was a following of Canning's lead.

This portion of Lord Palmerston's career may be dismissed with the record of two more facts. The first is that on the 8th of April, 1818, as he was mounting the stairs of the Horse Guards, a pistol was fired at him by a half-pay lieutenant named Davies. He was only slightly hurt, the ball striking him above the hip and causing nothing more serious than a contusion. It was said that had he not turned quickly round when passing the corner of the baluster the bullet must have taken a fatal direction. The would-be assassin was tried, proved to be insane, and confined for life in Bedlam, where he only recently expired. The other fact to which we have alluded is of higher biographical importance, although our information with respect to it is rather general than particular. It is that Lord Palmerston joined with Croker and Peel in producing that series of satires against the Parliamentary Opposition which was published under the title of the *New Whig Guide*. How much he contributed to this work, which, after all, perhaps, did not do the Whigs any great damage, it is difficult to say; nor are we well informed as to those squibs of his which appeared in the *John Bull*. On the whole, the satire in which the Tories indulged in those days was more remarkable for its personality and bluffness than for either wit or elegance, and very little of it deserves to live. Satire is the great weapon of Opposition, and when a party firmly seated in power resorts to it they are generally driven to extremities, and goaded into anger. In that case they are apt to be unsparing in their abuse, they are inclined to tread on the opponent whom they have managed to trip, and they hope to win by bullying what they lose in fair fight. This is the character of most of those shafts launched by the Tories against the Liberal party; and if we are forced to make such a statement with regard to men of great ability, it is but right to add that much of what is so distasteful to us now was due, not to the coarseness of the men, but to the temptations of their position; and that had they changed places with the Whigs, the latter, even with such men as Sydney Smith and Thomas Moore among their number, might have been guilty of the same excesses. The Whigs were at a discount in the eyes of the nation; they were therefore compelled to be circumspect; they found it necessary to guard against the imputation of using insolence for invective and personality for logic; they were obliged to rest their cause on its merits, and to attack the Government with genuine arguments and genuine wit; whereas the Tories, rioting in power, were less nice in their choice of missiles, and found it for their interest to show upon some occasions that the sole difference between them and their opponents was one of personalities.

The turning point in Lord Palmerston's career was now fast approaching. Hitherto he had been a member of the Government only in a subordinate capacity; he had never been a member of the Cabinet. Lord Liverpool's Ministry was in its later years divided into two sections, the principal point of difference being solicited by the claims of the Catholics to emancipation. At the head of the one section was Canning, and he had followers in Mr. Robinson (Lord Goderich), in Huskisson, in Sir John Copley, and in Lord Palmerston. At the head of the other section was the Premier himself, while among those who sided with him were Lord Eldon, the Duke of Wellington, and Mr. Peel. Canning, it is well known, was the advocate of Catholic Emancipation – therefore, up to a certain limit, of Constitutional Reform; while, on the other hand, Peel bore the standard of commercial and juridical reform. The Canning party fully accepted the Peel reforms, but the Peel party had the utmost horror of any attempt to meddle with the Constitution, and were determined to stop the way. Therefore, when Lord Liverpool was struck down by paralysis, and when Canning, as the most popular man in the Cabinet, was requested to form a Ministry, his colleagues, who were opposed to the very small measure of constitutional reform implied in Catholic Emancipation, refused to stand by him, and he was compelled to look for aid in the first place from the subordinates of the Government, among whom was Palmerston, and in the second place from the more moderate Whigs, among whom were Lord Lansdowne and W. Lamb, afterwards Lord Melbourne. It was under these difficult circumstances, which forced Canning to the dubious expedient of a coalition, that Lord Palmerston was called to the Cabinet and put upon his mettle. Unfortunately the Coalition Ministry of 1827 shared the fate of all coalitions, and after it had put Canning to death, and Goderich, his successor, to his wits' end, it went the way of all flesh. It served its purpose, however, in preparing the way for a new race of Ministers, of whom by far the most remarkable was Lord Palmerston. Of all the Tory Ministers who on this occasion coalesced with the Whigs he was attached to his party by the fewest number of ties, and was drawn to his political opponents by the greatest number. He was ripe for a quarrel with the men who had hunted his friend Canning to death, and he was ripe for a union with the men who had been his own companions at College and had sat with him at the feet of the eloquent professor of Whiggism. At first, however, his junction with the Whigs was not such as to preclude, when the Coalition fell to pieces, an acceptance of office under the Duke of Wellington, whose Government was pledged to oppose Reform. In the Duke's Cabinet the Canningites found that they occupied by no means so high a place as in the previous Government; but it was less on personal grounds than on grounds of principle that Lord Palmerston felt the necessity of seceding from it;

and it may be worth while to trace the steps by which he was led finally to change sides.

The Canningites agreed with the Whigs in their desire to emancipate Dissenters, both Catholic and Protestant; but they agreed with the Tories in their opposition to Parliamentary Reform. It was the opinion of Huskisson and Palmerston that by mitigating the more palpable abuses – by, for example, giving a member to Manchester – it might be possible to stave off more Radical measure of Reform. 'I am anxious,' said the latter, 'to express my desire that the franchise should be extended to a great town, not because I am a friend to Reform in principle, but because I am its decided enemy. I think that extending the franchise to large towns is the only mode in which the House can avoid the adoption at some time or other of a general plan of Reform.' Therefore, when East Retford and Penryn were to be disfranchised, and the Opposition proposed that the power of electing members should be transferred to Manchester and Birmingham, it so happened that by a curious shuffling of the question at issue Huskisson and Palmerston found themselves in the division lobby voting against the Government of which they were members. The real point of difference between themselves and the Government was quite unimportant, since they were all agreed on the Tory side of the House to give to a large town – Birmingham was the favourite – the franchise which had been taken from one of the corrupt boroughs, and to give that which was taken from the other to the neighbouring hundred. But in the particular division to which we refer, Mr. Huskisson and the Canningites, as fate would have it, were found voting the franchise of East Retford to Manchester, while their colleagues were voting it to the hundred in which the borough was situate. Poor Huskisson, with considerable ability and the best possible intentions, was all his life a bungler. He was always in difficulties through his clumsiness, which was physical as well as moral. He was always stumbling over chairs, tripping against ropes as he landed from steamboats, breaking his shins upon stones, until at last he was knocked down and killed outright by the first railway train. On the present occasion he sent in his resignation and didn't send it in, explained and tried to retract without retracting. 'There is no mistake, there can be no mistake, there shall be no mistake,' said the Duke, in his most oracular style. Palmerston and some others followed Huskisson, and it will be observed that they had the credit of retiring from the Ministry as the advocates of a certain measure of Reform. When afterwards Palmerston became the member of a Whig Cabinet pledged to Reform, he could say this in his defence, that he had been anxious to avoid a Radical measure by the application of partial remedies, but that the time had long passed for piecemeal legislation, and that nothing less than sweeping changes would satisfy the country.

To sit in the House of Commons no longer as a Minister was a novelty for Lord Palmerston. It was also a novelty that he now turned his attention especially to foreign politics. How came this about? The care of foreign politics devolved upon him as the ablest of Canning's disciples. Upon him the mantle of the master fell. Add to this, that among the eventualities to be foreseen was the chance of his one day taking a seat in a Whig Cabinet. Which of the great offices of State could he hold in that Cabinet with most satisfaction to himself and to his colleagues? Evidently the post in which he should find himself most enjoying the sympathy of the party would be the Foreign Secretaryship. The Whigs were always enthusiastic in praise of Canning's foreign policy, and they would back Palmerston as the successor of Canning. In quitting the Tory ranks however, he was not all at once committed to the Whigs. The Duke of Wellington tried to win him back to the Cabinet, but although he might conscientiously, and even triumphantly, have joined it when its leading members came round to his opinions on Catholic Emancipation, the position of the Government was so unsatisfactory that he deemed it better to maintain his independence. It was in this independent character that he made two very able speeches – the first (June 1, 1829) on our foreign relations generally, the second (March 10, 1830), on the affairs of Portugal in particular – which at once marked him out as the exponent of a Liberal foreign policy. Before the year in which the latter speech was delivered had expired, the Whigs, with Lord Grey at their head, found themselves unexpectedly in power, – and to whom should the seals of the Foreign-office be intrusted but to Lord Palmerston? He stepped into the post as unquestionably the right man in the right place, and during that 10 years' run of power which the Reform Bill gave to the Whigs he stood forth as the most brilliant member of the Cabinet, the man of men, the Minister of Ministers, the type and the glory of England. No English Minister ever attained to more world-wide fame than he acquired in these and subsequent years of office. All over the globe his name was invoked as the symbol of English generosity and English omnipotence. The Bedouin of the Desert recognised in Palmerston Pasha a being whom Allah had endowed with more than mortal power. The negro on the Guinea Coast knew that Palmerston was his friend, and worked day and night against slavery. Brown in the back-woods of America, or in the gardens of Siam, felt that he had an infallible safeguard if he had Palmerston's passport to show. Palmerston, it was imagined, would move the whole force of the British empire in order that this Brown – *Civis Romanus* – might not be defrauded of his Worcester sauce amid the ice of Siberia, or of his pale ale on the Mountains of the Moon. He could do anything, and he would do everything. Nothing great was accomplished without being attributed to him. He was supposed to have his pocket full of constitutions, to have a voice in half the Cabinets of Europe, to have monarchs past reckoning under his thumb. He humbled the Shah, he patronized the Sultan, he abolished the Mogul, he conquered the Brother of the Sun, he opened to the world the empire which had been walled round for centuries by impregnable barriers, he defied the Czar, and the

Emperor of the French felt safe when he received the assurances of the brilliant Foreign Secretary.

The foreign policy of Lord Palmerston has given rise to much controversy. Many a fierce debate has it kindled in both Houses of Parliament. Its author was said to be the firebrand of Europe, the destroyer of peace, a luckless lucifer match, the plague of the world, the Jonah of England, which was always in a storm when he was in the Cabinet. The question has been so stirred by political passions, and has been whipt into such a froth by the eloquence of interminable discussions, that there are very few of us indeed who know what is the real point at issue. And the perplexity is heightened by the fact that, after 20 years of opposition to his policy, Lord Aberdeen, his great rival, coalesced with him in 1853, and defended the coalition with the memorable statement 'that, though there may have been differences in the execution, according to the different hands intrusted with the direction of affairs, the principles of the foreign policy of the country have for the last 30 years been the same.' The cardinal doctrine of our foreign policy in those years was, as it is now, the principle of non-interference. There was not one of our statesmen who did not give his adhesion to this principle; and where, then, it may be asked, was the ground of dispute? In order to understand this fully from Lord Palmerston's point of view we must grasp his ruling idea in politics. If anybody will take the trouble to read his speeches from beginning to end he will be struck with the prevalence of one great idea running through them all like a thread of gold, and serving as a clue to every inconsistency. He saw in Public Opinion a force and a meaning which no statesman before him had realized, and which Peel only of his contemporaries acknowledged with anything like the same clearness. On two great occasions Peel sacrificed to Public Opinion. But all through his political life Lord Palmerston bowed to this deity, recognized its power, and used it as he could. He saw that opinion often creates a right where no right previously existed, – that it not seldom makes good evil and evil good. It has this peculiarity, too, that, exerting an enormous power it acts informally, beyond control and beyond rebuke. All the armies in the world cannot put down an opinion, which is a silent influence that remains even when the holder of the opinion is down in the dust. We may compel our neighbours to change their tactics, but we cannot compel them to alter their estimate of us; we cannot even quarrel with them for thinking as they do. We must submit to opinion, and though there are men who do not care for what other people say, yet those in whom the social instinct is strong are powerfully moved by it. The sociable nature of Lord Palmerston felt this deeply. The force of Public Opinion was a great fact, and he raised it into a great doctrine. Opinions in his view were more than opinions – they were deeds – they were title-deeds. All through his speeches we find him insisting on opinion as the source of political power, a moral influence which survives every physical force, and which, although more formidable than armies, we can bring into action without danger of hostilities. People said, – 'What is the use of his expressing sympathy for oppressed nationalities when he declines to fight for his opinions? He is a sham; he has only words to offer; he says one thing and does another; his talk is in favour of liberty, but his inaction is in favour of tyranny.' Lord Palmerston, in effect, said, – 'No, our principle is non-interference with foreign Governments; we have no right to appeal to the arbitrament of the sword; it is no business of ours to dictate to others. But we cannot help having our opinions; I express mine frankly; let it go for what it is worth; I believe that the opinion of an English Minister is worth something – is more than words, and, giving my voice to the side of freedom and justice, I leave the despots to their own intelligence, to conscience, and to God.'

And while thus, on the one hand, he was attacked by those who saw an inconsistency between his words and his work, and who wished him not only to sympathize with freedom but also to undertake a crusade in behalf of it, he was attacked, on the other hand, by those who, like Lord Aberdeen and Sir Robert Peel, agreed in the policy of non-interference, but thought that he was not consistent, that he was not honest in carrying out that policy, since he did not abstain from the expression of opinion as well as from the declaration of war. The expression of opinion, the offer of advice, they said, is in effect dictation and interference. There is no middle course. We have no right to interfere with the domestic affairs of other countries unless some clear and undeniable necessity arises from circumstances affecting the interests of our own country, and the attitude of non-interference is that of interested, it may be, but silent spectators. 'It is my firm belief,' said Peel, in the last speech which he delivered, 'that you will not advance the cause of Constitutional Government by attempting to dictate to other nations. If you do, your intentions will be mistaken, you will rouse feelings upon which you do not calculate, you will invite opposition to Government; and beware that the time does not arrive when, frightened by your own interference, you withdraw your countenance from those whom you have excited, and leave upon their minds the bitter recollection that you have betrayed them. If you succeed, I doubt whether or no the institutions that take root under your patronage will be lasting. Constitutional liberty will be best worked out by those who aspire to freedom by their efforts. You will only overload it by your help.' It was in this speech, delivered the day before he fell from his horse, that Sir Robert Peel, in spite of so emphatic a condemnation of Lord Palmerston's policy, passed upon him, or rather upon the speech in which Lord Palmerston defended his policy, the cordial eulogium – 'We are all proud of the man who delivered it.' The House of Commons, by a majority of 46, pronounced against Sir Robert Peel, and in favour of the foreign policy which he condemned.

Lord Palmerston insisted upon it that there is a middle course between interference and absolute silence. We are not stocks and stones – our non-interference is not that of lifeless blocks. Let the foreign States have the liberty of acting, but we surely have the liberty of thinking. If it is criminal to have our opinions, it is the crime of possessing intelligence; if it is criminal to express our opinions, it is the crime of possessing freedom. We cannot help having our opinions, and we should despise ourselves were we to conceal them. An English Minister has no right to dictate to foreign States, but it is very hard, indeed, if he alone is to be tongue-tied – if he alone is to see no difference between right and wrong, if he alone is to express no sympathy with suffering and no dissatisfaction with wrong. Besides which, it may well be asked whether non-interference, in the extreme sense of the word, be a possible thing. We know that silence may be eloquent, and that, as the world is constituted a sympathetic world, to hold our peace and to restrain our sympathies may, to all appearance, be the condonation of tyranny and the casting of our influence into the scale of the oppressor. In point of fact, Lord Aberdeen, who carried out the policy of non-interference in the most determined manner, obtained thereby the reputation of being partial to the continental despotisms, and of looking with an evil eye on the struggling liberties of Europe. Being one of the most liberal-minded men in England, he by reason of his liberality – we mean, by reason of his strict adherence to the principle of non-interference – gave the whole weight of his influence to the despotic Governments of the Continent, and withdrew his countenance entirely from the popular cause. In that first great speech on our foreign relations which Lord Palmerston delivered (June 11, 1829,) in Opposition, and which marked him out as the future Foreign Secretary, he laid down principles which afford the key to his subsequent conduct in office. 'There are two great parties in Europe,' he said; '*one which endeavours to bear sway in the force of public opinion*, another which endeavours to bear away by the force of physical control; and the judgment, almost unanimous, of Europe assigns the latter as the present connexion of England. The principle on which the system of this party is founded is, in my view, fundamentally erroneous. *There is in nature no moving power but mind; all else is passive and inert. In human affairs this power is opinion, in political affairs it is public opinion; and he who can grasp the power with it will subdue the fleshy arm of physical strength and compel it to work out his purpose.*' This was the weapon of weapons; Lord Palmerston had faith in its power; he believed also in the right of every man to have this weapon at his side and to use it as he could. If any statesman refused to arm himself with this power, he had but one other weapon to depend upon – he ranged himself definitely with those who had but the one resource of brute power, the one baptism of blood and fire.

These are the principles of foreign policy which were discussed through 20 long years, while Lords Aberdeen and Palmerston were rivals. If interest will lead us to side more frequently with Lord Aberdeen, every generous feeling will incline us to take the side of Lord Palmerston; although in the long run there is perhaps not much difference between these statesmen. At all events, from the general statement which we have thus given, the reader will be able to determine for himself how far the floods of eloquence that have been exhausted in endless debates on this question are important or unimportant; and we save ourselves the trouble of going over the history of Lord Palmerston's foreign policy in detail. It will be enough if we state some of the results, and foremost among these must be mentioned the establishment of Belgium as an independent kingdom with free institutions. We who now behold in Belgium a State which knows how to unite liberty with order, and which preserves its dignity in spite of limited means, are apt to forget in the midst of so much prosperity and quiet what anxiety the establishment of this little kingdom gave to the Ministers who had to conduct the negotiations, what interminable discussions in the Legislative Assemblies, what hosts of prophecies, what odious taunts, what waggonloads of despatches it called into being. Lord Palmerston came in for a good share of the abuse. His 'little experimental Monarchy' was a never-failing subject of jest. Through himself and Talleyrand the negotiations were principally conducted; and if the caricatures of 'H. B.' may be taken as a faithful index of the popular opinion, we should leap to the conclusion that our Foreign Secretary was a mere tool in the hands of his wily adversary. He was pictured as a blind man led by a French poodle to a precipice; again, as a blind man carrying a lame one who points the way; as a fly listening to the blandishments of the spider; as a cat held by a monkey, after the manner of Landseer's picture, in which the monkey makes use of the cat's-paw to get the chestnuts out of the fire. The caricatures were amazingly clever, and Talleyrand had such a reputation for cunning and success that people were ready to believe anything to his glory, and to the disadvantage of a younger adept who ventured to cope with him. If we may judge, however, by the facts, we do not see how Lord Palmerston could have acted differently; and if we may judge from results, it does not appear that France has gained anything by the transaction, while Europe has the advantage of possessing one more State which presents a favourable example of Constitutional government. It may be added that Talleyrand himself gave his opinion of Lord Palmerston in the phrase, '*C'est un homme qui n'a pas le talent du raisonnement*,' – which really means that he found his opponent proof against all his arguments and not to be deceived by all his talk.

But the establishment of what has been termed The Quadruple Alliance was still more fiercely canvassed. This was a treaty of alliance negotiated by Lord Palmerston between England, France, Spain, and Portugal; and the object of it was the defence of the existing monarchies in the Peninsula, that of Donna Isabella in Spain, and that of Donna Maria in Portugal, against all attempts to displace them. Don Carlos laid claim to the Spanish throne, and Dom Miguel to the Portuguese. Their claims were really false, but, besides the weakness of their titles, they were obnoxious to the English statesman on account of their antipathy to Constitutional government. The claims of the two Queens to their respective crowns were asserted by the Liberal Cabinets at Paris and London, and for the preservation of their rights the Quadruple Alliance was established. More than this, Lord Palmerston placed certain English forces at the disposal of the Peninsular Governments, and consequently engaged in armed as well as moral interference in the Affairs of two foreign States. Here was an opening for the enemy. Lord Aberdeen objected entirely to The Palmerstonian policy, and pertinently asked how the Foreign Secretary could work out the Quadruple Treaty, supposing – what was not at all unlikely – that Don Carlos should make his way to Madrid, should seize upon the throne, and should expel his niece from the country? What right had we to interfere in such a case? What business was it of ours to impose a Sovereign upon a foreign State? What voice had we in the election of a Peninsular potentate? The logic of debate evidently belonged to Lord Aberdeen; but Lord Palmerston had the still more convincing logic of success. He violated the principle of neutrality; but the principle could never be absolute; the violation was necessary, and it proved to be beneficial. In defending his policy long afterwards, in that great speech which he delivered in the Don Pacifico debate, Lord Palmerston observed:– 'As long as England is England, as long as the English people are animated by the feelings, and spirit, and opinions which they possess, you may knock down twenty Foreign Ministers one after another, but, depend upon it, none will keep the place who does not act upon the same principles.'

The most brilliant of Lord Palmerston's exploits, however, during the first period of his Foreign Secretaryship was an armed interference to prevent the dismemberment of the Turkish Empire. It is well known that Mehemet Ali, from being the mere vassal of the Grand Seignior, had by his great ability raised himself as Pasha of Egypt into a position of real, though not nominal independence. Not content, however with the Pashalic of Egypt, he wished to add to it Syria, and, with the assistance of his son Ibrahim, proceeded to carry out his plans. Turkey, which had from its weakness been for many years an object of anxiety to European statesmen, was apparently in a very critical position. It had practically lost Egypt, and it was now to lose another great province. The beginning of the end seemed to have come, as more than a dozen years later it seemed to have come again, when the Emperor Nicholas proposed that the European Powers should dispose of the sick man's effects. Lord Palmerston determined to avert this catastrophe if it were possible, and he made the utmost efforts to draw the great Powers into a league for the preservation of the Ottoman Empire in its integrity. Thiers at that time held the portfolio of Foreign Affairs in Paris, and, probably from some lingering sympathy with the Napoleonic designs on Egypt, kept aloof from the movement while he continued to play with it. The results of all M. Thiers's objections and doubts and despatches, however was that Mehemet Ali was gaining time; he was planting himself firmly in Syria, and the object for which the league was started was slipping from their grasp. Lord Palmerston saw through this Fabian policy, and set to work to counteract it. A treaty was suddenly signed by England, Austria, and Turkey, on the strength of which a fleet was sent to the Syrian coast with orders to co-operate in driving the Egyptian troops out of the country. The squadron was principally composed of English ships, and was under the command of Sir Robert Stopford, with Sir Charles Napier as second in command. In a very short time the intruders were driven from every position which they held in Syria, with the exception of the fortress of St. Jean d'Acre; and the defences of this town were so very strong that the Admiral declined the responsibility of an attack upon it. Sir Charles Napier's plans for its reduction, however, were forwarded to Lord Palmerston, who, at once accepting the responsibility, took the unusual course of giving orders to Sir Robert Stopford for the attack in accordance with the views of his second in command. Who does not know the rest? The fortress, which had defied Napoleon, was taken in the most brilliant style, and Mehemet Ali was finally driven from the country and compelled to give up his claims.

The rapidity with which the exploit was conceived and executed, the daring of the attempt, and the magnitude of the result gave a lustre to the reputation of Lord Palmerston, and rendered him at once the most popular statesman in England. The energy and skill which he displayed on this and other occasions were really marvellous, and we can have little idea of it unless we remember at the same time the precarious condition of the Government to which he belonged. With a straggling party, which barely contrived to present the appearance of a majority, Lord Melbourne's Administration was by its weakness forced into inaction and the most miserable expedients. The dashing Foreign Secretary, however, so far from acting as the member of a tottering Cabinet, went to work as if he had invincible majorities at his back, and could boast of being the most formidable Minister in Europe. He was, perhaps, the most active Minister then living, and his activity was felt in ways which but seldom came under the observation of the public. His exertions for the suppression of the slave trade, to give a single example, were of the most effectual, but also of the most unobtrusive, kind. He worked in that cause with the warmest zeal; others might wax cold in their endeavours, or might change their opinions, but he never altered – his interest in the negro never flagged, his desire to suppress the nefarious traffic amounted to a passion; and those who are fond of showing their own wisdom by talking of Lord Palmerston's insincerity in the cause of constitutional liberty might acquire a further insight into his character by turning their attention to his ceaseless but silent efforts in this sacred cause. To crown all, let it be added that in the midst of all these labours Lord Palmerston found time to marry. The most active Minister in the world was the lightest of heart and the freest from care. He married in 1839 the sister of Lord Melbourne, and the widow of the fifth Earl Cowper. There never was a happier union, and Lord Palmerston owed to it not only the comfort of a happy home, but also much of that public influence which comes of an extended social intercourse and which in the end raised him to the Premiership. It was delightful to see him in public with his wife, and to note the interest which the pair excited. At the opera a thousand glasses would be levelled at his box, and all his little attentions to Lady Palmerston would be studiously observed, and criticized as if he were different from other men. If he differed from other men in this respect, it was in being the most devoted and attentive of husbands and in asserting his resemblance to those conjugal models, the first Lady Palmerston and the second Lord Palmerston.

At length the Whigs were driven from office; Peel became Premier, and Lord Aberdeen ruled at the Foreign-office. Sir Robert Peel had no sooner attained the object of his ambition than Lord Palmerston made a remarkable prediction, which we must record in his own words. 'The right hon. baronet,' he observed, 'has said that he is not prepared to declare that he will never propose a change in the Corn Laws, but that he certainly shall not do so unless at the head of a united Cabinet. Why, looking at the persons who form his Administration, *he must wait something near five years before he can do it.*' Lord Palmerston waited something near five years, and, perhaps, to his own astonishment, beheld the prediction verified. It will be remembered that when Sir Robert Peel proposed to abolish the Corn Laws he soon felt the necessity of handing over that work to the Whigs and of resigning his Premiership, but that the Whigs were unable to form a Government, through the refusal of Lord Grey to sit in the same Cabinet with Lord Palmerston. The first Earl Grey was the only one of the Whigs who stubbornly refused to coalesce with the Canningites in 1827, and now his son imitated his example by refusing to become the colleague of the last of the Canningites, if the direction of the Foreign-office was to be in his hands. This was too much for Lord Palmerston, who expressed his willingness to retire from office altogether, but insisted on being placed in the Foreign-office if he was to have a place at all. In the following year Lord Grey got over his scruples, and, under Lord John Russell, a Whig Ministry was formed, with Lord Palmerston as Foreign Secretary. But, this preliminary complication seemed to indicate that even his colleagues began to doubt the policy of him who was at once the most popular and best abused statesman in England; and in the end Lord John Russell's Cabinet was overturned through its resistance to Lord Palmerston. Six years of office, however, is a long lease of power as Cabinets go; and in Lord Palmerston's department they were six very eventful years. The repeal of the Corn Laws had sweetened the political atmosphere of England, and had removed all anxiety from the administration of our domestic affairs. But, unfortunately, that which had brought peace and plenty to England – the repeal, which had done so much to alter the face of the country – had, by contrast, been the signal for revolution and disturbances of every kind throughout Europe. Lord Palmerston had scarcely received the seals of the Foreign-office, when he found himself in the midst of a Swiss difficulty. A majority of the Cantons had ordered the Jesuits to retire from Switzerland; the Catholic-Cantons resisted the order, and the Catholic States seemed not unwilling to assist the minority by force of arms. By very skilful negotiations, and by a promptitude and decision which distanced every attempt to keep up with him, Lord Palmerston settled the difficulty, holding the Catholic States back with a promise of joint intervention, until the Protestants of Switzerland had fairly put down their adversaries, scattered their forces in a single engagement, and left no question open for the interference of an European Congress. Then came the affair of the Spanish marriages, in which Louis Philippe was supposed to have outwitted the Foreign Secretary. If in this business Louis Philippe had a triumph, it was a short lived one; for in the following February the dynasty which he thought to strengthen and make sure for ever was banished from France. In that tempestuous year 1848 every one of the Continental Thrones was shaken, the oppressed nationalities of Europe arose, and there seemed to be every likelihood of universal Democracy. The attitude which our Foreign Secretary assumed in this conjuncture was that of 'a judicious bottle-holder,' to use a term which was constantly applied to him, – in plain English, was that of cautious sympathy. He was too sympathetic to please those whose watchword was the law, and who frowned on constitutional liberty, – he was too cautious, too much a friend to order, too little disposed for forcible interferences, to please those who wished for subsidies as well as opinions, soldiers as well as advice, and so falling between two stools, his conduct gave satisfaction to very few on the Continent. The Germans sang –

'Hat der Teufel einen sohn,
So ist er, sicher, Palmerston,'

because he refused to help them. So, also, he gave his support to Turkey when Austria and Russia with threats demanded the extradition of Kossuth and other refugees who had fled to the dominions of the Sultan, and he ventured to express great sympathy with the Hungarians; but, because he would not consent to go further, and wage war with Austria in behalf of the Hungarian and Italian nationalities he was denounced as a traitor. His conduct in the affair of Pacifico gave still greater offence on the Continent and not a little offence at home. He sent a powerful fleet to Athens in order to compel the Greek Government to pay up the 'little bill' of a certain Jew of the Ionian Islands, and of some others, for losses which they had sustained through outrages committed by the Greeks. There was something so amusingly disproportionate in the spectacle of the British fleet being sent to bombard Athens in order to force the payment of a disputed debt – of a British fleet dunning a Royal city for the recovery of a Jew's pots and pans and chamber crockery – that nobody can wonder at the earnestness with which the policy that led to such a result was assailed in both Houses of Parliament. The debates on Lord Palmerston's foreign policy which arose out of this incident are among the ablest and most important upon record, and, although his policy was entirely condemned in the House of Lords, it received the sanction of the House of Commons by a considerable majority. It was in reference to the vote of censure passed in the Upper House that Lord John Russell made the memorable statement – 'So long as we continue the Government of this country, I can answer for my noble friend that he will act not as Minister of Austria, or of Russia, or of France, or of any other country, but as the Minister of England,' – a statement which seemed to suggest that the question in dispute was something much deeper than that of a petty debt, and infringed on far more important rights affecting our relative position in the balance of power. The question was decided by the speech of Lord Palmerston himself, which was the ablest oration he ever made; and a very masterly, as well as very eloquent exposition of his whole foreign policy it is. The peroration is particularly effective, and when he came to that concluding passage in which he compared the British to the Roman citizen, reminded his audience of the protection which the latter could invoke in the simple phrase – '*Civis Romanus sum*' – and asked why the former should not claim a similar protection in a similar formula, the enthusiasm of his supporters rose to its height, he was tumultuously cheered, and for that night the debate closed with this miracle of a speech, which, said Sir Robert Peel, 'made us proud of the man who delivered it.'

Lord Palmerston gained the day, but the seeds of distrust were sown in the Cabinet, and soon bore their fruit. In December, 1851, he was forced to resign, because on his own authority he had pronounced in favour of Louis Napoleon when he assumed the dictatorship of France. It had been arranged that no important step in our foreign affairs should be taken without the assent of the whole Cabinet as well as of the Queen, and Lord Palmerston had – perhaps without knowing it – violated this arrangement, which was a restriction upon his powers. Lord John's Cabinet, however, did not long survive the dismissal of the Foreign Secretary, who quietly kicked it over on a Militia Bill. Lord Derby's Government succeeded, when, strangely enough, the Premier offered to Lord Palmerston that very post in the Foreign-office from which he had been dismissed by Lord John Russell, and for his conduct in which the House of Lords had, at the instigation of Lord Derby, passed a vote of censure. Lord Palmerston declined the offer, chiefly on account of the equivocal position which the Tory party maintained on the subject of Free Trade; and the consequence was that the Derby Ministry only held office until the more Liberal statesmen could compose their differences and make up an alliance. An alliance was soon formed under the auspices of Lord Aberdeen, who entered upon office at the head of the strongest Cabinet which has ever controlled the destinies of England. Lord Palmerston consented to serve in the Home-office under his old rival, while to propitiate the Whigs, Lord Clarendon was placed in the Foreign-office. The Russian War was the leading incident of this coalition. It finally broke down in consequence of those Crimean disasters which introduced an element of strife between the Conservatives and Liberal sections of the Ministry. In the meantime Lord Palmerston was plodding at the Home-office as if there were no such thing as foreign politics, and as if smoke nuisances and sewer nuisances were the only great themes of Ministerial anxiety. He dilated upon manure, and informed the world that dirt was only 'a good thing in the wrong place;' he discussed the subject of the cholera, and informed the English public that cleanliness is a more certain preventive than prayer. In this last piece of administration it was wittily said that the Foreign Secretary peeped out – he treated Providence as a foreign Power. There were not a few who in those days wished that he were indeed Foreign Secretary, – that he occupied a post which would bring more directly under his control the real work of the Aberdeen Cabinet, either the conduct of our negotiations for peace or the conduct of our military operations; and when he succeeded Lord Aberdeen as Prime Minister he more than justified the public expectation by the vigour which he threw into the war and the tact with which he concluded a peace.

It was certainly a proud day for him when, in answer to the long series of attacks upon him, he was elevated to the highest office in the State, as the only man able and ready to carry out that very policy of a war with Russia and an alliance with the French Emperor, which had been the source of misunderstandings innumerable and recriminations without end. It showed also immense courage on his part that he was willing to undertake this arduous task with the assistance of a Cabinet which Lord Brougham is said to have characterized as 'a staff of eleventh-rate men.' He was feebly supported both in administration and in debate; and the effects soon became visible in little incidents which do not come before the public, but which in the undercurrents of the Legislature tell with great force on the credit of a Government. The weakness of some of his colleagues compelled them into occasional discourtesies, which were nothing more than the natural refuge of incapacity, but which left a bad impression on political opponents and wavering allies; and the Prime Minister had so much to do to cover the deficiencies of his Cabinet that he was known to have given offence to certain of the Liberals by the assumed airiness of his manner and the levity of his answers to serious questions, while others reported to his discredit that he, the kind of heart and light of soul – he who had not one particle of bitterness in his nature – he who had been notorious for his good humour under the most trying circumstances – he who had won the hearts of the country gentlemen by refusing to side with the rest of the Liberal party in demanding from them a humiliating confession of the advantages of Free Trade, had on one occasion lost his temper and spoke angrily. The House of Commons was slipping from his grasp, and on the Chinese question he lost his majority. Nor did he recover it without an appeal to the country, from which he received the most enthusiastic support. He returned to Parliament with an enormous increase of power, and it seemed that, spite of the feebleness of his coadjutors, his term of office would be coincident with his life. Unfortunately, the same series of causes which deprived him of his majority in the previous Parliament gradually tended to deprive him of his majority in that which had been newly summoned. On a mere question of form the vote went against him. It is useless to say that there was anything really offensive to the country in his conduct to the French Emperor. The Tories voted in favour of his policy one day and against it the next. When they succeeded to power they but carried out the Palmerstonian policy. There was no real difference between Lords Derby and Palmerston on this question. A slight informality in the mode of conducting our foreign correspondence was seized as a fit opportunity for the annoyance of the Government, and the annoyance proceeded to the extent of placing Lord Palmerston in a minority. A minority in a Parliament summoned to support himself was a serious matter, and he instantly resigned.

Lord Derby, who ruled in his stead, did not long enjoy power. In about a year the whole of the Liberal party combined, agreed to sink their differences, and to cope with the Tories for victory. By a small majority they won, and Lord Palmerston was installed in office. If, however, one inquires why the Whigs again came in, it would be difficult to show any reason, save that of personal confidence in their chief. Nominally, Lord Derby's Cabinet was ousted because it was not sufficiently reforming, and because its foreign policy was not safe. But the new Government failed to carry a Reform Bill, and the new Secretary for Foreign Affairs distinctly declared after he got into office that his policy did not differ from Lord Malmesbury's. As far as we can see, the change of Government is to be explained only in one way. The Italian war broke out; there was an uneasy feeling in the country; and politicians of every shade wished to see the reins of Government in the hands of the most able, the most popular, and the most experienced statesman in the land. So Lord Palmerston was again raised to the chief office in the State. His Government carried us through the danger of the Italian war, united us through the treaty of commerce in a closer alliance with France, carried out reforms in India that led to its comparative prosperity, remodelled our bankruptcy law and our educational system, and steered through the difficulties raised by the American war and by the Polish rebellion. Amid these and other perplexities, which are so recent that they will be in everybody's recollection, it was constantly apparent that nothing but the personal popularity and adroitness of Lord Palmerston saved the Government from going to wreck in the House of Commons. While he sat on the Treasury Bench everything went on smoothly. Whenever an attack of gout compelled him for an instant to leave the guidance of the House of Commons, even to such an accomplished orator as Mr. Gladstone, defeat and disaster were the consequence. Again and again the Government were saved from ruin only by the marvellous popularity and address of its chief, who has been a Prime Minister for a greater number of years than any man in this century, with the exception of Lord Liverpool.

Nor was it merely his fame, his dexterity, and his good humour that thus succeeded; he worked hard for success even in extreme old age. As a young man he did less than his friends expected of him; as an old one he did far more. It was amazing to see how he could sit out the whole House of Commons in its longest sittings. At 3 or 4 o'clock in the morning he was the freshest and liveliest man there, ready with his joke or a clever explanation to appease the irritability of a worn assembly. Besides the toil of debate and incessant watching in the House of Commons, his office work was enormous. His despatches, all written in that fine bold hand which he desired to engraft upon the Foreign-office, are innumerable. His minutes upon every conceivable subject of interest in the last 50 years would fill many volumes, and it is to be hoped that some of them will be published. Moreover, in private, he was always ready to write for the information of his friends, and he always wrote well. We may add, in a parenthesis, that generally he wrote standing. To get through this immense amount of work he lived during the Session what most men would regard as an unwholesome life. Four days a week, when the House sat at night, he dined at 3 o'clock; on other days at half-past 8. When his dinner was late he took no lunch; when it was early he seldom took any supper. While young men went off from a debate to enjoy a comfortable meal, he sat on the Treasury Bench all night and never budged from it except to get a cup of tea in the tea-room, where he liked a gossip with whoever was there. For, with all his official labours, he kept his hold on society and enjoyed life like a youth. Lord Palmerston – and in this Lady Palmerston resembles him – was in his very nature genial and social. They loved society – not necessarily their own society, but all men and women. In the country, as in town, their hospitality was unbounded. A large family circle continually gathered about them, reinforced by whoever was remarkable for political or literary or artistic eminence, for sport, for travel, for military or naval exploits. All were welcome, and all found in both host and hostess a sympathizing audience. Yet they were never rich until latterly, and even at last their means were as nothing when compared with the opulence of many who never open their doors except to the members of a coterie. All this was the result of a prodigious vitality. Any doubts on that score might be settled by seeing Lord Palmerston at a public dinner – he sat down to it with the zest of an Eton boy; or by seeing him on horseback – when nearly an octogenarian he would ride some 15 miles to cover and think nothing of it. His mind never lost its interest in whatever was new. He was as keen as any young man about the coming 'Derby,' and would rather have won it then gained any political triumph. These things are worth mentioning, for they are elements of political success. Great as Pitt was, he was said to have lost much through deficient sociability. Lord Palmerston lost nothing in this way, but gained a great deal. He owed, indeed, so much to his social tact, that superficial observers have seen in it the whole secret of his power. There is no mistake more common than this. A dark and heavy writer is supposed to be profound; a pompous and reserved statesman gets the credit of wisdom. A clear writer is regarded as shallow, and a light-hearted statesman is said to have nothing in him. We, however, who breathe a religion the Founder of which was set at naught for His social habit, because He came eating and drinking, may learn not to think the less of a statesman because of his geniality, his ready jest, and his open house.

As this full, appreciative and observant obituary makes clear, Palmerston was a 'late flowering plant' who retained his zest both for life and for politics until his dying day. Latterly he may have been inclined to doze both in the Commons chamber and in Cabinet but in the July of last year of his long life he dissolved Parliament and increased his majority at the subsequent general election. As an Irish peer, who had succeeded to his title in 1802, Palmerston was able to sit in the House of Commons, representing a series of different constituencies for some fifty-eight years. The obituarist is well aware of Palmerston's widespread *rapport* with the general public, though he plays down his frequent disagreements over foreign policy with Queen Victoria and, above all, Prince Albert. His mistakes, notably his overt sympathy with the Confederate States during the American Civil War, are played down and there is also no hint of the womanising that inspired his nickname: 'Lord Cupid'. A twentieth-century Prime Minister, Harold Wilson, described him as 'undoubtedly the greatest "character" Downing Street has seen . . . Not all Prime Ministers enjoy the job; few enjoyed it more than Palmerston.'

MICHAEL FARADAY

Natural scientist: 'Disinterested zeal and lofty purity of life.'

25 AUGUST 1867

THE WORLD OF science lost on Sunday one of its most assiduous and enthusiastic members. The life of Michael Faraday had been spent from early manhood in the single pursuit of scientific discovery, and though his years extended to 73, he preserved to the end the freshness and vivacity of youth in the exposition of his favourite subjects, coupled with a measure of simplicity which youth never attains. His perfect mastery of the branches of physical knowledge he cultivated, and the singular absence of personal display which characterized everything he did, must have made him under any circumstances a lecturer of the highest rank, but as a man of science he was gifted with the rarest felicity of experimenting, so that the illustrations of his subjects seemed to answer with magical ease to his call. It was this peculiar combination which made his lectures attractive to crowded audiences in Albemarle-street for so many years, and which brought, Christmas after Christmas, troops of young people to attend his expositions of scientific processes and scientific discovery with as much zest as is usually displayed in following lighter amusements.

Faraday was born in the neighbourhood of London in the year 1794. He was one of those men who have become distinguished in spite of every disadvantage of origin and of early education, and if the contrast between the circumstances of his birth and of his later worldly distinction be not so dazzling as is sometimes seen in other walks of life, it is also true that his career was free from the vulgar ambition and uneasy strife after place and power which not uncommonly detract from the glory of the highest honours. His father was a smith, and he himself, after a very imperfect elementary education, was apprenticed to a bookbinder named Riebau, in Blandford-street. He was, however, already inspired with the love of natural science. His leisure was spent in the conduct of such chymical experiments as were within his means, and he ventured on the construction of an electrifying machine, thus foreshowing the particular sphere of his greatest future discoveries. He was eager to quit trade for the humblest position as a student of physical science, and his tastes becoming known to a gentleman who lived in his master's neighbourhood, he obtained for him admission to the chymical lectures which Sir Humphry Davy, then newly knighted and in the plenitude of his powers, was delivering at the Royal Institution. This was in 1812. Faraday not only attended the lectures, but took

copious notes of them, which he carefully re-wrote and boldly sent to Sir Humphry, begging his assistance in his desire 'to escape from trade and to enter into the service of science.' The trust in Davy's kindliness which prompted the appeal was not misplaced. Sir Humphry warmly praised the powers shown in the notes of his lectures, and hoped he might be able to meet the writer's wishes. Early in 1813 the opportunity came. The post of assistant in the Laboratory in Albemarle-street became vacant, and Sir Humphry offered it to Faraday, who accepted it with a pleasure which can be easily imagined, and thus commenced in March, 1813, the connexion between Faraday and the Royal Institution which only terminated with his life. Faraday became very soon firmly attached to Davy. The only instance of a suspension – for it was a suspension and not a breach – of his connexion with the Royal Institution occurred from October, 1813, to April, 1815, during which time he accompanied Sir Humphry as his scientific assistant and secretary in his travels on the Continent. His life after his return was devoted uninterruptedly to his special studies. In 1821, while assisting Davy in pursuing the investigation of the relations between electricity and magnetism, first started by Oersted, he made the brilliant discovery of the convertible rotation of a magnetic pole and an electric current, which was the prelude to his wonderful series of experimental researches in electricity. These investigations procured him the honour of being elected Corresponding Member of the Academy of Sciences in 1823, and Fellow of the Royal Society in 1825. In 1827 he published his first work, a volume on *Chymical Manipulation*; and in 1829 he was appointed Chymical Lecturer at the Royal Military Academy at Woolwich, a post he held, in conjunction with his duties at the Royal Institution, for many years. In 1831 his first paper appeared in the *Philosophical Transactions* on the subject of electricity, describing his experimental studies of the science, and from that time for many years the *Transactions* annually contained papers by Faraday giving the method and results of his investigations. These papers, with some others contributed to scientific journals on the same subject, were subsequently collected at different intervals in three volumes under the title of *Experimental Researches in Electricity*. The first volume appeared in 1839, and contained the contributions to the *Philosophical Transactions* up to that date. The second volume was published in 1844, and the third in 1855. It is not too much to say that by the experiments thus described Faraday formed the science of electricity. He established the identity of the forces manifested in the phenomena known as electrical, galvanic, and magnetic; he ascertained with exactness the laws of its action; he determined its correlation with the other primal forces of the natural world. While he was still pursuing the brilliant career of investigation which thus proved so successful, the chair of Chymistry was founded at the Royal Institution in 1833, and Faraday was naturally appointed the first Professor. In 1835 he was recommended by Lord Melbourne for a pension of 300*l.* a year, in recognition of his great distinction as a discoverer. From that time his career has been one of increasing honour. Oxford conferred on him an honorary degree upon the first occasion of the meeting of the British Association at the University. He was raised from the position of Corresponding Member to be one of the eight foreign Associates of the Academy of Sciences. He was an officer of the Legion of Honour, and Prussia and Italy decorated him with the crosses of different Orders. The Royal Society conferred on him its own medal and the Romford medal. In 1858 the Queen most graciously allotted to him a residence at Hampton Court, between which and Albemarle-street he spent the last years of his life, and where he peaceably died on Sunday. The belief in the disinterested zeal and lofty purity of life of the students of philosophy, which was one motive for Faraday's petition when a lad to Davy to enable him to become a servant in the humblest walks of science rather than to spend his days in the pursuit of trade, was redeemed by Faraday's whole life. No man was ever more entirely unselfish, or more entirely beloved. Modest, truthful, candid, he had the true spirit of a philosopher and of a Christian, for it may be said of him, in the words of the father of English poetry, 'Gladly would he learn, and gladly teach.'

The cause of science would meet with fewer enemies, its discoveries would command a more ready assent, were all its votaries imbued with the humility of Michael Faraday.

Faraday, born the son of an artisan near the Elephant and Castle in London, was yet another of the 'Self Helpers' so admired by Victorian social moralists. He was not only a first-rate scientist in his own right but also a pioneer populariser of science during a key period of progress in the subject. Faraday was a lucid and much appreciated lecturer at the Royal Insitution in Albemarle Street where, from January to April, weekly lectures and laboratory demonstrations were open to subscribers. He died in his grace and favour residence at Hampton Court. Being a devout member of the Sandemanian sect (founded in Scotland by John Glas) he was interred at Highgate Cemetery rather than being offered a tomb at Westminster Abbey.

CHARLES DICKENS

Novelist: 'There was always a lesson beneath his mirth.'

9 JUNE 1870

WE FEEL SURE that a thrill of sorrow as well as of surprise will be felt by our readers when they hear of the sudden death of Mr. Charles Dickens. On Wednesday evening he was seized with a fit, at his residence, Gad's Hill-place, Higham, near Rochester, between 6 and 7 o'clock, while at dinner. Mr. Stephen Steele, a surgeon at Strood, was sent for, and promptly arrived. He found Mr. Dickens in a very dangerous state, and remained with him for some hours. A physician was summoned from London yesterday morning, and Mr. Steele was also in attendance. Unfortunately, there was no improvement in the patient. In the afternoon Mr. Steele was again summoned from Strood. The reports in the after part of the day were discouraging, and shortly after 6 o'clock the great novelist expired.

There is no one, we are sure, of the men of the present day whose name will live longer in the memories of English readers, or will be more thoroughly identified with the English language, than the inimitable author of *Pickwick*. But the story of his life is soon told. The son of Mr. John Dickens, who held at one time a position in the Navy Pay Department, Charles Dickens was born at Portsmouth in the month of February, 1812. The duties of his father's office obliged him frequently to change his residence, and much of the future novelist's infancy was spent at Plymouth, Sheerness, Chatham, and other seaport towns. The European war, however, came to an end before he had completed his fourth year, and his father, finding his 'occupation gone,' retired on a pension and came to London, where he obtained employment as a Parliamentary reporter for one of the daily papers. It was at first intended that young Charles should be sent to an attorney's office; but he had literary tastes, and eventually was permitted by his father to exchange the law for a post as one of the reporters on the staff of the *True Sun*, from which he subsequently transferred his services to the *Morning Chronicle* then under the late Mr. John Black, who accepted and inserted in the evening edition of his journal the first fruits of the pen of Charles Dickens – those 'Sketches of English Life and Character' which were afterwards reprinted and published in a collective form under the title of *Sketches by Boz* in 1836, and the following year.

These *Sketches* at once attracted notice, and the public looked with something more than curiosity for the time when the successful author should throw off his mask and proclaim himself to the world. To adopt the phrase of an epigram which appeared in the *Carthusian*,

'Who the Dickens "Boz" could be
'Puzzled many a learned elf;
'But time unveiled the mystery,
'And "Boz" appeared as Dickens' self.'

Almost simultaneously with these *Sketches* appeared a comic opera from his pen, entitled *The Village Coquettes*.

The graphic power of describing the ordinary scenes of common life, more especially in their more ludicrous aspects, did not escape the notice of Messrs. Chapman and Hall, then of the Strand, but now of Piccadilly, and they accordingly requested 'Boz' to write for them a serial story in monthly parts; the result was the publication of the *Posthumous Papers of the Pickwick Club*. It is said that a portion of the rough outline of the work was the result of a suggestion thrown out by Mr. Hall, one of the firm above-mentioned; but be that as it may, the subject was treated by 'Boz' in a manner at once so easy, so graphic, and so natural, and yet with such a flow of genuine humour, that the author found himself raised almost at a single step to the highest pinnacle of literary fame. Illustrated at first by poor Seymour, and afterwards by Mr. Hablot K. Brown ('Phiz'), the *Pickwick Papers* found an enormous sale from their first appearance, and Mr. Charles Dickens presented himself to the world as their author in 1838.

The great success of *Pickwick* naturally led to offers being made to Mr. Dickens by the London publishers; but the author wisely consulted his own reputation, and confined himself to the production of *Nicholas Nickleby* in a similar style and form. The work was written to expose in detail the cruelties which were practised upon orphans and other neglected children at small and cheap schools, where the sum charged for the board of hungry and growing lads, with everything included, ranges from 16*l.* to 20*l.* a year. Mr. Dickens tells us, in the preface to this book, as it stands republished in the collective edition of his works, that it was the result of a personal visit of inspection paid by himself to some nameless 'Dotheboys'-hall' amid the wolds of Yorkshire; and the reader who has carefully studied it will with difficulty be persuaded that Mr. Squeers and Mr. John Browdie are not taken from living examples. The work was published in 1839.

About the same time he commenced in the pages of *Bentley's Miscellany*, of which he was the first editor, a tale of a very different cast. *Oliver Twist* lets the reader into the secrets of life as it was, and, perhaps, still is, to be found too often in workhouses and in the 'slums' of London. When finished it was republished as a novel in three volumes, and in that shape too enjoyed an extensive sale. The following year Mr.

Dickens undertook the production of a collection of stories in weekly numbers. The series was entitled *Master Humphrey's Clock*, and it contained, among other tales, those since republished under the names of *The Old Curiosity Shop* – famous for its touching episode of 'Little Nell,' – and of *Barnaby Rudge*, which carries the reader back to the days of the Gordon Riots.

The pen of Mr. Charles Dickens was henceforth almost incessantly at work. About the time of the publication of *Master Humphrey's Clock* appeared his *Memoirs of Joseph Grimaldi*, the celebrated Clown, almost his only production which deals with the plain prose of facts, and with everyday life divested of all imagination. Though much interest attaches to the work, we shall not be suspected of any intention of depreciating the author's reputation when we say that his imaginative powers rank far higher than his skill as a biographer. In fact, while *Pickwick* and *Nickleby* live, *Grimaldi* is forgotten. After completing *Master Humphrey's Clock* Mr. Dickens visited America, where he was received with extraordinary honours. On his return, in 1842, he published the materials which he had collected in the United States under the title '*American Notes for General Circulation.*' Many of its statements, however, were controverted by American pens in a book entitled *Change for American Notes.*

In 1844 he published *Martin Chuzzlewit* in numbers, like *Pickwick* and *Nicholas Nickleby*, and in the summer of the same year visited Italy and Rome. An account of much that he saw and heard in this tour he gave afterwards to the world in the columns of the *Daily News*, of which he became the first editor. Its first number appeared on January 1, 1846; but after a few months Mr. Dickens withdrew from the editorship, and returned to his former line of humorous serial publications, varying, however, their monthly appearances with occasional stories of a more strictly imaginative cast, called 'Christmas Books.' Of these the first, *A Christmas Carol*, was published so far back as 1843; the second, the *Chimes*, appeared at Christmas, 1845; the third, the *Cricket on the Hearth*, followed in 1846; the fourth, the *Battle of Life* in 1847; and the fifth, the *Haunted Man and the Ghost's Bargain*, in 1848.

Besides these Mr. Dickens has published *Dealings with the Firm of Dombey and Son*, the *History of David Copperfield*, *Bleak House*, *Little Dorrit*, *A Tale of Two Cities*, *Our Mutual Friend*, the *Uncommercial Traveller*, *Great Expectations*, and last of all the *Mystery of Edwin Drood*, of which only three numbers have appeared. In 1850 Mr. Dickens projected a cheap weekly periodical which he called *Household Words*, and which was published by Messrs. Bradbury and Evans; but, difficulties having arisen between author and publisher, it was discontinued in 1859, and Mr. Dickens commenced in its stead its successor, *All the Year Round*, which he continued to conduct to the last.

Mr. Dickens was one of the founders of the Guild of Literature, and was an ardent advocate of reforms in the administration of the Literary Fund. He was also an accomplished amateur performer, and often took part in private theatricals for charitable objects. Of late years he had frequently appeared before the public as a 'reader' of the most popular portions of his own works, of which he showed himself to be a most vivid and dramatic interpreter. He retired from this work only in March last, when his reputation stood at its highest. His renderings of his best creations, both humorous and pathetic, of his most stirring scenes and warmest pictures of life, will not readily be forgotten. Men and women, persons and places, we knew all before in the brilliant pages of his novels; but the characters lived with a new life, and the scenes took the shape of reality in the readings of the master. America had an opportunity of appreciating his powers in this direction on the second visit he paid to that country in 1868. That is all over now; but Mr. Dickens, in bidding his last audience farewell, consoled them with the promise that his retirement would be devoted all the more to his original and higher art. His words have scarcely had time to allow of their fulfilment in the way and in the degree in which, doubtless, he hoped to be able to fulfil them. It may be well here to place on record his parting speech on the occasion of his last reading at St. James's-hall:–

> 'Ladies and Gentlemen, – It would be worse than idle, it would he hypocritical and unfeeling, if I were to disguise that I close this episode in my life with feelings of very considerable pain. For some 15 years, in this hall and in many kindred places, I have had the honour of presenting my own cherished ideas before you for your recognition; and, in closely observing your reception of them, have enjoyed an amount of artistic delight and enjoyment which, perhaps, it is given to few men to know. In this task, and in every other I have ever undertaken as a faithful servant of the public, always imbued with a sense of duty to them, and always striving to do his best, I have been uniformly cheered by the readiest response, the most generous sympathy, and the most stimulating support. Nevertheless, I have thought it well at the full floodtide of your favour to retire upon those older associations between us which date from much further back than these, and henceforth to devote myself exclusively to the art that first brought us together. Ladies and gentlemen, in but two short weeks from this time I hope that you may enter, in your own homes, on a new series of readings at which my assistance will be indispensable, but from these garish lights I vanish now for evermore, with one heartfelt, grateful, respectful, and affectionate farewell.'

While *Pickwick* charms us with its broad humour, it is in *Nicholas Nickleby* and *Oliver Twist* that the power of Charles Dickens's pathos shows itself. In those two works he evinced a sympathy for the poor, the suffering, and the oppressed which took all hearts by storm. This power of sympathy it was, no doubt, which has made his name a household word in English homes. How many a phase of cruelty and wrong his pen exposed, and how often he stirred others to try at least to lessen the amount of evil and of suffering which must be ever abroad in the world, will never be fully known. There was always a lesson beneath his mirth.

It only remains for us to add that he married in 1838 a daughter of the late Mr. George Hogarth, a musical writer of some eminence in his day, and a man of high literary attainments – who was formerly the friend and law agent of Sir Walter Scott, and well known in private life to Jeffrey Cockburn, and the other literary celebrities who adorned the society of Edinburgh some 40 or 50 years ago.

> The relatively scant information about Dickens's early life which was available to the general public during the novelist's lifetime seems to have been scrupulously edited by Dickens himself. This obituary therefore makes no mention of his father's shameful financial embarrassments and confinement in the Marshalsea Prison, of Dickens's fragmented education and, above all, of his acute misery when he was employed as a twelve-year-old drudge at Warren's Blacking. These facts were not exposed until Dickens's friend John Forster published them in the first volume of his *Life of Charles Dickens* in 1872. Detailed revelations about the break-up of the novelist's marriage to Catherine Hogarth and his subsequent intense relationship with the young actress Ellen Ternan were not made until the second third of the twentieth century. Dickens had given his last Public Reading at St. James's Hall in Piccadilly on 15 March 1870 to the largest audience ever assembled there. Hundreds more had been turned away at the doors. The hall was demolished in 1905.

GENERAL ROBERT E. LEE

American soldier: 'one of the noblest soldiers who have ever drawn a sword in a cause which they believed just.'

12 OCTOBER 1870

EVEN AMID THE turmoil of the great European struggle the intelligence from America announcing that General Robert E. Lee is dead will be received with deep sorrow by many in this country, as well as by his followers and fellow-soldiers in America. It is but a few years since Robert Lee ranked among the great men of the present time. He was the able soldier of the Southern Confederacy, the bulwark of her northern frontier, the obstacle to the advance of the Federal armies and the leader who twice threatened by the capture of Washington to turn the tide of success, and to accomplish a revolution which would have changed the destiny of the United States. Six years passed by, and then we heard that he was dying at an obscure town in Virginia, where, since the collapse of the Confederacy, he had been acting as a schoolmaster. When at the head of the last 8,000 of his valiant army – the remnants which battle, sickness, and famine had left him – he delivered up his sword to General Grant at Appomattox Court House, his public career ended; he passed away from men's thoughts; and few in Europe cared to inquire the fate of the General whose exploits had aroused the wonder of neutrals and belligerents, and whose noble character had excited the admiration of even the most bitter of his political enemies. If, however, success is not always to be accounted as the sole foundation of renown, General Lee's life and career deserve to be held in reverence by all who admire the talents of a General and the noblest qualities of a soldier. His family were well known in Virginia. Descended from the Cavaliers who first colonized that State, they had produced more than one man who fought with distinction for their country. They were allied by marriage to Washington, and previous to the recent war were possessed of much wealth; General, then Colonel, Robert Lee residing, when not employed with his regiment, at Arlington Heights, one of the most beautiful places in the neighbourhood of Washington. When the civil war first broke out he was a colonel in the United States' army, who had served with distinction in Mexico, and was recounted among the best of the American officers. To him, as to others, the difficult choice presented itself whether to take the side of his State, which had joined in the secession of the South, or to support the Central Government. It is said that Lee debated the matter with General Scott, then commander-in-chief, that both agreed that their first duty lay with their State, but that the former only put in practice what each held in theory. It was not until the second year of the war that Lee came prominently forward, when, at the indecisive battle of Fairoaks, in front of Richmond, General Johnston having been wounded, he took command of the army; and subsequently drove M'Clellau, with great loss, to the banks of the James river. From that time he became the recognized leader of the Confederate army of Virginia. He repulsed wave after wave of invasion, army after army being hurled against him only to be thrown back beaten and in disorder. The Government at Washington were kept in constant alarm by the near vicinity of his troops, and witnessed more than once the entry into their entrenchments of a defeated and disorganised rabble which a few days previous had left there a confident host. Twice he entered the Northern States at the head of a successful army, and twice in decisive battles alone preserved from destruction the Federal Government and turned the fortune of the war. He impressed his character on those who acted under him. Ambition for him had no charms; duty alone was his guide. His simplicity of life checked luxury and display among his officers, while his disregard of hardships silenced the murmurs of his harassed soldiery. By the troops he was loved as a father as well as admired as a general; and his deeply religious character impressed itself on all who were brought in contact with him and made itself felt through the ranks of the Virginian army. It is said that during four years of war he never slept in a house, but in winter and summer shared the hardships of his soldiers. Such was the man who in mature age, at a period of life when few generals have acquired renown, fought against overwhelming odds for the cause which he believed just. He saw many of his bravest generals and dearest friends fall around him, but, although constantly exposed to fire, escaped without a wound. The battles which prolonged and finally decided the issue of the contest are now little more than names. Antietam, Fredericksburg, Chancellorsville and Gettysburg are forgotten in Europe by all excepting those who study recent wars as lessons for the future and would collect from the deeds of other armies experience which they may apply to their own. To them the boldness of Lee's tactics at Chancellorsville will ever be a subject of admiration; while even those who least sympathize with his cause will feel for the General who saw the repulse of Longstreet's charge at Gettysburg, and beheld the failure of an attempt to convert a defensive war into one of attack, together with the consequent abandonment of the bold stroke which he had hoped would terminate the contest. Quietly he rallied the broken troops; taking all the blame on himself; he encouraged the officers dispirited by the reverse, and in person formed up the scattered detachments. Again, when fortune had turned against the Confederacy, when overwhelming forces from all sides pressed back her defenders, Lee for a year held his ground with a constantly diminishing army, fighting battle after battle in the forests and swamps around Richmond. No reverses seemed to dispirit him, no misfortune appeared to ruffle his calm, brave temperament. Only at last, when the saw the remnants of his noble army about to be ridden down by Sheridan's cavalry, when 8,000 men, half-starved and broken with fatigue, were surrounded by the vast net which Grant and Sherman had spread around them, did he yield; his fortitude for the moment gave way; he took a last farewell of his soldiers and, giving himself up as a prisoner, retired a ruined man into private life, gaining his bread by the hard and uncongenial work of governing Lexington College. When political animosity has calmed down and when Americans can look back on those years of war with feelings unbiased by party strife, then will General Lee's character be appreciated by all his countrymen as it is now by a part, and his name will be honoured as that of one of the noblest soldiers who have ever drawn a sword in a cause which they believed just, and at the sacrifice of all personal considerations have fought manfully a losing battle. Even amid the excitement of the terrible war now raging in Europe, some may still care to carry their thoughts back to the career of the great and good man who now lies dead in Virginia, and to turn a retrospective glance over the scenes in which a short time ago he bore so prominent a part. – *Pall Mall Gazette*

In a letter to *The Times*, Lieutenant-Colonel Arthur Fremantle of the Coldstream Guards suggested that Lee was 'the greatest soldier that America has produced'. The present obituary, printed after Fremantle's letter on 15 October 1870, three days after Lee's death, appeared as the Franco-Prussian War was drawing to a bloody close and as the Communards were defeated in Paris. This generous obituary offers a balanced appreciation of Lee, who, after the defeat of the Army of Northern Virginia, had retired, not to a schoolmastership, but to the ill-paid Presidency of Washington College (now Washington and Lee University) at Lexington, Virginia. Honourable to the end, he had earlier refused an offer of $10,000 from a Virginia insurance company that sought to use his name. Lee had petitioned the government in Washington for the restoration of his US citizenship. His application, which had apparently been mislaid, was only granted in the 1970s.

CHARLES BABBAGE, F. R. S.

Mathematician: 'The Father of the Computer.'

18 OCTOBER 1871

OUR OBITUARY COLUMN on Saturday contained the name of one of the most active and original of original thinkers, and whose name has been known through the length and breadth of the kingdom for nearly half a century as a practical mathematician – we mean Mr. Charles Babbage. He died at his residence in Dorset-street, Marylebone, at the close of last week, at an age, spite of organ-grinding persecutors, little short of 80 years.

Little is known of Mr. Babbage's parentage and early youth, except that he was born on the 26th of December, 1792, and was educated privately. During the whole of his long life, even when he had won for himself fame and reputation, he was always extremely reticent on that subject, and, in reply to questioners he would uniformly express an opinion that the only biography of living personages was to be found, or, at all events, ought to be found, in the list of their published works. As this list, in Mr. Babbage's own case, extended to upwards of 80 productions, there ought to be no dearth of materials for the biographer; but these materials, after all, as a matter of fact, are scanty, in spite of an autobiographical work which he gave to the world about seven years ago, entitled *Passages in the Life of a Philosopher.*

At the usual age Mr. Babbage was entered at the University of Cambridge, and his name appears in the list of those who took their Bachelor's degree from Peterhouse in the year 1814. It does not, however, figure in the Mathematical Tripos, he preferring to be Captain of the Poll to any honours but the Senior Wranglership of which he believed Herschel to be sure. While, however, at Cambridge he was distinguished by his efforts, in conjunction with the late Sir John Herschel and Dean Peacock, to introduce in that University, and thereby among the scientific men of the country in general, a knowledge of the refined analytic methods of mathematical reasoning which had so long prevailed over the Continent, whereas we in our insular position, for the most part, were content with what has been styled 'the cramped domain of the ancient synthesis.' The youthful triumvirate, it must be owned, made a successful inroad on the prejudices and predilections which had prevailed up to that time. Keeping this object steadily in view, in the first place they translated and edited the smaller treatise on the Calculus by Lacroix, with notes of their own, and an Appendix (mainly, if not wholly, from the pen of Sir John Herschel) upon Finite Differences. They next published a solution of exercises on all parts of the Infinitesimal Calculus, a volume which is still of great service to the mathematical student, in spite of more recent works with a similar aim. To this publication Mr. Babbage contributed an independent essay on a subject at that time quite new, the solution of Functional Equations.

By steps and stages, of which the records at our command are scanty, these pursuits gradually led Mr. Babbage on to that practical application of mathematical studies which may justly be considered to be his crowning scientific effort – we mean, of course, the invention and partial construction of the famous calculating engine or machine which the world has associated with his name. As a writer in the *Dictionary of Universal Biography* remarks:–

> 'The possibility of constructing a piece of mechanism capable of performing certain operations on numbers is by no means new; it was thought of by Pascal and geometers, and more recently it has been reduced to practice by M. Thomas, of Colmar, in France, and by the Messrs Schütz, of Sweden; but never before or since has any scheme so gigantic as that of Mr. Babbage been anywhere imagined.'

His achievements here were twofold; he constructed what he called a Difference Engine, and he planned and demonstrated the practicability of an Analytical Engine also. It is difficult, perhaps, to make the nature of such abstruse inventions at all clear to the popular and untechnical reader, since Dr. Larduer, no unskilful hand at mechanical description, filled no less than twenty-five pages of the *Edinburgh Review* with but a partial account of its action, confessing that there were many features which it was hopeless to describe effectively without the aid of a mass of diagrams. All that can here be said of the machine is that the process of addition automatically performed is at the root of it. In nearly all tables of numbers there will be a law of order in the differences between each number and the next. For instance, in a column of square numbers – say, 9, 16, 25, 36, 49, 64, 81, &c.– the successive differences will be 7, 9, 11, 13, 15, 17, &c. These are differences of the first order. If, then, the process of differencing be repeated with those, we arrive at a remarkably simple series of numbers – to wit 2, 2, 2, 2, &c. And into some such simple series most tables resolve themselves when they are analyzed into orders of differences; an element – an atom, so to speak – is arrived at, from which by constant addition the numbers in the table may be formed. It was the function of Mr. Babbage's machine to perform this addition of differences by combinations of wheels acting upon each other in an order determined by a preliminary adjustment. This working by differences gave it the name of the 'Difference Engine.' It has been repeatedly stated that the construction of this machine was suddenly suspended, and that no reason was ever assigned for its suspension. But the writer in the *Dictionary* already quoted above thus solves the mystery in which the matter has hitherto been shrouded:–

> 'In spite of the favourable report of a Commission appointed to inquire into the matter, the Government were led by two circumstances to hesitate about proceeding further. Firstly, Mr. Clements the engineer or machinist employed as his *collaborateur*, suddenly withdrew all his skilled workmen from the work, and what was worse, removed all the valuable tools which had been employed upon it.'

– an act which is justified as strictly legal by Mr. Weld in his *History of the Royal Society*, though a plain common-sense man of the world may reasonably doubt its equity, as the tools themselves had been made at the joint expense of Mr. Babbage and the Treasury. 'Secondly,' says the same authority, 'the idea of the Analytical Engine – one that absorbed and contained as a small part of itself the Difference Engine – arose before Mr. Babbage.' Of course he could not help the fact that 'Alps upon Alps should arise' in such matters and that, when one great victory was achieved, another and still greater battle remained to be faced and fought. But sooner did Mr. Babbage, like an honest man, communicate the fact to the Government that the then Ministers, with Sir Robert Peel and Mr. H. Goulburn at the head of the Treasury, took alarm, and, scared at the prospect of untold expenses before then, resolved to abandon the enterprise. Mr. Babbage, apart from all help from the public purse, had spent upon his machine, as a pet hobby, no small part of his private fortune – a sum which has been variously estimated between 6,000*l.* and 17,000*l.* And so, having resolved on not going further into the matter, they offered Mr. Babbage, by way of compensation, that the Difference Engine as constructed should remain as his own property – an offer which the inventor very naturally declined to accept. The engine, together with the drawings of the machinery constructed and not constructed, and of many other contrivances connected with it, extending, it is said, to some 400 or 500 drawings and plans, was presented in 1843 to King's College, London, where we believe they are to be seen in the museum, bearing their silent witness to great hopes dashed down to the ground, or, at all events, to the indefinite postponement of their realization.

In speaking at this length of Mr. Babbage's celebrated machine, we have a little anticipated the order of events, and must return to our record of the leading facts of his life. In the year 1828 he was nominated to the Lucasian Professorship of Mathematics in his old University, occupying in that capacity a chair which had once been held by no less a man than Sir Isaac Newton. This chair he held during eleven years. It was while holding this Professorship, namely, at the general election of November, 1832 – which followed on the passing of the first Reform Bill –

that he was put forward as a candidate for the representation of the newly-formed borough of Finsbury, standing in the advanced Liberal interest, as a supporter not only of parliamentary, financial, and fiscal reform, but also of 'the Ballot, triennial Parliaments, and the abolition of all sinecure posts and offices.' But the electors did not care to choose a philosopher; so he was unsuccessful, and we believe never again wooed the suffrages of either that or any other constituency.

We have mentioned the fact that Mr. Babbage was the author of published works to the extent of some 80 volumes. A full list of these, however, would not interest or edify the general reader, and those who wish to study their names can see them recorded at full length in the new library catalogue of the British Museum. Further information respecting them will be found in the 12th chapter of Mr. Weld's *History of the Royal Society*, which we have already quoted. One or two of them, however, we should specify. The best known of them all, perhaps is his *Ninth Bridgewater Treatise*, a work designed by him at once to refute the opinion supposed to be implied and encouraged in the first volume of that learned series, that an ardent devotion to mathematical studies is unfavourable to a real religious faith, and also to give specimens of the defensive aid which the evidences of Christianity may receive from the science of numbers, if studied in a proper spirit.

Another of his works which has found a celebrity of its own is a volume called *The Decline of Science*, both the title and the contents of which give reason to believe that its author looked somewhat despondingly on the scientific attainments of the present age. The same opinion was still further worked out by Mr. Babbage in a book on the first Great Exhibition, which he published just 20 years ago. Another of his works which deserve mention here is one on *The Economy of Manufactures*, which was one result of a tour of inspection which he made through England and upon the Continent in search of mechanical principles for the formation of Logarithmic Tables.

It is about 40 years since Mr. Babbage produced his Tables of Logarithms from 1 to 108,000, a work upon which he bestowed a vast amount of labour, and in the publication of which he paid great attention to the convenience of calculators, whose eyes, he well knew, must dwell for many hours at a time upon their pages. He was rewarded by the full appreciation of his work by the computers not only of his own, but of foreign countries; for in several of those countries editions from the stereotyped plates of the tables were published, with translations of the preface. Notwithstanding the numerous logarithmic tables which have since appeared, those of Mr. Babbage are still held in high esteem by all upon whom the laborious calculations of astronomy and mathematical science devolve.

Mr. Babbage was one of the oldest members of the Royal Society at the time of his death; he was also more than fifty years ago one of the founders of the Astronomical Society, and he and Sir John Herschel were the last survivors of that body.

He was also an active and zealous member of many of the leading learned societies of London and Edinburgh, and in former years at least an extensive contributor to their published *Transactions*. His last important publication was the amusing and only too characteristic autobiographical work to which we have already referred as *Passages in the Life of a Philosopher*.

> Shortly after this obituary appeared on 23 October 1871 Babbage's nephew wrote to *The Times* to point out that the mathematician had been born in 1791 not 1792. His father, a banker who owned an estate at Bitton in south Devon, was at his death resident at 44 Crosby Row in the Walworth Road in south London. Babbage had been baptised at St Mary's, Walworth, on 6 January 1792. He was educated at a succession of schools in Devon and London, matriculating at Trinity College, Cambridge, in October 1810 and transfering to Peterhouse in 1814. Without taking any examinations, he was granted an honorary MA in 1814. In his lifetime Babbage's vastly innovative calculating machines seem to have been considered enigmatic. His first Difference Engine weighed an ungainly 15 tonnes. His second was not fully constructed until 1989–1991 when the Science Museum proved the accuracy of its calculations. Had it been realised in the nineteenth century his Analytical Engine, using punch cards, would have been the first programmable computer. Babbage was instrumental in establishing the standard gauge used on British railways and is credited with the invention of the 'pilot' or cow-catcher affixed to railway locomotives. A crater on the moon was named after him.

EMPEROR NAPOLEON III

Emperor of the French: 'History will find much to reproach him with, but it is certain his contemporaries have been very unjust to him.'

9 JANUARY 1873

It is with regret we announce the death of the Emperor Napoleon yesterday. Although the fate of the illustrious patient's general health and the critical nature of the operation performed on him naturally excited uneasiness as to the ultimate result, yet there was little apprehension of immediate danger. Indeed he had slept so soundly through the night and awakened comparatively so strong in the early morning that it had been decided to undertake a further operation at noon. He sank, however, suddenly, and in a very short time all was over.

In the singular career of the late Emperor, as in that of most remarkable men, there are breaks which divide it into distinct periods, without injuring the general dramatic unity. He was born seemingly to greatness. Apparently it threatened to elude him. He struggled after it in the face of adverse circumstances from the time he attained to years of discretion. He partly achieved it, partly had it thrust upon him, and after a success which should have satisfied his wildest dreams, he ended his active life an exile, as he had begun it. It would not be enough to say that Charles Louis Napoleon Bonaparte was born in the purple. His cradle was at the Tuileries Palace, in the closest vicinity to the Throne. He was the youngest son of Louis, King of Holland, and of Hortense Beauharnais, the Empress Josephine's daughter. His father was Napoleon's third brother; but the descendants of Joseph were excluded from the succession by their sex, and those of Lucien by the disfavour under which that stern Republican had fallen; so that, at the date of Louis Napoleon's birth, the 20th of April, 1808, the heir-apparent was sought among the scions of the younger branch. Whether, in the event of the Emperor's dying without a son, preference would have been given to Louis Napoleon over his elder brother Napoleon Louis, and what reasons might have determined such a choice, it would now be useless to inquire. Suffice it to know that the Emperor evinced a strong predilection in favour of this younger son of his step-daughter, Hortense. 'His name,' we are told, 'was written down at the head of the family register of the Napoleon dynasty.' His baptism was put off for more than two years and a half, till the 10th of November, 1810, when the Emperor and his newly-married Empress, Maria Louisa, soon to be a mother, held him at the font; and although the birth of the King of Rome, five months later, disappointed the hopes of his immediate succession, the infant of Hortense still held for several years a most important position in his uncle's household, and was treated with all the honours due to an heir presumptive. He was seven years old when he stood by his uncle's side at the great gathering on the Champ de Mai during the Hundred Days, and, after Waterloo, he clung to his uncle's knees when the Emperor left La Malmaison, struggling against separation, as if instinct had told him that with the Emperor his own fortunes and those of the House were overshadowed.

The young Prince, reduced, with his mother, to a private station, spent eight years then at the Augsburg Gymnasium; then six more as a student under domestic tutors at the Castle of Arenenberg, in the canton of Thurgau, on the Lake of Constance, became proficient in history and mathematics, skilful in fencing, horsemanship, and swimming, and curious about military affairs; joining the ranks of the Swiss Militia, and making the acquaintance of the Federal General Dufour. Next to the pale reminiscences of Court pageantries in his early childhood, nothing, perhaps, so powerfully contributed to form the character of the future Emperor as the influence of the mother in whose house he grew up as an only child. The marriage of Hortense with Louis Bonaparte was, by his confession, 'forced and ill-assorted.' Seven months before the birth of their third son the Royal couple parted never to be re-united. It was not without contention that the ex-King of Holland, now Duke of Saint Leu, made good his claims to his elder son, leaving the younger in the undisputed possession of the mother. Chagrined as she seemed with her retirement at Arenenberg, Hortense, however, not unfrequently spent the winter in Italy, chiefly at Rome. It was not under the ascendancy of such a mother that the aspiring youth could learn resignation to a humble lot. Louis Napoleon was taught to look for a change with as full a confidence as he would expect daylight at the close of the natural period of darkness. It little mattered when, where, or by what means the turn in his fortunes might come. Enough that an opening would be made. The Man was there; he would not have to wait long for the Hour.

The July Revolution in Paris was hailed as the dawn, but it was only a momentary and deceitful twilight. The Prince's advances met with no favour from the men at the head of the movement in France, but a chance soon offered itself in Italy. The outbreak in the Roman States in February, 1831, found both the sons of Hortense in arms under the Italian tricolour. There was a bloodless campaign – a mere promenade under Sertognani from Foligno to Otricoli; then a journey to Forli, where the elder brother died of the measles on the 17th of March. Louis Napoleon, attacked by the same complaint at Ancona, was tended by his mother, smuggled away to Marseilles and Paris, and hence, after vain endeavours to obtain a resting-place, conveyed, a convalescent, to Arenenberg. On the downfall of the Italian cause, the Prince was seized with enthusiasm for Polish independence. He travelled through Germany on his way to Warsaw, but the tidings of the final catastrophe met him in Saxony, and for four years, from 1832 to 1836, he was forced back to his life of expectant leisure on the Bodensee. While, in all probability, the future candidate for power, at the early stage of his career, sought only for distinction as a soldier and a patriot, more than one short cut to fortune seemed to present itself to him. At Foligno and Forli he was emphatically hailed as 'the Prince;' Polish Generals tempted him with the proffered command of their legions; at the London Conference his name, it is said, was brought forward as a candidate for Belgian Royalty, and he was even, it would be difficult to say with what truth, put down among the suitors for the hand of Maria da Gloria of Portugal. Any ambitious views of that nature he, however, invariably disclaimed. To struggling nations he would only bring a volunteer's sword; and as to France, 'the hope to be able to serve her as a citizen and soldier was in his eyes worth more than all the thrones in the world.'

His devotion to France, however, was stimulated by other considerations than those of disinterested patriotism. The Duke of Reichstadt had died at Schönbrunn, and the Prince was now the acknowledged head of the Napoleon dynasty. Notwithstanding the greatest dissimilarity of mind and heart, his intense admiration for his uncle led him to a strange identification of himself with the great conqueror. His landing at Cannes, and 'the flight' of the Imperial Eagle from steeple to steeple, till 'it folded its wings on the towers of Nôtre Dame,' were, he thought, feats only to be tried again to meet with the same success. Nor was he altogether out of his reckoning. From 1831 to 1848 Bonapartism in France had made common cause with Republicanism. The First Empire, it was argued, had been an era of war and despotism; but it had peace and freedom in reserve. There was no limit to which 'Napoleonic ideas' could not be stretched; no degree of perfectibility incompatible with their full development. Of these ideas the young enthusiast at Arenenberg made himself the high priest and interpreter with an earnestness of faith of which he was, possibly, the first dupe. Those ideas, it must be borne in mind, were not altogether peculiar to the Prince. They were the great delusion of the age. The memory of the First Napoleon was no sooner released from the pressure under which the senseless reaction of the Bourbons vainly attempted to hold it than it was idealized into a myth. Napoleon was no longer the man of the *Dix-huit Brumaire*, of the *Levée en masse*. What men remembered of him were the Code Civil, the Alpine roads, the Legion of Honour. His name was, above all things, associated with the liberal *Acte Additionel* of 1815. He was the man with whose good intentions the courtyard of the villa at Longwood was paved. It was from this Prometheus bound that the young Pretender professed to hold his commission. He came to repair and to fulfil; he stood forth as the redeemer of the great man's dying pledges, the executor of his last will and testament. Louis Philippe, who dreaded the Pretender and honoured him with the crown of proscription was all the time playing into his hands. From beginning to end the July Monarchy laboured at the apotheosis of

Imperialism. Aware of the nature of the people's complaint, their rulers hoped to overcome it by ministering to it homeopathically. They inoculated the virus already creeping in the nation's veins. From the restoration of the bronze statue on the top of the Vendôme column in 1831 to the laying of the granite coffin beneath the dome of the Invalides in 1840, France was being turned into a vast Napoleonic monument. The Press teemed with little else but Napoleonic literature. The attack on the Strasburg barracks in 1836, and the landing at Boulogne in 1840, were only egregious blunders in so far that they took France by surprise. There was neither preparation nor opportunity. Nations are not easily roused in cold blood. Popular movements must be in a great measure dependent on time and place. It was not because the Prince had any reason to believe that he would be particularly welcome in Alsace or in Picardy that he made choice of a city on the Rhine or of a seaport on the Channel. It was because those places happened to be each at a different period nearest at hand – the one nearest to him as he came up from Switzerland, the other opposite to him as he steamed from the English coast. The precedent at Cannes bewildered him. He acted in obedience to that blind idolatry of his uncle, to that servility of imitation, which, as may be seen in the sequel, marred not less than it made him. Strasburg and Boulogne were in every respect poor parodies of the Return from Elba. They were also clearly a rehearsal of the *Coup d'Etat* on a small scale. In 1836 and in 1840 Louis Napoleon had forgotten all his disclaimers of 1831. He no longer aspired to the glory of a mere French citizen and soldier of France. He was already a full-grown Cæsar, not with the tricolor merely, but with the crown, sceptre, and eagle. His notions about the sovereignty of the people were sufficiently plain and consistent. The people were to be free – free to choose him. At Strasburg and Boulogne he evidently took the nation's consent for granted. His appeal was to the soldiers; his faith was in them. Had the barracks realized his expectation, had his cry '*Vive l'Empereur*' found an echo in the ranks, the *plébiscite* would have followed as a matter of course.

Those miserable failures at Strasburg and Boulogne darkened the prospects of Bonapartism apparently for ever. They deprived the Pretender of all initiative in revolutionary movements. Henceforth the Prince would have to watch the tide. The quarry might be his yet, but only when others had struck it down for him. Those very failures, however, were instrumental in revealing no less than in forming his character. Placed in the power of his enemies, after Strasburg, from the 30th of October to the 21st of November, 1836, and, after Boulogne, from the 4th of August, 1840, to the 25th of May, 1846, he gave proof of fortitude and dignity. In his intercourse with his captors, judges, and gaolers, he managed to have himself treated as a Monarch, though a vanquished one. He repaid Swiss hospitality by a spontaneous departure from Arenenberg in August, 1838, when the gallant Confederacy professed its readiness to run the risk of a quarrel with France for his sake.

Neither his six years' confinement in a State fortress – his 'course of studies at the University of Ham,' as he termed it, nor the two distinct periods of his not ungenial exile in London – 1838 to 1840, and 1846 to 1848, were lost upon him. Amid the gloom of a captive's life, as among the dissipations of a small if not quite select society, the activity of his mind was uncommon. He studied England; he conceived for this country that quiet but steady attachment which seldom fails to spring up in the heart of those who spend a summer and winter among us. Among the French the Prince generally sought tools and accomplices; of the English he made friends and companions. He was stanch rather than choice in his connexions. The consciousness of the loftiness of his ends rendered him indifferent to the lowness of his means. The best instrument in the schemer's hand was the most passive, hence, if necessary, the most unscrupulous. His knowledge of men seldom failed him, and commensurate with his knowledge was his indulgence to their foibles, and his sympathy with their moods. He accepted devotion with all its burdens and drawbacks. He was a friend *à toute épreuve.* A partisan might have to be disavowed, but no one was ever sacrificed; nor was the least act of kindness shown to the Pretender in adversity ever forgotten by the Sovereign in his prosperity.

Eighteen hundred and forty-eight came. The faintheartedness of a King and the infatuation of a Minister left France to her own mastery. A handful of dreamers and schemers pulled down the whole social edifice. From February to June of that year the disorganization, though less violent and bloody, was far more thorough than during the worst period of the Reign of Terror. In an evil day France had been taken by surprise. On the morrow she was appalled at the results of her own supineness and improvidence. On the third day she was anxious for reaction, on the look-out for a man who could save society. That task was morally fulfilled by Lamartine with a happy phrase; materially by Cavaignac with an awful massacre. By biding his time Louis Napoleon reaped the benefit both of the poet's and of the soldier's work. In February he made a tender of his services; but in April and in June he still declined the seats which were offered to him in the National Assembly. On the memorable 10th of April, as the world remembers, Prince Louis Napoleon was still doing duty as special constable in King-street, St. James's. He 'wished to undeceive those who charged him with ambition,' but he 'would know how to fulfil any duty which the people might lay upon him.' He said this on the 15th of June; ten days later the revolution was crushed. On the 26th of September he crossed the Channel and made his first appearance in the Assembly. Clear as the ground was before him, actively as his friends exerted themselves in his behalf, he still felt his way cautiously, almost timidly. Republicanism was in the mouth of all; monarchic restoration in the hearts of most men. Lamartine, Cavaignac, any of the so-called Republicans *du lendemain*, would keep the seat warm for a Prince either of the elder or of the younger Bourbon branch; but Louis Napoleon, if he took it, would be sure to keep it for himself. Hence there was, doubtless, considerable mistrust of and illwill towards him. Aware of this feeling, and with but little confidence in his debating powers, the Pretender limited himself to a defensive policy in the Assembly. His rare attempts to speak were neither brilliant nor successful. He sat down unmoved, in sullen, silent discomfiture, trusting to the *prestige* of his uncle's name to plead his cause among the people. Whether dictated by choice or necessity, his course was the wisest. On the 10th of December, 1848, Cavaignac had a million and a half of the people's votes for the Presidency of the Republic. Prince Napoleon had above six millions. Upon that vote the supreme power of the Pretender could have been legally and peacefully founded for ever. Up to the close of the year 1848 no good whatever was known about the newly-elected President. Ridicule is apt to kill the most honourable names in France, and the Prince's name was only associated with the farces of Strasburg and Boulogne. The vast majority of the national representation, the whole wealth and worth of the country, were dead against him; yet the mass of the people had, with very little solicitation and hardly any exertion on his part, pronounced for him. Henceforth the President had possession – nine-tenths of the law – on his side.

For the best part of the next two years the President and the still hostile Assembly were busy with the task of killing the dead. Republicanism had no friends, and no quarter was to be given to it. All efforts were turned to the re-establishment of that compact, centralized administration which, in normal times, constitutes the strength and pride of France. The sword of the State was being tempered; no matter who might be destined to wield it, every one was interested in the keenness of its edge and the sharpness of its point. In the meanwhile, however, its hilt was in the President's hand and every repressive measure tightened his grasp upon it. Louis Napoleon was sure that the 'union of the two powers – legislative and executive – was indispensable to the tranquillity of the country.' The Assembly perceived, too late, that the President was bringing his theory into practice. They strove to limit his powers, to circumscribe his influence; they attempted to curtail his expenditure; they set up a permanent committee; they proposed to take from him the command-in-chief of the Army, and to invest it with the President of the Assembly. Goaded into action by imminent danger, the so-called 'old parties' – Bourbonists and Orleanists – were accused of a design to hasten a Restoration, which, if not absolutely impossible, was, at least, premature. In their visits to Claremont after Louis Philippe's death, and to Wiesbaden at the time of the Count de Chambord's stay in that place, the friends of the exiled Princes were supposed to be negotiating a fusion between the two branches of the Bourbon family – a negotiation which remains unfinished to the present time. Changarnier, the General in command of the Army of Paris and of the National Guard of the Seine, was pointed out as the French Monk who was to enable the legitimate dynasty to come by its own again. There may have been much or little in these surmises, but Louis Napoleon knew how to make the most of them. The President fought his battles with indifferent success in the Chamber, but his very defeats paved the way for his victories in the country. Nothing could be more daring than his self-assertion; nothing more open than his plans of operation. The Bonapartist conspiracy embodied in the *Société du Dix Decembre* was carried on with the cards on the table. 'In extreme dangers,' said the President, 'Providence not unfrequently trusts one man with the safety of all.' At the reviews of St. Maur and Satory the soldiers hailed the President with that cry of '*Vive l'Empereur!*' to which the garrisons of Strasburg and Boulogne had refused to respond years before.

From the beginning of 1851 everything was being made ready for a final conflict. Early in January Changarnier was removed from his command. In October and November the President laid his ultimatum – first before his Ministers, then before the Assembly. He proposed the repeal of the law of May 31, 1850, by which universal suffrage had been restricted. 'That measure,' said the President, 'was tantamount to the disfranchisement of 3,000,000 electors.' Had even the law really had such sweeping effects the President had but little to fear from an appeal to the people. Had even that law been in force in December, 1848, the balance of the votes would still have been decisive in his favour. Nothing, however, but the certainty of an overwhelming majority could allay his apprehensions. To insure it he resolved on the *Coup d'Etat* of the 2d of December. He laid a violent hand on his most dreaded opponents. He dispersed the less dangerous. He dissolved the Assembly and the Council of State. He abrogated the law of May 31, and re-established universal suffrage. He then called together the 'Comitia of the nation.' In the mean time he declared Paris in a State of Siege; he deluged its streets with blood; he terrorized France by wholesale transportation. He finally asked for a sanction or condemnation of his deed of violence. Seven millions and a half of Frenchmen against little above half a million gave sentence in his favour.

The Second Napoleon had thus his *Deux Decembre*, as the first had his *Dix-huit Brumaire*. The elevation of Louis Napoleon under any circumstances appeared so certain that one is almost tempted to fancy that wanton display of uncalled-for energy to have only been prompted by the nephew's blind obligation to tread in his uncle's footsteps. Every subsequent act of his, at any rate, was sheer repetition. From the 2d of December, 1851, to the same day and month of the following year, the Imperial Revolution went through the same phases which it exhibited from the 10th of November, 1799, to the 18th of May, 1804; only the more recent catastrophe was limited within a narrower cycle. There was the same impatient stir in the Departments; the same obsequious solicitations of the Senate; the same martial pageantries on the Champ de Mars; the same triumphal progress of the Cæsar. The Constitution was a paltry copy. The history on the coins was identical. Even the fortuitous coincidence of the assassin's dagger and of the infernal machine was not wanting. It was only in the number of votes that the new generation outdid the old.

And now, at last, Louis Napoleon was back at the Tuileries. It would be to little purpose if we were to endeavour to realize his sensations, as, at the mature age of 44, the pale reminiscences of thirty-seven years since crowded upon him on the threshold of that lately desecrated palace. Verily, the man's faith had its reward! That faith which never forsook him at the gloomiest periods of his career; that faith which, at a distance, raised a sneer at his expense, yet cast a magnetic spell over all who came within his reach – that faith proved to have been founded on unerring instincts. The Pretender's claims were admitted. He had aimed no higher than his stubborn will could lift him. That intense yearning by which the uncle had been haunted all his lifetime had certainly fallen to the nephew, whatever other parts of the rich inheritance might have been denied to him. The words by which that undefinable feeling found utterance in the strain of the Italian poet apply with equal force to the two aspiring relatives. There was in both cases 'the stormy, trembling joy of a great purpose, the longing of a heart fretting as it impatiently thirsted for empire, and attaining it at last, and grasping a prize for which it had seemed madness to hope.'

In the magnitude of the result people easily lost sight of the means by which it had been achieved. The cold shiver which had followed closely upon the revolutionary fever heat of 1848 had scarcely passed away three years later, and, under its fit, men were ready to go any length in the way of reaction. The cry was everywhere for strong Government; and, somehow, the *Coup d'Etat*, whatever might be the grounds of justice or expediency on which it was made to stand, was hailed as evidence of its author's energy, and accepted as a pledge of social security. The hand which had displayed so much vigour in seizing the reins of government might surely be relied upon to hold them with equal firmness. Even for men swayed by more rigid notions of right and wrong, the moral question how the supreme power had been obtained was absorbed in the other far more momentous problem – what uses it would be put to. The ends of Providence are often fulfilled in inscrutable ways; and it little mattered, after all, by what means another Napoleon had ascended the throne of France, if men could only ascertain how much of the good or the evil of the old Napoleonic era would be reproduced in the new.

We have already expressed our opinion that the nephew carried the worship of the uncle's memory to the verge of superstition. He was, however, aware that there was a weak no less than a strong side to old Imperialism. He announced the coming not of the Caesarean but of the Augustan age. The Second Empire brought not a sword but peace. In the mind of the French people the mere reappearance of the Eagle, the revival of the name of Napoleon, constituted a victory over allied Europe.

The *Deux-Decembre* had avenged Waterloo. France had broken through the dynastic arrangements of 1815, and her ancient enemies had not a word to say against her achievement. This negative homage being paid to her vanity, France had no longer an interest in the disturbance of the common tranquillity. Questions about natural frontiers, about oppressed nationalities might, indeed, arise; but moral ascendency could now, perhaps, accomplish more than the edge of the sword. France would be no less true to her mission because she put off its fulfilment by violent means till she was convinced of the inefficiency of all other arguments. There was, at the outlet, perfect harmony between the views of the French people and those of their new Sovereign with respect to foreign politics. There was faith in the undisputed, though pacific, ascendency of the Empire over the council of nations – in the necessity for a revision of existing Treaties, for a remodelling of the map of Europe, for the emancipation of enslaved nations, for the protection of minor States, of those especially which had shown the greatest devotion to the cause of Imperial France and had been involved in its downfall; of States like Belgium, Denmark, and Saxony; of nations like Italy and Poland. Over and above these general French sympathies, the Emperor brought with him, as peculiar to himself, a genuine regard for England, our own estimate of the true bases of national greatness, our notions of a free commercial policy. It is not a little remarkable that the first enterprise of real magnitude in which France was engaged, after panting for so many years to avenge Waterloo, should have been planned in concert with the very country upon which vengeance for that defeat was to be mainly wreaked. Yet the Crimean War of 1854 was waged not only in obedience to what the majority of the French people were inclined to consider as English views, but also in subservience to what they regarded as English interests. It was the Emperor's own war, and Napoleon only brought it to a sudden end when we refused to mix up with the original quarrel those French schemes about Poland and the Rhine in which he found it difficult to withstand his people's aspirations. Against the same rock were wrecked, in later times, 1864, all hopes of a cordial co-operation of the two great Western Powers in behalf of invaded Denmark. As to the immediate relations between the two nations, there is no doubt that against the half-smothered animosities of French Chauvinisim nothing availed us so much as the Emperor's stout determination, not only not to be driven into hostilities but to strengthen the bonds of amity with us at any price. Neither the vapouring and blustering of the Press nor the famous address of the Colonels were able to shake the Emperor's determination to maintain the cordial understanding between the two countries; and the conclusion of the Commercial Treaty and the abolition of passports in favour of English travellers must be traced to his sole initiative.

Equally sincere and unbounded was the Emperor's sympathy with the land which had witnessed his earliest exploits – Italy; and he never, perhaps, spoke more in earnest, never did greater justice to the generosity of his impulses, than when in 1859, calling upon the Italians to be men, he offered his help to free their country from the Alps to the Adriatic. The scheme of the Unity of the Peninsula did not, indeed, appear practicable to him any more than to some of the wisest and noblest Italian Liberals; and he, doubtless, conceived that the independence of Italy, although it might imply the complete severance of that country from Austria, need not therefore exclude some bond of alliance between the freed nation and its deliverer – a bond of alliance which might easily have been strengthened into a compact of indirect allegiance. In all this, however, the welfare of Italy, as he understood it, was the object nearest to the Emperor's heart; and, with a self-denial of which, in trying moments, he never failed to give evidence, and with respect to which his cold and deliberate nature stands forth in strong contrast with the wilful and headlong character of his uncle, he gave up his own opinions in deference to those of the Italians; he accepted 'accomplished facts,' and not only never willingly opposed the spread and growth of Italian nationality, but actually screened it from the attacks to which, in its helplessness, it would repeatedly have succumbed.

True, he extinguished the Roman Republic in 1849; he exacted the cession of Savoy and Nice in 1860; he accepted from Austria the temporary gift of Venetia in 1866, and he re-occupied Rome in 1867. All these, however, were not the spontaneous acts of the Emperor's own mind. He was influenced by what he considered due to French susceptibilities; to the claims of the Great Nation to her 'natural frontiers;' to her jealousy of her immediate neighbours; to her assumption of paramount authority as universal arbitrator; finally, to her half-chivalrous, half-selfish pretentions as Eldest Daughter of the Church. By most of these considerations he was also and much more forcibly moved in the policy he pursued with respect to Germany. That the instinct of Union was at work across the Rhine as well as south of the Alps the Emperor was fully aware, and he was also convinced that what the German nation firmly and unanimously willed it was not in the power of French jealousy to gain-say. He had been somewhat awed by the attitude of Germany, both in the full tide of his success after Solferino and in the furtherance of his designs in behalf of Poland and Denmark. It was not by opposing German Union, but by taking advantage of German disunion, that the Emperor hoped to secure the command. When the Germans had torn each other to pieces, when the victor lay on the battle-field as exhausted as the vanquished, to snatch from their grasp that Rhenish frontier which would free France from all uneasiness in that quarter would prove, as the Emperor conceived, no more impracticable an undertaking than it had been to rectify the border-line on the Italian side. The conditions which were peremptorily laid down at Plombières need hardly be as much as hinted at Biarritz. In Italy it was the help of France that was solicited. In Germany all that was required of her was neutrality. Mere looking on would do as much for her in the second case as stout fighting had done in the first. In all these calculations the Emperor relied on 'the irresistible logic of events.' But events were too quick for him. Germany achieved her unity in 1861; and France came in too late to claim her share of the spoil.

Before Sadowa and Nikolsburg the Emperor's European policy appeared faultless in the eyes of the vast majority of the French people. But the first check naturally prompted a review of its course from the outset, and encouraged that criticism which is always extremely easy after the event. The main difficulty for the Emperor lay between conceding too much or too little to the warlike and domineering spirit of the French nation. The French had hailed with satisfaction the Bordeaux announcement of October, 1852, that 'the Empire was Peace;' but they were no less delighted with the subsequent assurance that 'not a gun should be fired in Europe without the assent of the Tuileries.' France had no objection that 'the universe should be tranquil,' but only on condition that 'she herself should be contented.' The Third Napoleon was called upon to exercise by mere moral ascendency that sway over the European councils which the First failed to establish by might of arms; and for many years there is no doubt that he acquitted himself of the task with unparalleled success. But he pressed that success beyond its due limits; he fretted himself about Congresses and Conferences, the only object or result of which was to be the enhancement of his own importance. There is no doubt that he suffered the notion that it was at all times necessary to busy and, so to say, to amuse the French people to gain too strong a hold upon his fancy. The scheme of diverting public attention from domestic affairs by distant expeditions to China, Japan, Syria, and, finally, to Mexico, had little to recommend it on the score of originality. The rulers who preceded Napoleon III had found a vent for the superfluous activity of French enterprise in Algeria, and it was only unfortunate that the gradual pacification of that colony should have deprived the Second Empire of a convenient safety-valve so near home. Most of the Emperor's Quixotic undertakings beyond sea proved, as was to be expected, barren of results, but one, as might have been feared, turned out fatal. The project of a Mexican Empire, the scheme of the exaltation of the Latin races on the American continent, would have been sheer failures, even if the Emperor's belief that the breach in the United States was incurable had been correct; for a European Power has little chance of obtaining a footing anywhere across the Atlantic, except as a tool in the hands of some of the native factions, and these turn out mere quicksands under those who would build upon them. But the result of the Mexican experiment was not brought even to this test. The Americans recovered sufficient strength to make a stand for the Monroe doctrine; and France had to back out of her Mexican position with a hurry in which her very dignity was not consulted.

Independently of success, however, it may be fairly admitted that the general tendency of the Emperor's foreign policy was moderate and pacific; but it would not be equally easy to clear it altogether from the charge of disingenuousness and irresolution. The Emperor's diplomacy was unlike that of any other man. No Sovereign ever came to the Throne with so large a crowd of ready-made agents and advisers; none attained power by so long a series of underhand manoeuvres. Louis Napoleon had been for half his life a conspirator. Necessity, no less than habit, made him a plotter on the Throne. Bent upon bringing into his hands all legislative and executive authority, upon exacting from all and each of his subordinates the fullest responsibility to himself alone, the Emperor had, properly speaking, no Ministers, but simply Heads of Departments, blind and passive tools to be taken up or cast off at his own pleasure. But, behind his responsible Cabinet, behind his acknowledged Council of State, there was always a little knot of more trusted and devoted instruments, chosen chiefly among the faithful followers of the Pretender's obscure fortunes, men upon whom, in the gloomy isolation of absolute power, he must needs rely for his knowledge of that public opinion to which he denied all free utterance, and among whom he must seek such executors of his will as would rather guess than question his motives – men who would allow him all the merit of success, and take upon themselves all the blame of miscarriage; men between whom and himself there must be such a bond of freemasonry as to give them the intimate consciousness of their employers unfailing support, even under the cloud of his affected displeasure or the storm of his formal disavowal. It was in obedience to these necessities, created no less by the origin than by the nature of his government, that the Emperor, in his relations with foreign States, was frequently induced to give preference to indirect and clandestine negotiation; to intrust to extra-official agents messages un-meet for the conveyance of regularly accredited Envoys; to reserve for unwitnessed interviews the transaction of affairs of which no tangible document should be allowed to remain. Not satisfied with these not very dignified acts, which for some time established his credit for consummate dexterity, the Emperor also seemed to stake his reputation on a suddenness of action commensurate with his maturity of deliberation. He was perpetually taking the world by surprise. A Government ushered in by a *Coup d'Etat* was carried on by a succession of *Coups de Théâtre*. Whether a declaration of war was to be conveyed in a New Year's greeting to a foreign Ambassador, or peace to be announced in an after-dinner speech to a Provincial Magistrate; whether the revelation of the Imperial mind was to take the shape of a mysterious pamphlet, or whether his mind was to be intimated in a familiar letter – the aim as well as the result invariably was to give the Emperor's policy a 'sensational' character. 'The Emperor,' as his flatterers observed, 'allows himself no rest.' Perpetual activity and almost actual ubiquity seemed to be as indisputable attributes of an Imperial Providence as omniscience and omnipotence. Wherever the Emperor might go he must be in pursuit of some hidden object; his simplest act must proceed from some far-fetched motive. A morbid expectation was created to which it daily became more difficult to minister. The Emperor's speech and his silence were invested with an equally awful significance. Such overweening assumption must, however, be borne out by deeds of corresponding magnitude. The mere *prestige* of moral ascendency is soon brought to the test of material success. The world grew tired of all that solemn emphasis and oracular ambiguity. It looked for the results of all that profound statescraft, and saw it foiled by Cavour's superior cunning; thwarted by Bismarck's steadier resolve; it saw it wrecked against the Pope's passive obstinacy; it saw it everywhere frustrated by the combination of unforeseen circumstances, by a series of irresistible catastrophes. It heard it acknowledging the force of a fatal necessity by alluding to the presence of dark spots on the horizon. And it was, be it observed, not so much to error of judgment as to infirmity of purpose that the repeated failures of the Emperor were imputed. Hesitation and inconsistency were the bane of his political conduct. He would have been equally powerful to create a United or a Federal Italy. He might as easily have upheld as pulled down the Papacy. He might have checked all Germany in the Danish War of 1864. He might have backed one-half of it against the other half during the seven weeks' campaign of 1866. He might have done much less in Mexico, or he could have gone much greater lengths against the United States. His fault consisted in an excess of caution and circumspection. He seemed everywhere to arrive one day too late, and only to make up his mind when he had missed his opportunity. His Ministers were twitted in the Legislature by emboldened opponents, who asserted that there 'was not one fault left for the Imperial Government to commit,' and thus challenged them, as it were, to remain in office without a vital change in their policy. Two courses were open to the Emperor Napoleon after Sadowa – to make up by brute force what he had lost by unsuccessful manoeuvre, or else to acquiesce in the inevitable, to put a cheerful countenance on a losing game, and even to claim credit for a consummation which he had been unable to prevent. For nearly two years the Emperor wavered between the two resolutions. To rush into war before Nikolsburg or after Prague was declared to be impossible, owing to the unreadiness of the French military forces. Yet to accept and even to applaud the rise of a rival nation close on the Rhine frontier, especially after all that had been said about territorial compensations, natural boundaries, and popular aspirations, was, perhaps, to inflict too sore a wound on French susceptibilities. Hence there began that tentative, faltering, fidgeting policy; those abortive negotiations at Berlin, at the Hague, at Munich, at Vienna; those mysterious journeys and ominous interviews, which at first bewildered and dismayed, and at last half-amused, half-wearied Europe. At Paris and at Lille, the Emperor talked of peace. At Luxembourg, Salzburg, Copenhagen, he sought allies and nursed pretexts for war. Unequal to single-handed action, France affected to look for confederates. The real object was, if not to win partisans, at least to gain time; but both purposes were defeated. France revealed her unprepared condition at the same time that she widened and completed her isolation.

War, except on the most hazardous conditions, was clearly out of the question. Could, then, the Emperor resolve on peace? Peace he could certainly have with the world if he could only have it with France. The Emperor Napoleon was not cast in the mould of heroic conquerors. He was cold, cautious, even to the extreme of moral timidity. He had no love for war, at least for war's sake and on a large scale. He had a great respect for 'the odds' in any game. He never would launch France on an equal duel with Germany. The difficulty lay in preventing France from dragging him into such a war against his better judgment. All his sayings and doings since Sadowa had but one object – to humour, to soothe, to reassure French opinion. Faith in his infallibility, he conceived, was shaken in others as well as in himself; that his wonted good fortune had to some extent forsake him, that black spots were looming in the horizon, he had himself deemed it necessary to avow. It was now important for him to allay the apprehensions he had himself created, to restore the confidence which his words had undermined as much as his deeds.

The real question, however, lay in the estimate the Emperor could arrive at with respect to the state of public opinion. He had lived for many years away from the Throne; he was a man of the world, a cool, shrewd observer, and might form a correct judgment of whatever came before his eyes. But for the last twenty years he was labouring under the 'curse of Kings.' He had deprived France of free utterance. He must either take her at a rude guess or see her through the medium of that cumbrous scaffolding of official administration which he had reared between himself and the nation instead of the regular edifice of a responsible Government. Besides the France he had studied in the writings of M. Thiers, or in the *Mémorial de Sainte Héléne*, or that he had contemplated through the bars of his prison windows at Ham, he only knew the France which Messrs. De Morny, Persigny, or, at the utmost, Messrs. Billault and Rouher chose to describe to him; a France more Imperialist than the Emperor, more illiberal than the *Deux Décembre*. The only safety out of his embarrassing position could be found in his abdicating absolute power. Atonement for the errors of the past could best be made by relinquishing undivided responsibility for the future. To make up to the nation for its somewhat tarnished glory abroad it was before all things advisable to restore its liberties at home. His first movement upon having to acknowledge 'the force of irresistible circumstances' was to throw himself upon his people. The first result of the disaster of July, 1866, was the letter of January, 1867.

Between the 'Elected of December,' however, and the millions of his electors there was a conditional, though an irrevocable, compact. The French nation – or, at least, that part of it which constituted a majority resulting from the experiment of universal suffrage – had accepted its ruler on his own terms. The alternative lay between order and freedom, and he said 'Order at all events; Freedom whenever it might be.' As a President and as an Emperor, Napoleon always deemed the perfection of government to lie in the combination both of legislative and executive power in the same hand. His notions of a Constitution were those of the Consulate and the First Empire, and he seemed to forget that the concentration of all power in one hand had only been deemed advisable by the First Napoleon when he aspired to grasp France as a sword, and that the system had broken down, by confession of its original inventor, towards the close of his reign. With a new Empire which was to be 'Peace' there was no longer a necessity for the same strong military organization, and liberty should, therefore, have been compatible with it. But the tendency of the people, like that of their ruler, at the time was towards energetic repression. Society had to be saved. War to the bitter end was to be waged – not against foreign enemies, but against domestic parties. Even for such a war a Dictatorship was found indispensable. The State was constituted in the shape of a pyramid, with nothing between the electing masses at the base and the elected Autocrat at the point. Yet something like regret and misgiving seemed at times to assail the Sovereign in the awful solitude of his elevation. It was not for his own sake, not from personal ambition, he hinted, that so unbounded a power had been placed in his hands. He held it simply on trust. The people's liberties were only in abeyance. Indeed, a show was made now and then of slackening the reins of Government. Imperialism was described as by its nature progressive. It was considered as a temporary structure – a means to an end; the application of force to the establishment of legal authority. When the end was attained, when order could be pronounced quite safe, the superstructure should be removed, and the 'crowning of the edifice' would follow.

It is difficult to say to what extent the Emperor deceived himself or others. But, whatever his intentions might be, they could not be carried into effect without far greater resolution than seemed at any time to be at his command. His rule had sprung from the masses; it was identified with the multitude. He had ascended the Throne as the 'Working Man's Friend; the Emperor of the Peasant.' The millions who reigned through him were not as ready to resign their supremacy as he, perhaps, might have been. The Senate consisted of his own nominees; the Legislative Body was elected by constituencies over which his Administration was supposed to exercise almost absolute control. But there was in that Senate, in that Elective Assembly, in that Administration, in that vast mass of voters, a party, a vastly predominant party, which would stand up for Imperialism even against the Emperor. With such a Constitution as the Emperor framed mere legislative improvement must needs be illusory. It was impossible to get over the fact that in a State like the France of the present day the mass of the nation overrode its intelligence; the body crushed the soul. The reign of the upper and middle classes had come to an end in that country with the first and second revolution. It was now the turn of the multitude, and the only question was whether the Government should be in the hands of a mere mob or in that of a mob-delegated despot. With all its purple and gold the Imperial Government was heir to the communistic notions of the Red Republican *régime*. The Emperor's mission was to tax the rich for the benefit of the poor. By his arbitrary control over the price of bread, by his promotion of public works, the Emperor was perpetually bringing back his authority to its original sources. Put that authority to the test of a hundred elections, and the suffrage would always give the same results.

This assurance of almost boundless popular support was a source of weakness no less than of strength. With the exception of a few ambitious statesmen, and still fewer more or less devoted friends of the fallen dynasties, there were no elements for wholesome legal opposition in France. Hence the various proposals of the Emperor for an extension of constitutional liberties could hardly find sufficient support from the enlightened classes to overcome the mutinous ill-will of the mob-majority. It required the personal influence of the Sovereign to force even such paltry measures as the Press and Public Meetings Bill through a Legislature otherwise too ready to endorse all other Imperial Acts of home and foreign policy.

A Government placed so widely above all check or hindrance had it certainly in its power to achieve much, and twenty years of Imperial rule have not been without most splendid results for the general welfare of France. Within its own boundaries the country had never known a period of greater material progress. Beyond them, till very recent times, it had exercised an ascendency grounded on a moral *prestige* more than commensurate with its actual strength. The recognition of the advantages of Prussia's military system came most inopportunely for the Emperor to confirm a favourite saying of his, 'That a nation's influence is gauged by the number of soldiers it can bring into the field.' The Army Bill was no doubt a disastrous measure for him, but he had been drifting into a most difficult dilemma. He had to choose between resigning himself to a condition of comparative weakness, which must infallibly be exposed sooner or later, and a measure that levied 'a tribute of blood' on the classes where he found his warmest supporters. The dilemma was a difficult one. The Emperor had, indeed, asserted his ascendency by a pretension of controlling circumstances which had passed almost unchallenged. He had biased the policy of Europe by merely indicating the attitude of France. But the state of affairs had been insensibly shifting, until he had become conscious of a pressure he was powerless to resist. He had been led by Cavour, and the astuteness of the Italian statesman had betrayed him into positions where his only safety lay in pressing onwards. Now he was being forced by Bismarck. As Germany grew strong Europe was threatened with a change of masters, and it seemed that in the future the impulses in European politics might come as probably from Berlin as from Paris. The Emperor's sense of the change was indicated by his language. He affected to consider the disruption of the German Confederation as a weakening of Germany. One of those inspired pamphlets that appeared from time to time traced the parallel between the First and the Second Empires to the advantage of the latter. Napoleon III and his uncle had been revolving in identical historical cycles. But the pamphleteer stopped short in his comparisons. He neglected to point out that Sadowa, with its disclosures more than its successes, was the Moscow of that Second Empire which was paying the penalty of the domineering pretensions of the First. The Seven Weeks' War demonstrated the results of that military system which France had forced upon Prussia after the crowning victory of Jena. Now the Emperor recognized that, thanks to the apathy or irresolution he had certainly not borrowed from his uncle, the regular standing armies of France had to count with a nation of civilian-soldiers, trained, armed, and organized. He felt there was truth in the invectives of those political opponents who, appealing to the pride of France, told him he had blundered away France's commanding influence. It must be proved sooner or later whether he or they were in the right, and, with a belief in his destiny which had begun to falter, he set himself to prepare for the inevitable test.

At that time, too, he was already a prey to the painful malady to which he yesterday succumbed, and no doubt bodily suffering enfeebled the resolution which had once been believed indomitable. Radical and Republican pamphleteers and journalists gloated over his ailments in language that outraged decency and humanity. Rochefort's *Lanternes* became a feature in Parisian life; the noble turned Socialist shot his daily flight of poisoned arrows, and respectable Paris laughed, as its wont is, forgiving the coarseness of the scurrility for the sake of the keenness of the sarcasm. It became clear that things were ripening for a crisis, unless the credit of the Emperor was to be saved by his death; yet none but fanatic Red Republicans, ready to believe in everything they longed for, could have fancied the end of the Empire so imminent.

The year '68 must have been one of great searchings of heart at the Court of the Tuileries. The interview of the German Emperors at Salzburg, although followed by all manner of satisfactory assurances, kept minds uneasy as to the new relations of France with her neighbours, and stimulated the audacity of those reckless men who fish for profit and popularity in troubled waters. Ugly omens multiplied towards the close of the year, urging the Emperor towards some decided if not desperate resolution. The incident in the Hall of the Sorbonne, when, at the distribution of prizes, young Cavaignac refused to receive his at the hands of the Imperial Prince, must have shaken the Emperor's faith in the hold Imperialism had on the upper classes, while of a sudden the turbulent democracy discovered a martyr in Baudin, one of the victims of the *Coup d'Etat*, and even the eminent veteran Berryer contributed a letter and a subscription to the agitation.

The Emperor's resolution was taken. He would use his personal power and what remained of his *prestige* to promulgate a scheme of comprehensive Constitutional reform. Judging by the course of events, we may well doubt whether the resolution would have served him had he taken it earlier. As it was, he was late then, as he had so often been before. It seemed as if he was graciously making a gift of the power he felt slipping through his fingers; and after all, the gift, such as it was, was in a degree illusory. For the future his Ministers were to be responsible to the Chambers; they were to be chosen by the party that commanded a parliamentary majority, they were to hold office by the votes of the House, as in England. But so long as the Empire maintained its traditional electoral machinery the Emperor assured himself an enormous working majority, happen what might. The masses of the rural voters were drilled by obsequious Préfets on their promotion, and the different circumscriptions were manipulated, so that in most instances the votes of the stolid and loyal country should swamp those of the feverish radical towns. In the towns, if the voters were not bribed, and bought with hard cash, they were delicately conciliated by the concession of serviceable public works – town-halls, lines of railway, free bridges. The Autocratic Empire had consolidated its popularity on a system of corruption; it would have been simply suicidal had it reformed and become pure all of a sudden. There had been another unlucky coincidence for the shaking Empire. The Assembly had been dissolved, and there had been a general election. Of course, the Government obtained its commanding majority; but, unfortunately, Paris and the great cities had returned Opposition members as a rule. The logical deduction was obvious – the intelligence of the country is opposed to Imperialism, and the Opposition represents a moral force out of all proportion to its numerical strength. It is notorious that in France, the inert masses are swayed to one side or the other, as they receive the impulse, and it became clear that any day an accident might derange the existing equilibrium. The various chiefs of the Opposition attacked, with the whole weight of their eloquence and their influence, the vicious electoral system that made politics a comedy and falsified opinion. Excited mobs in the town shouted for the Republic and Rochefort. The Emperor was being forced towards abdication or a *Coup d'Etat*. He decided again for the *Coup d'Etat*, but this time it was altogether a Constitutional one. Cæsar proposed a '*senatus consultum*,' which resigned the power he had held in trust into the hands of the people, from whom it had flowed originally, and charged responsible Ministers with the exercise of the people's authority. The stanch Imperialist Ministers shook their heads at this putting new wine into old bottles. Rouher, Duruy, Lavalette, and Baroche resigned. Prince Napoleon made a remarkable and characteristic speech, which gave some colour to the theory of certain political seers that, with the assent of the head of his house, he held himself in reserve in case of a political catastrophe that should prove fatal to his cousin. The Prince approved the measure in the main, although, in his opinion, it was not sufficiently thorough. He avowed that he was not one of those who believed the Empire incompatible with the most absolute liberty, and he boldly touched all those burning topics which the official orators had carefully shunned. It was remarked at the time that the daring speaker had a long interview immediately afterwards with his Imperial cousin, and it was understood that they separated on the most cordial terms. It is probable the Emperor, having lost self-confidence, was in painful uncertainty as to the direction in which unforeseen circumstances might hurry him. The Home Minister, M. Forcade de la Roquette, proclaimed the programme of the Court in language sufficiently precise. The Empire hoped to succeed in solidly founding liberty, where the Governments of the Restoration and of July had failed, 'because its principle is stronger and more popular; because it rests upon the national will several times proclaimed, and because it defies surprises.' At that moment it felt so strongly that its existing titles were discredited that already it was thinking of a fresh appeal to the democracy; while it was the suspicion of surprises in store that had suggested its present attitude. Weakened and compromised by the secessions, the last genuinely Imperialist Ministry resigned, and the Emperor had recourse to the flexible Liberals, as represented by Emile Ollivier and his colleagues.

We may judge him with tolerable confidence after the event, and, enlightened by results, we may estimate pretty fairly the formidable difficulties against which he precipitated himself. The fact remains that at that time men who would rather have been rid of the dynasty believed it so firmly established that the best and most patriotic course was to come to an understanding with it. Men patriotic or ambitious, like Ollivier, Buffet, and Daru, accepted office and undertook the execution of the new programme. Yet the signs of the times were thickening. Not the least significant was the retirement of Haussmann, whose magnificent schemes – half developed, and arrived at a stage where perseverance might have been the truest economy – had so terribly embarrassed the finances of the capital. It was an acknowledgment that the Empire had reached the limits of its lavish expenditure and pushed to an extreme the fatal principle of national workshops. Yet it was plain that if the men who had so long been subsidized became idle, needy, and discontented, the streets of the capital would be crowded with turbulent *émeutiers*, ready to swell the ranks of the Reds, and to force the hand of the Government when prudence and patriotism should alike suggest a cautious game. A sinister incident occurred on the very day when the Chambers met the new Ministers. Prince Pierre Bonaparte shooting Victor Noir at Auteuil threw a weapon into the hands of the Red Republicans which they were not slow to lay hold of. Rochefort's language in his *Marseillaise* exceeded all measure. Noir was made a martyr, and the Empire was in more imminent danger on the day of his funeral than men suspected at the time. Had Rochefort been as daring in action as in speech, had his nerves not failed him before the starting of the funeral *cortége*, and had the impetuous Flourens taken his place at its head, it is hardly doubtful that there would have been a sauguinary collision in the Champs Elysées. The Empire would have triumphed for the day, for it was well prepared. But in its discredited condition a second carnage among the citizens of Paris could scarcely have failed to be a fatal defeat for it.

On the eve of the famous *Plébiscite* the position of the Olivier Ministry was more treacherous than ever, and the attitude of the Government was visibly ill-assured. The Ministry trembled between Liberalism and extreme Imperialism, and one of its genuinely liberal measures had terribly multiplied its difficulties by allowing full licence of language to all its most unscrupulous enemies. In throwing the rein to the Press, Olivier had said that they trusted it in future to the control of a healthy public opinion. It is hard to believe that either the Minister or the Emperor could have had any such confidence. Opinion had so long been stifled and gagged that it was debauched and thoroughly diseased. It was inevitable that the *régime* of repression should be followed by the reaction of excess, and the Empire suffered from the vice of its origin, and paid the penalty of the system by which it had hitherto succeeded. Now that writers could speak out, they reverted with justice to those crimes of the *Coup d'Etat*, when the President for motives they assumed to be purely selfish, had violated the oath of the Constitution, and abused the responsibilities he had solemnly accepted. They raked up the details of all those high-handed proceedings that had necessarily been received at the time in sullen silence. They denounced the sensational foreign policy that had been dictated by dynastical motives. They attacked the luxury and extravagances the people, and especially the middle classes, had been taxed for. They had facts enough at command, which needed scarcely to be distorted or overcoloured, to make up a damaging indictment. But they did not stop at facts. They made unsparing use of every calumny and falsehood perverted ingenuity could invent, and the condemnation of Pierre Bonaparte to a simple fine gave the demagogues of the democracy a standing text for philippics against the family with which he had so little in common. The virulent energy of the Opposition Press was swaying opinion; the organized agitation which was being fed with unfaltering activity might spread from the cities to the Conservative *bourgeoisie* of the towns, and from the towns to the loyal country people, who were drilled and directed by Préfets and Maires in the country. The *Plébiscite* was pressed on, lest delay should reduce the Government majority. Henceforth the Constitution, drawn in the most democratic sense, was only to be revised by the masses of the people on the initiative of the Sovereign. The Sovereign, in having his election confirmed by an overwhelming assent of his constituents, was to receive a retrospective act of oblivion for all the misdemeanours he had been charged with; he was to have a deed of indemnity for all the blood and the treasure the Empire had spent at home and abroad. The Emperor had urged on the step with feverish impatience, in opposition, it was understood, to the advice of the Achitophels by whom he had been wont to be guided. He waited the result with intense anxiety, although the vote was a foregone conclusion. With his superstitious cast of mind and his belief in destiny, he must have felt he had come to one of the turning points in his career, and no doubt he sought his horoscope in an analysis of the voting list, as soothsayers used to search for the omens on some solemn national ceremony. The omens were sinister, and although there were seven millions of ayes as against a million and a half of noes, the forebodings were confirmed which had induced him to tempt his fate. Not only was the vote against him in Paris and most of the great cities, in the centres of industry, intelligence, and political intrigue, but 50,000 of his soldiers were with the enemy. The shock was severe; what was Cæsar in the face of adverse circumstances if he could not count on the fidelity of the legions? Nothing could give more striking proof of the extreme impolicy of a measure which invited the soldiers to discuss the conduct of the master who relied upon their bayonets. As one blunder leads on to another, the Emperor, in his haste, advertised to the world his uneasiness at this military vote in a letter written to Marshal Canrobert and intended for publication to the Army, in which he made ostentatiously light of it. From that time the suspicions that his power was declining turned to convictions confirmed by electoral statistics. It appeared he could not even reckon on that backing from brute force, in the last resort, with which even his enemies had hitherto been inclined to credit him.

The *Plébiscite* had been presented to the country as a vote of peace, as the commencement of a new era of sound Constitutional progress, and as giving a fresh impulse to domestic prosperity. It is just possible it might have turned out so, had the voting answered the Emperor's hopes or dreams. As it was, it could scarcely fail to prove a vote of war sooner or later. That jealousy of growing German influence must become a question more dangerous to the dynasty than ever, now that the Emperor's power seemed to be tottering. Now that there was a *Fronde* in the Army, must there not be a foreign war to divert the minds of politicians of the canteen? Almost simultaneously with these events had come a change in the Cabinet, which had been nearly as freely commented on in Germany as in France. Daru and Buffet had retired from the enfeebled Ministry. After the *Plébiscite*, the former statesman had been replaced at the Foreign Office by the Duc de Gramont. We may be very certain that Napoleon, who had been given to hesitation in his best days, was hesitating now more painfully than ever over that question of a war with Germany.

But, taking the Gramont appointment in connexion with all that followed on it, we can scarcely doubt that at that time he inclined to war. Had it been his settled resolution, or even his ardent wish, to preserve peaceful relations, he could hardly have made so unfortunate a choice. Not only was the Duke by no means the man to direct the Foreign Office, where susceptibilities had become so sensitive, but his Prussian antipathies were notorious. Nor should the fact that he came straight from Vienna have been a recommendation in the circumstances. The suspicion that he might have been selected on account of his excellent relations in the Austrian capital would, doubtless, have strengthened the Emperor's hands had he decided upon war, by giving Europe the idea that Austria was prepared to revenge Sadowa. But if it was desirable to preserve peace, nothing could have been more injudicious than to give Prussia a pretext for taking the initiative in war, by persuading her that she was threatened by a danger which promptitude might best avert.

It is idle to speculate on what might have happened had the Emperor decided to play the patriot at all hazards – to accept facts abroad, and try to induce his subjects to accept them; to stake the fortunes of his family on his domestic policy. We have the authority of M. Thiers for asserting that the Empress urged him to make war for the sake of her son, and the assertion seems not improbable. It is certain that a knot of the most Bonapartist of the Bonapartists unceasingly pressed war on him for the most strictly personal reasons. They deluded themselves with the idea of the military preponderance of France; they believed the victory to be assured beforehand; the blood and treasure it might cost were nothing to them so long as they were assured a fresh lease of prosperity. The Emperor cannot altogether have shared these delusions, although doubtless to some extent he was deceived and willing to be deceived. But the successes that had once been matter of congratulation were now crowding their consequences upon him. He was being driven to seek for safety in provoking Providence; he was paying the penalties of a political *vie orageuse*. The *Coup d'Etat* had cut him loose from relations that should have been his security in time of danger, had he held his throne by a more legitimate title. But his interests already were trending far apart from those of his subjects; the events of the night of the 2d of December had left him few conscientious advisers, and limited his choice of capable military instruments. He had able creatures and subordinates who were bound fast to him; but the most eminent politicians of France, the men who might have had the confidence of the country, were in opposition or retreat, while disinterested veterans like Changarnier and Trochu were banished from his councils of war. The interests of an individual and of something far smaller than a faction were to decide on the destinies of the country at the moment when its fortunes were trembling in the balance. But no man, even in that extremity, would have rushed blindly on ruin to escape the dangers which menaced him. Did the Emperor believe he could enter on the war with reasonable hopes of success? Leboeuf might have deceived him so far with that unhesitating answer – 'We are ready, and more than ready.' But, after Leboeuf, there should have been no better judge of the situation than the Emperor himself. His master rolls might have been falsified, yet, all deductions made, he could roughly estimate the effective strength of his forces. At least, he knew the numbers Germany could put on foot in a given number of days, for the German military statistics were open to the world, and there was Stoffel at Berlin shrewdly noting everything and duly transmitting his Cassandra-like despatches to Paris. He must have been aware that, unless he could strike before those nine days of mobilization were accomplished, even Northern Germany would have a great numerical superiority in the field. The probability is that he taxed his ingenuity to combat the remonstrances of his common sense. In trying to deceive himself, he had plausible grounds to go upon. There was the reputation of those troops who had been the terror of Europe since the days of his uncle. They had only been repulsed by a combination of all the armies of Europe, when exhausted by unparalleled exertions. They had sustained that reputation in his own time, although he might have taken warning from the considerations which persuaded him to sign in haste the unlooked-for Peace of Villafranca. Then there were the chasse-pots, the mitrailleuses, and those new rifled cannon of bronze. *Moral* and armaments might compensate for lack of numbers, fortresses which could not be taken might be masked, and the French *élan* might carry him into Germany before the more sluggish Teutons had settled their plans or combined their operations. The communications once cut between the North of Germany and the South, he might hide his allies in the enemy's country, and beat Prussia, as his uncle had done, with South German auxiliaries. It was the Emperor's misfortune that he was doubly deceived, – that he was alike ill served in military affairs and in diplomacy. Had he been informed of the real spirit of Germany, he might have dismissed his notion of German alliances as the most extravagant of dreams; but his envoys to the minor German Principalities accepted the temper of the Courts as representing the spirit of the people. As is the manner of Frenchmen, they spoke no German. They reported that if France won a first success she might count on enlisting on her side South German jealousies of Prussia. It is less surprising that the Emperor received the fable at the time, since a man so intelligent as Edmond About repeats it confidently to this very moment. Moreover, as it appears now, the new Foreign Minister was persuaded that he had secured the adhesion of Austria. What he had to tell the Emperor probably confirmed such false reports as came from Courts like Würtemberg and Hesse Darmstadt.

Thus we may understand the Emperor's mental attitude early in the year. It was with anything but a light heart that he looked forward to this war looming on his horizon, yet to a certain extent he had succeeded in persuading himself that the venture was not so very desperate. Did not Leboeuf answer for the army? Had not De Gramont and his colleagues reassured him as to German alliances? Meanwhile, men were speaking of peace, while a sense of coming troubles was spreading, and there were rumours of war in the air. The country, and even the obsequious Chamber, became dangerously susceptible. Stanch Imperialists like Baron Jerome David held strange language. The project of a railway over the Alps threatened to create a conflagration in Europe. For a time there was a lull, but the heavens were lowering. Ollivier's voluble assurances in the debate on the Army Bill made most people uneasy; the barometer was falling fast, and men felt somehow by the movements of the ship of State that the hands which steered it were beginning to falter.

Early in July the squall of the Hohenzollern-Sigmaringen candidate for the Spanish Crown blew up. The Emperor found himself suddenly forced towards the resolution over which he had been hesitating so long. Let us judge his conduct and that of his Cabinet as we may, it is idle to say they regulated their policy on considerations of the dignity of France. The dignity of France was saved, and more than saved, when the King of Prussia formally approved the withdrawal of the objectionable candidate. But for the sake of the Emperor, of the dynasty, and the Bonapartist place-holders, it was deemed necessary there should be a diplomatic triumph to compensate the humiliation of Sadowa, by offering French vanity a brilliant satisfaction. The Emperor himself doubted and hesitated; if France was to be flattered by a triumph, Germany must smart under a defeat. But, in place of grasping at the reprieve which was offered him, doing his best in the circumstances, and giving himself time for reflection, he was tempted to push his success, and try if he could insult Prussia without having previously beaten her. Probably his judgment was remonstrating all the time. But we may believe that prolonged suspense was wearing a nature which had been tried by reaction of ill-luck after an extraordinary flush of prosperity. The Emperor saw that safety lay in waiting, had waiting been possible; but he had no longer either the resolution or the time to hold by his old maxim – 'Everything comes to him who waits.' The matter was precipitately discussed with the brutal bluntness of the telegraph. The most momentous questions were decided by the readiest pen in Cabinet Councils held standing, and in feverish exaltation of spirits. Stories were invented and facts deliberately misrepresented by officials with the idea of provoking popular enthusiasm. On the 19th of July the die was cast, and war was declared by Ministers almost as thoughtless as the *gamins* who raised the cry of '*A Berlin*' upon the Boulevards.

The war was declared, and the Emperor could have prevented or delayed it, but the French were never more unjust than when they subsequently insisted on holding him solely responsible. It was not only that seven millions of them, men like M. Guizot included, had voted the affirmative in the *Plébiscite*, but organs of all shades of opinion had been stimulating their jealousy of German unity, and the illustrious Thiers himself had published his gospel of war and revenge in his *History of the Consulate and the Empire.* Had it not been for the tone held by French writers for many years before, the Emperor would never have dreamt of the German war-path as the shortest way to regain his lost popularity; and it is matter of little consequence whether the cries on the Boulevards which followed the declaration of war came from his paid police agents or his enfranchised voters of the faubourgs.

Every one should be familiar with the history of the war, so far as it can be gathered from the conflicting testimony of the leading actors in it. The error of declaring it once committed, the Emperor became only secondarily responsible for the disasters which cost him so dearly. The *moral* and material efficiency Leboeuf had pledged himself for was lacking. A multitude of men who had been carried on the rolls were missing, and those who were actually under arms were never in the right place at the critical moment. The boasted *Intendance* system utterly broke down; magazines were found unfurnished, and supplies ran short. There was recrimination, disunion, and discontent among the leaders of the several *corps d'armée.* Time was lost when time was everything, and instead of France breaking ground with the swift advance that alone could have extenuated her precipitate declaration of war, her attenuated armies stood echeloned in a long line of observation along her assailable frontier. The plan attributed to the Emperor, of an aggressive movement that should sever Germany at once strategically and politically, had broken down before it could even be attempted. Had it been attempted it may be doubted whether it would not have proved more disastrous, if possible, than the one actually adopted.

The last pageants in which the unfortunate Emperor figured as the favourite of fortune were the arrival with the Army of Metz and the war rehearsal on the heights above Saarbrück, where his son received his 'baptism of fire.' While the world was expecting that, whatever might be the issue of the war, victory at first would incline to France, the Emperor was figuring as Commander-in-Chief of all the armies in the field. Had things gone well he would have accepted laurels of ceremony like the Grand Monarque when he travelled in his lumbering coach to see a town taken by one of his Marshals. But in reality, so far as the truth can be arrived at, it seems he only accompanied his troops in the capacity of spectator and adviser, perhaps as arbitrator in the last resort in some vexed question of combinations. Had all gone as well as in Italy, Cæsar's chariot or charger would have moved along in the middle of his victorious columns, through triumphs and ovations, and over roads strewed with bloody laurels. The great object of the war would have been attained, and Louis the Younger would have been presented to France and Europe as the spoilt child of Victory and Fortune. It was the dream of some such result which led the Prince's father to tempt this desperate game when he felt the odds were against him. His first proclamation, written in what should have been the flush of sanguine excitement, had somewhat chilled the more ardent spirits. He warned the troops of the formidable work that awaited them on their march in the country 'bristling with fortresses.' The anxiety that address shadowed out had more than realized itself. After the famous '*Tout peut se rétablir*' that followed the defeats of Woerth and Forbach, nothing can be conceived more deplorable than the position of the Emperor. Conscious of an irretrievable error, and moving despondently in the shadow of the approaching end, among disorganized and half-mutinous troops, who in their looks or language made him responsible for their misfortunes, surrounded by Generals who had lost head and heart, and had no comfort to offer to their master, he could do nothing by staying where he was, while he was sure to be made answerable for the defeats which impended when these demoralized troops of his should again be opposed to the disciplined and victorious Germans. The only thing more miserable than the scenes that were passing around him was the news which came from the capital. Paris would only receive him victorious; therefore, Paris would never receive him again. This was where he had been landed by revolving in that vicious circle which had commenced with the *coup d'etat.* This was the end of the years of strong personal government when he had boasted himself omnipotent for good or evil. It was but a year or two since he had declared that France was the arbiter of Europe, implying that he had the power to enforce her judgments; it was but a year since he had confidently answered for domestic order. Now the Germans were in France, and Paris, as he knew, was on the brink of a revolution. For him and for his son there was no safe home in his wide dominions but the head-quarters of a beaten and retreating army. He had no choice left him when he turned back with Mac-Mahon in that Quixotic enterprise of releasing Bazaine. Mac-Mahon, with candid chivalrousness, has acquitted his master of responsibility for that wild bit of strategy, but the surrender at Sedan must have come as a relief from a situation that was growing intolerable.

Thenceforward the Emperor's life has a personal rather than a political interest. The surrender of his sword to the King of Prussia symbolized nothing. He had ceased actually to be Emperor when Jules Favre had dared to demand his deposition three weeks before. The Palikao Ministry was Provisional rather than Imperial; it was understood that its precarious tenure of existence depended altogether on the news from the seat of war. With the capitulation of Sedan it ceased to be; the Empress sought safety in flight from Paris, not an hour too soon, and 'the gentlemen of the pavement' scrambled into authority over the fresh ruins of the personal power.

A howl of obloquy pursued the Emperor over the Belgian frontier to his seclusion at Wilhelmshöhe. It was not unnatural. The war was in great measure his; it had brought unspeakable suffering and bitter humiliation on the country, and his accomplices execrated him for not influencing them for their own good, in virtue of the authority their votes had vested in him. But dispassionate spectators regarded the fallen man with very different feelings. It was not only that such startling reverses might well have silenced harsh judgment, but the manner in which he bore them commanded involuntary respect and esteem. People who had called him a charlatan at the Tuileries confessed him to be a man when they saw him in the depths of misfortune. The wonderful result of his ambitions had been blighted so late in his life, that all hope was over for him; his pride was stung by the thought that his career had closed in humiliation; that posterity would denounce him as an impostor who had owed his rise and reputation to luck rather than genius; that the son, like the father, would begin life in proscription and exile, and find it the harder to repeat his father's successes among opponents forewarned by his father's example. With reflections so bitter gnawing at his mind, with his physical maladies conspiring to produce intense depression, he not only preserved his apparent serenity, but displayed invariably that dignified courtesy which denotes a mind too stable to be easily shaken. Nor was the effort merely a passing one. It has lasted from then till now. Beset by a mortal malady which would have made most men irritable and captious, the Emperor has shown himself invariably calm and strong. Nothing, perhaps, is so admirable in the life of this remarkable man as the silence he has consistently preserved with regard to those whose ill-advised counsels, incapacity, and self-interested falsehoods contributed so largely to his ruin. Ungrateful *protégés,* from whom he should have been sacred, have sought to make him their scapegoat, as he has been abused and calumniated by bitter enemies. He has neither remonstrated nor recriminated in person or by deputy. The wranglers might tell their stories as they would, they might be sure enough he would never contradict them. History will find much to reproach him with, but it is certain his contemporaries have been very unjust to him.

We have lingered long on the last year of his reign, pregnant as it was with events which have shifted the landmarks of history. We may dismiss his sojourn at Chislehurst in a line or two. His life passed there uneventfully and in apparent tranquillity. Silent, self-reserved, and self-controlled, he did not take the world into the secret of his regrets or remorse. If his party raised their heads again and bragged of a new revolution to their profit while France was struggling still in the social and financial chaos into which they had cast her, we have no reason to believe he gave them encouragement. Disappointed adventurers might talk and act madly when life was short. But the Emperor returned to England, whose life and people he had always liked, and lived like an English country gentleman, whose shattered health condemns him to retirement and the society of a few intimates. There were attached friends with him when he died, and if constancy should command friends few men deserved friends better.

It was unfortunate for his reputation that he was spared to live out his life. Had he succumbed some years ago to the first attacks of the disease he died of, he would have found eulogists enough to justify his policy by its brilliant success, and to deny that the Imperial system carried the inevitable seeds of dissolution. Had it collapsed after his decease they might have urged that the collapse was but a proof the more of his unrivalled genius, – that such a man could leave no successor to develope the ideas he had originated. As it is, it can hardly be doubted that his contemporaries will do him injustice, and that his memory will be, in a measure, rehabilitated by posterity. Unless absorbing ambition is to be pleaded as an excuse by Pretenders born in the people, we must judge his political morality severely. The *Coup d'Etat* was an offence almost more venial than the systematically relaxing and demoralizing nature of the rule that followed it. His best excuse was that he honestly believed himself and his system better adapted to the French than any other that could be substituted for it; and subsequent errors seem to have shown that he was not altogether wrong. In considering himself to the best of his lights, he did the best he could for his country. His foreign policy was generous and consistent, until personal motives compelled him to arrange a series of sensational surprises. His enlightened commercial ideas cost him some popularity among the Protectionist supporters of his dynasty. England at least had nothing to reproach him with, and the firmness with which he had held to her friendship assured him a friendly welcome when he sought refuge on her shores.

As might be presumed from the marvellous vicissitudes of his career, few men showed stranger or subtler contrasts in their nature. He owed his rise to the unflinching resolution with which he pursued a fixed idea; yet he hesitated over each step he took, and it was that habit of hesitation that ruined him in the end. His strong point was that no disappointment discouraged him, and so long as he felt he had time to wait, his patience was inexhaustible. Confined at Ham, in place of dashing himself against his prison bars, he turned quietly to his studies, and educated himself for the destinies in store for him. After the ridicule of his failures on the frontiers and in the Chamber of Deputies, he tried again as if nothing had happened. It was significant of the man that he succeeded in France in spite of ridicule, yet there may have been cool policy in the deeds that changed ridicule to terror on the 2d of December.

With his unquestionable ability and some extraordinary gifts, it must be confessed he owed much to fortune. She repeatedly did wonderful things for him when his circumstances were critical. He came to count with too great confidence on her favours when they were showering down on him, and he drew recklessly on his *prestige* instead of nursing it against gloomier days. It had been his aim to persuade his subjects that he was something more than mortal; when his mishaps proved his mortality, they resented the deception he had practised on them, and trampled their idol in the dust. It is not in our province now to speculate as to the influence of his rule on France, or to examine how far France is to be blamed for the vices and corruption of the Empire. If he misunderstood the people he governed when he treated them rather like children than men, we can only repeat, the fault was a venial one. Had he been born in a station beneath the influence of those ambitions that tempt men to become criminal, he would have lived distinguished and died esteemed. As it is, if the circle of his devoted friends has sadly dwindled since his fall and abdication, we trust for the honour of human nature that there are many who mourn him sincerely, in common gratitude.

The Times had been concerned for days with the former Emperor's deteriorating condition. His death, following an emergency operation designed to break up his kidney stones, was announced on 10 January 1873. Five days later his supporters issued a manifesto, stating that 'the Emperor is dead but the Empire is living and indestructible'. All hopes of reviving the Empire died when Napoleon's son, Eugène Louis, the Prince Imperial, was killed in Zululand, fighting with the British army, on 1 June 1879. Following his detention in Germany, the deposition of the Bonaparte dynasty and the declaration of the Third Republic in September 1870, Napoleon and his family had retired to Camden Place at Chislehurst in Kent. It was here that he died. In 1881 the Empress Eugénie moved to Farnborough in Hampshire, where she constructed a flamboyant domed mausoleum for her late husband and her son in 1887. She herself was interred there after her death in 1922. As this obituary consistently suggests, British responses to Napoleon III's policies as Emperor were at best ambiguous, and at worst suspicious and antipathetic. He and Eugénie had forged an amicable personal relationship with Queen Victoria, but many British critics, including this otherwise fair-minded obituarist, seem to have found the term 'charlatan' an appropriate description of both the Emperor and his régime.

WILLIAM CHARLES MACREADY

Actor: 'A deep and subtle insight into the shades and peculiarities of character.'

27 APRIL 1873

IT SOUNDS A little strange, even to the ear of veteran playgoers, to record the death of Macready, the favourite of half-a-century ago, the contemporary of the Keans and the Kembles, more than 20 years since his retirement from the stage. As our obituary of yesterday mentioned, William Charles Macready died on Sunday at Cheltenham, at the ripe age of 80 years.

The son of a gentleman who had not been very fortunate as lessee and manager of one or two provincial theatres, he was born in the parish of St. Pancras, London, on the 3rd of March, 1796. He was educated at Rugby, with a view to following one of the learned professions, probably either the Bar or the Church. But it was not his destiny to become either a Judge or a Bishop. His father was suffering from pecuniary embarrassments, and it became necessary for the son to turn his hand to some line of life where he could be earning money, instead of spending it. Accordingly, he appeared on the boards for the first time at Birmingham in June, 1810, performing the part of Romeo, when he had little more than completed his 17th year. His appearance is traditionally said to have been successful, and he remained with his father's Company until the year 1814 or 1815, performing at Bath, Birmingham, Chester, Sheffield, Birmingham, and Glasgow, and in other large provincial towns, with similar results. In September, 1816, he made his first appearance on the boards of a London theatre, performing Orestes in *The Distressed Mother*, at Covent Garden. Here, too, his success was undoubted, but he had difficulties to overcome. To use the words of a writer in the *English Cyclopedia*, 'Kemble, Young, and Kean had taken a sort of exclusive possession of the characters of Shakespeare in which, at a later period, Macready was destined to display such excellence. With a resolute industry, however, a deep and subtle insight into the shades and peculiarities of character, and a style at once original and simple, he made a certain range his own. He won applause as Rob Roy and Gambia; but it was in the *Virginius* of Sheridan Knowles that his true position was first fully demonstrated.'

From this time he continued to rise steadily in the favour of the public; and he increased his reputation abroad by well-timed visits to America and to Paris in the years 1826–28.

It was in the autumn of 1837 that he added to his many engagements and responsibilities by undertaking the post of lessee and manager of Covent Garden Theatre. Here his labour was immense. In the words of the writer already quoted, 'he did not overlay the drama by too gorgeous scenery or by too minute attention to the details of costume, as though they were to be the principal attractions, but strove to make them appropriate to the situation and feeling of the scene as a whole.' He also endeavoured to purify the atmosphere of his theatre by the exclusion of immoral characters and of all that could justify the suspicions and attacks of the enemies of drama. It cannot, however, be said that the financial results corresponded to his praiseworthy attempt; and at the end of two years he resigned his management. At the close of his management, however, his friends not only entertained him at a public dinner, but presented him with a more solid 'testimonial' of their sympathy.

After a short performance at the Haymarket, we find him next undertaking the management of Drury Lane, undeterred by his experience at the rival house. His management here was distinguished by the introduction of musical dramas set forth in the highest style of scenic illustration, among which we ought to particularize *Acis and Galatea* and *The Masque of Comus.* It also marked the introduction of new dramas to the public, including many of the best pieces of Serjeant (afterwards Mr. Justice) Talfourd, Sheridan Knowles, and the late Lord Lytton, then better known to the world by the familiar name of Bulwer, who was his firm and fast friend for many years, and who wrote for him both *Richelieu* and the *Lady of Lyons.* As the great French Cardinal Macready achieved one of his chief histrionic triumphs; but still, with reference to financial results, his management was not successful. Accordingly, he resigned it at the end of a second season; and it is not a little remarkable that in his parting address he took occasion to denounce the injurious operation of the dramatic monopoly which then prevailed. This step he followed up by a petition to Parliament for its removal, and before long he had the satisfaction of seeing his wishes realized.

In 1849 Macready again paid a professional visit to North America; and on this occasion it will be remembered that a quarrel raised by the well-known American actor named Forrest, lately deceased, gave rise to a riot in the Astor Opera-house at New York while the performance was going on, in which Macready's life was endangered. The riot was not suppressed until the military were called out; shots were fired, and several persons killed.

Returning to England towards the close of the same year, Mr. Macready entered upon his last engagement at the Haymarket; but his health was not good, and he soon after retired, fortunately in good time to enjoy his professional honours in private life, but not until he had completed the representation of all his principal characters. It was in February, 1851, that he took his formal farewell of the stage and was entertained at a public dinner in London, the chair being filled by his old friend Sir E. Bulwer Lytton, whom he has now followed to the grave.

After his retirement from public life, he took up his residence first at Sherborne, in Dorsetshire, and subsequently at Cheltenham, where, as we have said, he breathed his last on Sunday. At Sherborne he employed his leisure time in literary pursuits, and nothing pleased him better than to deliver lectures at the local Mechanics' Institutes and other similar institutions for the benefit of the humbler classes of society; and both there and at Cheltenham he did his best to promote the cause of popular education. About 25 years ago Mr. Macready published an edition of the poetical works of Pope, which was originally prepared and privately printed by him for the use of his children, to whom it is dedicated.

Despite being born into the theatre, Macready had claims to be a gentleman and, as this obituary argues, he consistently strove to render both his profession and his art as an actor and manager 'respectable'. Gradually emerging from the long shadows cast by his popular contemporaries, Edmund Kean and John Philip Kemble, he achieved a singular reputation in playing non-Shakespearian roles. He remained the victim of professional jealousy, notably during his visit to New York in 1849 when the American actor, Edwin Forrest, fomented a riot at the Astor Opera House. Macready barely escaped with his life, and the military had to be called in to suppress the disturbance in which seventeen men were killed and thirty wounded. He was manager of Covent Garden 1837–1839 and of Drury Lane Theatre 1841–1843. It was as part of a series of important revivals of Shakespeare plays at the former theatre that Macready mounted a production of *King Lear* in January 1838. It was the first stage performance since the seventeenth century to dispense with Nahum Tate's happy ending and to reintroduce the character of the Fool. Macready took leave of the theatre in a farewell performance of *Macbeth* at Drury Lane on 28 February 1851 and retired to Cheltenham, where he died on 27 April 1873.

DAVID LIVINGSTONE

Missionary and explorer: 'Fallen in the cause of civilization and progress.'

1 MAY 1873

THE FOLLOWING TELEGRAM, dated Aden, the 27th inst., has been received at the Foreign Office from Her Majesty's Acting Consul-General at Zanzibar:–

> 'The report of Livingstone's death is confirmed by letters received from Cameron, dated Unyanyembe, October 20. He died of dysentery after a fortnight's illness, shortly after leaving Lake Bemba for eastward. He had attempted to cross the lake from the north, and failing in this had doubled back and rounded the lake, crossing the Chambize and the other rivers down from it; had then crossed the Luapuia, and died in Lobisa, after having crossed a marshy country with the water for three hours at a time above the waist; ten of his men had died, and the remainder, consisting of 79 men, were marching to Unyanyembe. They had disembowelled the body and had filled it with salt, and had put brandy into the mouth to preserve it. His servant Chumas went on ahead to procure provisions, as the party was destitute, and gave intelligence to Cameron, who expected the body in a few days. Cameron and his party had suffered greatly from fever and ophthalmia, but hoped to push on to Ujiji. Livingstone's body may be expected at Zanzibar in February. Please telegraph orders as to disposal. No leaden shells procurable here.'

A plain Scottish missionary, and the son of poor parents, David Livingstone yet came of gentle extraction. The Livingstones have ever been reckoned one of the best and oldest of the Highland families. Considering that his father and himself were strong Protestants, it is singular that his grandfather fell at Culloden fighting in the Cause of the Stuarts. And that the family were Roman Catholics down to about a century ago, when (to use his own words) 'they were made Protestants by the laird coming round their village with a man who carried a yellow staff' to compel them, no doubt, to attend the established worship. More recently the Livingstones were settled in the little island of Ulva, on the coast of Argyleshire not far from the celebrated island of Iona, so well known in the annals of medieval missionary enterprise.

Dr. Livingstone's father, one Neill Livingstone, who kept a small teadealer's shop in the neighbourhood of Hamilton, in Lanarkshire, is represented by him, in

David Livingstone

a biographical sketch prefixed to his volume of *Travels*, as having been too strictly honest and conscientious in his worldly dealings ever to become a rich and wealthy man. The family motto, we are told by one writer, was 'Be honest.' He was a 'deacon' in an independent chapel in Hamilton; and he died in the early part of the year 1855. His son was born at East Kilbride, in Lanarkshire, in or about the year 1816. His early youth was spent in employment as a 'hand' in the cotton-mills in the neighbourhood of Glasgow; and he tells us, in the book to which we have already referred, that during the winter he used to pursue his religious studies with a view to following the profession of a missionary in foreign parts, returning in the summer months to his daily labour in order to procure support during his months of renewed mental study.

While working at the Blantyre mills, young Livingstone was able to attend an evening school, where he imbibed an early taste for classical literature. By the time he was 16 years of age he had got by heart the best part of both *Horace* and *Virgil*. Here also he acquired a considerable taste for works on religion and on natural science; in fact, he 'devoured' every kind of reading, 'except novels.' Among the most favourite books of his boyhood and early manhood, he makes special mention of Dr. Dick's *Philosophy of Religion* and *Philosophy of a Future State*. His religious feelings, however, warmed towards a missionary life; he felt an intense longing to become 'a pioneer of Christianity in China,' hoping that he might be instrumental in teaching the religion to the inhabitants of the Far East, and also that by so doing might 'lead to the material benefit of some portions of that immense empire.' In order to qualify himself for some such an enterprise he set himself to obtain a medical education, as a superstructure to that which he had already gained so laboriously; and this he supplemented by botanical and geological explorations in the neighbourhood of his home, and the study of Patrick's work on the *Plants of Lanarkshire*.

We next find him, at the age of 19, attending the medical and Greek classes in Glasgow in the winter, and the divinity lectures of Dr. Wardlaw in the summer. His reading while at work in the factory was carried on by 'placing his book on the spinning-jenny,' so that he could 'catch sentence after sentence while he went on with his labour,' thus 'keeping up a constant study undisturbed by the roar of machinery.' Having completed his attendance on Dr. Wardlaw's lectures, and having been admitted a Licentiate of the Faculty of Physicians and Surgeons, he resolved in 1838 to offer his services to the London Missionary Society as a candidate for the ministry in foreign parts. This step he was induced to take, to use his own words, on account of the 'unsectarian character of that society, which sends out neither Episcopacy nor Presbyterianism, but the Gospel of God, to the heathen.' In this 'unsectarian' movement he saw, or thought he saw, realized his ideal of the missionary life as it ought to be. The opium war, which then was raging, combined with other circumstances to divert his thoughts from China to Africa; and from the published accounts of the missionary labours of Messrs. Moffat, Hamilton, and other philanthropists in that quarter of the globe, he saw that an extensive and hopeful field of enterprise lay open before him.

His offer was accepted by the society, and having spent three months in theological study in England, and having been ordained to the pastoral office, he left these shores in 1840 for Southern Africa, and after a voyage of nearly three months reached Cape-Town. His first destination was Port Natal, where he became personally acquainted with his fellow countryman, the still surviving Rev. Robert Moffat, whose daughter subsequently became his wife and the faithful and zealous sharer of his toils and travels, and accompanied him in his arduous journey to Lake Ngami.

From Natal he proceeded inland to a mission station in the Bechuana country, called Kuruman, about 700 miles distant from Cape-Town, where, and at Mahotsa, he was employed in preparatory labours, joined with other missionaries down to about the year 1845. From that date for about four years more he continued to work at Chenuane, Lepelole, and Ko'obeng, aided and supported by no larger staff than Mrs. Livingstone and three native teachers. It was not until 1849 that he made his first essay as an explorer, strictly so called, as distinct from a missionary; in that year he made his first journey in search of Lake Ngami. In 1852 he commenced, in company with his wife, the 'great journey,' as he calls it, to Lake Ngami, of which a full and detailed account is given in the work already quoted above, and which he dedicated on its publication to Sir Roderick Murchison, as 'a token of gratitude for the kind interest he has always taken in the author's pursuits and welfare.' The outline of this 'great journey' is so familiar to all readers of modern books of travel and enterprise that we need not repeat it here. It is enough to say that in the ten years previous to 1855 Livingstone led several independent expeditions, into the interior of Southern Africa, during which he made himself acquainted with the languages, habits, and religious notions of several savage tribes that were previously unknown to Englishmen, and twice crossed the entire African continent, a little south of the tropic of Capricorn, from the shores of the Indian Ocean to those of the Atlantic.

In 1855 the Victoria gold medal of the Geographical Society was awarded to Livingstone in recognition of his services to science by 'traversing south Africa from the Cape of Good Hope, by Lake Ngami, to Linyanti, and thence to the western coast in 10 degrees south latitude.' He subsequently retraced his steps, returning from the western coast to Linyanti, and then – passing through the entire eastern Portuguese settlement of Tete – he followed the Zambesi to its mouth in the Indian Ocean. In the whole of these African explorations it was calculated at the time that Livingstone must have passed over no less than 11,000 miles of land, for the most part untrodden and untraversed by any European, and up to that time believed to be inaccessible.

In 1856 Livingstone returned to England, to use the eloquent words of his firm friend, the late Sir Roderick Murchison, –

> 'As the pioneer of sound knowledge, who by his astronomical observations had determined the sites of various places, hills, rivers and lakes, hitherto nearly unknown; while he had seized upon every opportunity of describing the physical features, climatology, and even geological structure of the countries which he had explored, and pointed out many new sources of commerce as yet unknown to the scope and enterprise of the British merchant.'

The late Lord Ellesmere bore similar testimony to the importance of his discoveries, adding his warm approval of the 'scientific precision with which the unarmed and unassisted English missionary had left his mark upon so many important stations in regions hitherto blank upon our maps.'

It may possibly be remembered that in a letter published in our columns on the 29th of December, 1856, Dr. Livingstone publicly stated his views and convictions upon the question of African civilization in general, and strongly recommended the encouragement of the growth of cotton in the interior of that continent, as a means towards the opening up of commercial intercourse between this country and the tribes of Southern and Central Africa. Such measures, if adequately supported, he considered, would lend, in the course of time, to the graduate but certain and final suppression of the slave trade, and the proportionate advancement of human progress and civilization.

Early in the spring of 1858 Livingstone returned to Africa for the purpose of prosecuting further researches and pushing forward the advantages which his former enterprise had to some extent secured. He went back with the good wishes of the entire community at home, who were deeply touched by his manly, modest, and unvarnished narrative, and by the absence of all self-seeking in his character. He carried with him the patronage and encouragement and the substantial support of Her Majesty's Government (more especially of Lords Clarendon and Russell), and of the Portuguese Government also; and before setting out on his second expedition in that year he was publicly entertained at a banquet at the London Tavern, and honoured by the Queen with a private audience, at which Her Majesty expressed, on behalf of herself and the Prince Consort, her deep interest in Dr. Livingstone's new expedition. In the meantime a 'Livingstone Testimonial Fund' was raised in the city of London by the liberal subscription of the leading merchants, bankers, and citizens, headed by the Lord Mayor. Within a very few months from the time of leaving England, Dr. Livingstone and his expedition reached that part of the eastern coast of Africa at which the Zambesi falls into the ocean; her two small steamers were placed at their disposal, and they resolved to ascend the river and thence make their way into the interior. Passing over the details of the expedition, a full account of which is given in the *Narrative* published by himself and his brother in 1865, we may state that in these journeys Livingstone and his companions discovered the lakes Nyassa and Shirwa, two of the minor inland meres of Africa, and explored the regions to the west and north-west of Lake Nyassa for a distance of 300 miles – districts hitherto unknown to Europeans, and which lead to the head waters of the north-eastern branch of the Zambesi and of several of that river's tributaries. The geographical results of the expedition, then, were the discovery of the real mouths of the Zambesi and the exploring of the immense territories around that river and its tributary, the Shire – results which not only possess much interest, but may prove hereafter of great value if this part of Africa can be brought within the sphere of civilization and commerce. It was hoped, indeed, at one time, that this exploration of the Zambesi would lead to a permanent settlement of Christianity on the banks of that river; but the first head of that mission, sent out mainly by Oxford and Cambridge – Bishop Mackenzie – soon fell a victim to the climate; and the mission itself was abandoned as hopeless by his successor, Bishop Tozer. The fact was that we had endeavoured to plant the tree before the land was dug up and prepared to receive it.

In this second work, the *Narrative*, which was written in the hospitable abode of Newstead Abbey, in the autumn and winter of 1864–65, the author tells his own story with a genuine modesty and yet a native force which carries the reader irresistibly onwards. Like its precursor, it obtained a sale of upwards of 30,000 copies. In its pages he sums up the positive results of his researches as the discovery of a large tract of fertile soil, rich in cotton, in tobacco, and in timber, though subject to periodical droughts, and also the establishment of an excellent port, the capacities of which had been overlooked by previous travellers. It is only fair to add that some of those results have been disputed by independent writers, who, however, have never visited those parts. Still, it is no slight thing to be able to boast, as Dr. Livingstone could boast, that by means of the Zambesi a pathway has been opened towards Central Highlands, where Europeans, with their accustomed energy and enterprise, may easily form a healthy and permanent settlement, and where, by opening up communications and establishing commercial relations with the friendly natives, they may impart Christianity and that civilization which has for centuries marked the onward progress of the Anglo-Saxon race. This expedition, it is right to add, originated among the members of the Geographical Society, and Livingstone was aided in it from first to last, not only by the support of Her Majesty's Government, but by the counsel of Captain Washington, the Hydrographer to the Admiralty, Commander Bedingfield, R. N., Dr. Kirk, of Edinburgh, Mr.

Baines, of African and Australian fame, and by his ever faithful friend and companion, his devoted wife. By their assistance he was enabled, to use the expression of Sir R. Murchison, 'to reach the high watersheds that lie between his own Nyassa and the Tanganyika of Burton and Speke, and to establish the fact that those lakes did not communicate with each other; and that, if so, then there was, to say the least, a high probability that the Tanganyika, if it did not empty itself to the west, through the region of Congo, must find an exit for its waters northwards by way of the Nile.'

This leads us to the third and last great journey of Dr. Livingstone, the one from which such great results have been expected, and in which he has twice or thrice previous to the last sad news been reported to have lost his life. Leaving England at the close of 1865, or early in the following year, as our readers are probably aware, he was despatched once more to Central Africa, under the auspices of the Geographical Society, in order to prosecute still further researches which would throw a light on that mystery of more than 2,000 years' standing – the real sources of the Nile. Of his explorations since that date the public were for several years in possession of only scanty and fragmentary details, for it must be remembered that Dr. Livingstone was accredited in this last expedition as Her Britannic Majesty's Consul to the various native chiefs of the unknown interior. This post, no doubt, gave him considerable advantages connected with his official status; but one result was that his home despatches have been of necessity addressed, not to the Geographical Society, but to the Foreign Office. It was known, however, that he spent many months in the central district between 10 deg. and 15 deg. south of the Equator, and Dr. Beke – no mean authority upon such a subject – considers that he has solved the mystery of the true source of the Nile among the high tablelands and vast forests which lie around the lake with which his name will for ever be associated.

Although we cannot travel quite so rapidly in our inferences as Dr. Beke, we are bound to record the fact that Dr. Livingstone claims to have found that 'the chief sources of the Nile arise between 11 deg. and 12 deg. of south latitude, or nearly in the position assigned to them by Ptolemy.' This may or may not be the case; for time alone will show us whether this mystery has been actually solved, or whether we are still bound to say, as Sir R. Murchison, said in 1865,– 'We hope at the hands of Dr. Livingstone for a solution of the problem of the true watershed of that unexplored country far to the south of the huge water-basins which, we know, contribute to feed the Nile, the Victoria Nyanza of Speke and Grant, and the Albert Nyanza of Baker.'

During the last year or two our news of Dr. Livingstone has been but scanty, though from time to time communications – some alarming and others, again, reassuring – have reached us from himself or from other African Consuls, officially through the Foreign Office and privately through Sir Roderick Murchison. It will be remembered, more especially, that in the Spring of 1867, a letter from Dr. Kirk, dated Zanzibar, December 20, 1866, was received by Sir R. Murchison and Mr. Bates, giving an apparently circumstantial account of Livingstone's death by an attack of a band of Matites, some miles to the west of Luke Nyassa. The news rested mainly upon the testimony of some Johanna men, who declared that they had with difficulty escaped the same fate; and for some days half London believed the sad story to be true; but Sir Roderick Murchison, with a keen insight which almost amounted to intuition, refused to believe the evidence on which the tale was based and gradually the world came round and followed suit. The story, as told in the *Times of India*, March 13, 1867, ran as follows:–

> 'It would appear that Dr. Livingstone had crossed Lake Nyassa about the middle of September last, and had advanced a few stages beyond its western shores, when he encountered a horde of savages of the Matite tribe. He was marching, as usual, ahead of his party, having nine or ten personal attendants, principally boys from Nassick, immediately behind him. The savages are said to have set upon them without any provocation and with very little warning. Dr. Livingstone's men fired, and before the smoke of their muskets had cleared away their leader had fallen beneath the stroke of a battle axe, and his men speedily shared the same fate. Moosa who witnessed the encounter and the death-blow of his master from behind a neighbouring tree, immediately retreated and meeting the rest of the party they fled into the deep forest, and eventually made their way back to Lake Nyassa, whence they returned to the coast with a caravan. When the news of Dr. Livingstone's sad death reached Zanzibar, the English and other European Consuls lowered their flags, an example which was followed by all the ships in the harbour, as well as by the Sultan. It may be worth while to remark that Dr. Livingstone himself had a strong presentiment that he would never return from the expedition which has terminated thus disastrously; and this presentiment he frequently expressed to the officers of Her Majesty's ship Penguin, who were the last Europeans he saw before starting for the interior.'

It will be within the memory of our readers also that in 1867 an expedition was sent out by the British Government, in concert with the Geographical Society, under Mr. E. D. Young, R. N., and Mr. H Faulkner, in order to ascertain the fate, and, if still alive, the position of Dr. Livingstone. The result of this expedition was that they found sufficient traces of his recent presence at Mapunda's and Marenga's towns on the Lake Nyassa, to negative entirely the melancholy rumour of his murder, by showing that these Johanna men had deserted him while still pursuing his travels, and that, consequently, he was alive when he and they parted company. It was in this westward journey that he was said to have been killed in the autumn of the year 1868; but the story as soon as it reached London was discredited, both by Sir R. Murchison and by the city merchants, as inconsistent with the known dates of his movements, and afterwards happily proved to be false.

In July, 1869, Dr. Livingstone resolved to strike westwards from his head-quarters at Ujiji, on the Tanganyika Lake, in order to trace out a series of lakes which lay in that direction, and which, he hoped, would turn out eventually to be the sources of the Nile. If that, however, should prove not to be the case, it would be something, he felt, to ascertain for certain that they were the head waters of the Congo; and, in the latter case, he would probably have followed the course of the Congo, and have turned up, sooner or later, on the Western Coast of Africa. But this idea he appears to have abandoned after having penetrated as far west as Bainbarro and Lake Kamolondo, and stopping short at Bagenya about four degrees west from his starting point. At all events, from this point he returned, and which, in the winter of 1870–71, he was found by Mr. Stanley, he was once more in the neighbourhood of his old haunts, still bent on the discovery of certain 'fountains on the hills,' which he trusted to be able to prove to be the veritable springs of the Nile, and to gain the glory of being alone their discoverer – to use his own emphatic words, 'So that no one may come after and cut me out with a fresh batch of sources.'

During the last two years or so, if we except the sudden light thrown upon his career by the episode of Mr. Stanley's successful search after him, we have been kept rather in the dark as to the actual movements of Dr. Livingstone. Mr. Stanley's narrative of his discovery of the Doctor in the neighbourhood of Ujiji is in the hands of every well-informed Englishman, and his journey in company with him round the northern shores of Lake Tanganyika (with some hint of a possible modification of his opinion as to the connexion between that sea and the Nile) was recorded in the address delivered by Sir Henry Rawlinson, the President of the Geographical Society, last summer. On that occasion the President remarked:–

> 'Our knowledge of Livingstone's present whereabouts is not very definite. He appears to have been so thoroughly impressed with a belief or the identity of his triple Lunlaba with the Nile that, in spite of earnest longings to revisit his native land, he could not persuade himself to leave Africa until he had fairly traced to their sources in the southern mountains the western branches of the great river that he had explored in Manyema. Awaiting accordingly, at Unyanyembe the arrival of stores and supplies which were partly furnished by Mr. Stanley, and partly by our own First Relief Expedition, no sooner had they arrived than he started in September last (1872) for the further end of Tanganyika, intending

from that point to visit a certain mound in about 11 deg. South latitude, from which the Lufira and Lulua were said to flow to the north, and the Leeambye and Kafué to the south. Hence he proposed to return northwards to the copper mines of Katanga, in the Koné mountains, of which he had heard such an extraordinary account. Later still he was bent on visiting Lake Lincoln, and following the river which flowed out of it, and which, under the name of the Loeki or Lomanae, joined the Lualaba a little further down, to the great unexplored lake at the Equator. His expectation seems to have been that this lake communicated with the Bahr-el-Gazal, and that he might thus either return home by the route of the Nile or retrace his steps to Ujiji but if, as we hope will be the case, either the one or the other of the expeditions which are now penetrating into the interior from the East and West Coast respectively should succeed in opening communication with him before he is called on to decide on the line of his return journey from the Equatorial lake, it is far from probable that, with the new light thus afforded him, he will continue his journey along the Congo, and emerge from the interior on the Western Coast.'

We fear that these forecastings have been falsified by the event, and that we must now add the name of David Livingstone to the roll of those who have fallen in the cause of civilization and progress.

It is impossible not to mourn the loss of a missionary so liberal in his views, so large-hearted, so enlightened. By his labours it has come to pass that throughout the protected tribes of Southern Africa Queen Victoria is generally acknowledged as 'the Queen of the people who love the black man.' Livingstone had his faults and his failings; but the self-will and obstinacy he possibly at times displayed were very near akin to the qualities which secured his triumphant success, and much allowance must be made for a man for whom his early education had done so little, and who was forced, by circumstances around him, to act with a decision which must have sometimes offended his fellow-workers. Above all, his success depended, from first to last, in an eminent degree upon the great power which he possessed of entering into the feelings, wishes, and desires of the African tribes and engaging their hearty sympathy.

As the best memorial of such a man as Livingstone, we would here place on permanent record his own eloquent words, in which he draws out his idea of the missionary's work in the spirit, not merely of a Christian, but of a philosopher and statesman:–

'The sending of the Gospel to the heathen must include much more than is implied in the usual picture of a missionary, which is that of a man going about with a bible under his arm. The promotion of commerce ought to be specially attended to, as this more speedily than anything else demolishes that sense of isolation which is engendered by heathenism, and makes the tribes feel themselves to be mutually dependent on each other. Those laws which still prevent free commercial intercourse among civilized nations appear to me to be nothing but the remains of our own heathenism. But by commerce we may not only put a stop to the slave trade, but introduce the negro family into the body corporate of nations, no one member of which can suffer without the others suffering with it. This in both Eastern and Western Africa would lead to much larger diffusion of the blessings of civilization than efforts exclusively spiritual and educational confined to any one tribe. These should, of course, be carried out at the same time where possible – at all events, at large central and healthy stations; but neither civilization nor Christianity can be promoted alone; in fact, they are inseparable.'

In conclusion, our readers will forgive us for quoting the following testimony to Livingstone's character from the pen of Mr. E. D. Young, whom we have mentioned above: 'His extensive travels place him at the head of modern explorers, for no one has dared as yet to penetrate where he has been; no one, through a lengthy series of years, has devoted so much of his life to the work of searching out tribes hitherto unknown and I believe that his equal will rarely, if ever, be found in one particular and essential characteristic of the genuine explorer. He has the most singular faculty of ingratiating himself with natives whithersoever he travels. A frank openhearted generosity combined with a constant jocular way in treating with them carries him through all. True, it is nothing but the most iron bravery which enables a man thus to move among difficulties and dangers with a smile on his face instead of a haggard, careworn, and even a suspicious look. Certain it is, also, that wherever he has passed, the natives are only too anxious to see other Englishmen, and in this way we must crown him "the King of African Pioneers." '

This obituary never doubts the nature and enterprise of Livingstone's missionary work in Africa. Although it portrays the man as one who early on in his life raised himself above his humble origins by education and a sure sense of vocation, it also seems to rejoice in suggesting that there may be a significance in his distinctive Highland ancestry. This is 'self help' with an added degree of genetic determining. Livingstone, a meticulous observer and recorder of the topography of the continent on which he laboured, is honoured as a pioneer explorer of territory unknown to Europeans and as one who earned the respect of the Africans amongst whom he worked. After his death on 1 May 1873 from dysentery in what is now Zambia, his body, accompanied as far as

Zanzibar by his two most faithful servants, was brought back to Britain for burial in Westminster Abbey. His posthumous reputation was fostered by Henry Morton Stanley.

JOHN STUART MILL

Philosopher and political theorist: 'the most candid of controversialists.'

8 MAY 1873

LIKE MANY OF his most distinguished contemporaries – like Charles Buller, Macaulay, Buckle, Dickens, Thackeray, George Cornewall Lewis, Sydney Herbert, Lytton – John Stuart Mill has died when many years of thought and action might still have been confidently anticipated for him by his friends. He was born in 1806, and may be cited as one of the strongest confirmations of their theory by those who maintain the hereditary nature of genius or capacity; for he was the son of a man eminently endowed with the same qualities of mind by which he himself rose to be one of the most remarkable writers and thinkers of his generation. James Mill, the father, popularly known as the historian of British India, was the author of a great variety of essays on morals, government, and philosophy; among others of an essay on *Education*, in which he takes for granted, as an indisputable fact, 'that the early sequences to which we are accustomed form those primary habits, and that the primary habits are the fundamental character of the man. The consequence is most important, for it follows that as soon as the infant, or rather the embryo begins to feel, the character begins to be formed, and that the habits which are then contracted are the most pervading and operative of all.'

The 'primary habits' of the infant or embryo disciple of Bentham were formed with especial reference to this principle. His education was in every sense private and paternal. He was hardly allowed to breathe out of the utilitarian atmosphere, he was swathed in metaphysics, he was dieted on political economy; and, instead of lisping, like Pope, in numbers, he lisped in syllogisms. His father, before going to the India House, had him up at 6 in the morning to dictate the tasks of the day, which included classics and modern languages, besides other branches of knowledge. He was, by all accounts an extraordinary child; and it is within our personal knowledge that he was an extraordinary youth when, in 1824, he took the lead at the London Debating Club in one of the most remarkable collections of 'spirits of the age' that ever congregated for intellectual gladiatorship, he being by two or three years the junior of the clique. The rivalry was rather in knowledge and reasoning than in eloquence: mere declamation was discouraged; and subjects of paramount importance were conscientiously thought out. He was already a frequent contributor to the *Westminster Review*, and a prominent member of the long defunct party, the Philosophic Radicals, whose sayings and doings in its heyday have recently been revived by Mrs. Grote. He must have been a boy in years when a foolish scheme for carrying out the Malthusian principle brought him under the lash of the satirist. In Moore's Ode to the Goddess Ceres we find:–

'There are two Mr. Mills, too, whom those who like reading
'What's vastly unreadable, call very clever;
'And whereas Mill senior makes war on *good* breeding
'Mill junior makes war on all *breeding* whatever.'

Coleridge, in his *Biographia Literaria,* plausibly suggests that literature will be most efficiently pursued by those who are tied down to some regular employment, official or professional, apart from and independent of it. Such employment, he thinks, exercises a steadying and bracing influence upon the mind. 'Three hours of leisure, unannoyed by any alien anxiety, and looked forward to with delight as a change and recreation, will suffice to realize in literature a larger product of what is truly genial than weeks of compulsion.' During the entire period of his greatest intellectual efforts John Stuart Mill held an important office under the East India Company, and discharged its duties in a manner to make his retirement a real loss to the public when, in 1868, he declined a seat in the Indian Council offered him by the present Lord Derby. The despatches and other documents drawn up by him would entitle him to a high rank among those it is the fashion to call 'closet statesmen.'

The first edition of his *System of Logic,* the work on which his reputation would be most confidently rested by his admirers, appeared in 1843. 'This book,' he says in his preface, 'makes no pretence of giving to the world a new theory of the intellectual operations. Its claim to attention, if it possess any, is grounded on the fact that it is an attempt, not to supersede, but to embody and systematize the best ideas which have been either promulgated on its subject by speculative writers or confirmed by accurate thinkers in their scientific inquiries.' It is a book which no one would read for amusement, hardly; indeed, except as a task; his style, always dry, is here at its driest, and the circumstance of the work having reached an eighth edition in 1872 is, therefore, a conclusive proof of its completeness as a system and a text-book. The same praise may be granted to his *Principles of Political Economy,* from which the existing state of the so-called science may be learnt; but in this work, instead of confining himself to the collection of known and recognized theories or facts, he has propounded sundry doctrines of dangerous tendency and doubtful soundness, which have laid him open to suspicion and attack – for instance, his doctrine of property in land, which, he maintains, is the inalienable inheritance of the human species, and may at any moment be wholly or in part resumed from considerations of expediency.

We need hardly add that many of his opinions on society and government have been generally and justly condemned; and that, in his more appropriate domain of mental and moral philosophy, he was engaged in unceasing feuds. He was, however, the most candid of controversialists, and too amiable to indulge in scorching sarcasm or inflict unnecessary pain. He was often a wrong-headed, but always a kind-hearted man. After conversing with some Oxford tutors in 1863, Mrs. Grote sets down:–

> 'Grote and Mill may be said to have revived the study of the two master sciences – History and Mental Philosophy among the Oxford undergraduates. A new current of ideas, new and original modes of interpreting the past, the light of fresh learning cast upon the peoples of antiquity; such are their impulses given, by these two great teachers, that our youth are completely kindled to enthusiasm towards both at the present time.'

Mill's election for Westminster in 1865 was an honourable tribute to his character and reputation, as his rejection in 1868 was the natural consequence and well-deserved penalty of his imprudence in exhibiting an uncalled-for sympathy with Mr. Odger and otherwise recklessly offending the most respectable portion of the constituency. He was well received in the House of Commons, and, although wanting in most of the physical requisites of an orator, he seldom failed to command attention when he rose. Indeed, he made a better figure even as a debater than was expected from his former appearances in that capacity, and the proof is that a well known writer produced a carefully finished parallel between him and Mr. Lowe *apropos* of some passages of arms between them during the Cattle Plague debates:–

> 'Mr. Lowe takes by preference the keen, practical common-sense view of his subject; Mr. Mill the philosophical, speculative and original view. Mr. Lowe's strength lies in his acquired knowledge, memory, and dialectic skill; Mr. Mill's in his intellectual resources and accumulated stores of thought. Their reading has been in different lines, and employed in a different manner; Mr. Lowe being the much superior classic, and Mr. Mill (we suspect) more at home in legislation, morals, metaphysics, and philosophy. Books, ancient and modern, are more familiar to Mr. Lowe, and have been better digested by Mr. Mill. The one has most imagination, the other most wit. The one almost rises to genius, whilst the palm of the highest order of talent must be awarded to the other. The one fights for truth, the other for victory. In conflict it is the trained logician against the matured thinker; not that the logician wants thought, or the thinker logic. A set combat between them would resemble one between the *retiarius* or

> netman of the Roman arena and a swordsman; and the issue would depend on whether Mr. Lowe could entangle his adversary in the close meshes of his reasoning by an adroit throw, or whether Mr. Mill could evade the cast by an intellectual bound, close, and decide the contest by a home thrust.'

We do not reproduce this parallel as agreeing with it, but as strikingly presenting some illustrative trait of each.

Of late years Mill has not come before the world with advantage. When he appeared in public it was to advocate the fanciful rights of women, to propound some impracticable reform or revolutionary change in the laws relating to the land; but, with all his error and paradoxes, he will be long remembered as a thinker and reasoner who has largely contributed to the intellectual progress of the age.

This is a deeply grudging notice of the career of a man whose work was to exert a profound influence over succeeding generations. The obituarist evidently draws on Mill's *Autobiography* of 1873 but he eschews mention of what latter-day readers might consider his most significant works: *On Liberty* (1859), *Representative Government* (1861), *Utilitarianism* (1863) and *The Subjection of Women* (1869). Mill had entered Parliament as an Independent MP for Westminster in July 1865. During his time in Parliament he was an outspoken advocate of liberal reform and of women's rights and acted as a supporter of George Odger, a shoemaker and trades unionist who made five unsuccessful attempts to become a working class MP. In 1851 Mill married the newly widowed Harriet Taylor, with whom he had been intimate for twenty-one years. Her tuberculosis obliged the couple to retire to Avignon for her health. She died there in 1858. Mill is buried beside her.

SIR EDWIN LANDSEER

Painter: 'His paintings are known . . . through the length and breadth of the land.'

1 OCTOBER 1873

WE HAVE TO announce, with deep regret, the death yesterday morning, at 10.40, of Sir Edwin Landseer. Sir Edwin had been long known to be in a most precarious state of health, but the news will not the less shock and grieve the worlds both of Art and of Society, in which he was an equal favourite. The great painter never, however, courted publicity; he was singularly reticent about all that concerned himself, and it is astonishing to find how little was known to his contemporaries respecting his early career.

The grandfather of Sir Edwin, we are told, settled as a jeweller in London in the middle of the last century; and here, it is said, his father, Mr. John Landseer, was born in 1761, though another account fixes Lincoln as his birthplace, and his birth itself at a later date. John Landseer became an engraver, rose to eminence in his line of art, became an Associate of the Royal Academy, and, having held that position for nearly 50 years, died in 1852. He was largely employed in engraving pictures for the leading publishers, including Macklin, who engaged him on the illustrations to his 'Bible;' this employment led to his marriage with a Miss Pot, a great friend of the Macklins, and whose portrait as a peasant girl, with a sheaf of corn upon her head, was painted by Sir Thomas Lawrence. The issue of this marriage consisted of three daughters and also of three sons – Thomas born in or about the year 1795; Charles, born in 1799; and Edwin, the youngest, in 1802. In 1806 Mr. John Landseer delivered to large audiences at the Royal Institution in Albemarle-street a series of lectures on engraving, in which he laid down broader, higher, and truer views of that branch of art than those which had hitherto prevailed. His name will also be remembered by many as the author or *Observations on the Engraved Gems brought from Babylon to England by Mr. Abraham Lockeit* in 1817; *Saboean Researches*, another work on the same subject; and a *Description of Fifty of the Earliest Pictures in the National Gallery*. He subsequently edited the *Review of the Fine Arts* and the *Probe*. Later in life he exhibited at the Academy some water-colour studies from Druidical Temples, and finally engraved his son Edwin's 'Dogs of St. Bernard,' of which he wrote also a small explanatory pamphlet. The chief work, however, of John Landseer lay in bringing up his three sons, of whom the eldest is as well known by his engravings as was his father, and the second was elected keeper of the Academy in 1851. The artistic education of Edwin Landseer was commenced at an early age under the eye of his father, who, after the example of the greatest masters, directed him to the study of nature herself, and sent him constantly to Hampstead-heath and other suburban localities to make studies of donkeys, sheep, and goats. A series of early drawings and etchings from his hand, preserved in the South Kensington Museum, will serve to show how faithful and true an interpreter of nature the future Academician was even more than half a century since, for some of his efforts are dated as early as his eighth year, so that he is a standing proof that precocity does not always imply subsequent failure. Indeed, he drew animals correctly and powerfully even before he was five years old!

His first appearance, however, as a painter dates from 1815, when, at the age of 13, he exhibited two paintings at the Academy; they are entered in the catalogue as Nos. 443 and 584; 'Portrait of a Mule' and 'Portraits of a Pointer Bitch and Puppy,' and the young painter appears as: Master E. Landseer, 33, Foley-street. In the following year he was one of the exhibitors at 'the Great Room in Spring-gardens,' then engaged for 'the Society of Painters in Oil and Water Colours,' along with De Wint, Chalon, and the elder Pugin; about the same time, too, we find him receiving regular instruction in art as a pupil in the studio of Haydon, and the residence of the family in Foley-street was the very centre of a colony of artists and literary celebrities. Mulready, Stothard, Benjamin West, A. E. Chalon, Collins, Constable, Daniel, Flaxman, and Thomas Campbell all lived within a few hundred yards of John Landseer's house; and from their society young Landseer, we may be sure, took care to draw profit and encouragement. He also derived considerable assistance from a study of the Elgin marbles at Burlington-house, where they lay for some time before finding a home in the British Museum. These ancient treasures he was led to study by the advice of his teacher Haydon. In the same year (1816) he was admitted as a student to the Royal Academy. In the following year he exhibited 'Brutus, a portrait of a Mastiff,' at the Academy, and also a 'Portrait of an Alpine Mastiff;' at the Gallery in Spring-gardens already mentioned.

With the year 1818 commenced an important epoch in the life of Landseer. His 'Fighting Dogs Getting Wind,' exhibited this summer at the rooms of the Society of Painters in Oil and Water Colours, excited an extraordinary amount of attention; and, being purchased by Sir George Beaumont, it set the stream of fashion in his favour. Sir David Wilkie, writing to Haydon at this date, remarked, as much in earnest as in jest, 'Young Landseer's jackasses are good.'

'The Cat Disturbed' was young Landseer's chief picture in 1819; it was exhibited at the Royal Institution; here, also, were exhibited about the same date his 'Lion enjoying his Repast,' and a companion picture, a 'Lion disturbed at his Repast.' In these paintings it is not fanciful or absurd to say that an educated eye can detect the hand of the designer of the Lions which guard the Nelson Monument in Trafalgar-square. His opportunity for studying the anatomy of the lion had arisen shortly before, we are told, through the death of one of the old lions in Exeter 'Change, and his subsequent dissection in Landseer's presence.

In 1821 he exhibited at the Academy his 'Ratcatchers,' which was subsequently engraved by his brother Thomas; and at the British Institution another sporting picture, entitled 'Pointers Soho.' In 1822 he was fortunate enough to obtain the premium of 150*l.* from the directors of the British Institution for his celebrated picture 'The Larder Invaded.' This was followed next year by 'The Watchful Sentinel,' contributed to the Exhibition of the British Institution, now in the Sheepshanks Gallery at South Kensington, and styled 'The Angler's Guard.' It represents a large brown and white Newfoundland dog and a white Italian greyhound seated and keeping strict watch and ward over a fishing-rod and basket. In 1821 he exhibited, also at the Royal Institution, 'The Cat's Paw,' which, we believe, hangs, or hung, in the dining-room at Cashiobury, the seat of Lord Essex in Hertfordshire. 'Taking a Buck,' 'The Widow,' and a stray 'Portrait' were Landseer's contributions to the Academy in 1825, and in the same summer his 'Poacher' was hung on the walls of the British Institution. In the following season was shown at the Academy his 'Hunting of Chevy Chase,' an important picture which has often been exhibited since. In the same year Landseer removed to the house in St. John's-wood-road, where he fixed his studio to the last. In 1826 he exhibited at the Royal Institution the picture of 'The Dog and the Shadow,' which is now at South Kensington. If we may trust the compiler of the monograph on *Sir E. Landseer's Early Works*, published by Messrs. Bell and Daldy in 1869, it was about this time that, being asked by Lord and Lady Holland to sit for his portrait to Landseer, Sydney Smith sent the well-known reply, 'Is thy servant a dog that he should do this thing?'

It can scarcely be supposed that it was merely the exhibition of 'Chevy Chase' which led to Edwin Landseer's election at this time to an Associateship of the Royal Academy. The fact is that the honour was anticipated long before, and that the election was made almost as a matter of course immediately on his attaining the age of four-and-twenty – the limit prescribed by the laws of the Academy. It may be interesting to our readers to know that the only other artists to whom a like compliment has been paid are Sir Thomas Lawrence and Mr. J. E. Millais.

It was in this year that Landseer paid his first visit to the Highlands – a district of which it may be said with truth that for more than 30 years he was the prophet and interpreter, and from which he drew more subjects than from any other, illustrating its men, its animals, and its landscapes with almost unvaried success. 'The Chief's Return from Deer stalking,' exhibited at the Academy in 1827, may be regarded as the first fruits alike of this northern tour and of his Associateship. Together with this appeared his 'Monkey who had seen the World,' showing the reunion of 'Pug' and his untravelled friends at home. Meantime, in spite of his election to the Academy, he proved that he did not forget his acquaintances and friends at the British Institution, to which he contributed, in the same year, another picture of 'Chevy Chase,' and 'A Scene at Abbotsford' representing Sir Walter Scott's favourite dog Maida reclining by a piece of ancient armour. The year 1828 was one of comparative rest to Landseer – at all events, it was productive of no contribution to the exhibitions of the day; but in 1829 he produced his 'Illicit Whisky Still in the Highlands,' and 'A Fireside Party' (now at South Kensington), in which the terriers which figure as the principal characters are said to have been the original 'Peppers and Mustards' so graphically described in the *Antiquary* by Sir Walter Scott.

The year 1830 witnessed the election of Landseer to the full honours of the Academy; and from that date to the end of his long career there is little for a biographer to do but to chronicle a long and regular catalogue of pictures year by year exhibited either at the British Institution or else on the walls of the Academy at Somerset House, in Trafalgar-square, and at Burlington House. Of these the best known and most popular are his 'High Life' and 'Low Life' (comprised in the Vernon gift, and now at South Kensington); 'Poachers Deer-stalking;' 'Too Hot;' 'A Lassie Herding Sheep;' 'Spaniels of King Charles' Breed' (also at South Kensington); 'The Cavalier's Pets,' a picture which, it is said, was painted in two days; 'Jack in Office;' 'Suspense ;' 'A Highland Dog rescuing Sheep from a Snowdrift;' 'Bolton Abbey in the Olden Time' (now at Chatsworth); 'The Drover's Departure; a scene in the Grampians' (part of the Sheepshanks' gift, and now at South Kensington); 'The Tethered Rams' (ditto); 'Comical Dogs' (also at South Kensington); 'Odin,' a portrait of a Scotch Deerhound; 'The Highland Shepherd's Chief Mourner;' 'There's Life in the Old Dog yet;' 'Dignity and Impudence' (a noble contrast of the heads of a magnificent bloodhound and a small terrier, bequeathed by Mr. Jacob Bell to the nation, and now at South Kensington); 'A Distinguished Member of the Humane Society;' 'Her Majesty's favourite Dogs and Parrot;' 'The Return from Hawking;' 'The Hooded Falcon;' 'Favourites, the property of his Royal Highness Prince George of Cambridge;' 'A Highland Breakfast;' 'Deer and Deerhounds in a Mountain Torrent;' 'Corsican, Russian, and Fallow Deer;' and 'Spaniels belonging to Lord Albemarle.'

These were all exhibited, with many others, by Landseer during the first ten years after he began to write the letters 'R. A.' after his name. They were almost all of them great favourites at their first appearance, and are well known to the world by the engravings of them. They may be regarded as marking the perfection of Landseer's style. To the next decade of Landseer's life belong 'Horses taken in to Bait;' 'Macaw, Terrier, and Spaniel Puppies belonging to Her Majesty;' 'Laying down the Law;' 'Otters and Salmon;' 'The Highland Shepherd's Home;' 'Brazilian Monkeys;' 'The Otter Speared;' 'Horses, the property of Mr. W. A. Wigram;' 'Shoeing;' 'Coming Events cast their Shadows Before;' 'Time of Peace;' 'Time of War,' – a pair in well marked contrast, to whose lessons it would be well if certain Kings and Emperors of late had listened; 'The Stag at Bay;' 'Pincher;' 'Alexander and Diogenes' (the philosopher of the tub being, of course, a four-footed one); 'A Random Shot;' 'The Desert;' 'The Forester's Family;' 'The Free Church;' 'Collie Dogs;' 'Evening Scene in the Highlands;' 'Good Doggie;' and 'A Dialogue at Waterloo.' In these, too, as in the productions of Landseer in the previous decade, we see the canine element and also the Highland element well represented; but, upon the whole, we should say that these works have never gained the hold on the popular estimation which confessedly was accorded to those of 1830–1840.

With the year 1851 the Highland sketches occur less frequently, and there is a corresponding increase in ideal subjects in the published list of Landseer's works. Among the pictures exhibited by him at the Academy in 1851–60, we may particularize his 'Fairy Scene from *Midsummer Night's Dream*;' 'A Group at Geneva;' 'The last Run of the Season;' 'Night' and 'Morning,' a pair; 'The Children of the Mist;' 'Twins;' 'Dandie Dinmont,' an old skye terrier of the Queen; 'Saved,' dedicated to the Humane Society; 'Highland Nurses,' dedicated to Florence Nightingale; 'Rough and Ready;' 'Uncle Tom and his Wife (two dogs, of course) for Sale;' 'Deer-stalking;' 'The Maid and the Magpie;' 'Doubtful Crumbs;' 'The Prize Calf;' 'Bran, Oscar, and the Deer;' 'A Kind Star;' and lastly 'A Flood in the Highlands' – his only contribution to the Academy Exhibition in the last-named year, and a picture which will long be remembered for its pathos and truth to life.

The closing decade of Landseer's artistic career shows but little falling off from the preceding, either in the number or in the power of its productions. 'The Shrew Tamed;' 'The Fatal Duel;' 'Scenes in Lord Breadalbane's Highland Deer Forest;' 'Windsor Great Park;' 'Pensioners;' 'Man Proposes, God Disposes;' 'Déjeuner a la Fourchette;' 'Prosperity' and 'Adversity' a pair; 'The Connoisseurs;' 'Mare and Foal in an Indian Tent;' 'The Prayer of Lady Godiva;' 'The Chase;' 'The Stag at Bay;' 'Odds and Ends;' 'Deer at Chillingham;' 'Wild Cattle at Chillingham;' 'Rent-day in the Wilderness;' 'Her Majesty at Osborne in 1866,' a picture which will be remembered as a thorough contrast to the rest of his works; 'Eagles Attacking the Swannery;' 'The Queen Meeting the Prince Consort on his return from Deer-stalking;' two 'Studies of Lions;' and 'A Doctor's Visit to Poor Relations at the Zoological Gardens' – one of the best illustrations of monkeydom. These and many others will crowd with more or less vividness and freshness on the reader's memory as he peruses this brief biography of him who in his day was deservedly called 'the Shakespeare of the world of dogs.' It appears from the annual catalogues that from the very first Landseer was one of the most regular and constant exhibitors at the Academy, for from his first appearance on its walls in 1815 down to the present date, his name is absent on only seven occasions – namely, in 1816, 1841, 1852, 1855, 1862, 1863, and 1871. But even this statement fails to do justice to his indefatigable industry as a painter, for, between 1818 and 1865, he exhibited at the British Institution no less than 90 pictures, including (besides those already mentioned) some of his most popular efforts, such as 'The Twa Dogs;' 'The Sleeping Bloodhound;' 'The Eagles Rest;' 'Well Bred Sitters;' and 'Dear Old Boz,' painted for Her Majesty. To this list must be added four other pictures exhibited with the Society of British Artists between the years 1826 and 1832, and also nine more exhibited in his early days, between 1816 and 1820, on the walls of the Society of Painters in Oil and Water Colours, in Spring-gardens. His contributions to the Royal Academy Exhibition in 1870 were five in number, 'Voltigeur,' the winner of the Derby and St. Leger; 'Deer: a Study;' 'Lassie: a Sketch;' and two pictures already mentioned. The name of Sir Edwin Landseer does not occur in the catalogue of 1871, as illness had then paralyzed his powerful and charming pencil. He exhibited in 1872, and even last summer, but the works were scarcely worthy of his fame and reputation.

It is not our purpose, nor, indeed, would it be possible, here to enter into any minute and detailed criticism of the works of Landseer. His paintings are well known in the household of every educated man through the length and breadth of the land. His Lions at the foot of the Nelson Column in Trafalgar-square, his only known effort in the sister art of sculpture, are so well known to the public, and were made the subjects of so much criticism in the columns of the newspapers at the time of their completion, that we need only allude to them here.

It only remains to add that he received from Her Majesty, in 1850, the honour of knighthood. He received also the large gold medal from the authorities of the Universal Exhibition of Paris in 1855. A few years ago, upon the death of Sir Charles Eastlake, he was offered the Presidency of the Royal Academy, but his modesty led him to decline the distinction. In private life he was one of the most kind and courteous of men, and the warmest of friends; and, in very many circles, from Royalty downwards, people will miss with regret his round, merry, genial face, his white hair, and his pleasant smile.

Landseer was a regular exhibitor at the Royal Academy but his paintings became 'well known in the household of every educated man', largely due to the medium of engraving. More than half of his substantial annual income came from the copyrights on these engravings. His animal paintings delighted generations of Victorians and were especially esteemed in Royal circles. His largest, and most taxing composition, the four bronze lions for the foot of Nelson's Column were commissioned in 1857 and finally installed ten years later. Landseer's 'precarious state of health' in his last years was the result of chronic nervous disturbance accentuated by alcoholism. After his death on 1 October 1873 Queen Victoria noted that 'for the last three years he had been in a most distressing state, half out of his mind, yet not entirely so.' He was accorded a public funeral at St Paul's Cathedral where he is buried beside Reynolds, Lawrence and Turner.

* * *

HARRIET MARTINEAU

Social and economic critic and novelist:
'A great new light has arisen among English women.'

27 JUNE 1876

WE REGRET TO announce the death of Miss Martineau on Tuesday evening, at her residence, The Knoll, near Ambleside. She had just completed her 74th year. So far back as the year 1832, Miss Lucy Aikin wrote to Dr. Channing, 'You must know that a great new light has arisen among English women,' and a still greater authority, Lord Brougham, remarked to a friend about the same time:—

> 'There is at Norwich a deaf girl who is doing more good than any man in the country. You may have seen the name and some of the productions of Harriet Martineau in the "Monthly Repository;" but what she is gaining glory by is a series of "Illustrations of Political Economy" in some tales published periodically, of which nine or ten have appeared. Last year she called on me several times, and I was struck with marks of such an energy and resolution in her as, I thought, must command success in some line or other in life, though it did not then appear in what direction. She has a vast store of knowledge on many deep and difficult subjects – a wonderful store for a person scarcely 30 years old; and her observation of common things must have been extraordinarily correct as well as rapid. I dined yesterday in the company of Mr. Malthus and Miss Martineau, who are great allies. She pursues her course steadily, and I hear much praise of her new tale on the Poor Laws. I fear, however, that it is the character of her mind to adopt extreme opinions upon most subjects, and without much examination. She has now had a full season of London "lionizing," and, as far as one can judge, it has done her nothing but good. She loves her neighbours the

better for their good opinion of her; and, I believe, she thinks the more humbly of herself for what she has seen of other persons of talent and merit.'

Harriet Martineau was born at Norwich on the 12th of June, 1802. In her biography of Mrs. Opie she gives us a picture of life in this eastern cathedral city in the early part of the 19th century, when its Bishop was the liberal and enlightened Dr. Bathurst; and she tells us how the proclivities of the city, alike towards clerical exclusiveness and to intellectual stagnation, were largely corrected by the social gatherings of one or two highly-cultivated families, and by a large infusion of French and Flemish manufacturing industry, the result of the revocation of the Edict of Nantes. The Martineaus were among the families whom that measure drove to our shores; and at Norwich they had flourished for the best part of a century, part of the family devoting itself to silk weaving on a large scale, while other members were in practice as surgeons, enjoying a high reputation in the city of their adoption. Not much is known of Harriet's father, who died early, except that he had eight children, of whom she was the youngest. Her education was conducted under the supervision of her uncle, one of the most eminent surgeons in the east of England, and who took every means to give his nephews and nieces the best instruction Norwich could afford. Like most persons of a high order of intellect, however, young Harriet Martineau at an early age resolved to walk alone, and not in educational leading-strings, and practically taught herself history and politics while her brothers and sisters were reading their 'Goldsmith' and 'Mrs. Markham.' Not that she had any lack of teachers or instructors; but from a child she resolved to practise the virtue of self-reliance and to fit herself for life in earnest by such literary exertions as sooner or later, she felt, would at least make her independent.

She was barely of age when she appeared before the public as an author. Her first work, however, was not one which gave any scope to literary talents, and must be regarded rather as a proof of her internal piety, on the model of the Unitarian school in which she had been brought up, than as a criterion of her intellectual ability. It was entitled 'Devotional Exercises for the Use of Young Persons,' and was published in 1823. It was, however, the harbinger of a long series of far more important works which were destined to appear thenceforth in rapid succession. In 1824 and the following year Miss Martineau came before the public as the authoress of two tales, entitled 'Christmas Day,' and a sequel to it, 'The Friend;' these she followed up with several other stories all more or less dealing with social subjects, and more especially illustrating by argument and by example the rights and interests of the working classes. The best known of these are 'Principle and Practice,' 'The Rioters,' 'The Turn Out,' 'Mary Campbell,' and 'My Servant Rachel.' It is needless to add that in these the work of helping the weaker and poorer members of society is not only enforced upon the wealthier classes as a duty, but shown to be no less the common interest of both the one and the other. These publications carry down the story of the life of our author to about the year 1830 or 1831.

With this period we come to a new era in the literary career of Miss Martineau. This is shown by her choice of more elevated subjects, and possibly a more elevated tone is to be discovered in her treatment of them also. Her first publication after that date was a charming collection of 'The Traditions of Palestine,' and her next, if we remember right, her 'Five Years of Youth.' About the same time also she made her name known far more widely than before by gaining three prizes for as many separate Essays on subjects proposed by the Unitarian Association. The subjects were independent of each other, though mutually connected in their plan; and on opening the sealed envelopes, containing the names of the writers, it was found that on each of the three subjects the successful competitor was a young lady, just 30 years of age, named Harriet Martineau. The three subjects were respectively, The Faith as unfolded by many Prophets; Providence, as manifested through the dealings of God with Israel; and the Essential Faith of the Universal Church. These Essays were published, and thoroughly established the writer's claim to the credit of being a profound thinker and reasoner upon religious as well as social questions.

The next subject to which she applied her fertile and versatile pen was a series of 'Illustrations of Political Economy,' in which she attempted to popularize, by familiar and practical illustrations and examples, the principles which – speaking generally – Adam Smith, Jeremy Bentham, and Romilly, and other men of original minds, had laid down in an abstract and strictly philosophical matter. These 'Illustrations' extended to above 20 numbers; they were afterwards republished in a collective form, and, having since been translated into French and German, have helped perhaps more than any other work of modern times to spread abroad, in other countries as well as in our own, a knowledge of that science which till our own day had been so little known and studied. These she followed up by two similar series, on cognate subjects – 'Illustrations of Taxation' and 'Illustrations of Poor Laws and Paupers.'

In the year 1834 Harriet Martineau paid a visit to the United States, whither she found that the fame of her social writings had travelled before her. There she met with a most cordial reception from the leaders of thought and action on the other side of the Atlantic; and on her return to Europe she published her comments on the social, political, and religious institutions of the United States, under the title of 'Society in America,' and her observations on the natural aspects of the Western world and its leading personages, under that of 'A Retrospect of Western Travel.' On returning to England she found awaiting her plenty of offers of literary engagements from the leading publishers; but she chose to throw in her lot mainly with

Mr. Charles Knight, who was then in the zenith of his high and well-earned reputation, as the publisher of the Society for the Diffusion of Useful Knowledge, under the auspices of such men as Lord Brougham, Grote, Thirlwall, and Lord John Russell. To Charles Knight's series of cheap and popular publications she contributed a most useful little manual called 'How to Observe,' which she followed up by others, respectively intended as guides for the Housemaid, the Maid-of-all-Work, the Lady's-maid, and the Dressmaker. With the object of lightening her literary labours by variety, she next employed her pen on a series of tales for children, which she gave to the world under the title of 'The Play-fellow.' Of these graphic tales the most popular were 'The Crofton Boys,' 'The Settlers at Home,' 'The Peasant and the Prince,' and 'Feats on the Fjord.' At the same time she addressed to children of a larger growth two novels of a very marked and distinctive character, called 'Deerbrook' and 'The Hour and the Man,' the latter of which works passed through several editions.

About this time her health, which was never of the strongest, appears to have suffered so much from the continual strain of her literary exertions, that she was obliged to lay aside her pen, and Lord Melbourne offered and, we believe, even pressed upon her acceptance a literary pension. But she was either too proud or too independent to accept it; and possibly also even a higher motive came into play; at all event in declining it she was largely influenced by a feeling that 'she could not conscientiously share in the proceeds of a system of taxation which she had reprobated in her published works.' Her illness lasted several years; but she found means to turn even sickness to account by writing and publishing her 'Life in a Sick-room,' – a book suggested by her own experiences of suffering, and, therefore, appealing powerfully to the sympathies of many of her readers.

In 1844, soon after her restoration to health and strength, we find Miss Martineau once more at work upon her favourite themes – social subjects – and publishing three volumes of tales and sketches, illustrative of the evil effects of our 'Forest and Game Laws,' which she followed up with a more fanciful work, 'The Billow and the Rock.' In 1846 she varied the monotony of her quiet and laborious life by a visit to the East; and she recorded her impressions of the scenes and countries through which she travelled in a book which she published in 1848, and which is still most justly popular – namely, 'Eastern Life, its Past and Present.'

In 1850 or 1851 appeared a work by Miss Martineau of a totally different character from all its predecessors – namely, a volume of 'Letters on the Laws of Man's Nature and Development,' which had passed between herself and a philosophic friend named Atkinson; and it was this work which gave the public a hint that when she had reached something more than middle life she was inclined to adopt the teachings of the 'Positive' school of philosophy, founded by Auguste Comte. Two or three years later she still more thoroughly identified herself with this school of thought and faith by giving to the world a condensed version of Comte's 'Positive Philosophy.' But while thus employed in the study of scientific and semi-religious subjects, she found time to devote to her 'History of England during the Thirty Years Peace,' a book which is to be admired for its singular clearness and the studied impartiality of its views.

We next find the indefatigable pen of Miss Martineau employed in contributing to the 'People's Journal,' and her essays in that periodical soon came to be so widely in demand that they were subsequently republished under the title of 'Household Education.' About the same time she employed her leisure hours in compiling a work of less pretension – we mean her 'Complete Guide to the Lakes,' which appeared in 1854, and for which her long residence at the pretty cottage near Ambleside, which she made her home during her declining years, eminently qualified her. From and after this date it was mainly as a contributor of leading articles, and of biographical and other literary papers to the *Daily News*, and as a writer of social articles, 'historiettes,' and graphic personal reminiscences of the celebrities of the present century, in the early volumes of 'Once a Week,' that we must look mainly for evidence of Miss Martineau's literary activity; but the weight of increasing years began to tell heavily upon her, and after a long illness in or about the year 1865 she almost entirely withdrew from those engagements. Her biographical contributions to the *Daily News* and 'Once a Week' were republished in a collected form in the early part of 1869.

In this brief sketch we have had no space to mention the other works, mostly of a more or less ephemeral character, which are identified with the name of Harriet Martineau. Of these the best known, perhaps, are her 'Essay on British India' (1851); 'The Factory Controversy; a Warning against Meddling Legislation' (1855); 'Corporate Tradition' and 'National Rights and Local Dues on Shipping' (1857); 'Endowed Schools in Ireland' (1859); 'England and her Soldiers' – a work on the vexed question of Army reform (1859); and 'Health, Husbandry, and Handicraft,' a collection of stray papers contributed to some of the leading serials of the day.

At her charming home in Ambleside, so long as health and strength remained to her, Miss Martineau rejoiced to entertain a circle of attached literary and political friends, and to receive the visits of such strangers, both English and foreign, as cared to travel in order to gratify some higher interests than those of mere pleasure. From mere pleasure, apart from the business of life, and to mere pleasure-seekers and idlers and triflers, she had an unconquerable aversion; but if any one sought to benefit his fellow creatures, high or low, rich or poor, and to lead a useful life as a social being, and a member of the busy hive of English labour, or, indeed, of humanity at large, to him or to her the doors of Miss Martineau's house and of her heart were at once open. To the last, in spite of a painful chronic illness, she took the greatest interest in every movement which had for its object the social, physical, and moral improvement of the world in which her lot was cast, and she corresponded largely with various leaders of such movements, who seldom sought in vain for her counsel and advice. If any lady in the 19th century, in England or abroad, may be allowed to put in a claim for the credit of not having lived in vain, that woman, we honestly believe was Harriet Martineau.

Martineau was, as this generous obituary notice remarks, an indefatigable writer who had a considerable impact on the social and political debates of her time. She came from a distinguished Unitarian family and inherited a considerable degree of intellectual earnestness. In 1830 the British and Foreign Unitarian Association offered premiums for the best essays on what even then must have seemed the unpromising subject of the 'Introduction and Promotion of Christian Unitarianism among the Roman Catholics, the Jews and the Mahometans'. Martineau submitted three essays and won prizes from three separate groups of arbitrators. Her later commitment to Utilitarianism, and particularly her series of didactic Benthamite stories *Illustrations of Political Economy* (1832–35) and *Poor Law and Paupers Illustrated* (1833), may well have persuaded some wavering readers of the virtues of the 1834 Poor Law, but otherwise certainly did much to provoke Dickens into writing the even more persuasive *Oliver Twist*. It is as a writer of fiction, however, that Martineau has a lasting claim to fame, but the obituarist strangely gives scant mention of her *The Hour and the Man* (1841), an historical romance about the Haitian revolutionary Toussaint L'Ouverture, or her fine three-volume modern novel of 1839, *Deerbrook*.

SIR TITUS SALT

Industrialist and philanthropist:
'He was not unmindful of his more public obligations.'

29 DECEMBER 1876

WE REGRET TO announce the death of Sir Titus Salt, which occurred yesterday afternoon at Crow Nest, his seat near Bradford, after a lingering illness. His age was 73.

Sir Titus Salt was born on the 20th of September, 1803, at the old Manor-house, Morley. His father, who was a woolstapler, moved with his family from Morley to Crofton, near Wakefield, and at Heath Grammar School, near that town, his son received his education. It was just at the time when the worsted manufacture was beginning to rise from a domestic operation to a factory institution; and as the change was distasteful to the older stuff manufacturers in the district around Wakefield, the trade shifted its quarters and settled at Bradford. Among those who moved with it were Daniel Salt and his family. The father continued to confine himself to the purchase and sale of wool. The more ambitious son determined to attempt the manufacture of stuffs, and gave the first indication of his speciality in the utilizing of raw materials heretofore unappreciated. The wool called 'Donskoi,' from the south-eastern parts of Russia, grown on the banks of the River Don, was a coarse and tangled material, then considered unavailable for purposes of manufacture. How to overcome the difficulties of spinning and weaving this article was the first problem Mr. Titus Salt set himself to solve. For this purpose he set up his machinery in what was known as Thompson's Mill, Silsbridge-lane, Bradford. Successful in this enterprise, he extended his operations in this and other branches of the worsted manufacture, and added a large factory in Union-street. His trade grew rapidly under his hands, and in a few years he was carrying on his works not only in the two places just named, but also at Hollings' Mill, Silsbridge-lane; at Brick-lane-mill, and in Fawcett-court. It was in the year 1836 that he achieved his greatest success, in becoming for practical purposes the discoverer of the wool or hair now known in almost all parts of the civilized world as alpaca. The existence of the animal called the paca, or alpaca, had indeed been known nearly 300 years before, and its long fleeces were boasted of by the Spanish Governors of Peru in the 16th century. But no one in England had operated upon the article with much success, and it was shown to Mr. Salt by a Liverpool broker as a novelty in 1836.

While thus founding his private fortunes, he was not unmindful of his more public obligations. He was elected Mayor of Bradford in 1848, and discharged the duties of that office with punctuality and efficiency. Meanwhile his reputation as a manufacturer was advancing, and the increased demand for his goods rendered necessary improved facilities for their production. Accordingly, in 1851, the year of the 'Great Exhibition,' the works at Saltaire were commenced. They were opened on the 20th of September, 1853, the anniversary of their owner's birthday, on which occasion he gave in one of the vast rooms of the factory a banquet, at which he entertained 2,500 workpeople. The works started with such *eclat* received subsequently various additions and improvements, and furnish employment to a very large number of persons, for whose accommodation he erected the dwellings now grown into the town of Saltaire. These comprised, at the last census taken, 820 houses, occupied by 4,389 persons. In 1859 he erected the Congregational Church at Saltaire. In 1863, by erecting buildings for baths and washhouses, he provided for the cleanliness and consequent self-respect of his workpeople. He had before this furnished them with facilities for the education of their children by building a large schoolroom; but as, with the extension of his works and the increase in the numbers of his workpeople, this provision had made his judgement become inadequate, he built a fresh range of schoolrooms in 1868, with accommodation for 750 scholars. During the past summer a new Sunday school was built by Sir Titus in connexion with the Saltaire Congregational Church, costing with site, nearly £10,000. It may be mentioned also that he contributed in a munificent manner towards the cost of the handsome Congregational Church at Lightcliffe, and has very recently offered a site for a Board school at Saltaire. A hospital and infirmary have also been added to his erections, so that the needs of the sick might be relieved; while for the widows and aged he provided 45 alms-houses, with a lawn and shrubbery in front, all so neatly kept as to be models of cleanliness and comfort. The married couples receive 10s. per week, the unmarried inmates 7s. 6d. In 1871 a beautiful park, 14 acres in extent, on the banks of the River Aire, and within an easy distance of the factory and the town, was given by Sir Titus Salt for the use of the public; and in November of the following year a large and handsome building was provided by him to serve as a Club and Institute, where a large library is to be found, evening classes assemble, lectures on science and literature are delivered, and the games of chess and billiards may be played.

In the year 1859 he was elected member of Parliament for the borough of Bradford. So long as he filled this post he attended regularly the sittings of the House of Commons, but the post was somewhat of an irksome one to him, and he resigned his office in 1861 and came back to his admiring followers and friends. Previous to entering Parliament, however, he had filled a number of important public offices. Besides being a magistrate for the borough of Bradford, he was appointed on the commission of the peace for the West Riding, and was also made a deputy lieutenant of the Riding. In 1857 he filled the office of President of the Bradford Chamber of Commerce. In September, 1869, the Queen conferred a baronetcy upon him – an act which was universally recognized as a well-merited bestowal of the Royal favour. During the last few years he has lived in retirement at Crow Nest, although never relinquishing his connexion with the works at Saltaire. During the 23 years over which the history of Saltaire now extends, there have been many public manifestations of the high esteem in which Sir Titus Salt was held both by his own workpeople and the public generally. On the 20th of September, 1856, a marble bust of Sir Titus, executed by Mr. T. Milnes, was presented to him by the people of Saltaire. In July, 1869, the residents of the almshouses presented him with a pair of gold spectacles and a silver mounted staff. In September, 1870, two silver-plated corner dishes were given to him by the children of Saltaire. An oil portrait of himself, painted by Mr. J. P. Knight, R. A., was subscribed for in 1871, and on the 26th of August in that year was presented to him in the Bradford Mechanics' Institute, along with an address expressing in flattering terms the affection and esteem of the subscribers. In 1829 Sir Titus married Caroline, daughter of Mr. George Whitlam, of Grimsby, by whom he had a family of 11 children. Several of his sons have become partners in the firm now known as 'Sir Titus Salt, Bart., Sons, and Co.,' and have shown an activity in carrying on the gigantic works at Saltaire, and a zeal in promoting the welfare of the workpeople that are warmly appreciated. The eldest son and the successor to the title is William Henry Salt, who was born in 1831, and is magistrate for Leicestershire and the West Riding of Yorkshire. Sir William married, in 1854, Emma Dove Octaviana, only child of Mr. John Dove Harris, of Ratcliffe-Hall, Leicestershire, and has, with other issue, Shirley Harrison, born 1867. He resides at Maplewel, near Loughborough, Leicestershire.

Sir Titus Salt's public donations during the last quarter of a century have amounted to many hundred thousand pounds. The estimate of a man's charitableness of nature is not, of course, to be formed merely from the money value of his gifts. But those who were best acquainted with Sir Titus Salt knew that he felt genuine compassion for distress, however much it might be unconsciously veiled by an outward appearance of impassiveness and reserve. Though unable, from advancing years and physical infirmity, to take a prominent part in public matters, his influence and his purse were ever at the disposal of patriotism and benevolence. He remained true to the Liberal political opinions he had formed in his youth. He had been a Radical reformer ever since he attained to manhood, and he was not a person to give up convictions that had become part of his character. A conscientious Dissenter when comparatively poor, he would not throw aside his religion when he got rich. And, having always sympathized with the sufferings of his fellow creatures, his practical manifestations of the feeling increased with his power of exhibiting them.

The obituarist is at pains to point out that Sir Titus, unlike many of his rich fellow Dissenters, had remained fiercely loyal to his Congregationalist roots. Salt was already a very rich man when he resolved to develop Saltaire, which would be laid out according to plans drawn up by the Bradford architects Lockwood and Mawson. The first sketch for his mill was rejected as not being large enough. When told a larger building would cost more than £100,000 he replied off-handedly, 'Oh, very likely.' The architects consequently designed expansively. Apart from the great T-shaped Mill, the Institute and the Italianate Congregational Church, Saltaire contains 895 stone dwellings designed to house both mill workers and their managers. There were originally no public houses at Saltaire.

* * *

WILLIAM HENRY FOX TALBOT

Pioneer photographer:
'The new art, which has since been named photography.'

17 SEPTEMBER 1877

The Discoverer of Talbotype.

Mr. W. H. Fox Talbot, F. R.S., of Laycock Abbey, Wiltshire, whose death was recorded in our columns on Friday, as having happened on Monday, September 17, at his country residence, at the age of 77, was the eldest son of the late Sir William Davenport Talbot, by his marriage with Lady Elizabeth Theresa Fox-Strangways, eldest daughter of Henry Thomas, second Earl of Ilchester. He was born in February, 1800, and received his early education at Harrow, then under Dr. Butler, afterwards Dean of Peterborough, the father of the present head master. In due course of time he was removed to Trinity College, Cambridge, where he gained the Porson Prize for Greek Iambic verse in 1820, and took his degree in the following year as Chancellor's Medallist.

He does not appear to have been called to the bar, or in fact to have followed any learned profession; but he took a delight in chymistry and in chymical experiments, with which he combined a zeal for archaeology and antiquarian studies. Elected as a Liberal for the borough of Chippenham at the general election which followed on the passing of the first Reform Bill, he held his seat for two years, but then withdrew from political life. His motives for so doing we can gather from his own writings. Mr. Talbot tells us, in his 'Pencil of Nature,' that in the month of October, 1833, when trying to sketch the scenery along the shores of the lake of Como, by the aid of a camera lucida, and wearied by many successive failures, he was 'led to reflect on the inimitable beauty of the pictures painted by the hand of nature, pictures which the glass lens of the camera throws upon the paper in its focus,' and further, 'to consider whether it would be possible to make these pictures permanent.' He was aware that paper might, by chymical means, be made sensitive to the action of light, and he resolved to try and follow up the idea by experiments. By a long and elaborate course of these experiments, which it would be useless now to enumerate in detail, he had nearly arrived at a result satisfactory to himself, when he read one day in a scientific journal that his own solution of the mystery had been, if not anticipated, at all events rivalled, by the parallel researches of M. Daguerre. To use his own words, 'An event occurred in the scientific world which in some degree frustrated the hope with which I had pursued during nearly five years this long and complicated but interesting series of experiments – the hope, namely, of being able to announce to the world the existence of the new art, which has since been named photography.' This was, of course, the publication of an account in January, 1839, by M. Daguerre of what was termed the daguerreotype process after its discovery. Mr. Talbot lost no time in communicating to the Royal Society the details of his own independent process, which he called at first photogenic drawing, and afterwards calotype. Sir David Brewster, however, perceived at once its value and importance, and therefore proposed that it should be called Talbotype – and the name was to some extent adopted, until, with the full consent of its modest discoverer, it became popularly merged in the more comprehensive term of photography.

The two rival processes, though one in their design and object, differ very largely in matters of detail. As a writer in the *English Cyclopaedia* observes:–

> 'In Daguerre's process the image was produced upon metal plates; in that of Mr. Talbot the same image was obtained upon paper, and neither the one nor the other could claim to be the first who had obtained sun-pictures upon a surface previously rendered sensitive, the principle having been perceived and announced by Thomas Wedgwood in his "Account of the Method of Copying Paintings upon Glass, with Observations by Sir Humphrey Davy," which was published in the "Transactions" of the British Institution as far back as 1802, and later by M. Niépce, who had made known in London in 1827 his own experi-

> ments in obtaining sun-pictures. But in none of these was the image either distinct or permanent; so that M. Daguerre and Mr. Talbot were the first to apply the principle practically, and from them the photographic art may be said to date its origin. It is probable that this statement does justice to all who were concerned in this discovery, both theoretically and in the application of theory to practice.'

Mr. Talbot's invention, however, remained for some months in a very imperfect state; and it was not till the autumn of 1840 that he made the discovery, which 'laid the foundation of the photographic art in its present form' – namely, that sensitive paper, during the first few seconds of its exposure to the light, receives an invisible image perfect in all respects, and that, in order to render the image visible, it is sufficient to wash the paper over with gallic acid or with some other astringent liquid. In 1842 Mr. Talbot was presented with the gold medal of the Royal Society in recognition of the part which he had taken in the discovery of photography. Already – namely, in 1841 – he had taken the necessary steps for securing to himself by patent the commercial profits which were likely to accrue from this novel use of the suns rays; but upon second thoughts and becoming convinced of the various public and private uses to which the art might be made subservient, and at the request of several members of the Royal Society, he consented to forego the profitable privilege and to throw open to the public his discovery, with what results is known now to all the world, with one single reservation – that of taking portraits. This, however, he afterwards waived, the legal question having been raised and somewhat unsatisfactorily decided in one of the superior courts.

In 1851 Mr. Fox Talbot presented to the Royal Society and also to the Académie des Sciences at Paris an account of sundry further experiments which he had made in the direction of obtaining instantaneous photographs; and two years later he published a notice of some successful experiments in the application of photography to the work of engraving on steel plates.

Of late years Mr. Fox Talbot employed much of his time in the study of languages, and especially in the work of deciphering the cuneiform inscriptions on Assyrian monuments. He was also the author of several valuable works, such as 'The Pencil of Nature,' quoted above; 'Legendary Tales;' 'Hermes, or Classical and Antiquarian Researches;' 'New Arguments of the Antiquity of the Book of Genesis;' and 'English Etymologies.' He also contributed largely to the papers read at meetings of the Society of Biblical Archaeology, and of other learned Societies.

Mr. Fox Talbot married in 1832 Constance, youngest daughter of the late Mr. Francis Mundy, of Markeaton, Derbyshire, by whom he has left a family to lament his loss.

The obituary hails Talbot as 'the discoverer of Talbotype' in order to distinguish him from his fellow pioneer and rival, Louis Daguerre (for whom the Daguerreotype was named). A gifted scientific experimenter, Talbot published his first paper – 'On the Properties of a Certain Curve Derived from the Equilateral Hyperbole' – at the age of 22. He was elected a Fellow of the Royal Society in 1831. His early experiments with silver salts, which were darkened by light, paralleled those by Thomas Wedgwood and Nicéphore Niépce, but it was Talbot who produced the first true negatives. The earliest surviving negative, dated August 1835, shows a bay window in the South Gallery at Lacock Abbey in Wiltshire. Daguerre's public announcement on 7 January 1839 of the success of his experiments with silver-plated copper plaques obliged Talbot to publicise his own invention. Michael Faraday welcomed the discovery at the Royal Institution on 25 January, showing examples of the new 'photogenic drawings', and on 31 January Talbot himself presented a paper to the Royal Society entitled 'Some Account of the Art of Photogenic Drawing; or the Process by which Nature's Objects May be Made to Delineate Themselves without the Aid of the Artist's Pencil'. The paper was published on 9 February. In September 1840 Talbot perfected the 'Calotype' process (which his friends called the 'Talbotype') by sensitising paper with gallo-nitrate of silver and exposing it to light in a camera for one to three minutes. Positives were obtained from the resulting negatives. In 1937 thousands of Talbot's earliest photographs were discovered in a cupboard at Lacock Abbey and were presented to the Science Museum.

POPE PIUS IX

Pope: 'No man of the present generation can imagine what frenzy seized the generation of 31 years ago.'

7 FEBRUARY 1878

THE LONG SUFFERINGS of the Pope, Pius IX, are at last at an end. We have outlived the longest and one of the most eventful Pontificates on record. The name of Pius IX will probably be the last in the roll of the Pope-Kings, but it will be added to the number of the Pope-Saints – a high compensation, for the canonization of Roman Pontiffs has been an extremely unfrequent occurrence during the long lapse of centuries since Peter's successors added to the Bishop's mitre a Monarch's diadem. Pius IX will take his place among the Pope-Martyrs by the side of the many of his predecessors who underwent persecution, waged home and foreign wars, were the victims of conspiracy and rebellion, made experience of dethronement, restoration, exile, and captivity, of the various vicissitudes to which earthly sovereignty is liable – all calamities partly owing to the storms of the transitional period in which it was his lot to live, but partly, also, the consequences of the rashness and waywardness of his own physical and moral temperament, and of his attempts at unpractical and dangerous innovation. He lived 'to see the years of Peter,' an unprecedented distinction, and hailed as miraculous, violating a rule to which time had given almost the consistency of a destiny, and portending a change which marked the close of an exploded system and laid open the prospect of a new order of things. It was only as head of a Church, not as ruler of an ecclesiastical State, that Pius IX exceeded his allotted span of 25 years, and thus broke the spell of that fatal tradition. It was no longer a temporal sovereignty that he, in compliance with the solemn oath taken at his accession, was able to hand down 'intact' to his successor, but merely a spiritual dominion, to which he endeavoured to give a worldwide extension, and which he exposed to contests the issue of which will long be doubtful. A failure as a prince, Pius IX aspired to achieve transcendant success as a priest. With a mind of no breadth, and a character of no real firmness, he flattered himself that he could crown the edifice of which the genius of Hildebrand had laid the foundation. It was only when the sceptre broke in his hand and the Royal mantle fell from his shoulders that he put forth his claims to the authority of a King of Kings. His ambition rose in the same measure as his territory dwindled; his pretensions expanded in proportion as his sphere of activity was limited.

Pius IX was born at Sinigaglia in the Marches, a Province in the States of the

Church, on the 13th of May, 1792, or, according to other accounts two years earlier. His name was Giovanni Maria Mastaï-Ferretti, and his family, of Lombard extraction, belonged to that provincial nobility, ancient but impoverished, the number of which is prodigiously great in Italy, and especially in the Roman and Neapolitan districts. His brothers, whose number was considerable, and among whom longevity seemed to be the rule, were destined to a military career; and some of them achieved distinction in their youth in those wars of the First Napoleon in which the Italians had to take part now with one, now with the other, of their foreign invaders. Giovanni, as one of the cadets, is also said to have served either under French or Austrian colours, or perhaps both; but this could only be for a short time, and the real particulars of his life at this period are involved in some rather unaccountable obscurity. For such education as he received he was indebted to the Ecclesiastical College of Volterra, not a very renowned institution, where it seems he spent five or six years, and which he quitted in 1810. On the restoration of Pius VII, five years later, he entered the Guardia Nobile of the Vatican, but probably the limited fortunes of his family, and the impression wrought upon him by an epileptic fit, apparently the first attack of a complaint which became chronic, induced him to make choice of the ecclesiastical profession; he was ordained, said his first Mass, and lived in Rome for a few years as a chaplain or spiritual director of some hospitals, and generally employed in deeds of charity, thereby winning, as it is stated, the good will of Pius VII, though filling no post at his Court.

In 1823 he went out in the suite of Monsignor Muzi, who was appointed Apostolic Vicar in Chili, and travelled over a considerable extent of South America. He came back not long after the death of Pius VII, and found equal favour with the new Pontiff, Leo XII, who appointed him a Prelate in his household, gave him a Canonry in Santa Maria di Via Lata, and seconded the inclination of young Mastaï to deeds of charity by naming him President of St. Michael's Hospital in Via Grande.

In 1827 Monsignor Mastaï-Ferretti was created Archbishop of Spoleto, and five years later was transferred to the See of Imola. In the interval Leo XII had died (1829) and had been followed by Pius VIII, after whose death, in February, 1831, Gregory XVI came to the throne. Those were years of great political commotion in France and throughout Europe, and especially in Italy and in the Roman States, where the successors of Pius VII, needing the support of Austria, had departed from the mild and wise rule introduced at that Pope's restoration by Cardinal Consalvi, and hardened their hearts against their subjects, aggravating temporal misrule by the reckless exercise of spiritual tyranny. The accession of Gregory XVI, whose election was well-known to have been favoured by Austrian influence, was the signal for an outbreak in Central Italy, where the insurrection, triumphant at Parma, Modena, and Bologna, overran the Papal territory as far as Otricoli and up to the very walls of the Pontifical stronghold of Civita Castellana. Mastaï-Ferretti, who, in his diocese of Spoleto, had to stand the brunt of this overwhelming movement, had no little trouble in assuaging the violent passions which raged around him, and was greatly aided in this arduous task by the reputation he had established as a man of liberal and benevolent opinions. 'On one occasion,' his biographer says, he 'harangued the rebels in circumstances of personal risk, and peaceably disarmed them.' The revolutionary attempt of 1831, which had been secretly stirred up by French intrigue, was crushed by the Austrians in the month of March in the same year, but broke out again in the following spring of 1832 upon the withdrawal of the foreign bayonets, determining a new enterprise of Austria, which was in this instance seconded – under pretence of opposing it – by a French expedition to the Adriatic and the occupation of Ancona, much to the astonishment of the world and to the utter disappointment and discouragement of the Italian patriots.

It was at the end of these turmoils that Mastaï-Ferretti was made to pass from the See of Spoleto to that of Imola, a strange promotion from an Archbishopric to a Bishopric, which clerical writers, after the event, described as 'a first step towards the Papacy, as Imola had already given two Popes – Alexander VII, in 1667, and Pius VII, in 1800 – to the Church. It is by no means unlikely that this falling-off in the episcopal dignity was owing to displeasure given to Pope Gregory by Mastaï-Ferretti's humane and enlightened views of the duties of a Pontifical Government; and those views, whether sincerely entertained or merely imposed by the exigencies of his perilous position, could hardly fail to be confirmed by the sense of his undeserved punishment, and by the atmosphere, as it were, of his new diocese, where about half a century before another Bishop, Chiaramonti, afterwards Pope Pius VII, had edified his flock by homilies which Botta quotes as specimens of Catholic Democratic eloquence, and which won the Prelate of Imola the appellation of the Ecclesiastical Jacobin. At Imola Mastaï-Ferretti is said to have remained true to his liberal convictions, to have shone as a reformer of abuses, to have encouraged the development of a more extensive knowledge in his diocesan seminary, and to have founded an *Accademia Biblica* somewhat on the plan of the Protestant Bible Societies, aiming at the diffusion of Hebrew history and the discussion of Scriptural subjects. He had also the credit of founding an orphan asylum and one for discharged convicts, bestowing some of his own money on these and similar institutions. As a reward he enjoyed a high popularity among his flock, who hailed him as 'the Good Bishop,' and held him up as a model for the edification of other Prelates. He was during this period sent on a temporary mission to Naples, where his Nunziatura coincided with the year of the cholera, 'when, in a spirit worthy of San Carlo Borromeo, he disposed of his plate, furniture, and equipage, employing the produce of the sale for the relief of the poor sufferers, observing that "when God's poor were dropping down from sickness in the streets, his ministers ought not to be going about in their carriages."'

At last, whatever might be the disposition of mind of Pope Gregory and of his Secretary of State, Cardinal Lambruschini, towards Mastaï-Ferretti, they deemed it expedient to give in to popular opinion by raising the Bishop of Imola to the Cardinalate in December, 1840, when he assumed the title of St. Peter and St. Marcellinus. He, however, continued to reside in his diocese till the year 1846, when, upon the death of Gregory XVI, on the 1st of June, he repaired to Rome to attend the Conclave.

Nothing could be more deplorable than the condition of the Ecclesiastical States at this juncture. Pope Gregory, who, after the removal of the French garrison from Ancona, relied for existence on Austrian support, and made himself a passive tool of Imperial policy, was seconded in his blind reactionary work by his State Secretary, Cardinal Lambruschini, a truculent, narrow-minded, avaricious Genoese monk, whose influence was irresistible both in Church and State, and was but feebly counteracted by Pellegrino Rossi, an Italian exile, formerly a Professor at Bologna, then filling at Rome the place of French Ambassador to the Holy See, and by the Diplomatic Agent of Charles Albert, of Sardinia, who was then won over to the views of the Piedmontese Liberals and bent on resisting the pressure of Austria by appealing to the national aspirations of the people throughout the Italian Peninsula. The Cardinals, in Conclave assembled, felt that the deceased Pope had not only, by his despotic rule, diminished the ascendancy, but also, by his indulgence in ignoble pleasures and by his subjection to unworthy favourites, compromised the dignity of the Holy See; they had become aware of the necessity of rehabilitating a declining and, indeed, rapidly sinking institution by the election of a Pontiff who should correctly interpret the spirit of the age, and take the lead in the way of thorough political reforms. The Party displaying the most earnest zeal in this movement was called the Roman Party, and was headed by Cardinal Gizzi, an accomplished churchman and a thorough man of the world, who would have secured in his favour a sufficient majority of suffrages had it not been for his pursuit of gallant adventures. The votes of this portion of the Sacred College eventually centred, therefore, on the Bishop of Imola, against whose elevation no other obstacle was apprehended than the well-known and uncompromising enmity of Austria. The Party among the Cardinals, bent on resistance to all innovation, and disposed to cling to the old system in all its repulsiveness, mustered under the leadership of Cardinal Lambruschini, the Secretary of State (from whom it took the name of the Genoese Party), and looked upon him as their own candidate for the Tiara.

The Conclave was opened on the 14th of June, and only lasted 50 hours. Cardinal Lambruschini, who, with all his aptitude for intrigue, was too violent and impetuous to wait for the arrival of some of his partisans then on their way to Rome, attempted to carry his election by a *coup de main*, by which he determined the prompt action of his Liberal opponents, and alienated the support of Cardinal Franzoni, and of a considerable knot of his Conservative colleagues. The result was the return of Mastaï-Ferretti by a majority of 36 votes out of the 50 electors present; thus more than fulfilling the exigencies of the rule followed in all Conclaves, which requires a candidate to have secured at least two-thirds of the suffrages. On the following day, the 17th, the expected Cardinals arrived, and among them Cardinal Gaysruck, Archbishop of Milan, who was the bearer of the secret instructions of the Court of Vienna to veto the elevation of the Bishop of Imola. Gaysruck came in too late by 12 hours, the election of Mastaï-Ferretti having already been publicly announced on the previous night at midnight. Had the Milanese Prelate been more expeditious in his movements, or had post-horses served him better, Mastaï-Ferretti would have lost his chance, and the course of Roman, Italian, and, indeed, of the world's history would probably have been something very different from what has now to be written.

The election of Mastaï-Ferretti, who took the name of Pius IX in honour of his early benefactor, Pius VII, was decided on the 16th of June, 1846. His coronation followed on the 21st. The intelligence of his exaltation took Rome and the world by surprise, because the common expectation was that the choice of the Conclave would fall upon Cardinal Gizzi, and because the name of the Bishop of Imola, though revered and beloved in his diocese, was obscure beyond its limits, and almost utterly unknown even to many of the members of the Sacred College. But it was soon understood that Mastaï-Ferretti was the candidate of the Gizzi Party, and his many virtues, as well as his Liberal politics, were easily taken on credit. It is an old maxim in Rome that a new Pope should usher in his reign by undoing whatever has been done by the old Pope; and in this case there was a general conviction that a continuation of the system on which the Government had been carried on under the three last Pontiffs would be fraught with inevitable ruin both to Church and State. Pius IX was advised that it behoved him to strike out an untrodden path; and to begin he threw open the prisons into which his predecessors had crowded as many as 2,000 political offenders. The decree, bearing date the 18th of July, was a *bonâ fide* general amnesty, releasing all prisoners, recalling all exiles, and restoring them to their civil rights on the sole condition of their signing a simple declaration of allegiance. It took away the world's breath. The deed of mercy was interpreted as an act of retributive justice. The vanquished, it was understood, were henceforth to have their *revanche*; the prisoners on their deliverance were expected to become the rulers; and they were numerous, and almost strong enough to impose themselves upon the Pope, to haunt and beset him as a legion of monsters of his own creation, and to hurry him into a headlong career of reform – to plunge him into deep waters, neither himself nor anyone knowing whether he would sink or swim. The Holy See was actually taken by storm. The Bishop of Imola had attempted improvements;

the new Pope should try reforms. The Bishop had founded academies; the Pontiff should inaugurate Constitutions. The clamour of the multitudes was deafening and bewildering; it electrified Rome; it crazed all Italy; it spread throughout Europe. Never had there been so universal or so genuine a commotion in the Catholic, or even in the Protestant, world. There was no limit to political aspirations; none to religious expectations. The Millennium was at hand. Not only were Rome and Italy to be free and independent; not only was a new era to begin for all suffering nations, but there was to be a reconciliation of all creeds, a healing of all schisms, a recantation of all heresies, a Church of true, universal Christian charity, a regenerated world, with a 'benevolent Pope' for its soul. No man of the present generation can imagine what frenzy seized the generation of 31 years ago; no one could believe how powerful, how wonder-working a talisman there was in those three words, '*Viva Pio Nono!*' The new Pope's portraits, his plaster casts, his tin medals, became household gods in huts and palaces; libertines and infidels were seen at masses and benedictions; the *Te Deum* was sung in all churches, in all chapels; even ranting Radicals began to think that their business was over – that a priest would take the bread out of their mouths. Mazzini apostrophized the Liberal Pope with those words, '*Abbiate fede, Santo Padre, siate credente*;' and Carlyle, the hero-worshipper, acknowledged that 'the Old Chimera was rejuvenized.'

Pius IX was, indeed, 'benevolent,' but he was weak and vain; he had many of the virtues and some of the faults which are supposed to be peculiar to a feminine character. He had been modest, somewhat timid, as a Prelate. The world's acclamation naturally inspired him with faith in himself. Greatness was thrust upon him; he was determined to achieve greatness. He made up his mind that his Pontificate should be memorable; that it should be an epoch of epochs in the annals of the Church and of the world. In all that admirable accord of cheering voices, however, the Pope, or the well-meaning advisers he had at first by his side, soon detected a jarring note. The Austrian Ambassador wore an ominous frown at all that pageant of Roman festivities. The French Envoy, that same Pellegrino Rossi, who had been recommending reforms to Pope Gregory, shook his head and looked grave as he heard of the intended reforms of Pope Pius. These were the last years of Louis Philippe, who, when asked by Charles Albert of Sardinia, in 1831, whether, in the event of his granting a constitution to his subjects and thereby incurring Austria's displeasure, he could always rely on French support, answered that 'he, the Citizen King, was too sorely plagued with his own constitution to trouble his head about those of other people.' In obedience to the same views Rossi was now instructed to give the Pope to understand that if His Holiness ventured beyond mere milk-and-water reforms, why, he would have to take the consequences.

France was not encouraging, but Austria was hectoring and bullying. She stood on her rights to keep her garrisons at Ferrara and Comacchio which she had occupied during the disturbances of Romagna, in 1845, really upon the *J'y suis, j'y reste* principle, but nominally on the ground of the Treaty of Paris of 1815, which empowered her to take possession of those strongholds whenever it might be needful. But the new Pope protested that this occupation could only be at the request of the Court of Rome, and for its benefit; and that, as the new Pontificate had now no occasion for foreign aid, it had a right to demand the immediate evacuation of its territory and the removal of the obnoxious garrisons. It was a pretty quarrel, and the Pontiff was well-nigh expected to make good his words by deeds, and, as a new Julius II to don Scipio's helmet, ride at the head of his Guardia Nobile, and reduce the citadels of Ferrara and Comacchio by siege or storm. Austria showed at that juncture the best part of valour – she withdrew across the Po, but the impression remained that in the event of a collision between Italian patriotism and foreign domination, Pius IX and the flag of the Cross Keys would not fail to take their place at the head of the national ranks.

Events, meanwhile, were maturing. Charles Albert of Sardinia, wounded in his pride by Austrian ill-treatment, and bent on recovering a popularity which the early years of his reign had grievously compromised, made his peace with his subjects by concessions which greatly exceeded whatever had been hitherto attempted in Rome, and assumed towards Austria a dignified attitude, which, backed as it was by a valiant and tolerably well disciplined army, was entitled to more serious consideration than a mere unarmed Papal protest. In Naples and Sicily at this same period, King Ferdinand tried all that fire and sword could do to quell the rebellious spirit of his subjects, and, though successful on the mainland, he met with repeated failures in the island. The eventful 1848 now dawned. The Throne of Louis Philippe was overthrown in February. German monarchs strove to prop their own by free charters, and Constitutionalism was now the word throughout Italy. The first movement was made by King Ferdinand in Naples; it was followed in self-defence by Charles Albert in Turin; by Leopold II in Tuscany; and the Pope, who had vainly endeavoured to keep his ground in his people's affections by an abortive *Consulta*, summoned a lay Ministry about him, and directed them to draw up a scheme of representative Government with two Chambers, a free Press, a national guard, and all the trappings with which people wished to be harnessed in those days.

Constitutions, however, were not all the Italians wanted; it was by no means what they most particularly wanted. Their wish was to drive out the Austrians, to be masters in their own houses, to rule the destinies of their country, establish its independence, and give it some bond of union or unity. The first interpreters of these national aspirations were the Milanese, who overpowered Radetszky within their own walls after the fight of their five ever-memorable March days. Next followed Charles Albert, who led his victorious Piedmontese to the Mincio, thereby determining the success of the Revolution throughout the Lombardo-Venetian Kingdom. With him the youth of all Italy came up to the rescue, and in their rear, and not without reluctance, the Royal Army and Fleet of the Neapolitan Bourbon. Pius IX was a Liberal, he was a patriot, he was all that his subjects wished him to be; but he was a Sovereign, he was a priest, he was a man. As a Sovereign he considered that his gain in any military enterprise could never be as large as that of the Piedmontese King, who already showed a decided inclination to secure the lion's share for himself. As a priest, he found out that his sacred ministry forbade him to shed blood and to wage war against any Christian nation, a theory which did not prevent his using a neighbour's armies to go to war with his own subjects. He seemed also to have been startled by some pointed warnings from Vienna that, if he persevered in his national crusade, Austria would also, for her part, nationalize her own Church and withdraw her bishops from all spiritual allegiance to Rome. As a man, besides, and a vain man, the Holy Father was hurt by the visible turn the tide of public opinion had taken in Italy, where the shouts of '*Viva Carlo Alberto!*' were rapidly out-crowing the now bated cry of '*Viva Pio Nono!*'

The benevolent Pontiff yielded to a fit of petty feminine spite. He sent an order to Durando, who, with 12,000 Pontifical troops and volunteers had already joined Charles Albert, to recross the border instantly – an order to which his General, of course, could not and would not attend, and he issued that fatal Encyclic of April 23, the moral of which was that his office as a Pontiff was not compatible with his duty as an Italian.

The sequel was sorrowful. Charles Albert, forsaken by Naples, harassed by Mazzini, and clogged by his own military incapacity, was overpowered in Lombardy. Freedom in Naples, in Tuscany, in Parma, in Modena, was stifled in blood with or without Austrian aid, and Pius IX found himself face to face with his subjects, bound by his own rash engagements to an impracticable, impossible Constitution, thoroughly disgusted with his own work, and fully determined to undo it, if skill and opportunity could be of any avail. He built up one Ministry after another, and at last made choice of Rossi, who, after the fall of Louis Philippe, had remained at Rome in a private capacity, and who, as a *doctrinaire* of the Guizot school, was paradoxical enough, after all recent experience, to conceive that he could reconcile the theory and practice of Constitutional freedom with the pretensions and privileges of the Roman Catholic Church. But he fell the victim of a cowardly assassination at the door of the Parliament he was going to open on the 15th of November, and after his death all the fiends of anarchy ran riot in the streets of Rome, and the Pope, threatened by the mob at his own Palace at the Quirinal, where his secretary was shot by his side on the balcony from which the Pope attempted to address the multitude, saw no way of safety except in flight, which he effected by the help of the Bavarian Minister, or his wife, the Countess Spaur, who smuggled him away in her carriage disguised as a domestic or as a common priest, and conveyed him safely across the frontier on the 24th of November, 1848. Some of the Pope's biographers give the credit of saving him at this crisis to the French Ambassador, d'Harcourt. Matters did not mend in Rome in the Pope's absence. The Mamiani Ministry which he had left behind him broke down at once. Men of extreme views and of no scruple came into power, and a Roman Republic was proclaimed in February, 1849, of which Mazzini was invited to take the direction as one of the Triumvirate on the 30th of March. This did not suit the Government and Assembly of the sister Republic of France, whose President, Louis Napoleon, making himself the interpreter of the national will, organized an expedition to Rome under Oudinot, by whom, after a first repulse, the Italian patriots, who fought with heroism under Garibaldi, were overpowered. The city was compelled to surrender on July 3, and everything was made ready for the restoration of the Papal Government and for a return of the Pontiff, who, however, put off his entrance into his capital till the beginning of April, 1850.

The choice of Naples – Gaëta at the beginning, and Portici towards the close of his exile – as a land of refuge, in preference to France, Austria, or English Malta which were equally open to him, was an earnest of the frame of mind in which the Pope quitted Rome and returned to it. He brought back the spirit of his host, the Bourbon King. Those who gave him credit for 'benevolence,' for the mildness and clemency befitting the name of Pius, by which he chose to go down to posterity, merely judged from the set smile on his dimpled face, from the pleasing gentleness of his voice and address, and from an habitual jocularity which was not always good-natured or amiable. But the truth is that he was, or became, at least, at this period of his life, both obstinate and vindictive. He had been subjected to ill-treatment and outrage by some of his subjects, it is true, and the punishment of the assassins of Rossi and of Monsignor Palma, as well as of the other authors of the November movement, would have been just, however severe. But the Pope did not seem to consider that upon his departure his people were scarcely any longer responsible for their doings – that their allegiance had passed from him to the Government which, whatever might be thought of its origin or of its constitution, upheld that national principle which the Pope had first proclaimed and then abjured, and stood up in defence of their country's territory against an invader who made religion a pretext for political party manoeuvre. The Pope drew no distinction between the innocent and the guilty among his people. He betrayed an indecent joy at the defeat of his adversaries, and applauded Prince Doria, who raised the monument to the memory of Frenchmen who had come to slay Italians without provocation and without good cause for a quarrel on their own part. Those who were by the side of Pius IX at his return, those who saw and heard him even in what should have been his guarded moments, never allowed him the merit of that meek and forgiving temper which ought to be the badge of every Christian, and ought especially to become the head of Christianity. The fact is he never forgave himself for having once said, '*Benedite o Sommo Iddio all' Italia!*' Repentance of that short whim, or *velléité*, of patriotism and liberalism sank deep in his heart, and he seemed determined that the penance should fall on his subjects, and that his Government should be like that of King Bomba – that of a Sovereign at war with his subjects.

It must be said, also, by way of exculpation, that his rule had, on his return, lost much of its personal character, and the responsibility of the worst acts of his Government weighs in a great measure on the men, or man, to whom, in his estrangement from temporal interests, he intrusted the management of public affairs. The Cardinals upon whom, out of gratitude for their support at the Conclave, Pius IX had at first bestowed the highest offices in the State – such as Bernetti and Gizzi – had fallen away from him in their alarm at the subversive policy into which their Sovereign was being urged by his longing for popularity. Among the members of the Sacred College who showed the greatest readiness to share his adverse fortune, no one made himself so conspicuous as Antonelli, a man who had already risen to influence in the Councils of Gregory XVI, and whom Pius himself had raised to the Cardinalate, and to a place in the Ministry in June, 1847. Antonelli was the inseparable companion and sole adviser of his master at Gaëta and Portici, and enjoyed his unlimited confidence on his return, even before he was raised to the supreme dignity of Secretary of State, in September, 1850. The Secretary was from first to last rather feared than loved by his master, who was nevertheless only too happy to leave him all the odium of the reactionary policy upon which there was perfect agreement between them. To all the solicitations of his subjects, to the remonstrances of his wiser and more humane councillors, and to the incessant warnings, and even threats, of the Emperor Napoleon, who had to answer at Paris for the misrule of his *protégé* at Rome, the invariable answer of the Pope was a reference to his Prime Minister; and this man, whose ability was unquestionable, but who was restrained by no scruple, was at no loss for plausible arguments by which he could justify as necessary the conduct to which the stubborn will of his Sovereign never failed to give a tacit approval. The ascendancy of Antonelli in all State matters outweighed all the joint efforts of those disinterested friends who had crowded the Pope's ante-chambers in the early stage of his career, and whom now death, or disgust, or intrigue removed from his side, and who were gradually superseded by Court minions, whose business was complaisance to the master and subserviency to the useful servant. Only in one instance was Pius IX advised to perform the part of a personal temporal ruler, and this was in 1857, when he made the tour of his dominions 'for the purpose of seeing with his own eyes, and hearing with his own ears, what were the wants of his people;' but the result, as might be expected, was only to add to the irritation of the Pontiff, and to widen the breach between him and his subjects. The tour only added to the public dissatisfaction, and extinguished such sparks of the Pope's popularity as might still linger in those provinces in which Cardinal Mastaï-Ferretti's 'good intentions' were still a matter of innocent belief.

In his heart of hearts, and in spite of the suggestions of pernicious flatterers, Pius IX felt that his political career on the throne had been a failure; but no disappointment could cure him of the fond conceit that his Pontificate was destined to eclipse the glory of his most renowned predecessors. Full of this ambition, and impelled by the restlessness of his nervous temperament, he now turned to the Church that attention which before his flight and banishment he had almost exclusively bestowed on the State. He summoned Jesuit theologians to his side; he recalled and reconstituted their discomfited and scattered order; he canonized Saints, lavished indulgences, countenanced miracles, attempted and enforced conversions, marked out new dioceses in Protestant communities, and at last ventured on subtle polemic discussions and daring definitions of new dogmas. An absolute ruler by all his instincts, he liked to surround himself with all the pageant of a large retinue, and, not satisfied with his ordinary Court, he sought every opportunity of calling together a full array of his hierarchy. It was now for the hallowing of the Japanese martyrs, now for the proclamation of the dogma of the Immaculate Conception, now for the 1800th anniversary of the death of St. Peter, that the Bishops of all Christendom were invited to assemble round the tomb of the Apostles; and it was from this series of great solemnities, from the gratification which the homage of so many Prelates ministered to his overweening vanity, that the idea of an Ecumenic Council, vague at first and undefined, but irrepressible, sprang up and grew and absorbed all the Pope's faculties.

A Council, he well knew, was a Church Parliament. Its institution had become an anachronism since, at its last meeting at Trent in the sixteenth century, a packed majority of Latin, chiefly of Italian, Prelates, had made over all the powers of the hierarchy to its supreme head, and virtually abolished the Constitution of the Church, submitting it to a close, absolute, Pontifical government. The Vatican Council of 1869 was originally intended as a mere pageantry, like all the other previous festivities. There was no programme for this great priestly gathering; no notion of discussion, or of any opposition to such Order of the Day as it might please the *Curia*, the knot of Roman Monsignors, to propose. The dogma of Papal Infallibility was an after-thought, a subtle cavil, and quibble of some of the Pope's Jesuits, a Passaglia or a Curci, who thought on these subjects as Italians, and held that, as the infallibility of the Church was universally accepted by all Catholics, this divine gift, which resided in the whole establishment or in its Councils so long as the Church was a free or representative community, had become vested in the

Pontiff since, by the act of the Synod of Trent, the Holy Father had been empowered to say, *'l'Église c'est moi.'*

The Jesuitic Cabal at Rome, and its uncompromising partisans abroad, had, indeed, good reason to be surprised and alarmed at the storm which the first announcement of these arrogant designs of the Papacy raised beyond the Alps, and especially in the German and Austrian Dioceses. But they were re-assured when they saw that, trusting in the justice of their cause and in the soundness of their arguments, the Prelates of the Opposition consented to travel to Rome and to take their seats in the Sacred Assembly, and that, waiving for the sake of union and harmony the fundamental question, they limited their objections to matters of expediency, such as the opportuneness of the discussion at this crisis, the unfriendly disposition of their flocks, and the displeasure of the lay potentates, whose presence at such gatherings had been an almost invariable rule, and who had hardly ever suffered them to be held without their approval. The Pope and his advisers, however, relied on the enormous majority of the Latin, and especially of the Italian, Episcopate. They had not the best of the argument, but they carried everything by their overwhelming vote, and reduced their opponents to a loud but unavailing protest, which they were soon compelled to repent and abjure; and in July, 1870, Pius IX had the consolation of proclaiming that 'the Roman Pontiff, when he speaks *ex cathedrâ* – *i. e.*, when in discharge of the office of pastor and teacher of all nations he defines a doctrine regarding faith or morals to be held by the universal Chuch – is, by the divine assistance promised to him in the person of the blessed Peter, possessed of that infallibility with which the Divine Redeemer willed that his Church should be endowed in defining doctrines regarding faith or morals, and that, therefore, such definitions of the Roman Pontiff are of themselves, and not from the consent of the Church, irreformable.'

It was a great achievement, and its magnitude will, perhaps, be better understood, its importance better tested, and its consequences, good or bad, better developed under some of the successors of Pius IX. The result, in so far as that Pontiff himself was concerned, was considerably affected by the political vicissitudes in which his reign was involved only two months later.

The restorer of the Papal Throne in 1849 had ample leisure to appreciate the effect of his own work in subsequent years. Beset by the cares of his precarious position, bewildered by the maze of his wavering, tentative policy, the Emperor Napoleon looked upon his occupation of Rome as an incubus of which he vainly wished to rid himself on any terms. His suggestions to the Pope's Ministers of measures by which they should remove the scandal of the ecclesiastical rule, were met in every instance by Antonelli with his inexorable *Non Possumus.* It became evident to Napoleon III that the Pope either must remain the same as he had always been or must cease to be. The time came when, to the difficulties by which the

Emperor was hampered at home, no other remedy suggested itself than some *coup de tête* of an adventurous enterprise abroad. *Il lui fallut déborder*; and Italy was chosen as the field of his compulsory activity. The victories of Magenta and Solferino determined the occupation of the Papal Legations, which were not allowed to return to their allegiance at the peace of Villafranca and Zurich in 1859. In the following year France, won over by the cession of Savoy and Nice, countenanced the further spoliation of the Marches and Umbria and their annexation to the Italian Kingdom, which soon extended its sway over Naples and Sicily, including the Papal enclaves of Benevento and Pontecorvo. The Pope's dominions were now reduced to the City of Rome and its Province, together with St. Peter's patrimony, Viterbo, and the district of Velletri. Further than this the Pope's patron did not mean that Italian encroachment should extend. In his anxiety to wash his hands of the Pope and to withdraw from Rome his protecting garrison, the successor of Pepin and Charlemagne extorted from the feeble Italian Government the Convention of September, 1866, implying a removal of the Italian capital to Florence, and a more or less openly acknowledged renunciation of the claim to Rome. The French tricolor was thus let down from the Castle of St. Angelo, and the Pope was left to the protection of his own Zouaves. Rattazzi's intrigues and Garibaldi's rashness broke through that Convention, and the bands of adventurers which had overthrown the Bourbons in the two Sicilies pressed forward into the shrunken Papal territory till they were in sight of St. Peter's dome. Here, however, the French Emperor again interposed; the tide of invasion was forced back by De Failly's chassepots at Mentana, on the 3d of November, 1867, and M. Rouher pronounced that emphatic '*Jamais!*' which was meant to assure the Pope from all future molestation. Less than three years later Napoleon surrendered his sword at Sedan; the French Imperial Zouaves again filed off at Porta Pancrazio, and, presently, on the 20th of September, 1870, the *Bersaglieri* of General Cadorna burst in at Porta Pia.

Thus ended the Temporal Power, and the actual reign of Pius IX, in the third month of its 24th year. The Pontificate outlasted the years of St. Peter, even reckoning the time of his Government of the Church at Antioch. The Pope was left in possession of the Vatican, and his independent position was insured by the Law of Guarantees, establishing the inviolability of his person as well as of his attendants, and of his postal and telegraphic correspondence, with a free diplomatic intercourse, and all the honours and privileges becoming a Sovereign rank, with a competent Civil List of 200,000L yearly. Pius IX ignored the Guarantees, declined the assignment, and maintained a sullen, hostile attitude, allowing his partisans to declare that he was under restraint, and considered himself a prisoner in the Vatican. To that Palace and its garden he, in fact, confined himself with great determination year after year.

The incessant bickerings between the apostolic recluse and those whom he designated as his sacrilegious persecutors, the endless complaints of the Pontifical retinue, and the petty gossip and scandal of the rival diplomatic establishments which France, and after her example, if not at her instigation, the other Catholic Powers accredited to the two hostile Courts of the Vatican and the Quirinal, kept up a ferment in Rome which would have been repeatedly attended by violent collision, had it not been for the marvellous discretion and long suffering of the Italian authorities on the one side, and, on the other, for the timely intervention of the soundest party among the Pope's advisers, and especially of the wary and worldly-wise Antonelli during his lifetime. It was by the crafty and temporizing astuteness of the latter that the Pope was at first dissuaded from venturing on so desperate a course as a second flight from Rome would have been, a resolution from which His Holiness, whatever might be his inclination, was in later days debarred by advancing age and infirmity, which put any thought of his again setting out on his travels altogether out of the question. Advised, or compelled, to stay where he was, the Pope was determined to make the most of his position, and to turn his alleged captivity to the best account. He filled the world with his grievances, and vented his withering displeasure in those endless jeremiads of his allocutions and encyclics, which, freely printed in every newspaper in Italy and abroad, made a display of his scribe's eloquence, and won him a reputation which was not acquired without some detriment to his dignity. His complaints found, however, very ready sympathy throughout the Roman Catholic world, and especially among the Ultramontane Party, which studied everything that could enliven the Pontiff's solitude and soothe his weariness and chagrin by incessant visits, by pilgrimages, and by the tender of pecuniary subventions which made both himself and his vast *entourage* independent of Italian bounties, and heaped treasures at the Vatican which strangely contrasted with the destitute condition of the Italian National Exchequer. Through all these years of hope-deferred and disappointment, the faith of the sanguine old man never deserted him. To the very last he cherished the expectation that something would turn up; that Providence would interfere on behalf of a cause which, in his opinion, was the cause of Heaven. In his deep conviction that the independence of the Church was bound up with the existence of the Temporal Power, he looked for friends among all those nations which he fancied inimical to Italian interests; and he shaped his ecclesiastical policy by the dictates of his worldly views. Thus it happened that he almost invariably found himself committed to the losing cause, and gave his countenance to the Party against which fortune, or, as he called it, Providence, gave sentence; and this so constantly, so perseveringly, that he was at last suspected by the vulgar multitude in Rome of having the 'evil eye,' and bringing misfortune to all those upon whom his favour rested. It is thus that Francis Joseph of Austria, Napoleon III of France, Queen Isabella of Spain, Don Carlos, the Sultan, MacMahon, and many others came to ill-fortune as soon as they were known to rely on the Pope's support and to have secured his blessings. Not satisfied with the open war he was waging against Italy, he brought upon himself a variety of other quarrels, chiefly arising from the pretensions he grounded on the newly established principle of his own Infallibility. The most formidable of these was connected with the solidarity established by their common interests between the Italian and the German nationality, and the apprehended determination of France to make the disruption and subjugation of the weaker country a stepping-stone to that revenge which she was supposed to meditate against the stronger one. With Russia, with the Latin Churches in the Levant, and even with the Spanish Republics of South America, some of which, as that of Ecuador, voted half their yearly revenue to be consecrated to the Pope under the denomination of Peter's pence, the Court of the Vatican did, at various times, within the period of its worldly dethronement, contrive to be at strife. In France the Vatican Court was the chief cause of that dissension between the Republic and its President of which the Pope could scarcely hope to live to see the permanent termination, or even the immediate consequences; and in Turkey his predilection for the Mussulman cause, or his ill-will to the Greek Church, led to the grievous distress of his own Treasury and of the purses of his supporters; large sums of Ultramontane money having improvidently been invested in the Ottoman funds.

As years and infirmities advanced, and the Pope began to apprehend that the fulness of the times to which he looked forward with most persevering confidence was no longer likely to be accomplished during his own life, he was haunted by some anxiety as to the condition in which the Church would find herself upon the Holy See becoming vacant; and he debated in his own mind, and discussed with his advisers, the project of attempting to influence the choice of his successor. The number of Cardinals who had attended the Conclave of 1846, which had led to his own elevation, had been reduced by death to three or four; and the ranks of the hundred or more whom he had created at various stages in his career had been so rapidly thinned from the same cause that, in the year 1874, the Sacred College consisted of only 45 members. As six years had elapsed without any distribution of Red Hats, it began to be surmised that the Pope had an object in his proceedings; that he thought his authority in attempting to influence a future Conclave would be more easily exercised on a small number of voters, and especially on the majority of those he had at hand in Rome – *Cardinali di Curia*, as they are called, habitual frequenters of the Vatican, and men accustomed to an almost unbounded submission to the Pontiff's behests. The votes of a sufficient majority of these were supposed to have been secured on behalf of a Papal nominee, and it was stated, moreover, that a sealed brief, or Bull, in the Pope's hand, was laid in some of His Holiness's drawers whence it would be drawn out by a trusty hand the moment the breath was out of his body, the seal broken, and the contents of this Papal last will and testament communicated to the knot of Cardinals, whose compliance could be reckoned upon as fully as their discretion.

The Bull, however, had probably no existence, except in the fervid brain of some quidnuncs, and it was long before the death of Cardinal Riario Sforza, Archbishop of Naples, whose name was mentioned as that of the candidate of the Pope's choice, that Pius IX, at once changing his mind, or, at least, his conduct, began to create one batch of Cardinals after another with such good effect that before the middle of the year 1877 the members of the Sacred College were 62, and there was every appearance of the Pope's intention to reach the full number of 70. It was also observed that while, in 1868, the roll of the foreign Cardinals was limited to one-fifth of the whole College, being thus kept within the proportions established by usage, the Pope from that date seemed to deal more liberally towards the foreign Prelates, the proportion being 26 foreign out of a roll of 62 Cardinals; a line of conduct on his part leading to the surmise that he had abandoned all hope of being able to bias the minds of those who were to gather in Conclave round his death-bed, as the election could now no longer be held, as it were, *en famille*, and he could not presume to find so large an assembly as the next meeting must be, amenable to his posthumous suggestions, nor could he count on the compliance of so many men placed by the duties of their office in distant dioceses altogether beyond reach of his influence.

In the midst of these plans for the future, and of the anxiety of mind attendant upon their discussion, the Pope's body was gradually, but perceptibly, succumbing to the infirmity of which the end had long been predicted. Gifted with a marvellous vitality, in spite of his liability to an illness which so often counterfeited death, he contrived to battle, and, so to say, to dodge the enemy and almost to reach the age to which nature seemed to entitle the majority of the members of his family. Deprived during the summer months of the power of locomotion, then, as the autumn advanced, denied the benefit of the free air of his garden, to which the mildness of the climate allowed him to be carried in his arm-chair, he was at first condemned to a sitting, then to a recumbent position, till it was at last understood that he would never leave his bed, except to be removed to his coffin. From that prostrate state he had short intervals of apparent recovery; but a restoration to the free use of his limbs was out of the question. Little rest was permitted to him even at the last stage of his sufferings; for of all men a Pope is the one whose active personal rule can be least dispensed with, the one whose infallibility can least be deputed to a proxy, the one whose sovereignty least admits of a regency; the one on whom the duty of dying in harness is most inexorably incumbent. In the case of Pius IX the freshness and lucidity of mind, which never forsook him to the last, and his jealousy of a power of which he loved at least the semblance, precluded the possibility of those delusions and juggleries by which the will of a dying Pontiff has been in many instances forged by the bystanders. Pius IX died with all his wits about him.

The repeated failures of Pius IX, both as a Spiritual and a Temporal ruler, were in some measure redeemed by his character as a private man. He was benevolent, liberal, affable in his general intercourse, sharpwitted, sanguine and cheerful, chatty and sociable, never so happy as when he could doff his Apostolic dignity and come down from his Pontifical pedestal. Even among the stiffness of his State receptions he would indulge in a little by-play, and would turn to his trusty attendants with an occasional aside, which did not always escape the visitors among whom he chose the butts of his humorous shafts. At the fag-end of one of these levées his Chamberlain informed him that some young ladies were still in the ante-chamber waiting to be admitted to the honour of kissing the Apostolic ring, and the Pope, nodding his consent and looking towards the door, presently descried the damsels who were being ushered in, conspicuous for the towering headgear with which Fashion, at that season, cumbered her female votaries. '*Santo Padre,*' said the Chamberlain preceding and announcing the fair bevy, '*Le Signorine Guerrieri!*' '*Me ne sono accoto dai cimieri,*' quoth his Holiness, and forthwith he put on his most winning smile, and bestowed on the high-crested maidens his most solemn benediction. There was almost something personal in the puns and quibbles he was fond of perpetrating, even at the expense of his best friends, and quite without a shade of bitterness or malice. He wondered at De Angelis, the Cardinal Bishop of Fermo, '*da tanti anni in-fermo senza morir mai.*' The dying state of Cardinal Barili suggested to him the consolation that *Se anche si perdesse il barile rimarrebbe sempre la botte,* the 'butt' or cask in the case being the Falstaff-like corpulence of Cardinal Bartolini. The jokes were harmless and almost childish; but it should be borne in mind that Pius IX was 86 years old, and that sternness, or even great earnestness, was no part of his idiosyncrasy.

Naturally joyous and buoyant as was his disposition, the Pope was, however, subject to fits of sudden irritability, touchy and impatient, and above all things he was resentful of any presumption on his condescension, any approach to disrespect towards his person or dignity. He was easily ruffled by direct and frank contradiction. If it came to any divergence of views, who should know better than the Infallible? His instincts tended to goodwill to all men, and in youth he had friends; but there was something indiscriminate and somewhat instable in his affections, and, after his elevation, he was too full of himself to be capable of much expansion to other men. It was attested to his credit that he was free from the besetting sin of other Popes; he was no Nepotist; but it is well to observe that, after his return from Gaëta, it was not he who would not befriend and promote his relations; the estrangement was owing to his brothers, who condemned his reactionary policy, and would not come near him. On the Throne Pius IX found solitude. That same necessity of his position which compelled him to put up with men whom he feared, like Antonelli, closed his heart against those whom he might have felt prompted to love.

On the other hand, he was severe and even terrible to those who had justly or unjustly incurred his displeasure; but it must be said, in justice to him, that the implacability of his enmity arose from his consciousness of his unerring judgment, and from the conviction that opposition to him was as unpardonable a sacrilege as rebellion to Heaven. The world has not forgotten his treatment of Cardinal D'Andrea, but has not heard much of his harshness to more obscure persons, upon whom his wrath was poured out with even more unsparing measure. Not naturally strong in argument, and not provided with a large stock of knowledge, the Pope relied on vehemence for the means of overcoming his adversaries in controversy. Many of the Italian and even some of the foreign Prelates were convinced against their will about the dogma of infallibility; some because unable to withstand his cajoling, some because unwilling to expose themselves to his wrath and reproaches.

The Pope's health, after declining throughout the summer, threatened to give way in the autumn, and on the 23d of November he was deprived of the use of his limbs, and never rose from his bed except to be laid in an arm-chair in a reclining position. Even in that state, however, he held two Consistories, created new cardinals, appointed bishops, and received the visits of diplomatists and other distinguished personages. In the early part of the present year the illness and death of Victor Emmanuel caused him deep emotions, and awakened sympathies which induced him to send words of forgiveness and gave rise to some vague hopes of reconciliation between Church and State. But the hostile suggestions of uncompromising Ultramontanes again hardened the old Pontiff's heart and one of his last acts is said to have been to prepare an allocution protesting against the accession of Humbert as King of Italy.

This generally sympathetic, but far from uncritical, obituary opens with reference to Pius IX's singularly long but troubled reign. His successors might have ceased to mourn the loss of their temporal sovereignty, but none saw fit to proclaim his sainthood or insisted on his status as a martyr. This was a Pope who, despite losing control of the Papal States, and ultimately of Rome itself, was the fosterer of the dogma of the Immaculate Conception, the promoter of the feast of the Sacred Heart, the introducer of new Catholic hierarchies in England and the Netherlands, the presider over a major Church Council, and, above all, the first Pontiff to be declared Infallible. He met opposition, both inside and outside the Church, over all these contentious issues. He had been forced into temporary exile by a Revolution in Rome. Between 1850 and 1870 he had ruled some 3,000,000 unwilling subjects merely on the strength of French military support. After 1870 he sulked in the Vatican, pronouncing anathemas on the new King of Italy reigning from the erstwhile Papal palace on the Quirinal and, moreover, on an antipathetic modern world. What that English Ultramontane, Cardinal Manning, saw as 'the beauty of inflexibility' seemed uglier to those nineteenth-century progressives who strove for plural answers and open or compromised conclusions. Pius IX's pontificate was the longest in the Church's history. It was also amongst the most contentious. He was interred in the rebuilt narthex of the Basilica of San Lorenzo Fuori le Mura.

GEORGE GILBERT SCOTT

Architect: 'His hands have been more than full.'

27 MARCH 1878

WE REGRET TO announce the almost sudden death of the eminent architect, Sir George Gilbert Scott, R. A., which occurred yesterday morning at his residence, Courtfield-house, South Kensington. The grandson of the Rev. Thomas Scott, the author of a 'Commentary on the Bible,' he was born at Gawcott, in Buckinghamshire, of which place his father was the incumbent, in 1811. In early life he showed a taste for making drawings of ancient churches, and his father eventually placed him in an architect's office. The taste referred to might have been taken as a sign that his talents lay in a different direction, but the event proved that the Rev. Mr. Scott had not made a mistake. Gothic architecture was then attracting general attention, and when Mr. Scott became an architect on his own account he was one of its most fervent advocates. In 1841, during a brief partnership with Mr. Moffatt, Mr. Scott designed the Martyr's Memorial at Oxford, and soon afterwards the new church at Camberwell. In 1842 the church of St. Nicholas at Hamburg was destroyed by fire, the architects of Europe were invited to compete for the privilege of rebuilding the edifice, and, to the astonishment of all save those to whom his previous works were familiar Mr. Scott's design was accepted. This work has not long been completed, the spire being 478ft. high, or the highest in the world until those of Cologne Cathedral are completed. The honour he had thus won gave him a wide reputation, and since that time his hands have been more than full. In 1848 he was requested to furnish a design for the Cathedral Church at St. John's, Newfoundland. He did so, but even now the building is unfinished. In 1855, though some of the most renowned architects in Europe were his competitors, he was selected to erect the proposed Hotel de Ville and Senate House at Hamburg, and afterward, superintended the restoration of the parish church of Doncaster. In the meantime he had been appointed official architect to the Dean and Chapter of Westminster, and had written his 'Plea for the Faithful Restoration of our Ancient Churches.' It would take some time to enumerate the works he has accomplished within comparatively recent memory. He restored the Cathedrals of Ely, Lichfield, Hereford, Ripon, Glocester, Chester, St. David's, St. Asaph, Bangor, Salisbury, Exeter, Peterborough, Worcester, Rochester, and Oxford. He rearranged the choir, including new screen and pavement and pulpit, at Durham Cathedral, and was engaged with Mr. Slater in the reconstruction of the central tower and spire at

Chichester. He designed the new Abbey Gatehouse and the buildings on the north side of Westminster Abbey, to say nothing of many desirable improvements in the venerable edifice itself. Subsequently he made the Chapter-house what it is now. In addition to restoring old churches and erecting new ones in all parts of the country, he carried out many secular works, such as Kelham-hall in Nottinghamshire, Lee Priory in Kent, the Town-hall at Preston, Walton-house in Warwickshire, the Infirmary at Leeds, Hafodanos-house in North Wales, the Midland Railway terminus at St. Pancras, and the National Memorial to Prince Albert. He was the architect of the new Foreign Office and the new Home and Colonial Offices, and, in conjunction with Sir Digby Wyatt, designed the new India Office. The Home and Colonial Offices are complete except as regards the main angles, for which, as we learn by a letter written by him not many weeks ago, he never succeeded in obtaining the orders. He also restored Exeter, Merton and New Colleges at Oxford, made many alterations in St. John's College at Cambridge, and entirely rebuilt the University buildings at Glasgow. Though his time was more than sufficiently occupied, he occasionally found time to write upon the art to which his life was devoted. In 1850 he published some 'Remarks on Secular and Domestic Architecture,' in 1862 his 'Gleanings from Westminster Abbey,' and in 1864 his 'Conservation of Ancient Architectural Monuments.' The Architectural Museum, too, owes much of its prosperity to the interest he took in its welfare. Honours, as may be supposed, flowed in upon him from many quarters; he was elected R. A. in 1860; it was at the wish of the Queen that he received the appointment of architect to the National Memorial to the Prince Consort; and finally he received the honour of knighthood. Towards the close of his life he was engaged in erecting the new cathedral at Edinburgh, in re-roofing and re-arranging the Chapel of New College, Oxford, and in carrying out the restoration of the Cathedral at St. Alban's.

Scott's achievement, as this obituary emphasises, was phenomenal even by Victorian standards. As a civil and ecclesiastical architect, he had left his mark on virtually every county in England and, as a restorer, he had refaced, repointed, rebuttressed and in some cases virtually rebuilt many of the finest cathedrals, abbeys and parish churches in the land. He had also reordered their interiors and designed many of their noblest fittings. This did not stand him in good stead with a sprinkling of his contemporaries (William Morris referred to his 'coarseness of manners and morals') and a steady stream of his successors. Scott was also virtually demonised by twentieth-century critics until the revival of a serious appreciation of Victorian architecture after the 1960s. Properly enough, no mention is made in this obituary of Scott's undistinguished early work as a designer of Union Workhouses and the obituarist skirts over the rejection by Lord

Palmerston of his Gothic design for the Foreign Office in Whitehall. Scott had defended his original scheme in letters to *The Times* in 1859 and would later complain of the Prime Minister's 'poor buffoonery which only Lord Palmerston's age permitted'. Scott's self-justifying autobiography, *Personal and Professional Recollections*, was published posthumously in 1879.

* * *

JOHN THADEUS DELANE

Editor of The Times: 'The man who worked *The Times*.'

22 NOVEMBER 1879

THE BRITISH PUBLIC has finally lost one of the oldest, most devoted, and most meritorious of those who may be called its own special servants. Mr. Delane died on Saturday evening at his residence at Ascot, having not long completed his sixty-second year. In the summer of 1877 it became painfully evident to Mr. Delane's friends, and not less to himself, that near 40 years of incessant work had told on a vigorous Constitution and powerful nerve, and that it would be well for him to seek rest while still able to enjoy it. The result showed that the determination was not arrived at too soon, and Mr. Delane has not survived more than two years his release from the continuous round of daily and nightly duties. Perhaps it is not more than public men have a right to expect. Soldiers and sailors, if on the one hand liable to be cut off in mid career, are much more generally rewarded with half a life of honourable rest and pleasant retrospection. But as a rule they who have once entered the political strife never quit it willingly or become deaf to the old challenges and familiar rallying ones. They would be ready to die in harness if they could only persuade their colleagues that the old is still better than the new.

John Thadeus Delane was born at Bracknell, which all our readers may not know to be a pleasant spot, half town, half village, in the favoured and residential part of Berkshire, included so recently as the beginning of this century in Old Windsor Forest. While he was still in his boyhood his father, a solicitor, received from the late Mr. Walter an appointment in *The Times* Office. The conductors of

John Thadeus Delane

this journal very early saw in young Mr. Delane the industry, the quickness of apprehension, the eagerness for information, and the accessibleness to new impressions and ideas which might qualify him for a place in its future management. He was educated therefore, it may be said, for the purpose, and if Mr. Delane owed much to himself, few men have owed so much to favourable circumstances and to the kind and provident care of their friends. After learning about as much as boys usually learn at a private school, and perhaps more than is usually learnt at a private tutor's, in Lincolnshire, he was admitted to Magdalen Hall, in the University of Oxford, where the present Bishop of Chester was Tutor and Vice-Principal, under Dr. Macbride. Mr. Jacobson's thorough scholarship and genial temper converted not a few of his pupils, from very different schools, into attached friends and Mr. Delane was one of them. Perhaps this and his friendship with Sir G. Dasent were the special gains of his University career which he ever most appreciated. Immediately on leaving Oxford, indeed before taking his degree, Mr. Delane was qualifying himself for almost any profession he might finally decide on, under good direction, with a view to the better discharge of the post eventually assigned to him. He walked the London hospitals for several terms, and, having a natural taste for the art of medicine and for operative surgery, he made more real progress than many who have no other aim than the exercise of the medical profession. He kept his terms at the Middle Temple, where he was called to the Bar. He reported both on Circuit and at the House of Commons, where for two years he took his turn in the gallery. There was no necessary training which he did not undergo with as much spirit as if his career was to begin and end there; – an example to those who imagine that important positions are to be jumped into or had for the asking, and that luck is the arbiter of eminence. When he entered the Editor's room he had the advantage of an able and accomplished chief, and of excellent instruction and advice as to the traditions and policy of this journal. As he did his work well, it grew in his hands till, by the successive deaths of two colleagues, he became in 1841 the recognized Editor of *The Times*, and so continued till the autumn of 1877.

After stating the special advantages and qualifications Mr. Delane had for his position, we shall be only adding to his merits when we allude to deficiencies which some would think insurmountable. He had not had the thoroughly classical education then to be obtained only in one of our old public schools. He was out of the 'ring' which for a long time had claimed the monopoly of orthodox literature. What was more, he never was a writer; he never even attempted to write anything except what he wrote much better than most writers could do – reports and letters. These he had to do and he did them well. He had a large staff of writers, and it was not necessary he should write except to communicate with them. This was, indeed, the greatest of his numerous advantages. He immediately started with a number of able and educated men, found for him by those who were, above all things good judges of character. When it is considered that he was, at least in early years, younger than most of the men he had to deal with, and that while they were practised writers he was not, it is no slight testimony to his success in the discharge of his delicate office that none of these writers ever disputed the value of his criticisms, or failed to agree cordially in his revisions, alterations, and suppressions. Thousands of times when in the heat and haste of writing expressions had been employed which the writer had some little doubt about and felt to be weak points in his composition, he has found the Editor's pen falling with sure discernment on the faulty passage and justifying the writer's own suppressed misgivings. The advantage of this process was mutual. To criticize freely and to submit to criticism is to learn and improve. The greatest writers in our language, in this and in former ages, if they have not themselves admitted that they had published much which would have been the better for a previous censure, have at least left their readers to say it in stronger language. One of the greatest of living writers has often stated that every man ought to have a reviser. It is not without its cost to the person charged with the duty. The almost exclusive practice of critical revision is not favourable to original writing, for it developes fastidiousness. When Lord Beaconsfield said that critics were unsuccessful writers he ingeniously inverted the natural order of the fact. It is too true that if a man's life work is criticism, it is likely to take away freedom and freshness of expression except in those familiar utterances in which he is not trammelled by the obligations of style.

The work of an Editor can only be appreciated by those who have had the fortune to have had some little experience of it. The Editor of a London daily newspaper is held answerable for every word in 48, and sometimes 60, columns. The merest slip of the pen, an epithet too much, a wrong date, a name misspelt or with a wrong initial before it, a mistake as to some obscure personage only too glad to seize the opportunity of showing himself, the misinterpretation of some passage perhaps incapable of interpretation, the most trifling offence to the personal or national susceptibility of those who do not even profess to care for the feelings of others, may prove not only disagreeable, but even costly mistakes; but they are among the least of the mistakes to which an Editor is liable. As it is impossible to say what a night may bring forth, and the most important intelligence is apt to be the latest, it will often find him with none to share his responsibility, without advisers, and with colleagues either pre-engaged on other matters or no longer at hand. The Editor must be on the spot till the paper is sent to the press, and make decisions on which not only the approval of the British public, but great events, and even great causes, may hang. All the more serious part of his duties has to be discharged at the end of a long day's work, a day of interruptions and conversations, of letter reading and letter writing, when mind and body are not what they were 12 hours ago, and wearied nature is putting in her gentle pleas. An Editor cannot husband his strength for the night's battle with comparative repose in the solitude of a study or the freshness of green fields. He must see the world, converse with its foremost or busiest actors, be open to information, and on guard against error. All this ought to be borne in mind by those who complain that journalism is not infallibly accurate, just, and agreeable. Their complaints are like those of the Court lord who found fault with the disagreeable necessities of warfare.

Since Mr. Delane became Editor of this journal there have been 13 Administrations, all founded necessarily on some new concurrence of circumstances. At the beginning of this period Lord Melbourne was in power. Since his time Sir R. Peel was in power once, Lord Russell twice, Lord Derby three times, Lord Aberdeen once, Lord Palmerston twice, Lord Beaconsfield twice, and Mr. Gladstone once. Every one of these 13 Governments has been typical of some new phase of opinion, some new policy, or some new idea, and in every instance a new mass of particulars amounting, it seems to a new volume of political history, had to be accurately mastered, justly appreciated, and carefully kept in view. An Editor, it has often been said, sometimes not very seriously, must know everything. He must, at least, never be found at fault, and must be always equal to the occasion as to the personal characteristics, the concerns, the acts and utterances of those who are charged with the government of this great Empire. But this is only one of many points, some even more difficult, because more special and more apt to lie for a time out of the scope of ordinary vigilance. Since the year 1841 the world has seen unprecedented improvements in naval and military material and tactics; not slowly making their way as curiosities that might take their time, but forced into notice by frequent reminders of their necessity. Europe has seen not only two or three but many revolutions, wars unexampled for their dimensions, their costs, and their results; many dynasties overthrown, an Empire rise and fall, another all but finally dismembered amid a scramble over the spoil, and several re-unifications effected beyond even the hopes of former times. Scientific discovery in every department of knowledge has been more than ever active, and that in the practical bearings which claim the notice of the public from day to day. Never before have the earth and the sea so freely revealed their resources and their treasures. Continents supposed to be protected from intrusive curiosity by intolerable heat, by untameable savagery, or by national jealousy, have been traversed in all directions by explorers whose volumes have been as familiar as our Continental Handbooks. Within this period have been the gold discoveries and the new communities founded on them. It is commonly said that the English never really learn geography or history till forced upon their acquaintance by wars or other disasters. This shows how much has to be learnt if any one has to keep pace with events. The American Civil War, our own Indian Mutiny, and the occupation of France by the German Armies are events which the future student of history may find comprised in a few paragraphs, but the record and explanation of them day by day for many months involved particulars sufficient to fill many bulky volumes. With a large class of critics, a small mistake counts as much as a large one, but everybody is liable to make mistakes, and an Editor labours under the additional danger of too readily accepting the words of writers, some of whom will always be too full of their ideas to pay needful attention to such matters. These are days of Blue-books, of enormous correspondence, of tabular returns, of statistics twisted into every possible form, of averages and differences always on supposition to be carefully remembered, of numerical comparisons everybody challenges if they are not in his own favour, and of statements that if they possess the least novelty or other interest are sure to be picked to pieces. Reference has been made to the severe conditions under which all this work has to be done. It frequently happens that a long night's work has to be thrown away, including many carefully revised columns of printed matter, to make room for an over-grown Parliamentary debate, a budget of important despatches, or a speech made in the provinces by some one, may be, who did not love this paper, and to whom it owed nothing but public duty. Often has it been said at 2 in the morning that a very good paper has been printed and destroyed to make way for a paper that very few will read, none perhaps except a few Parliamentary gentlemen looking out for passages which, if they don't read well, must have been incorrectly reported. As an instance of what may happen to an editor the Quarterly Return of the Revenue once came with an enormous error, an addition instead of subtraction, or *vice-versa*. The writer who had to comment on it jotted down the principal figures and the totals, which were unexpected, and returned the original for the printers. It was not till an hour after midnight that, on a sight of the return in print, the error was perceived, and corrected, without a word of remark, by the paper. Of course, the comments had to be re-written and carefully secured from error.

It is not in man not to have a bias, personal as well as political, and this bias is even more inevitable where there is a considerable acquaintance with the subject or the person concerned. As with the Editor, so with his indispensable informants, subordinates, and other colleagues. Great as is the audacity of inner consciousness in these days, its place is not in an editor's room. For the materials, and, to a great extent, for the use made of them, he has to depend on others, and very often upon persons at a great distance, surrounded by influences amounting sometimes to a sort of compulsion. At high heat, the most honourable combatants or controversialists are conscious of nothing but their own case, and can tolerate no other. Partizanship has to be reduced to impartiality, rancour to fairness, and one-sided statements to approximate truth, in the editor's room. This delicate process has often to be performed after midnight, as a mere episode in the continual press of ordinary, but still exigent matters. How far 'The man who worked *The Times*,' as Mr. Delane would sometimes describe himself, for near 40 years has done this successfully is a point on which people will claim opinions of their own. It cannot be pretended, however, that any other person can be put in competition with him, as having had an equal task, as having been so long at it, and as having achieved such a preponderance of success. What is the measure and proof of that success? It is not far to seek. He is the best General, the Great Duke said, who makes the fewest mistakes. For the long period of time named above the British public took up what may be called their favourite 'broadsheet' every morning, not expecting, or intending, or even wishing to agree constantly with what they found in it, yet with the utmost confidence that they would find the great questions of the day fairly and fully stated, that nothing would be added or left out from malice or carelessness, and that they were at least furnished with all the materials for forming opinions of their own. The great work in which Mr. Delane has borne the chief administrative part has not been done in a corner. It has been before the whole world. The course of this paper has been the course of this nation and of the world. If that course be a failure, if England is but the wreck of what it was 40 years ago, if it has lost wealth, happiness, grandness, and whatever else constitutions, governments, statesmen, patriots, and soldiers are made of, then Mr. Delane has assisted to lead public opinion the downward road of decline and decay. If, like most Englishmen, we believe the course of public affairs to have been upwards rather than downwards, we must credit our departed friend with a long and victorious service in a cause vastly more important than that of ordinary conquerors.

Mr. Delane had in a remarkable degree several qualities which are indispensable to success in all business of importance. He was capable of long application and concentrated attention. After hours of work, under harassing and perplexing circumstances, he had ample reserve of strength for those critical emergencies which make the greatest demand on the powers of apprehension and judgment. He could always seize on the main point at issue and lay his hand on that upon which all the rest depended. It seemed a kind of intuition that enabled him to foresee at once the impending fate of a cause or the result of a campaign, but it was a practical and methodical power. He could distinguish between the relevant and the irrelevant in the calculation of probabilities as well as in the conduct of an argument. In a continual experience of mistakes and disappointments – for, as we have said, the nightly birth of the broadsheet is not without its agonies and mishaps – he maintained more equanimity and command of temper than most people do under the petty harasses of private life. Compelled as he was occasionally to be decisive even to abruptness, and to sacrifice the convenience of contributors and subordinates to the paramount interest of the public, he never lost the respect or affection of those who could sympathize with him in his work, make due allowance for his difficulties and think less of themselves than of the great issues at stake. In these days a great man is expected to master a bulky report in one day and deliver it in flowing sentences the next; but the former process is performed in the quiet of a study, and the latter with the comfortable feeling that so long as the orator is on his legs he has possession of the audience. If he is not clear, he can be diffuse; if he misses the point himself, he can take care that his hearers miss it too; he can at least lead his foes a dance as well as his friends and admirers. Mr. Delane could always, at a moment's call, give a succinct epitome, in terse, telling English, of any speech or debate, any book, any correspondence he had read or listened to; and many a writer and speaker might have been thankful to learn from him for the first time the real purport and drift of all the sentences or facts they had been stringing together. He did this without being either tedious or slapdash, if we may use the word, for his was an honest attempt to do justice even to those with whom he did not agree. The facility with which he did this, and the sometimes marvellous manner in which he would present the real substance of addresses beyond the patience of ordinary hearers or readers, made him most welcome, almost too welcome, in every society in this country. The self-denying ordinance Mr. Delane had to submit to is not to be estimated simply by the usual repugnance to put business before pleasure, work before play, or by the natural and universal preference shown by educated men for what is called good society. There were features in Mr. Delane's character which made the sacrifice specially painful. He had the instincts of family affection almost to excess for in no one was more exemplified the old saying that blood is stronger than water. A warm and, in this matter, almost impulsive nature found vent in friendships which lasted many years, and passed, in many instances, from the parents to the children, and embraced a widening circle. It cost no small management, as well as self-denial, to divide days and hours, body and soul, between friends and a country equally unwilling to take a denial. It is the ordinary martyrdom of public men in this country, but of even our best and great men few can estimate what it was for Mr. Delane to withdraw as unobservedly and as early as he could from the assembled guests, 'before they had joined the ladies,' to spend many hours selecting materials, pruning redundant paragraphs, fining down tedious narratives, deciphering manuscripts, correcting proofs, harmonizing discordant intelligence, discovering the sense of telegraphic riddles, and often finishing by sacrificing the editorial labour of many hours to make room for some bulky and important, but very late arrival, that must be published at whatever cost. It is curiously said that most Englishmen accept the glorious phenomenon of sunrise on the authority of the poets who describe it and the astronomers who prove it, for they have never seen it themselves, except now and then on the walls of the Royal Academy. For nearly half the year Mr. Delane saw it every morning, not after what it is a mockery to call his night's rest, but before it.

The most jealous rival would not venture to dispute that Mr. Delane did honour to his singular position as the chief of English journalists. He held his own amid temptations, solicitations and interferences of a less gentle kind, and, though an affectionate friend and a pleasant companion, could deny the unreasonable requests incessantly made, in one form or other, to all who are believed to have anything to do with public opinion. As is universal with British statesmen and politicians his one idea of dignified happiness was that of a country gentleman. For many years his delight was to go down on the Saturday and bury himself for a few hours in a rather dull cottage, in a corner of his native parish, and feel himself once more at home. Some 20 years since he bought one of two pieces of barren heath near Ascot that an enthusiastic freetrader had bequeathed to Mr. Cobden. Here he eventually built a mansion and reclaimed the surrounding sands with the usual economical results. A stranger who might see Mr. Delane here, surrounded by his relatives, and ready to enter into any question that might afford a topic of common interest and unite friends in pleasant companionship, would little suppose that he had been credited for years with a power as great as that of Governments and Legislatures. However that might be, he had borne his honours meekly and could easily bear to resign a burden of which none had known more than he the weight and anxiety. At Ascot-heath, within a short drive of his birthplace, surrounded by home associations, amid the fir plantations and evergreens that redeem the otherwise sterile waste, he looked back on 40 years of incessant toil, not without a sense of shortcomings and failures, and desiring no other record of him than that he had done his best.

> In the nineteenth century as in our own day journalists have exhibited a tendency to have a somewhat elevated view of their profession and of their political influence. In Delane's case that influence was real. When his long and distinguished career was commemorated in this obituary it took up three and a half page-length columns of print and was edged in black. Delane had made *The Times* into a great and highly influential newspaper, one worthy of its nickname: 'The Thunderer'. In 1849 it was he who had obliged Lord Palmerston to apologise to the Neapolitan Government for assisting insurgents and he who maintained criticism of the Government's mishandling of the Crimean War. Ill health had forced his retirement from Printing House Square in 1877.

GEORGE ELIOT

Novelist: 'A woman of rare and noble endowments, a great figure in our literature.'

22 DECEMBER 1880

A GREAT ENGLISH writer has suddenly passed away. 'George Eliot,' to give her the name by which Mrs. Cross was known wherever the English language is spoken or English literature is prized, died on Wednesday evening, after only three days' illness. On Sunday evening last she received the visits of several old friends at the house in Cheyne-walk which she and her husband (to whom she was only married last May) had lately occupied, and when they left her she was apparently in good health and spirits. That night, however, she was seized with a sudden chill, which first attacked the larynx. On the following day, at Dr. Andrew Clark's request, Dr. G. W. Mackenzie, of Lowndes-square, saw Mrs. Cross, that he might report on the case, and not until Wednesday evening, about 6 o'clock, when Dr. Andrew Clark visited her for the first time with Dr. Mackenzie, did the case appear to assume an alarming aspect. It was discovered in the course of their examination that since the morning inflammation had arisen in the pericardium and heart, and that death was not only inevitable, but near at hand. The heart rapidly losing power, Mrs. Cross became insensible, and died about 10 o'clock, without either agitation or pain.

For the biography of George Eliot few materials exist. Many apocryphal stories have been told, not the least remarkable of which is one concerning the authorship of 'Adam Bede,' to which we shall presently refer, and some few of these can be corrected; but the time has not yet come for that full record of her private life and literary history which, as we may hope, may some day be given to the world. Marian Evans – whom all the world knew as 'George Eliot' – was born, we believe, in Warwickshire, little short of sixty years ago. She was not, as has often been stated, the daughter of a poor clergyman, nor is it true that she was adopted in early life by another clergyman of greater wealth, who gave her a first-class education. Her father, Robert Evans, was a land agent and surveyor, who lived in the neighbourhood of Nuneaton, and served for many years as agent for the estates of more than one old Warwickshire family; he is still remembered as a man of rare worth and character by many neighbours in the Midlands. The father of George Eliot is the prototype of more than one character in the writings of his daughter. Of these 'Caleb Garth' in 'Middlemarch' will be recognized as the chief example; but the same note of character – the craftsman's keen delight in perfect work – is struck in 'Adam Bede' and in the little poem on Stradivarius. George Eliot's early years were spent in the country of Shakespeare. The sleepy life of the rural Midlands before the time of the Reform Bill, their rich and tranquil scenery, their homely and old-world inhabitants all left an indelible impress on her imagination – most strongly felt, perhaps, in 'Adam Bede' and 'The Mill on the Floss,' but reappearing with a difference in 'Middlemarch,' and inspiring one or two passages as tender and graceful as anything she ever wrote in 'Theophrastus Such.' It is not very clear when she left her father's home, nor where her education was acquired, but she seems to have come to London almost as a girl, and to have devoted herself to serious literature in a manner far more common among women of the present day than it was nearly 40 years ago. She became associated with many of the writers in the *Westminster Review*, with John Stuart Mill, Mr. Herbert Spencer, George Henry Lewes, Mr. John Chapman, and others. She was a frequent contributor to the *Review*, and at one time, we believe, she edited the section devoted to 'Contemporary Literature' in that periodical. Her first serious work was a translation of the celebrated Strauss's 'Life of Jesus,' published in 1846, when she must have been barely 25 years of age. Of this almost forgotten effort it was said at the time that it exhibited an equal knowledge and mastery of the German and English languages. Seven years afterwards, in 1853, Miss Evans published a translation of Feuerbach's 'Essence of Christianity,' the intervening period being that of her greatest activity as a contributor to the *Westminster Review*. Soon after this Miss Evans began to turn her attention to fiction. It is said that the manuscript of 'Scenes of Clerical Life,' her first imaginative work, was sent anonymously to *Blackwood's Magazine* by George Henry Lewes, and was eagerly accepted by the editor, who discerned in it the promise, since abundantly fulfilled, of rare and pre-eminent genius. It was not, however, until 'Adam Bede' was published in 1859 that the world at large discerned that a new novelist of the first rank had appeared. 'Adam Bede' made the name of George Eliot a household word throughout England, and set curiosity at work to discover the real name and sex of the author. Those who had studied 'Scenes of Clerical Life' at all closely felt sure that the writer was a woman, notwithstanding the masculine tone and breadth conspicuous in 'Adam Bede.' A singular controversy arose in our columns on the subject. On April 15, 1859, a few days after we had reviewed 'Adam Bede,' and conjectured that the author, whether man or woman, could neither be young nor inexperienced, we received and published the following letter:–

> 'Sir, – The author of "Scenes of Clerical Life" and "Adam Bede" is Mr. Joseph Liggins, of Nuneaton, Warwickshire. You may easily satisfy yourself of my correctness by inquiring of any one in that neighbourhood. Mr. Liggins him-

self and the characters whom he paints are as familiar there as the twin spires of Coventry. Yours obediently, H. ANDERS, Rector of Kirkby.'

This produced on the next day the following rejoinder from the real George Eliot:–

> 'Sir, – The Rev. H. Anders has with questionable delicacy and unquestionable inaccuracy assured the world through your columns that the author of "Scenes of Clerical Life" and "Adam Bede" is Mr. Joseph Liggins, of Nuneaton. I beg distinctly to deny that statement. I declare on my honour that that gentleman never saw a line of those works until they were printed, nor had he any knowledge of them whatever. Allow me to ask whether the act of publishing a book deprives a man of all claim to the courtesies usual among gentlemen? If not, the attempt to pry into what is obviously meant to be withheld – my name – and to publish the rumours which such prying may give rise to, seems to me quite indefensible, still more so to state these rumours as ascertained truths. – I am, Sir, yours, &c., GEORGE ELIOT.'

Notwithstanding this protest, the secret soon leaked out. Long before 'The Mill on the Floss,' the second great novel of the series which has immortalized the name of George Eliot, was published in 1860, it was well known, in literary circles at least, that George Eliot was none other than Marian Evans, the Westminster Reviewer and translator of Strauss, better known to her intimates as Mrs. Lewes; for by this time was established that close association and literary friendship with the gifted George Henry Lewes, which terminated only with the death of the latter a little more than two years ago. 'The Mill on the Floss,' in which some critics discerned a falling-off from 'Adam Bede,' and others the richer maturity of a splendid genius, was followed, in 1861, by 'Silas Marner,' the shortest, but as many think, the most perfect, of all George Eliot's novels. 'Romola' – that marvellous tale of Florence in the time of Savonarola, in which the author essayed a task harder by far than that of Thackeray in 'Esmond,' and accomplished it triumphantly – followed in 1863. In 'Felix Holt,' published in 1866, George Eliot returned to English life, but somehow failed to recover that sureness of touch and blitheness of humour which gave Mrs. Poyser and Mrs. Tulliver to the world. After a silence of five years, broken only by several poems, not, indeed, unworthy of her genius, but still deriving more repute from her name than they conferred upon it, George Eliot returned to fiction with 'Middlemarch,' which was published in numbers during 1871 and 1872. 'Middlemarch' carried the reader back once more to the Midlands, and gave us the family portrait of Caleb Garth, and perhaps a sketch in his daughter of the early life of the author herself; but the satire was more copious and less kindly than in the earlier novels, and the humour, though still abundant, was not so genial as it had been. 'The Legend of Jubal,' with other poems, followed in 1874, and 'Daniel Deronda,' the author's last novel, was published in 1876. 'Daniel Deronda' was 'caviare to the general;' none but George Eliot could have written it, perhaps, but we almost may hazard the conjecture that if any other had written it few would have read it. It is the great work of a great writer, very instructive and profound, but regarded as a novel it commits the unpardonable sin of failing to entertain. The last work of George Eliot was 'Theophrastus Such,' published in the course of last year. Fiction, in its ordinary sense, is here abandoned for the heavier and less attractive style of the essayist and thinker. Here and there occurs a gem of humour or of thought worthy of the author of 'Adam Bede' but the imagination is cold and no longer attempts to fuse the mass of thought into a luminous and consistent creation.

The life of George Eliot is, as we have said, little more than the history of her literary activity. A mere catalogue of her writings will stir many memories, and far better than a critical estimate of their value will remind her innumerable readers of the keen and innocent pleasure she has afforded them, of the stirring and elevated thoughts she has lavished on their entertainment. Those who only knew her books will deplore an irreparable loss to English letters, while those who also knew the writer will feel that a great and noble spirit, supreme in intellect as in culture, as tender as it was strong, has passed away from the world. The friends of George Eliot have long recognized her rare and commanding gifts both of intellect and character, and it was impossible even for casual acquaintances to pass a few minutes in her society without falling under the spell of a strangely fascinating and sympathetic personality. Her gracious manner, condescending as became her genius, but never either patronizing or indifferent, overcame at once the diffidence of any who approached her, and her winning smile irradiated and softened features that were too strongly marked for feminine beauty. Those who have seen her either in private or in public, as at the Popular Concerts, at which she was a constant attendant, cannot but have been struck with her resemblance to Savonarola as he appears in the portrait by Fra Bartolommea at Florence. She is gone, and the pen which drew Savonarola with all the strength of a man, and Romola with all the tenderness of a woman, which has produced a gallery of English portraits almost unrivalled in fiction, is laid aside for ever. But her memory lives in the gratitude of countless thousands of readers, and the thought of the life of a great and noble woman suddenly cut off in the promise of renewed happiness will sadden many a household in the midst of Christmas rejoicings.

The editorial comment which accompanied this obituary eulogised 'a woman of rare and noble endowments' though it felt constrained to comment that her later books exhibited 'too scientific a temper' and an 'excessive intrusion of extraneous matter'. The editorial also complained that as a poet Eliot had 'the aspiration' but 'none of the inspiration of song'. Both the editorial and the obituary proper maintain the custom of referring to the novelist by her pseudonym 'George Eliot' rather than by the name she had used privately for most of her career: 'Marian Evans Lewes'. Mary Ann Evans had set up home with the already married George Henry Lewes in October 1853. Thereafter, she had customarily been addressed as 'Mrs Lewes' though the nature of their liaison meant that they were often shunned by the more punctilious members of society. As the obituary suggests, however, once the secret of the authorship of *Adam Bede* and *The Mill on the Floss* was out, Eliot was steadily honoured for the 'stirring and elevated thoughts' contained in her novels. Lewes died on 30 November 1878. To the surprise of many, Eliot then accepted a proposal of marriage from John Walter Cross and married him at St George's, Hanover Square, on 6 May 1880 and the couple moved to a house at Cheyne Walk in Chelsea. After her death on 22 December, the Dean of Westminster wrote suggesting that this 'woman whose achievements were without parallel in the previous history of womankind' should be interred in the Abbey. She was instead buried close to Lewes in the unconsecrated section of Highgate cemetery. Cross's *George Eliot's Life as related in her Letters and Journals* was published in 1885.

THOMAS CARLYLE

Historian and philosopher:
'A great man of letters, quite as heroic as any of those whom he depicted.'

5 FEBRUARY 1881

THOMAS CARLYLE died at half-past 8 on Saturday morning at his house in Cheyne-row, Chelsea. He had been for some years in feeble health, and more than once in 1879 and 1880 his recovery seemed doubtful. Of late even his friends saw little of him. He could not bear the strain of prolonged or exciting conversation, and growing weakness, approaching, as he himself said, almost constant pain, had compelled him to give up very much his old habit of taking long walks every day. But since early manhood he had been frequently subject to ailments; dyspepsia and kindred weaknesses had been his scourge since his college days; he had rallied more than once from severe attacks of illness; and it was not supposed until quite recently that his end was near. The announcement of his death will bring home to every educated Englishman its significance. A chasm opens between the present and the past of our literature, a whole world of associations disappears. No recent man of letters has held in England a place comparable to that which for at least a quarter of a century has been his without dispute, and authors of all kinds and schools will feel that they have lost their venerable doyen. A great man of letters, quite as heroic as any of those whom he depicted, has passed away amid universal regret. The close has come of a well-ordered, full, stately, and complete life.

About eight months before Robert Burns died, and within but a few miles of Dumfries, the scene of his death, was born the most penetrating and sympathetic interpreter of his genius. Carlyle's birth-place was Ecclefechan, an insignificant Dumfriesshire village, in the parish of Huddam, known by name, at least, to readers of Burns, and memorable for an alehouse which was loved only too well by the poet. There Carlyle was born on the 4th of December, 1795. He was the eldest son of a family of eight children; his brothers were all men of character and ability; one of them, Dr. John Carlyle, was destined to make a name in literature as the translator of Dante. Mr. Carlyle's father, James Carlyle, was the son of Thomas Carlyle, tenant of Brown-Knowes, a small farm in Annandale, and of Margaret Aitken. At the time of his eldest son's birth James Carlyle was a stone mason, and resided in Ecclefechan; but he became afterwards tenant of Scotsberg, a farm of two or three hundred acres, which is now occupied by Mr. Carlyle's youngest and only surviving brother. James Carlyle was a man of rectitude, worth, and intelligence, and in many

ways remarkable. His son once said, 'I never heard tell of any clever man that came of entirely stupid people,' and his own lineage might well have suggested this saying. Carlyle never spoke of his father and mother except with veneration and affection. Of the former especially he liked to talk, and he once made the remark that he thought his father, all things considered, the best man whom he had ever known. There were points of strong likeness between them. The father was a man of energy and strong will; and he had in no small measure the picturesque and vivid powers of speech of the son, and liked to use out-of-the-way, old-fashioned, sharp, and pungent words. His pithy sayings, occasionally prickly and sharp, ran through the countryside. His favourite books were the Bible and an old Puritan divine. He was, said his son on one occasion to a friend, 'a far cleverer man than I am, or ever will be.' An elder in the Kirk, and a man of established character for probity, he was one who, to use again his son's description of him, 'like Enoch of old, walked with God.' All extant testimony goes to show that Mr. Carlyle's father and mother were of the finest type of Scotch country folk – simple, upright, and with family traditions of honest worth. Carlyle learnt to read and write in the parish school of Hoddam, where he remained until his ninth year. The parish minister, his father's friend, taught him the elements of Latin. From the parish school he passed to the Burgh School of Annan, six miles distant, where he saw Edward Irving, 'his first friend,' as he once called him, who was some years his senior. Lads still go very young to Scotch Universities; 60 years ago they went still younger, and were wont to quit them with their degrees, if they cared to take any, which they rarely did, at an age when an English youth has not quitted a public school. Carlyle was barely 14 when he entered the University of Edinburgh. It was then in its glory. Some of its professors possessed a European reputation. The eloquent and acute Dr. Thomas Brown lectured on moral philosophy; Playfair held the chair of natural philosophy; the ingenious and quarrelsome Sir John Leslie taught mathematics; and Dunbar was professor of Greek. They were a group of men likely to impress much a susceptible lad of genius, and especially one who had a strong bias towards mathematical studies. But Carlyle was not so impressed. For Dr. Brown – 'Miss Brown,' or 'that little man who spouted poetry,' as he derisively called him – he had no liking. Against Playfair he had a grudge, because, after having worked hard at the class studies, on calling at Playfair's house for the certificate to which he was entitled, he found the document worded in a somewhat niggardly spirit. The only professor for whom he seems to have had much regard was Sir John Leslie, who had some points of affinity to his pupil; and the feeling was returned. Carlyle made few friends at the University. He was lonely and contemplative in his habits. He took no part in the proceedings, and his name is not to be found on the list of members of the Speculative Society, which every clever student was then expected to join. In after years he laid it down that 'the true University of these days is a collection of books,' and on this principle he acted. Not content with ransacking the College Library, he read all that was readable in various circulating libraries – among others, one founded by Allan Ramsay – and acquired knowledge which extended far beyond the bounds of the University course. He left the University with no regret. 'Had you anywhere in Crim Tartary,' he observes with reference to the University at which Teufelsdröckh studied, but probably with a covert glance at his own Alma Mater, 'walled in a square enclosure; furnished it with a small, ill-chosen library; and then turned loose into it eleven hundred Christian striplings, to tumble about as they listed, from three to seven years: certain persons, under the title of professors, being stationed at the gates, to declare aloud that it was a University, and exact considerable admission fees – you had not, indeed, in mechanical structure, yet in spirit and result, some imperfect resemblance of our High Seminary.' Still Carlyle profited much by the four years spent at college. He read hard, even to the point of injuring his health; he acquired a sound and, for his years, unusual knowledge of mathematics, and he might have boasted with Gibbon, but without the qualification which Gibbon appended, that he had attained a stock of erudition that would have puzzled a doctor. Having passed through the arts curriculum of the University, Carlyle ought, in the natural course of things, to have proceeded to the study of theology, for he had been destined by his father to be a minister. There is some tradition that matters had gone so far that it had been arranged in what church Carlyle should appear as a 'probationer.' But he did not carry out his father's intentions. 'Now that I had gained man's estate,' to quote his own account of this crisis in his life, 'I was not sure that I believed the doctrines of my father's kirk; and it was needful I should now settle it. And so I entered my chamber and closed the door, and around me there came a trooping throng of phantasms dire from the abysmal depths of nether-most perdition, doubt, fear unbelief, mockery, and scoffing were there; and I wrestled with them in agony of spirit.' The end of all this storm was the settled conviction that he could not enter the Church. Carlyle at once turned his hand to work by which he could earn his bread, and for a year or two he taught mathematics in the burgh school of Annan, where he had but lately been a pupil. He remained there only two years; at their close he was appointed teacher of mathematics and classics in the burgh school of Kirkcaldy. At the other end of 'the lang toun' was a private adventure school, called the Academy, where Edward Irving taught some of the known tongues and mathematics. The two young men of genius were already acquainted with each other; indeed, it was at Irving's instigation, and with a view to be near him, that Carlyle went to Kirkcaldy. There, however, were riveted the bonds of a friendship destined to be tested by trials, some of them of a very personal character. These bonds were sometimes stretched, but never broken, not even when Carlyle saw with sorrowfulness his gifted friend pass into the regions of darkness and chaos whence he never returned. Teaching Fifeshire boys was not Carlyle's vocation. After staying about two years in Kirkcaldy he quitted it, leaving behind him the reputation of a too stern disciplinarian to begin in Edinburgh the task his life as a writer of books. At that date the capital of Scotland was still another Weimar. Men of letters had not yet deserted it for London. 'Maga' was in its glory. Lockhart, John Wilson, Maginn, were in their brilliant prime; Jeffrey was at the head of the *Edinburgh;* and the stalwart form of Scott, not yet bent by the load of misfortune and toil, might be seen occasionally in the streets. Carlyle tried his 'prentice hand in Brewster's 'Edinburgh Encyclopaedia,' to which he contributed many articles on geographical and biographical subjects; among others, articles on Sir John Moore, Dr. Moore, Nelson, the elder and younger Pitt, Montaigne, and Montesquieu. These first essays at authorship have never been republished, and they do not, perhaps, deserve to be so. They give but faint, uncertain promise of the author's genius and of those gifts which made his later works as individual as a picture by Albert Dürer or Rembrandt. But they indicate patient industry and research and minute attention to details; and they show that the author was accumulating those stores of varied knowledge upon which his imagination was to work in after years. Here and there is a stroke of force and felicity. Occasionally the confidence of his later style is anticipated, as, for example, when he refutes Montesquieu's theory of the influence of climate on race and history. We recognize the author of 'The French Revolution' in the vivid description of the philosopher as a cheerful and benign sage, talking with the peasants under the oak at La Brède. At the instance of Sir David Brewster he translated Legendre's 'Geometry and Trigonometry,' prefixing to the treatise a short and modest introduction on Proportion. Brewster's name was put to the translation. Carlyle received for his work £50, a sum not unimportant in those days. He was always proud of his essay on Proportion, and with good reason. De Morgan pronounced it 'a thoughtful and ingenious essay, as good a substitute for the fifth book of Euclid as could be given in speech,' and it is certainly clear, concise, and direct. Carlyle about this time mastered German; his brother was studying in Germany, and the letters from Dr. Carlyle heightened his interest in its language and its literature, which was then in full blossom. The first fruits of this knowledge was an article contributed to the *New Edinburgh* on 'Faust,' a subject to which he was so often to return. For some time after leaving Kirkcaldy, and until a year or two before his marriage, he acted as tutor to the brilliant and amiable Charles Buller, teaching him, if not then, at least afterwards, some other things besides mathematics, as those who remember Buller's views on pauperism, emigration, and colonization will admit. About this period of Carlyle's life the once famous John Scott was editing the *London Magazine* and had gathered round him a group of clever writers; Hazlitt, Lamb, Croly, Cary, and Allan Cunningham were a few of them. Carlyle joined them. Here appeared, in 1823, the first part of the 'Life of Schiller.' No name was attached to it. Those who knew that it was Carlyle's work predicted great things from a writer who, in youth, exhibited noble simplicity and maturity of style, and who had conceptions of criticism very rare in those times. In the following year he published, again anonymously, a translation of 'Wilhelm Meister's Lehrjahre' with misgivings, not strange or unjustified, as to how his countrymen would receive a book so repugnant in many ways to the dominant taste. Goethe was then no prophet out of his own country. He was known to no Englishman but De Quincey, Coleridge and a few students of German literature. The novel was sneered at, and the savage, elaborate invectives which De Quincey hurled at Goethe did not spare the translator. Carlyle's style was sharply criticized. Maginn, in after years, complained that Goethe had been translated from 'the Fatherlandish dialect of High Dutch to the Allgemeine Mid Lothianish of Auld Reekie,' and that Carlyle was seeking to acclimatize 'the roundabout, hubble-bubble, rumfustianish (*hübble-bubblen, rümfüsteanischen*), roly-poly, gromerly of style, dear to the heart of a son of the Fatherland'. Undeterred by sneers and remonstrances, Carlyle published in 1827 several volumes entitled 'German Romance,' containing translations from the chief writers of the romantic school, such as Musæus, La Motte Fouqué, Tieck, Hofmann, and Richter, with short biographical notices. This work was, as he himself admitted, 'mere journeywork,' not of his own suggesting or desiring – mere preparation for the true occupation of his genius. Before putting out his full strength he seems to have felt the necessity of retiring to some secluded spot where he might mature and arrange his seething and tumultuous thoughts. The occasion of doing so presented itself. In 1827 he married Miss Jane Welsh, the only daughter of Dr. Welsh, of Haddington, a descendant of John Knox. She had inherited a farm lying remote and high up among the hills of Dumfriesshire; and there Carlyle found the Patmos which his perturbed spirit needed. To the farmhouse of Craigenputtock – a plain, gaunt two-story dwelling, with its face blankly looking towards the hill, up which the little gooseberry garden runs, partly sheltered on one side from the fierce winds by a few badly-grown ash trees, almost cut off from the world by a morass, and reached only by a rough cart-road – to this peaceful and simple abode, some 15 miles from town or market, came Carlyle and his bride in 1828. Here for six years he lived with this one friend and companion – a companion worthy of him; a woman of much character and practical wisdom, given to silence when he talked, but a talker scarcely inferior to himself, as those who knew her well could testify; a woman, as he himself termed her, of 'bright invincibility of spirit.' Here for these years he wrote and read much – 'a whole cartload of French, German, and American and English journals and periodicals piled upon his little library table' – meditating or holding much high converse with his wife as they wandered on foot or horseback over the black and silent moors and unending hills – an expanse of bleak, sour uplands, watered by nameless rills and shadowed by mists and rolling vapours, yet not wholly wanting in rugged and tender beauties congenial to his spirit . . .

Carlyle toiled hard in this temple of industrious peace. In these obscure youthful years, he wrote, read, and planned much, and made incursions into many domains of knowledge. Writing in December of 1828 to De Quincey of his occupations, he says:–

> 'Such a quantity of German periodical and mystic speculation embosomed in plain Scotch peat-moss being nowhere that I know of to be met with . . . We have no society, but who has in the strict sense of that word? I have never had any worth speaking about since I came into the world. . . . My wife and I are busy learning Spanish; far advanced in "Don Quixote" already. I purpose writing mystical reviews for somewhat more than a twelve-month to come; have Greek to read, and the whole universe to study (for I understand less and less of it).'

In a bare, scantily furnished room of the farmhouse, now shown with pride to visitors, he pursued this plan and wrote essay after essay and did much of his best work. Here were composed his essays on Burns, Goethe and Johnson, Richter, Heyne, Novalis, Voltaire and Diderot. 'Sartor Resartus' was composed here; the manuscript to be laid aside until some other time. It was here, too, while, as Mr. Lewes remarks, Carlyle was rambling over the wild moors 'with thoughts at times as wild and dreary as those moors,' that he conceived the notion of sending to his master at Weimar a birthday present as a token of gratitude and affection on the part of himself and a few other English admirers of Goethe. The memento was a seal, designed by Mrs. Carlyle; it was accompanied by a letter written by Carlyle himself. The epistle runs:–

> 'We said to ourselves, as it is always the highest duty and pleasure to show reverence where reverence is due, and our chief, and perhaps our only benefactor, is he who by act and word instructs us in wisdom; so we, the undersigned feeling towards the poet Goethe as the spiritually taught towards their spiritual teacher, are desirous to express that sentiment openly and in common; for, which end we have determined to solicit his acceptance of a small English gift, proceeding from us all equally, on his approaching birthday; so that while the venerable man still dwells among us some memorial of the gratitude we owe him, and we think the whole world owes him, may not be wanting. And thus our little tribute, perhaps among the purest that men can offer to man, now stands in visible shape, and begs to be received. May it be welcome and speak permanently of a most close relation though wide seas flow between the parties.'

In this happy mountain home Carlyle was not wholly cut off from the world. Fame came to him, though thus secluded, and thither from time to time journeyed strangers desirous of seeing and holding converse with a man whose written words in the *Edinburgh* and *New and Foreign Quarterly* had made them feel that a new teacher had come into the world. Sometimes an Edinburgh man of letters would travel by coach to Dumfries and walk or ride the 15 long Scotch miles to Craigenputtock, making, perhaps, unexpected demands on the resources of the hospitable household, and compelling Mrs. Carlyle to mount a pony and set out in search of provisions. Thither came, among many other strangers, Emerson, who had read and admired in New England what Carlyle had written, and who went away full of amazement at his host's bright, vivid talk, full of lively anecdote and streaming humour, which flooded everything it looked upon. Carlyle contributed to the *Edinburgh Review*, which was still under the management of Jeffrey. The relationship was not perfectly smooth or entirely satisfactory to either editor or writer. It was difficult to adjust the boundaries of the respective provinces, Carlyle being apt to take offence at the ruthless hacking and hewing of his work in which Jeffrey indulged, and the latter being cut to the quick by the eccentricities of style displayed by his contributor, and surprised that Carlyle was not grateful for efforts to impart trim grace and polish to his articles. Jeffrey once told Charles Sumner, who had made some remark about the deterioration in Carlyle's style since the publication of the essay on Burns, that there had been, in fact, no change, and as much as suggested that the earlier writings owed their grace to his careful revision. In the recently published correspondence of Professor Macvey Napier we can see the feeling of Jeffrey and Carlyle toward each other. It was by no means unmixed friendliness. 'I fear Carlyle will not do,' writes the Aristarchus of Craigcrook to his sorely-bullied and much-suffering successor in 1832, 'that is, if you do not take the liberties and pains with him that I did, by striking out freely, and writing in occasionally. The misfortune is that he is very obstinate and, I am afraid, very conceited.' 'It is a great pity, for he is a man of genius and industry, and with the capacity of being an elegant and impressive writer.' Carlyle was, alas! never fated to become the 'elegant writer' whom Jeffrey saw in his critical mind's-eye. Jeffrey lived to see his awkward contributor take rank as a classic, but that consummation of elegant authorship which he desired he was never to behold. With Professor Napier, on the other hand, Carlyle's dealings were much to his satisfaction, and he preferred to write for the *Edinburgh*.

'Sartor Resartus,' that unique collection of meditations and confessions, passionate invective, solemn reflection, and romantic episodes from his own life, was composed at Craigenputtock in 1831. It had a difficulty in seeing the light. It is not a little astonishing that this book, every page of which is stamped with genius of the highest order, failed at first to find admirers or appreciators. The publishers would have nothing to do with it. One declared that the author lacked 'tact' which was probably true. Another pronounced the humour too Teutonic and heavy – a piece of criticism not without point. Even John Stuart Mill who afterwards delighted in the book, admitted that when he saw it in manuscript he thought little of it. The general impression seemed to be that much genius and German had made the author mad. He himself was at times a little disheartened by repeated rebuffs. 'I have given up the notion,' he says of 'Sartor,' in 1832, 'of hawking my little manuscript book about any further; for a long time it has lain quiet in a drawer waiting for a better day. The bookselling trade seems on the edge of dissolution; the force of puffing can no further go, yet bankruptcy clamours at every door; sad fate! to serve the Devil, and get no wages even from him! The poor Bookselling Guild, I often predict to myself, will ere long be found unfit for the strange part it now plays in our European world; and will give place to new and higher arrangements, of which the coming shadows are already becoming visible.' Not for seven years after its composition did 'Sartor' appear as a volume. It 'had at last,' says its author, 'to clip itself in pieces, and be content to struggle out, bit by bit, in some courageous magazine that offered.'

Strengthening and helpful and rich in fruit were these years in his Nithsdale hermitage. They were the seed-bed of his future achievements. There he unravelled the tangled skein of his thoughts. There he laid up stores of knowledge, of health, of high resolutions for the work lying before him. There, in a solitude peopled only by books and thoughts and the companionship of his wife, and converse with some congenial stranger, he laid the sure foundations of a life which was destined to be so complete. But the time came for him to leave Craigenputtock. A historian, a critic, a biographer must needs have libraries within his reach. He must know men if he is to instruct them; and on a hill-side or bleak moor he cannot find to his hand all the materials which are necessary when he essays to write the history of the French Revolution. Some ties which bound Carlyle to Dumfriesshire had been severed. His father had passed away full of years, and it became fit, and even necessary, that Carlyle should leave his mountain seclusion and betake himself to London. He settled in Cheyne-row, in a small three-storied house, which he never afterwards quitted. The part of Chelsea which he chose had associations interesting to him as a man of letters. Dr. Smollett's old house, Don Saltero's coffee-house, and Nell Gwynne's boudoir were close at hand. He had Leigh Hunt as a neighbour. He was, as he himself says in a letter written shortly after he went to his new home, encompassed by a cloud of witnesses – good, bad, and indifferent. Chelsea has changed much since 1834. Let any one recall the enthusiastic terms in which Leigh Hunt speaks of his escape from the noise and dust of the New-road to the repose and quietude of a corner of Chelsea, where the air of the country came to refresh him, and where only pastoral cries of primroses and cowslips were to be heard in the streets. Carlyle lived to know Chelsea in very altered circumstances. The fields which he could see from the windows of the attic, which was his study and place of work, were swallowed up by all-devouring brick and mortar, and hideous noises which came with increase of population vexed and distracted him, and were among the serious discomforts of his life.

Carlyle was a man of mature years when he removed to London. He had then done comparatively little. His intellectual growth had been far from surprisingly fast. He was born a few months before Keats, and by 1821 Keats had sung his last song, and was at rest in his grave at Rome; Shelley, born only three years before Carlyle, had made himself an immortal name, and passed away in 1822. Had Carlyle died thus early what would he have left but the memory among a few friends of brilliant but uncertain promise? His genius was a fire which, slowly lit, slowly died. The first years after his coming to London were the most fruitful of his literary life. Essays, histories, lectures, biographies poured from his brain with surprising rapidity. No book-hack could have surpassed the regularity and industry with which he worked, late and early, in his small attic. A walk before breakfast was part of the day's duties. At 10 o'clock in the morning, whether the spirit moved him or not, he took up his pen and laboured hard until 3 o'clock; nothing, not even the opening of the morning letters, was allowed to distract him. Then came walking, answering letters, and seeing friends. One of his favourite relaxations was riding, in an omnibus. In the evening he read and prepared for the work of the morrow. Success did not visit him at once. His form of genius not being readily classed under any of the established categories, repelled ordinary readers of the time; he was not the mere popularizer of ideas already accepted; he had a gospel of his own to preach and disciples to convert and teach before it could be spread abroad. His best books were by no means instantaneously successful. Even the 'French Revolution,' with all its brilliancy and captivating *élan*, had to wait for a publisher. His 'broad Brobdingnagian grin of true humour' was not relished. One *North British* Reviewer seemed inclined to take southern opinion before committing himself to being amused. Another writer pronounced 'Sartor Resartus' a 'heap of clotted nonsense.' Carlyle's style was held up as a fearful warning. He found his first warmest admirers on the other side of the Atlantic. The enthusiasm which his works excited in a few minds was not always tempered with intelligence, and we have come across an American literary periodical of those times which warns its readers that the author of 'Sartor Resartus' is not to be confounded with Mr. Carlisle, now deceased, who was a confident and avowed champion of infidelity. Before fame in its common form had come to him, men whose private opinions were to be future public opinion had conceived the highest notion of his powers and the future before him; and the little parlour in Cheyne-row had become the gathering place, the favourite haunt of many literary men. At different times between 1837 and 1840, Mr. Carlyle delivered at Willis's Rooms and Portman-square courses of lectures on some of his favourite subjects – 'German Literature,' 'The History of Literature,' 'The Revolutions of Modern Europe,' and 'Heroes and Hero-Worship.' Each of these lectures was a considerable event in literature. Their effect was such as it is difficult now to conceive. The audience included most of the chief men of letters of the day. 'The accomplished and distinguished, the beautiful, the wise, something of what is best in England, have listened patiently to my rude words' is his own account of his hearers. They were alternately shocked and entranced. There was uncertainty whether his burning words, delivered in an odd sing-song and unquestionable Doric, were wild rhapsodies or the sublime mutterings of a true prophet, who had a message to deliver to modern society. But, at all events, it was a man of a wholly new order who spoke, and people of all shades and schools – the Parthians, and Medes, and Elamites of London – were amazed. Crabbe Robinson, who attended the whole of one course, says of a certain lecture, 'It gave great satisfaction, for it had uncommon thoughts, and was delivered with unusual animation.' 'As for Carlyle's Lectures,' writes Bunsen, 'they are very striking, rugged thoughts, not ready made up for any political or religious system; thrown at people's heads, by which most of his audience are sadly startled.' 'Attended Carlyle's lecture,' writes Macready, '"The hero as a prophet," on which he descanted with a fervour and eloquence that only complete conviction of truth could give. I was charmed, carried away by him. Met Browning there.'

'The French Revolution,' the first work to which Mr. Carlyle put his name, appeared in 1837. It would have been published sooner but for the famous disaster which befell the manuscript of the first volume. The author had lent it to Mr. John Stuart Mill; the latter handed it to Mrs. Taylor, his future wife. What became of it was never exactly known. Mrs. Taylor left the manuscript for some days on her writing table: when wanted it could nowhere be found; and the most probable explanation of its disappearance was the suggestion that a servant had used the manuscript to light the fire. Carlyle at once set to work to reproduce from his notes the lost volume; he swiftly finished his task, but he always thought that the first draft was the best. Though welcomed, as it deserved to be, by Mill and Stirling, the 'French Revolution' was not at once successful. The bulk of readers did not hail it as the great prose poem of the century. They were not enraptured by the Iliad-like swiftness and vividness of the narrative, the sustained passion, as if the whole had been written at a sitting, the full flow of poetry, with touches of grandeur and tenderness: and those pages like the pictures from Salvator Rosa's brush, in which a flash of lightning reveals, side by side, the horrors of Nature and her pastoral sweetness. Landor, indeed, hailed 'The French Revolution' as the best book published in his time, and recognized the coming of a new literary potentate; but his vision was exceptionally acute. The incongruities, monstrosities of style, and the author's disdain for what an admirer called the 'feudalities of literature' struck all readers and it was only some of them who thought much more of the intrinsic beauty of the jewel than of the strange setting.

About 1839 began a new phase of activity. Mr. Carlyle had imbibed a deep distrust and even abhorrence of all the somewhat mechanical expedients for the amelioration of society then in fashion. The favourite schemes of social reform were then even more crude than they generally are; Mr. Carlyle despised them all. The philanthropists whom he met with were not the most practical or the wisest of their kind; Mr. Carlyle thought them, for the most part, mealy-mouthed, engaged in ineffectual dallying and parleying with the stern, invincible verities of life, and coaxing and coddling those upon whom Nature had pronounced her irreversible sentences of extermination. From the depths of society, from torchlight meetings held by Chartists in Birmingham and other towns, from the agricultural counties where 'Swing' was burning ricks or throwing down toll gates, from Ireland, where an overgrown population no longer found potatoes enough to satisfy its simple wants, came sullen mutterings of discontent, ominous signs of commotions to come, perplexity, tribulation, and distress among nations. There was no lack of nostrums or social doctors. Mr. Carlyle pronounced them one and all vain and unprofitable. In a series of works published from 1839 to 1850 – in 'Chartism,' 'Past and Present,' and 'Latter-day Pamphlets' – he poured unmeasured scorn and contumely on the false teachers and blind guides of the time. It was the kernel of his philosophy that legislation, Reform or Ballot Bills, statutory measures of social improvement of any kind, would do of themselves next to no good. Reforms to be effectual must go deeper than an English Parliament, of whose perfect wisdom he had grave doubts, was likely to tolerate. 'Christian philanthropy and other most amiable-looking, but most baseless, and, in the end, most baneful and all-bewildering jargon;' 'philanthropisms' issuing 'in a universal sluggard and scoundrel protection society'; the crowds of amiable simpletons sunk in 'deep froth oceans of benevolence;' Bentham, a 'bore of the first magnitude,' with his immense baggage of formulae, and his tedious iteration of 'the greatest happiness of the greatest number;' the political economists mumbling barren truisms or equally unfruitful paradoxes about supply and demand; Malthusians preaching to deaf ears the most unacceptable of gospels; so-called statesmen collecting with impotent hands information about the Condition of England Question which they could not apply, and letting things slide to chaos and perdition; Ireland sluttishly starving from age to age on Act of Parliament freedom; the braying of Exeter Hall; the helpless babbling of Parliament; and liberty made a pretext, in the West Indies and elsewhere, for flying in the face of the great law that, if a man work not, neither shall he eat – these were some of the butts of his scorn and contempt. It would be scarcely worth while to try to measure the exact value of these jeremiads. Mr. Carlyle was much too eloquently wrathful. His criticisms were often grotesque caricatures. They abounded in contradictions, and it was always pretty clear that Mr. Carlyle found it much easier to rail at large than to suggest any working substitutes for the systems which he despised. De Quincey was unanswerable when he said to Carlyle, 'You've shown or you've made another hole in the tin kettle of society; how do you propose to tinker it?' Harsh and crude judgments are to be met with in almost every page, and much of the teaching, so far as it is intelligible and consistent, is preposterous and impracticable. But, dismissing all expectation of finding precise suggestions, it is astonishing to note how, under uncouth, rhapsodical phraseology, lie many ideas which are now the common property of most educated men. The novelties and paradoxes of 1840 are, to a large extent, nothing but the good sense of 1881. Who would not now echo Mr. Carlyle's protests against the supposed omnipotence of Parliament or of the possibility of saving nations by the use of the ballot box? Who now believes that men can be instantaneously reformed in battalions and platoons, or that human nature can be remade by any order of the Poor Law Commissioners? Who does not own that the change in our colonies from servitude to idleness and squalor, temporary, it is true, was not an unmixed blessing to those most concerned? If all wise men are now haunted by a sense of the impotence of legislation to effect deep changes for good, and of the necessity of working out reformations really worth anything in the souls of individuals, to whom do they owe this so much as to Mr. Carlyle? Who recognized the duty of spreading education earlier and more clearly than he? We say nothing of the keen eye for the detection of rogues and impostors, under all disguises, which Mr. Carlyle's political pamphlets reveal; or of those ingenious epithets of his which, attached to some blustering, swelling piece of fraud, acted like a stone tied to the neck of a dog flung into deep water. It is enough to say that again and again he reminded, in his own way, his generation of stern truths which it was in danger of forgetting.

In 1845 he published 'Oliver Cromwell's Letters and Speeches, with Elucidations.' The work was well received. It passed rapidly through several editions. In a petition addressed in 1839 to the House of Commons on the subject of the Copyright Bill, Mr. Carlyle had said of his literary labours that they had 'found hitherto, in money or money's worth, small recompense or none,' and he was by no means sure of ever getting any. His 'Oliver Cromwell,' however, was at once widely read; and in his preface to the second edition he thought proper to admit that, contrary to his expectations, 'the work had spread itself abroad with some degree of impetus.' No one could fail to see how the great Protector, as he really was, had at last been disinterred from beneath Pelions and Ossas of calumny and rubbish, heaped upon him by generations of detractors. We are familiar enough by this time with the process of historical whitewashing. None of the attempts of the kind have, however, stood the test of time so well as Mr. Carlyle's. From the gibbet on which Cromwell had hung for nearly two centuries he has been taken down for ever. In 1850 appeared the 'Latter-day Pamphlets.' Mr. Carlyle's next work, published in 1851, was the life of his friend, John Sterling, one of the most charming biographies in the language. Why Sterling's Life should have been again written, after Archdeacon Hare had told the simple, uneventful story was *à priori* anything but clear, but posterity would not willingly lose this record of a beautiful friendship. Carlyle had first met Sterling accidentally at the India Office in company with John Stuart Mill. The talk on this occasion laid the foundations of a lasting intercourse. Sterling's mother took to Mrs. Carlyle in a kindly, maternal way, and the two families formed many ties. 'We had unconsciously made an acquisition which grew richer and wholesomer every new year, and ranks now, even seen in the pale moonlight of memory, and must ever rank, as among the precious possessions of life.' The personal feeling which guided Mr. Carlyle's pen gave a lighter touch and more genial glow to the style; the book is full of sunny sketches of men and things; and a benign fate, similar to that which descended upon young Edward King, the hero of 'Lycidas,' has given to John Sterling in these pages an immortality which his fugitive writings and his amiable virtues and beautiful endowments would not have procured him.

Between 1858 and 1865 appeared the ten volumes of Mr. Carlyle's laborious history of Frederick the Great. On this work Mr. Carlyle spent more time and trouble than on any of his other books. It is a marvel of industry. He has not been outdone by the German writers on the subject – and Ranke, Preuss, and Droysen are in the field – in minute and painful investigation. Every accessible memoir and book bearing on the subject was read and collated. Mr. Carlyle went to Germany in 1858 for the sake of his book. He visited Zarndorff, Leuthen, Liegnitz, Sorr, Mollwitz, Prague, and many other places famous in the wars of Frederick; and the vivid descriptions to be found in the later volumes – for example, the description of the scenes of the battles of Chotusitz and Dettingen – we owe to this journey. In none of his works is more genius discernible. Nowhere does his humour flow more copiously and brilliantly. Who that has read his Tobacco Parliament will ever forget it? The figures of Wilhelmine, Old Papa, Excellency Robinson, Old Dessau, and a dozen other characters, move about vividly as they did in life. And yet the ten volumes are painful to read. Peculiarities of diction, embarrassing in others of Mr. Carlyle's books, have grown to be wearisome and vexatious; little tricks and contortions of manner are repeated without mercy; miserable petty details are pushed into the foreground; whole pages are written in a species of crabbed shorthand; the speech of ordinary mortals is abandoned; and sometimes we can detect in the writer a sense of weariness and a desire to tumble out in any fashion the multitude of somewhat dreary facts which he had collected. When he visited Varnhagen von Ense in 1858, he told his host, as we gather from Von Ense's 'Tagebücher,' that his 'Friedrich' was 'the poorest, most troublesome, and arduous piece of work he had ever undertaken.' 'No satisfaction in it at all, only labour and sorrow. What the devil had I to do with your Frederick?' As to which Von Ense observes, 'It must have cost him unheard-of labour to understand Frederick,' adding in his snappish, cantankerous way, 'if he does understand him.'

Since his 'Frederick' was published Mr. Carlyle had undertaken no large work. But he had not been altogether silent. During the American War was published his half-contemptuous, we had almost said, truculent, account of the issues in his 'Ilias in Nuce,' enunciating his old predilection for the peculiar institution. In 1865 he was elected Rector of Edinburgh University. Next year he delivered an address to the students on 'the choice of books.' It was full of serene wisdom, the apt words of one who looked benignly down from the summit of a life well spent on the beginners in the struggle. Those who remember the old man's appearance, as he talked to the lads before him with amiable gravity of manner, his courageous, hopeful words, did not expect that in a few hours exceeding sorrow would befall him. During his absence from London his wife died. Her death was quite unlooked for; while she was driving in the Park she suddenly expired. When the coachman stopped he found his mistress lifeless. Carlyle might well say that 'the light of his life had quite gone out;' and the letters which he wrote to his friends are full of exceeding sorrow, and were at times the voice of one for whom existence has nothing left. 'A most sorry dog kennel it oftenest all seems to me, and wise words, if one even had them, to be only thrown away upon it. *Basta, basta,* I for the most part say of it, and look with longings towards the still country where at last we and our beloved ones shall be together again. Amen, amen.' 'It is the saddest feature of old age,' he wrote, just a year after the death of his wife, in a letter to his friend, Mr. Erskine of Linlathen, 'that the old man has to see himself daily growing more lonely; reduced to commune with inarticulate eternities, and the Loved Ones, now unresponsive, who have preceded him thither. Well, well, there is blessedness in this too, if we take it well. There is grandeur in it, if also an extent of sombre sadness which is new to one; nor is hope quite wanting, nor the clear conviction that those whom we most screen from sore pain and misery are now safe and at rest. It lifts one to real kinship withal, real for the first time in this scene of things. Courage, my friend, let us endure patiently, let us act piously, to the end.'

In 1867 the discussions about Parliamentary Reform revived in Mr. Carlyle his old thoughts about democracy, and he published in *Macmillan's Magazine* 'Shooting Niagara, and After?' Through our columns, he gave to the world in 1870, his trenchant views on the Franco-German War, denouncing 'the cheap pity and newspaper lamentation over fallen and afflicted France,' and expressing his opinion that it would be well for her and everybody if Bismarck took Alsace and so much of Lorraine as he wanted. Mr. Carlyle's last published writings were some contributions in 1875 to *Fraser's Magazine*, on John Knox's portrait. His active literary life had thus extended over about half a century.

Mr. Carlyle has shunned many literary honours which were always within his reach. He did not accept the Grand Cross of the Bath, and on the death of Manzoni, in 1875, he was presented with the Prussian Order 'for Merit' – an honour given by the Knights of the Order and confirmed by the Sovereign, and limited to 30 German and as many foreign Knights.

It was knowing Mr. Carlyle imperfectly to know him only by his books. One must have talked with him, or, to be more accurate, allowed him to talk, in order to understand how his influence had burnt itself so deep into all men who knew him well. In his prime, strangers of all sorts came from the ends of the earth to the little house at Chelsea, just to hear this genial Timon inveigh and harangue against shams, wiggeries, and other customary themes. His talk was in many respects like his writings – equally picturesque, vehement, lit up with wayward flashes of humour, abounding in song-like refrains, rarely falling into those ingeniously grotesque entanglements of phraseology which disfigure his later pages, and set off by his homely Scotch accent, rugged, peasant-like as the day when first he quitted Nithsdale. There were not many greater pleasures than to sit by his arm-chair and hear him tell, as he loved to tell, when years came on, of old Annandale folk and ways, or descant on his favourite themes, turning round sharply every now and then upon the listener while he uttered some crashing dogma, such as 'Lies – lies are the very devil'. There have been men of more astonishing powers of talk – men with more, varied information at their command; men who could quote chapter and verse in a way which was not distinctive of him. But Mr. Carlyle's talk had a charm of its own which no one could resist. He put so much genius, so much of himself, so much aggressive fervour into a talk with a friend or a stranger who was to his mind. It was natural to him, as natural as it was to Dr. Johnson, to talk well. Let us quote on this head the testimony of Margaret Fuller, herself no mean talker, and, with all her admiration, a little vexed as we may see, at Mr. Carlyle's inability to let others shine. In spite of its transcendental twang, the description will serve to show how he looked in 1846 to a clever woman:–

> 'His talk is still an amazement and splendour scarcely to be faced with steady eyes. He does not converse only harangues. Carlyle allows no one a chance, but bears down all opposition, not only by his wit and onset of words, resistless in their sharpness as so many bayonets, but by actual physical superiority, raising his voice and rushing on his opponent with a torrent of sound. This is not in the least from unwillingness to allow freedom to others no man would more enjoy a manly resistance to his thought. But it is the impulse of a mind accustomed to follow out its own impulse as the hawk its prey, and which knows not how to stop in the chase . . . He sings rather than talks. He pours upon you a kind of satirical, heroical, critical Poem with regular cadences and generally catching up near the beginning some singular epithet which serves as a refrain when his song is full . . . He puts out his chin till it looks like the beak of a bird of prey, and his eyes flash bright instinctive meanings like Jove's bird.'

Scarcely less interesting than his talk were his letters. They are models of what letters ought to be. Even those which were written in his old age were little infected with the vices of manner which spoiled his published writings. We have lying before us letters written in as pure and liquid a style as that of the essay on Burns or on Goethe. They will no doubt be gathered together; and if, as is understood, he has had more than one possible Boswell, who knows that his memory may not have the fate of Johnson's – his pithy sayings being remembered and quoted when Carlyle-ese is forgotten as much as Johnsonese? He was a copious letter-writer, and answered readily and with rare forbearance the frequent miscellaneous appeals made to him. His clever young countrymen, coming to London with unborn projects in their heads, were apt to believe that they had a prescriptive right to lay before him their difficulties and plans, and to claim full and precise, counsel. He rarely failed to respond with affectionate solicitude and many a young author has owed to him wise advice which saved him from making shipwreck. Mr. Carlyle's purse was open, but his charity was of a rarer kind than that which is content with occasionally subscribing a few pounds. He would enter into details and give counsel at once precise, minute, and judicious.

In early life he was a swift writer. Later, however, his habits of composition changed. It is said that the sight of the manuscript of a well-known author, with numerous interlineations and erasures, was a revelation to him of the pains which were necessary for the best workmanship. Certain it is that he corrected and re-corrected his later works; pieces of manuscript were interpolated or pasted in, and the finished production was sometimes very wonderful in appearance.

This is not the fit time to try to measure Mr. Carlyle's services or the worth of his works. They have stood many years before the world; each one has long ago had his say about them; the general judgment of mankind on their shortcomings and faults has been pronounced. It will scarcely be questioned that the quantity of the ore of pure truth to be extracted from them is small. Precise definitions, reservations, and qualifications are not in his way; he is too eager and too much afire to be particular about these things; he will not tarry over the niceties of attorney logic. He does not travel by the common highways; he is on the wing; and there is neither obstacle nor boundary thought of in his flight. Justness of view as a critic is not to be expected of him. His prejudices have always been immense and wayward. You must not look for sober, well-ordered reasoning; for him the time of argument is always past; his business is to make good his victory, to force upon you his conviction. As Johnson refuted Berkeley by 'striking his foot with mighty force against a stone' so with equal cogency Mr. Carlyle has disposed of many disagreeable theories by dubbing their authors M'Crowdy or M'Quirk. His books are a sort of puritanical syllabus, not less condemnatory of the modern spirit than that which issued from the Vatican. His social and political theories are, in the main, but aspirations after impossible ideals – vain attempts, heroic, but ineffectual, to bring back the past and yet to retain the richest fruits of progress. His extravagances of style lie on the surface, and his disciples have found it easy to copy and outdo his tricks and foibles of manner and his recurring touches of grotesqueness. They have not always copied also the sound sense which made atonement and which controlled all that he did. Many historians have fancied that they were following in Mr. Carlyle's footsteps because they poohpoohed the operation of general causes and principles, paraded some trumpery scrap of information about the clothes or 'property' of their heroes, ostentatiously cleared up a wretched date, or struck out a new mode of spelling an unimportant name. We have seen clumsy imitators who cumbered their pages with meaningless and garish details, or interpolated laboured rhapsodies, which were feeble reminiscences or hollow echoes of Sauerteig. The commonplaces of Mr. Carlyle have been the stock-in-trade of a terribly wearisome group of writers, who assumed the nod of Jove, but could not hurl his thunderbolts. Unfortunately they aped other and graver faults, and supposed that they were animated by Mr. Carlyle's spirit when they applauded every exhibition of brute force and insulted the weaker but not less noble elements of human nature. Mr. Carlyle is responsible for much in modern literature which it is not pleasant to look upon; and some of his own pages, with their exultant *vae victis* over fallen causes, are not edifying. But what are these defects to the good which he has done? To whom has he not been a salutary teacher? Kingsley, Froude, and Ruskin have sat at his feet, and a host of others, scarcely a leading mind of our time excepted, have felt his influence. Wherever, in truth, men have turned their minds for the last quarter of a century to the deep relations of things his spirit has been present to rebuke frivolity, to awaken courage and hope. No other writer of this generation ever cast so potent a spell on the youth of England. They might outgrow him; they might travel far from the region of his thoughts; they might learn to see in the teacher of their early days only the iconoclast whose work was done. They could never wholly get outside the circle of his spell, and to take up one of his books and read but a page or two was sure to recall a flood of old memories and influences even as will the sound of distant bells or a snatch of a once familiar song. To many he was always a teacher. He brought ardour and vehemence congenial to their young hearts, and into them he shot fiery arrows which could never be withdrawn. What Hazlitt said of Coleridge was true of him – he cast a great stone into the pool of contemporary thought, and the circles have grown wider and wider. He was early enough in the field to deal the last blows to expiring Byronism. It was his fortune to be for most educated Englishmen the discoverer of the literature of Germany. In what state did he find literary criticism here? What did it not become under his hand? How many heaps of dry bones in history have been quickened and made to rise and walk? How many skeletons have been clothed with flesh at his touch? And yet in all his varied activity, from first to last, he was something of the inspired peasant. The waves of London life came up to and about him; but they had never overwhelmed him or had power to alter him one jot. With all his culture and nearly 50 years of residence in the south, he was to the end substantially unchanged; his ways were his forefathers' ways; his deepest convictions were akin to theirs; and it needed but a little stretch of the imagination to suppose him a fellow worker with Knox or the friend and companion of Burns.

This is a full and generally just tribute to a man who was adulated by generations of influential Victorians. As the obituarist reminds us, however, he was a contemporary of the second generation of Romantics and only gradually made his mark on the Victorian nineteenth century. Only with his move to London in the spring of 1834 and with the publication of *The French Revolution* in 1837 did he become established as a real force in English letters. He was the esteemed friend of many of the most eminent of his contemporaries and the mentor of many more. This did not prevent him being acidly critical of their opinions, their manners and their published work. Carlyle was a great, if occasionally taxing, writer of experimental prose. The obituarist, in common with many other Victorian critics, expresses some reservations about the tricks, contortions, complexities and whimsies of Carlyle's style and admits to finding the six 'laborious' volumes *The History of Frederick II of Prussia, called Frederick the Great* (1858–65) 'wearisome and vexatious'. Details of Carlyle's often fraught relationship with his long-suffering wife, Jane, would not be revealed until the publication by JA Froude of Carlyle's *Reminiscences* in 1881 and the *Letters and Memorials of Jane Welsh Carlyle* in 1883.

BENJAMIN DISRAELI, FIRST EARL OF BEACONSFIELD

Statesman and novelist: 'The time will come when you will hear me.'

19 APRIL 1881

YESTERDAY CAME TO an end one of the most extraordinary careers recorded in our political annals. It is hard to say what makes a great man; conceptions of greatness differ so widely when gauged by individual ideas. Lord Beaconsfield's own definition was 'one who affects the mind of his generation; whether he be a monk in his cloister agitating Christendom, or a Monarch crossing the Granicus and giving a new character to the Pagan world.' The definition has the disadvantage of being somewhat vague, for there are moral influences, indirect as well as direct, through which every veteran politician of commanding position must obviously have acted on the mind of his nation. But whether the late Premier may fairly be called great or not, the achieving pre-eminence in political life in the face of exceptional obstacles is the infallible test of a remarkable man. The career of a statesman who was emphatically a partisan can scarcely be dispassionately criticized when he has just departed. His character as well as his conduct, his actions, in their motives as in their consequences, will be considered more or less leniently or harshly according to the bias of those who judge them. It was Lord Beaconsfield's fortune to lay himself more open to unfavourable construction than most of his contemporaries, even in an age when charges of inconsistency are bandied freely and plausibly among the most eminent of our statesmen. It must be remembered, however, that in the most generous concessions of the Conservative leader to Liberal impulse he invariably asserted his consistency, appealing, in proof of the harmony of his convictions, to writings that embodied the professions and indicated the progress of his political faith. How far he did justice to himself or received hard measure at the hands of others we shall inquire later. There can be no question, at least, about the force of character and brilliancy of talent which assured him a lasting triumph over obstacles that are matters of fact and history; which placed him in a position to defy, if not to vanquish, prejudices of inborn feeling which secured his leadership of a party who regarded him distrustfully till he dazzled them with his latest triumphs, and yet followed him docilely if doubtingly to divisions the most eventful.

Lord Beaconsfield was of alien, although not obscure, extraction; he came of the

Benjamin Disraeli, First Earl of Beaconsfield

separate people which, since it has been scattered from a land of its own, has been persecuted or ostracized by Christian intolerance. His family was ancient; allied, it is said, with that high Hebrew aristocracy of Spain that embraced individuals of the stamp of his own Sidonias, it traced its descent through merchant princes of Venice to a stem that had been transplanted from the East in very early days. But, like other privileges, such claims of blood came under the head of Jewish disabilities, and did less than nothing to help him in the struggle towards a position that seemed practically beyond his dreams. Now that he has pioneered the way for his people, blunting in 50 years of hard fighting the prejudices that at every step opposed themselves to his own advance towards power; now that Jews sit as matter of right among the representatives of the country, legislating for interests in which they have a common concern with their fellows – it is difficult to measure the distance that then divided the young aspirant from the Premiership of England. Nor was his birth his only obstacle. His training had been directed to less splendid destinies. It is true that by literature his father and grandfather had made their names known far beyond literary circles, and, as events showed, the subject of our notice inherited their cultivated tastes with more than their literary talents. But his father, who intended him for a Government office, only gave him a private education, and early articled him to an attorney by way of preliminary preparation. Born in 1805, he was sent into the City when those who became his contemporaries in public life were matriculating at the Universities. In place of being educated, he very much educated himself, although it may he questioned whether what must have been a loss to many did not in the end prove a gain to him. The irresistible bent of his inclinations soon burst the bonds of circumstances; the consciousness that it must rest with himself to create his future hardened him into a man while most men are still boys. He not only knew his value, and perhaps overrated it, but he had the happy faculty of impressing the sense of it on others. The art of making himself indispensable was the secret of his successful life. Imperturbable self-sufficiency, founded on a profound consciousness of equality or superiority, was the talisman by which an able man might force the doors that were held against him. The tactics which gave Vivian Grey a fabulous supremacy with mythical celerity became, when gradually modified by sense and experience, precisely those with which Disraeli anticipated the lofty patronage of Whig leaders, and asserted himself later with his colleagues of the Tory aristocracy. The clever book gained its author the ear of the novel-reading public, and attracted the attention of society. In 1827 he made a classical tour in Italy and Greece; in 1830 a religious pilgrimage to Syria and the Holy Land, where he found or fed the Oriental fancies that inspired his fantastic romance of 'Alroy.' Then, also, he travelled through the sacred scenes which he revisited afterwards with Tancred and Lothair.

He came back to England to find the country in the vortex of the Reform agitation. With the old landmarks being swept away before the rising flood of democratic feeling, with his ambition catching fire at the prevailing excitement, one has only to read 'Coningsby' to conceive the eagerness with which he panted to make his way into the arena. He set himself with characteristic determination to enter public life. Few men, starting from nothing to win everything, have met with more discouragement at the outset. His first attempt was on the Buckinghamshire borough of High Wycombe, and the names of his sponsors are vouchers sufficient for the principles on which he stood. Joseph Hume and Daniel O'Connell promised and vowed on his behalf; yet a Whig held his ground against the Radical, and the name and interest of the Hon. Charles Grey carried the election against Disraeli. Sent back to private life during the eventful year of the Reform Bill, he occupied his leisure and energy in the production of 'Contarini Fleming,' pronounced by Heine one of the most original of works. 'Contarini Fleming' was followed speedily by 'Alroy,' and by 'What is He?' an answer to a question asked half-contemptuously in political clubs, and in which, appearing as a political pamphleteer, he gave evidence of those powers of sarcasm which did him and his party such service afterwards. Next his versatile talents turned themselves to poetry, and the 'Revolutionary Epic' was, perhaps, the only failure he never tried to redeem. In 1836 he reappeared on the hustings at High Wycombe with no better fortune than before, and in the following year, standing for Taunton as a Conservative, was defeated by Mr. Labouchere. When he alluded later to the easy politics of his early years, he dismissed them lightly as the wild oats of his political life. Yet Mr. Disraeli all along enunciated ideas of his own as to the natural alliance of Toryism with democratic progress. In his 'Vindication of the English Constitution,' published in 1831 and dedicated to Lord Lyndhurst, he struck the keynote to the explanations he afterwards consistently offered of all his apparent inconsistencies. In that *brochure* he boldly averred that since 1831 the political power of the Tories had only 'been maintained by a series of democratic measures of the greatest importance and most comprehensive character.' Compelled to accept a Reform Bill, they insisted forthwith upon widely extending its operation. They rescued the freemen of England from threatened political annihilation, and they organized societies throughout the country for the general promotion of registration, 'three great democratic movements quite in keeping with the original and genuine character of Toryism.' The plain comment on such rhetorical subtleties is that, in detaching words from the ideas popularly attached to them, they must strike at the very roots of the system of government by party; that their logical results must be party struggles for place on identical principles, and that in voting Liberal measures the practice of professing Conservatism may keep pace with the proposals of Radical reformers. That the practical deductions which came naturally from such assertions may prove dangerous was demonstrated in the history of Mr. Disraeli's own Reform Bill when the unexpected flexibility of the Government of the minority carried the moderate men of the majority much further than they intended. That some years after the passing of the Bill, the Conservatives secured a brilliant electioneering victory proves nothing in favour of its author's principles, whatever it may say for his tactics. Granting that the measure was wise in itself, yet, coming from the Conservatives when it did, it strained and discredited our Parliamentary system. Granted that the Conservative leader had shrewdly foreseen that the new distribution of forces might prove a positive gain to his friends on their next appeal to the country, that is but the argument of an electioneering agent, unworthy to weigh with a patriot or statesman. But Mr. Disraeli's was just the mind to let itself be persuaded by some ingenious sophistry of its own, when yielding conviction to it would chance to forward his views. Whether in action or in speech, a paradox had always a charm for him. A consummate and versatile tactician, he was quick to see his party's advantage in some sudden evolution of surprise, as he was skilful to reconcile the startling move to the consciences of his followers. But, however his ingenuity might contrive to reconcile the apprehensions of Toryism with the encroachments of democracy, he was sufficiently consistent through life in his dislike and denunciations of the Whig oligarchy. Political convictions apart, it was natural enough that an ambitious and unfriended young politician should feel little attraction towards the exclusive caste which regarded Government posts as its inalienable birthright – as so many close seats transmitted by descent. In the 'Letters of Runnymede,' contributed to this journal, and republished in 1836 with a dedication to Sir Robert Peel, he passed the leaders of the Whig party in fierce and unflattering review.

It was in 1837 that he took his seat in the House of Commons. Instead of studying to conciliate prejudice, he set himself to provoke and defy it. Chalon and Maclise have preserved that striking exterior, strongly suggestive of foreign blood and foreign taste, that St. Stephen's has since had time to familiarize itself with. The matter of his speech seemed almost as affected as its manner to an audience accustomed to the severe simplicity and unimpassioned delivery of model English orators. It was in the debate on the Irish election petitions that the member for Maidstone rose to break down in his famous maiden speech. He followed the Irish Liberator, his former patron, now his bitter personal enemy. The scandal of their recent quarrel, an encounter of shillelaghs rather than a passage of rapiers, was still fresh in every one's recollection, and, as was generally the case with those who fell foul of O'Connell, the Irishman had had the last word, and left his adversary the ridicule. The Tory candidate for Taunton had gone out of his way to make a violent attack on the Agitator in an election speech. The latter had retorted with that bitter surmise as to his assailant's descent from the impenitent thief, and, for once, Disraeli's usually impassive nature had been stung into madness. Disraeli had vowed revenge 'when they should meet at Philippi,' and now the meeting had come and he had his opportunity. When O'Connell resumed his seat it was the new member who caught the Speaker's eye. The story of his failure has been often told. In spite of the habitual consideration of the House for a novice, the orator's style and manner were irresistible. Smiles broke into laughter, and at last the oration came to a premature standstill amid shouts of merriment – so far as it went, an almost unparalleled episode; but the peroration of that maiden failure was the most remarkable of the many telling perorations delivered by the speaker, for it contained the secret as well as the promise of his long series of triumphs. 'I am not at all surprised at the reception I have experienced. I have begun several times many things, and I have often succeeded at last. I shall sit down now; but the time will come when you will hear me.' To think this and say it next day would have been nothing. To say so, not so much in the petulance of temper as with the calm earnestness of conviction, at a moment when most men would have been crushed helplessly under the load of ridicule, and stung beyond power of reflection by the disappointment of cherished hopes, gave evidence of unexampled strength of will and presence of mind and of the overweening self-confidence it went so far to justify.

As it did not crush him, it is probable that first mishap helped him. The House was disposed to listen with interest and even favour to a man who showed he had reason for his audacious defiance of its judgment. During the next few years Mr. Disraeli spoke at intervals, and was listened to with growing attention as he learnt to tone down his style and gestures in deference to the sentiment of his critics. But he kept himself before the public rather as a writer than a speaker, and added more to his literary than his political reputation. It was then he wrote some of his most successful fictions, till at last in his 'Coningsby,' a political novel of the day, he embodied the doctrines of a new school of political thought. In it he criticized the great party leaders, and with brilliant epigram, metaphor, and antithesis delineated their party strategy from his own sarcastic point of view. Rigby, Tadpole, and Taper were recognized everywhere as telling portraits, and few but those supposed to have stood for them were prepared to set them down as caricatures. If in other sketches the resemblances to individuals was occasionally vague, there could be no question of their being vivid reproductions of representative types. In Lord Henry Sydney, Buckhurst, Milbank, the group of rising talent and advanced thought which clustered round Coningsby, men might study the 'Young England' party with whom the clever author acted. One of the band, at least, has since sat more than once in the same Cabinet with his leader. It is worth while reverting to 'Coningsby,' because in the guise of fiction it gave deliberate expression to opinions, and this is the definition by the future Conservative leader of the Conservatism of Sir Robert Peel:–

> 'Conservatism was an attempt to carry on affairs by substituting the fulfilment of the duties of office for the performance of the functions of Government, and to maintain the negative system by the mere influence of property, reputable private conduct, and what are called Government connexions. Conservatism discards Prescription, shrinks from Principle, disavows Progress; having rejected all respect for antiquity, it offers no redress for the present, and makes no preparation for the future. It is obvious that for a time, under favourable circumstances, such a confederation might succeed; but it is equally clear that on the arrival of one of those critical conjunctures that will periodically occur in all States, and which such an impassioned system is even calculated ultimately to create, all power of resistance will be wanting; the barren curse of political infidelity will paralyze all action; and the Conservative Constitution will be discovered to be a *caput mortuum*.'

The attacks which Disraeli, as a member of the 'Young England' party, made on the Premier commenced in 1844, the year in which 'Coningsby' made its appearance. It must be confessed the ground he then took up was more in harmony with the language of his novel than with the positions towards which he executed his daring strategical movement – when he made himself the mouthpiece of the Protectionist malcontents. In 1844 he attacked the Premier rather for illiberality in commercial and religious matters than for over-advanced ideas on those questions; and it is difficult to believe that, had his choice been unbiased, his intellect would not have enlisted him as an advocate of Free Trade. Undoubtedly both his natural feelings and his personal circumstances disinclined him to anything like bigotry. Twice he came to what might have been a turning point in his career, opening to him, perhaps, a shorter cut to a more solidly established eminence than he even attained in 1874. Twice, certainly, the fortunes of a great party depended on the attitude of this comparatively obscure member of the House. The first time was when Sir Robert Peel succeeded to power in 1841, the second in 1846, when Disraeli went into systematic opposition to the Minister. On the first occasion the option did not rest with him, and it is doubtful whether the Premier ever seriously entertained the idea of offering the member for Shrewsbury – Disraeli had exchanged Maidstone for Shrewsbury in 1841 – a position he might not unreasonably have aspired to. Had Disraeli been given some minor post in the Ministry, his action must have been fettered by party ties; gratified ambition and the responsibilities of office might have conspired with his natural leanings to make the Thersites of Protection the Ulysses of Free Trade. But Peel had no presentiments, and few sympathies with his future enemy. There was little in common between the grave sense and cumbersome fluency of the one and the subtle speculation and volatile brilliancy of the other. Peel probably undervalued talents so antithetical to his own, for there can be no doubt he, of all men, would have shrunk from the wearing struggle before him could he have foreseen the danger he provoked. Peel, in his intense conscientiousness, provoked that which gave the sting to his enemy's attacks. No man was more sensitive on the point of public as of personal honour; and, whatever the pressure which had modified his convictions, he knew he had come into power the pledged champion of Protection. To be presented or misrepresented to men whom it had been his pride to lead, to whose opinion he was still keenly susceptible, as an unscrupulous renegade and the organizer of 'the organized hypocrisy' was unspeakably bitter to him. He might retort, or repeat explanations, but reiterated charges were addressed to ears ever ready to receive them – to the men who had seen their trusted leader pass over to the enemy at the critical moment of the campaign. Disraeli had chosen his points of attack with that instinctive judgment which made his enmity so damaging; yet the audacity which singled out for unremitting hostility the Minister 'who played on the House like an old fiddle,' although characteristic enough, was, perhaps, more apparent than real. Addressing himself on plausible grounds to passions fiercely excited, to principles unexpectedly scandalized, and prejudices rudely ruffled, to a party smarting from the sense of having been hoodwinked and betrayed, he awoke the enthusiastic sympathy that insured success to his philippics, and he bid for the support of a formidable following. We have said the fate of a party twice depended on his attitude. The second time was when Sir Robert formally intimated his conversion and the impending doom of the Corn Laws. Party ties were dissolved, the Premier's change of views and schemes offered high precedent for the imitation of humbler men, and Disraeli stood less committed than most. The ground he had taken hitherto was one on which he was as little as possible committed, circumscribed, or embarrassed, and any one of three paths lay open to him. He had often held language that might be construed into leaning towards free trade in corn and liberty in religion, and he might have easily waived unimportant differences and tendered his support to Peel. But such welcome as he might reasonably look for was hardly likely to tempt him to the sacrifice of more ambitious hopes. At best, he must have been content to remain the lieutenant of a man whose nature had little in common with his own; while in choosing differently he might aspire to lead either a Whig or Tory Opposition. His avowed democratic inclinations might, with slight violence, have softened into decorous Liberalism, and he would have had to step little out of his way to attach himself to the Whigs. But, putting principle out of the question, his objections to that course sprang from feeling as much as calculation. Detestation of the Whigs appears to have been among the most deeply-rooted of his sentiments, and the Reform Bill of 1867 was only the last of a long series of deadly moves directed to the discomfiture of his natural enemies. As matter of calculation he saw their front rank formed of men of high Parliamentary reputation, although the party might be weak in rank and file. Before pitting himself against their great opponents, he must force his way to the front through a line of dangerous rivals, leaving himself exposed to side shafts from a party whose notorious vice was jealousy of stranger talent. Casting in his lot with the Protectionists, pre-eminence was assured him at once. They were a scattered mob, hesitating between desperate and timid counsels; but they offered the nucleus of a formidable force to a leader who knew how to rally them. They had position, consideration, and wealth, and at their back was an amount of feeling in the country inadequately represented even by their considerable numbers. They were struggling silently with the bitter indignation that sought an utterance. Hope for the moment was gone, but, as Disraeli has told us himself in his memoir of Lord George Bentinck, their longing was for vengeance. That vengeance he could offer them and count on their gratitude. Their support would be given as a matter of course to the man who made himself necessary to them, and their instrument must inevitably become their leader. The story of an express bargain between him and his future supporters – a compact that he should attack while they should applaud – is improbable, if not incredible. From the moment he made his decision the arrangement was natural and necessary; the success of his studied sarcasms was assured in advance, and when the orator shaped the feelings of his faction into winged words, each man behind him cheered his own sentiments to the echo. It is a question still whether Conservatives or Liberals have most cause to be grateful to him for his choice of sides. It is certain that, at a critical moment, he saved his party from dissolution, and commenced the training that carried it through some fruitless victories to a very substantial one. It is equally certain that he acquired that undemonstrative but irresistible influence which completed its liberal education with a measure so democratic that Conservatism seemingly had little left to preserve, at least according to its old notions, whoever might be the constitutional advisers of the Crown. The Moltke of his party, his prompt facility of resource and rare talent of strategical combination were speedily recognized by the chiefs he acted with and the leader they followed. To him must be ascribed the tactics which, on the theory that young whelps need to be blooded, won the Treasury benches for the 'large-acred squires and men of metal' to whom place was comparatively indifferent, and his must be the credit of the measures that kept them there, very often to the scandal of their constituents. Thus the first speech the member for Shrewsbury launched at Peel's re-constructed Cabinet of December, 1845, marked an epoch in our political history.

One of the most graphic and characteristic chapters in the 'Political Biography' is that in which the writer describes the opening of the debate on the Corn Laws, with the speech in which the Minister announced his intentions. The matter-of-fact trivialities by which Peel made his approaches to the crushing climax – embodying what half his hearers regarded as their sentence of ruin – his leading up to the duties on corn through soap and candles, by boot-fronts and shoe leather – the emphatic pathos of his declaration, 'I believe it is impossible to over-estimate the importance of promoting the fattening of cattle' – all lend themselves to Mr. Disraeli's happiest vein of irony. But in his narrative of the events, in which he might say '*Pars magna fui*,' the violent language of his philippics as the Protectionist champion finds no echo. His own reorganization of his party and his displays in the House; his energy, his eloquence, and their pregnant results, are either passed over in silence or subordinated almost unfairly. His book is a frank and generous tribute to the merits of his self- sacrificing friend and colleague. The vindication of the tactics he directed demanded the impeachment of Peel, and we have no leisure now to analyze the justice of his indictment; but he closes with a graceful tribute to that statesman's memory. Shiel said, with some justice, that the sudden death of Sir Robert left Disraeli in the position of an anatomist whose subject has been snatched away. Politically, it was true; morally it gives a false impression of his character. Doubtless Disraeli lost a convenient object which was always there to serve for an effective declamation; he missed the ladder by which he had mounted to the place he filled. But he left his party enmities behind him at St. Stephen's; he delivered and received thrusts of debate as matters of business, like the gladiator who carouses in friendship with his fellows while in training for the deadly combat, and goes back from the arena, should he survive, to pledge them amicably in the wineshop. Few men, it must be confessed, have dealt more freely in exchanges of personalities, and yet we only recall two instances where he showed any sign of soreness on the morrow. The one was when he challenged Mr. Maurice O'Connell for the savage sarcasm of O'Connell the elder; the other when he wreaked old wrongs, in 'Lothair,' on the head of 'the Oxford Professor.' On the other hand, not a few can vouch for the cordiality with which he used to grasp the hands of his opponents in many a fierce faction fight when they met after the recess on the eve of fresh combats. Be it to his credit or the reverse, we must record our opinion that, amid all the virulence of his attacks on Peel, few men in the House were likely to construe more leniently the Premier's conduct; he fiercely assailed the politician without a shade of malice to the man.

We have remarked that, like a man of spirit and shrewdness, in his writings as in his speeches, Disraeli boldly prided himself on his Jewish descent and the glories of his race. Jews rich in gifts as in gold are the mythical heroes of the Utopias in his fictions. But this most eloquent defence of his people against the prejudices of Christendom is to be found in that chapter of the 'Political Biography' which precedes the explanation of Lord George Bentinck's conduct with respect to the Jewish disabilities. In ingenious arguments, more sophistical than satisfactory, he seeks to demonstrate that these prejudices are neither historically true nor dogmatically sound, and urges characteristically that we owe the Jews a large debt of gratitude for becoming the instruments to carry out the great doctrine of the Atonement. That he felt more than natural sympathy, that he took a genuine pride in his people, there can be no doubt whatever, and as little that he had no bigoted prejudice against religious emancipation in the abstract. Yet, when Lord George Bentinck resigned the leadership of his party rather than countenance its intolerance on the question of Jewish disabilities; when he not only voted, but exerted himself, under great physical suffering, to address the House on behalf of the Jews, Mr. Disraeli took a different view of his duty. It is impossible not to suspect that here, as elsewhere, he sacrificed conscience and inclination alike to what he considered as the paramount claims of party.

In 1847 Mr. Disraeli had obtained the seat for Buckinghamshire he retained till his elevation to the peerage. It was in 1849 he succeeded his friend Lord George Bentinck in the leadership of the Country party. In 1852 his genius for opposition had succeeded in landing that party in power, and the Chancellorship of the Exchequer was the post assigned in the Derby Cabinet to one whose reputation was rather brilliant than solid. In July of that year, his speech at Aylesbury had committed him to 'new principles and new policies.' As Chancellor of the Exchequer he set himself to redeem his pledges in a Budget that satisfied neither friends nor enemies. It was rejected with the 'new-fangled' novelties it contained, although the speech in which it was introduced and defended unquestionably evidenced the attention its author had bestowed on financial questions since he had held a responsible position. The faults and merits of the Budget were at least distinctively his own; had he studied more the feelings and opinions of his party in its composition, its reception might have been different even on the part of his enemies. It contained a series of startling surprises, and Englishmen are slow to be surprised out of old habits of transacting money matters. The Ministry of the minority was outvoted, but February, 1858, saw it again in power. On the former occasion the Government had been professedly provisional, avowedly sacrificing itself to patriotism when public affairs seemed at a deadlock. In 1858 the Conservatives had modified their action to accord with the only principles which promised them a lease of power. The feeling of the nation had pronounced in favour of a measure of Reform, as it had been loudly expressed before for an abolition of the protective duties. As it chanced, the Conservative leaders for the time had no strong motive for resisting the popular feeling. They had few scruples to overcome. Lord Derby had been a Liberal. Mr. Disraeli, as we know, had always preached the union of Toryism with Democracy, and declared that the soundest basis of the former was on substantial concessions to the latter. It was a question between power on sufferance and prolonged abdication. The choice was soon made where feelings argued plausibly in favour of expediency. But it was the most transparent of fallacies to assert that Conservative measures could only be carried by a Conservative Ministry when that Ministry took office to do the work the more moderate of its political opponents shrunk from. When Lord Derby – or rather Mr. Disraeli – declared for Reform, the leverage in favour of a subversive measure became irresistible; for, once assured that the cause was prejudged, no man cared to damage himself by futile opposition to the claims of the inevitable constituencies. Even Liberals felt that the impulse came from the wrong side, that the bit had slipped out and was doing the work of the spurs. When Disraeli declared for Reform he challenged the other party to enlarge their views and increase their offers. When he tendered a £10 county franchise Liberals were bound to outbid him. When the Conservatives comprehended disfranchisement in their measure, the Whigs could not possibly omit the schedules. The Bill of 1859 doomed Conservatism and condemned the Whigs. Execution on one or the other might be deferred, but it could not ultimately be evaded.

Mr. Disraeli had a theory of his own as to the conditions under which Reform could be safely conceded, a pet recipe for perfecting his favourite idea of a Democratic Conservatism. He was disposed to the amplest concession so long as the equilibrium between county and town could be preserved. His Bill of 1859 would have added materially to the registration rolls, but it attempted guarantees by which town votes should be polled only for town members. His 'fancy franchises' were designed to enlist impecunious intelligence on the side of property. The practical objection to them was that they embarrassed general rules with invidious exceptions for results totally inadequate to their intention. He did not oppose the second reading of the rejected Reform Bill of 1860, but Mr. Gladstone's measure of 1866 was introduced under better auspices and threatened to be more formidable. As it struck at what Mr. Disraeli regarded as the essential Conservative element in Reform, and threatened to swamp the county constituencies in the rising tide of urban voters, he would naturally have opposed it, independently of party considerations. Whether the Cave of Adullam would have filled as it did had its occupants foreseen the coming events that were beginning to cast their shadows; whether the refinements of reasoning that satisfied Mr. Disraeli would have convinced the logical judgment and secured to the Conservative cause the incisive eloquence of Mr. Lowe, is another question. Next year Lord Derby took his leap in the dark, and there can be little doubt as to who had the chief share in urging him to it. It is certain Mr. Disraeli's enemies might have addressed to him the taunts he had himself levelled at the illustrious convert to Free Trade, and taxed him with running away with the Liberals' clothes while the wearers were bathing. It is not so sure he would have ventured to maintain that this fourth great democratic movement, the one of which he was the promoter, and which gave us virtual household suffrage, was altogether in keeping with the original and genuine character of Toryism. It might be so, but if it were, after all Mr. Disraeli had done to teach his party, they still remained hopelessly confused between old words and their new meanings. The memory of these events is still so recent that it is superfluous to dwell on them, or to recall the details of a campaign when the army were kept to their colours while made to manoeuvre in the dark; where the officers had their instructions in cipher, or made solemn terms with the enemy only to have them disavowed. Never did the Conservative chief show such consummate strategy or so amazing a versatility of resource as in this appropriate crowning of a career whose triumphs were won by science against numbers. He took his orders from his adversaries with perfect taste, temper, and dignity, and gained one battle for himself while winning another for them. It was a triumph of the Conservative party and of the Liberal principles.

The resignation of the Disraeli Cabinet at the close of 1868 gave him the opportunity of paying a graceful tribute to one to whom he owed a debt of gratitude he was never slow to acknowledge. We did not interrupt our notice of his political career to chronicle his marriage, which took place in 1839. Mrs. Disraeli was the wealthy widow of Mr. Wyndham Lewis, his former colleague in the representation of Maidstone; and to the fortune she brought him, and the influence she exercised on his character and career, he was in no small measure indebted for his brilliant success. The glorification of the strength of woman's influence in 'Lothair' embodied the fortunate experiences of the author, and the promise of conjugal sympathy in the union between Corisande and the hero had, notwithstanding a considerable disparity of years, been fully realized by Disraeli in his long wedded life. He could not yet spare himself from the House where he had so long played a leading part, but the honours offered the retiring Minister were accepted for his wife, and Mrs. Disraeli was raised to the peerage by the style of Viscountess Beaconsfield.

In the meantime the next trick in the great game fell to Mr. Gladstone. If he did not trump Mr. Disraeli, he followed suit with Disestablishment, rallying his party to the cry of justice to Ireland. The powerful majority of his rival, acting together generally with extraordinary harmony, gave Mr. Disraeli little opportunity for anything else than his familiar attitude of patient observation. He was forced to content himself with manoeuvring for some insignificant concessions, until the blundering and the menacing activity of his opponents gave him an opening for the display of special abilities. He had been chary of his words before, and now that he lifted his voice in grave warnings, he contributed greatly to the increasing unpopularity of the Ministry and to the growing uneasiness as to what they might do next. A Government inclined to hurry too fast and too far, which had begun to live by the excitement of harassing and sensational measures, could scarcely have found a more formidable critic. Mr. Disraeli pounced upon the weak points of schemes that had gained on Mr. Gladstone's convictions after his ardent fancy had fallen in love with them at first sight. The epigrams and sarcasms he had always at command must often have done useful service afterwards, although at the time they seemed merely the sparkling fireworks of debate. The definition of the Irish Disestablishment as 'legalized confiscation and consecrated sacrilege' was remembered at the ensuing elections when the friends of Church and property wanted a telling cry. Sarcastic sneers like that at the 'sweet simplicity' of Mr. Lowe's transformed Budget of 1871 passed current among many people as certificates to the shortcomings, if not the incapacity, of prominent Liberals. Next year opportunities were multiplied for the stinging censor of the Government as champion alternately of the spirit and letter of the Constitution. The Collier appointment was followed by the Ewelme Rectory case, and the 'Government began to live in a perpetual blaze of apology.' The Session of 1873 may be said to have been a decisive one, although the dissolution was deferred to the following spring. Certainly it illustrated in striking contrast the characters of the chiefs of the opposing parties. Mr. Gladstone had proposed to complete a triad of measures for Ireland with his University Bill. Considering that it dealt with those religious questions which ruffle the susceptibilities of the least excitable politicians and on which the various sections of his majority were almost irreconcilably divided, it was a delicate measure to carry at best. Playing into his opponents' hands and doing the last thing Mr. Disraeli would ever have dreamt of doing, he declared that a settlement of the question was vital to the honour and existence of the Government, and that he was resolved to stand or fall by the Bill. Then the Conservative leader felt assured of winning his waiting game. He had only to persist in his habitual tactics, to give his enemies rope enough, and let them trip each other up. The Bill was a marvel of ingenuity and a startling illustration of its author's want of political tact. At first sight and in theory it seemed plausible; practically, it was impossible to please alike the Liberal Protestants and the Irish Catholics. Beaten by a narrow majority, Mr. Gladstone resigned, and expressed characteristic resentment at Mr. Disraeli declining to accept the logical consequences of his victory and accede to power. Mr. Disraeli saw things were working in his favour, and that this last defeat of the once powerful Government on a vital question must precipitate the process of disintegration. He had no idea of being hurried to the country by way of softening the catastrophe the Liberal leader had provoked. With quiet irony he enunciated his views on the Constitutional point. Neither Constitutional doctrine nor Parliamentary etiquette compelled him to take office on the strength of an accidental majority due to the casual desertion of the Irish Roman Catholic irregulars from the ranks of the enemy. But he urged his most unanswerable argument in turning to his own purpose the taunts that had often been addressed to him. He had had some personal experience of government by minority, and it had convinced him 'that such an experiment weakened authority and destroyed public confidence.' His arguments against the alternative of a dissolution were, perhaps, sound, as they were certainly plausible. His speech was a forcible exposition of constitutional principles founded upon long experience, and with his conduct it was an admirable commentary on his philosophy of Parliamentary tactics. In declining to have his hand forced, in restraining the impatience of his jubilant friends, he showed his customary political prescience. The tide of public opinion had fairly turned, and through the recess of 1873 it ran steadily against Ministers. One marked exception there was, and if a Liberal won the seat at Bath it was partly owing to an indiscretion of Mr. Disraeli. He addressed the famous 'Bath letter' to Lord Grey de Wilton, in which, strange to say, he appeared to crowd blunder on blunder, line after line, making the communication as much a mistake in point of policy as of taste. He gave the Conservative candidate a strong certificate to character, put impolitic pressure on the judgment of the enlightened electors of Bath, and denounced the Ministers and their course of 'blundering and plundering' in language rather befitting a reckless Old Bailey counsel than the responsible chief of a great party at a critical turn of its fortunes. If the letter proved anything more than the truth that the most astute and self-controlled of men are liable to indiscreet impulses, it showed that Mr. Disraeli was more able in Parliament than out of it, and understood the feelings of parties in the House better than the temper of the country. But Liberal victories like Taunton and Bath had come to be regarded rather as accidents than otherwise, so universal and radical had been the change since Mr. Gladstone had entered on his Irish campaign in 1868 with his commanding majority. The returning a Conservative at Stroud in place of a distinguished member of the Liberal Government was the straw that broke the camel's back and wore out the waning patience of the Minister. In 1874 Mr. Gladstone surprised the country with the Greenwich letter, announcing a dissolution in mid-Session for no obvious or immediate reason. Impulsively he put his fate to the test, and yet at the same time, with what had the semblance of a shortsighted piece of astuteness, he tendered the electors a bribe in the shape of a promised remission of the income-tax. The answer of the country was unmistakable. It seemed to vindicate the shrewdness with which Mr. Disraeli had suspected the results of a household suffrage. No longer the Minister of a minority existing by sufferance, he found himself with a compact working majority of over 50, and for the first time had the free control of his actions. With characteristic imperturbability, he declined to be pressed. He protested against the theory that a new Ministry, surprised into the acceptance of office, is bound to be provided with 'a cut and dry policy;' and he practically assumed that his mandate from the country meant the cessation of that 'meddling and harassing,' 'blundering and plundering,' which he had so consistently denounced and which had wearied even restless spirits into a longing for repose.

As it happened, besides, domestic measures were subsequently thrown into abeyance by the state of affairs in Europe and Asia. The Prime Minister found himself face to face with the troubles that were speedily to reopen the Eastern question and shake the Ottoman Empire to its foundations. The position of England was difficult and embarrassing in view of events that must nearly affect her. Her navy was formidable, though the late Mr. Ward Hunt on his accession to office had talked of a 'phantom fleet;' but the army, distributed all over the world, had relatively shrunk into insignificance compared to the gigantic armaments of Continental Powers. Moreover, while the Gladstone Ministry was busy with home reforms, England had been steadily losing influence abroad, if not deliberately effacing herself. Nothing could show more unpleasantly the slight regard in which she was held than the independent action of the 'Three Emperors,' when their Chancellors decided on the terms of the Berlin Memorandum, merely telegraphing to the Western Powers for their approval. But Mr. Disraeli had determined from the first that England should play a part that became her, and not only speak, but be respectfully listened to. That he made mistakes when each step was beset with embarrassments can scarcely be denied, that he was less successful than he might have been is only saying that he was the constitutional chief of a divided Cabinet and that he had inherited from his predecessors a legacy of difficulties. But we believe that impartial historians will do him the justice of having been guided by a noble and farsighted patriotism, and will make large allowance for the untoward circumstances which compelled him to alter or modify his plans. The line he took or desired to take was merely a return to traditions which had made the greatness or assured the safety of the Empire in times of general convulsion. But a long continuance of tranquillity and prosperity had wrought certain changes in the national feeling. Responsible politicians carried their advocacy of non-intervention to a point at which prudence became cowardice and folly; while a noisy sect of popular orators clamoured for peace at any price. Action that would have appeared inevitable to a Chatham or a Pitt was denounced as a flashy display of 'Imperialism.' As the impression had been spreading on the Continent that nothing short of actual invasion would force England to fight, language of the kind was as dangerous as it was unseasonable And the impression received some official confirmation when a member of the Cabinet in a most critical moment declared that England would never be guilty of another Crimean war. It is probable that the increasing indignation at the pretensions of Russia might have sufficiently strengthened the hands of the Minister to enable him to override such opposition. As events proved subsequently, he had touched the real pulse of the nation and knew how it was beating. But then occurred those 'Bulgarian atrocities,' which brought philanthropy into conflict with patriotism and evoked an outburst of generous indignation. Horrible as they were, they were exaggerated by sensational writers, and the nation was misinformed as to their origin. Lord Beaconsfield's sagacity saved him from the trap which a Russian envoy was believed to have prepared with coldblooded astuteness. From the first he never doubted of the truth that the rising that was so savagely suppressed had been provoked by foreign agents. It was a deplorable accident, but it ought not to outweigh the considerations that had hitherto governed our policy in the East. The truth was, that while a great body of Englishmen had their minds full of the misdeeds of the Turks Lord Beaconsfield had his eye on the Cabinet of St. Petersburg. The excesses of some bands of savage irregulars were no sufficient reason for sacrificing the interests we had hitherto defended. We had never fought for Turkish misgovernment, but for the barriers that were opposed to the ambition of Russia. But Turkey's attitude of stolid resistance made it as difficult to help as it was impossible to sympathize with her. She did her best to put those who would have befriended her in the wrong when she rejected the concessions that Europe recommended; and Lord Beaconsfield had to do the best he could in difficult and most embarrassing circumstances.

His last utterances in the House of Commons were in August, 1875, when he was questioned upon Eastern affairs immediately before the close of the Session. Next day came the announcement of his acceptance of the peerage, which he had declined for himself when his wife was ennobled. We may regret that the Lower House lost a leader so admirably fitted to deal with the Obstructionists, but no doubt he felt that his party could spare him, since his leadership had given them a commanding majority, and he had well-earned the comparative repose of the calmer atmosphere of the Lords. There the brilliant debater and orator chiefly distinguished himself by his reticence, and even his enemies must admit the dignified self-control which submitted in silence to misconstruction and was content to wait for justification by results. Not only had he to face the legitimate criticism of fair opponents who differed from his measures, but he was fiercely attacked in the Press and on the platform with a rancour embittered by honest, though perverted philanthropy. His motives were misconstrued as facts were frequently misrepresented; and even Mr. Gladstone deigned to indulge in language which is happily exceptional in recent political warfare. Very few men could have been capable of such calm self-restraint, and it is especially remarkable in a character like Lord Beaconsfield's. For his political credit was as the breath of his nostrils to him, and the verdict of his countrymen could hardly have been flattering had he died while his policy seemed a humiliating failure. Yet all the time his increasing popularity showed even the worldly wisdom of the course he had pursued. The answer he had waited for was the revised terms of the Treaty of Berlin, and these were received no doubt with exaggerated enthusiasm. But meantime the Russians had declared war and, after many checks and humiliating discomfiture, were threatening Erzeroum and advancing on Constantinople. Whether Lord Beaconsfield if he had been in the position of a Bismarck would have boldly taken the bull by the horns and openly sided with the Turks is a question. Had he done so, it is probable the Russians would have drawn back; it is certain that with English generalship on the Danube the Turks would have anticipated the invasion of Roumania and changed the whole course of the war. But, in fact, considering the excitement of the country over the Bulgarian massacres and the feelings of some influential members of his Ministry, he had no choice in the matter. As it was, much of his apparent vacillation was doubtless due to the presence of Lord Derby in the Cabinet. When Lords Derby and Carnarvon seceded later, he paid a touching tribute to the necessity which compelled him to break with the son and political heir of his former friend and patron. The presence of the English fleet in the Bosphorus which followed the secession of the dissenting statesmen went far to impose moderation on the Russians. It was a sign that England was ready to act, and the vote of the six millions for military preparations showed that it was at least possible that we might repeat the 'guilt and folly' of the Crimean war. The bringing a contingent of the Indian army to Malta was a characteristic, but far more questionable piece of policy; and it was promptly answered by the counter-stroke which involved us in hostilities with Afghanistan. But in the meantime it had sensibly lowered the tone of the Russian Press, and we heard no more of privateering cruisers to be fitted out in American ports. From the time the British squadron passed the Dardanelles, Lord Beaconsfield was forced forward into the proud position of champion of neutral Europe and the rights of nations. The independent foreign Press unanimously approved his conduct; and though they may have written with some selfish *arrière pensée*, yet they must have expressed the dispassionate judgment of Europe. It was owing in great measure to our vigilant watching of the negotiations that the exorbitant pretensions of the Treaty of San Stefano were submitted to revision in the Congress of Berlin. Lord Beaconsfield decided to represent the country in person with Lord Salisbury for his colleague; and we may suppose that nothing flattered him more in his long career than the cordiality of his reception by the admiring Germans. His task at Berlin would have been greatly simplified had their Chancellor sympathized with the popular feeling. But the understanding of the Emperors still subsisted, and no Continental Power had personal reasons for setting limits to the acquisitions of Russia in Asia. As Lord Beaconsfield reminded the House of Lords when defending the terms of the treaty, he had a delicate game to play with indifferent cards. Russia had lavished blood and treasure, and had a right to claim the fruits of her victories; while England had chosen to confine herself to despatch-writing. He hinted at the understanding between the three Emperors, and maintained that, all things considered, we had good reason to be satisfied. It is, perhaps, too soon even now to judge of the treaty by its results, and unquestionably it would have been more dignified to have gone to Congress with hands unfettered by secret engagements. But, on the whole, Lord Beaconsfield was justified in the memorable boast that the Plenipotentiaries had brought back 'peace with honour.' The treaty restored to Turkey much valuable territory, did its best towards securing the independence of the detached provinces, and offered the Porte one more opportunity of saving what remained to it by necessary reforms. The most effective clause was that which, by bringing Austria into Bosnia and Herzegovina, opposed a counterpoise to Russian aggression beyond the Balkans. The private convention with the Porte was of more doubtful advantage, and gave some handle to those who declared that it was intended as a salve to English vanity. As for the acquisition of Cyprus, it is difficult not to associate it with a passage in 'Tancred,' and, at all events, the coincidence is curious. The passage runs thus:– 'The English want Cyprus and they will take it as compensation . . . The English will not do the business of the Turks again for nothing.'

It might have been well for Lord Beaconsfield – as many people are of opinion that it might have been well for England and the world – had he made his appeal to the constituencies in the triumph of the return from Berlin. It is at least probable that he would have been sent back to power with an undiminished majority, and had the opportunity of shaping out the plans he had conceived; and of continuing the alliances he had commenced. As it was, he was over-persuaded to delay, and we know how disastrous the delay proved to the Conservatives. We do not care to go back upon events which are fresh in the recollection of everybody; nor need we do more than make passing allusion to the Afghan and Zulu wars. The one was the legacy of our antagonism to Russia in the East; the other was imposed on a reluctant Government by the precipitate decision of a strong-willed subordinate. After the return from Berlin, the head of the Ministry, though never shrinking from responsibility for the policy he originated and directed, left its defence chiefly to the heads of the Indian and Colonial Departments. Since then, indeed, he has spoken seldom. But he was moved for once from his usual apparent indifference to personal attacks by the fiery oratory of Mr. Gladstone when that right hon. gentleman brought his damaging indictments against Ministers in his famous Mid-Lothian progress. Nevertheless, and notwithstanding some discontent with the Afghan and South African imbroglios, and some disappointment with the slow settlement of Eastern affairs, the Conservative prospects seemed satisfactory in the beginning of 1880, as the Parliamentary strength of the party was unbroken. Few but those who are wise after the event had any suspicion of the surprise that was being prepared by the constituencies in answer to the appeal to them in the spring of the year. That it was a shock and bitter grief to Lord Beaconsfield in more ways than one we have no reason to doubt. It not only broke up the great majority that had rewarded him for the patient labours of many years, condemning him besides to absolute impotence while he saw the reversal of the plans he had most deeply at heart, but it must have shown him that he had been deluding himself when he cherished the belief that lowering the franchise might not be necessarily opposed from his particular point of view either to Conservatism or to the permanent interests of the country. Moreover, the revolution wrought by the elections demonstrated to foreign States that henceforward their understandings with England might be altered at any moment by the decision of a popular vote following on some party division. But Lord Beaconsfield when he resigned carried into his retirement the respect and admiration of the most honourable of his political opponents; nor can we do better than quote the graceful expressions of Lord Hartington in one of the happiest passages of his speeches in North-East Lancashire:–

> 'It may be said that Lord Beaconsfield is ambitious. I should like to know what man who has attained the position which he has attained in the political life of his country is not actuated by feelings of ambition. No one certainly can attribute any mean or unworthy feelings to Lord Beaconsfield. We disagree with his politics, but we must admire the genius and talent which the man has shown under the disadvantages he has laboured under. I firmly believe that Lord Beaconsfield has had in view what he believes to be the greatness of his country and the power of the Sovereign whom he serves.'

And we may add that few statesmen ever deserved more generous consideration at the hands of their opponents, since he never embarrassed them by the shadow of factious opposition when he felt the dignity or interests of the country to be at stake. A party leader before everything, on critical national questions he invariably rose superior to party; and we may remember on a recent occasion, when he spoke and voted in the Lords against Mr. Gladstone's Irish Disturbance Bill, that the honesty of his action was amply vindicated by the rejection of the measure by the Liberal peers.

Had he never turned to politics Lord Beaconsfield must have made himself a brilliant reputation as a literary man. But, in truth, he was a born politician; his most vigorous fictions took the shape of political manifestoes; his women inspire his heroes to public actions and feats of oratory, and dismiss them from sighing at their feet to save their country and do battle with the dragon of faction. He went further than Mr. Trollope, and not only held a Parliamentary career the necessary culmination of a distinguished Englishman's life, but, in his eyes, it was the only life worth living. The greater comprehended the less, and all minor ambitions merged themselves in that of making your mark in public. All his 'men' were men of thought or speculation, of action or the capability of action. Like Vivian Grey, having nothing else to look to, they made ambition their profession, set their feet on the ladder before they had well left school, with their eyes riveted on the highest rung, and studied every human being they came across as possible foothold. Or like Coningsby, sustained by powerful connexions and hedging on influential friendships, they afforded themselves the luxury of abnegation, and, sacrificing wealth and commonplace prospects to independence, found themselves rewarded with the possession of one and the other. Like the Young Duke, they vindicated their manhood by a heroic effort when they seemed hopelessly succumbing to temptations, tore themselves from the arms of sirens and left the gaming-table to shake the Senate. We might multiply parallel instances down to Lothair, who, having been well-nigh persuaded to discredit his Church by a perversion so notorious, redeems the passing weakness by consecrating his life and fortune to her support. The inevitable result of the tone and spirit of the novels was to limit their popularity to a class. They were no mere stories of fashionable life, stories which none read more greedily than those hopelessly beneath the charmed circles. They identified themselves only with the feelings and instincts of the high-born, the intellectual, and the ambitious, yet even by these they were severely criticized. They were too didactic for the many, expatiating on topics in which the masses do not care to be instructed; they were too speculative for the sagely practical; the tenets they advocated were too advanced alike for quiet-going Whigs and for Conservatives who thought their traditionary thoughts and inherited family opinions. As pictures of society the earlier novels were cleverly painted by a brilliant young artist drawing freely on his imagination, although the colouring gradually sobered down, and in 'Lothair' and 'Endymion' at last came compositions from the life. Yet from the first there was the originality, lightness, and sparkle which will carry off any quantity of improbability or even absurdity, and a good deal of mysticism or dulness to boot. Few writers have succeeded better in hitting off a character in an epigram, in making a speaking likeness of a caricature. Lord Beaconsfield was fond of seeking his models in well-known men, reproducing them with a realism sometimes repugnant alike to art and to good taste. We have alluded to the political portraits in 'Coningsby,' and there could be still less mistake about the Byron and Shelley of 'Venetia.' In 'Lothair' his more cultivated judgment dealt in compositions rather than photographs; and, with a single exception, the characters were representative men more than the men themselves. In it, too, there was little or nothing of the satirist who relies on human weakness for his best effects. Rather you had the genial philosopher, who took for granted the evil of the world and its countless follies, but who had come to see there was good in everything and in most people, and who had learnt to take more pleasure in seeing things on their sunny side.

Lord Beaconsfield was less an orator than a debater, and his reputation as a speaker will diminish as death thins away the men who listened to him and saw him in action. Notwithstanding his lucidity of statement, brilliance of fancy, and marvellous command of language, his set speeches are comparative failures. Sarcasm and irony were his natural weapons; he never showed to more advantage than when forced to betake himself to them in repelling a sudden attack. He had the presence of mind that is seldom taken at a disadvantage, great quickness of perception, a natural gift of detecting the flaws in his adversaries' armour, while few men knew better the weak points in his own or how best to cover them. With his imperturbable coolness of manner he could fight out a desperate campaign in a pasteboard visor, while to friends and foes he contrived it should show like tempered steel. It had been his fate in the early part of his career to combat from a false position as well against as in favour of the great measures of his time. He advocated Protection when he had been to a certain extent compromised against it by his own admissions. He opposed Reform although he often avowed his sympathies with democratic progress; he had to champion it afterwards amid apologetic appeals to the opinions of his supporters. Proud of his race and lenient to its creed, he only tardily assented to the removal of its disabilities; and in Ireland he had to defend a Church doomed beforehand, which he had himself pronounced and doubtless believed an anomaly. Until the time arrived when he became the exponent of a definite foreign policy, and himself the chief actor in it, till his last accession to power we can scarcely recall a single great occasion on which he could have thrown himself without *arrière-pensée*, and in the fulness of conviction, into anything that rose above the nature of a party speech. If earnestness is the soul of oratory, it would be strange indeed if we could bestow higher praise than brilliancy on most of the speeches of Mr. Disraeli. His character and special gifts plunged him into battle and cabal; his talents in council and skirmish would have rusted in peace, and were fatal to the dignity of repose. Few men's political character has been more harshly attacked, and few statesmen ever addressed their protestations of patriotism and principle to more distrustful ears. If we grant some justice in the common sentiment, we must recollect that there is much extenuation for the relaxation of political morality when authority was so often detached from responsibility. What power he exercised was during the greater part of his career in Opposition, and then it was chiefly critical or obstructive. While on the Treasury benches he had long to accept his impulse from Liberal Opponents, or conciliate the opposition of extreme Radicals. At length a time arrived when he could actually direct the national policy. With a powerful Parliamentary majority, and the absolute confidence of his Sovereign, he may be almost said to have swayed for a time the councils of Europe. It is by his use of that ascendancy that posterity will chiefly judge him. Undoubtedly since then he has held a very different place in the public estimation. In his last Ministry the world recognized a resolute and consistent fulfilment of purposes deliberately formed and matured. It may be said of him, inverting the words of Tacitus, *Omnium consensu incapax imperii nisi imperusset.* Whatever may be the estimate of his public policy, in his personal career he has left an example of successful industry and determination that should encourage every one who looks to work and progress as the rule and end of life. He has left his mark and set his name on great public measures, and now that he is gone and they have passed into history, we can judge more charitably of motives to which his enemies frequently did grave injustice. We repeat again, what we said before, that often, where we believe him to have been mistaken and ill-advised, often when he changed his ground with a celerity unusual even in these days of rapid conversions, a subtle power of self-deception was at work that kept his acts and conscience in honest harmony. This remark applies to his long and arduous labours as an English party-leader, by which he gradually converted a dismayed and disorganized mob into a successful army. His foreign policy needs no such excuse. That policy was a consistent effort directed towards definite ends, and having for its object the maintenance and augmentation of the Empire, avoiding even the appearance of weakness, and deliberately preferring the risk of war to making even trivial concessions if they could be represented as involving national humiliation.

As this obituarist makes plain, Disraeli was 'a born politician' but not one who came from the traditional mould of British parliamentarians. It was through 'the force of character and brilliancy of talent which assured him a lasting triumph over obstacle that are matters of fact and history'. His Jewish birth and his relative lack of a formal education are properly dwelt upon, but there is no mention of his father's distinguished, if dilletantist, literary career and no estimate of the significance of Isaac D'Israeli's withdrawal from the Bevis Marks synagogue in 1817 and the subsequent baptism of his son. Disraeli was not strictly a self-made man but, as much of his fiction serves to suggest, he was certainly a self-fashioned one. His fascination with the Near East, which determined so much of his foreign policy and which has a direct bearing on significant elements in his novels, was almost certainly influenced by his experience of Syria and the Holy Land in 1830. From the time of his uneasy first appearances in the House of Commons he was determined to scale pre-existing political and social ladders in order to claim his place at the heart of the constitutional Establishment. He left the Commons when he was created Earl of Beaconsfield in 1876. He was made a Knight of the Garter in 1878. As a country landowner in Buckinghamshire he restored Hughenden Manor without any trace of architectural exoticism, he planted trees, paid for the reconstruction of the parish church and was accorded the rare honour of a private visit from Queen Victoria.

DANTE GABRIEL ROSSETTI

Painter and poet:
'There is in his best work a depth and a subdued glow of colour.'

9 APRIL 1882

MR. DANTE GABRIEL ROSSETTI died on Sunday evening, at Birchington-on-Sea, near Margate, where he had been staying some weeks for the improvement of his health. Mr. Rossetti was born in London in May, 1828, the son of Gabriel Rossetti, the famous Italian poet and Dante scholar, who had come to England as a refugee after the Neapolitan revolution in 1821. He showed artistic gifts at a very early age, and for a short time became a pupil of the Royal Academy. His first important picture was entitled 'Mary's Girlhood,' with one exception, the only work ever exhibited in London by the painter. Another early work, a triptych called 'The Seed of David,' is in the Cathedral of Llandaff. Mr. Rossetti's name became familiar to the public in connexion with the so-called Pre-Raphaelite movement, a style of painting founded essentially upon the early Florentine school, in combination with a strict adherence to nature, and strongly opposed to the platitudes of academic art as practised in those days. The revival of medievalism, initiated by such men as Mr. Madox-Brown, in whose studio Mr. Rossetti worked for some time, Mr. Millais, Mr. Holman Hunt, and later on Mr. Burne Jones, has exercised a profound influence on English art. The eccentricities of the school were treated with merciless ridicule by the critics, but the discussion thus raised tended in the end to attract public attention to subjects previously looked upon with indifference, and no amount of abuse was able to crush the fundamental principle of the new movement or the genius of the artists, who, as they grew into maturity, spontaneously abandoned their early mannerisms. Mr. Rossetti's individual bias – his speciality, if the term may be used – is traceable partly to his Italian origin, and partly to the associations of his youth. His father, as has already been said, was a lover of Dante, and his curious mystico-political explanation of the '*Divina Commodia*' still counts some adherents, especially among French commentators. The worship of the great Italian poet was with Mr. Rossetti hereditary, and from the 'Divine Comedy' and the '*Vita Nuova*' some of his finest pictorial ideas were derived. The large picture of Dante's vision of the dead Beatrice, recently purchased by the Liverpool Corporation, belongs to this class of subjects, and deserves, by its elaboration and deep poetic import, to be classed among the artist's finest works. Scarcely less beautiful, although less finished, is the early picture, which represents the first meeting of the poet with the lady of his love. Mr. Rossetti may be broadly stated to have been a colourist rather than a draughtsman. In the former respect he was, perhaps, unrivalled, certainly unsurpassed, by any living painter. There is in his best work a depth and a subdued glow of colour which surround his figures with an atmosphere of beauty, whatever the subject may happen to be. Apart from this, Mr. Rossetti had realized a very high type of female beauty, which, albeit somewhat monotonous, could never fail to rouse the admiration of those not satisfied with the prettinesses and clevernesses of conventional modern art. Such a picture as the 'Proserpine,' one of the artist's latest works, although consisting only of a single figure, is instinct with all the pathos of the antique legend, which would be fully understood even without the beautiful Italian sonnet which the artist has added by way of explanation. And this leads us to the second side of Mr. Rossetti's genius, which in him was inseparable from his artistic gift. He was as pictorial a poet as he was a poetic painter. His first literary effort also was inspired by Dante. It took the form of a collection of translations from 'The early Italian poets, from Ciullo d'Alcamo to Dante Alighieri, together with Dante's *Vita Nuova*,' published in 1861, and re-issued under the title of 'Dante and his Circle' in 1874. Both the spirit and form of the originals are rendered with marvellous fidelity, the translator's skill being shown in the prose portions of the '*Vita Nuova*,' perhaps, even more brilliantly than in the sonnets and canzoni. Mr. Rossetti's first original volume of 'Poems' was published in 1870 and at once established his reputation. The pictorial beauty of 'The Blessed Damozel,' the dramatic force of 'Sister Helen,' a ballad of genuine popular ring, the deep pathos of 'Jenny,' and the profound symbolism of the sonnets could not fail to impress all lovers of serious poetry, while the rhythmical charm of the shorter lyrics was as music in the ear. In addition to this, the absolute originality of these effusions could not be contested by those who were acquainted with the history of the Pre-Raphaelite or medieval movement in poetry. Mr. Rossetti, as we recently pointed out, was the originator of that movement, and his poems were produced and read by the few long before those of younger writers which preceded them in date of publication were thought of. That work of this class could not escape adverse criticism of a more or less reasonable kind might have been foreseen, and Mr. Rossetti had his full share of both admiration and abuse. He was, and partly is still, held responsible for the excesses of imitators who have caught his manner without his spirit. Even the vulgarities and affectations of the so-called 'aesthetes' have been gravely cited against him – with what degree of justice students of modern poetry may decide for themselves. It was, perhaps, partly owing to these misrepresentations that Mr. Rossetti waited ten years before publishing a second volume of poems which in many respects evinced even greater and more fully matured powers than the first. Of this book, entitled 'Ballads and Sonnets,' we have recently spoken, and need, therefore, not return to it, beyond expressing an opinion that the two narrative poems 'Rose Mary' and a 'King's Tragedy' the short lyric, 'Cloud Confines,' and some of the sonnets are likely to take permanent rank with the best poetic work of our time. Mr. Rossetti's death will be deeply felt by the admirers of his art and his poetry, and by his personal friends. Although well-read and an excellent talker, he shrank from general society, and in his latter years, when ill-health confined him to his house, his circle of acquaintance grew more and more limited. Only a few old friends used to frequent his studio in the quaint Elizabethan house in Cheyne-walk, Chelsea. As an artist he was very sensitive to criticism – favourable or unfavourable – and he seldom exhibited his pictures, although they were occasionally seen in public, chiefly in provincial towns. It is a curious fact that a painter should on this principle have achieved a reputation scarcely inferior to that of the most popular favourites of the day.

> There was an exoticism about Rossetti which enthralled his friends and delighted the many Victorian admirers of his work. He never really needed to exhibit and never felt obliged to pander to public taste, but his paintings sold well. His poetry, like his pictures, consistently drew inspiration from his Italian roots, and, above all, from Dante. Both were also shaped by the founding principles of the Pre-Raphaelite Brotherhood. The Brotherhood, formed in September 1848, had aimed to produce an art with a 'serious and elevated invention of subject, along with earnest scrutiny of visible facts, and an earnest endeavour to present them veraciously and exactly'. The Brotherhood fell apart in the early 1850s. The obituary makes little reference to Rossetti's complex private life. He had married his long-term but ailing model, Elizabeth Siddal, in 1860. In May 1861 she gave birth to a still-born child, and was found dead in February 1862 (the verdict at the inquest was accidental death). In October 1862 he moved to Tudor House, 16 Cheyne Walk in Chelsea (an eighteenth-century house, though once assumed to have been of sixteenth-century origin). Here the increasingly isolated painter set up his model Fanny Cornforth as housekeeper, amassed a collection of porcelain and antiques, and kept a menagerie of exotic animals. In the later 1860s he turned increasingly to his poetry and began an intense sexual relationship with William Morris's wife, Jane. His last book, *Ballads and Sonnets*, appeared in 1881 and, in debt and addicted to the drug chloral, he retired to Birchington-on-Sea in Kent. He died there on Easter Day, 9 April 1882. He is buried in Birchington churchyard.

CHARLES DARWIN

Naturalist: 'One must seek back to Newton or even Copernicus to find a man whose influence on human thought and methods of looking at the universe has been as radical.'

19 APRIL 1882

EXACTLY A YEAR to a day has separated the deaths of two of the most powerful men of this century, some have said of any century; and those who care for the task will find some very curious analogies between the progress and the ultimate results of the work of the two men, totally different as were the spheres in which they exercised their remarkable powers. On April 19, 1881, all the civilized world held its breath at the news of the death of Lord Beaconsfield; not less must be the effect upon the most civilized part of the civilized world when the announcement of the death of Charles Darwin flashes over the face of that earth whose secrets he has done more than any other to reveal. All who knew anything of Mr. Darwin know that, massive as he seemed, it was only by the greatest care and the simplest habits that he was able to maintain a moderate amount of health and strength. Mr. Darwin had been suffering for some time past from weakness of the heart, but had continued to do a slight amount of experimental work up to the last. He was taken ill on the night of Tuesday last, when he had an attack of pain in the chest with faintness and nausea. The latter lasted with more or less intermission during Wednesday and culminated in his death, which took place at about 4 o'clock on Wednesday afternoon. He remained fully conscious to within a quarter of an hour of his death. His wife and several of his children were present at the closing scene. During his illness he had been attended by Dr. Norman Moore, Dr. Andrew Clarke, Dr. Moxon, and Dr. Alfrey, of St. Mary Cray. Mr. Darwin leaves besides his widow a family of five sons and two daughters. It has not yet been decided when his remains will be interred, but the place of burial will be in the quiet churchyard of the village of Down, near which place Mr. Darwin spent the last forty years of his life.

Fifteen volumes lie before us and nearly as many memoirs large and small, the product of 45 years' work – a product which, in quantity, would do credit to the most robust constitution. But when we consider Mr. Darwin's always feeble health and his deliberately slow method of work, never hasting but rarely resting, the result seems marvellous. But wonderful as this is under the circumstances, it is not by mere quantity that Mr. Darwin's work will be judged; the quantity is of chief

importance in respect of the multifarious channels through which his influence has spread.

On the great principle of hereditariness, of which he himself was the prophet and expounder, Mr. Darwin could not help being a remarkable man. Through his father descended from Erasmus Darwin, one of the most remarkable and original men of his age, and through his mother from Josiah Wedgwood, a man in his own line of scarcely less originality, Mr. Darwin was bound, under favourable surroundings, to develop powers far beyond the average. Charles Robert Darwin (he seldom used the second name) was the son of Robert Waring Darwin, the third son by his first marriage of Erasmus Darwin, best known to the general reader by his scientifico-poetic work 'The Botanic Garden.' The late Mr. Darwin's father was a physician at Shrewsbury, who, although a man of considerable originality, devoted his powers almost entirely to his profession; his mother, as we have said, was a daughter of Josiah Wedgwood. He was born at Shrewsbury on February 12, 1809, so that he has died in his 74th year. Mr. Darwin was educated at Shrewsbury School under Dr. Butler, afterwards Bishop of Lichfield. In 1825, he went to Edinburgh University, therein following the example of his grandfather, where he spent two sessions. Here, among other subjects, he studied marine zoology, and at the close of 1826 read before the Plinian Society of the University two short papers, probably his first, one of them on the Ova of Flustra. From Edinburgh Mr. Darwin went to Christ's College, Cambridge, where he took his Bachelor's degree in 1831, proceeding to M. A. in 1837. The interval was of epoch-making importance. We believe that Darwin, like Murchison, was a keen fox-hunter in his youth, and that it was in the field that his great habits in observation were first awakened. In the autumn of 1831, Captain Fitzroy having offered to give up part of his own cabin to any naturalist who would accompany Her Majesty's ship Beagle in her surveying voyage round the world, Mr. Darwin volunteered his services without salary, but on condition that he should have entire disposal of his collections, all of which be ultimately deposited in various public institutions. The Beagle sailed from England December 27, 1831, and returned October, 28, 1836, having thus been absent nearly five years. In more ways than one these five years were the most eventful of Mr. Darwin's life. During these five years the Beagle circumnavigated the world, and it is not too much to say that single-handed, Mr. Darwin during the voyage did more for natural history in all its varied departments than any expedition has done since; much more when we consider the momentous results that followed. No one can read the simple, yet intensely interesting 'Naturalist's Voyage Round the World,' without tracing in it the germs of all that Mr. Darwin has subsequently done in natural science. Simplicity and freedom from technicality have been the leading characteristics of all Mr. Darwin's best known and most influential works, and in this volume on the Voyage of the Beagle there is scarcely a page that will not interest any ordinarily intelligent man, and many pages that must claim the attention of the mere reader of stories of adventure. Full of incident it is, especially during the author's lone sojourn in South America and in the vicinity of Magellan's Straits. Mr. Darwin's phenomenal genius as a scientific observer is seen throughout – when watching the method of catching and taming the wild horses of the

Pampas, as when investigating the structure of the coral reefs of the Pacific. The first edition was published early in 1845, and the second was dedicated to Sir Charles Lyell, who, with his usual acuteness, early perceived the remarkable originality of the young naturalist, and to whom the latter was indebted for much wise counsel and help, as is evident from the recently published Life and Letters of the great geologist. That was not the only immediate result of this great voyage; under the superintendence of Mr. Darwin, and with abundant description and annotation by him, the Zoology of the expedition was published before the narrative, in 1840, with Professor Owen, Mr. Waterhouse, the Rev. L. Jenyns, and Mr. Bell as contributing specialists. Not only so, but still also before the general narrative, Mr. Darwin published his first original contribution to science in his 'Structure and Distribution of Coral Reefs' (1842). This work for the first time shed clear light upon the method of work of the tiny creatures whose exquisite fabrics are spread over the face of the Pacific. True, quite recently Mr. Murray has broached a new theory, or rather modification of Darwin's theory, which is beginning to find acceptance; but even if universally accepted it will not detract from the original estimate of the work of the Beagle naturalist. Still further, we have as direct result of the voyage in a volume, published in 1844, on the 'Volcanic Islands visited during the Voyage of the Beagle,' and in 1846, 'Geological Observations in South America.' Both these works are even now referred to by geologists as classical, and as having suggested lines of research of the highest fertility. In the Transactions of the Geological Society, moreover, other memoirs suggested by the results of the voyage will be found, one as early as 1838. But even that is not the earliest important paper of the great observer. Just a year after his return, in November, 1837, he read to the Geological Society a paper, to be found in its Transactions, 'On the Formation of Vegetable Mould.' This paper gave the result of observations begun some time before, observations only completed in his latest published work, that on 'Earthworms,' reviewed in these columns only a few months ago. Experiments were arranged for, we then pointed out, which took 40 years to ripen. Such far-seeing deliberation can only be the attribute of the greatest minds, which can see the end from the beginning. Other results of the voyage in botany and entomology we could refer to were it needful.

But, the greatest result of all was probably that on the mind of the naturalist himself. Passing over a generation, the spirit of his grandfather seems to have re-appeared in Charles Darwin with intensified power and precision. We need not here enter into the delicate distinctions which exist between the developmental theories of Erasmus, which were prematurely sown in unfruitful and unprepared soil, and those of his greater grandson, which have revolutionized research and thought in every department of human activity. The inherited germ was doubtless rapidly and fully developed during the splendid opportunities presented by the voyage of the Beagle. Throughout all his subsequent work the influence of this voyage is apparent, and continued reference is made to the stores of observation laid up during those eventful five years. Mr. Darwin's subsequent life was totally uneventful. Three years after his return, in the beginning of 1839, he married his cousin, Emma Wedgwood, and in 1842 he took up his residence at Down, Beckenham, Kent, of which county he was a magistrate. There he has lived since; and there on Wednesday he died. It is known to his friends that Mr. Darwin never quite recovered from the evil effects of his long voyage. He himself tells us that during nearly the whole time he suffered from sea-sickness, an affliction which no constitution could altogether withstand. As we have said, it has only been by the quietest living and the greatest carefulness that Mr. Darwin was able to keep himself in moderate health and working order. His habits and manners were of childlike simplicity, his bearing of the most winning geniality and his modesty and evident unconsciousness of his own greatness almost phenomenal. In sending a letter or contribution to a journal, he asked for its insertion with a doubting hesitancy, rare even in a tiro. His personal influence on young scientific men can with difficulty be calculated; his simple readiness to listen and suggest and help has won the gratitude of many an aspiring observer.

Since he took up his residence at Down, Mr. Darwin's life has been marked mainly by the successive publication of those works which have revolutionized modern thought. In 1859 was published what may be regarded as the most momentous of all his works, 'The Origin of Species by means of Natural Selection.' No one who had not reached manhood at the time can have any idea of the consternation caused by the publication of this work. We need not repeat the anathemas that were hurled at the head of the simple-minded observer, and the prophecies of ruin to religion and morality if Mr. Darwin's doctrines were accepted. No one, we are sure, would be more surprised than the author himself at the results which followed. But all this has long passed. The work, slowly at first, but with increasing rapidity, made its way to general acceptance, and its anathematizers have been bound to find a *modus vivendi* between their creeds and the theories propounded in the 'Origin of Species.' The revolution in scientific doctrine and scientific method brought about by the publication of this work was ably pointed out by Professor Huxley two years ago in his lecture on 'The Coming of Age of the Origin of Species.' Mr. Huxley says:–

> 'In fact, those who have watched the progress of science within the last ten years will bear me out to the full when I assert that there is no field of biological inquiry in which the influence of the "Origin of Species" is not traceable; the foremost men of science in every country are either avowed champions of its leading doctrines, or at any rate abstain from opposing them; a host of young

and ardent investigators seek for and find inspiration and guidance in Mr. Darwin's great work; and the general doctrine of Evolution, to one side of which it gives expression, finds in the phenomena of biology a firm base of operations wherein it may conduct its conquest of the whole realm of nature.'

But it is not only in physical and natural science that the revolutionary influence of the 'Origin of Species' is seen. It is not too much to say that the doctrines propounded in this volume, on 'The Descent of Man,' and other subsequent works, have influenced thought and research in every direction. It has been said, perhaps prematurely, that one must seek back to Newton or even Copernicus, to find a man whose influence on human thought and methods of looking at the universe has been as radical as that of the naturalist who has just died. Of course Mr. Darwin's originality has been assailed. Kant, Laplace, Buffon, Erasmus Darwin, and others, and of course Lucretius, have been brought forward as the real originators of the fertile idea which has taken its name from Mr. Charles Darwin. Give these old-world worthies all the credit which is justly their due, and it is not little; let it be granted that Darwin received the first initiative in his fertile career of research from a study of what they had done by his predecessors; and yet how comes it that these old theories fell comparatively dead and bore no substantial fruit. One reason must be that, as propounded by Mr. Darwin, the theory of evolution had a mature vitality which compelled acceptance, and the phenomenal vigour of which is seen in the results. Mr. Darwin's great theory, in some of its parts, may require modification; he himself latterly, we believe, did not seek to maintain it in all its original integrity. As has been suggested, some greater law may yet be found which will cover Darwinism and take a wider sweep but, whatever development science may assume, Mr. Darwin will in all the future stand out as one of the giants in scientific thought and scientific investigation.

All Mr. Darwin's subsequent works were developments in different directions of the great principles applied in the 'Origin of Species.' Between 1844 and 1854 he published through the Ray and other societies various monographs, which even his greatest admirers admit do not do him the highest credit as a minute anatomist. His next great work, published in 1862, was that on the 'Fertilization of Orchids;' this, with the work on 'Cross and Self-Fertilization of Plants' (1876), and that on the 'Forms of Flowers' (1878), and various papers in scientific publications on the agency of insects in fertilization, opened up a new field which in his own hands and the hands of his numerous disciples have led to results of the greatest interest and the greatest influence on a knowledge of the ways of plants. Other works belonging to this category are those 'On the Movements and Habits of Climbing Plants,' 'Insectivorous Plants,' and 'The Movements of Plants' (1881), all of which opened up perfectly fresh fields of investigation, and shed light on the most intimate workings of nature. Mr Darwin's influence in these, as in others of his works, has acted like an inspiration, leading men to follow methods and attain results which a quarter of a century ago were beyond the scope of the most fantastic dream. But, perhaps, the works with which the name of Mr. Darwin is most intimately associated in popular estimation, and indeed the works which have had the deepest influence on the tendencies of modern thought and research in those departments in which humanity is most deeply interested, are those bearing on the natural history of man. Nine years after the publication of the 'Origin of Species,' appeared (1868), in two volumes, the great collection of instances and experiments bearing on the 'Variation of Plants and Animals under Domestication.' We have called this a collection of facts, and the same term might be applied, with greater or less exactness, to all the other works of Mr. Darwin. This is the characteristic Darwinian method. Years and years are spent in the accumulation of facts with open-minded watchfulness as to the tendency of the results. The expressed inferences in Mr. Darwin's works are few; he piles instance on instance and experiment on experiment, and almost invariably the conclusion to which he comes seems but the expression of the careful and unbiassed reader's own thought. Nowhere is this more signally evident than in the work on Domesticated Animals and Plants. The results which were brought out in those volumes were full of significance, while at the same time they afforded abundant occasion for the opponents of Darwinism to scoff and pour harmless contempt on the whole line of inquiry; forgetting or wilfully shutting their eyes to the fact that the results which Mr. Darwin showed were possible *in petto* bore no proportion to the gigantic efforts of nature through untold ages. The chapters on Inheritance in this work were full of significance, and seemed a natural transition to the work which followed three years later (1871) – 'The Descent of Man and Selection in relation to Sex.' Even greater consternation was caused in many circles by the publication of this work than by 'The Origin of Species.' And the reason of this is obvious. Not only did it seem directly to assail the *amour propre* of humanity, but to imperil some of its most deeply cherished beliefs. With wonderful rapidity, however, did men of all shades of belief manage to reconcile themselves to the new and disturbing factor introduced into the sphere of scientific and philosophical speculation. All sorts of halfway refuges were sought for and found by those whose mental comfort was threatened, and, again, as before, there was little difficulty in finding a *modus vivendi* between two sets of doctrines that at first sight seemed totally irreconcilable. After all, what have the highest aspirations of mankind to fear from the investigations and speculations of a man who is capable of writing as Mr. Darwin does in the concluding pages of his 'Descent of Man.' 'Important as the struggle for existence has been, and even still is, yet as far as the highest part of man's nature is concerned, there are other agencies more important. For the moral qualities are advanced either directly or indirectly, much more through the effects of habit, the reasoning powers, instruction, religion, &c., than through natural selection; through to this latter agency may be safely attributed the social instincts which afforded the basis for the development of the moral sense . . . For my own part I would as soon be descended from that heroic little monkey who braved his dreaded enemy to save the life of his keeper, or from that old baboon who, descending from the mountains, carried away in triumph his young comrade from a crowd of astonished dogs – as from a savage who delights to torture his enemies, offers up bloody sacrifices, practices infanticide without remorse, treats his wives like slaves, knows no decency, and is haunted by the grossest superstition. Man may be excused for feeling some pride at having risen, though not through his own exertions, to the very summit of the organic scale; and the fact of his having thus risen instead of having been aboriginally placed there may give him hope for a still higher destiny in the distant future. But we are not here concerned with hopes or fears, only with the truth as far as our reason permits us to discern it; and I have given the evidence to the best of my ability. We must, however, acknowledge, as it seems to me that man with all his noble qualities, with sympathy which feels for the most debased, with benevolence which extends not only to other men, but to the humblest living creature, with his godlike intellect which has penetrated into the movements and constitution of the solar system – with all these exalted powers, man still bears in his bodily frame the indelible stamp of his low origin.' Among scientific men themselves, among those who welcomed the Darwinian method and the distinctive doctrines of Darwinism, none of the master's works have probably met with more criticism than that on the Descent of Man. Not that the naturalists of the highest standing have any hesitation in accepting the general principles illustrated in the 'Descent of Man;' the ablest and most candid biologists admit that in that direction the truth seems to lie; but that the various stages are so incomplete, the record is so imperfect, that before stereotyping their beliefs it would be wise to wait for more light. The general conclusion is not doubted, but how it has been reached by nature is by no means evident. And in this connexion we cannot do better than quote the words of Professor Huxley in the lecture already alluded to, and which, we are sure, Mr. Darwin himself would have endorsed with all his strength.

> 'History warns us, however, that it is the customary fate of new truths to begin as heresies and to end as superstitions; and, as matters now stand, it is hardly rash to anticipate that in another 20 years, the new generation, educated under the influences of the present day, will be in danger of accepting the main doctrines of the Origin of Species with as little reflection, and it may be with as little justification as so many of our contemporaries 20 years ago, rejected them. Against any such a consummation let us all devoutly pray, for the scientific

> spirit is of more value than its products, and irrationally-held truths may be more harmful than reasoned errors. Now, the essence of the scientific spirit is criticism. It tells us that to whatever doctrine claiming our assent we should reply, Take it if you can compel it. The struggle for existence holds as much in the intellectual as in the physical world. A theory is a species of thinking, and its right to exist is co-extensive with its power of resisting extinction by its rivals.'

As a sort of side issue of the 'Descent of Man,' and as throwing light upon the doctrines developed therein, with much more of independent interest and suggestiveness, 'The Expression of the Emotions in Men and Animals' was published in 1872. This is, perhaps, the most amusing of Mr. Darwin's works, while at the same time it is one which evidently involved observation and research of the most minute and careful kind. It is one, moreover, which shows how continually and instinctively the author was on the watch for instances that were likely to have any bearing on the varied lines of his researches.

To attempt to reckon up the influence which Mr. Darwin's multifarious work has had upon modern thought and modern life in all its phases seems as difficult a task as it would be to count the number and trace the extent of the sound-waves from a park of artillery. The impetus he has given to science, not only in his own, but in other departments, can only find a parallel in Newton. Through his influence the whole method of seeking after knowledge has been changed, and the increasing rapidity with which the results are every day developed becomes more and more bewildering. To what remote corners in religion, in legislation, in education, in every-day life, from Imperial Assemblies and venerable Universities to humble board schools and remote Scotch manses, the impetus initiated on board the Beagle and developed at the quiet and comfortable home at Beckenham, has reached, those who are in the whirl and sweep of it we are not in a position to say. Under the immediate influence of the sad loss we can only state a few obvious facts and make a few quite as obvious reflections; in time we may be able to realize how great a man now belongs to the past. That Mr. Darwin's work was not done nor his capacity for work exhausted was well enough seen in his recently-published work on Worms; and with the help of his able and congenial sons, Mr. George and Mr. Francis Darwin, we might have hoped for one or two more of the familiar green-covered volumes.

Mr. Darwin's elder brother, the faithful friend of Mrs. Carlyle, died about a year ago, leaving his younger brother his principal heir; the latter, however, has all along been in comfortable circumstances. It goes without saying that honours and medals were showered upon Mr. Darwin by learned societies all the world over: from Germany, where his disciples led by Häckel, have out-Darwined Darwin, he received a Knighthood of the Prussian Order of Merit.

From respect to the memory of Mr. Darwin, the Linnean Society yesterday adjourned after transacting formal business only. Sir John Lubbock, the president, addressing the meeting, said they would, no doubt, all have heard the sad news of the irreparable loss which science, the country, and their society had experienced in the death of Mr. Darwin. Only a few days ago they had the pleasure of hearing a paper of his – unhappily, his last – which showed no sign of any abatement of vigour. That was not the occasion to speak of the value of his scientific work, but he might say that while the originality and profound character of his researches had revolutionized natural history, he had also added enormously to its interest, and given, if he might so say, new life to biological science. Many of them, and no one more than himself, had also to mourn one of the kindest and best of friends. He begged to propose, as a small mark of respect to the memory of their late illustrious countryman, the greatest – alas, that he could no longer say of living naturalists, that, after the formal business was concluded, the society should adjourn.

Darwin was not to be buried at Downe, as this obituarist supposes, but in the North Aisle of Westminster Abbey, thanks to the influence exerted on the dean of Westminster by the then President of the Royal Society. His funeral took place on 26 April and was attended by, amongst many others, one of his earliest admirers, Thomas Hardy. As this substantial tribute suggests, Darwin's *On the Origin of Species by Means of Natural Selection* had shaken the scriptural foundations of nineteenth-century Christianity. It had also profoundly altered how many Victorians looked at themselves and at their civilisation. In the post-Darwinian world, philosophy as much as science had to adjust to the idea that chance begot order and that fortuitous events resulted in the physical law of natural selection. The Linnæan Society, mentioned at the end of the obituary, had been founded in 1788 and was incorporated in 1802. It was to the Society on 1 July 1858 that Darwin and Alfred Russel Wallace jointly presented the paper 'On the Tendency of Species to form Varieties; and on the Perpetuation of Varieties and Species by Natural Means of Selection'. Darwin, prompted by sight of a memoir by Wallace outlining parallel conclusions to his own, had agreed to this joint presentation in order to make his own theories public for the first time. The paper was printed in the Society's journal in 1858. *On the Origin of Species* was first published in November 1859.

ANTHONY TROLLOPE

Novelist: 'He was never guilty of the deadly mistake of becoming dull.'

6 DECEMBER 1882

OUR READERS WILL hear with deep regret of the death of Mr. Anthony Trollope. Seized suddenly at the dinner table, only a very few weeks ago, with something in the nature of a paralytic attack, from the first anxiety was felt as to his recovery. He rallied more or less and from time to time, thanks to a naturally vigorous constitution, but he cannot be said to have ever recovered either speech or perfect consciousness. Within the last day or two it had become evident that the end was drawing near, and he died at 6 o'clock last evening. The circumstances being as they were, this was hardly to be regretted. Had he lived or lingered on, the brilliant novelist would probably never again have been himself; and we can imagine no sadder fate to a man of his intellect and energy than renouncing the pursuit which had brought him both fame and fortune. As it is, he was removed in a lusty maturity, and before decay had begun to cripple his indefatigable industry or dull the brightness of his versatile fancy.

Mr. Trollope was far from being an old man, and might well have looked forward to further years of activity. He was born an the 24th of April in the famous 'Waterloo year,' and was a son of the gifted lady who wrote 'Widow Barnaby,' and whose observations on the manners of our Transatlantic kinsfolk caused such dire indignation to the citizens of the Union. He had been educated at Winchester and Harrow; and shortly after leaving school, was appointed to a clerkship in the Post Office. As he brought the strictest business habits to the constructions of his fictions, so he threw himself with characteristic earnestness into his official occupations. So much so, that in his later life, he was repeatedly chosen to negotiate delicate international postal arrangements with different Continental Governments. But although Trollope went steadily in official harness, the bent of his literary instincts was irresistible, and he yielded to it very early by way of distraction. We believe that the first of his acknowledged and republished novels were 'The Macdermotts of Ballycloran,' issued in 1841, and the more lively 'Kellys and O'Kellys,' which made its appearance in the following year, But we have Mr. Trollope's own authority for saying that he had written other novels before these, which, we presume, he had subsequently recognized as comparative failures. We can still read the melancholy story of the Macdermotts with interest, while there is a great deal of genuine Hibernian drollery in the lively social sketches contained in 'the

O'Kelly's.' Having felt his strength and discovered his vein, thenceforth Mr. Trollope has poured forth from his teeming brain an inexhaustible stream of popular fictions. The actual quantity of paper which he has covered must have been marvellous, putting quality out of the question. He used to boast, and we doubt not with reason, that he was the most prolific novelist of his day – which probably means the most prolific novelist this country has seen. Of the quality of his work we shall have to say a word or two by-and-by. And all the time, or at least until about eight years ago, when he resigned the appointment, he was tied day after day to his desk in the Post Office. Nothing could have carried him through the amount of labour he undertook, save a singularly happy combination of circumstances. He had an admirable constitution; he had an easy nature; he was the most methodical romance writer of whom we have ever heard, Mr. Charles Reade himself not excepted. Above all, he was blessed with the most remarkable literary temperament which has come within the range of our knowledge or experience. He had literally a 'five o'clock in the morning genius,' to parody the memorable saying of Napoleon; and setting himself down to certain hours of what might have seemed daily drudgery, he could fairly rely upon the average merits of his work. As a rule, he rose early and worked on till 11. Then, at the stroke of the clock, the pen was laid down, however lightly it might be turning off the sentences or though it might be working up to the climax of a sensational scene. What is remarkable, taken in connexion with our knowledge of his manner of work, is the wonderful uniformity of quality in each of his novels. Some were better; others very decidedly worse; but each was very much the same throughout. It appeared that when he had hit upon a happy idea or a constellation of good ideas, he might be trusted to turn them to excellent purpose. When he had been unfortunate in striking out the main scheme of a plot, or had been unlucky in his crude conceptions of his characters, no subsequent skill or efforts could retrieve the original mistakes. It may have been this which induced him to keep to those characters which had best pleased their creator and made the deepest impression on the public. Nay, we understand that he carried precision of idea and expression so far that he could write upon either side of each page, and that the very number of the words on the folio were duly counted and noted. But the work in the Post Office would hardly have gone forward so well, considering the briskness of the daily novel manufacture, had it not been for his hearty enjoyment of recreation. Mr. Trollope liked society, he delighted in his rubber at whist, but he was still more devoted to hunting. For long he had his residence in the country; for years he continued to hunt his three days in the week; and welter weight as he was, he managed to be well mounted. He turned his hunting experience and his knowledge of horse flesh to profitable purpose, as he did everything else. They resulted in a series of picturesque hunting sketches, and in innumerable touches true to the life which are scattered broadcast throughout all his novels.

Besides all that, he found time to travel, generally when his strength needed recruiting. His volumes on America, on Australia and South Africa were serious contributions to our acquaintance with those countries; and we need hardly say that the genial novelist was a welcome visitor wherever he went. But by far the best and most spirited of his books of travel was his little volume on the 'West Indies and the Spanish Main.' Nowhere do we remember to have seen more brilliant pictures of those islands in their decay, which the author of 'Tom Cringle' had described in their glory. In our opinion, they throw those in Kingsley's 'At Last' altogether into the shade; while his social sketches taken among the planters and his slightly caricatured portraits of the blacks, in their several ways are inimitable. Besides his books of travel, he found time to write, with more or less success, the biographies of Julius Cæsar and of Cicero; while among his latest productions is the little memoir of Lord Palmerston, which has received almost universal commendation from critics of very opposite politics.

But it is by his novels, after all, that he will live and must be judged; and of his novels we must say something more before concluding. Their general level throughout remained much the same. He was never guilty of the deadly mistake of becoming dull by aiming at being over-deep or metaphysical, and he had carefully cultivated the faculty of being entertaining. And within certain definite limits, though the limits were by no means narrow, the range of versatility was wonderful. The books that first brought him substantial profit and fame were 'The Warden,' and 'Barchester Towers,' novels which are ecclesiastical rather than religious. We might have fancied that the author had been swaddled in surplices and cradled to the cawing of the rooks in some shady cathedral close. When asked how he managed to make himself so thoroughly at home among the clergy, he answered that he had trusted less to knowledge than to invention. If it were so, we can only say that his speculations are worth the best information of most other writers. Then, if we pass from cathedral chapters or divinity to law, we have only to assist at the famous trial in 'Orley Farm' to be half persuaded that the author must be a practising barrister or a solicitor notorious in the Criminal Courts. As for his doctors, he more seldom needs to go into the technicalities of physic; but what can be better than his representations of consultations and death-bed scenes, with their Filgraves and Thornes and Sir Omicron Pies. The inimitable Dr. Thorne is, of course, a personage by himself; and is familiarized to us by the very decided idiosyncrasy which is merely coloured by his professional pursuits. And talking of Dr. Thorne leads us to remark that Trollope can boast of one rare distinction which is a conclusive proof of his standing in his craft. He has enriched our English fiction with characters destined to survive. As to how many of these there may be, no doubt there will be differences of opinion, but we can dare to name several whose titles are altogether incontestable. To begin with, there is that venerable Warden of Hiram's

Hospital; with the softness and firmness so blended in his nature, and the gentle spirit that was nevertheless too high to stoop to anything that might trouble his sensitive conscience. There is that very different type of clergyman – though a scarcely less admirable one – the Rev. Mr. Crawley, learning, in the depths of his despondent and much enduring misery, the lesson from the bricklayer that 'it is dogged that does it.' There is that most autocratic among-ecclesiastical dignitaries, the Rev. Mrs. Proudie the very much better half of the Bishop of Barchester. Next we have the motley group of statesmen and politicians, with Plantagenet Palliser at their head, become Duke of Omnium and Premier; and the consistency of whose attributes is so excellently developed and preserved in that comparatively recent novel of 'The Duke's Children.' There are fascinating scamps like Mr. Sowerby, and commercial travellers like Moulder; there are *nouveaux riches* like Scatcherd, and strong-minded spinsters like Miss Dunstable; and such embodiments of maidenly beauty and good-humoured innocence as Lucy Roberts and Grace Crawley and Lily Dale, which surprise us as being realized rather than idealized by a middle-aged gentleman. In our opinion and, we believe, in his own, the most perfect novel Mr. Trollope ever wrote was his 'Last Chronicle of Barset,' and its chief defect was the introduction of a subsidiary story to spin it out to the regulation three-volume length. Mr. Trollope has gone, and it will be hard to fill his place as the brightest among the contributors of fiction to our most popular periodicals. But those who will miss him most are the many personal friends to whom he was endeared by his kindly nature and his genial manners; and we cannot resist a melancholy suspicion that if he had relaxed a little sooner he might have been spared to us the longer. Anxiety rather than actual work may have been injurious, when he began to grow nervous under the strain of keeping engagements against time.

This appreciation of Anthony Trollope was not able to draw on Trollope's own account of his life, published in his quirky *An Autobiography* in October 1883, ten months after its author's death. Nevertheless, the obituarist's selective critical observations on Trollope's output as a writer generally stand the test of time. Although the obituary praises the novelist's supposedly intimate knowledge of the lives and concerns of his fictional clergymen, lawyers and doctors, there is significantly no discussion of Trollope's acute understanding of the workings of government and no mention of his abortive foray into politics as MP for Beverley. There is also no reference to his other claim to fame beyond his achievement as a writer: the introduction to mainland Britain of the pillar box.

RICHARD WAGNER

Composer: 'A star of the first magnitude . . . his work will have a lasting effect on the art of the present and of the future.'

13 FEBRUARY 1883

THE DEATH OF RICHARD WAGNER will be felt all the more deeply as it was entirely unexpected. Although in his 70th year, his vitality seemed unexhausted – inexhaustible. Quite lately a message full of life and cheerfulness reached his friends from Venice, where he was living in retirement for a few months to recover from the fatigue of the *Parsifal* performances in July last year. Wagner was staying at the Palazzo Vendramin Calergi with his wife and children, and Liszt, his father-in-law and dearest friend, was with them on a visit. 'Those who wish to see him,' Signor Filippi wrote in a musical contemporary a little more than a month ago, 'may find him nearly every day on the Piazza di San Marco, between 4 and 5, taking his daily walk, sometimes with his wife, at others preceded or followed by all his children. He often sits alone on one of the marble steps which support the Byzantine columns of the cathedral, meditating or resting from his work.' Madame Wagner's birthday falling on Christmas Eve, her husband intended to prepare a musical surprise for her. The long-lost manuscript of a juvenile symphony performed 50 years before at Leipsic had recently been re-discovered. This Wagner rehearsed with the orchestra of the Liceo Benedetto Marcello, and had it played for his wife and children, who, together with Liszt, were all the audience. Of this family celebration and of the symphony thus rescued from oblivion for a brief moment, Wagner gave an account in a letter addressed to an intimate friend, the editor of a German musical journal. Few who read that letter, written in Wagner's happiest vein, could have predicted that a little more than a month after it was penned the brain, so full of thought and humour and plans for the future, from which it flowed would be at rest for ever.

That the death of Wagner extinguishes a star of the first magnitude, and that his work will have a lasting effect on the art of the present and of the future, that he was indeed a great power – all this is acknowledged by those most hostile to the movement inaugurated by him. It may, indeed, be doubted whether a similar combination of gifts has ever been witnessed in the same individual. If it is remembered that the same man whose music has revolutionized the world of art was also the author of dramas considered by some as literary efforts of the highest order, and that he designed and superintended the rendering of those dramas down to the minutest details of scene painting and scene shifting, one may well be astonished at the energy and vastness of mental power required for those various tasks. The influence of a genius of this kind cannot be confined to one country; it is of its nature international. In England Wagner counts perhaps more genuine and unbiased admirers than in Germany itself. Last year the entire list of his works then in existence, from *Rienzi* down to *Götterdämmerung*, was performed in London within less than six months, before audiences including the various strata of society, from the Prince of Wales downwards, whose enthusiasm never seemed to flag. At Brussels a similar result was quite recently attained by the *Ring of the Nibelung*. In Italy the earlier operas have been given with much success, and the school of that country has not escaped the influence of the great German master. Verdi in his last and finest opera, *Aïda*, has paid undisguised tribute to Wagner's genius, and Boito, the most promising of the younger composers, is his stanch champion and the translator of his music-dramas. From the Paris stage Wagner is excluded by political animosities caused partly by his own fault. Smarting under the defeat of his *Tannhäuser*, hooted off the stage of the Grand Opera before it had been heard, the composer wrote during the siege of Paris a burlesque drama ridiculing the beleaguered city in terms neither generous nor witty. This breach of taste the Parisians have never forgiven him, and his works have been shut out from French theatres. But the audiences of the leading concerts in Paris – those of Pasdeloup, of Colonne, and Lamoureux – have for years applauded extracts from Wagner's operas to the echo, and one need only open the scores of the best French composers of our time to see that they have studied the works of the German master to some purpose. The design of Gounod's *Redemption*, to quote but one instance, is based upon the 'leit-motive' or representative theme, a device of dramatic characterization which the history of music will identify with the name of Wagner.

To determine the loss which the development of art has sustained by the composer's death at this juncture it would be necessary to enter the field of conjecture. It is impossible to say what a man of his indomitable energy would have done even at the age of 70. That he would have gone on working is not a matter of doubt. Whether such work as he might still have achieved would have added to his fame is a different question. Even the energy of a Titan must begin to flag at last, and to see Wagner's strength gradually decline would have been a sight sadder almost than that of his death in the full possession of his power. Hopes and fears such as these have now been set at rest. The fact remains that Wagner's life-work, such as it is, is in itself a complete and perfect thing. He believed himself charged with a mission, and that mission is fulfilled. Whether dramatic music is a better or a worse thing for what he has made it, certain it is that it can never again be what it was before him, no more than a river can flow back to its source. Even those most adverse to Wagner's art must grant him the place of a great reformer in the history of art. As to the nature of the reform initiated by him, there can be little doubt. The composer himself has elucidated the point in those theoretical writings which his enemies believed to be fatal to his claims as a spontaneous creator. Such an opinion, it may be parenthetically stated, is founded upon a misconception of psychological and historic facts. It is an entire mistake to think that Wagner wrote his operas according to and in illustration of a preconceived scheme. His most important theoretical work, *Oper und Drama*, was written about 1850. Ten years before his practical reform of the opera had begun with the *Flying Dutchman*, and it was further developed in *Tannhäuser* (1845) and *Lohengrin* (1849). It was from these works spontaneously conceived as well as from those of other composers that Wagner deduced his theory and not *vice versa*. The *Flying Dutchman*, so far from being the outgrowth of a doctrine, is perhaps the most subjective work in dramatic literature. It was written in the darkest period of Wagner's career, when in Paris homeless and friendless he was nearly brought to the verge of starvation. To express his mood in these circumstances the conventional pomp of the grand opera which he had introduced in *Rienzi* no longer sufficed him, and he had recourse to the pure mythical type of the weary mariner tossed by the waves of the ocean, homeless and friendless like himself. It was this transition from historic to mythical subject-matter which involved a commensurate change of musical treatment. For with Wagner poetry and music were always one, the latter flowing from the former with organic necessity. This is what he himself says on the point:–

> 'The plastic unity and simplicity of the mythical subjects allowed of the concentration of the action on certain important and decisive points, and thus enabled me to rest on fewer scenes with a perseverance sufficient to expound the motive to its ultimate dramatic consequences The nature of the subject, therefore, could not induce me, in sketching my scenes, to consider in advance their adaptability to any particular musical form, the kind of musical treatment being in each case necessitated by these scenes themselves. It could, therefore, not enter my mind to engraft on this my musical form, growing as it did out of the nature of the scenes, the traditional forms of operatic music, which could not but have marred and interrupted its organic development. I never thought of contemplating, on principle and as a deliberate reformer, the destruction of the aria, duet, and other operatic forms, but the dropping of these forms followed consistently from the nature of my subjects.'

These words contain the gist of the reformatory or negative tendency of Wagner's art. The positive or reconstructive side of that art is not as easy of explanation, although much more important. Wagner has abolished, as far as the opera is concerned, the entire apparatus of absolute musical form. But he has put in its place another form, founded upon the necessities of the dramatic action, and inspired by poetry alone. In other words, he uses all the devices of polyphony and harmony developed by the classical masters with unrivalled skill. But these devices are in every instance made subservient to the dramatic purpose, and thus gain a new and deeper significance. It is by this feature that the affinity between Wagner and the music of Beethoven's third and grandest period is established. That greatest of all masters also felt that music might have a higher mission than that of charming the ear with 'concord of sweet sounds.' In his ninth symphony, where the art in its absolute form reaches its highest climax, he calls the human word to his aid to express what music in its separate condition could not embody. Again in Beethoven's last quartets and sonatas there are, as Wagner points out, passages, such as long recitatives for the instruments, which find their explanation only in the presence of some occult idea struggling for self-consciousness, or, if it may be, expression. The next step would have led to the music-drama, but that step Beethoven was never to take, because he did not succeed in finding a poem adapted to his sublime purpose (*Fidelio*, his only opera, belongs to a much earlier period than that here referred to). Wagner's conclusions in this respect have been the subject of fierce and prolonged controversy. Kinship to Beethoven has been claimed by and for many other masters. When Schumann raised the banner of 'Romanticism,' it was to Bach and Beethoven that he looked up as his models. Mendelssohn, and in our time Brahms, upholders of 'abstract form' though they are, would scarcely disown the influence of Beethoven's poetic idea. That idea, on the other hand, is believed by their adherents to be consistently developed in the symphonic poems of Berlioz and Liszt. But who, we asked on a former occasion, is the right heir to this much discussed 'poetic idea' which the master bequeathed to future ages? The only answer we were able to give was that whereby the cautious Jew Melchisedek evaded Sultan Saladin's questions as to the true religion in Boccaccio's story of the three rings. There are three sons, and each declares that he has received the true miraculous ring from their common father. 'Ciascuno la sua eredità, la sua vera legge, e i suoi comandamenti si crede avere a fare, ma chi se l'abbia, come degli aneli ancora ne pende la questione.' This was all we ventured to say while Wagner was still living and striving. Now that death has put, as it were, the seal of finality upon his achievements, we may, perhaps, go a little further. Lessing, in his *Nathan the Wise*, continuing the fable of Boccaccio, says that the true ring had the quality of making its owner beloved by gods and men; he, therefore, should he acknowledged as that owner who could prove himself to be the best friend of his friends and of mankind. On the same principle, one might say, Let that composer be the true heir of Beethoven who has moved most hearts, and has moved them most deeply and most lastingly. We think that Wagner's admirers may cheerfully accept such a test.

The life of Wagner differs essentially from that of most musicians and literary workers. He was essentially a man of action, of action restless and extending over many branches of thought and passion. A story might be told of him very different from the ordinary summary of an artist's career; 'He lived, worked, took a wife, and died.' That story has been written by the most competent of all hands which could have undertaken it. Several years ago a few privileged friends were permitted to hear the composer read a few chapters of his autobiography. The manuscript even then seemed to extend to several bulky volumes, and there is every reason to hope that it has been continued, and will in due course be given to the world. For the present Wagner's career is too much interwoven with the fate of living persons to allow of detailed notice. We must limit ourselves to supplying a few dates and facts which should be looked upon only as the skeleton of a future biography.

Wilhelm Richard Wagner was born at Leipsic on May 22, 1813, and received his first education at the Kreuzschule, Dresden. In addition to the ordinary course of classical study, he had lessons on the piano, which all his life he played very badly. His first attempt at musical composition was made in connexion with poetry – a significant fact in the life of the future representative of the 'poetic idea' in music. At the age of 11 he had written a stupendous tragedy – a 'kind of compound of *Hamlet* and *King Lear*' he calls it. 'The design,' he adds, 'was grand in the extreme. Forty-two persons died in the course of the piece, and lack of living characters compelled me to let most of them re-appear as ghosts in the last act.' Suddenly the idea struck him that so grand a work ought to have a befitting musical accompaniment, and immediately he set to work to supply that want, regardless of his very imperfect knowledge of the art. These wild attempts, continued through several years, eventually led to serious study. Wagner took Beethoven for his model, and the works of that master he studied with what one of his early friends calls a genuine *furor Teutonicus*. He also went through a course of counterpoint under Cantor Weinlig, and his proficiency in that difficult branch of art was shown in the symphony written and performed at the Gewandhaus Concerts in 1832 and revived a few weeks ago at Venice. In the meantime the *res angusta domi* compelled Wagner to turn his art to more practical account, and about 1835 he became conductor of the theatre of Magdeburg in Prussia, where a juvenile opera, the *Novice of Palermo*, founded on Shakespeare's *Measure for Measure*, was performed without success. It has totally disappeared, with the exception of a single melody, which was subsequently embodied in *Tannhäuser*. In 1839 Wagner became conductor at Riga, and here he began his first acknowledged opera, *Rienzi*, which he destined for Paris. For that city he sailed in the same year without friends or introductions to open the way to the great theatres for the unknown foreigner, but trusting in his stars with that absolute confidence in his own resources which never left him through life. All his attempts at having his opera performed proved in vain, and Wagner was compelled to undergo the most miserable drudgery to gain the necessaries of life for himself, his wife – an actress, whom he had married at Magdeburg – and an enormous Newfoundland dog, with whom, in spite of his poverty, he refused to part. During this time he finished *Rienzi* (in November, 1840) and the greater part of the *Flying Dutchman* (1841), the idea of which had come to him during his stormy voyage from Riga to London on his way to Paris. *Rienzi*, all but repudiated by the composer in later life, was the first stepping-stone to his final triumphs. It was accepted by the Dresden theatre and performed in 1842 with such signal success that the post of conductor of the Royal Opera, one of the most important and lucrative musical appointments in Germany, was offered to the composer. In that position he remained for seven years, during which time he composed *Tannhäuser*, first performed in 1845, and *Lohengrin*, finished in 1849. Before the latter saw the light of the stage, the composer was an exile, having been involved in the revolutionary movement of the eventful years 1848 and 1849. The first performance of *Lohengrin* is connected with one of the brightest episodes of Wagner's chequered career, his friendship with Liszt, which death alone has been able to sever. The history of this remarkable artistic companionship Wagner has embodied in a sketch of his life written in 1851, which may follow here *in extenso* both on account of its interesting nature and as a specimen of the composer's power as a writer of prose:–

> 'I was thoroughly disheartened,' Wagner says, 'from undertaking any new artistic scheme. Only recently I had had proofs of the impossibility of making my art intelligible to the public, and all this deterred me from beginning new dramatic works. Indeed, I thought that everything was at an end with my artistic creativeness. From this state of mental dejection I was raised by a friend. By most evident and undeniable proofs he made me feel that I was not deserted, but, on the contrary, understood deeply by those even who were otherwise most distant from me. In this way he gave me back my full artistic confidence. This wonderful friend has been to me Franz Liszt. I must enter a little more deeply into the character of this friendship, which to many has seemed paradoxical. Indeed, I have been compelled to appear repellent and hostile on so many sides that I almost feel a want of communication with regard to this our sympathetic union. I met Liszt for the first time during my earliest stay in Paris, and at a period when I had renounced the hope, nay, even the wish of a Paris reputation, and, indeed, was in a state of internal revolt against the artistic life I found there. At our meeting, Liszt appeared to me the most perfect contrast to my own being and situation. In this world, to which it had been my desire to fly from my narrow circumstances, Liszt had grown up from his earliest age, so as to be the object of general love and admiration at a time when I was repulsed by general coldness and want of sympathy . . . In consequence, I looked upon him with

suspicion. I had no opportunity of disclosing my being and working to him, and, therefore, the reception I met with on his part was altogether of a superficial kind, as was, indeed, quite natural in a man to whom every day the most divergent impressions claimed access. But I was not in a mood to look with unprejudiced eyes for the natural cause of his behaviour, which, friendly and obliging in itself, could not but hurt me in that state of my mind. I never repeated my first call on Liszt, and, without knowing or even wishing to know him, I was prone to look upon him as strange and adverse to my nature.

'My repeated expression of this feeling afterwards reported to Liszt just at the time when my *Rienzi* at Dresden attracted general attention. He was surprised to find himself misunderstood with such violence by a man whom he had scarcely known, and whose acquaintance now seemed not without value to him. I am still touched at recollecting the repeated and eager attempts he made to change my opinion of him, even before he knew any of my works. He acted not from any artistic sympathy, but led by the purely human wish of discontinuing a casual disharmony between himself and another being; perhaps he also felt an infinitely tender misgiving of having really hurt me unconsciously. He who knows the terrible selfishness and insensibility in our social life, and especially in the relations of modern artists to each other, cannot but be struck with wonder, nay, delight, by the treatment I experienced from this extraordinary man. Liszt soon afterwards witnessed a performance of *Rienzi* at Dresden, on which he had almost to insist, and after that I heard from all the different corners of the world where he had been on his artistic excursions how he had everywhere expressed his delight with my music, and indeed, had I would rather believe unintentionally, canvassed people's opinions in my favour.

'This happened at a time when it became more and more evident that my dramatic works would have no outward success. But just when the case seemed desperate, Liszt succeeded, by his own energy, in opening a hopeful refuge to my art. He ceased his wanderings, settled down at the modest Weimar, and took up the conductor's baton, after having been at home so long in the splendour of the greatest cities of Europe. At Weimar I saw him for the last time, when I rested for a few days in Thuringia, not yet certain whether the threatening prosecution would compel me to continue my flight from Germany. The very day when my personal danger became a certainty I saw Liszt conducting a rehearsal of my *Tannhäuser*, and was astonished at recognizing my second self in his achievement. What I had felt in inventing the music he felt in performing it; what I wanted to express in writing it down he proclaimed in making it sound. Strange to say, through the love of this rarest friend, I gained, at the moment of becoming homeless, a real home for my art, which I had longed for and sought for always in the wrong place . . .

'At the end of my last stay at Paris, when, ill, miserable, despairing, I sat brooding over my fate, my eyes fell on the score of my *Lohengrin*, totally forgotten by me. Suddenly I felt something like compassion that this music should never sound from off the death-pale paper. Two words I wrote to Liszt. His answer was the news that preparations for the performance were being made on the largest scale the limited means of Weimar would permit. Everything that men and circumstances could do was done in order to make the work understood. Errors and misconceptions impeded the desired success. What was to be done to supply what was wanted so as to further the true understanding on all sides, and with it the ultimate success of the work? Liszt saw it at once, and *did* it. He gave to the public his own impression of the work in a manner the convincing eloquence and overpowering efficacy of which remain unequalled. Success was his reward, and with this success he now approaches me saying – "Behold, we have come so far; now create us a new work that we may go still further."'

The first performance of *Lohengrin* was given in 1850. Wagner at that time was settled in Switzerland, where he had sought refuge on his flight from Germany, and where during his enforced severance from the active life of the operatic stage, he wrote his two most important theoretical works, 'Opera and Drama,' and 'The Work of Art of the Future,' the latter probably the origin of the nickname, 'Music of the Future,' applied to Wagner's music by one of his enemies, the late Professor Bischoff, and subsequently adopted by his friends as an omen of lasting fame. In 1855 he accepted the conductorship of the Philharmonic Society, which he held for one season only, his reading of some of the classical works being at variance with English tradition, and, therefore, violently assailed by the Press. With his orchestra, however, Wagner was a great favourite, and some of the performances are still remembered by musicians and amateurs. M. Sainton, at whose suggestion the post had been offered to Wagner, remained his staunch friend during his stay in London. Of the band which played under Wagner in 1855 four members still belong to the present Philharmonic Orchestra, and will take part in the Dead March in *Saul*, which will be played at the Philharmonic concert to-night in memory of the society's whilom conductor.

In addition to his theoretical works, Wagner conceived during the first years of his exile the plan of his greatest, or, at least, most colossal work, the tetralogy of the *Ring of the Nibelung*, which occupied him for a quarter of a century. The drama in its present form was completed as early as 1852, and during the three following years Wagner wrote the music to the *Rhinegold* and the *Valkyrie*. Before continuing the composition of the tetralogy he undertook a new work, *Tristan und Isolde*, his masterpiece as far as unity of design and sustained passion are concerned. This great work, finished in 1859, and first performed in 1865 at Munich, was partly written at Venice, the city where many years later death awaited the master. In 1861 *Tannhäuser* was given at the Grand Opera, Paris, with what disastrous results has already been indicated. The causes of this world-famed fiasco are said to have been partly political. Prince Metternich, the Austrian Ambassador, had taken great interest in the matter, and induced the Emperor to command the performance of the work – sufficient reason for the Legitimists of the Jockey Club to damn the work *à priori*. Nothing daunted by this ill-success, Wagner returned to his solitude and his work. The tetralogy made steady progress, and in 1867 a new opera, *Die Meistersinger von Nürnberg*, was finished and performed in the next following year at Munich. To that city Wagner himself had been called in 1864 by the young and enthusiastic King Ludwig II of Bavaria, who remained his friend and patron to the last. It was the assistance of King Ludwig also which enabled Wagner to realize the boldest dream of his life, the performance of his *Ring of the Nibelung* at a theatre erected for the purpose at Bayreuth. This event took place in the summer of 1876, before a representative audience, including the Emperor of Germany and leading artists from all countries of the civilized world. It marked the climax of Wagner's career, but by no means the end of his incessant labours in the service of art. In 1877 he paid a visit to London and conducted a series of concerts at the Albert-hall. Herr Richter, the greatest living conductor, assisted on that occasion, and soon afterwards founded the concerts known by his name, which have become so important for the progress of musical taste among us. Last year was an epoch in the history of Wagnerism in this country. The works of his later period, the *Ring*, *Tristan*, and *Die Meistersinger* were for the first time heard in England, and made a profound impression on the public. In July of the same year Wagner's last opera, *Parsifal*, was produced at Bayreuth. A full account of that interesting event appeared in *The Times*. The entire series of his other operas also has been the subject of recent and comprehensive notice in our columns, and it would be needless to return once more to the subject. A few general remarks as to the permanent position Wagner's music is likely to take in the history of art will suffice. As to certain points with regard to that music, there is practically but one opinion. Friends and enemies agree in calling Wagner the greatest master of the orchestra the world of art has seen. He treats the band as Liszt and Mdme. Schumann treat the pianoforte, setting forth its strength and its delicacy with singular judgment, and producing effects of which no previous composer had dreamt. His style as a contrapuntist and harmonist, if the term may be used, has undergone great changes in the course of his career. The occasional crudeness, not to say coarseness, of writing which is found in *Rienzi* and less frequently in the *Flying Dutchman* and *Tannhäuser* has disappeared in *Lohengrin*, and in his later works, notably in *Die Meistersinger*, Wagner has given examples of contrapuntal skill of which John Sebastian Bach himself need not have been ashamed. That, moreover, his design is always grand and noble and his execution marvellously powerful the composer's most persistent detractors would scarcely venture to deny. It is curious, however, that those detractors have tried to discover Wagner's weakness in the point where his greatest strength really lies. It is a common saying among people who have no ears to hear, that Wagner is not a tuneful composer, that he lacks spontaneous invention. We believe that when the mists of prejudice have cleared away it will be found that the world owes to Wagner more beautiful melodies than to any other composer, with the exception perhaps of Schubert.

The following is a list of Wagner's operas, with the dates of first performance and of production in England attached : *Rienzi, der letzte der Tribunen* – first performed, under Wagner, 1842, Dresden (in England, 1879); *Der Fliegende Holländer* – first performed, under Wagner, 1843, Dresden (in England, 1870); *Tannhäuser* – first performed, under Wagner, 1845, Dresden (in England, 1876). *Lohengrin* – first performed under Liszt, 1850, Weimar (in England, 1875); *Tristan und Isolde* – first performed, under Bülow, 1865, Munich (in England, 1882, under Richter); *Die Meistersinger von Nürnberg* – first performed, under Bülow, 1868, Munich (in England, 1882, under Richter); *Der Ring des Nibelungen, ein Bühnenfestspiel; Das Rheingold* – first performed, 1869, Munich; *Die Walküre* – first performed, 1869, Munich; *Siegfried, Götterdämmerung* – the entire work first performed under Hans Richter, at Bayreuth, 1876 (in England, 1882, under Seydel); *Parsifal, ein Bühnenweihfestspiel* – first performed at Bayreuth, 1883, under Levi. Wagner's literary works, collected in nine volumes, have been published in Leipsic, 1871. 'Die Kunst und die Revolution,' 'Das Kunstwerk der Zukunft,' 'Oper und Drama,' and 'Beethoven' are the titles of his most important treatises. In the last-named the philosophy of Schopenhauer is discussed in as far as it bears upon the aesthetic basis of music.

We have received the following telegram, dated February 14, 1883, from Herr Angelo Neumann, on behalf of the Richard Wagner Theatre, Aachen:–

'The startling news of the death of the great master had induced the direction of the Richard Wagner Theatre to close the building to-day. Having regard, however, to pressure of circumstances, and the want of the necessary authority, this order to close the theatre was perforce cancelled, and the performance will, therefore, be given as usual.

'Richard Wagner, in the last letter which he addressed to the director of the theatre, on the 13th of January last, perhaps with some foreboding of his approaching end, expressed a wish to establish, during the space of life which might yet remain to him, an assured future for his only son Siegfried, who is still under age.

'In order to accomplish the fulfilment of this wish of the master, now that he has passed away, the direction of the Richard Wagner Theatre intends to devote the entire receipts of this evening's performance as the foundation of a capital sum to be secured for the benefit of this young son of Richard Wagner.

'Moreover, that this evening's performance may lead in this way to the fitting celebration of the earthly end of this immortal genius, the direction of the Richard Wagner Theatre appeals to the directors of all the theatres of Germany to follow its example, and thus to erect to the memory of the great artist a monument which will carry out the one absorbing desire cherished by an anxious father during the last year of his life.'

Wagner first visited London in 1839, spending eight days recovering from the effects of a tempestuous crossing of the North Sea from Riga, but managing also to admire the workings of the Houses of Parliament (then still in temporary accommodation). Wagner later recorded that his voyage, via Norway, had given the legend of the Flying Dutchman 'a very definite and individual colouring'. He returned to London for four months in the spring of 1855, and made a further brief visit to conduct at the Royal Albert Hall in 1877. The enthusiasm with which, according to this obituary, his music was received in Britain did not stem from the immediate experience of Wagner the concert conductor, but derived from a steady and consistent appreciation of his extraordinary innovations as a composer of opera. *The Ring of the Nibelung*, which was first performed in Britain as a cycle by Angelo Neumann's company at Her Majesty's Theatre in May 1882 as part of the season of Wagner's work mentioned by the obituarist, had created a sensation. His last music drama, *Parsifal*, had to wait for its London première at Covent Garden until February 1914, by which time a Wagner 'cult' was firmly established. *Parsifal* had first been produced in the new Festspielhaus at Bayreuth 22 years earlier. There were 16 performances at Bayreuth after which, in August 1882, Wagner had retired exhausted to Venice. He died there of heart failure on 13 February 1883. His body was transported overland to Bayreuth and was buried on 18 February close to the Villa Wahnfried.

KARL MARX

Political philosopher and economist:
'An attack on the whole capitalist system.'

14 MARCH 1883

OUR PARIS CORRESPONDENT informs us of the death of Dr. Karl Marx, which occurred last Wednesday, in London. He was born at Cologne, in the year 1818. At the age of 25 he had to leave his native country and take refuge in France, on account of the Radical opinions expressed in a paper of which he was editor. In France he gave himself up to the study of philosophy and politics, and made himself so obnoxious to the Prussian Government by his writings, that he was expelled from France, and lived for a time in Belgium. In 1847 he assisted at the Working Men's Congress in London, and was one of the authors of the 'Manifesto of the Communist Party.' After the Revolution of 1848 he returned to Paris, and afterwards to his native city of Cologne, from which he was again expelled for his revolutionary writings, and after escaping from imprisonment in France, he settled in London. From this time he was one of the leaders of the Socialist party in Europe, and in 1865 he became its acknowledged chief. He wrote pamphlets on various subjects, but his chief work was 'Le Capital,' an attack on the whole capitalist system. For some time he had been suffering from weak health.

It is striking that this obituary notice is not only brief but also that it is the work of 'Our Paris Correspondent'; it is a reminder of how obscure a figure Marx was to many of his non-socialist contemporaries. In his last years Marx had lived in a villa in Maitland Park Road, Kentish Town in London. He died on 14 March 1883, and only eleven people attended his funeral in the unconsecrated section of Highgate Cemetery three days later. A clumsily translated version of Marx and Friedrich Engels's *The Communist Manifesto* of 1848 had been published in English in the Chartist newspaper the *Red Republican* in 1850. The first volume of *Capital*, much of which had been written in the reading room of the British Museum, had appeared in German in 1867, but it had to wait until the end of the century for an English translation. William Morris, who made a pilgrimage to Highgate Cemetery on the anniversary of Marx's death, read *Capital* in French in 1883, but was forced to admit that 'political economy is not my line, and much of it appears to me to be dreary rubbish'. Marx had come to London as a political refugee in May 1849 and had stayed in Britain for the rest of his life, supported for much of the time by Engels.

* * *

VICTOR HUGO

Poet, dramatist and novelist:
'Perhaps the finest literary spirit that France has ever produced.'

22 MAY 1885

BY THE DEATH of Victor Hugo yesterday, France loses the most variously gifted of her sons, and the world of letters its most brilliant ornament. From the universality of his genius he has frequently been compared with our own Shakespeare; but while his power over human passion, his vivid and capacious imagination, and his plastic intellectual energies may suggest and partially warrant such a comparison with the first of all poets, the great writer just deceased lacked the grand impartiality, the profound calm, and the serene and lofty judgment which are characteristic of Shakespeare and of the few great master spirits of the world. But, when this exception has been taken, the poet whose loss all humanity now mourns was not only one of the most remarkable figures of this generation, but perhaps the finest purely literary spirit that France has ever produced.

Victor Marie Hugo was born at Besançon, on the 26th of February, 1802. He is generally reputed to have sprung from a family which had been ennobled three centuries before, in the person of George Hugo, Captain of the Guard to the Duc de Lorraine. Joseph Leopold Sigisbert, the father of Victor Hugo, was a General in the French Army, and held important commands in France and Italy. Beginning his military career under the Republic, he rose rapidly during the Empire, distinguishing himself by his courage and his brilliant services. His wife was a native of La Vendée, and an ardent Catholic and Royalist; the character of both was strongly individualized, and the poet seems to have inherited many of their mental peculiarities. But the physical tenement of the child of genius was exceedingly frail, and none who saw him gave him as many days to live as he survived to number years.

While in an apparently moribund condition he was taken to the Mairie, and there his birth was registered. Years afterwards the poet celebrated in verse the care, the tenderness, and the love which were lavished upon him, and which made him in a two-fold sense the child of his devoted mother.

His earliest years were passed amid constant change and excitement. Before he had completed his fifth year he had travelled from Besançon to Elba, and thence into the province of Avellino, in Calabria, where his father was engaged in the extirpation of the brigand tribes, one of whose leaders was the famous bandit, Fra Diavolo. He also visited Florence, Rome, and Naples, and returned to Paris in the year 1809. Madame Hugo took up her abode at the old convent of the Feuillantines, and for two years the young Hugo led a quiet and studious existence, beginning his education under Lahorie, a proscribed general, and having near him his mother and the little child-friend Adèle Foucher, who was afterwards to become the poet's wife. Lahorie, having been betrayed, was imprisoned and put to death by the Imperial Government, and this melancholy event made a profound impression upon his little pupil. It contributed, together with the teachings of his mother, to develop in the mind of the child those strong Royalist sentiments which found expression in his youthful works. In 1811 Victor was called by his father to Spain, where he passed a year in the seminary of nobles. At the early age of ten he began to experiment in verse. Returning to Paris, he resumed the old life at the Feuillantines, and his studies here, under the direction of his mother, continued for three years unchecked. But during the period of the Hundred Days, although Victor Hugo had given clear proof of the bent of his genius, his father resolved upon placing him in a preparatory school, before sending him to the Polytechnic, with the view of adopting a military career.

Yet even in his new and uncongenial quarters the young poet did not neglect the muse. His literary precocity and fecundity were indeed marvellous. One writer states that during the years 1815–1818 – that is, from his 13th to his 16th year – he made every possible kind of verse, odes, satires, epistles, poems; tragedies, elegies, idylls, imitations of Ossian, translations from Virgil, from Horace, and from Lucan. There were other translations from Ausonius and from Martial, romances, fables, stories, epigrams, madrigals, logographs, acrostics, charades, enigmas, and impromptus; and he also achieved a comic opera. In 1816 he wrote the tragedy of *Irtamène*, to celebrate the accession of Louis XVIII, but not long afterwards this and other juvenile efforts he deemed it necessary to apologize for. He considerably puzzled the wise heads of the Academy in the year 1817, when he competed for the prize of poetry, the subject assigned being 'The Happiness derived from Study in every Situation in Life.' The examiners were struck with the merits of the poem, but refused credence to the statement of the author that he was but 10 years of age. In order to convince the sceptics, the young poet forwarded his certificate of birth, but instead of obtaining the prize he had to content himself with the honourable mention of the Academy. Many anecdotes are told respecting these early days. By his poem of 'Moses on the Nile,' Hugo won the prize, offered by the Academy of Toulouse. Having gained three prizes he was constituted Master of the Floral

Games, and at the age of 18 he became a provincial Academician. About this time he wrote the 'Ode to La Vendée,' and the curious story of 'Bug-Jargal,' which was published in the *Conservateur Littéraire*, a periodical founded by Victor and his two brothers. A singular example is furnished of the acuteness and foresight of Hugo's father. His talented son having on one occasion expressed himself strongly in favour of the Vendeans, the elder Hugo turned towards General Lucotte, and observed – 'Let us leave all to time. The child shares his mother's views; the man will have the opinions of his father.' This vaticination was strictly fulfilled. On the death of the Duc de Berry, Victor Hugo wrote an ode which became very popular in Royalist circles. Madame Hugo died in the year 1821, to the great grief of her already famous son, who was devotedly attached to her. In his sorrow he turned to the one being who had alone the power to comfort him, and in 1822, Mdlle. Foucher became the wife of Victor Hugo. He was but 20 years of age, while the bride was much younger. In this same year appeared the first volume of Victor Hugo's 'Odes et Ballades,' poems which united a classic form with romanticity of sentiment. For this work Hugo received 700f., and with the generous recklessness which distinguished him, he spent the whole sum on a French cashmere shawl, the gem of his wife's wedding trousseau. 'Han d'Islande' quickly followed the odes, and the first edition of this work produced him 1,000f. The realism of this novel created many enemies in literary circles. While critics admitted the wit, the learning, and the picturesque force which stamped it with a refreshing originality, they complained of manifest defects, and condemned the author for his attempt to satiate his ambition and his hopes with the reputation and the excitement of the present moment.

With the publication of the second volume of 'Odes et Ballades,' in 1826, it was obvious that a change was coming over the ideas of the poet. A literary revolution preceded the political one of 1830. Hugo was one of the chief spirits among a band of writers who charged themselves with the formidable task of regenerating French literature. They resolved to discard the old classical models, and, by the warmth of their imagination and the electrical fervour of their newly-emancipated spirits, to establish a new order of things in the realm of poetry. The monotonous Alexandrines were deposed, and irregular but powerful forms of verse usurped their place. Nor was it only in poetic form that they sought to effect a revolution. Matter must be changed as well as metre. Art must conform to Nature. Nature was mistress, and must be followed. The new school assumed the name of 'La jeune France,' but the outer world distinguished them by the generic title of the Romanticists, as opposed to their rivals and predecessors, the Classicists. Victor Hugo was the acknowledged head of the new movement, and the circle which was formed under the name of the Cénacle included such writers and critics as Saint Beuve, Boulanger, and the brothers Deschamps. A newspaper, *La Muse Française*, was established to advocate the new views. It was in 1827 that the first definite fruits of the literary revolution became apparent by the publication of Victor Hugo's drama of *Cromwell.* In composing the original draft of this drama, the author intended it for stage representation, with Talma as the chief character. But Talma died before the drama was completed, and, as ultimately finished, the author did not intend the drama for stage representation. In the preface, he unfolded his views upon the dramatic art. Briefly put, they were to this effect – that the stage is chiefly a reflex of society, a mirror in which the public should see its image faithfully reflected. The drama was not to be circumscribed by tragedy alone, but comedy was to render its share in the delineation of character. The author's resolve to make himself independent of the three unities led to much hostile criticism; but he was also not without his defenders. In 1828, M. Hugo published a series of odes entitled 'Les Orientales.' They contained much fresh and musical, but not very profound, verse, and advanced the author in the esteem of the public. He next engaged upon a play dealing with the history of Amy Robsart, but it was not given to the public, a pension granted by Louis XVIII to the author enabling the latter to keep back such works as his judgment recommended him not to issue.

The occasion of the next publication of Victor Hugo, 'Le Dernier Jour d'un Condamné,' furnishes an opportunity for referring to him in his character of a humanitarian. The abolition of capital punishment was a measure which he warmly and persistently supported, and his powerful writings had great influence in disgusting the French mind with the sickening details of public executions. The work above mentioned was a powerful protest against capital punishment, and it was followed up by an earnest and life-long advocacy of the same course. After the lapse of a quarter of a century he wrote 'Claude Gueux,' dealing with a convict of that name, whose reprieve had been appealed for in vain. In 1839 Hugo was successful in interceding for the life of Barbès, who had been co-leader with Blanqui in an insurrection; and 23 years later an interesting correspondence passed between the reprieved man and his benefactor. As a peer of France Victor Hugo sat in judgment in 1846 and 1847 on two men, named King and Lecomte, who had fired at the King, and in both cases he declined to vote for the capital sentence being executed. When the whole question of capital punishments was discussed by the Assembly in 1848, Victor Hugo delivered a brief but impassioned speech. 'In the first act of the Constitution that you vote,' he said, 'you have carried out the first thought of the people – you have overturned the throne. Now carry out the other; overturn the scaffold! I vote for the abolition, pure, simple, and definitive, of the penalty of death.' The friends of condemned criminals repeatedly besought the intercession of Victor Hugo, knowing his horror of capital punishment. In 1851, when the poet's eldest son, Charles Hugo, was summoned before the Court of Assize, for having protested in *L'Evénement* against an execution which had been accompanied by horrible circumstances, the father claimed the right to defend him, which was accorded. In the course of his very powerful address on that occasion, he exclaimed, with much emotion, 'The real culprit in this matter, if there is a culprit, is not my son. It is I myself – I who for a quarter of a century have not ceased to battle against all forms of the irreparable penalty – I who during all this time have never ceased to advocate the inviolability of human life.' The speech was thrilling and argumentative by turns. But the speaker, notwithstanding his fervid eloquence, failed to convert his hearers, and Charles Hugo was sentenced to six months' imprisonment. In 1854 the hanging of a man named Tapner, in Guernsey, created a great sensation. Victor Hugo laboured for his reprieve, but in vain; and he afterwards addressed a trenchant letter to Lord Palmerston, in which he recapitulated certain ghastly incidents which rendered the execution unusually horrible and repulsive. When John Brown, of Harper's Ferry celebrity, was condemned to death, Victor Hugo penned a stirring remonstrance to the United States. On many other occasions also he came forward to denounce the exaction of the death penalty. The power of his pen was so great that the Deputy Salverte declared it was owing to such 'execrable books' as 'The Last Day of a Convict' that France had adopted the plea of extenuating circumstances. To him also credit was given for the cry which arose in Switzerland for the abolition of the punishment of death, a letter which he wrote, and which was distributed widely throughout the cantons, having produced an immense effect.

To return to the literary efforts of M. Hugo. Having established a now dramatic school, it was but natural that he who was regarded as its founder should be urged to produce a work that should serve as a stage exposition of the new principles. This was forthcoming in the drama of *Marion Delorme.* This work was unquestionably original, and, in the opinion of some critics, as unquestionably immoral. It is full of excellent things, but the task which the author set himself in its composition was a difficult and delicate one. But for its delineation of human passion it must take high rank among stage efforts. The censor, M. de Martignac, who held by the old school, decided against it, both on literary and political grounds. He saw in the description of Louis XIII an unflattering allusion to Charles X. The author carried the matter to the King himself. Charles promised to look into the matter and give an immediate answer. He did so, but it was hostile to the play. Desiring to pacify Hugo, whose genius he admired, the King granted him a fresh pension of 4,000 francs, but the poet refused the bribe, and the *Consitutionnel* remarked upon this:– 'Youth is less easily corrupted than the Ministers think.' Another dramatic venture immediately succeeded, for Victor Hugo's was a restless and impulsive intellect, which sought only a fuller expression under a policy of repression. This time it was the famous drama of *Hernani* with which he delighted his friends and still further exasperated his enemies. The play was produced at the Théâtre Français on the 25th of February, 1830, amid a scene of great excitement. Some of the partisans for and against the drama came to actual blows, but the friends of the dramatist prevailed, and the piece was successful. Chateaubriand wrote a flattering letter to the author. After a few nights the enemies of the piece increased in numbers and violence, but still the theatre filled and money came pouring into the treasury. *Hernani* excited a *furore* that extended to the provinces. A fatal duel arising out of it was fought at Toulouse, and at Vannes a corporal of Dragoons died leaving this instruction in his will:– 'I wish to have it engraved on my tombstone, "Here lies one who believed in Victor Hugo."'

The poet now alternated his dramatic writing with the production of the remarkable romance, 'Nôtre Dame de Paris.' He had bound himself by agreement with a publisher to produce a novel within a given time, and unable to get sufficient leisure in any other way he shut himself up resolutely beyond the reach of the world. Investing in a bottle of ink and a thick gray worsted garment which enveloped him from the head to the heels, he locked up his clothes so that he should not be tempted to go out, and set to work. His friends thought very little of the portions of the novel which he read to them; but M. Alphonse Karr was so struck by the title which Hugo first thought of giving to his story, 'The Contents of a Bottle of Ink,' that he begged to be allowed to use it. The book was finished in less than six months, and although the great majority of the critics were strongly hostile to it, it became one of the most favourite romances with both French and English readers. And the strength of its characters, combined with the dramatic power it displays, may well justify the popular verdict in this matter. The author was pressed by the publishers for more novels, and for some time two titles were displayed before an eager public – viz., the 'Fils de la Bossue' and 'La Quiquengrogue.' But other work intervened, and these stories were never produced. The Revolution of 1830 did away with the old censorship of the stage, and a proposition was at once made by the Comédie Française to produce *Marion Delorme*. In the year following he consented to its performance, but gave it to the Théâtre of the Porte Saint-Martin. It achieved a fair success. In 1831 appeared a new volume of lyrical poems by Victor Hugo, entitled 'Les Feuilles d'Automne.' In these impressions of a poetic nature, thrown off when the author had banished from his mind the distracting outer world, there are many sweet and tender passages.

In 1832 Victor Hugo wrote *Le Roi s'Amuse*, and Baron Taylor secured it for the Théâtre Français. It was produced on the 22d of November, but immediately suspended by the Government. An attempted assassination of the King on the night of the first performance played into the hands of the censor, and made the alleged necessity for the suppression of the drama the more plausible. The play was not very well received, and on Victor Hugo being asked whether his name should be mentioned to the audience, he replied, 'Sir, I have rather a higher opinion of my play now that it is a failure.' The reason assigned for the suppression of the drama was that it was an offence against public morality. The author was exceedingly angry, and appealed to the Judges, but they decided against him. Although the Revolution had deprived M. Hugo of the pension of 1,000f. out of the privy purse conferred upon him by Louis XVIII, he still received the pension of 2,000f. allowed him by the Home Minister. The Ministerial journals now twitted him with attacking Royalty but at the same time taking pay from it. Upon this Victor Hugo wrote a letter to M. d'Argout, in which he stated that he had accepted the pension as a tribute to his literary work, but now that it was misunderstood he entirely relinquished it. M. d'Argout replied that he should still reserve the pension for the poet, but the latter never afterwards took it up.

Dramas from Victor Hugo's pen now followed each other in rapid succession. *Lucrèce Borgia* was performed in 1833, with Mdlle. Georges, M. Delafosse, and M. Frédéric Lemaître in the principal characters. The superb acting in the last scene called forth quite an ovation. The author was obliged to escape as best he could from the admiring crowds which besieged him on leaving. The receipts from the three first performances amounted to 84,769f. – a sum never approached under the management of the Porte Saint-Martin. *Marie Tudor* followed, but prejudice was created against this piece on the ground that it was more than ever a tissue of horrors; that Mary was a bloodthirsty creature, and that the executioner was perpetually on the stage. By the year 1834 it became manifest that a change had come over the political sentiments of Victor Hugo. In 'L'Etude sur Mirabeau' the Royalistic ideas of the early ballads were thrown over, and the celebration of the rights of the people had taken their place. The change had been arrived at gradually and honestly, but the poet felt that some statement of a semi-autobiographic character was due from him, and he gave the reasons for his new faith in his 'Littérature et Philosophie Melées.' It was impossible for a mind constituted like his, and susceptible at every point, to stand still; and he felt himself irresistibly urged upon the path of progress. *Angelo*, another new drama, was produced in 1835, and Mdlle. Mars sustained the chief character. We almost toil after this prolific writer in vain. Three volumes of poems – 'Les Chants du Crépuscule,' 'Les Voix Intérieures,' and 'Les Rayons et les Ombres' – appeared between 1835 and 1840, and testified not only to the poet's versatility but to his richness and wealth of diction. In July, 1837, Victor Hugo was appointed officer of the Legion of Honour. In 1838 was produced his drama of *Ruy Blas*. The manager of the theatre looked forward anxiously to the opening night, but the play succeeded admirably. The first four acts went off very well, but at the fifth act M. Frédéric Lemaître rivalled the greatest comedians. The drama achieved a genuine success – that is, a success emanating spontaneously from the public; and it was performed for 50 nights. The last of Victor Hugo's writings for the stage, *Les Burgraves*, was produced in 1848. Here, as in his other pieces, there was witnessed the same strong contrasts. He delighted in opposing human passions and in a strange commingling of comedy with tragedy which shocked the notions of those who held by the severity of the dramatic unities. But the effects which he managed to produce were undoubted; and, however people might urge that he was heterodox, all at least concurred in admitting that he was original. But he resolved to give up the theatre, and with the production of *Les Burgraves* our author shook the dramatic dust from under his feet and left the stage to pursue its own course.

With regard to the developments in his political and social views, while these excited surprise and animadversion in some quarters, upon those who had faithfully traced his career and his writings during his fourth decade these changes could have no effect. For example, although he fell in with the *régime* of Louis Philippe he made no secret of it that he regarded the Monarchy only as temporary – it was merely a prelude to the Republic. Yet he did not think that the Republic was at that moment ripe. But the keen and intuitive mind of Lamennais had read him rightly. 'I knew,' remarked that distinguished man, 'that you could not remain Royalist; but I place the Republic in the present and you foretell it in the future.' Though enthusiastic beyond measure in most things, Victor Hugo was willing to tolerate the existing Monarchy under the belief that it must lead to the Republic. In discoursing of Mirabeau in 1834 he had dwelt upon the necessity for the observant man to make allowances. By 1837 he had gone a step further, and defined his object to be to agree with all parties in what was liberal and generous, but with none in what was illiberal and mischievous. At this time also he regarded social reforms as by far the most necessary and the most pressing. In 1840 he claimed the following as his rule of action: – 'No engagement, no chain. Liberty should pervade both his ideas and his actions. He should be free in his goodwill towards those who are really working, free in his aversion towards those who are hurtful, free in his love towards those who serve, free in his pity towards those who suffer.' It required little in the nature of prophecy to indicate Hugo's future upon political and social questions. Emancipation, in the sense of democratic progress, was all that could be predicated of him.

Although the brilliant talents of Victor Hugo had given him a fame already extending far beyond his native country, they could not insure him a place among the 'Immortals.' That capricious corporation, the French Academy, looked askance when he knocked at its doors for admittance. For some years he was obliged to console himself with the fact that he was but one member of an illustrious band, beginning with Molière, all of whom had been passed over by this learned body. His first application as a candidate was in 1836, when the Academy preferred M. Dupaty; at the next attempt, three years later, M. Molé was the fortunate one; in 1840 the Academy chose M. Flourens in preference to the poet and dramatist; but on a fourth application, in 1841, the sacred doors were at length opened to him, and

Victor Hugo obtained the honours to which he had long ago become legitimately entitled.

Shortly after his election into the French Academy Victor Hugo made several foreign tours, among others one through Spain, whence he was suddenly recalled by a severe domestic affliction. His daughter Léopoldine and her husband, Charles Vacquerie, to whom she had but recently been united were drowned while out upon a pleasure excursion. The sad event made a profound impression upon the mind of the poet. On the 15th of April, 1845, Victor Hugo was created a peer of France by Louis Philippe, but the title of Count seems an anomaly when associated with such a name as his. The Revolution of 1848 called him to definite action. Elected to represent the city of Paris in the Constituent Assembly, his votes were given now to the Right and now to the Democratic party. He was re-elected to the Legislative Assembly, being the tenth among 28 candidates; and he now rapidly assumed the position of one of the leaders and chief orators of the Left. He spoke eloquently upon the affairs of Rome, the limitation of universal suffrage, the project for the revision of the Constitution, and other questions. But the passionate vehemence of his language, his strong personal attacks upon Montalembert, with whom he engaged in a Parliamentary duel extending over three years, and his frequent attacks upon the President of the Republic drew upon him the reproaches of the majority for his new-born republican zeal. The odes written in his youth, as well as the writings of maturer years, were quoted against him. At the same time also, the journal which he had founded, *L'Evénement*, and which had passed through the same changing phases of opinion as himself, was prosecuted, condemned, and suppressed, but only to reappear under the name of the *Avénement*. With MM. Schoelcher, Madier-Montjau, &c., Victor Hugo organized an abortive resistance to the *Coup d'État* of the 2d of December. With other members of the Extreme Left he was banished from France for life by Prince Louis Napoleon. Immediately upon his exile he signed, along with several of his colleagues, an appeal to arms, couched in extremely vehement language, and he followed this up by his scathing brochure 'Napoléon le Petit,' published in Brussels. In the following year, 1853, he further issued at Brussels a volume of poems under the title of 'Les Châtiments.' These works furnished the strongest invectives ever uttered against 'the man of December.' They exhibit a man of genius expending all his wealth of satire and denunciation in the white heat of passion. The work last named, which is as remarkable for its elegance of composition as for its intense political feeling, was destined, after a clandestine circulation of 18 years, and upon the fall of the Emperor in 1870, to prove the poet's best passport to a yet greater popularity than he had hitherto enjoyed. Withdrawing first to Jersey, the illustrious exile was not long allowed to remain there. Difficulties arose between the French and British Governments, and Victor Hugo ultimately settled in Guernsey, with which island his name has ever since been associated, and where he spent many years fruitful in literary effort. The first substantial result of the exchange of political for purely literary labours appeared in 'Les Contemplations,' published in 1856. The work was speedily very popular, and it has been described as the lyrical record of 25 years.

In 1859 appeared 'La Légende des Siècles.' Announced as a simple fragment of a yet greater poem – as the first part of a trilogy, of which the other two were to be called 'La Fin de Satan' and 'Dieu' – this work was yet far more striking than any of its predecessors for its brilliancy and energy, its literary skill, and its powerful conceptions. The Bishop of Derry has given a full and, on the whole, discriminating criticism of this remarkable work, and with some success has translated passages from it. But Victor Hugo's French is too peculiar and impassioned to be brought within the trammels of English verse.

On the 15th of August, 1859, a general amnesty was proclaimed. This was refused by Victor Hugo, Edgar Quinet, Louis Blanc, and others, who replied by a counter manifesto. When he was again pressed, ten years later, to accept a second amnesty, he refused with still greater warmth, answering his friend Pyat in these words – *S'il n'en reste qu'un, je serai celui-là.* He was blamed by some for adopting this attitude, and others affirmed that if he had stood forward in the time of peril as he ought to have done, the fatal day of Sadowa might have been averted, and the disastrous Ministry of M. Emile Ollivier, with its subsequent avalanche of ruin, might have been rendered impossible. This, at any rate, will suffice to show the power ascribed to the individual will of Victor Hugo. In the year 1862 appeared a new and powerful work by our author, and one in an entirely new groove – namely, the great social romance 'Les Misérables.' It was issued simultaneously in nine languages, and published in Paris, Brussels, London, New York, Madrid, Berlin, St. Petersburg, and Turin. The appearance of the work had been eagerly awaited. Its reception was peculiar. It was as warmly applauded by some as it was fiercely denounced by others for its social philosophy. But all critics acknowledged the genius which blazed in the pages of this romance, one writer affirming that it contained in dilution more colossal imagery than anything which had been produced in Europe since the 'Divine Comedy.' In 1865 was published the volume 'Chansons des Rues et des Bois,' in which so much power was expended over the infinitely little as to earn for the author the sobriquet of 'the Paganini of poetry.' A second important work dealing with metaphysical and social questions, 'Les Travailleurs de la Mer,' appeared in 1866. This romance has been compared with the *Prometheus* of Aeschylus. The plot is nothing; the development of a human soul everything. Gilliatt's battle with the devil fish is probably the most realistic thing ever penned. A third descriptive romance, 'L'Homme qui Rit,' appeared in 1869, the year following the death of Madame Victor Hugo at Brussels. Again the movement of life plays a subordinate part, and the real purpose of the work is seen to be a description of the battle waged in the individual breast, first with Fate, and then with those ancient enemies of man, the World, the Flesh, and the Devil. But, notwithstanding its evidences of power, this work failed to obtain that deep hold upon the public mind which was secured by its predecessors. The closing years of the Empire witnessed a great literary triumph for Victor Hugo in the reproduction of his *Hernani* at the Théâtre Français. During the time of the Paris Universal Exhibition in 1867 this drama was performed for the long period of four months with striking success.

At this time Victor Hugo was a frequent contributor to the *Rappel*, a journal which had been founded under his inspiration, and which was conducted by M. Vacquerie, the brothers Hugo, and M. Rochefort. It had gained a great ascendancy over the population of Paris. On the occasion of the *plébiscite* of the 8th of May, 1870, which ratified the new Constitution of the Empire, the poet published a protest in the *Rappel* entitled '*Non*; in three letters this word says everything.' The article was so strong a development of the writer's views on the subject of the Empire that he was cited for bringing the Government into hatred and contempt. With the disaster of Sedan the Empire fell, and the revolution of the 4th of September followed. Victor Hugo now returned to Paris, where he was received with great enthusiasm. He addressed a letter to the German people exhorting them also to proclaim a republic and to join hands with France. When the insurrectionary movement of the 31st of October occurred, his name appeared on the list of the Committee of Public Safety; but he disavowed the use made of his name, and on the ensuing 5th of November declined to become a candidate at the general election of the mayors of Paris; 4,029 suffrages, however, were accorded him in the 15th arrondissement. In the elections of February, 1871, he was returned second on the list with 214,000 votes, Louis Blanc coming first with 216,000, and Garibaldi third with 200,000 votes. Speaking in the National Assembly on the 1st of March, he powerfully denounced the ratification of the preliminaries of peace. On the 8th, during the debate which took place in the National Assembly on the election of Garibaldi, Victor Hugo ascended the tribune and said:–

> 'France has met with nothing but cowardice from Europe. Not a Power, not a single King, rose to assist us. One man alone intervened in our favour: that man had an idea and a sword. With his idea he delivered one people; with his sword he delivered another. Of all the Generals who fought for France, Garibaldi is the only one who was not beaten.'

Here there were violent interruptions on the Right, and the speaker declared he would give in his resignation. Being, subsequently asked by the President whether he adhered to the letter of resignation which he had laid upon the table, he replied that he persisted in his resolve, and forthwith left the hall. The next day M. Grévy read the following letter from Victor Hugo:– 'Three weeks ago the Assembly refused to hear Garibaldi; to-day it refuses to hear me. I resign my seat.' Louis Blanc expressed the profound grief caused by this resignation to all the political friends of Victor Hugo, and said that it was a misfortune added to the other calamities of the country.

A heavy domestic calamity befell the poet on the 13th of March, when his son Charles died of cerebral congestion. The bereaved parent brought the body to Paris on the 18th, the day of the insurrection in the capital. Civil war was now inaugurated, with all its horrors; but this period of outrage and assassination is matter of familiar history. Leaving Paris during the horrors of the Commune, the poet went to Brussels. On the 26th of May, while in this city, he wrote a letter protesting against the decision of the Belgian Government with regard to the insurgents of Paris. In this letter he offered publicly an asylum to the soldiers of the Commune, and, as the Ministry considered that the letter compromised the interests of Belgium, the writer was expelled from the country. Returning to Paris after the trial of the leaders of the Commune, he interceded, but in vain, with M. Thiers on behalf of M. Rochefort. He was again adopted as a candidate for Paris by all the Radical Press in the election of the 7th of January, 1872; but he declined the imperative mandate which the Radical clubs wished to impose upon him, while accepting the '*mandat contractuel*,' which he defined for the first time. He was defeated, receiving only 95,900 votes, as against 123,395 given to his opponent, M. Vautrain. During the siege of Paris a new edition was brought out of 'Les Châtiments,' a work, as we have seen, originally published in 1853. This reproduction consisted of more than 100,000 copies. The principal pieces in the collection were recited at the theatres, the proceeds being devoted to the works of defence, the ambulances, &c. Readings and recitations from the work were also given in the provinces, with a like object. Victor Hugo defended his own career in the work entitled 'Actes et Paroles,' written in 1870–72; and this was followed up by 'L'Année Terrible,' issued in the last-named year. Belonging to the same class or category of intellectual labour was 'La Libération du Territoire,' a poem published in 1873 and sold for the benefit of the inhabitants of Alsace and Lorraine.

In 1874 appeared the grand historical and political romance 'Quatre-vingt-treize,' which was published on the same day in 10 languages. This great prose epic, upon the most terrible year in modern history, 1793, excited the liveliest interest throughout Europe, and critics of all shades of opinion hastened to do justice to its extraordinary merits. To this work succeeded, in 1874, a pathetic sketch, 'Mes Fils,' and, in 1875–6, 'Avant l'Exil,' 'Pendant l'Exil,' 'Depuis l'Exil,' being a complete collection of Victor Hugo's addresses, orations, and confessions of faith, &c., during the preceding 30 years. 'Pour un Soldat' was a little *brochure* written in favour of an obscure deserter. Although the poet seemed temporarily to have abandoned political life, he had not forgotten his friends and the electors of Paris. Frequent letters published in the public Press proved this, as well as his presence as chairman at a number of democratic conventions, and the delivery of a number of public discourses, such as those pronounced at the funerals of M. Edgar Quinet, Madame Louis Blanc, and others. Preparatory to the first Senatorial elections, M. Clémenceau, President of the Municipal Council of Paris, waited upon the poet, and, in the name of the majority of his colleagues, offered him the function of delegate. M. Hugo accepted, and at once issued his manifesto, entitled 'The Delegate of Paris to the Delegates of the 36,000 Communes of France,' in which he reiterated, with redoubled energy, his old idea of the abolition of monarchy by the federation of the peoples. On the 30th of January, 1876, he was elected Senator of Paris, but after a keen struggle. He was only the fourth out of five, and was not returned until after a second scrutiny, when it was found that he had secured 114 votes out of a total of 216.

On the 21st of March, 1876, M. Hugo introduced in the Senate a proposal for granting an amnesty to all those condemned for the events of March, 1871, and to all those then undergoing punishment for political crimes or offences in Paris, including the assassins of the hostages. On the 22d of May he delivered an eloquent oration in support of his motion, but it was rejected, only about seven hands being held up for the amnesty. The poet-orator again pleaded the same cause in January, 1879, but his proposal was coldly received. In the following month, however, an Amnesty Bill was passed by the Chamber of Deputies.

To return to the literary record of Victor Hugo. Early in 1877 appeared the second part of the 'Legende des Siècles,' and shortly afterwards the poet was deeply gratified by Tennyson's greeting of him in the *Nineteenth Century* as 'Victor in poesy, Victor in romance.' In October, 1877, appeared another remarkable work by the deceased, 'L'Histoire d'un Crime.' It had been written a quarter of a century before in condemnation of the events of December, 1851, and now, when there were possible rumours of a *coup d 'État* of another kind, he deemed it absolutely imperative to publish it. As he remarked in his preface 'This work is more than opportune; it is imperative. I publish it.' In the following November appeared a lighter work, 'L'Art d'être Grandpère.' When the second part of 'The History of a Crime' appeared, at the beginning of 1878, France had fortunately passed through a period of great political excitement without those fearful consequences which have frequently followed such periods in her history. The continuation of Victor Hugo's work did not, consequently, create such popular fervour as it might otherwise have done. But the author was as scathing as ever in his invectives, and no one knew such strong depths of bitterness and indignation as he. On the 29th of April, 1878, appeared Victor Hugo's new poem – 'Le Pape.'

When the Voltaire centenary was celebrated in Paris in May, 1878, Victor Hugo was the chief speaker. The great meeting was held in the Gaîté Theatre, which was crowded to suffocation. While all the speakers at that meeting were warmly applauded, our Correspondent, writing on that occasion, observed that 'it was when M. Victor Hugo rose that the tempest of acclamation burst forth. Can a grander, a more striking, a more exaggerated scene be conceived than this association of Victor Hugo and Voltaire, of the most eloquent and the most touching of French orators, exhausting his mines of highly coloured epithets and colossal antitheses on the ironical head of Voltaire? A report of his speech does not suffice; the white head and apostle's beard, the inspired eye, the solemn voice, rolling as if it would sound in the ears of posterity; the involuntarily haughty attitude in vain striving to seem modest; the imperturbable seriousness with which he piles antithesis upon antithesis – all this must be realized.' Victor Hugo was enthusiastically cheered on taking the chair; but, waving his arm, he exclaimed, 'Vive la République!' – a cry which was then taken up with equal fervour. After the other speakers had been heard the distinguished chairman delivered his oration. He rapidly sketched the work accomplished by Voltaire, and concluded with an eloquent peroration.

The International Literary Congress, held in Paris in June, 1878, once more beheld Victor Hugo to the front upon a question in which he took much interest. His speech on that occasion was accepted by the Congress as forming the basis of its decisions. In the August following this conference a great working men's meeting was held in the French capital in favour of international arbitration, and Victor Hugo, unable to be present and to take the chair as he intended, sent a communication expressing his approbation of the objects of the meeting. 'The supreme future is with you,' he wrote. 'All that is done, even against you, will serve you. Continue to march, labour, and think. You are a single people. Europe and you want a single thing – peace.' In February, 1879, Victor Hugo furnished another illustration to many which had gone before of the liberality of his mind and his support of the doctrine of universal toleration by the publication of a poem entitled 'La Pitié Suprême.'

On the eve of the 78th birthday of the poet, February 25, 1880, which was also the 50th anniversary of *Hernani*, this famous play was produced at the Comédie Française. The performance of the piece was followed by the recitation of verses by M. Coppée, and by the crowning of the author's bust.

'Réligions et Réligion,' a work by Victor Hugo which appeared early in 1880, is an attack not only upon various systems of religion, but also upon those who attack all religion. 'L'Ane,' which was published some months later in the same year, is, as its name implies, a poem of a totally different order. Desiring to lash his kind, with Rabelais, the poet puts his denunciations into the mouth of an ass, which animal is taken to be the type of unsophisticated man. The work was regarded as a failure, in spite of the genius which played about its pages, the satiric power of Victor Hugo being one rather of fierce denunciation than that which consists in the perception of the incongruous in humanity. In 1881 appeared 'Les Quatre Vents de l'Esprit.' *Torquemada*, a drama written chiefly during Victor Hugo's exile in Guernsey, was published in 1882. The poet himself regarded it as one of his best efforts, and it certainly exhibits his glowing imagination and his power in depicting human misery at their highest. The great Inquisitor is drawn as a single-minded enthusiast who, following relentlessly to their conclusion the doctrines upon which he has been nourished since childhood, burns and tortures people from pure love of their souls, hoping thereby to save them. In 1883 Hugo issued the last part of his great work, 'La Légende des Siècles,' on the whole the finest, perhaps, of all his works, since it displays a disciplined imagination without revealing so prominently the defects apparent in so many other of the poet's compositions.

In addition to the works named, Victor Hugo was the author of 'Choix Moral des Lettres de Voltaire,' published in 1824, and afterwards incorporated with some modifications in the volume already mentioned, 'Littérature et Philosophie Mêlées;' of a number of articles, poems, and translations which appeared in the Conservateur *Littéraire*, the *Revue des Deux Mondes*, and the *Globe*; of three discourses pronounced before the French Academy; a collection of poems relating to childhood, published in 1858, and entitled 'Les Enfants, Livre des Mères,' 'William Shakespeare,' an anonymous work published in 1864; 'Paris,' being an introduction to the Paris Guide, published by M. Ulbach; and the 'Voix de Guernesey,' a poem which appeared at Brussels in 1868, and was inspired by the engagement of Mentana. It is also well known that the deceased was a skilful artist, and M. Théophile Gautier published in 1863 a collection of his designs. The poet is understood to have left behind him a considerable number of important works in manuscript, which will be published in accordance with his instructions.

Few monarchs have received such an ovation as was accorded to Victor Hugo by the city of Paris on the 27th of February, 1881. The day before, the poet had completed his 70th year, and by the French people this is regarded as entitling to octogenarian honours. A celebration took place which was compared with the reception of Voltaire in 1788. The Avenue d'Eylau, where Victor Hugo resided, was densely thronged, and the poet, being recognized with his children and grandchildren at an upper window of his house, was cheered by a vast multitude, estimated by unsympathetic observers at 100,000. The Municipality had erected at the entrance to the avenue lofty flagstaffs decorated with shields bearing the titles of his works, and supporting a large drapery inscribed '1802, Victor Hugo, 1881.' Early in the morning the avenue was thronged with processions consisting of collegians, trades unions, musical and benefit societies, deputations from the districts of Paris and from the provinces, &c. A deputation of children, bearing a blue and red banner with the inscription 'L'Art d'être Grand-père,' and headed by a little girl in white, arrived at the house, and were received by Victor Hugo in the drawing-room. The little maiden, who recited some lines by M. Mendes, was blessed by the venerable poet. Among other incidents of the day, the Paris Municipality drew up in front of the house, when Victor Hugo addressed them in praise of the city of Paris. A stream of processions then began to file past the house, those of the musical societies alone exceeding 100. The entire avenue, nearly a mile long, was crowded with spectators, and the conduct of this immense gathering was most exemplary. At the Trocadéro a musical and literary festival was held, when selections from Victor Hugo's works were sung or recited by some of the leading Paris *artistes*, and the 'Marseillaise' was performed by a military band. M. Louis Blanc, who presided, said that few great men had entered in their lifetime into their immortality. Voltaire and Victor Hugo had both deserved this, one for stigmatizing religious intolerance, the other for having, with incomparable lustre, served humanity. In the evening of the day there was a Victor Hugo concert at the Conservatoire, and at many of the theatres verses were recited in his honour. On the night of the 25th a special performance was given at the Gaîté of *Lucrèce Borgia*, which had not been produced there for 10 years. The house was filled, all the notabilities of Paris being present, while the poet himself also appeared for a short time. The celebration generally was one triumphant success.

On the occasion of Hugo's 80th birthday, in February, 1882, the French Government ordered a free performance of *Hernani* at the Théâtre Français; 2,300 persons squeezed themselves into accommodation intended only for 1,500. On the day following the committee of the previous year's grand celebration presented Hugo with a bronze miniature of Michael Angelo's Moses. In responding for the gift, in the presence of 5,000 persons, the poet said:–

> 'I accept your present, and I await a still better one, the greatest a man can receive – I mean death; death, that recompense for the good done on earth. I shall live in my descendants, my grandchildren, Jeanne and Georges. If indeed I have a narrow-minded thought it is for them. I wish to insure their future, and I confide them to the protection of all the loyal and devoted hearts here present.'

On the 22d of November, 1882, a jubilee performance of *Le Roi s'Amuse* was given at the Théâtre Français. Fifty years before, as we have seen, it was produced amid such tumults that the Government forbade its further representation. Now it was produced with great favour, the utmost interest having been manifested for weeks previously. Our Correspondent stated at the time that if there had been 10,000 seats in the house instead of 1,500 there would still have been an insufficiency of places to satisfy the demand. M. Got achieved a great triumph in the part of Triboulet.

In private life and character Victor Hugo was one of the noblest and most unselfish of men. Many are the anecdotes related of his generosity and kindliness of disposition. One who had every opportunity of studying his private life states that when residing at Hauteville-house, Guernsey, he organized a poor children's repast twice a week, to which he invited the poorest of the poor, giving them roast beef and good wine to invigorate them. He likewise adopted the rather Quixotic measure of reserving a room in his house for the use of any literary person in temporary distress; and this hospitality would last sometimes for two, three, or even six months. The befriended ones were not allowed to feel the irksomeness of their position; they had their place at table with the poet, and free rooms were granted them. The poet had a special talent for organizing Christmas parties, and was never happier than when surrounded by his grandchildren. He mingled in all their games and even shared their troubles and their punishments. When his favourite little grandchild was put on dry bread for bad conduct the grandfather was so unhappy that he would take no dessert. His pleasures were as simple as his mind was great. He has been accused of being an infidel; but those who knew him best maintain strongly that he was a firm believer in God and in a future state. Even when in his octogenarian period it was the poet's habit to rise with the day, summer and winter, and to work until 9. He then allowed himself an hour's rest for breakfast and his morning constitutional, after which he again sat at his desk, mostly pursuing his intellectual labours, till 5 in the afternoon. Work being concluded, he dined at half-past 6, and invariably retired to rest at 10. On one occasion, speaking of his future works, the poet said:– 'I shall have more to do than I have already done. One would think that with age the mind weakens; with me it appears, on the contrary, to grow stronger. The horizon gets larger and I shall pass away without having finished my task.'

It may be stated that a magnificent national edition of Victor Hugo's works is being prepared, which, when completed, will extend to 40 volumes of square quarto form. Each volume will contain five etchings from designs by Baudry, Constant, Boulanger, Gérôme, Henner, and other distinguished artists; and, in addition, the work will contain altogether 2,500 illustrations in the text. All that art and the printers and publishers can do is being essayed to make this edition worthy of the poet's reputation.

We have now reached the close of our survey of a remarkable career. This is not the place in which to cast the horoscope of this great name. It is not for us to say what will perish and what will remain of that vast mass of intellectual treasure which Victor Hugo has left behind him. But it must be obvious to all that with the passing away of the great head of the romantic school there is lost to French literature one of its mightiest and most operative forces. Victor Hugo's is a colossal figure in that literature. His mind was one of the most powerful and original that ever illumined its brilliant pages. Yet that mind had its weaknesses. Superb in wealth of fancy and power of language, the very gift of speech itself proved a snare to him. He lacked concentration. Who could have predicted for Shakespeare the same kind of immortality he now enjoys if he had bequeathed to us an intellectual legacy ten times larger than that which we have received? As it is, in spite of its infinite variety, we can, as it were, stretch our hands over the whole Shakespearian keyboard and bear within our recollection his exquisite notes of sadness and of joy. We can never gauge the depths of his heart and intellect, but we can make his every line immortal. With Victor Hugo it is different. Passing in review the prodigious list of his works, we may use the words of Scripture and ask, 'Who shall say which shall prosper, this or that, or whether both shall be alike good?' That much will live, however, and live permanently, we may rest assured. He has a niche to himself in that temple of fame assigned to the world's great poets; and that niche is a high and an honourable one. For the present, to change the figure, we can only add our tribute of regret that one of the greatest luminaries of our time has sunk below the earthly horizon.

The problem for many nineteenth-century British admirers of Hugo's work was that it was inextricably bound up with Hugo's contorted and sometimes contradictory politics. He was, as this obituary notice remarks, of mixed Bonapartist and Monarchist parentage, and the political fissures in post-Napoleonic France continued to mark both Hugo's life and the tenor of his literary work. He was a tacit supporter of the Bourbon Restoration but accepted a peerage from Louis-Philippe (while making no secret of the fact that he regarded the July monarchy as only a temporary constituional experiment). His subsequent Republicanism rendered him an exile on Guernsey under Napoleon III. Having declined to return to France under the general amnesty issued in 1859, he continued to relish his high international profile as a dissident writer, and delighted in the huge success of the revival of *Hernani* during the Paris Universal Exhibition of 1867. The further tergiversations of his political career after 1870 are well described in the obituary. Such a career cannot possibly be paralleled by that of a contemporary British writer. If Hugo's highly Romantic verse dramas never had quite the same impact on the English stage that they had in Paris, his fiction was extraordinarily well received on both sides of the Channel. Hugo died in his house in Paris in the avenue d'Eylau (now avenue Victor Hugo) on 22 May 1885. He was buried with great pomp in the Panthéon.

SIR MOSES MONTEFIORE

Philanthropist: 'Piety, loyalty, and benevolence.'

28 JULY 1885

SIR MOSES MONTEFIORE passed away peacefully yesterday afternoon at his house of East Cliff, near Ramsgate. It would be out of place to use the conventional terms of regret with regard to one who has died so full of years and honours. His life has gradually and painlessly waned away since his neighbours and friends, the latter to be found in the most diverse ranks, religions, races, and climates, celebrated on October 28, 1884, the completion of the 100th year of his singularly prolonged and memorable existence. He retained intermittently to the last great mental clearness and activity which he enjoyed alternately with long periods of passive expectancy waiting for the end; and it is satisfactory to know that he was cheered and positively sustained by being told from time to time how the good works he had set on foot prospered, and by learning the universal interest felt in his health and the long continuance of his days. He was, in particular, greatly cheered to hear Dr. Hermann Adler's good report of the well-being of the tenants of the dwellings which he had promoted in and about Jerusalem; and he was much occupied with the wedding present which he was privileged to present to Princess Beatrice. On this he caused to be engraved the verse from Proverbs, 'Many daughters have done virtuously, but thou excellest them all,' which he had never tired of applying to his own wife. When he no longer possessed the energy for conversation he was sometimes heard repeating under his breath verses in Hebrew from the Psalms, and it may truly be said that his last thoughts were occupied with the duties of piety, loyalty, and benevolence, which it had been his aim during the century to fulfil. To the Jews it may well seem as if with him the central pillar of their temple had fallen; but those who calmly contemplate his life will understand that the example of his useful and benevolent career has done its work.

Moses Montefiore was born, the eldest son of a not very wealthy merchant, on the 24th of October, 1784. His ancestors had dwelt in Ancona and Leghorn, cities in which by special, and then exceptional legislation, Jews had been permitted to trade. His grandfather, Moses Haim Montefiore, had settled in England, where he had nine sons and eight daughters, and was a near neighbour and associate of Benjamin Disraeli, the grandfather of Lord Beaconsfield. Joseph Elias, fourth son among the 17 children, married a daughter of the house of Mocatta, a family of

Moorish or Spanish Jews, who had left their tombs in the Lido at Venice and in the graveyard of Amsterdam. Joseph Montefiore's wife accompanied him to Leghorn whither he went to buy for the English market, and there in the Via Reale she gave birth to the first of her eight children, Moses Haim, the subject of this notice, whose name was registered as born on October 24 (the eve of Heshvan 9th), 1784, in the books of the synagogue. Returning to England with his parents, Moses Montefiore was educated privately, articled to Mr. Robert Johnson, a wholesale tea merchant in Eastcheap, and afterwards entered the Stock Exchange, where his uncle purchased for him for £1,200 the right to practise as one of the 12 Jewish brokers. No greater number than that was permitted by the City of London, although a more enlightened body than most of the English communities of that day, to compete with the stock-brokers of the orthodox confession. Moses Montefiore joined a Surrey volunteer regiment (he lived at Kennington-terrace), and rose to the rank of captain. He became very popular on the Stock Exchange, and much consideration was shown for him when, in consequence of the default of another person, he had to ask for a few days' time, which was cheerfully accorded him, to deliver some Exchequer Bills. He began the publication of a regular price-list of securities, was joined in business by his brother Abraham, and became connected in business and by marriage with Nathan Mayer Rothschild, whose name is still signed on the cheques of the great house in New-court. The two friends married sisters, daughters of Levy Barent Cohen, a merchant of Dutch descent, greatly respected for his wealth and benevolence. Abraham Montefiore wedded Henrietta Rothschild, sister of the great financier, and thus established another bond of union between the families. It is fitting that in Sir Moses's will this time-honoured connexion is still recognized. Lord Rothschild, whose elevation to the peerage during the last few weeks of Sir Moses's life was a sign of the completeness of the emancipation for which the Rothschilds and Montefiore battled so long, is named as one of the executors, the others being Mr. Joseph Sebag, Mr. Arthur Cohen, Q. C., and Dr. Loewe. Mr. Joseph Sebag, as the senior surviving nephew, is the senior executor; Mr. Arthur Cohen is a nephew of the late Lady Montefiore; and Dr. Loewe is the linguist and Orientalist who accompanied Sir Moses and Lady Montefiore on their journeys to the East. Moses Montefiore married in 1812. It was in 1813 that Mr. Rothschild brought out the British loan for £12,000,000 for warlike operations against Napoleon Bonaparte; and henceforward the brothers Montefiore were associated with the transactions of the house of Rothschild. He lived next door to Mr. Rothschild, and has himself described how 'N. M. Rothschild,' as Sir Moses was wont to call his brother-in-law in speaking of him to other persons, roused him at 6 o'clock in the morning to give news of the escape from Elba, which Mr. Rothschild was able to communicate to the Ministry. The carrier, on being told the message he had brought in a sealed despatch, cried 'Vive l'Empereur' and his interlocutors were able to frame from his enthusiasm a shrewd estimate of the temper of the French.

In 1824 Mr. Montefiore had retired from business and settled in Park-lane, Mr. Rothschild removing at about the same time to Piccadilly, where he long occupied a house now the property of the Savile Club. 'Thank God, and be content,' was his wife's behest to Mr. Montefiore, and he was henceforth only occupied with duties of a semi-public nature, as in founding, in conjunction with his friends, the Alliance Fire, Life, and Marine Insurance Office, the Imperial Continental Gas Association, and the Provincial Bank of Ireland. The Alliance Office was successful from the first, profiting as it did in its life department by the greater average of longevity among its Jewish clients, who were admitted at the ordinary rates, based on actuarial calculations embracing both Jew and Gentile. The Gas Association, though its shares stand now at a high premium, had as hard a struggle for existence as the electric light companies which are now striving to soften the heart of the Board of Trade. In connexion with the Irish banking business Sir Moses went twice round Ireland, and was presented with the freedom of Londonderry. He was for a short time a director of the South-Eastern Railway, and in memory of this connexion received in 1883 from the then directors a gold pass, a purely honorary distinction in the circumstances.

It was in 1827 that Mr. Montefiore undertook the pilgrimage which coloured the whole of his future existence. He had been known as a pious and benevolent man, and as one who, while reverent of tradition, controlled it by good sense, as in seeking his wife from among the 'German' Jews, although himself a member of the Sephardic or Spanish synagogue. But his life-long devotion to the cause of his oppressed brethren in the East dates from his visit to Palestine in 1827. The way to Palestine then lay through Egypt, as that to Cairo now passes by Constantinople. The record of the journey, as told by Mrs. Montefiore in her diary, is interesting. Mr. and Mrs. Montefiore drove to Dover, had their travelling carriage placed on the Boulogne steamer, and posted to Turin. At Radicofani Mr. Montefiore, a man of 43, and ignorant that he himself would exceed a century of existence, gave the curate a dollar for the oldest person in the place, who, writes Lady Montefiore, 'had only the heavens for his covering and the earth for his couch.' They were rowed from Messina to Malta, and took in their convoyed ship which they chartered for Alexandria three poor Greek women, whose husbands had fallen at Missolonghi. The meeting with Mehemet Ali laid the foundations of a lasting friendship, but Mr. Salt, the British Consul, warned the travellers strongly against proceeding to Palestine. They would be sold for slaves; he trembled to think what would become of Mrs. Montefiore. This pair of travellers, however, were not easily frightened. They sailed to Jaffa and rode into Jerusalem, 'a fallen, desolate and abject' city, as Lady Montefiore describes it. They found the Jews very poor and miserable, dwelling like conies in the clefts in the rocks, oppressed by officials, paying £300 a year for the melancholy privilege of weeping at the wall which is called the Wailing Place of Jerusalem. After administering bountiful alms, and making still more fruitful inquiries into the possibility of a permanent amelioration of the condition of the people by stimulating industry, the Montefiores returned to Alexandria, where they heard Arab women lamenting in the street the defeat of Navarino. Afterwards they themselves brought home some of Codrington's despatches.

Immediately on his return from this visit to the East, Mr. Montefiore joined the Board of Deputies of British Jews, a body of representatives elected by the synagogues, and this council for many years afterwards under his direction took a lively interest in the welfare of its foreign brethren. The English Jews had, however, on their own part a struggle to maintain for political emancipation. Wealthy, well-educated, and often honoured socially, they were excluded by their religion from sitting in either House of Parliament and from most public offices. The battle for the privileges and duties of citizenship had to be won by showing themselves conspicuously worthy of these rights and able to fulfil these duties. David Salomons, the friend of Montefiore, being a candidate for the shrievalty, was told that if a criminal were reprieved from hanging on a Saturday, his Sabbath, his religion would prevent him from announcing the commutation of the sentence. He refuted so absurd a charge and was elected sheriff of London and Middlesex, but was unable to take the qualifying oath, and accordingly exercised but an imperfect jurisdiction, till Lyndhurst passed a Bill to relieve him. This was in 1835; in 1837 Montefiore came forward and became the second Jewish sheriff. A year before, he had been elected a Fellow of the Royal Society. As sheriff at the Coronation Moses Montefiore was knighted by the Queen, to whom as Princess Victoria he had already been enabled to offer the courtesy of the use of his grounds at Ramsgate, the agreeable gardens attached to his house at East Cliff at which he lived for over 60 years and at which he ultimately died. By his energy, popularity, and his own munificence, Sir Moses Montefiore made unprecedentedly large collections for the City charities during his year of office as sheriff. He was also able to secure the pardon of the only criminal whom it would have been his duty to cause to be put to death. Immediately after he had served his year Sir Moses and Lady Montefiore departed on their second pilgrimage to the Holy Land. They visited on the way the seven synagogues of Rome, making benefactions to the congregations; and while they fulfilled the responsibilities of life did not forget its graces. They met Prince Coburg and the Duchess of Sutherland at a reception at the Duke of Torlonia's, saw Severn's pictures, Gibson's statues, and the museums, bought works of art, entertained a Papal monsignor and a French abbé, and sent Passover cakes to their friends. At Malta, where Prince George of Cambridge (now his Royal Highness the Field-Marshal Commanding-in-Chief) arrived during their stay, news met them that the plague was raging at Jerusalem. Sir Moses accordingly proposed to proceed alone. 'This' writes Lady Montefiore 'I peremptorily resisted, and the expressions of Ruth furnished my heart at the moment with the language it most desired to use "Entreat me not to leave thee, or to return from following after thee; for whither thou goest I will go, and where thou lodgest I will lodge."' This time they were received in Jerusalem with the most brilliant ceremony as the friends of the Egyptian ruler, and the benefactors of all. After distributing funds entrusted to him by the Chief Rabbi, Sir Moses returned to Beyrout impressed with the necessity of introducing agriculture among the Jews of the Holy Land. He obtained from Mehemet Ali a decree authorizing the Jews to acquire land, and was preparing an extensive scheme for farming the soil of Palestine by the descendants of those who anciently possessed it, when political disturbances overturned all the plans formed, and rendered valueless the privileges acquired. The Sultan sent his armies against Syria, Acre was bombarded, and the rule of Mehemet Ali was destroyed.

In 1840, the blood accusation, the terrible and lying charge that the Jews offer up human sacrifice, was stirred against them in Rhodes and Damascus. In both these places the populace demanded the blood of the Jews, and the local authorities were not averse to imprisoning such as could afford ransom. Some of these victims perished in captivity. Sir Moses Montefiore called upon his fellow-citizens to express their disbelief in the charge and their sympathy with the oppressed Israelites. The Lord Mayor presided over a public meeting at the Mansion-house, Lord Palmerston received a deputation, Sir Moses Montefiore proceeded to Alexandria and Constantinople to demand a fair trial for the accused. Political complications made a public hearing at Damascus impossible but the surviving prisoners were released; the Rhodian charge fell to the ground; and the Sultan in response to Sir Moses's appeal issued the firman of 12th Ramazan, 1256, which discusses the inveterate calumny, refers to the Biblical maxim which prohibits Jews from using the blood even of animals, and dismisses as groundless the charge that they employ human blood. The firman goes on to declare the equality before the law of the Jewish nation with the other subjects of the Commander of the Faithful, and forbids any molestation of them in their religious or temporal concerns. During his visit to Constantinople Sir Moses found that few of the Jews could read or write the language of the country, although they were by no means illiterate so far as concerned Hebrew and the strange dialect compounded of Spanish and Hebrew which their ancestors had brought away in exile from the Iberian Peninsula. He conferred with the leaders of the congregations, and suggested that the Turkish language should be taught in their schools. 'I am quite satisfied' he writes 'it will be greatly useful, as it will fit our people for employments and situations from which they are now excluded.' This expectation has been signally fulfilled. At that time no Jew was in the public service. Now many have attained high military or civil rank.

The result of the mission of 1840 was felt to be so momentous that it was proposed in Germany to institute a new Purim in its honour. In England the Queen granted to her Knight-errant, who had ridden abroad redressing human wrongs, the right of bearing supporters, an honour usually reserved to peers and the knights of orders.

Sir Moses Montefiore's next mission was to Russia. In the wintry weather of February and March, he travelled to St. Petersburg to induce the Czar to recall a ukase which he had issued ordering the removal into the interior of all Jews living within 50 versts of the frontier. With the good offices of the Court of St. James, and the commercial results of the measure being foreseen, it was recalled. Great risks had been run from wolves and ice during this journey, and the eloquence, or rather the sincerity of Sir Moses Montefiore, and the effect of his bearing as a representative Israelite, and at the same time an English gentleman of high standing, had entirely prevailed. On his return several members of the Royal House attended a reception given in his honour by the late Charlotte Baroness de Rothschild, at Gunnersbury, and the Queen conferred upon him a baronetcy.

In 1858 Sir Moses travelled to Rome and had his unsuccessful encounter with Cardinal Antonelli, who refused to give up the child Mortara, surreptitiously baptized by a nurse and stolen from his mother, who died of grief. The refusal, perhaps, hastened the fall of the temporal power.

In 1860 Montefiore headed the subscription for the relief of the misery of the Christians of Syria, who had been attacked by the Druses of Mount Lebanon. His letter appeared in our columns on July 12, and resulted in the collection of more than £22,500. We cannot describe all his journeys to the Holy Land, which he visited seven times in all, on the last occasion when he was more than 90 years of age. Whole cities went out to meet him on the way, sermons were preached, odes composed in his honour. In Palestine he endowed hospitals and alms-houses, set on foot agricultural enterprises, planted gardens, built synagogues and tombs. Besides his own benefactions he was often chosen to administer the charities of others, as, for example, by Juda Touro, of New Orleans, who left large sums at his disposal for improvements in Jerusalem. He pleaded with a later Czar (Alexander II) in St. Petersburg and with the King of Roumania at Bucharest for his brethren, crossed the great desert on a litter to the city of Morocco and procured a milder treatment for Jews tortured by barbarians. From his bedroom at East Cliff he sent letters to every member of the Hungarian Legislature exposing the iniquity of the false blood accusation at Tisza Eslar, and corresponded with Lord Beaconsfield and the present Prime Minister on the subject of the Jews of Roumania, whose condition he believed in vain to have been permanently regulated and improved by the Treaty of Berlin. Judith, Lady Montefiore, the dear companion of his travels died in 1862. He built in her memory a college at Ramsgate, where rabbis maintained by his benevolence pass their days in prayer and study of the law. He also founded in her memory scholarships and prizes for girls and boys. The mausoleum at Ramsgate in which she at present lies alone is a model of the building called the tomb of Rachel on the road from Bethlehem to Jerusalem, which he had often visited with her who was as dear to him as Rachel was to his ancestor.

Sir Moses's entry into his 100th year on the 8th of November, 1883 (corresponding with 8th Heshvan, 5643), was celebrated as a public holiday at Ramsgate, where his liberal but discriminating charities, administered by the local clergy of all denominations, and his unfailing courtesy and hospitality, had made him most popular. The occasion became, by reason of the widespread public interest aroused, one of national significance, and the Queen herself telegraphed, 'I congratulate you sincerely on your entering into the hundredth year of a useful and honourable life.' The Prince of Wales, the Duke of Edinburgh, the City of London, and hundreds of representative bodies sent similar messages. At Jerusalem and among the Jewish congregations throughout the world special prayers were offered up and services held. The Lord Mayor attended the special service held last year (October 20, 1884) in London on the completion of Sir Moses's century of existence, and the commemorations at Ramsgate and throughout the country and the world in churches and synagogues were still more striking than that of 1883. The excitement of receiving so many congratulations was great for a centenarian, but on the whole it had a beneficial effect upon his health. Sir Moses had ardently desired to see his hundredth year, and that wish had been fulfilled. We have since then chronicled in Dr. Woodman's bulletins his gradual and peaceful decline. He passed away without a struggle yesterday at 4.30 p.m. His nearest relations had been summoned by telegraph early in the morning.

The funeral has been appointed to leave East Cliff-lodge, Ramsgate, precisely at 2 on Friday for the mausoleum already described, where Sir Moses Montefiore will be laid beside the body of Judith, his wife.

Having amassed a fortune as a stockbroker, Montefiore retired from business in 1824. To the Victorian age, he was a man admired for his generosity and respectability as much as for his energy and his uncommon longevity. As a devout Jew he lived to see not only the growing confidence and strength of the British Jewish community, but also the steady opening up of all aspects of civic life to his co-religionists. As the obituary makes clear, the aged Montefiore was prepared to lend both his voice and his fortune in support of Jews oppressed or slighted by foreign regimes. In 1858, the year that saw his friend, Baron Lionel de Rothschild, take his seat in the Commons, Montefiore travelled to Rome to plead the case of Edgar Mortara, a Jewish boy purportedly baptised by a servant and taken from his parents by order of the Archbishop of Bologna. Montefiore visited Jerusalem for the seventh and last time in 1875.

* * *

FRANZ LISZT

Composer and pianist:
'Hungary had produced a deep impression on his fancy.'

31 JULY 1886

THE DEATH OF FRANZ LISZT on Saturday night at Bayreuth will throw a gloom over the entire musical world. In England it will be felt by many as a personal loss. If it had happened before his memorable visit to this country all lovers of serious music would have deplored the death of a famous musician, who in his person represented a link between the past and the present and the future; as it is, we regret him as a friend whom we recently welcomed among us and who at parting gave us hope of another and longer visit. It will be remembered that the reception given to Liszt assumed this entirely personal character. Many people who knew little or nothing of his music, down to the very cabmen in the street, were impressed by the venerable appearance of the great musician, and submitted to the indefinable kind of fascination exercised by Liszt over all sorts and conditions of men. Few of those who saw him and heard him for the first time on that occasion could have foreseen that the vital force which seemed to sustain his frame would so soon have been exhausted. He seemed indefatigable, going from concert to concert, from entertainment to entertainment, attending the rehearsals of his *St. Elizabeth* and giving valuable hints to Mr. Mackenzie, the conductor, and the principal vocalists engaged in the performance. Those, however, who had known Liszt even a few years before could not help noticing the marked change which had come over him. His gait, formerly full of elasticity and vigour, had become older; his eyesight was impaired, and – ungracious though it would have been to say so at the time – his playing had lost some of its old indescribable charm, apart from the natural decline of physical strength and agility. To them in short Liszt for the time appeared an old

Franz Liszt

man, little fitted to sustain the wear and tear of a London season without serious danger to his life. These apprehensions were destined to be realized only too soon. From London Liszt returned to Paris, where further ovations and another performance of *St. Elizabeth* were in store for him. Thence he returned to Weimar to recruit his strength for the Wagner performances at Bayreuth, from which he was never absent. He went to Bayreuth in the beginning of last month, to witness the marriage of his grand-daughter, and remained for the festival plays. There death has at last overtaken him; and it could not have found him in a more classical, one might almost say hallowed, atmosphere, or among friends more devoted. In this as in all other respects he was a favourite of fortune, and the gift of enthusiasm was only the crowning mercy of a career almost unique in its unbroken continuity of successful endeavours.

That Liszt would occupy a prominent position among the artists of his age might have been predicted when, as a child nine years old, he appeared for the first time before the public; and the boldest prophecies then ventured upon by his admirers have since been more than verified. Among modern *virtuosi* Paganini alone was equal to Liszt in the irresistible, almost personal fascination he exercised over his audience; of all his eminent followers in the art of pianoforte playing many of whom were also his pupils, none equalled or even approached the genius over which age till quite recently seemed to have no power. This was admitted in the midst of his London triumphs by Rubinstein, who shares together with some of Liszt's greatest artistic qualities, his generous appreciation of other men's merits. As a composer Liszt's excellence has been less generally acknowledged. Perhaps his earlier fame as an executant was against him. For the public is slow to admit merits different from those it has once discovered and appreciated in its favourites. Here, however, also, the undaunted energy of Liszt proved in the end victorious, and he lived to see his great choral and orchestral works not only performed but also imitated by a band of admiring disciples. Both as a composer and an executant, Liszt has left a marked impress on the artistic development of our time. But perhaps still more important was the personal influence he exercised over the minds of young musicians, uniting their efforts to a common aim, guiding them in their studies, calling their attention to all that is best and greatest in ancient and modern art. For Liszt was no fanatic preacher of a narrow doctrine. His taste was eminently catholic; Italian and French and German music found in him an admirer and interpreter. He advocated and practically illustrated the supreme merits of Beethoven's pianoforte music when other *virtuosi* scorned it as unpopular; he shares with Schumann and Mendelssohn the merit of having rescued Schubert's works from undeserved oblivion; he was as enthusiastic in the cause of Bach as he was successively in those of Berlioz, of Schumann, and of Wagner. It was, indeed, by keeping pace with the changes and developments of his art that he preserved his freshness of mind and his influence over the rising generation of musicians. His executive power also remained unabated almost to the last, and whenever he was of late years induced to play at a concert his reception was as enthusiastic as when his young genius astonished the world more than half a century ago. His appearances in public in his latter days were always caused by the motives of charity, to which Liszt all his life was accessible to an almost exaggerated degree. From the career of a *virtuoso* he retired many years ago to devote himself to composition. That he was inclined to do this when his fame and his pecuniary success were at their highest is perhaps the noblest trait in his artistic character.

Liszt, successful in everything else, has not been fortunate in his biographers. His life, interesting and full of incident, remains to be written. Among his numerous disciples, there was, as far as one knows, no Boswell, no Schindler – *carat vate sacro*. There are, it is true, many sketches of his life and criticisms of his works, but not one of them is of permanent value. Of an extensive biography by L. Ramann only one volume has appeared which closes with the year 1840, before Liszt's activity as a composer had begun.

Franz Liszt was born at Raiding, near Oedenburg, in Hungary, October 22, 1811. His father was a Magyar, his mother a German, the mixture of races being distinguishable in the artistic disposition of their son. Adam Liszt, the father, held an appointment on the estates of Prince Esterhazy – a name well known in the history of music in connexion with Haydn, Schubert and other great composers. Although not a trained musician, Adam Liszt had sufficient taste and knowledge to recognize the genius of his son evinced at a very early age, and to undertake his first education in the art. So rapid was the progress of the boy that at the age of nine he was able to play in public at Oedenburg, and soon afterwards at Pressburg, with such success that six Hungarian noblemen on the spur of the moment guaranteed a sufficient sum for the cultivation of his extraordinary talent during six years. This enabled the family to go to Vienna, where young Liszt continued his studies under Salieri, the rival of Mozart and Czerny, a famous pianist of the time. Here also his success in public was as brilliant as it was instantaneous, among the admirers of the young *virtuoso* being Beethoven, who, after one of Liszt's concerts, strode on to the platform and kissed him before the audience. Soon afterwards Liszt's father determined to take his son to Paris, at that time the musical centre of Europe, and for that city they accordingly started in 1823, giving concerts by the way. The boy's desire to enter the Conservatoire was frustrated by a regulation excluding students of foreign origin, and Cherubini refused to make an exception in his favour in spite of the urgent recommendations of so powerful a patron as Prince Metternich. Liszt accordingly took private lessons from Reicha, and Paër, the operatic composer, and besides this continued his triumphs as a *virtuoso* in the concert-rooms and salons of the French metropolis. He also made various concert tours abroad, and visited

England for the first time in 1824. Here, as everywhere, his reception was enthusiastic. He had to play before George IV at Windsor, and a few days afterwards the King was present at Liszt's concert at Drury-lane Theatre, where he honoured the young *virtuoso* with an encore.

After his third visit to England in 1827, Liszt lost his father, and had henceforth to rely upon his own resources for the support of himself and his mother. He settled in Paris, which for a number of years became his home. Here his character as an artist and a man developed itself in the familiar intercourse with the leading spirits of French literature and art, with Lamennais and George Sand and Alfred de Musset and Berlioz. Here, also, he went through the youthful struggles and tribulations of a poetic and deeply religious mind, wavering at various periods between the sentimental mysticism of Chateaubriand and the advanced doctrines of Saint-Simon. At Paris, also, he met the Countess d'Agoult, well known in the literary world as 'Daniel Stern,' who for years remained attached to him. By her he had three children – a boy who died in infancy, a daughter, also dead, who married Emile Ollivier, the statesman who went into the Franco-German war 'with a light heart,' and a second daughter, the widow of Richard Wagner, who survives her father. To follow Liszt on his artistic tours between the years 1839 and 1847 would be only to repeat an unvaried record of triumphs offered to him by every capital of Europe from Madrid to St. Petersburg. At last he grew himself tired of the weary reiteration of his successes, and resolved to leave that great world for the modest but famous city of Weimar, where the post of Court chapel-master and conductor of the opera was offered to him. Here he gathered round him a group of young and gifted musicians, to whom he communicated his own ideas of the high aims and possibilities of musical progress. He also trained a number of pianists of the first order, Dr. von Bülow, the late Charles Tausig, and others among the number. The opera at Weimar, under his leadership, became the home of such works as were written regardless of immediate success, and therefore had little chance of a hearing elsewhere. Schumann's *Genovefa*, Schubert's *Alfonso and Estrella*, Berlioz's *Benvenuto Cellini*, and Wagner's *Lohengrin*, among other works, saw the light under Liszt's auspices at Weimar. The last-named event leads us to say a few words of the friendship between Liszt and Wagner, which remained undisturbed for many years, to be parted only by death. Wagner's own account of that friendship may find a place here. He writes:–

> 'I met Liszt for the first time during my earliest stay in Paris (1839), at a period when I had renounced the hope, nay, even the wish, of a Paris reputation, and, indeed, was in a state of internal revolt against the artistic life which I found there. At our meeting he struck me as the most perfect contrast to my own being and situation. In this world, into which it had been my desire to fly from my

narrow circumstances, Liszt had grown up, from his earliest age, so as to be the object of universal love and admiration, at a time when I was repulsed by general coldness and want of sympathy . . . In consequence, I looked upon him with suspicion. I had no opportunity of disclosing my being and working to him, and, therefore, the reception I met with on his part was altogether of a superficial kind, as was indeed natural in a man to whom every day the most divergent impressions claimed access. But I was not in a mood to look with unprejudiced eyes for the natural cause of his behaviour which though friendly and obliging in itself, could not but wound me in the actual state of my mind. I never repeated my first call on Liszt, and without knowing, or even wishing to know him, I was prone to look upon him as strange and adverse to my nature. My repeated expression of this feeling was afterwards told to him just at the time when my *Rienzi* at Dresden attracted general attention. He was surprised to find himself misunderstood with such violence by a man whom he had scarcely known, and whose acquaintance now seemed not without value to him. I am still moved when I remember the repeated and eager attempts he made to change my opinion of him, even before he knew any of my works. He acted, not from any artistic sympathy, but led by the purely human wish to dissolve a casual disharmony between himself and another being; perhaps he also felt an infinitely tender misgiving of having really hurt me unconsciously. He who knows the selfishness and terrible coldness of our social life, and especially of the relations of modern artists to each other, cannot but be struck with wonder, nay delight, by the treatment I experienced from this extraordinary man . . . At Weimar (1849) I saw him for the last time, when I was resting for a few days in Thuringia, uncertain whether the threatening prosecution would compel me to continue my flight from Germany. The very day when my personal danger became a certainty, I saw Liszt conducting a rehearsal of my *Tannhaüser*, and was astonished at recognizing my second self in his achievement. What I had felt in inventing this music he felt in performing it; what I wanted to express in writing it down he expressed in making it sound. Strange to say, through the love of this rarest friend I gained at the moment of becoming homeless, a real home for my art, which I had hitherto longed for and sought for always in the wrong place . . . At the end of my last stay at Paris, when ill, miserable, and despairing I sat brooding over my fate, my eye fell on the score of my *Lohengrin*, which I had totally forgotten. Suddenly I felt something like compassion that this music should never sound from off the death-pale paper. Two words I wrote to Liszt; his answer was the news that preparations for the performance were being made on the largest scale the limited means of Weimar would permit (1851).'

In 1859 Liszt abandoned his official position, and has since resided at intervals at Rome, Pesth and at Weimar. His time to the last was occupied in producing the compositions on which his permanent fame must mainly rest. Of the merits of those compositions this is not the place to speak. Of all of them detailed accounts have appeared in *The Times* as they were produced at the concerts of Mr. Walter Bache, Liszt's most devoted disciple in London, at the Crystal Palace, at the Richter concerts, and elsewhere. Of their final position in the history of music it would be premature to judge. Liszt is distinctly an innovator, not to say a revolutionist. In his symphonies or symphonic poems, as he calls them, he endeavours to develop the mighty poetic impulse given by Beethoven in his later works, and carried to its ultimate dramatic consequences by Wagner. Whether in this he has succeeded, and whether the new form created by him, and imitated by many younger composers, will prove to be durable the future must show. In the meantime one cannot but acknowledge the high purpose pervading such works as *Mazeppa* or *Tasso's Lament and Triumph*, and at the same time the technical mastership with which that purpose has been realized by the music. Among the religious works which take a prominent place among Liszt's creations, the *Graner Messe*, the oratorio *Christus*, and the sacred cantata *St. Elizabeth* are the most important. Liszt's minor compositions, his transcriptions and arrangements for the pianoforte, and his songs also should not be forgotten. The former have developed the technique of the instrument to a degree previously undreamt of, the latter frequently show depth and tenderness of lyrical feeling and a rich vein of genuine melody. Liszt's literary work is marked by critical discernment and wealth, sometimes redundancy, of expression. He generally took up the pen to interpret and praise the work of others. With that view he wrote 'Lohengrin et Tannhäuser de Richard Wagner,' and his biographical sketches of Chopin and Robert Franz, the former in French, the latter in German. More interesting even than these is his account of the gipsies and their music in Hungary. Here he was thoroughly at home. In his childhood the wild rhythms of the gipsies' dances played at fairs and wedding feasts in Hungary had produced a deep impression on his fancy, and the echo of that impression is audible even in his mature work.

As this obituary suggests, Liszt was generally better known to his contemporaries as a virtuoso pianist than as a composer. He first visited England as a boy prodigy in June 1824, performing at the Argyll Rooms and at Drury Lane on the newly perfected Erard pianoforte. The following year he played before George IV at Windsor, and gave a concert at Manchester. It was, however, as the composer of his sacred oratorio on a Hungarian theme, *The Legend of St Elizabeth*, that Liszt revisited London in 1886 for the first time since 1841. He attended rehearsals and a performance of *St Elizabeth* at the St. James's Hall, conducted by Alexander Mackenzie. He then travelled to Paris and on to Bayreuth in early July for his granddaughter's wedding, and to see performances of Richard Wagner's *Parsifal* and *Tristan and Isolde*. He died there of pneumonia on 31 July and was buried close to his son-in-law, Wagner. A correspondent to *The Times* records him as saying of his last visit to England: 'England is the home of music', adding with a laugh, 'At least it is the home where musicians are best treated'.

* * *

MATTHEW ARNOLD

Poet and essayist: 'To a certain number of readers he has as a poet a place apart; a place in the inmost shrine of their affections.'

15 APRIL 1888

WE DEEPLY REGRET to record that Mr. Matthew Arnold died suddenly on Sunday afternoon. On Thursday last he was in Leicestershire at the funeral of a brother-in-law; on Friday he was in London, conversing with many friends at the Athenaeum, and showing no signs of failing health or of any lack of power. That afternoon he went down to Liverpool to meet his married daughter, who was expected to arrive on Saturday or Sunday in the Aurania from New York. All Saturday he was as happy and bright as he always was when with his family, and on Sunday morning, after a good night, he attended service at a Presbyterian church, and then walked back to the house of his sister, with whom he was staying. After luncheon he wrote a note and then started with his wife for the landing-stage to meet the ship. While waiting for the tram-car he fell forward; they carried him to a doctor's house, and before an ambulance could be brought to take him home he was dead. For several years he well knew that his heart was seriously affected, and more than once, especially during his last visit to America, he had received a severe warning of the danger in which he perpetually stood. But although from time to time he was troubled with somewhat painful symptoms, and although he had to take special care of himself, he had lately been, on the whole, remarkably well, and neither himself nor those around him had the least suspicion that the end was so near.

He was the eldest son and second child – the eldest being Mrs. W. E. Forster – of the Rev. Thomas Arnold, D. D., and was born on December 24, 1822, at Laleham, near Staines, where his father was at the time taking private pupils. In 1827 Dr. Arnold was appointed to the headmastership of Rugby, and thither the family migrated in the following year. From this time down to the year 1845, when Matthew Arnold was elected Fellow of Oriel, the story of his life is best told in the words of one who was his constant companion throughout those years:–

'For some years previously to 1836, Matthew Arnold was under the care of the Rev. J. Buckland, the brother of the celebrated geological professor and Dean of Westminster, who kept a flourishing private school at Laleham. The astonishingly copious repertory of school-boy slang which the future poet brought home with him at the commencement of his first holidays, and poured into the ears of his brothers and sisters in the school-room at Rugby, is still within the recollection of some of them. On entering Winchester, in August, 1836, he was put at once in "Senior Part," and was consequently under Dr. Moberly. An unfortunate remark made to the doctor at a breakfast where he and several of his form-fellows were present, relative to the light character of the work which they had to do, being ill-naturedly repeated, caused him to incur much unpopularity in the school, and he was subjected to that singular form of ostracism known as "cloister-peelings," when the victim was led out before the whole school, and exposed for some minutes to a rain of "pontos," round missiles made of the crumb of new bread. But this unpopularity soon passed away, and when he was adjudged to have obtained the palm of rhetoric over the whole school by his declamation of the last speech of Marino Faliero in Byron's drama, every one was well pleased. It had never been his father's intention to leave him at Winchester longer than was necessary to make him familiar with a system which had inwoven itself into the very nature of the elder man; and in the summer of 1837 Matthew Arnold was removed from Winchester and entered at Rugby. Several uneventful years followed, during which he worked his way nearly to the head of the school, obtaining an exhibition in 1841. Before this, in November, 1840, he had won the open scholarship at Balliol College with great *éclat*, but was permitted to postpone the period of his coming into residence to the autumn term of the following year. His first rooms were on the second floor of the corner staircase in the inner quadrangle. His perfect self-possession, the sallies of his ready wit, the humorous turn which he could give to any subject that he handled, his gaiety, exuberance, versatility, audacity, and unfailing command of words made him one of the most popular and successful undergraduates that Oxford has ever known. In his first academical year he won the Hertford scholarship, given by the University for proficiency in Latin. He won the Newdigate, the subject being "Cromwell"; in the final schools he was disappointed, and only obtained a second class. In 1845 he was elected Fellow of Oriel, just 30 years after the election of his father. Dean Church, Dean Burgon; Fraser, the late Bishop of Manchester; Buckle, now Canon of Wells; Earle, the present professor of Anglo-Saxon, and Arthur Hugh Clough were among his colleagues at the then famous college. It was the year in which Newman, himself a Fellow of Oriel, after long deliberation took the final step and seceded to Rome. The intimacy of Matthew Arnold with Clough was of the closest character. During all the early part of 1846 Clough used every Sunday to entertain at breakfast a small party of friends, consisting of Matthew, his brother of University, and Theodore Walrond.' Clough himself Arnold always loved, though he cared little for his poetry; and their friendship, as all readers of English poetry know, received its final seal in the exquisite elegiac poem of 'Thyrsis' – that poem which Mr. Swinburne has placed by the side of 'Lycidas' and 'Adonais,' and which contains the very spirit of the Oxford of those days.

Matthew Arnold never felt any desire for the life of a college tutor, and, indeed, such a career was at that time almost impossible except under the condition of Holy Orders, and these he was not disposed to take. An opening in London presented itself two years after his election, in 1847, when the late Lord Lansdowne, the veteran Whig leader, offered him the post of private secretary. He was thus transplanted to the very centre of political and social life in London, but it is evident that neither politics nor society absorbed him, for it was in the next year (1848) that there appeared the now famous little volume, 'The Strayed Reveller, and Other Poems, by A.' Here the note was struck, which vibrated to the last through Mr. Arnold's poetry and through much of his prose; here was a sensibility and an inward experience intensely modern, expressed with a luminousness and a perfection of form that was purely Greek. Three years after the appearance of the 'Poems by A' Mr. Arnold married the daughter of Mr. Justice Wightman, and, as he lately told the Westminster school teachers, when they made a presentation to him on his retirement, it was in consequence of his marriage that he left his private-secretaryship and accepted the post of Lay Inspector of Schools. In the interval he worked for a short time as assistant master at Rugby. At that date, as is well known, the State organization of elementary instruction was but just beginning; the antagonism between the Church schools and the Dissenting schools was still acute, and it was even necessary to have separate staffs of inspectors for the one and for the other. Mr. Arnold had assigned to him what were called the British Schools, under which short title the schools of the British and Foreign School Society were known; and it was in travelling about the country examining these schools that he learnt his business and formed besides those views as to the nature of British Nonconformity and of the mental and moral horizon of the middle class, to which in later years he often gave so trenchant an expression. His work as a school inspector – which, it may here be said, only ceased two or three years ago – was laborious, and a few of those who have been charmed and consoled by his poetry, or stimulated and amused by his prose, have reflected that what they were reading was produced in the intervals of drudgery such as, it might be thought, would have sufficed to dull the edge of genius.

And here we may pause to say something of Matthew Arnold's strictly professional work as a school inspector and as a reformer of education. The most direct outcome of it is to be found where few people outside the official circle have ever looked for it – viz., in the Annual Reports published by the Committee of Council on Education. In those Blue-books it has been the habit to print a certain number of the most striking reports annually sent in by the school inspectors, and among these a large number were written by Arnold. It need not be said that these reports of his are excellent reading, and that they abound in telling phrases and in piquant statements of opinion. More than this, they are full of wisdom; of views based upon wide observation and solid reflexion, of pleas for the steady and practicable improvement of elementary education. They hold up a high ideal, but one which an observation of what has been done in other countries had shown the writer to be attainable. For, as is well known, his educational work was not confined to inspecting the schools in his own country. In 1859, when the public conscience had begun to be seriously stricken with respect to the state of our primary schools, and when such a measure as was afterwards brought into being by Mr. Forster had begun to loom before the minds of statesmen, Mr. Arnold was sent abroad as Foreign Assistant Commissioner to inquire into the state of education in France, Germany, and Holland. Six years later he went again with a special mission to inquire into the state of middle-class education abroad, and in 1867 a volume appeared embodying his investigations into this subject. These professional tours had an immense effect upon his mind. They gave him an answer to the question how to make the English middle class less contented with commonplace ideals, or, in the phrase which he was the first to make popular, less Philistine. He never till the end of his life ceased from efforts to carry into practical effect his desire to get our middle-class education, our secondary schools, better organized. It was to his mind the one crying want of English civilization. He traced to the chaotic condition of our middle-class schools by far the larger part of the moral, social, and political faults which, with all his love for England, he could not help seeing in her. '*Porro unum est necessarium!*' he cried, and that one thing was to be education for the middle class, organized as well as the education for the working class is now organized, and as well as middle-class education itself is organized in Germany and in France. 'Schools for the licensed victuallers, schools for the commercial travellers, schools for the Wesleyans, schools for the Quakers – to educate a middle class in this way is to doom it to grow up on an inferior plane, with the claims of intellect and knowledge not satisfied, the claim of beauty not satisfied, the claim of manners not satisfied.' One of the chief causes of his discontent with English party government was the fact that both parties alike thought the organization of secondary schools no business of theirs. The Conservatives would not undertake it, and 'at this hour,' wrote Mr. Arnold a few years ago, apropos of an article of the Liberal leader, 'in Mr. Gladstone's programme, of the 22 engagements of the Liberal party there is not one word of middle-class education. Twenty-two Liberal engagements, and the reform of middle-class education not one of them!' It is one of Mr. Arnold's chief titles to the regard of his countrymen that in spite of the indifference of party leaders he continued to the end to press, with all the force of exhortation and of irony of which he was master, for this most penetrating of all reforms.

It is time, however, to turn from this aspect of Mr. Arnold's work to those achievements by which he is and will continue to be most widely known – his achievements in literature. The 'Poems by A.' made a profound impression upon the very limited class of readers who cared for scholarly poetry. In 1853, five years after the appearance of the first little volume, he published 'Empedocles on Etna, and Other Poems,' but in a very short time, becoming dissatisfied with the poem that gave its title to the book, he withdrew the volume from circulation, so that it is now, as all bibliophiles know, extremely rare. Next year he published in his own name a new volume of poems, partly new and partly selected from those issued already, and a second series followed soon afterwards. The impression made by these in academical circles was so great that in 1857 he was elected to a Chair which he was destined to raise to a position of greater importance and influence than it had ever reached before – the Chair of Poetry at Oxford. Next year appeared *Merope*, a tragedy after the Greek manner, which was in itself perhaps not quite successful, but which gave him the opportunity of writing a preface that contained one of the most valuable expositions of the principles of criticism ever produced in England. Then followed the 'Lectures on Translating Homer' and the 'Last Words,' in both of which he put forward his plea for the English hexameter. That plea has not generally been allowed, but every one who heard the lectures, or has since then studied those scarce little volumes, was struck with the breadth and the enlightenment of their tone, at that time so new to English criticism.

The 'Essays in Criticism,' a collection of articles and lectures, appeared in 1865, 23 years ago. How faintly does the young writer of to-day, to whom its methods and maxims have almost unconsciously become the commonplaces of his literary education, realize all he owes to that modest little volume! But as one traces back the stream of thought, as one recalls Hazlitt and Leigh Hunt and Macaulay, as one thinks of the older *Quarterly* and *Edinburgh* and the lumbering conscientiousness of the *Retrospective Review*, one gradually becomes aware of all that the Essays and their successors have done for us. The critic, by that book, acquired a new dignity and importance. It both enlarged his functions and abated his pretensions. Thenceforward criticism, among those who aspired to any eminence in it, was to be a much humbler and sincerer thing than it had been in the omniscient days of Jeffrey and Croker; and at the same time it was to deal with a wider world than that of which Lamb or Hazlitt had had knowledge. 'A disinterested endeavour to learn and propagate the best that is known and thought in the world' – so Mr. Arnold originally defined his task, and his whole literary life has been an effort to fulfil it. The Essays themselves were an adequate comment on such a definition. To many persons even of the reading class such studies as those on Joubert, on Eugénie and Maurice de Guérin, or on 'The Literary Influence of Academies' were a revelation. 'All can grow the flower now, for all have got the seed.' But 25 years ago Mr. Arnold by such work opened new worlds of thought and feeling to those who had eyes to see and ears to hear; he taught us sympathy with fresh and varied forms of thought, and so made us think for ourselves in a fruitful way. He bade us shake off convention, and see 'the thing in itself,' without prejudice and without conceit, personal or national. And, on the way, what beauties of perception and style, what felicities of manner! Who that has read it will easily forget the address to Oxford – 'home of lost causes, and forsaken beliefs, and unpopular names, and impossible loyalties' – which closes the Preface, or the translation of Maurice de Guérin's 'Centaur,' or the summing up of Heine and Byron with which the Heine article ends, or the delicate truth and originality of all that moral observation in which the Joubert essay abounds? To look at these passages again is to understand, even apart from Mr. Arnold's poems, what Sainte-Beuve meant when five or six years before he drew the attention of the French public to a young English writer, 'dont le talent réunit la pureté et la passion.'

Mr. Arnold was of course re-elected at the end of his five years, and at the end of ten many were the complaints in Oxford that the statutes did not permit a 'third term.' More than once, as vacancies occurred in later years, efforts were made to induce him to come forward as a candidate once more, but by that time he had made himself, or believed that he had made himself, unpopular with the clergy, and he shrank from the danger of what he used to call 'an odious contest.' So he never stood again, and, though he now and then lectured at the Royal Institution, in provincial towns, and during two visits to America, Oxford knew him officially no more. But he loved Oxford to the end; 'that sweet city' which he celebrated in 'Thyrsis' and in the famous preface to the Essays always continued to exercise her spell upon him, and he was interested to the last in watching the part that she played in the life of England, in the men who were conspicuous in her colleges, in the books that she produced, in the 'movements' which from time to time passed over her. But after he ceased to be Professor of Poetry the subjects of his critical writing underwent a change. He would not have been his father's son had he not been profoundly interested in religion; he would not have been the open-minded critic that he was had he not seen that upon many classes in modern England religion was losing its hold. Therefore, he set himself to consider whether a way might not be found of preserving what was essential in religion while giving up whatever modern criticism had shown to be untenable. His fastidious taste revolted against the crude attempts of some modern reformers of religion, and in what we believe to have been his earliest writings on these subjects, certain articles published in *Macmillan's Magazine*, he dealt rather unmercifully with the mechanical methods of Bishop Colenso. His own views he expounded some ten or twelve years later in the book called 'Literature and Dogma;' in its successor 'God and the Bible;' and in 1877, in the volume of collected papers called 'Last Essays on Church and Religion.' It is remarkable that the latest but one of his writings was an article in the March number of the *National Review* on Disestablishment in Wales; so impossible did he find it to keep his hand and his pen from touching subjects of pressing ecclesiastical or theological interest.

Mr. Arnold must be pronounced to have been much less successful as a theologian than as a critic and a poet. Undoubtedly his own object was to preserve the Bible against the consequences of a purely destructive criticism. But to many he seemed to destroy the substance of religion, while he preserved merely a kind of aroma or tradition. Even those, however, who deplore his rejection of dogma, and see a lamentable want of logic in his argument, can admire the spirituality of his work, and the salutary manner in which he constantly dwells on the importance of 'conduct' in life. It is a tribute to the wide effect produced by his principal work of this class, 'Literature and Dogma,' that many of the phrases with which it abounds have passed into common speech, although much of its metaphysics is more than questionable, and the Hebrew scholarship of this and the other volume avowedly second-hand.

We have reserved to the last Mr. Arnold's work in poetry – that work which is represented by the five or six little early volumes so dear to collectors, or by the two volumes of 'Complete Poems' issued in 1876, or by the three volumes, containing these and fortunately a few more recent verses, which Messrs. Macmillan published two or three years ago. It is worth while here to quote a judgment written 20 years ago by a brother poet, a judgment of which it is easy to discount and to pardon the enthusiasm, and which, after all, tells the truth, if it tells it too forcibly. 'For some years past,' wrote Mr. Swinburne, 'the fame of Mr. Matthew Arnold has been almost exclusively the fame of a prose-writer. Those students could hardly find hearing – they have nowhere of late found expression that I know of – who with all esteem and enjoyment of his essays, of the clearness and beauty of their sentiment and style, retained the opinion that if justly judged he must be judged by his verse and not by his prose – certainly not by this alone; that future students would cleave to that with more of care and of love; that the most memorable quality about him was the quality of a poet. Not that they liked the prose less, but that they liked the verse more. His best essays ought to live longer than most, his best poems cannot but live as long as any, of the time.' The statement that comparatively few of Mr. Arnold's readers cared for his poetry was quite true in 1867; it is less true now, though it would be inaccurate to say that he is a popular poet. His Muse is too austere, the subjects with which he deals are too remote from the ordinary superficial interests of the many. But to a certain number of readers he has as a poet a place apart; a place in the inmost shrine of their affections. To them, the early poem 'Resignation,' with its Wordsworthian severity, its air of bracing moral freshness, as though newly blowing from the Westmoreland fells; to them 'Dover Beach,' with its noble music and the grave stoicism of its tone; to them 'The Strayed Reveller,' with its magical realization of the Greek spirit, 'The Sick King in Bokhara,' and 'Sohrab and Rustum,' which profess to be pictures of the mysterious East, and are so much more; to them 'Heine's Grave,' 'Rugby Chapel,' the 'Lines written in Kensington Gardens' – all these are among the most precious, the most abiding gifts that any modern mind has bequeathed to the English race. But it is invidious to name some poems and leave the others. When, some ten years ago, Mr. Arnold made a 'Selection' of his own poems for the Golden Treasury series, and when his friends complained to him of the omission of one or other of their favourites, he laughingly answered, 'Of course, if I had consulted my own taste I should have inserted everything.' And, indeed he would not have been far wrong; for so carefully modelled and welded are his poems, so sincerely are they felt, that there are hardly a dozen among the whole that one could wish away.

Mr. Arnold was personally one of the most charming of men. On first acquaintance, indeed, there was something in his manner which might set matter-of-fact people against him; but if they were sensible they soon got over what was in reality purely superficial. His geniality and kindness of nature, his tolerance, his humour soon won their way; and hence there were few men who had more or warmer friends. Even the egotism of which readers who did not know him used to complain was, for the most part, a rhetorical device; and where it was not, it was so frank, so good-natured, that it was soon forgiven. No one could be more missed in London than he, though for many years he had not actually lived in London. While his boys were growing up he lived at Harrow, that they might go to the school; of late years he occupied a pretty cottage at the foot of Pain's-hill, near Cobham. He loved the country; he had a strong affection for animals (who does not remember his poem 'Geist's Grave'?); and his love for flowers was keen. In all family relationships he was admirable; and it may be of interest to mention that a vast number of letters from him to various members of his family are in existence, which are full of the personal and the literary charm that attaches to the best of his writings.

His funeral will take place on Thursday, at noon, at Laleham, near Staines, where he was born, and where three of his sons lie buried.

Matthew Arnold almost certainly inherited his congenital heart condition from his father, Thomas. He also inherited a moral earnestness, and a clear sense of defined rights and wrongs, which is evident in much of his written work. Writing of his father in the poem 'Rugby Chapel', Arnold speaks of a man who, beyond the grave, 'upraisest with zeal The humble good from the ground, Sternly repressest the bad. Still, like a trumpet, dost rouse Those who with half-open eyes Tread the border dim Twixt vice and virtue'. What Matthew lacked was his father's religious conviction. As hard-working Inspector of Schools and as a critic of the Victorian educational system and of nineteenth-century culture, the younger Arnold continued not only to tread borders but also to define them. The obituarist, who begins by citing Swinburne's opinion of Arnold's verse, moves on to suggest that his ultimate claim to fame will rest on his poetry, despite its 'austerity'.

GEORGE CHARLES BINGHAM, 3RD EARL OF LUCAN

Field-Marshal: 'It was chiefly in relation . . . to the memorable charge of the Light Brigade . . . that Lord Lucan's name became historic.'

10 NOVEMBER 1888

WE REGRET TO announce the death, which occurred on Saturday after a short illness, of the Earl of Lucan at the patriarchal age of 88. His lordship was the oldest officer of the British Army and had attained the exceptional rank of Field-Marshal. The name of the gallant peer, who had served his Sovereign and country for more than 70 years, was most famous at the time of the Crimean War, of which he was rightly considered one of the heroes. During that campaign he commanded the cavalry division of Lord Raglan's army, and, long as he had lived in the profession of arms, his military experiences in the field were limited to one campaign in the service of Russia – that of Diebitsch, in Bulgaria, in 1828 – and our war with that Power in 1854–56.

George Charles Bingham, third Earl of Lucan, and son of the second Earl and of the daughter of the last Earl of Fauconberg, was born on April 16, 1800, and, after passing several years at Westminster School, entered the Army in 1816 as an ensign in the 6th Foot. Two years later he exchanged into the Foot Guards, and in 1822 he joined the 1st Life Guards, of which at his death he was colonel. From that time his service was exclusively in the cavalry. The long peace which followed the Waterloo campaign gave English officers no opportunity of distinction in Europe for 40 years, and it was evidence of his military spirit that, when the war between Russia and Turkey broke out in 1828, he should have volunteered to serve on the staff of the Russian army, which, under the able leadership of General Diebitsch, invaded Turkey and overthrew the Sultan's forces in several engagements, until Constantinople itself seemed to lie at its mercy. For the part he took in this war Lord Lucan received the Commandership of the Order of St. Anne of Russia. By this time he had attained the rank of lieutenant-colonel in the English Army, and, on his father's death in 1839, succeeded to the family titles. He had given some attention to politics before this, having been returned in the Conservative interest for Mayo in 1826. Immediately after his accession to the earldom he was elected one of the representative peers of Ireland, which he continued to be until his death. But the part he took in political questions was always subordinate to his interest in the Army and military questions, although on one occasion he came forward prominently in connexion with what promised to be a grave dispute between the two Houses of Parliament.

When the war with Russia broke out in 1854, and it became necessary to send a large army to the Black Sea, Lord Lucan, who had reached the rank of major-general in 1851, was appointed to the command of the cavalry division with the local grade of lieutenant-general. In that capacity he was present at the battles of Alma and Inkermann, as well as throughout the covering operations intrusted to the cavalry during the siege of Sebastopol. But it was chiefly in relation to the events of the day on which Balaclava was fought, and the memorable charge of the Light Brigade was made, that Lord Lucan's name became historic. Probably the exact truth as to the orders given which resulted in that brilliant, if unnecessary, display of English gallantry will never be known, but it is at least strange that the principal persons blamed should have been intimately connected with each other – Lord Lucan having married Lord Cardigan's sister in 1829 – and that both should have carried away honourable scars from the fray. After that encounter few opportunities presented themselves to the cavalry of gaining distinction, although to the end of the war they had to bear their share in the hard work of the siege. Lord Lucan received at the conclusion of peace the Commandership of the Bath, the Legion of Honour, and the Medjidie of the 1st class, besides the English and Turkish medals. He was also appointed colonel of the 8th Hussars. In 1858 he became lieutenant-general. His subsequent steps in the Army may here be mentioned. In 1865 he was nominated colonel of the 1st Life Guards, and a few months later attained the rank of full general. In 1869 he received the Grand Cross of the Bath, and last year he was somewhat tardily, when the length of his service and seniority are considered, awarded the much-coveted baton of a field-marshal.

After the Crimean War, Lord Lucan again devoted himself to politics and became a regular attendant in the Upper House. Although he did not take a very prominent part in its debates he was a vigilant observer of the course of public events, and when the two Houses came into collision on the subject of Lord John Russell's Bill for removing the Jews' disabilities in taking the oath, and there seemed no way out of the difficulty, Lord Lucan got up and proposed a very simple and, as it proved, practical compromise. This was merely to add a clause to Lord John's Bill allowing either House to modify the form of oath required of its members at its pleasure. The suggestion was favourably taken up by both sides as a happy way of getting out of the embarrassment into which the collision of the two Houses had involved them. If Lord Lucan was not an active politician, he showed himself at least on this occasion a shrewd and discriminating man of the world, and as such a useful member of his party.

Lord Lucan married, in 1829, the sister of Lord Cardigan, as has been said, and by her, who died in 1877, he had two sons and one daughter, Lady Alington, who survive him, and three daughters who predeceased him. He is succeeded in his titles by his eldest son George, Lord Bingham, who was born in 1830, and who, after serving in the Crimean War as aide-de-camp to his father, retired from the Army with the rank of Lieutenant Colonel. Lord Bingham was member for Mayo from 1865 to 1874, and married, in 1859, Lady Cecilia Gordon Lennox, sister of the present Duke of Richmond, by whom he has a large family.

There is a considerable poignancy in this obituary. Tennyson claimed that he had written his poem 'The Charge of the Light Brigade' 'in a few minutes, after reading . . . *The Times* in which occurred the phrase "some one had blundered"'. Delane's editorial in *The Times* of 13 November 1854 had in fact spoken of 'some hideous blunder'. Some three weeks earlier, on 25 October, Lucan, in command of the cavalry at the Battle of Balaclava, had received an order from Lord Raglan, the British Commander in the Crimea, to advance into the valley between the Fedyukhin Heights and the Causeway Heights. The ambiguous order was passed to Lucan's brother-in-law, Lord Cardigan, who led the disastrous cavalry charge towards the Russian guns. When the news reached London it created a furore. In an extraordinary edition of the *London Gazette* Raglan blamed Lucan 'for some misconception of the order to advance'. In March 1855 Lucan was recalled to England and proceeded to publicly repudiate Raglan's charge, calling it 'an imputation reflecting seriously on my professional character'. In an acrimonious correspondence in the pages of *The Times*, Lucan continued to blame Raglan and his aide-de-camp, Captain Nolan, who had carried the order and who had died in the charge. He also forcefully restated his case before the House of Lords on 19 March. Lucan never again saw active duty, but the remainder of his military career, his steady promotion and the honours accorded to him are outlined in the obituary.

WILKIE COLLINS

Novelist: 'A model of all that is most sensational, most thrilling, and most ingeniously probable in the midst of probability.'

23 SEPTEMBER 1889

WE MUCH REGRET to announce the death of Mr. Wilkie Collins, the well-known novelist, which took place yesterday morning at his house in Wimpole-street. He had never completely rallied from the stroke of paralysis which attacked him some months ago, when he was apparently enjoying his usual vigorous health of mind and body. But, though confined to the house, he had recently been able to leave his room. The improvement continued until the close of last week, when Mr. Collins contracted a fresh cold, which brought on a relapse, which terminated fatally yesterday.

William Wilkie Collins was the eldest son of William Collins, R. A., the celebrated landscape painter, and was born in 1824, two years after the marriage of his parents. He may be said to have inherited a literary strain on the father's side, for his grandfather, William Collins the elder, was himself, in his way, a man of letters. He was by profession a picture dealer, but he is still known to the curious in such matters as the author of a rather dull poem on the Slave Trade, and of a curious, rambling, ill-digested, but, after all, interesting book called 'The Memoirs of a Picture' (London, 1805), one of the volumes of which is devoted to a first-hand account of the life of George Morland. Of William Collins the painter it is not necessary to speak here, for his position in the world of art is still as high as ever it was, and his best pictures, like Lord Lansdowne's 'The Bird-Catchers,' are nowadays as greatly admired when they appear in the winter exhibitions of the Royal Academy as they were when the artist first exhibited them. William Collins died in 1847, leaving two sons, the subject of the present memoir and Charles Allston Collins, who essayed both painting and literature with some success. It should here be mentioned that a contemporary of these two brothers, Mortimer Collins, was not, as has often been supposed, a member of their family. Wilkie Collins, whose Christian name was given him in memory of his father's intimate friendship with his brother Academician, Sir David Wilkie, did not receive any very thorough education; he went first to a private school, then spent two years with his parents in Italy, then was articled to a firm in the tea trade, then became a student at Lincoln's Inn, and finally, after his father's death, found his true path in the profession of letters. His first work was a biography of his father, which was published in two

volumes in 1848 a very respectable performance for a young and comparatively untrained man, but somewhat diffuse in style, and giving little promise of the future literary eminence of the author. In 1850 he published his first novel, 'Antonina, or the Fall of Rome,' a book inspired by his residence in Italy. Then followed several more books of little importance, and one, 'Basil, a Story of Modern Life' (1852), which had a deserved success, being certainly the best of the early works of the writer.

Soon after this Mr. Collins became intimately acquainted with Charles Dickens, and the friendship had a profound effect upon the whole of Collins's later life. He began to contribute to *Household Words*, and wrote in that magazine 'After Dark' (1856) and 'The Dead Secret' (1857). 'The Queen of Hearts' followed in 1859, but still the public, though they had learnt to know Collins's name, saw no reason to rank him among the leading novelists of the day. In 1860, however, he had his success – a remarkable success, and one most eminently deserved – on the publication of that striking story 'The Woman in White.' This book had first appeared in *All the Year Round*, and in it Wilkie Collins had shown the most extraordinary skill as a writer of a serial story, which, it must be observed, is a special skill, not necessarily the same as that which goes to the composition of a novel that is first published as a whole. There is no necessity to dwell upon the characteristics of 'The Woman in White,' for everybody has read it, and many people have read it several times over; but we may not be going too far in pronouncing it to be the first of English novels of plot and situation. It is avowedly a sensational story; it is a story of mystery, of intrigue, of secret plotting, of crime, and of thrice-ingenious discovery; but it is at the same time something more. It differs, for instance, from Gaboriau's novels in one essential particular. They are police novels pure and simple; their interest wholly depends upon the riddle that is asked in the first chapter and that is slowly answered through the succeeding pages. But 'The Woman in White' is a novel of character as well, and Count Fosco is a creation almost of the first order. Since the publication of this book many other writers and the author himself have endeavoured to rival and surpass it, but none have achieved quite the same brilliant combination of plot and character as Collins did in this central effort of his life. Of course, it is easy to see the influences that were at work upon him when he wrote it, and especially to recognize the influence of Dickens; but, on the other hand, there is reason to believe that Collins had nearly as much influence upon the last works of the greater writer as Dickens had upon him.

In 1862 there followed 'No Name,' a curious story, which neither deserved nor obtained anything like the success of its predecessor, but which still had a certain quality of its own. 'Armadale' came next, in 1866, having first appeared in the *Cornhill Magazine*; and then, in 1868, there followed the second of Collins's great successes, 'The Moonstone.' From some points of view, indeed, this book may be placed higher than 'The Woman in White,' for while the interest was kept up quite as skilfully, the original plan was even more ingenious than that of the earlier novel. There were elements of mysterious poetry about the three Indian priests, and the last chapters of 'The Moonstone' will remain, so long as sensation novels are read, as a model of all that is most sensational, most thrilling, and most ingeniously probable in the midst of improbability. The stories that followed – 'Man and Wife' (1870), 'Poor Miss Finch' (1872), 'Miss or Mrs.?' (1873), and several others – were read by multitudes of people, but in none of them, excepting in 'The New Magdalen,' did it seem that the hand preserved its cunning. This last-named book, however, was a moving and an interesting story, and on the stage it has awakened in many an audience something very like enthusiasm. The late Mr. Matthew Arnold, who was not a great admirer of sensation novels as such, always spoke in terms of the highest praise of the play of *The New Magdalen.* It might, indeed, be said that Wilkie Collins's gifts in general were of a dramatic character. He was a master of plot and a master of dramatic situations; his style was rather rapid and nervous than literary. He was fond of the theatre and of actors, his affection for them dating from the old days of Tavistock House and the days of his collaboration with Dickens. Often they acted together on the private stage, and, though they never actually wrote a play together, their tastes in this respect were alike; they enjoyed and understood the world of the theatre perhaps better than they understood the world of real life. Of Collins's plays that have been performed in public we may mention *The Frozen Deep* (1857), *The Moonstone* (1877), *Rank and Riches,* which failed in 1883, though it succeeded well in America, *The New Magdalen, The Woman in White,* and *Man and Wife,* the last of which was produced by Mr. and Mrs Bancroft in the old days of the Prince of Wales's Theatre in Tottenham-street. Mr. Collins was at work till the last; a novel of his is now appearing in the *Illustrated London News.*

The funeral will take place at Kensal-green Cemetery on Friday, at noon.

Collins had entered Lincoln's Inn in 1846 and had been called to the bar in 1851. His first published work was a biography of his painter-father (1848), but, as this obituary properly acknowledges, his reputation will always rest on the much admired fiction he wrote between 1860 and 1870. It is he who took what his contemporaries styled 'sensation fiction' to new heights and effectively invented the detective novel. No mention is made of Collins's unconventional domestic circumstances. He never married, but had lived openly since 1858 with Caroline Graves and her daughter. When Mrs Graves left him in 1868, he fathered three children by Martha Rudd. Caroline Graves resumed her relationship with him in 1870 and remained his partner until his death. Collins's last novel, *Blind Love,* left unfinished at the time of his death, was completed by Walter Besant and published posthumously in 1890.

ROBERT BROWNING

Poet: 'Browning's muse has been for the lifetime of most educated Englishmen a kind of poetical wheel of fortune giving forth.'

12 DECEMBER 1889

ROBERT BROWNING has died in the plenitude of years, fame, and affection. He has breathed his last in the land associated with his most glowing dreams of human happiness, and in a city he fondly loved. His family was by his side, and he knew that the sympathy, not of one nation alone, but of nations, was with him. Sickness had scarcely, except at one point, touched his physical faculties, and had in no respect whatever affected his mind. He retained unimpaired his courage, his clearness of insight, even his gaiety and sense of the zest of life. As if to crown the whole, the applause bestowed on the latest effort of his minstrelsy was echoing around his death-bed like the cries of triumph borne to the ears of the general expiring on the field of victory. Such an end to a career would have been pronounced by the sage and lawgiver of old the sum of earthly prosperity. Nothing seems wanting to its close; and the life itself, as this generation has perceived it, has abundantly answered to that close in pleasantness and charm. Not to many natures is it given to explore, like Robert Browning, the depths of thought, and, like him, at the same time to gather the best flowers and sweets of everyday social existence. The curiosity of his character was the interweaving of an innocent mundane tissue with the resolve to grapple continually with the most intricate mysteries of being. He could cease at any instant to be, as it appeared, the inspired poet, the profound philosopher, and became the delightful and equal companion. If there be a defect in his story, it might almost be imagined by his younger contemporaries to be the absence of difficulties overcome. Troops of friends, devotion, enthusiasm, the choice of everything most agreeable in common life, the taste for enjoying all, with no lawless propensity to excess requiring to be checked, plentiful means without the burdens of riches, cheerfulness, health, and the experience of old age, with none of its infirmities, make up a total of even fortune relieving a character from the demands upon its resources which reveal its height and breadth. Literary memoirs of twenty years back show another picture, in which all the necessary shadows are represented in profusion. For a quarter of a century or longer no poet met with more scant and grudging recognition. For years he received no other tribute than jeers. Obscure or ridiculed, he laboured on, content to possess his own soul. Only very gradually did the general reading public become aware of

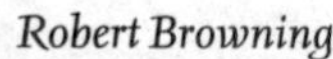

Robert Browning

his existence. Neither indifference nor renown shook him from the tenour of his intellectual movement. But certainly the author of 'Paracelsus' and 'Sordello' cannot be accused of having walked in nothing but sunshine.

He must have had infinite courage to go on singing with few or none to listen. When the prospect brightened about him and he had won the laurel, he must have had as much strength of will to withstand the temptation to develop one side of his poetic genius rather than the other. Throughout he has had to an extraordinary degree two veins of inspiration remarkably diverse. He was endowed with the gifts at once of a Lucretius and of a ballad writer, each in perfection. Both powers were always in him; and, so far as the owner of any intellectual wealth is free, he was free to exert one or the other: The difference in the results as he must have been conscious, was that, whenever he chose to open the one chamber of his brain, and tell of the Pied Piper of Hamelin, of the bringing of the Good News from Ghent to Aix, of Clive, or of a Soliloquy in a Spanish Cloister, the world cheered, cried, or laughed, as he would; he was its master; and its emotions waited upon his. When he resorted to the other chamber, he was left with an audience, select it might be, but exceedingly small. Yet thither he went always by preference, and there he stayed for four-fifths of his poet's term. That he chose his course thus, and would appeal straight to the thought of his hearers, and not to their ears, indicates a noble independence in the man; it renders it peculiarly hard to foresee whether the splendour of his poetic celebrity will wax or wane. Melody and action in literature are sure of their future. The thinker who wrestles with the enigmas of time and eternity may grow unintelligible, inaudible, or obsolete. Robert Browning added to the stumbling-blocks in the way of his own continued supremacy by a method of work which for his disciples has always intensified its fascination. He thought out his problems before them. Each printed page is a photograph of his brain at its toil. Not merely the finished edifice is there, but the scaffolding. For the purposes of mental study no poems have ever been more deeply interesting than his. Their drawback, as creations which ought to live, is that they cannot be enjoyed properly, or be rightly profitable unless the reader follow the process step by step, and attend upon his guide through every stage. That is a homage which only a minority can be expected to bestow. But Robert Browning never courted allegiance which implies no mental toil, and would not have deprecated the loss of such as came by haphazard to him. He desired to be heard by those who will dive deep and soar high. If heroic aims in philosophic speculation, and thrills of emotion stained by no spot of earthy sensualism can insure a poet's immortality, he has earned it.

He is gone, and has left a void impossible to fill. For the moment it is beyond understanding that the literary horizon keeps in store behind it no more fruits of his many-sided genius. At any season for fifty years past there was the chance that a 'Christmas Eve and Easter Day,' a 'Bishop Blougram,' a 'Pippa Passes,' a 'Sordello,' a 'Ring and the Book,' a 'Balaustion's Adventure,' a 'Sludge the Medium,' a 'Hervé Riel,' a 'Fifine at the Fair,' a 'Ferishtah's Fancies,' an 'Asolando,' might be emerging to astonish, rejoice, anger or bewitch and bewilder. An element of uncertainty was constantly present. Whether the poet were inspired in one mood or in another could not be conjectured, least of all from the title, and scarcely from the volume, till the whole had been read and digested. Robert Browning's muse has been for the lifetime of most educated Englishmen a kind of poetical wheel of fortune giving forth; it may be, none but prizes, but prizes of the most strangely dissimilar characters. One common feature, however, all possessed; and that was a note of sovereignty in each successive and changing phase. From the day he was disclosed to the world of letters, he was acknowledged lord of his domain, though it might contain but a single subject. Whatever ground he occupied was of his own discovery; and no flag had ever floated over it but his. With time his borders widened, and thousands instead of tens offered him fealty. In his obscurity and in his fame, at any moment within the present generation, no less before half his life's work had been fulfilled than this week, his death would have been felt to be the extinction of a vast and distinct intellectual force. The loss is more painful now for losses which have preceded it. As years have passed since first his ascendancy within his special limits began to be understood, other and not unequal lights have gone out, till at length, not merely in poetry, but in literature, he and one besides have been shining alone. The Anglo-Saxon book-world is served, and well served; by many knights and squires. Till Thursday night it had two kings, fit to be reckoned in the universal golden roll of letters. One of them has passed away. Who will venture to lift, and has the right to hold, the vacated twin sceptre?

Browning died in the Rezzonico Palace in Venice on 12 December. It was first mooted that he should be interred next to his late wife in the Protestant Cemetery at Florence, but it was finally agreed that his body should be repatriated and buried in Westminster Abbey. The funeral service was held on 31 December, his pallbearers including Tennyson's son, Hallam, and Frederic Leighton. Suggestions that Elizabeth Barrett Browning might be buried by him at some future point were never brought to fruition (largely due to their son Pen's opposition to the idea). Browning's collected *Poetical Works* had appeared during 1888–89, and his last volume of verse, *Asolando*, was published in London on the day of his death. As this appreciative obituary suggests, it had taken some time to firmly establish Browning's reputation with the reading public, and he had retained a distinctive talent for 'thinking out his problems' in front of his readers – the word 'difficult' often crops up in Victorian commentaries on his work. When they married in September 1846, Elizabeth was probably the better-known poet. The obituarist evidently feels no need to re-tell the story of their extended courtship, their elopement and their period at Casa Guidi in Florence, which ended with Elizabeth's death in May 1861.

JOHN HENRY NEWMAN

Cardinal and theologian: 'Two lines can be forever approaching without falling together, but it is not so when the heart is concerned.'

11 AUGUST 1890

WE HAVE TO record, with feelings of the most sincere regret, the death of his Eminence Cardinal Newman. He died last evening at the Oratory, Edgbaston, in his 90th year, after less than three days' illness. The Cardinal has for many years manifested the feebleness of advanced age, although he has fully retained his mental faculties, and has rallied in a wonderful manner from more than one severe illness. His last sermon at the oratory church was delivered three years ago last Easter, although he made a few comments on the 1st of January, 1889, with reference to the Pope's sacerdotal jubilee. Since then his physical weakness has developed, and he has had to depend upon the support of two of the Fathers of the Oratory in entering and quitting the chapel when assisting at the sacred functions. The last ecclesiastical function in which he took part was the solemn triduò which was celebrated on July 18–20, in honour of the beatification of Juvenal Ancina of the Roman Oratory. His feebleness on that occasion was specially noticed, and at the opening service he was carried into the church seated on a chair. At the Saturday and Sunday services his Eminence was not carried through the church, but had his seat placed at the entrance to the St. Philip's Chapel, which has private communication with the Oratory. On the Saturday he gave the Benediction to the congregation with the relics of the Saint. Two evenings later – namely, on the 22d ult., the Cardinal was among the company who witnessed the Latin play – at this time the *Andria*, arranged by himself – which is annually performed by the pupils of the Oratory school. He also distributed the prizes to the pupils, addressing a few remarks to each. From that time until Saturday last there was nothing abnormal in the Cardinal's condition, and his medical attendant (Dr. Blunt) went to Blackpool, leaving his illustrious patient in charge of Mr. C. H. Jenner Hogg. On Saturday night the Cardinal had an attack of shivering, followed by a sharp rise of temperature, and the symptoms indicative of pneumonia rapidly supervened and became acute. Dr. Blunt was telegraphed for and arrived from Blackpool the same evening. During the day Cardinal Newman, though rapidly becoming worse, was able to speak to those about him, and in the afternoon, at his request, the Rev. W. Neville recited with him the Breviary. Yesterday morning he fell into an unconscious condition. He was heard, in a mechanical way, to whisper 'William,' the Christian name of his secretary, Father Neville, but he gave no signs of understanding any questions addressed to him. The Oratory Fathers were then informed that he was sinking, and that the prolongation of his life was to be measured by hours. Upon this the rite of extreme unction was performed by the Rev. Austin Mills, in the presence of such members of the community as were at the time in the Oratory, four of their number being away from Birmingham. Owing to the patient's comatose condition the Viaticum was not administered, but he received Holy Communion on Saturday. Information of the Cardinal's condition was telegraphed to the Oratory, in London, and also to the Right Rev. Bishop Illsley. The latter visited the Cardinal early in the afternoon, and spent some time with him, and made the 'commendation of his soul' in the presence of the oratory Fathers. There was an appointment on the part of the doctors to meet for consultation at 8 o'clock last evening. At that time it was seen that life was fast ebbing away, and both medical men remained until 12 minutes to 9, when Cardinal Newman quietly breathed his last. He died in the presence of the Fathers of the congregation, and there is every reason to believe that his death was painless.

The medical attendants have issued the following account of their patient's last illness. 'The Oratory, August 11, 1890. His Eminence Cardinal Newman was seized with inflammation of the right lung at 2 o'clock a. m. on Sunday, August 10.He very rapidly became worse until this evening at 8.45, when he expired. His Eminence expressed himself as feeling quite well an hour before this attack occurred. – G. Vernon Blunt, M. D.; C. H. Jenner Hogg, M. R. C. S. E.' The private prayers of the congregation were asked for the Cardinal at the Oratory Church on Sunday, and in the evening there were numerous and anxious enquiries respecting him. He will be buried at the little country retreat of the Oratorians, at Rednall, where there is a private cemetery and chapel. The body will be exposed in the Oratory from noon to-day until it is removed for burial. The date of the funeral is not yet fixed.

The greatest name in that matter which most occupies, most unites, and most divides men is now resigned to history. Cardinal Newman is gone to that rest which for him will not be happiness if it does not give work to be done. His disappearance from the stage of life is no sudden event. It is not as if an army had lost its commander in mid-battle, or as if the tongue of the orator had become suddenly mute, or the lyre had dropped from the poet's hand. It is not a future that has vanished with the past, or a cataract of life that has been arrested in full flow. The truth is the great Cardinal has occupied so exceptional a place in human affairs that, while he has largely influenced them, he has had himself to discover and even to recognise that they could go on without him. Standing apart from the world, he has long been on excellent terms with it, and they part in peace. Rome, wisely and happily for its credit and its influence, eleven years ago added his name to its highest list of honour; but, otherwise, Cardinal Newman may be said to have been without a place in the earth's pedigrees and successions; to have been left out of common reckoning, tied by no allegiance, complicated by no secular ties, 'without father or mother,' in the link of causation and the rolls of time. Forty years have now shown that the Church of England can pursue its course without his guidance or his warnings; still more have they shown that it is not such men the Church of Rome most trusts and employs. The Cardinal has long taken his position as a 'Father' of we know not what century in that constellation of acute and saintly minds that still illumines the dark interval between ancient and modern civilization. It was his own choice to be *Athanasius contra mundum.* Whether from his ashes will rise the avenger, to do for him the work he has not seen done with his own eyes, and so reverse the judgment of time, is beyond even conjecture. For the present a mighty man has fallen, yet we are much as we were.

John Henry Newman began his life with the century, for he was born in the city of London on February 21, 1801. His father was a partner in two successive banking firms, from the French Revolution to the disastrous crisis of 1816, when his firm, like a crowd of others, had temporarily to suspend payment. His mother was of a Huguenot family long resident in London, and remarkable for ingenuity and enterprise. Two of her brothers brought over, perfected, and established the paper-making machine. John H. Newman, with his not less remarkable brother Frank, was sent to Dr. Nicolas, at Ealing, the best private school in England, at a time when the tide of opinion had turned against public schools. Newman was easily and soon the top boy of the school. He had already shown a decided taste for music, becoming at 13 a proficient on the violin, and composing a sort of opera. Music was in the blood, and also in the Newman circle of friendship. At 15 he received the impulse, ever after credited with the formation of his career. This was through Mr. Walter Mayers, who had much talk with him, and lent him books, which were devoured, probably, as they had never been before. As far as Englishmen can be described in Continental terms, this excellent and very amiable clergyman was a Calvinist. Through him, and especially through one of Scott's works lent by him, Newman felt himself converted. From that year he ever dated his spiritual life, or his 'regeneration.' In his 'Apologia' he utterly ignores the first 15 years of his life, including all that father, mother, brothers, sisters, clergymen, or other friends might have done for him. In so doing he has given scope for inferences for which he seemed not to have been quite prepared. Of course, he learnt the Church Catechism, but he also read the Bible thoroughly, and acquired a great liking for it, which is by no means a matter of course in boyhood. Did he read it, also, without profit? Did he return again and again to the study of the Word without being yet a child of grace? That at 15 he might be persuaded to think little of himself is likely enough, but it is strange to find so little felt, at least said, for his natural teachers. Yet every one who has had to do with the teaching or training of boys must be painfully aware that in one sense it is a most thankless task. At about 15 there is such an expansion of mind and real development of character that in the new vision of life the old is forgotten. A grown-up man looks back and sees himself emerging out of the bright mist separating boyhood from youth. That is the beginning of his mental history.

Still under these novel impressions, Newman went to Trinity College, Oxford. About the same time the family came down from affluence to simple competency, and Newman, who had been destined for the Bar, felt a higher calling. His own religious feelings disposed him to friendships in what were then the not very large or very distinguished, or, indeed, very refined Evangelical circles. But the college system operates as a cross division in all social matters, and just as it brings together different classes, so it gives to different schools of opinion the opportunity of friendly disagreement, and sometimes final approximation. Newman's Trinity friendships were his longest and, perhaps, his deepest; but they were out of the Evangelical circle in which he first appeared at Oxford. As all the world knows, and as has happened to many others from whom great things were expected, Newman failed for honours. His reading, he used to say, had been too discursive. His health, however, had broken down. He was only 19, the age at which many men now enter the University. Much also depended on the examiners. Perhaps it may be added that Newman's independent and autocratic nature might easily put him out of the groove of an examination. He certainly was more likely to say things his own way than in the way expected by an Examiner; and, if the Examiner could only understand things in his own way, there would ensue a continual misunderstanding. It was as a Scholar of Trinity, and residing in that very pleasant college, that Newman, together with his friend John Bowden, wrote and published the now famous poem on St. Bartholomew's Eve. The Cardinal was always proud of that work, perhaps as his first-born, and he even took the pains to put on record his share of it. This might be to show that it was from no ignorance of Rome, or early learning, that he finally submitted to her and became her foremost champion.

Three years after taking his degree Newman was elected Fellow of the College with which his name will ever be associated, and which is proud to place him by the side of Raleigh, Butler, and, we may add, Copleston in the highest rank of its worthies. Though evidently not understood by the last-named, who was then Provost, and who measured men by the figure they made in a literary tournament, Newman rapidly won a place in the hearts of many good men. It was here, and in this interval of peace and quietness, that he became Whately's ally and Vice-Principal and the longest attached friend of Keble, Pusey, Froude, and Robert and Henry Wilberforce. It was here that he learned to love and revere Edward Hawkins, in whose long and steadfast course the Cardinal's Oxford career seems but a brief episode. Dr. Hawkins was a member of Oriel College 70 years, Provost 55. Though

Newman lived long in a short time, his whole connexion with the College only extended to twenty-three years. His mental acquaintance with the future Provost began as early as his own undergraduate days, when he heard the latter's sermon on 'Unauthoritative Tradition,' which sent his thoughts in a new direction. When he became better acquainted with the preacher he learnt from him to weigh his words and to be cautious in his statements. Hawkins bestowed friendly and useful criticisms on the first sermon he wrote. He lent Newman Sumner's treatise on Apostolical teaching, which Newman says dispelled his remaining Calvinism. If he did not receive this creed till 15, he could easily dismiss it at 23. The doctrine of 'Apostolical Succession,' he said, he received from Mr. William James, a very good and very sensible Fellow of the College, but not the man one would expect to change the current of a national theology. Long before this, in his unconverted state as he afterwards deemed it, he had employed himself with evidence, reading 'The Age of Reason,' Hume's Essays, and Voltaire. Later on he wrote a long but now forgotten article on the miraculous story of Apollonicus Tyanæus, to distinguish between false miracles and true.

Of all his contemporaries, or early friends, the one whose relations with him have excited the most curiosity is Keble. Newman has put on record that Keble was shy of him at first and for some time. Being where they then were they had every reason for being shy of one another; but the truth is Keble was shy of everybody at first, and at that time Newman was also. At this distance of time it seems almost inconceivable that for several years the most constant and familiar member of Oriel society was that very interesting, but very singular personage, Blanco White, with his medieval lore and his philosophical ideas. Like many other brooding spirits, he deeply felt the power of music and, though an indifferent performer, had frequent quartettes with Newman at his lodgings.

At 23 Newman was ordained deacon, and took charge of the Trasteverine parish of St. Clement's for four years. There is a certain mystery about his preaching during this period, for all his published sermons bear St. Mary's on their face. The old church of St. Clement's was a mean little structure, on the eastern slope of the well-known bridge, which of late years had had to sacrifice its picturesque features to give space to a tramway. Newman had to see to the building of a new church on a conspicuous but not very accessible site. His preaching excited some curiosity, not so much in the University at large as in Evangelical circles, where close agreement and familiar phrases were wont to be expected, and could not be missed without suspicion. In 1825, on the death of Peter Elmsley, Whately became Principal of St. Alban's Hall, and invited Newman to share the teaching of his small and awkward squad as Vice-Principal. Whately always liked to have somebody about him ready and competent to receive his emanations. The habit is a good one, but risky, and Whately had his failures. To judge by the sequel, Newman was one of these. For the present, however, they appreciated one another, and there was even a time when Newman had a better opinion of Whately's orthodoxy than Whately of his. Very quickly, however, Newman made the discovery that Whately's turn of mind was negative and destructive; that logic was the one thing not to be found in his book on that subject, and that he could only lash the waters, without having his net ready to secure the fish. Yet in after years Newman felt he had to thank Whately for weaning him from the Erastian views of Church polity which he believed to have been part of his own original composition. Up to 1826 Newman had held loyally to the ideal of Church and State as shown in Hooker's Ecclesiastical Polity; but at this day he and all Oxford were greatly stirred by an anonymous pamphlet, generally ascribed to Whately, and never repudiated by him, to the effect that this was a double usurpation and a double injury.

In this year Newman became tutor of his college in place of Jelf, who was now tutor to Prince George of Cumberland. Lloyd, whose private theological lectures Newman had been attending, sent for him first, but finding him two years under the stipulated age, had to pass him over for Jelf. Few will now doubt that the latter was the better adapted for the purpose. It would, indeed, have been hard to find any one better adapted. Up to that date the undergraduates of Oriel had been equally divided between four tutors, each of whom stood in *loco parentis* to his own men, a score perhaps. The relation was variously understood, and variously carried out, but it was a tradition of the University that the office admitted of a large significance. Newman immediately let it be known that he was only too willing to give his pupils all the direction, advice, assistance, and actual instruction they might desire, and some half-dozen or more gladly availed themselves of the invitation. There ensued in most instances a life-long friendship. Two younger tutors, as they succeeded to office, followed the example, and there was a time when the greater part of the College stood thus restored to what was really the original idea. Newman was soon after appointed a public examiner in *Lit. Hum.*, and for a year he was to be seen every day in High-street in the velvet-striped gown indicating a Pro-Proctor.

The year after Newman had taken his tutorship, Copleston was called to St. Paul's and Llandaff, and a new Provost had to be elected. No election has ever been more discussed; no choice ever more wondered at, perhaps unnecessarily. Keble had just presented himself as the Christian poet of the age, an age that had come to think the Christian faith incompatible with poetry. He was also a scholar of a high and then expiring class. He had been a tutor for some years, and his name was great in provincial circles. There was no doubt of his readiness to resume his Oxford residence. By the light of other times we all see that he and Newman were well-nigh brothers in theology. Why was he not elected as a matter of course? There was another candidate, Tyler, recently appointed rector of St. Giles, a sound working scholar, and a good, hearty, honest man, who could get on well with everybody. The choice fell on Hawkins, and it has always been stated, without contradiction, that Newman turned the scale. We are not aware whether this has ever been stated as a fact by any one who could certainly know it. But it is hardly necessary to reopen the whole question, when the choice has really justified itself. There can be no doubt Dr. Hawkins was the better man for the almost unparalleled difficulties to be encountered. They required strong practical powers, perfect command of temper, strict impartiality, fondness for business, and knowledge of the world. In these and other points Hawkins was known to excel, while even his failings, it may be said, leant on virtue's side, for without a prompt, critical, and decisive style of expression and action, coupled with a reasonable jealousy of interference and tenacity of power, he could not have maintained his ground so long, and with so much credit. It has sometimes been said that he sought power at the cost of love, but it was a time of war, when love had not fair scope.

Very soon after his election there arose the 'little cloud' which eventually deluged the land. The three tutors who were of one mind wished to remodel the whole system of tuition, both as to the men and as to the books. The new Provost took a defensive position, and was impracticable. He probably felt he would be nowhere in the College if he ever left the tuition entirely to the tutors. As they persisted, he announced that for the future no young men coming to the College would be entered in their names or assigned to them as pupils. As this would give him pupils without tutors, and none of the younger Fellows were immediately ready to accept office, the Provost took what was then the very extraordinary step of inviting Hampden, a married Fellow, with a family, taking private pupils in Oxford, to fill the gap. He complied, and walked into the College every morning to take his class, which done, he walked out again. If the confederate Fellows were surprised, or if they even felt aggrieved, theirs was only the common case of those who, upon the inducement of some momentary advantage, drive an opponent to bay, without remembering the counsels of despair to which they are driving him. Hampden was a hard-working, able, and conscientious man, after his light and his fashion, and was more than equal to the demands made on him. The three Fellows were checkmated, at least they gave up the game, and the Provost, before long, had the tuition wholly under his control and upon his own lines. On the other hand, upon becoming Provost, Hawkins had had to leave to Newman what proved, in his hands, the far more important and influential position of vicar of St. Mary's, including the parochial occupancy of the pulpit from which the University sermons were delivered. Hawkins himself had shown the use that could be made of it, for he always had full congregations, and they included many members of the University. This latter feature increased rapidly under Newman's preaching. His sermons became the staple of many a college conversation; admired by all, though here and there the objects of an indefinite suspicion.

His first public act was in a strictly Anglican direction. He was secretary of the Oxford branch of a religious society – the Church Missionary, we believe – of a liberal and comprehensive character. In this capacity he found himself allied with persons taking small account of Episcopal authority and organization. He resigned the office and circulated a pamphlet explaining his reasons for so doing. About the same time he heartily responded to a call to protect the Church of England from attack, or, at least, from indignity, in another direction. The mode in which Catholic emancipation was suddenly forced on the Church, like the springing of a mine, set Oxford in a blaze; and when Peel placed his seat at the disposal of the University, the majority of Convocation were resolved that he should be taken at his word, and full use should be made of the opportunity. Looking down the Christ Church list they found in Sir R. H. Inglis an eminently genial, safe, and respectable representative. As a dispensation rather than a boon, Newman and his friends accepted the choice, and thenceforth Sir R. H. Inglis became the type of old Oxford.

The year 1831 – that is, the year after the 'July Revolution' at Paris – saw some great beginnings in this country. The Reform Bill was introduced into Parliament and battled over for a twelvemonth. Nothing else was read or thought about. There were those, however, who saw a rift in the political storm. Newman undertook to prepare for a theological 'series' a handy volume for the Church councils; and Blanco White, on the same day and hour, undertook the 'Inquisition.' The subject was new to Newman, and overtaxed his time and strength. The compass of his thoughts and the range of his design expanded every day, and in that visit to the buried past he roused the ghost that ever pursued him, and finally drove him to seek shelter in Rome. The meaning of this statement, afterwards repeated at much greater length and in various forms, was that the study of the Fathers could no more lead to truth than the study of the Scriptures, without an infallible guide. Newman simply lost himself in a task for which a lifetime had been insufficient. Laying his foundation deep in the centuries, and resolved to prejudge the question at issue, he does not arrive at the first Œcumenical Council till the 270th page. To the Council itself he gives six pages. He then wanders at large in a succession of biographical sketches and generally lamentable incidents, till, at page 416, he comes to the second Œcumenical Council, to which he gives four pages, and then closes the volume with a thundering anathema on the Papal Apostasy. Whether on Mr. Rivington's line or his own, whether as history or as theology, the work is an utter breakdown. Tone and style, however, carried the day. The work has only to be compared with any other history or theology, or of the Church, to account for its enthusiastic reception, and its effect on the rising movement. Such is the work generally, but incorrectly, known as the 'History of the Arians.' Newman was now a 'Select preacher,' and it was when he had just plunged out of his depth – indeed, out of all human depth – into anti-Nicene controversy that he made a great sensation by a University sermon on 'Personal Influence, the means of propagating the Truth.' In this he compared the continual transmission of the light of faith from age to age to the beacon fires described in a Greek play. If any one sermon is to be credited with the first start of the 'Movement' it is this, preached January 22, 1832.

After completing his task – or rather leaving it scarcely begun – Newman started with Froude on a tour of several months on the Mediterranean, seeing much and having many interesting experiences. It is evident that Newman, at least, if not Froude also, shrank from Rome, as from one whose charms were dangerous and well nigh irresistible. It is not the ordinary English tourist who avoids all religious ceremonies and functions, who will not be entrapped even into a momentary act of united worship, and who comes home with his mouth full of hot things against Rome. It is the man with much sympathy for that from which he violently recoils. Two men, however, the travellers saw and conversed with at Rome, and even liked, as far as can be seen, pretty equally. These were Bunsen and Wiseman. While Newman's heavier labours were necessarily suspended these six months, the outpourings of his heart were fresh and abundant at every stage of his wanderings. Most of his contributions to the 'Lyra Apostolica,' including several pieces that have won a world-wide acceptance, were written at this time. Retracing his course alone from Rome to Sicily, for a more leisurely contemplation of its manifold beauties, Newman caught a fever, in which he was nursed by a monk, and the traces of which were still upon him when he returned home. It was not to the 'sweet home' of song and story that he returned, for all the minds, all the pens, and all the tongues were there contending for the glory of regenerating this isle, and Newman came in, so to speak, on the top of a scramble. Hurrell Froude was before him, thundering and lightning, out-talking and out-doing everybody, but compelled soon to collapse within the dimensions of his frail earthly tenement. Strange as it now may seem, thus far, the event that most angered Newman and drove him into an irreconcilable course was the suppression of ten Irish bishoprics. A see once founded he believed to be indestructible.

Hugh James Rose was then the tallest, grandest, and, his contemporaries say, the most winning figure in the Church of England. Round him gathered A. P. Perceval, Froude, and another, at what came to be called the 'Hadleigh Conference.' After considering various suggestions, they agreed that something should be done, and that everybody was to do and say what he thought best, without inviting the criticism or expecting the agreement of others. On this basis of a wide authorization and personal liberty Newman at once proceeded to write and issue the 'Tracts for the Times,' of which the first famous words were, 'I am but one of you, a presbyter.' At this distance of time it costs an effort to conceive how these simple and very offhand productions should stir up a whole Church and rend it almost in twain. As a matter of fact they did. Tract after tract was read, though they inculcated much that was impracticable, not to say impossible. Everything that came from Oxford was read. The Christian public wanted and waited, and could hardly be supplied quick enough. Even when the heat and stir of the movement had somewhat abated, it was found strong enough to give a wide circulation, and even a popularity, to bulky volumes on the distinctive doctrines of the Church of England, to endless 'catenas,' series, and 'libraries.'

As soon as Newman saw the vast superstructure of religious literature arising upon his first flaming tracts, he felt that the fire stood some chance of being stifled under its smoke, so he opened a new crater of his own in a succession of volumes of sermons preached at St. Mary's. Hitherto he had been rather shy about publishing sermons, but such scruples do not last long. Immediately all the world read his sermons, and few other. To educated men they still hold their ground, and may be said to have eclipsed and superseded all sermons of an earlier date, unless a man can gird his loins and prepare himself to read a sermon by Jeremy Taylor, or one of the few that Ken has left us. But the most ardent admirers of John Henry Newman must still admit a defect of fatal significance dimly observed 50 years ago, known by its fruits now. That defect it is needless to describe, were it even possible. These sermons have not reached the hearts and understanding of the masses, who, upon any theory, are the persons most to be considered, and for whom Divine ordinances and human institutions are most designed. We now see, and are not even surprised to see, that Newman has not carried the people of England with him; and when we look to his works we see that he was not likely to do so. However, in the three years following the first stir of the movement, its progress was rapid and brilliant.

Meanwhile the Provost of Oriel was loyal and constant to his friend in need, and the College now saw the influence and patronage which the usage of the University leaves to the heads of Houses heaped upon the unwelcome intruder. Hampden realized and utilized his position, seeing within his grasp both an academic and a political harvest. He delivered the famous Bampton Lectures, which have yet to be read, understood, and fairly estimated. To make sure he translated some of his hieroglyphics into language which 'they that run can read,' and if he did not propitiate Dissenters, he much troubled Church people. He was admitted into the then Sacred College of Heads of Houses as Principal of St. Mary Hall. By the favour of his fast friend, he became Professor of Moral Philosophy. The two antagonist leaders of thought were at close quarters. Hampden was lecturing and writing; Newman was preaching, writing and talking, within a few yards of one another. Hampden had secured the Hall, Newman the Church, included in the foundation of the College. The latter had also the hamlet of Littlemore, three miles out of Oxford, the ancient nunnery of which was the true founder of St. Mary's, of Oriel College, and of a great part of the University. Here he built a church. Two such opposite personalities, acting, growing, developing side by side, within sight and hearing, could not but come into collision. The inevitable hour arrived in 1836, when Lord Melbourne recommended Hampden for the Chair of theology vacated by Burton's premature death. The note of alarm had already been sounded in the metropolis, and most provincial centres, and now the worst had come to pass. The anti-liberal members of the University, in much haste, confusion, and prejudice, met and agreed on a proposal to meet the Premier – that is, the Crown – with a statute disabling the nominee of the Crown to the utmost in their power. The non-resident members of Convocation responded to the appeal, and after a temporary hitch, caused by a procuratorial veto, this violent and probably illegal resolution was carried, and the Crown deprived of more than half the substance of that which it had supposed itself, there was more insult in it than injury. The authorities took Hampden's side, and his friends had no reason to complain of exclusion from the University pulpit. When the opportunity arrived, they acted as lawlessly as the other side had done; if one Canon of Christ Church was not allowed a voice in the selection of preachers, another found himself excluded from the University pulpit.

But the greater the noise, the greater the disturbance, the greater the lawlessness, just in the same proportion was the growth of the 'Oxford party.' It was idle to fight about the occupation of the University pulpit, when not only that very pulpit every Sunday afternoon, but some thousand other pulpits, were open to a party that courted persecution, and would have been disappointed had they not been paid in their own coin. The remembrance of that time suggests a terrible misgiving as to the true nature of the centuries in which the magnificent fabric of Christian theology was elaborated and finally established. The present generation, that knows of the Cardinal chiefly in the comparatively quiet retreat of the Oratory and in the continual ovation everywhere and by almost all people accorded to his pre-eminent character, can be little aware of the inexhaustible energy and indefatigable industry with which he fought, what no doubt he believed the fight of faith. It would be exceeding the limits of our space to do common justice to his manifold labours. He was incessant in correspondence; he was always accessible to visitors; he kept journals and wrote 'mémoires justificatives:' he read, translated, analyzed, and abstracted; he wrote and delivered sermons of the most intense originality; he lectured, he kept account of his army of followers. Before the publication of the Tracts, he wrote letters till he had taxed to the utmost its forbearance and its space. Some years afterwards, upon the occasion of Sir R. Peel's delivering a 'march of wind' address on the opening of Tamworth Reading Room, he wrote, with the signature of Catholicus, a series of letters in this journal, read with eager interest by many who never guessed the author, still less that he would one day be a member of the 'Sacred College.' He and his friends were large contributors to the *British Magazine*, which somehow came to an end in the conflict between the new and the old materials now to be found in it. All that is now remembered of either is the 'Lyra

Apostolica,' reprinted from its pages. While still enjoying liberty of thought and of action, Newman 'lectured' alike Romanists and Dissenters from St. Mary's. He preached and published six volumes of 'Parochial Sermons' that have not yet lost their hold on the religious public, and that have been republished by an old and early friend within the last few years. In 1837 he published 'Romanism and Popular Protestantism,' or, to give the volume its full title, 'Lectures on the Prophetical Office of the Church viewed relatively' to these two systems. Were it true that a lady's meaning is to be found in that postscript, or that the best way to read a book is, as Whately once suggested, to begin at the end, then we might believe that Newman, at the above date, loved Rome as little as he did Arianism and Dissent. His work on 'Justification' was either very right, or very wrong, for the Evangelical party at once pronounced that the author had confounded, or misplaced, justification and sanctification. A work on 'Development in Matters of Doctrine,' though the theme has been since extensively enlarged upon, was a great shock to the fixed ideas and conservative instincts of English Churchmen. The *British Critic*, the old-established organ of the 'High and Dry,' now lay athwart the path of the movement. It was in the hands of an amiable and even brilliant writer seeking peace in a mid course. By successive encroachments, one involving another, Newman became editor, and for five or six years under his direction, or influence, the *British Critic* kept the Church of England in one long agony of surprise and alarm as to the results of its trenchant criticisms and reckless speculation. Though Rome was repeatedly the subject of an enormous protest, and the Church of England warned against her seductions, it was still felt that the underlying mass of feeling and of argument was moving towards her. In mathematics two lines can be forever approaching without falling together, but it is not so when the heart is concerned, or when every day gives new birth to new motives.

The 'Tracts for the Times' pursued what can hardly be called their steady course. If some of them might kindly give repose, and even sleep, whenever Newman's pen took its turn all were roused from their tranquillity or their slumber. Taking the Bible in one hand and the mediæval Church in the other, he would command his readers to accept both or neither. Culling from the indictments or the declarations of his antagonists their most felicitous and irresistible arguments, he would hurl them at the sacred object of their common reverence, the inspired Scriptures themselves – the only Rule of Faith. The stoutest Protestant ceased to throw stones when he found them falling on his own head. Reason itself, the old foe of authority, seemed now a good renegade. There still remained, however, a good many thousands in the land who could hold to the faith of their fathers, without the aid of reason or the pomp of a scientific theology. The publications of the day were equally divided between the Tractarian and the anti-Tractarian writers. Learned clergyman, who but for the 'Movement' would have read and dozed in their studies, produced heavy octavos. Religious novelists supplied lighter stuff. The Bishops were bound to make an appearance, and they did. All must have felt the father's yearnings for the son that only erred by excess of zeal – Bishop Bagot certainly did – but they had to stand by their own order and law. Some delivered censures at once unscientific and unmitigated. No historian describes the order of attack, for it told its tale in the result. At length No. 90 challenged the forbearance of the Church and University to the utmost, for had it been endured there was nothing that might not plead the example. At the invocation of 'Four Tutors,' one of them the late Primate, the Vice-Chancellor and Heads of Houses exercised that domestic authority with which they are armed for matters affecting the discipline of the undergraduate crowd. They pronounced a public censure of the Tract without waiting for a defence, and evidently without caring to know what the author might have to say about it. This seemed very harsh, and is still so thought by many. But power and authority cannot afford to be always logical. Newman's case was the historic fact that the Thirty-nine articles are older than the decrees of the Council of Trent, and were meant to be comprehensive. Accordingly, as he maintained, they only condemned certain popular abuses or excesses, and cannot be interpreted as in direct conflict with existing Roman Catholic doctrine. This was a question which neither Oxford, nor the Bench of Bishops, nor the people of England were willing to entertain. Newman bowed to the censure, and perhaps felt it a deliverance. He professed to be always guided by circumstances. It was for the Church of England, not himself, to pronounce it no longer Catholic. The 'Tracts for the Times,' which had now attained to the bulk of five octavo volumes, and which, in the original editions, are now hardly to be got at any price, were stopped. This, however, only created a new position, with new opportunities, which Newman was quick to discover. Rome had as yet made few or no converts. The Tracts taught that Christians had all they wanted in the Anglican Communion. Deny this, and you drive them to Rome. The sequel seemed to bear this out. At the very time that the scheme of comprehension propounded in No. 90 was formally condemned, there was suddenly started another scheme of comprehension in the Jerusalem bishopric, aiming to combine in one communion Anglicans and German Protestants. Against this Newman made a solemn public protest, to which his own position now gave the greater influence and authority.

Newman held on for a time at St. Mary's, and then, step by step, withdrew to Littlemore, where he finally ensconced himself with a small band of faithful adherents.

The end of one question was now the beginning of another. Was a new Anglican Church to rise on this spot of mysterious and immemorial sanctity? Had the nuns of Littlemore, the true founders of half the University, been heard to invoke *nostris ex ossibus ultor* to avenge their wrongs? A great University was thrown into alternative paroxysms of curiosity and terror by a new neighbour, somewhat resembling the *epipolis* thrown up for the occasion by a besieging host. Was this to be a new Oxford? Fate has otherwise ordered. Littlemore is now best known for its county lunatic asylum, while a couple of miles off the military centre has transformed the neighbouring plain into a gay and busy suburb. What has been called the crash of the party had now begun. 'Ideal Ward,' as he came to be called, from the most irreconcilable of his many utterances, provoked his fate with an impetuosity that could not be resisted, and he was finally stripped of his degrees and consequently of his Fellowship, by an assembled University, only to appear at the altar of the English Church with a beautiful young bride a few weeks after. By a happy intervention the University was saved the disgrace of an ill-considered sentence on Newman's own work, as had been proposed. Nor was there occasion for such a step. A few months afterwards, Newman sent for a foreign monk of the Order of St. Dominic, and through him submitted to the Church of Rome.

As the greater part of the English public had long been expecting the news, and could not understand a position between two rival and antagonistic Churches, nobody now asked what had finally decided Newman. It was his way, however, to assign to every act its own proper occasion and motive, and it is stated that an article by Dr. Wiseman on the Donatists turned the scale. This would imply that the chief obstacle in Newman's mind, up to this time, had been the moral scandals affecting the Church of Rome, alike priests and people. These the Donatists, who were the Protestants of their day, held to vitiate orders, nullify ordinances, and destroy authority. But Newman had no need to go to the pages of the *Dublin Review* to learn that a mixture of good and bad is a universal condition of human life. Calumny itself was silenced by the very act that might be accepted as its justification. Before this, controversialists had freely charged Newman with a secret intention. In after years Newman was frequently consulted by young people 'on the move,' but not prepared to face the difficulties of a decision. He uniformly counselled against concealment and reserve, or any course that would be one thing to the actor, another to the world.

From that hour the Church of England has regarded Newman at an increasing distance, but with an increasing favour. Yet is has been but a cold and profitless regard; a just pride and a high admiration, but little more. As a nation and a race we now boast to have contributed to Rome one of her greatest minds and one of her best men. Yet we do not follow. The captain has led the way, but the column lags behind. The following has been almost wholly confined to the educated and refined, to the classes to whom religion is a luxury, an amusement, an agreeable relief from the frivolities and vulgarities of the hour. Several thousand have thus accompanied Newman, not into the wilderness, but into magnificent churches, and into well furnished and well frequented drawing rooms. But that multitude which responded to the Gospel-call on the shores of Gennesareth holds aloof and hears not the voice of a shepherd. The wise and prudent are many in the crowd that has left us, but of the babes there are none. As soon as he had crossed the Rubicon, Newman, like the conquered kings of antiquity, had to show himself at Rome. He appears to have wished to remain and study there, but he was sent back to work on the English masses, if haply he could break or soften them.

The Pope then, or soon after, gave Newman the degree of D. D., and it is a remarkable fact that this addition to his name had the effect of raising the degree in English estimation. Up to that date any aspirant for the merely nominal honour was credited with sheer vanity, or some pecuniary motive, and any one of high standing would much rather be called Canon than D. D. Englishmen are no longer ashamed of a title which places them next to saints in the celestial Hierarchy.

Newman must himself have suggested Birmingham, for it was one of Froude's ideas, possibly because to an Oxford man the most repulsive and self-denying that could be imagined. There Newman founded the Oratory; a society, not an order – and under a comprehensive engagement to do all kinds of duty and kindness to all sorts of people, at all times, and as much as possible in all places. Another branch, we presume, was founded in King William-street, Strand; and more recently by the one magnificently housed in Brompton-road, and for a long time under Father Faber. There could not be a stronger test of sincerity, or a higher proof of devotion, than for a great theologian and scholar to resign Oxford and Littlemore, and bury himself in the throng, smoke, and din of a great manufacturing centre. Newman retained his hold of the place ever after, though he did not reside there constantly. In the year 1854 he accepted the Rectorship of the Catholic University at Dublin, and persevered through the manifold and growing difficulties of that position six or seven years. The Irish never get on well under Englishmen, and Newman is said to have found his position neither easy nor always agreeable under a board of management consisting of his superiors in rank and authority, if not always in other respects. At one time there went round a story that, in order to save his dignity, and enable him to take his due share in the management, he was to be made a Bishop *in partibus*; but this was not done. Newman did his best during his brief sojourn to educate the Irish mind up to his ideas of a University, and he made some attached friends, but on the whole he thought it best to leave Ireland to the Irish. One old friendship he found to be lost beyond recovery. After some ineffectual attempts at mutual civility, he and Archbishop Whately found it more convenient to pass without recognition, painful as it might be to both of them.

The Irish failure, as it might be called, was a great disappointment, for the turn of Newman's mind was always rather academic than ecclesiastical. From the time of his 'conversion' to Rome, at least from the date of his visit to the Holy See, he earnestly desired to see a Roman Catholic college at Oxford, no doubt under his presidency. For this he worked, canvassed, and obtained flattering assurances, but in vain. A party of his own friends at home, headed by Ward, continually counteracted his efforts, and whether they were right from a Roman point of view it is not easy or necessary to say. But it was the disappointment that most preyed on Newman's mind, and that extorted from him some rather hard sayings upon the Italian notions of veracity, to which he preferred the English. Returning to Birmingham, Newman found no difficulty in winning the love, if not the obedience, of a population specially addicted to having a way of its own, and to take that way. No doubt they were proud to have so great a man among them. But a residence in the provinces is a sort of banishment, even if it be accompanied with important work; and Newman's retirement to Birmingham has been regarded by the public generally much as his retreat from Oxford to Littlemore. He established a school for Catholic noblemen and gentlemen, and his pupils have succeeded in due time to their hereditary positions; but it can hardly be said that any have brought with them the traces of a great teacher. They are 'good Catholics,' and no more. He has published sermons, lectures, treatises, and theological works, but they have not penetrated into the Church of England, not at least beyond a circle of devoted admirers. His lectures on 'Anglican Difficulties' may have helped to unsettle some hundred clergymen. His lectures on the office and work of Universities would seem to have had no other result than further to liberalize Oxford and Cambridge, and provoke the godly jealousy of the Congregationalists. His history of the Turks, on the spur of a sudden occasion, is an amazing feat, but as a contribution to the politics of the day it is far too much on the 'bag and baggage' line. It is not every great author who will venture to write tales. Newman did. His 'Callista' and his 'Loss and Gain' were received with great interest, necessarily confined to those who feel dogmatic truth the supreme object of every inquiry. The 'Grammar of Assent' which is said to contain some wonderful passages and to develop the principles of No. 90 and some other Tracts were written; but the mass of ore out of which the precious metal is to be extracted is immense. Newman often overtaxed the time and patience, as well as the subtlety, of his readers, and, like some other great men, he may be found in after times buried under the pile of his own works, or represented by one small volume or two out of half a hundred.

On several occasions was Newman dragged out of his provincial security. In 1851, in the course of some lectures delivered at Birmingham, he delivered a tremendous phillipic against one Achilli, an Italian monk, who had been driven out of Italy and his Church, and was now declaiming against them, much to the delight of our Protestant gentlemen and ladies. The man had now to fight for dear life. They brought an action for libel against Newman, and, as he also had friends, he brought over a host of witnesses. There was no doubt as to the libel, and the truth of the libel was no defence. Newman was fined £100, but the expenses were many thousands, and they were cheerfully subscribed for him. The only result of the action has been to write on the role of history a character and career which Englishmen will henceforth be apt to associate with mountebanks of Achilli's description. In January, 1864, Kingsley, under some unaccountable, perhaps quite momentary, impulse, writing for a magazine, charged Newman with teaching that truth need not be a virtue to the Catholic clergy, and, indeed, ought not to be; that cunning is the proper weapon of the saints; and that, whether this notion be doctrinally correct or not, it is historically true. Newman at once demanded a justification of this libel, which Kingsley found himself unable to produce. Instead of proofs he went into generalities, into which Newman followed him. After a long stage of personalities, as they must be called, happily the assailed party changed his key and ascended into the most interesting of all his writings, and the one which put him once more in accord with the English public. The 'Apologia' is a household word in this country; nor is the interest of it diminished by the fact that it is the history of a mind rather than a course of events; and that it is the inner life of one man without much attempt to enter into other personal experiences. It is Newman, and very little more. Even Hamlet, monopolist as he is, leaves more room and more honour to inferior personages. But, whatever the faults, if faults they be, the 'Apologia' will ever hold its ground in English literature. At the time of the 'Œcumenical Council' Newman was said to be adverse to an authoritative definition of Papal infallibility. His objections were so delicately and mildly expressed that to an ordinary English eye they looked more like a pious performance necessary to the idea of a discussion rather than a real opinion. Indeed, most Englishmen will think it a matter of indifference how infallibility is defined, one definition in an impossible matter being as good as another. It must be considered, however, that Newman's whole life had been one long controversy, and where there is no beginning there is likely to be no end. A definition, if it be worth anything, must preclude some alternatives, and so far stop discussion. But, as there were said to be more than 60 distinct definitions of Papal infallibility before the year 1870, it can hardly be supposed that one more will make a material difference. The Vatican council was such a grand and imposing demonstration, and as such it has told on the open field of human affairs.

Eleven years ago a great omission was repaired, a great inequality removed. So high was the regard that England had for Newman, on whatever grounds, that it felt really aggrieved at what seemed to be the denial of a Cardinal's hat. Englishmen are apt to talk and write on stilts, so to speak, and in this vein they do not take too much account of Cardinals. But nature will come out. We have all been children in our time, and the child never wholly departs from our nature. So all England was delighted when Newman went to Rome, which, at his age and in his infirm health, was a service of danger, and came back with his long-due decorations. Already his own first college at Oxford had been proud to restore his name to its books and to raise him from a scholar to an Honorary Fellow. Fastidious critics observed that he had left Oxford a believer and returned to it in the guise of a liberal; the change, however, was in the University, not in himself; and in this country we give everybody licence to avail himself freely of its varying and not entirely consistent opportunities. Things must be done by hook or by crook, or not at all. Yet it is an amazing sign of the times that a Cardinal should head the list of names in an Oxford College. The chief feature of the visit was a call on Dr. Pusey, for a long interchange of guarded sympathies and old memories. Two years after he paid Oxford a second visit, for a large garden party at his college, and to preach a sermon at the new Roman Catholic Chapel. Newman never lost a friend if he could help it, and always took care that it was not he that cut the sacred tie, as he deemed it. About this date he travelled into the western counties, seeing old friends in the way, and full of old thoughts and feelings. On this occasion he had to seek in vain for an admission to Exeter Cathedral at an hour when he had fair reason to expect it would be open to strangers, as the Continental churches are. Oddly enough, the single reason of his exclusion was that the cathedral authorities, with a large party of invited friends and partisans, were engaged in a discussion upon the unhappy reredos, which proved a bone of contention between Bishop Temple and the Chapter. At Edgbaston he was always most easy of access, and ready to see an old friend, or a stranger, even to the interruption of some important work, or of the brief midday repose. When much pressed, or worn, he retired for a short holiday to a cottage at Rednal, on the Lickey Hills, a few miles from Birmingham.

Now, for many years, all Englishmen have vied in rendering the proper homage, whatever it might be, or whatever its worth, to the most conspicuous and interesting name in our theological or literary annals. Unless it be on some rare occasions and instances, Newman was singularly free from the weaknesses and misfortunes that so often make polemics a plague and literature a grief. There are great and even good men who repel sympathy, and even forfeit it; Newman could not do either. With all his faults – for all have faults – England has loved him still. The truth is we are a nation of hero-worshippers, sometimes to the extent of holding one hero as good as another, though they may have considerable differences to settle between themselves. Such feelings, often the suggestions of the hour, have to stand the severer test of years to come. Will even the next generation read Newman's now voluminous works? Will it enter upon a course the termination of which is already historical? Every work of man is measured by its results. The narrow range of human power and opportunity has to be taken into account. Near home, on this very spot, we have frequent and melancholy experiences of the fate that may await the fruits of industry and genius. As one hour succeeds another, important matter has to give way to the latest arrival, and has to be first minished, and then, perhaps, finally squeezed out of our columns. Enter any good old-fashioned library that has had the rare luck to escape fire, the auction-room, and the waste-paper store. In long rows are the works of the 20 or 30 great divines, the delight and the support of their respective generations. Of most of these good men, so great in their day, it is now rare to find anybody who has read even a page, or can so much as say what manner of men they were, or what were their distinctive opinions, or where they preached or wrote, or where they lived and died. Over every library, even such as those now annually scattered, volume by volume, over all lands, may be written the warning not to work for posterity, but for the present day, and for those that share it with us.

Newman was received into the Roman Catholic Church on 9 October 1845 by Father Dominic Barberi (a Passionist not, *pace* this obituary, a Dominican). To Newman himself this seemed to be the climax of an inexorable intellectual progress. The reasoning behind his decision is carefully delineated both in his novel *Loss and Gain* and in his *Apologia pro vita sua*. The soul-searching occasioned by his defection is well caught in fiction by Anthony Trollope in the account of Dr Arabin's early career in *Barchester Towers*. This obituary dwells on Newman's Anglican years and readily recognizes the distinctive and supple genius which had so influenced the contemporary Church of England and which was to bear so deeply on Catholic theology after his death. As the evidently Anglican obituarist notes, despite the perceived danger that he and his disciples presented to the religious status-quo Newman did not 'carry the people of England with him' when he converted. Nevertheless, as a prominent Catholic he had not proved the sort of man 'the Church of Rome most trusts and employs'. Newman had introduced the Oratorian Order in England under directions from Pius IX. It was in their first London Church, in converted premises off the Strand, that Newman delivered his lectures on *The Difficulties of Anglicans* in 1850. Despite having devoted much of his energy to establishing the Birmingham Oratory, which moved to Edgbaston in 1850, and despite his celebrity, Newman's presumed theological liberalism had denied him promotion to a bishopric. He was belatedly accorded the Church's highest priestly honour when Pope Leo XIII made him Cardinal Deacon of the ancient Church of St Giorgio in Velabro in Rome in May 1879. He is the only figure in this book to be a candidate for sainthood.

CHARLES BRADLAUGH

Freethinker and politician:
'He was a remarkable figure of a somewhat obsolete type.'

30 JANUARY 1891

YESTERDAY DIED CHARLES BRADLAUGH, the junior member for Northampton. In his robust frame had been sown long ago the seeds of disease. In the Session of 1889 it had become painfully apparent that he had lost his old vigour and elasticity. A visit to India appeared for a time to restore him to health; but the recovery was only partial. His friends have for a long time been aware that his public work was over. He became seriously ill a week or two ago, and had not been in full possession of his senses since Friday evening last week. On Thursday there was thought to be a possibility of his recovery, owing to the continuance of a slight improvement which had appeared in his condition on the previous evening; but he became worse later on, and passed away peacefully and quietly at half-past 6 o'clock yesterday morning.

Charles Bradlaugh was born September 26, 1833, at Hoxton. His father was a lawyer's clerk, and, according to the testimony of his son William Bradlaugh, 'one of the kindest, noblest, and best men that ever lived.' His son Charles was, for a time, employed in the same office as his father. He subsequently acted as a wharf clerk, and in the course of his many employments he was successively a coal merchant and a traveller for a manufacturer of buckskin braces. He was precociously intelligent, and at a very early age he was an active Sunday-school teacher under the Rev. Mr. Packer, of St. Peter's Hackney-road. He fell under the influence of the friends and disciples of Richard Carlile, the once famous editor of the *Republican and Prompter*, and the hero of half a dozen prosecutions for blasphemy and sedition; and by 19 Bradlaugh had become known on Hackney-downs and in Victoria Park as a fluent advocate of free thought. He did not prosper in business, and he gladly availed himself for some months of the hospitality of Mrs. Carlile, the widow of Richard Carlile. In his distress he decided to enlist as a soldier, and the 7th Dragoon Guards welcomed the tall, stalwart recruit. About this part of Mr. Bradlaugh's life, and, in fact, about many passages in his early years, there is obscurity – his own accounts of them are not always quite consistent. There are traditions that while with his regiment in Kildare and Dublin he read much, that once at least he distinguished himself as a pugilist, that he was an earnest advocate of teetotalism, and a champion of popular rights. What is certain is that he became orderly clerk, that he disliked soldiering, and that he managed to purchase in 1853 his discharge, taking with him a good character from his colonel. He returned to London, and again got, apparently with some difficulty, employment as a lawyer's clerk. The first of the Common Law Procedure Acts was then coming into operation; in the applications made at Chambers there was an opportunity for adroitness and astuteness; and Bradlaugh was quick to profit by the chance. At all events, he picked up that knowledge of legal forms and processes of which he made effective use in later years. While in the office of Mr. Rogers, of Fenchurch-street, and other solicitors, he lectured on religious subjects. In a few years he ceased to be a lawyer's clerk, and as 'Iconoclast,' the representative of pugnacious, aggressive atheism, he began that career of pamphleteering and lecturing which made his name repulsive to the majority of his countrymen. From town to town he travelled preaching free-thought, and was the chief figure in little-edifying platform encounters, in which well-meaning, ill-advised advocates of orthodoxy were persuaded to take part. He aspired to the place which Paine, Richard Carlile, Robert Taylor, and Charles Southwell had successively occupied; and he succeeded. He possessed considerable powers of speech, and the courage needed to face an angry mob or a hostile audience. The hard, reckless way in which he touched sacred themes, his arrogance and ever present egotism, made him offensive even to many who thought as he did. But he won platform victories; and he elicited a certain admiration by his ingenuity in his far from few legal difficulties – for example, when he foiled the Devonport authorities by lecturing from a boat moored in deep water only a few yards from a large audience ranged along the shore. In the Hall of Science and the pages of the *National Reformer* he advocated Republicanism and Secularism, and inflamed the not inconsiderable number of his followers with hopes of what he would accomplish when he entered the House. Several times he tried, without success, to get a seat. At last, in April, 1880, he was returned for Northampton.

Then began a long course of litigation, which had the effect of making Mr. Bradlaugh known to those who had scarcely heard of 'Iconoclast.' He had always been prone to show his legal acumen. He sued in 1861 the superintendent of police at Devonport for interfering with his lectures but recovered only a farthing damages, and for the first time figured in the law reports – wherein his name was afterwards so prominent – by moving unsuccessfully in the Court of Common Pleas for a new trial. He was more successful in defying the Inland Revenue in an attempt to enforce an obsolete Act against the *National Reformer*. In 1877 he and Mrs. Besant were indicted for publishing an obscene book, 'The Fruits of Philosophy,' and they were sentenced to six months' imprisonment and a fine of £200. The conviction, however, was ultimately quashed on technical grounds; the pleader had omitted to set out in the indictment the entire book, or so much of it as was complained of. While in Parliament Mr. Bradlaugh spent most of his time for several Sessions in trying to remove the barrier opposed to his taking his seat by the form of the oath of allegiance. When elected he claimed to be entitled to affirm under the Parliamentary Oaths Act, 1866, and the Evidence Acts, 1863 and 1870. A Select Committee, by a majority of one, reported against his claim. Then, to the amazement of his friends, he claimed on May 21 the right to take the oath. A Select Committee decided against his competence and the House proceeded to pass a resolution denying his right either to take the oath or to affirm. Refusing to recognize the authority of the House, he was removed by the Sergeant-at-Arms. An action for enormous penalties, for having sat and voted without having first taken the oath, was begun. It is unnecessary to recall all the subsequent intricate steps of the struggle waged from 1880 to 1885, the athletic performances in the House of Commons whereby he sought to secure his seat, or the memorable 21st of February 1882, whereon, before an amazed House, he stepped to the table, drew a Testament from his pocket, and administered the oath to himself. Successively excluded by the House and invariably re-elected by his constituents, he was allowed in 1886 to take the oath, and two Sessions afterwards the principles for which he had contended triumphed by the passing of the Oaths Act. In that interval Mr. Bradlaugh was rarely out of litigation, which he conducted with rare skill, but with a clever layman's weakness for dwelling *inter apices juris* and for pushing technicalities to extremes. In 'The Queen v. Bradlaugh,' 'Clarke v. Bradlaugh,' 'Bradlaugh v. Erskine,' and 'Bradlaugh v. Gosset' he showed remarkable acuteness. The decision of the House of Lords in 'Clarke v. Bradlaugh' was that the writs against him were so much waste paper. A scarcely less important victory was that which he achieved in the action which he brought with success against Mr. Newdegate for maintenance.

Since he was permitted to take his seat Mr. Bradlaugh has been less heard of. But the part of his life to he regarded with most satisfaction was the last. The junior member for Northampton had little resemblance to 'Iconoclast,' the lecturer of the Hall of Science, or the Republican editor of the *National Reformer*. Of late and especially since his visit to India, he sought to become the champion of Hindoo claims for representation; and if his advocacy of this cause showed no great knowledge, it was conducted with no needless acrimony. To one of his last Speeches of importance in the House of Commons, on the report of the Select Committee on Perpetual Pensions – his favourite theme of denunciation – no exception could be reasonably taken. He grew in moderation and decorousness. He kept his religious opinions in the background. He learned perhaps to understand much of what he had scoffed at; and more than once he set an example to those who ought to have known better. With Socialism he had no sympathy and he declined to purchase support by flattering it. He showed by his conduct in regard to the Employers' Liability Bill, and, more recently, in regard to the Eight Hours Movement, that he dared risk his popularity. His Parliamentary achievements, in a time unfavourable to the efforts of private members, were considerable and they were due to the qualities wherein his strength lay – a dogged perseverance and an eminently practical bent of mind – together with the respect which he succeeded in extorting from all parties in the House and which grew rapidly in the last few years. This feeling culminated in the unopposed motion carried on Tuesday last, whereby the House decided to expunge the resolution of June 22, 1880, which refused him permission to take the oath or to affirm. It was a pathetic circumstance that when the news of this arrived Mr. Bradlaugh had already passed into unconsciousness. Mr. Bradlaugh was not even a Wilkes, far less a Danton, as his flatterers told him. Nor was he the mediocrity which his many enemies among working men described him. He was a remarkable figure of a somewhat obsolete type.

This is not a particulary sympathetic obituary of a figure who managed, through determined bloody-mindedness, to change an important aspect of Parliamentary procedure in the United Kingdom. Dissenters and Roman Catholics had been given full civil rights in the late 1820s; Jews were finally admitted to Parliament, with an alteration to the requisite oath of allegiance to the Crown, in 1860. Having been elected Member for Northampton in 1880, Bradlaugh objected, as an atheist, to taking the oath. His offer merely to 'affirm' was rejected by his fellow MPs on 3 May, though a Parliamentary committee recommended that he should be able to merely take the oath 'as a matter of form'. He was further denied the right to affirm by a vote on 23 June, and Bradlaugh, having refused to leave the House, was taken into custody and confined in the Clock Tower, only to be released the following day. A resolution, moved by Gladstone, that affirmation should be accepted instead of an oath was passed on 2 July 1880, and Bradlaugh took his seat temporarily. A group of MPs, led by Lord Randolph Churchill, then forced a further vote which again excluded him, and he was taken to court (*Clarke* v. *Bradlaugh*, 1881), where he lost his case and was fined. Bradlaugh was re-elected in 1882, but in 1884 and 1885 was duly excluded from the House on each occasion (though in 1883 he managed to vote three times and was then fined £1,500 for voting illegally). He was finally allowed to swear 'as a matter of form' and take his seat in 1886. He remained MP for Northampton until his death, and was an outspoken advocate of what became the Parliamentary Oaths Act of 1888. Bradlaugh died on 30 January 1891. His funeral at Brookwood Cemetery was attended by 3,000 people.

CHARLES STEWART PARNELL

Irish patriot and politician:
'Broken down under such a load of obloquy and disappointment.'

6 OCTOBER 1891

MR. CHARLES STEWART PARNELL died at half-past 11 on Tuesday night at his residence, 10, Walsingham-terrace, Aldrington, near Brighton. The event was not, however, known locally until yesterday morning, when the news rapidly spread, causing everywhere the greatest astonishment. It had not even been known that Mr. Parnell had been ill, and the suddenness of the event led to the dissemination of sensational rumours, which, so far as could be ascertained, were altogether without foundation. Neither before nor after their marriage were Mr. and Mrs. Parnell much known in Brighton and Hove. Walsingham-terrace, where before the marriage they occupied adjoining houses, and where they had since resided, is a lonely row of houses near the sea some two miles westward of the town. It is not, therefore, surprising that Mr. Parnell's illness should have passed unnoticed. The facts, so far as they can be ascertained, appear to be as follows:– On Thursday Mr. Parnell returned from Ireland to Walsingham-terrace suffering from a severe chill. As he was not unaccustomed to similar attacks little was thought of it at the time. The following day, however, he was so much worse that he did not leave his bed. On Saturday some improvement was visible in his condition, but on Sunday he suffered a severe relapse. A Brighton doctor was sent for, and found him, it is said, in the greatest agony, suffering from acute rheumatism. According to another account, however, death is ascribed to congestion of the lungs and bronchitis. Mr. Parnell was nursed by his wife and one of her daughters, who happened to be staying at the time at the house next door, still kept up by Mr. Parnell. In addition to the doctor already in attendance, two other medical men were called in. Mr. Parnell remained, however, in the same condition until Tuesday afternoon, when a very rapid and startling change for the worse occurred, and after lingering for some hours in pain he died, as stated, at half-past 11. With the exception of Mrs. Parnell and her daughter, no relatives or immediate friends of the deceased were present. Mrs. Parnell is completely overcome by this sudden and heavy blow, and yesterday absolutely refused to see any one. At present, therefore, no arrangements for the funeral are known.

A Dalziel despatch from Brighton yesterday states: – The disease to which Mr. Parnell succumbed was not at first supposed to be dangerous. For some time past he had been troubled with rheumatism and the result of excitement and overwork. His wife and friends entreated him to suspend hard political work, but without avail. When he left here a week ago, to speak at Galway, his health was not at all good, and he was so afflicted with rheumatism that after sitting a while it was painful for him to walk. Nevertheless, he fulfilled the Galway engagement, and then returned from Ireland. From that time he became more and more indisposed, but no serious symptoms manifested themselves until last Friday. On that day he came home in much pain. He lay down immediately, complaining of pains in the head and back. On Saturday he did not leave his bed, but refused to have a doctor called in, as he was confident that he would be better next day. He remained in bed all day, the pains diminishing somewhat; but he complained of a dull feeling and heavy weight about the head. On Sunday morning he was so much worse that Mrs. Parnell sent for Dr. R. F. Jowers, who on arriving found that fever had set in, and that, generally speaking, the patient was in a very bad state. The disease appeared to be congestion of the liver, complicated with other disorders arising from a low state of the system. Dr. Jowers called in his father, who is a physician of considerable standing in Brighton, to assist him; but, despite their joint endeavours, the fever increased, and on Monday night the patient became delirious at times and unable to retain any food. All day yesterday he kept sinking, until at nightfall the gravest fears were entertained. There was no knowledge outside of the house of his dangerous state, and no people were present at the bedside except the physicians, the nurse, Mrs. Parnell and her daughter Miss O'Shea. Mr. Parnell died in their presence. He was conscious, but unable to speak. He left no directions, political or otherwise, so far as is known, his knowledge of his approaching death coming when he was already too weak for preparation.

The Press Association special correspondent at Brighton, telegraphing late last night, says:–

> 'I have just interviewed Mr. J. O'Kelly, M. P., at the Grand Hotel. He states that he only returned from France yesterday, and, on hearing of the death of Mr. Parnell, took the first train to Brighton. He saw the dead body of Mr. Parnell at Walsingham-terrace, and from the peaceful expression of the face it was difficult to believe that he was dead. When asked what his opinion as to the cause of death was Mr. O'Kelly said: – "I cannot say. I have not seen either of the medical men, and therefore am not in a position to state what was the cause of his death. To all appearances he died from natural causes." Mr. J. Nolan, M. P., has also arrived at Brighton.'

Charles Stewart Parnell, the eldest son of the late John Henry Parnell, high sheriff of Wicklow in 1836, was born at Avondale, in that county, in June, 1846. His mother was Delia Tudor, daughter of Admiral Charles Stewart, of the American Navy, who, as commodore, had been conspicuous in the naval struggle with England early in the century, when the United States struggled stoutly for the palm of naval supremacy. Mr. Parnell's family had long been settled in Cheshire, and from their seat there his great uncle, Sir Henry Parnell, whose motion on the Civil List turned out the Wellington Government in 1830, and who was afterwards Secretary for War and Paymaster of the Forces under the Whigs, took his title of Lord Congleton. The Parnells belonged to the 'Englishry' of Ireland; one of them, Dr. Thomas Parnell, an author now best known by his poem 'The Hermit,' friend of Pope and Swift, and the subject of a sympathetic biography by Goldsmith, used to bewail his clerical exile among the Irish, and, indeed, consistently neglected his duties as Archdeacon of Clogher; others, later on, during the period of Protestant ascendency were Judges, officials, and members of Parliament; Sir John Parnell, who joined with Grattan and other patriots of that day in fighting for an independence that secured a monopoly of power to their own creed and caste, was Chancellor of the Exchequer just before the Union. Sir John Parnell's grandson was Mr. John Henry Parnell, of Avondale, the father of the future chief of the Separatists, who thus inherited on the paternal side an antipathy to the Union, and on the maternal side the traditions of a bitter conflict with England. Mr. Parnell nevertheless received, like many scions of the Irish landlord class, an exclusively English education at various private schools, and afterwards at Magdalene College, Cambridge, where, however, he did not take a degree, and where, it is said, he was 'sent down' for some rather gross breach of academic discipline. Some surprise was expressed in Ireland when, in 1874, Mr. Parnell, then high sheriff of Wicklow, came forward to oppose in the county Dublin the re-election of Colonel Taylor, who had taken office as Chancellor of the Duchy of Lancaster in the Disraeli Government. He stood as an advocate of Home Rule, to which many of the Irish loyalists had temporarily attached themselves in their disgust at the success of Mr. Gladstone's disestablishment policy. But Mr. Parnell's 'Nationalism' proved to be of another type. If it had a sentimental origin in his family traditions, it was qualified and dominated by the cold temper and the taste for political strategy which he seems to have inherited from his American kinsfolk. Defeated by a large majority in Dublin county, he was more successful a little more than a year later when a vacancy was created in the representation of Meath by the death of John Martin, one of the 'Young Ireland' party and a convict of 1848, like his brother-in-law, John Mitchel. When Mr. Parnell entered the House of Commons in April, 1875, the Liberal Opposition was disorganized, the Conservative Government was both positively and negatively strong, and the Home Rule party, under Mr. Butt's leadership, was of little account. Mr. Parnell immediately allied himself with Mr. Biggar, who had struck out a line of his own by defying decency and the rules of Parliament, and, with more or less regular aid from Mr. F. H. O'Donnell and Mr. O'Connor Power, they soon made themselves a political force. How far Mr. Parnell saw ahead of him at this time, what his motives were, and what secret influences were acting upon him may, perhaps, never be revealed. He found, as he believed, a method of bringing an intolerable pressure to bear upon the Imperial Parliament and the Government of the day by creating incessant disturbances and delaying all business, and he persisted in this course in spite of the protests and the denunciations of Mr. Butt and the more respectable among the Irish Nationalists. To quote the triumphant language of one of his own followers, writing, almost officially, long afterwards, whereas obstructive tactics had been previously directed against particular Bills, 'the obstruction which now faced Parliament intervened in every single detail of its business and not merely in contentious business, but in business that up to this time had been considered formal.' The design was boastfully avowed that, unless the Imperial Legislature agreed to grant the Irish demands as formulated by Mr. Biggar and Mr. Parnell, its power would be paralyzed, its time wasted, its honour and dignity dragged through the dirt. In 1877 the whole scheme of obstructive policy was disclosed and exemplified in the debates on the Prisons Bill, the Army Bill, and the South Africa Bill. Speaking on the last measure, Mr. Parnell said that 'as an Irishman' and one detesting 'English cruelty and tyranny' he felt 'a special satisfaction in preventing and thwarting the intentions of the Government.' On one occasion the House was kept sitting for 26 hours by the small band of obstructionists. The rules of the House, even when cautiously strengthened at the instance of Sir Stafford Northcote, proved entirely inadequate to control men, like Mr. Parnell, undeterred by any scruples and master of all the technicalities of Parliamentary practice. Motions of suspension produced as little effect as public censure, nor was Mr. Butt, though he strongly condemned the policy of exasperation and lamented the degradation of Irish politics into a 'vulgar brawl,' able to stem the tide. He was deposed in the winter of 1877 by the Home Rule Confederation of Great Britain, a body including most of the 'advanced' wing of the Irish in England and Scotland; and though a *modus vivendi* was adopted in the Parliamentary party itself, and accepted by Mr. Parnell, as he said, in Mr. Butt's presence, on the ground that he 'was a young man and could wait,' it was felt that power had passed away from the moderates, of whom many were afraid to oppose the obstructives with a general election in sight, hoping, as the Parnellites said, to tide over the crisis and 'survive till the advent of the blessed hour when the return of the Liberals to power would give them the long-desired chance of throwing off the temporary mask of national views to assume the permanent livery of English officials.' History sometimes repeats itself with curious irony, and these words are almost textually the same as those lately used by Mr. Parnell of those most intimately associated with him in his campaign against Mr. Butt. The Session of 1878 emphasized the cleavage;

Mr. Butt practically resigned the lead to the extreme faction, and both spoke and voted in favour of the foreign policy of the Government. Mr. Parnell pursued his course of calculated Parliamentary violence. In 1879 Mr. Butt died, a broken man, and Mr. Shaw was chosen to fill his place as 'Sessional Chairman' of the party. But events were playing to Mr. Parnell's hands. He had been associated with some of the Radical leaders in the attack on flogging in the Army, and he had been chosen as the first president of the Land League, which was started at Irishtown, in Mayo, a couple of weeks before Mr. Butt's death, and which embodied the ideas brought back from the United States by Mr. Davitt after his provisional release from penal servitude, with three other Fenian prisoners, at the end of 1877. Mr. Parnell was at the head of the 'Reception Committee' which presented an address to these patriots, and the list of those associated with him contains, besides the names of Mr. John Dillon and Mr. Patrick Egan, those of James Carey, Daniel Curley, and J. Brady.

Up to this point there was nothing known to the public to show that Mr. Parnell was not pursuing a Parliamentary agitation by irregular and censurable methods. How far he had previously allied himself with those who had other objects in view and who worked by other methods remains obscure. At any rate, he quickly entered into the policy that Mr. Davitt had devised in America in co-operation with Devoy and others, and after taking counsel with the leaders of the Clan-na-Gael and of the Irish Republican Brotherhood. That policy had been originally sketched by Fintan Lalor, one of the '48 men, and was intended to work upon the land hunger of the Irish peasantry in order to get rid of the British connexion. Davitt and Devoy brought over the revolutionary party to their views, including extremists like Ford of the *Irish World*, an open advocate of physical force, whether in the form of armed rebellion or of terrorist outrage. Proposals for co-operation with the Parnellites on the basis of dropping the pretence of federation and putting in its stead 'a formal declaration in favour of self-government,' of giving the foremost place to the land agitation, and adopting an aggressive Parliamentary policy generally were transmitted to Ireland, and, though not formally accepted either by Mr. Parnell, for the moment, or by the Irish Fenians became, in the opinion of the Special Commissioners, 'the basis on which the American-Irish Nationalists afterwards lent their support to Mr. Parnell and his policy.' This 'new departure,' which Mr. Davitt advocated as widening the field of revolutionary effort involved Mr. Parnell's adoption of a more decided line on the land question and the opening up of closer relations with his allies beyond the Atlantic. In June, 1879, therefore, a few weeks after the establishment of the Land League, and in the teeth of the denunciations of Archbishop MacHale, Mr. Parnell, accompanied by Mr. Davitt, addressed a League meeting at Westport, told the tenantry that they could not pay their rents in presence of the agricultural crisis, but that they should let the landlords know they intended in any case to 'hold a firm grip on their homesteads and lands.' He added that no concession obtained in Parliament would buy off his resolution to secure all, including, as Mr. Davitt took care to say, the unqualified claim for national independence.

Mr. Parnell's advances to the Revolutionists in America had an immediate reward, not only in the removal of any remaining obstacles in the path of his ambition, but in the supply of the sinews of war for the work of agitation and electioneering. Mr. Davitt started the Land League with money obtained out of the Skirmishing Fund, established by O'Donovan Rossa in order to strike England 'anywhere she could be hurt' and then in the hands of the Clan-na-Gael chiefs. But much more was needed, and in October, 1879, Mr. Parnell started with Mr. Dillon for the United States. During the voyage he imparted his views to the correspondent of a New York paper, afterwards a witness before the Special Commission, and told him, among other things, that his idea of a true revolutionary movement in Ireland was that it should partake both of a constitutional and an illegal character, 'using the Constitution for its own purposes, but also taking advantage of the secret combinations.' He was cordially welcomed by most of the extreme faction, and gratified them with declarations quite to their own mind. He told them that the land question must be acted upon in 'some extraordinary and unusual way' to secure any good result and that 'the great cause could not be won without shedding a drop of blood.' He went even beyond this point in the famous speech at Cincinnati, which he subsequently attempted to deny, but which was reported in the *Irish World* and was held to be proved by Sir James Hannen and his colleagues. He then said that the 'ultimate goal' at which Irishmen aimed was 'to destroy the last link which kept Ireland bound to England.' The American wing were perfectly satisfied, and Mr. Parnell, when he was summoned back to Ireland by the news of the dissolution, felt that he could rely on their support, pecuniary and other. It was not, at first, so easy to convince the Irish Fenians – who had distrusted and abjured any form of Parliamentary action – that they ought to vote for Parnellite candidates; and one or two Parnellite meetings were disturbed by this element. But Mr. Parnell's speeches during the electoral campaign of 1880 showed them how far he was prepared to go in their direction, and how little inclined he was, to use his own phrase, 'to fix the boundary to the march of a nation.' It was at this time that Mr. Parnell told, with great applause, the story which became very popular on Land League platforms, of the American sympathizer who offered him 'five dollars for bread and 20 dollars for lead.' The leading spokesmen and organizers of the League, Sheridan, Brennan, Boyton, and Redpath, were either known Fenians or used language going beyond that of Fenianism; and the same thing may be said of Mr. Biggar, Mr. O'Kelly, and Mr. Matt Harris, members of Mr. Parnell's Parliamentary following. The policy which Mr. Davitt, acting as the envoy of the Irish extremists, thus used

Mr. Parnell to carry through, was developed in the announcement of the boycotting system in the autumn of 1880. Meanwhile, the alliance had already borne fruit at the general election of that year, when Mr. Parnell, aided somewhat irregularly by Mr. Egan out of the exchequer of the League, was returned for three constituencies – Meath, Mayo, and the city of Cork. He decided to sit for the last, and as 'the member for Cork' he has since been known. The overthrow of the Beaconsfield Government, which had appealed to the country to strengthen the Empire against Irish disorder and disloyalty, was an encouragement to the Parnellites, who had a narrow and shifting majority in the ranks of the Parliamentary party. Mr. Shaw was supplanted as chairman by Mr. Parnell, and an open separation between the two sections ensued. The Parnellites took their seats on the Opposition benches; the Moderate Home Rulers sat on the Ministerial side below the gangway. To the latter Mr. Gladstone seemed to incline most favourably, as he showed afterwards when he proposed to make Mr. Shaw one of the Chief Commissioners under the Land Act. The Liberals, though they took the opportunity of dropping the Peace Preservation Act, were not disposed to reopen the land question, and it was only under pressure that Mr. Forster hastily introduced the Compensation for Disturbance Bill, which was rejected in the House of Lords, and appointed the Bessborough Commission.

Mr. Parnell and his party seized the opportunities afforded by the distress in Ireland and the Parliamentary situation to push on the operations of the League. The policy of boycotting had been expounded and enforced early in the year in Mr. Parnell's speech at Ennis, a few days after Lord Mountmorres's murder, when he urged the peasantry if any man among them took an evicted farm to put the offender 'into a moral Coventry by isolating him from the rest of his kind as if he were a leper of old.' This doctrine was rapidly propagated by Mr. Dillon, Mr. Biggar, and the organizers of the League, and in the autumn the persecution of Captain Boycott and many other persons became a public scandal. This system of acting upon those whom Mr. Parnell had described as 'weak and cowardly,' because they did not heartily join in the refusal to pay rent, has been pronounced on the highest judicial authority to amount to a criminal and illegal conspiracy, devised and carried out to lower the rental and selling price of land and to crush the landlords. Mr. Parnell declared that he never incited to crime, but though he and his colleagues knew that boycotting and the unwritten law of the League led to outrages, wherever the organization spread, they took no effective measures to denounce and repress crime, and it is now plain that they could not do so without alienating the American support on which they were dependent. The ordinary law was shown to be powerless by the failure of the prosecution of Mr. Parnell and others for conspiracy in Dublin in the opening days of 1881, when the jury disagreed, and Mr. Parnell, in announcing the result to his American friends, telegraphed his thanks to the *Irish World* for 'constant co-operation and successful support in our great cause.' But the progress of unpunished crime, in which the American-Irish brutally exulted, and the paralysis of the law compelled Mr. Gladstone's Government to act. Early in the Session of 1881 Mr. Forster introduced his 'Protection of Persons and Property Bill' and his 'Arms Bill,' of which the former empowered the Executive to arrest and detain without trial persons reasonably suspected of crime. At the mere rumour of this Egan transferred the finances of the League to Paris. It was a part of Mr. Parnell's task, as he well knew, to fight the 'coercion' measures tooth and nail, but, though he led the attack, the most critical conflicts were precipitated by the passion and imprudence of less cold-blooded politicians. We need not here recapitulate the history of that struggle, in which obstruction reached a height previously unknown, and in which the knot had to be cut for the moment by the enforcement of the inherent powers of the Chair. The Parnellite members were again and again suspended, and at length, after several weeks, both Bills were carried. Mr. Parnell's party had by this time assumed an attitude towards the Government of Mr. Gladstone which was highly pleasing to the *Irish World* and the Nationalist organs in Ireland, but was ominous for the prospects of the Land Bill. They did not, however, venture to offer a direct and determined opposition to a measure securing great pecuniary advantages to the Irish tenants. They could not go beyond abstaining on the question of principle and denouncing the whole scheme as inadequate. Of course, if the Land Act had succeeded in accordance with Mr. Gladstone's sanguine hopes, it would have cut the ground from under Mr. Parnell's feet and deprived him of the basis of agitation on which his alliance with the Irish Extremists rested, and from which his party derived their pecuniary supplies. No sooner, therefore, had the Land Act become law than the word went forth from the offices of the League that the tenants were not to be allowed to avail themselves of it freely, but that only some 'test cases' were to be put forward. The penalties of any infraction of this addition to the unwritten law were well understood, for all this while terrorism and outrage were rampant. Mr. Gladstone was more indignant at the rejection of his message of peace than at the proofs, which had been long forthcoming, of the excesses of Irish lawlessness. He denounced Mr. Parnell at Leeds, in impassioned language, and declared that 'the resources of civilization against its enemies were not yet exhausted.' Mr. Parnell replied defiantly that Mr. Gladstone had before 'eaten all his old words,' and predicted that these 'brave words of this English Minister would be scattered as chaff' by the determination of the Irish to regain 'their lost legislative independence.' A few days later he was arrested and imprisoned in Kilmainham with Mr. Sexton, Mr. O'Brien, the editor of his organ, *United Ireland*, and several others. Egan, on the suggestion of Ford, at once issued a 'No-Rent' manifesto; the books of the Land League were spirited out of the jurisdiction of the Irish executive, and as a natural consequence the Land League was suppressed. But the struggle was carried on, with little substantial change, during Mr. Parnell's imprisonment. The Ladies' League nominally took the work in hand; American money was not wanting; boycotting was rigidly enforced, and was followed, as Mr. Gladstone had shown, by crime. For this state of things the incendiary journalism subsidized and imported by the Parnellites was, and long after remained, responsible. The *Irish World*, with its advocacy of dynamite and dagger, was used to 'spread the light' among the masses, and *United Ireland* was scarcely behindhand. *The Freeman's Journal*, which had opposed Mr. Parnell's extreme views on the Land Act, was compelled to come to heel, and the priesthood, who never loved him, as a Protestant and as a suspected ally of the Fenians, found their influence waning in presence of the despotism of the League. The secret history of all that went on during Mr. Parnell's imprisonment in Kilmainham is not yet revealed, though some light has been thrown upon it by the recent split among the Nationalists. Mr. Parnell, for instance, said the other day in the last speech he delivered that 'the white flag had been first hung out from Kilmainham' by Mr. William O'Brien. Be that as it may, it is evident that in the spring of 1882 both the Government and the Parnellites were anxious to compromise their quarrel. Mr. Gladstone was pressed by the Radicals to get rid of coercion, and the patriots were eager to be again enjoying liberty and power. Negotiations were opened through Mr. O'Shea; Mr. Parnell was willing to promise that Ireland should be tranquilized – for the moment and in appearance – through the agency of the League; Mr. Forster, refusing to become a party to this sort of bargain with those who had organized a system of lawless terrorism, resigned; Lord Spencer and Lord Frederick Cavendish went to Ireland as envoys of a policy of concession, including a Bill for wiping out arrears of rent. How long Mr. Parnell would have continued to give a *quid pro quo* for this can only be guessed at. A few days after the ratification of what became known as the Kilmainham Treaty, Lord Frederick Cavendish and Mr. Burke were murdered in the Phoenix Park by persons then unknown. Mr. Parnell expressed his horror of the crime in the House of Commons, but refused to admit that it was a reason for the Coercion Bill immediately introduced by Sir William Harcourt. This change of policy was forced upon Mr. Gladstone by the imperious demands of public opinion, which was exasperated by the defiant attitude of the Irish party. The forces of obstruction, however, were for the moment broken by the shock. The Coercion Act became law, and was at the outset vigorously administered by Lord Spencer and Mr. Trevelyan, who were, in consequence, attacked with the most infamous calumnies by *United Ireland* and other Parnellite organs. The authors of several wicked crimes were brought to justice in Ireland in spite of the clamour of the Parnellites against Judges and jurymen, and early in 1883 the invincible conspiracy, which had compassed the deaths of Lord Frederick Cavendish and Mr. Burke, was exposed by the evidence of the informer,

James Carey. Mr. Forster made this the occasion of a powerful attack on Mr. Parnell in the House of Commons, telling the story of the Kilmainham negotiations in the light of later disclosures, and pointing out that the language used without rebuke in Mr. Parnell's organs and by his followers plainly sowed the seed of crime. Mr. Parnell's callous defiance of the voice of public opinion shocked even those inclined to make allowance for him. Radical sympathy was withdrawn from him, while there was about this time also a widening breach with the Irish-Americans, who did not wish to have outrage even condemned by implication, and who were entering upon the dynamite campaign. Nevertheless, Mr. Parnell's hold on his own party was unshaken; from time to time there were movements of revolt; he had to speak scornfully once of 'Papist rats.' Mr. Dwyer Gray, Mr. O'Connor Power, Mr. F. H. O'Donnell, and Mr. Healy at different times tried to thwart him, but he swept all opposition away, and reduced his critics to subjection or drove them out of public life. The Land League was allowed to revive under the name of the National League, and, operating more cautiously on the old lines, secured Mr. Parnell's power. It was evident that the extension of the franchise would give Mr. Parnell the power of nominating the representatives of three-fourths of Ireland. The priesthood, trembling for their influence, came round to him. But he was unable to induce the Government either to repeal the Coercion Act or to tamper with the land question. It was when the Franchise Bill was introduced that Mr. Parnell's influence over the Government was first manifested. He insisted that Ireland should be included in the Bill and that the number of the Irish representatives should not be diminished, and on both points he prevailed. Meanwhile the alliance with the American-Irish had been renewed. The Clan-na-Gael captured the Land League in the United States, and in view of the elections in Great Britain funds were provided, Egan being now a member of the organization. Simultaneously a more active policy was adopted at home. As soon as the passage of the Franchise Bill had been made sure the Parnellites joined with the Conservatives to defeat Mr. Gladstone. Towards the weak Salisbury Administration that followed Mr. Parnell showed, during the electoral period, a benevolent neutrality, acting on the principle he had laid down several years before in Cork – 'Don't be afraid to let in the Tory, but put out the Whig.' He judged that he would be thus more likely to hold the balance of power in the new Parliament, and Mr. Gladstone held the same opinion when he asked for a Liberal majority strong enough to vote down Conservatives and Parnellites together. In an address to the Irish electors on the eve of the struggle the Parnellites fiercely denounced the Liberal party and its leader. Mr. Parnell had even amused Lord Carnarvon at a critical time with a deceptive negotiation.

The issue of the contest left Mr. Gladstone's forces just balanced by those of the Conservatives and Parnellites combined. He at once resolved to secure the latter by an offer of Home Rule, though he had up to that time professed his devotion to the Union, and though nine-tenths of his followers had pledged themselves to it. His overtures were, of course, welcomed, though without a too trustful effusiveness, by Mr. Parnell; the Conservative Government was overthrown on a side issue; Mr. Gladstone came into power and introduced his Home Rule Bill. Much was made of Mr. Parnell's unqualified acceptance of that measure. It now appears that he objected to several points in it, being, no doubt, aware of the view taken of it by his American allies, but he did not press his objections, fearing, as he said since, that the insistence on further concessions would deprive Mr. Gladstone of other colleagues and break up the Government. Mr. Parnell's temporary forbearance, which had no element of finality in it, did not save the Bill. In the Parliament of 1886 his numerical forces were nearly the same as those he previously commanded, but he was now allied with a greatly enfeebled Gladstonian Opposition. It was necessary to affect the most scrupulous constitutionalism, and for a time Mr. Parnell played the part well. The Irish-Americans took the cue from him, and were willing to wait. Dynamite outrages had ceased. But the necessities of the case urged him to insist on reopening the Irish land question, and in Ireland the National League continued to work on the old system. Boycotting and its attendant incidents increased, and, during Mr. Parnell's temporary withdrawal from active politics, Mr. Dillon and Mr O'Brien committed the party to the Plan of Campaign, which involved a pitched battle with the Executive and the law. The introduction of the Crimes Bill was the direct result of this policy, which Mr. Parnell privately condemned. His opposition to the Bill was of the familiar kind. But the tactics of obstruction which were then pursued were overshadowed in the public eye by the controversy on 'Parnellism and Crime' that arose in our own columns. Seeing that the alliance between Mr. Parnell and the Gladstonian Opposition was growing closer and closer, that it was employed to obstruct the Executive Government and to set at naught the law, and that the success of Home Rule would deliver over Ireland to a faction tainted by association with Ford and Sheridan, we thought it right to call public attention to some salient episodes in Mr. Parnell's career and to draw certain inferences from them. We also conceived it to be our duty to publish some documentary evidence that came into our hands, of the authenticity of which we were honestly convinced, and which seemed to us perfectly consistent with what was proved and notorious. Mr. Parnell gave a comprehensive denial to all our charges and inferences, including the alleged letter apologizing to some extremist ally for denouncing the Phoenix Park murders in the House of Commons. He did not, however, accept our challenge or bring an action against *The Times*, nor was it till more than a year later, after Mr. O'Donnell had raised the question by some futile proceedings, that he demanded a Parliamentary inquiry into the statements made on our behalf by the Attorney-General. We need not here recite the story of the appointment of the Special Commission and its result. The evidence of Richard Pigott broke down, and with it the letters on which we had in part relied, and Mr. Parnell's political allies claimed for him a complete acquittal. But the Report of the Commissioners showed that, though some other charges against Mr. Parnell were dismissed as unproved, the most important contentions of *The Times* were fully established. The origin and objects of the criminal conspiracy were placed beyond doubt; the association for the purposes of that conspiracy with the Irish-American revolutionists was most clearly made manifest, as well as the reckless persistence in boycotting and in the circulation of inflammatory writings after it was known in what those practices ended. Nor was it without significance that a confession was extorted from Mr. Parnell that he might very possibly have made a deliberately false statement for the purpose of deceiving the House of Commons. Indeed, on more than one point where Mr. Parnell's sworn testimony had to be weighed against that of other witnesses – as in the case of Mr. Ives and Major Le Caron – the Commissioners rejected it. Nevertheless, the Gladstonians went out of their way to affirm their unshaken belief in the stainless honour of Mr. Parnell, to accept him as the model of a Constitutional statesman, and to base upon his assurances their confidence that a Home Rule settlement would be a safe and lasting one. Mr. Parnell received the honorary freedom of the city of Edinburgh. He was entertained at dinner by the Eighty Club; Mr. Gladstone appeared on the same platform with him; his speeches were welcomed at Gladstonian gatherings in the provinces as eagerly as those of the patriarchal leader himself; and, finally, he was the late Premier's guest at Hawarden Castle, where the details of the revised Home Rule scheme, which has never been disclosed even to the National Liberal Federation, was discussed confidentially as between two potentates of co-equal authority.

But a cruel disappointment was in store for credulous souls. Mr. O'Shea, whose intervention had brought about the Kilmainham Treaty, instituted proceedings against Mr. Parnell in the Divorce Court. It was denied up to the last that there was any ground for these proceedings; it was predicted that they would never come to an issue. But when, after protracted and intentional delays, the case came on in November last, it was found that there was no defence. The adultery was formally proved and was not denied, nor was it possible to explain away its treachery and grossness. The public mind was shocked at the disclosure; but those who were best entitled to speak were strangely silent. Mr. Gladstone said nothing; the Roman Catholic hierarchy in Ireland said nothing; Mr. Justin M'Carthy, Mr. Healy, and the rest of the Parliamentary party hastened to Dublin to proclaim, at the Leinster-hall, their unwavering fidelity to Mr. Parnell. Mr. Dillon and Mr. O'Brien telegraphed their approval from America. On the opening day of the Session Mr. Parnell was re-elected leader. Meanwhile the Nonconformist conscience had awakened, and Mr. Gladstone responded to its remonstrances. His letter turned the majority round, and, after a violent conflict in Committee Room No. 15, Mr. Parnell was deposed by the very men who had elected him. He refused to recognize his deposition, and has fought a daring, but a losing, battle in Ireland ever since. The declaration of the Roman Catholic hierarchy against him, however, sealed his doom. The clergy have worked against him as they never worked in politics before. Mr. Dillon and Mr. O'Brien have taken the same side. He has been defeated in North Kilkenny, North Sligo, and Carlow, and though he has been battling fiercely down to a few days ago, the ground has been visibly slipping away from him. Even his marriage with Mrs. O'Shea, the only reparation for his sin, has been turned against him in a Roman Catholic country, and was the excuse for the defection of the *Freeman's Journal.* It is not surprising that a feeble constitution should have broken down under such a load of obloquy and disappointment.

Parnell, who had married the divorcee Kitty O'Shea on 25 June 1891, died in Brighton on 6 October. An editorial notice in *The Times* which preceded the present obituary compared the fall of Parnell with that of General Boulanger, the leader of the Boulangiste party in France, who believed that post-1870s France would be saved by three 'R's: Revenge on Germany; Revision of the Constitution; and the Restoration of the Monarchy. Having threatened a *coup d'état*, Boulanger had been accused of treason in 1889 and was forced into exile, initially in England. In September 1891 he had travelled to Brussels and had shot himself on the grave of his mistress in the Ixelles Cemetery. The parallels between Boulanger and Parnell might have seemed more striking in an age when being named a co-respondent in a divorce case could stir not only the British Nonconformist conscience but also, and far more significantly, that of the 'credulous souls' shepherded by the Roman Catholic hierarchy of Ireland. Boulanger may have threatened to disrupt the France of the Third Republic, but, a year before his fall, Parnell, 'the uncrowned king of Ireland', had come very close to achieving his goal, the repeal of the Act of Union and the radical renegotiation of Ireland's constitutional relationship with the rest of the United Kingdom.

THOMAS COOK

Travel agent: 'The originator of the excursion system.'

18 JULY 1892

MR. THOMAS COOK, the originator of the excursion system of railway travelling and founder of the well-known firm of Messrs. Thomas Cook and Son, whose headquarters are at Ludgate-circus, London, died at his residence, Thorncroft, Stonegate, Leicester, about midnight on Monday. His success in life was entirely due to his indomitable courage and energy under the most discouraging conditions. Born on November 22, 1808, at Melbourne, in Derbyshire, of very humble parentage, he had in his early years a severe struggle for the bare means of existence. He was only four years old when his father died, and he commenced to earn his daily bread at the age of ten, when he was employed in a village garden at the wage of 1d. a day. At this early age he contrived also to be of material assistance to his mother, who kept a small shop for the sale of books. Soon afterwards he took to hawking fruit and vegetables in Derby market place, and a little later went to learn wood-turning. Afterwards he went to Loughborough, where he entered the employment of Mr. John Winks, a printer and publisher of books in connexion with the General Baptist Association. In 1828 he was appointed a Bible reader and village missionary for the county of Rutland, and in the following year he travelled 2,692, miles, of which 2,106 miles were covered on foot. Having in 1832 married Miss Mason, daughter of a Rutland farmer, he removed to Market Harborough, where, in addition to his work in connexion with the Baptist Association, he carried on the business of a wood-turner. In 1836 he became a total abstainer, and he was an ardent temperance reformer for the remainder of his life. Subsequently he published a monthly paper called the *Temperance Messenger*, of which he was the editor. This was followed by the *Children's Temperance Magazine* in 1840. In 1841, while walking from Market Harborough to Leicester to attend a temperance meeting, he read in a newspaper a report of the opening of a part of the Midland Counties Railway, and the idea burst upon him that the new means of travel might be used for the benefit of the temperance movement. If, thought Mr. Cook, the railway company could be induced to run a special train from Leicester, many persons might be removed from the temptations of the races and great results might be achieved. He broached the subject to his friends, and arranged with the railway company for a special train to Loughborough on the 5th of July, 1841. This the first publicly advertised excursion train, conveyed no fewer than 570 passengers at 1s.

each. The event caused great excitement. The passengers were preceded to the Leicester Station by a band of music. At Loughborough they were met by a great crowd of people, and they were welcomed home with equal enthusiasm. The success of this trip induced Mr. Cook to combine the management of excursions with his book and printing business in Leicester, to which town he had removed. He organized trips to Derby, Nottingham, and Birmingham, and the business having grown so much that in several trips he conveyed between 4,000 and 5,000 people, he in 1844 entered into permanent arrangements with the directors of the Midland Railway to place trains at his disposal whenever they were required while he provided the passengers. Next year saw an extension of the system to Liverpool, the Isle of Man, and Dublin. He also about this period organized a trip to Scotland, and conveyed 350 passengers from Leicester and Nottingham to Glasgow, where the excursionists received a warm welcome. His next move was to provide hotel coupons for his patrons, and Scotland was the field of his first endeavours in this direction. Personally conducted tours to Ireland followed, and in 1851, Mr. Cook conveyed many thousands of people to the Great Exhibition in Hyde Park. The business began to extend in all directions in England and on the Continent. Mr. Cook's ambition was the institution of an annual tour round the world, which he successfully accomplished. His first tour round the world was in 1872, when he, with nine companions, started to make what he termed an exploratory tour. The tour was completed in 222 days. Mr. Cook retired from the firm in 1878, the business being then placed under the sole control of his son, Mr. John M. Cook. The jubilee of the firm was celebrated by a banquet in the Hotel Métropole in July last year. Mr. Cook's career as an excursion manager and the history of his operations form an agreeable volume written last year by Mr. Fraser Rae on the occasion of the jubilee. During the last few years of his life Mr. Cook was afflicted with blindness. On Monday evening he was walking about his residence apparently in his usual health, but shortly after 8 o'clock he was suddenly seized with paralysis in the side. Medical aid was at once summoned, but Mr. Cook never rallied, and passed peacefully away just before midnight.

> A Temperance excursion from Leicester to Loughborough in July 1841 might have sounded like an unpropitious beginning to one of the great business ventures of the nineteenth century, but no Victorian would have underestimated either the Nonconformist conscience or its contribution to 'Self Help'. Cook was one of the first to recognise the new freedom of movement that the railway system gave to men and women of modest means. Once the railways were established in Europe, and later across the globe, and once steamships crossed oceans at record speeds, the possibility of a world tour for Cook's more prosperous

customers became real. Jules Verne may have speculated about such a tour lasting eighty days in 1873; by 1872 Cook had already realised it for his clients for 222 days.

* * *

ALFRED LORD TENNYSON

Poet: 'The most brilliant light in English literature.'

6 OCTOBER 1892

THE DEATH OF LORD TENNYSON extinguishes the most brilliant light in English literature – a light which has shone to the last with unwaning lustre. He linked us with the golden age of the famous poets of the beginning of the century, and his loss, following on that of his old friend Browning, leaves a blank we can scarcely hope to fill. Though the late Laureate had kept his powers and much of his natural energy almost to the last, he has died in the fulness of years as of fame. He lived to a good old age; he did great and imperishable work; his name had long been a charmed household word around the hearths and in the hearts of his admiring countrymen, for he was eminently the poet of the feelings and the affections; and if he cared for lower honours and for riches, he had won enough of both to satisfy his ambition. The greatest or most conspicuous men are often the least to be envied; but we should say that few lots were more enviable than his. The son of a clergyman in affluent circumstances, life from the first was made smooth and pleasant to him. From the first he found delight in a congenial vocation; and his genius became his philosopher and guide in the boundless realms of the fancy. When most boys are still drudging at the *gradus*, or beginning to labour over the grindstone of Latin verse, he wrote flowing poetry, which is readable, and was full of promise for the future. The promise was promptly recognized by those who were nearest and dearest to him; and he had never to complain of that lack of encouragement which may chill the susceptible temperament of the poet. Perhaps the excessive partiality of his friends, though the triumphs of the future justified their foresight, may have helped to provoke the severity of unkindly critics. Yet many an aspiring and

Alfred Lord Tennyson

self-confident poet would have given much to secure such universal notice as was speedily bestowed upon Tennyson. Susceptible he might be, like all refined and original spirits, but nature had gifted him with sterner qualities as well. He had a self-confidence which some pronounced over-weening, and a resolute devotion to his art which rose superior to satire. If the one and the other served to blunt the shafts of the critics, they saved him as well from the injudicious flatteries of his enthusiastic admirers. At one time he seemed to stand at 'the parting of the ways;' and a weaker man might have chosen the worse, which would have led him downwards towards fluent mediocrity. Tennyson at that critical turning point gave proof of his good sense and worldly wisdom. On calmer thought he profited by the stinging criticisms which had provoked him at first into indiscreet outbursts of temper. That is proved by the suppression in subsequent editions of the poems which had been most mercilessly ridiculed. He meditated and laboured over his gracefully polished work: each melodious line and measured couplet was the deliberate expression of his feelings; he wrote slowly and published leisurely. The rich exuberances of fancy were lopped and pruned; his deepest sentiments were seldom obscure; the loftiest flights of his philosophical mysticism rarely carried him beyond reach of the perceptions of his intelligent worshippers. In short, his methods were the very opposite of those of the greatest of his rivals, and he had his full reward. His genius ripened steadily and surely. His reputation increased with the appreciative and sympathetic, as his popularity was widely extended among the crowd. With a single exception, which was soon forgotten or forgiven, each fresh publication was warmly welcomed as it had been eagerly expected. In the enjoyment of ample means, absolute master of his time and of his arrangements, he made his favourite recreation his regular occupation, writing just as much or as little as he pleased. He led the easy life of a country gentleman as he understood it, drawing inspiration for his scenery and his minutely exquisite painting of nature from the lanes and downs that surrounded his dwellings. He had the choice of two country residences in the fairest districts of southern England; he had books at will as the companions of his solitude when he cared for solitude; and we may add, though it sounds something of a bathos, he found unfailing solace in an inexhaustible tobacco-jar. He chose to hold aloof from the so-called 'society' that would have gladly courted and petted him, because he disliked anything in the shape of social dissipation. But from his school time and college days to extreme old age no one was more fortunate in the attachment of familiar friends, and had he not been as happy with his children as in his marriage, he might hardly have lived so much of a hermit. So far as we can know, the worst trouble of his later years was the notoriety that attracted troops of admirers to gaze at the roof that sheltered the Laureate, and, if possible, to force the *consigne* at his gates. It is said that he was fairly driven by obtrusive tourists from the home which lay near their beats in the Isle of Wight to pass the summer and autumn months in less accessible solitudes in Sussex. But if these were among his worst troubles, we may be sure we are right in pronouncing his lot a phenomenally happy one.

Alfred Tennyson was born on August 5, 1809, at Somersby, a small village in Lincolnshire. His father was rector of the parish, and remarkable for bodily strength and stature, which may help to explain his son's longevity and the perennial vigour of mind which prolonged his powers of giving pleasure beyond reasonable expectation. The rector, though living remote from the world, was not only a gifted but an accomplished man, and most of his many children took after him. Alfred was the third of seven brothers, and they all either turned naturally towards intellectual amusements or were trained to them. They read much and wrote habitually. The Rector of Somersby devoted himself to his children, and Alfred's education, like that of his brothers, began under the care of their father at the village school. All the time, whether as a child or a school boy, he was studying elsewhere than in printed books. He was reading and eagerly drinking in facts, fancies, and inspirations from the richly-illuminated volume of nature, and he never wearied of it. It was then he was grounding himself in those minute details of natural history and botany which he was to turn to such graceful account. He is said to have been no mean artist, too, and at all events the scenery and the landscapes about him were indelibly impressing themselves on his memory. Lincolnshire is not the most romantic of English counties, nor is the neighbourhood of Somersby especially picturesque. Nevertheless it is neither flat nor tame, and with its fields, fens, and marsh flowers it has characteristic charms of its own which have stamped themselves on the most pleasing pages of the Laureate's earlier poetry. There to the north of his native village rose 'the long dim wolds' of the ballad of 'Oriana' that were 'ribb'd with snow,' when the Norland whirlwinds were storming in the winter. Thence or from the neighbouring heights with the hero of his 'Locksley Hall' he overlooked

> – the sandy tracts
> And the hollow ocean ridges roaring into cataracts,

for the sea stretches away at no great distance. Around many a Lincolnshire hall and quaint old farm-house was such a moat as encircled Mariana's Grange, where

> About a stone-cast from the wall
> A sluice with blacken'd waters slept,
> And o'er it many, round and small,
> The clustered marish-mosses crept.

Each piece of minute description in the earlier poems seems to be the fond and vivid reflection of photographs on the memory. There are gray hills in the woodlands, with 'Hangers' like that of Selborne: the very numbers of the species of the trees standing before the rectory door are given exactly; but, above all, we may identify the brook with its surroundings – the brook that ripples and murmurs through many of his pieces, besides the 'Miller's Daughter' and the 'Ode to Memory.' It flowed at the bottom of the rectory garden, and like his Lotus-eaters he must have often dreamed away the summer days upon its banks, soothed by the drowsy melody of the water, as it 'purled o'er matted cress and ribbed sand.' We may remark, by the way, how fond he was from first to last of certain epithets, which are invariably suggestive and expressive. 'Ribbed sand', for example, though it might have been borrowed from Coleridge, is perpetually recurring. Then everywhere in those poems we recognize the natural history as well as the scenery of his native parish. We have 'the many-wintered crow that leads the clanging rookery home'; we have 'the wanton lapwing' and many another bird of passage that frequents the dreary moorland and the barren shore. Like Scott, who was observed making notes of the wild flowers on Greta banks, Tennyson was never content with picturesque generalization in his descriptions. As no one can talk a language like a native, who has not mastered it in his youth, so Tennyson could never have been so universally at home with nature had it not been for the close observations of the botanizing and bird-nesting rambles of his boyhood. He was as precocious in his study of nature as in his poetry. It is Mr. Holbrook, the old country gentleman in 'Cranford,' who quotes the phrase 'black as ash-buds in March' as a fact which he did not know 'till this young man comes and tells me.' So the marsh and moat-botany in 'Mariana' is almost perfect in its technical precision, and yet how wonderfully the creepers and the trailing water plants have interwoven themselves with the beauties of the verse. With unconscious, or, at least, imperceptible, effort his genius turns all it touches to his purpose; and the trailers on a wall, as a gardener might have catalogued them, are poetical as the figure of the Pleiads on a stormy night, glittering like a swarm of fireflies tangled in a silver braid. If we go down to the insect world it is always the same, for the lustre of his genius, like the microscopic lens, sets off the tiniest of objects in unsuspected beauty. He can brighten the stagnant surface of a mill-pond; and there are few more finely-expressed parables in his poems than that he draws from the glittering dragon-fly in 'The Two Voices':–

An inner impulse rent the veil
Of his old husk: from head to tail
Came out clear plates of sapphire mail.
He dried his wings; like gauze they grew;

Thro' crofts and pastures wet with dew
A living flash of light he flew.

If there be anything to surpass that in similar style in our English poets we should be glad to see it. And if we have dwelt at length on his education by nature, it is because its influence on his poetry is hardly to be overrated. Books are well; the intimacy with cultivated minds which Tennyson enjoyed and appreciated to the fullest extent is even better; but best of all for the poet is the familiarity with nature, which teaches him to read her very innermost soul, and to rejoice in singing her praises in her humblest works. We may add that that habit of close and searching observation became introspective and extended itself to mental phenomena as well. So much so, that at one time it threatened to become a snare to him, and to make much of his poetry metaphysical, if not mystic; although, fortunately for our pleasure as for the poet's popularity, healthier and more natural impulses prevailed.

From his village he was sent to the grammar school of Louth, in Lincolnshire, an establishment which, we believe, had even then a high local reputation. It was there that, in conjunction with his elder brother Charles, he produced the 'Poems by Two Brothers.' The little volume was so far a pecuniary success that the copyright was bought for £10 by a local book-seller. In point of merit there is little more than we might have expected to be said for it, considering the ages of the authors and their inexperience. But it is interesting as showing now and again the germs of ideas which were to ripen later, and still more as illustrating the width of the young writers' reading and scholarship. The Tennysons must have come far nearer than most young gentlemen of their years to Macaulay's typical and omniscient schoolboy. There are not only numerous quotations from the English and French poets, but there are evidences of a scholarly acquaintance with the choicest of the Roman classics. 'The Lover's Tale,' which was written in 1828, is a proof of the judicious self-restraint which tempered Alfred Tennyson's ambition and self-assurance. Though printed a few years after it was written, it was never published till 1879, and only then because garbled extracts had got abroad. Yet the genius that was still immature had made wonderful progress in the meantime, and in the 'Tale' we recognize the marked characteristics that were chastened down afterwards by thought and by exercise. We are struck already by the independence and originality of the youthful poet. It has been said, and no doubt said with truth, that the poem bears traces of the influences of Shelley, with whom in some respects Tennyson was much in sympathy. But, though the influence may be distinctly traced, there is no servile imitation, and there is the promise of not a few of the beauties that became very distinctively Tennyson's own.

In the year in which it was written the brothers went up to Cambridge, where they were entered at Trinity. There they were welcomed at once in as brilliant a circle of young and aspiring contemporaries as were ever assembled at that venerable seat of learning. We need only name among them Merivale and Spedding, Dean Alford, Archbishop Trench, Bishop Thirlwall, and Lord Houghton, Lord Stanley, Charles Buller, John Sterling, and the Lushingtons. Above all and dearest of all were Brookfield – to whom Tennyson was to dedicate one of the most beautiful of his lyrics – and Arthur Hallam, son of the historian, whose untimely death was the gain of literature, since it suggested the pathetic elegy of the 'In Memoriam.' The friendly intimacy of that gifted fellowship was to have a marked influence on his future and fortunes. That his mind was enriched we need hardly say by the cultured intercourse. But these youths, so many of whom were destined to high distinction, had formed themselves into what scoffers might call a mutual admiration society. They did justice, and more than justice, to Tennyson's poetical genius, and welcoming each fresh performance of his with affectionate sympathy and admiration, thenceforth they became the champions and guardians of his fame. It would have turned the head of a weaker man, and certainly it was no unmixed advantage to him, for Tennyson at no time undervalued his own powers. But, on the other hand, the ardent admiration of such critics was irresistible evidence of extraordinary talents; they set themselves to discover subtle or hidden meanings; they indicated the more conspicuous beauties with discriminating admiration, and, in short, they hurried the public judgment in the direction in which it must have drifted sooner or later. It is true, as we have remarked already and shall notice again, that their obvious and excessive partiality provoked a reaction. Even if their praise of the beauties was not exaggerated, they were inclined to pass the faults and blemishes over in silence; so it was certain that other and less friendly judges would charge themselves with the less grateful part of the critics' duty. When Hallam indulged in the *Englishman's Magazine* in almost unstinted laudation, a writer in the *Quarterly*, believed to be Lockhart, and Wilson in *Blackwood* seem to have felt bound to lay on the rod with extreme severity, greatly to Tennyson's displeasure and disgust. He had good reason to feel annoyed, if not aggrieved, for the *Englishman's Magazine* was a comparatively obscure periodical, with no such authority as either of the others. Yet the skirmish of the pens, and the slashes which left him smarting, contributed to bring him fame and fresh admirers.

The occasion of the articles by Hallam and Wilson was the publication of a volume of 'Poems Chiefly Lyrical,' which appeared in 1830, and contained not a few of the finest of his shorter effusions. Besides 'Claribel,' 'Lilian,' &c., there were 'Mariana,' 'Oriana,' and the 'Recollections of the Arabian Nights.' Hallam's article, obviously over-partial as it was, is still valuable for its delicately sympathetic appreciation. Tennyson, more than most, is a poet who should be read sympathetically; and Hallam was at home with the mind that had cherished and fostered those graceful fancies. He analyzes the distinctive features of the author's genius with fine discrimination, and in the main with a truth there is no disputing. But the article in *Blackwood* we must now take *cum grano.* It was written at a time when the rising Scotch periodical was waging relentless and unscrupulous war against what it denominated 'The Cockney School,' and all who were supposed in any way to be affiliated to that school. The critic gave his victim a good deal of advice, but hardly understood him. He merely vexed the poet's mind without fathoming it. But when Wilson turns from censure to praise, he shows as much critical prescience as good feeling. It was his habit to write in violent extremes, but no one could be more generously effusive. Even in his swing of reckless sarcasm he stops to say that the day may come when 'Tennyson's genius will grow up and expand into a stately tree, embowering a solemn shade within a wide circumference.' He gives the poet generous credit for fancy, imagination, and genius, and he comments upon the beauties he extracts by the page. From the 'Ode to Memory,' through 'Oriana,' to the 'Recollections of the Arabian Nights,' he rises from eulogy to something approaching rapture. What can be more graceful than the compliment to the cluster of beauties, the Isabels and the Claribels? 'We are in love, as an old man ought to be, as a father is with his ideal daughters – with them all.' Nevertheless, it is not to be wondered at that Tennyson, though he may have had the wisdom to profit by the advice, was provoked to bitter retort.

The volume which followed in 1833 contained, among others, the poems of 'Œnone,' 'The May Queen,' and 'The Dream of Fair Women.' It was then that the *Quarterly* article nipped without crushing him, for, indeed, it was already clear that he was a poet, and a poet of exceeding sweetness and rare endowments. There was the ring of rich music in his melodious measures; he had the instinct of strangely harmonious cadences, which chimed in marvellously with his subjects, as in the refrain of 'Mariana in the Moated Grange,' and, above all, in the wildly plaintive burden of 'Oriana.' He had a luxuriant imagination that rather needed to be pruned; the gift of most realistic and yet poetical description; a happy selection of gracefully appropriate metaphor. He had a sweet intelligence of love in its changing moods; he could analyze the passions and dramatize them in action; he had powers of pathos and sympathy that awakened and soothed the affections. Within a limited range his versatility was remarkable. He drew on memory and observation for the descriptions of the 'Moated Grange' or 'Locksley Hall'; on exuberant fancy for the gorgeous scenery in the Oriental visions of the 'Arabian Nights.' There is as much of antithesis as of similarity in the 'May Queen' and in 'Œnone'; yet the feeling in the one as the passion in the other are equally simply and pleasingly true to nature.

Though a fertile and a facile writer, Tennyson for one reason or another showed a self-restraint which poets who can afford it would do well to imitate. We know that he neither laid aside his pen nor let his faculties lie fallow, but for nearly 10 years after 1833 he printed little. In 1842 appeared an edition of his poems in two volumes, consisting in great measure of reprints, but with some noteworthy additions. They were warmly welcomed as they well might be. 'The Two Voices' in itself might have made a poet's reputation. Many consider it Tennyson's masterpiece. Melodiously metaphysical, without being mystically obscure, it leads up through softly flowing stanzas to the practical lessons that help us to carry the burdens of life; nor can anything be more artistic than the climax, which whispers consolation and lets the glimmer of the dawn break gently through the darkness. Wordsworth remarked when he read the book that in the higher spheres of poetry Mr. Tennyson afforded the richest promise. 'He will do great things yet, and ought to have done greater things by this time.' He was soon to do greater things, or, at least, to undertake more important work. In the fragment of the 'Morte d'Arthur' was the germ of the grand conception which was expanded in the 'Idylls' and 'The Holy Grail.' These volumes, like the former, were praised and blamed; but now the praise immeasurably predominated. The best judges delighted to honour the rising star, and the *Quarterly* made something more than the *amende honorable*, though in this case, the writer being one of Tennyson's friends, some of the savour may have been taken out of the incense. If he had taken parody as flattery instead of blasphemous desecration, assuredly he would have had no reason to complain. Aytoun and Martin, in their 'Bon Gaultier Ballads,' did much to popularize 'Locksley Hall' and the 'May Queen' among the classes who might have missed the beauties of the originals. His publishers paid him well; and he received besides a substantial tribute to his rising reputation in the shape of a pension of £200. We fear we must say that his prosperity provoked the envy of a man who should have been superior to petty jealousies. It was an unfortunate coincidence, to say the least, that in the very same year Lytton attacked Tennyson bitterly in the 'New Timon,' and the attack was directed against the pensioner as much as the poet. Discreditable personalities were too much the fashion in those days, as Lytton himself was to learn to his cost when Thackeray fell foul of him in the 'Epistles to the Literati.' And to do Tennyson simple justice, he was by no means behindhand when he answered his enemy's challenge in the pages of *Punch*. There was clever portraiture as well as rough caricature in the stanzas:–

> The padded man that wears the stays.

'The Princess' came out in 1847. It was the longest poem he had yet written, and he lost no reputation by it, if he gained little. It was a literal 'medley' in which the beauties predominate, and where many exquisite sentiments found harmonious expression. In a second edition he seems to have considered and laid to heart the severe strictures of some of the critics; although that does not necessarily follow, for he was in the habit of judging himself reflectively and dispassionately, recasting and polishing his work. He suppressed a few of the lines, he interpolated many others, and he introduced the brief lyrics dividing the chapters which are the sweetest and most attractive parts of the poem. He was in happier vein, and his warm affections had found a more congenial theme, when composing the 'In Memoriam' which appeared two years after 'The Princess.' Tastes must differ widely as to styles and subjects; but on the whole the 'In Memoriam' must be pronounced one of the finest, and the most finished, as it is the most thoughtful, of Tennyson's poems. Never did the memory of an unknown youth receive such signal honour, and by what appeared a sad and untimely death young Hallam secured a world-wide and deathless fame. The success of the 'In Memoriam' was wonderful, considering the sadness of subject. No idea could have seemed more morbid than that of ringing the changes in a monotony of lament for one long departed. There seemed something of affectation, too, in inviting the public to chime in with the unrestrained indulgence of a private grief. But these obvious objections were surmounted by the genuine pathos of the poet and by his masterly methods of treatment. There was nothing morbid in the course of the plaintive strains, bringing sweet consolation out of grief and hope out of despondency. The poet of the 'Voices' drew new lessons from the discipline of sorrow, and pointed the struggling victims of time to the glorious promise of a blessed eternity. If the ring of 'The Princess' was sometimes hollow and even harsh, nothing can be richer or more sonorous than the deep melodies of 'In Memoriam.'

The year 1850 was a memorable one for the poet as well as for his admirers. He was married in the early summer, and appointed Laureate in the autumn. The wedding was at Shiplake Church, in Oxfordshire; his wife was the eldest daughter of Mr. Henry Sellwood, and a niece of Sir John Franklin. It was shortly afterwards that the death of Wordsworth left the Laureateship vacant. It was scarcely flattering to Tennyson that the only competitor seriously put forward was Leigh Hunt, another of the poets, by the way, whom Wilson and Lockhart had satirized as singers of the Cockney school. Posterity will have no difficulty in deciding upon their comparative claims to precedence; and, indeed, the chief objection to the exercise of the Premier's patronage was that Tennyson was already a pensioner of the State. It may be doubted whether the Laureate's bays and mantle exercised a favourable influence on his poetry. In everything he has ever written we come as matter of course on fine ideas and noble passages. But no one of his Court ditties, except the welcome to the Princess of Wales, has risen in any great degree above the commonplace. Nor was 'Maud,' which came out in 1855, by any means one of his most successful efforts. Like 'The Princess' its welcome by the reviewers was less warm than usual, and he had struck a key and taken a tone which was unlikely to popularize the poem. With such exceptions as the 'Come into the Garden, Maud,' which at once seized on the fancy, we missed some of the accustomed melody. The poet of sentiment, of nature, and the domestic affections, was scarcely at home in singing the praises of war.

Whether or not he had sunk in 'The Princess' and in 'Maud,' he soared again in the 'Idylls of the King' in a more daring flight than he had hitherto attempted. It was the fault of the fragmentary design that he had to await the full triumph. The 'Idylls' in their completed form are in reality a grand epic. The cycle of the Arthurian legend had long engaged his fancy; he had touched it already in the 'Morte d'Arthur' and elsewhere. It offered singular attractions to the chivalrous side of his genius; it gave rare opportunities for his statelier and more severe forms of diction. His fancy might freely indulge its flights in gilding a national and favourite romance; imagination might make what it would of myth and legend. Tennyson's ideal Arthur was the star of chivalry, the soul of honour, and the prince of purity, as well as the best and bravest lance among his Paladins. Virtue went hand in hand with valour at a Court which stood fast on the foundations of faith and chivalry in the surging sea of heathenism and barbarism. In the spotless Arthur, with his mysterious birth, we have something, if we may say so, like the antitype of the Saviour. He wears the form and bears the weapons of humanity; but he is too good for the world; even the wife who should have known him best wearies of his spotless perfection. And in falling back upon Lancelot, she so far has our sympathy as a woman abandoning an unimaginable ideal for the noblest of frail and erring mortals. So that in our idea, save in the pathetic closing scene of forgiveness in 'Guinevere,' the very moral perfection of Arthur is a blemish, though, perhaps, an inevitable blemish, on the 'Idylls.' He fails to interest because we fail to conceive. As for meaner mortals, they are true enough to nature in the passions, the follies, and the caprices which are the common property of all ages and of men of every rank. We may say, indeed, that the passing brutality of Geraint to his wife, extenuated by that fierce outburst of suspicion, is far truer to probabilities in that barbarous age than the graceful deportment of the ladies or the stately courtesy of the knights. The seduction of Merlin, where the mighty sage and enchanter falls a victim to the wiles of a worthless siren, is unpleasing. But it is a scene of all times, and symbolical to boot; and by way of contrasts in companion pictures we have the gentle courtship of the knightly Geraint, and the death-love of the lily maid of Astolat. Yet, although the Arthur of the Idylls, the chivalrous champion of the holy Faith and of civilized order, had been purged of his impurities, yet in the blighting of friendship and love, and the darkening of his day-dreams, he was to expiate the faults of his hot youth. The earlier parts of the poem – which appeared the last – explain its full significance. The root of evil and bitterness springs up in Modred, the fruit of the good King's youthful follies. So the golden promise of 'The Coming of Arthur' is heavily clouded before the end. In 'Gareth and Lynette' the allegory is obvious. The young Hope and Faith which are to work marvels for the redemption of a world groaning in guilt and under the oppression of tyranny are personified in the chivalrous purity of the youthful knight-errant who gives full and perfect service to the master he adores. Going forward from 'Gareth and Lynette,' through the 'Enid' and onwards, we comprehend the scheme and moral of the connected epic, as we trace the growth of sin with the harvest of evils which bring sorrows and speedy expiations in their train. Sin and sorrow predominate in the 'Pelleas and Ettarre,' and they culminate in 'Guinevere,' in the crowning and most moving scene where Arthur, bending over his fallen Queen, tells her that it is his fate to love her always, and that it is their destiny to be reunited when she has been purged by suffering. Finally, in 'The Passing of Arthur,' the poet is at his grandest in painting the conflict of feelings in the wreck of hopes, when there is calm in the soul of the King amid the storms that are raging around him and beneath the black clouds that come drifting up. That group of idylls is a noble poem – rich in lofty lessons and noble thoughts; rich in scenes of romantic description that sparkle like gems in a golden setting; rich in melodious diction and picturesque fancies. And with the appearance of that volume of wonderful verse the author's reputation culminated likewise. The 'Holy Grail' did little for it, and, though 'Enoch Arden' and 'Aylmer's Field' were eagerly bought and widely circulated, we doubt if either has been often re-read. More remarkable and certainly more original were the two minor pieces of the 'Northern Farmer,' old and new styles, which were given to the public with 'Aylmer's Field.' They are not only notable as specimens of uncompromising provincial English, ingeniously moulded to the purposes of the poet; but there are strange depths of sad and cynical satire in the types of seemingly simple character that are photographed by unconscious self-revelation.

Before we pass from these, the best known of the Laureate's works, we may note that they contain a remarkable number of felicitous phrases, 'jewels five words long,' which have speedily become the common property of our literature. Many of them are so familiar, so classical, that one is apt to forget their origin; but 'the grand old gardener,' 'the supreme Caucasian mind,' 'the caste of Vere de Vere,' 'the falsehood of extremes,' 'the fairy tales of science,' 'the touch of a vanished hand,' 'sweet girl graduates,' 'the rosebud garden of girls,' 'mealy-mouthed philanthropies,' 'immemorial elms,' 'a stony British stare,' 'faultily faultless,' 'the little rift within the lute,' and the 'chorus of indolent reviewers,' – these, and many others, are Tennyson's.

As a dramatist Tennyson cannot take his place among the greatest masters, though there are scenes and passages in the plays which will not be easily forgotten. Within certain limits he shows great dramatic power, but his range was limited. He plays on the feelings with a masterly touch, and many of his characters are conceived with Velasquez-like realism and vigour. But he is conspicuously deficient in the flexibility of moods which lends itself lightly to changing attitudes, and identifies itself easily with an infinity of varying personalities. His finest piece is decidedly his *Queen Mary*, although even in that there is no great richness of dramatic fancy. Yet *Queen Mary* has many striking scenes, and would act well were it not too crowded with leading characters for good stage business. Mary is admirable, with her strong natural sagacity consciously subjugated to feminine weakness in spite of the warnings of her wisest counsellors, and her sister Elizabeth, though a slighter sketch, is perhaps even more spirited. Philip is represented, as we might imagine him in his youth, sensuous, yet cruel and a bigot in embryo, with an irrepressible disgust for the woman he is to wed, which he scarcely cares to conceal in his haughty selfishness. And Gardiner, a sturdy English patriot, though a zealot for the foreign faith, contrasts finely with the gentler Pole and the feebler but conscientious Cranmer. In *Beckett* there are at least two great characters – the Prelate and the King – though perhaps the incarnation of the encroaching power of Rome is relegated too decidedly to the second place. *Harold* in human interest falls far below the others, possibly because the dramatist is groping among more shadowy personages and in more mythical history. *The Cup* and *The Falcon* were slighter efforts; and the *Promise of May* was not a success. In *Robin Hood*, published so lately as last March, it was evident that the poet had kept his delicacy of touch, and that the wand of the dramatist had not lost its charm. The play was long and in parts it dragged, but there were many redeeming passages of singular grace, and it was brightened with sparkling songs which breathed the very spirit of the greenwood. Yet even the brightest of the songs provoked not altogether favourable comparison with the lays and lyrics in Love Peacock's 'Maid Marian.'

Tennyson's place among the poets was honourably recognized by the Universities many years ago. Oxford took the lead in 1855, instituting him a Doctor of Civil Law. Cambridge followed suit when the members of his own college placed the admirable bust by Mr. Woolmer in their library, and subsequently elected him to an honorary fellowship. In December, 1885, the Laureate was raised to the peerage as Baron Tennyson of Aldworth, in Sussex, and Freshwater, in the Isle of Wight. Doubtless he appreciated the unprecedented honour paid to English poetry in his person, yet the distinction did not, perhaps, give much additional dignity to the new peer considering the freedom with which titles of nobility have been lavished latterly. In the same year he brought out 'Tiresias and other Poems.' The poems were undated, and it is doubtful when they were written, but for the most part they appear to bear the mark of a ripe, if not an over-ripe, maturity. They sing the old and favourite themes in the old familiar manner, and though they show neither barrenness of fancy nor enfeebling of the imaginative powers, they define the limits of the poet's conception and illustrate the monotony of his inspiration. In 'Tiresias' he treads again the familiar classical ground, on the borderland between mythology and semi-mythical history, where human sympathies and passions are swayed by the unsympathetic gods, 'who love and hate with mortal hates and loves,' as they 'move unseen among the ways of men.' 'Tiresias,' although it gives the title to the volume, is short and slight. But there are fine passages in the impassioned appeal of the blind old prophet, who has still the vision of beauty that had blinded him burned in upon the brain, who is writhing under the sense of the predestined impotence, foreseeing calamities it is powerless to avert. 'Despair' is a daring and unpleasing theme; the poem ends abruptly, like 'Tiresias;' but in this case the abrupt termination, as it seems to us, is inartistic and eminently unsatisfactory. The poem breathes the raving despair of a would-be suicide saved sorely against his will from the sea that has swallowed his wife. It is the wail of a soul that foresees itself lost, and, anticipating the inconceivable horrors of hell, heaps curses on the cruel creed that has wrecked it. No ray of light breaks in upon the darkness, and the minister of religion to whom the ravings are addressed stands silenced and presumably self-convicted before the audacious blasphemer. 'Balin and Balan' supplies a missing link in the series of the Idylls of Arthur's Court. It comes in as the prelude to 'Merlin and Vivien,' and one of the wandering brother-knights falls a victim to the wiles of the fair enchantress, when on the quest of a demon in a haunted forest. Wild and fanciful beyond the common, the chivalrous Christianity of Arthur's Court is brought face to face with the insane asceticism of a superannuated recluse, and with the fiends and ministers of evil that are the survivals of expiring Heathendom. There is many a graceful fancy and many a melodious line; we remark again the Laureate's predilection for homely similes, and his extraordinary power of dignifying them in poetic dress, but we have never thought that 'Balin and Balan' added to the reputation of the author of the Idylls. On the other hand, he never wrote anything better in its way, he never showed a lighter or more sprightly touch, than in 'The Spinster's Sweet-Arts.' It will be remembered that it is in the homely dialect of 'The Northern Farmer.' There is subtle and delicious comedy in the firmly-drawn character of the old maid, who might have been married many times for her money, and is very glad she never married, as she sits musing among the cats she confounds with the sweethearts, after whom she has named them.

Perhaps 'Locksley Hall – Sixty Years After,' published in 1886, excited more attention if it did not win more praise than any of the later poems. Pleasant old memories were awakened by the old name and the old flowing measure; curiosity was excited over the probable changes in the poet's mind, since it had cynically, under the blight that had befallen the lovelorn hero, surveyed the world and society of sixty years before. Curiosity was gratified, if fond expectations were not altogether fulfilled. The jilted lover of the shallow-hearted Amy had learnt lessons of wisdom with gathering years, and was in charity with his old rival, just dead, whose virtues he somewhat contemptuously recognized. But the reckless cynicism of youthful despair had given place to the pessimism of sad experience, and in the character of the poet-prophet denouncing the decadence of his age his individuality is merged in that of Tennyson. This latter-day 'Locksley Hall' is a personal revelation; it expresses with a candour of earnestness there is no mistaking the political and social opinions, the prepossessions, the prejudices, the vain aspirations, and the vanished illusions of the venerable poet. Although now and again a couplet sounds unusually harsh; though here and there are gratuitous barbarisms of language, coined impetuously for the fiercer expression of burning indignation, on the whole it is a remarkable *tour de force*. The dominating idea is lofty and tragical. The poem is the wail of age over the sins and sorrows, the crimes, the follies, and the foul abuses of a world that is 'groaning and travailing' in misery and hastening downwards through democratic demoralization to decay. But the incidents and the details, as we have said, are often inevitably prosaic, and though scathing invective and stinging satire came readily enough, it was difficult to sustain the level of lofty verse in denouncing such real scourges of humanity and such social nuisances as the East-end sweaters or the Socialist stump-orators. Yet the Laureate, having decided to sing out his soul, was not to be deflected from his course by subsidiary difficulties, and sometimes he soars in one of the highest of his flights when we should have expected him to come to the ground with crippled pinions. One couplet we might quote as holding up to scorn with fine irony the fond dreamers and the self-seeking anarchists who shadow out an ideal world which they fill with their wild chimeras:–

> 'Hesper-Venus – were we native to that splendour, or in Mars,
> 'We should see the globe we groan in, fairest of their evening stars.'

Another poem, which recurs to the memory at the moment of the poet's death, is the beautiful lyric 'Crossing the Bar,' which closed the last published volume of verses, 'Demeter, and other poems.'

Extremely domesticated, the Laureate loved to relax with congenial talk in the society of congenial friends, and he delighted in doing the honours of the Sussex woodlands and the marine scenery which had so often inspired his muse. One of the surest ways to his heart was the admiration of that cherished scenery, and he says as much in his charming verses to General Hamley, the prologue to his ode on the Balaclava charge of the Heavy Brigade. Under pressure he would not infrequently read poetry of his own, though he much preferred to recite the poetry of others. But, with all his sympathetic appreciation, he was wanting in the gifts of an elocutionist, and his manner of reading was somewhat monotonous and unimpassioned. Since he rose into celebrity, his good nature had been overtaxed by correspondents who submitted their manuscripts for examination and revision. Repeatedly he raised a cry of expostulation in our columns, and so lately as December, 1885, we published a letter, declaring, once for all, that he was overwhelmed with such unscrupulous requests, and imploring immunity from them for the future. Another of the drawbacks to his world-wide reputation was the persecutions he had to endure from obtrusive notoriety-hunters. The familiar figure will long linger in the recollections of the sightseers who had the good fortune to catch a glimpse of the shy quarry they were stalking. They will remember him as he appears on the canvas of Millais, with the soft felt hat in the hand, and the thin gray beard falling over the well-worn Inverness cape, which is almost as much associated with the personality of Tennyson as their mantles with the memories of Moses or Elijah.

Lady Tennyson survives her husband. Of the poet's two sons, the elder, Hallam, who has been in latter years his father's constant companion and secretary, survives him, and succeeds to the title. He married, in 1884, Audrey Georgiana Florence, daughter of Mr. Charles John Boyle, and has two sons. The poet's younger son, Lionel, died in 1886, leaving a widow, the daughter of Mr. Frederick Locker-Lampson, and three sons. Mrs. Lionel Tennyson has since married Mr. Augustine Birrell, M. P.

At this moment many stories are being recalled of the retired habits of Lord Tennyson, and of the inconvenience to which he would sometimes put himself in order to elude sight-seeing excursionists. Prominent among these during the summer months, when the poet made Aldworth his home, were Americans, some of whom have been known to make a fortnight's sojourn in the neighbourhood with the sole object of catching a glimpse of him. He would occasionally be found rambling a little distance from his private grounds, but the approach of a vehicle invariably led to a hasty retreat or a sudden turn to the left on the part of the master of Aldworth. This beautiful residence of Lord Tennyson is situated on an eminence about 1,000ft. above the level of the sea. From the windows the unbroken weald of Surrey and Sussex, together with a beautiful panorama of the country between the North and South Downs, can be seen. The house is of Gothic design, with large windows and a stone porch. It was built nearly 30 years ago under the direction of Lord Tennyson. Probably nowhere else within easy reach of London could the poet have found a retreat so beautiful, and at the same time so secluded, as Aldworth.

This is a fine, observant and detailed appreciation of Tennyson's art as a poet, one which, unlike posthumous criticism, finds much to admire in his later work (though there is real reserve about the literary success of his plays). It might seem extraordinary to modern readers to find only scant mention of Arthur Hallam, in whose memory *In Memoriam AHH* had been written, and after whom Tennyson's eldest son was named. But then the obituarist expresses some reserve about the poem's 'unrestrained indulgence of private grief'. Hallam had not only been a close and supportive friend, he was also the young Tennyson's mentor and his first and most constructive critic. To find the Arthur of the *Idylls* referred to as 'like the antitype of the Saviour' seems somehow to miss the point that the Arthur of *In Memoriam* has a similar function. It seems likely that the praise of Tennyson as a 'fertile and facile writer' who nonetheless 'showed a self-restraint which poets who can afford it would do well to imitate' is a comment on the conspicuous lack of restraint in the work of the most talented of the younger poets who were left to dominate the literary scene in 1892: Swinburne. At Tennyson's funeral in Westminster Abbey, which Swinburne declined to attend, the nave was lined by men from the Light Brigade. He was buried next to Robert Browning in Poets' Corner.

LOUIS (LAJOS) KOSSUTH

Hungarian patriot: 'All lovers of freedom in every country, all admirers of valour, all men who had hearts to sympathize with the misfortunes of patriots mourned when the Hungarian cause was lost.'

20 MARCH 1894

IF FEW PEOPLE among the generation that has seen Kossuth die know more of him than his great name, the fault is wholly that of the man, whose ambition was of the kind which Quintilian has called the parent of the virtues. The abdication of a tribune is even rarer than that of a King, but Kossuth found that in his case integrity and self-interest lay far apart – Sidera terra / Ut distant et flamma mari, sic utile recto.

As Manzoni finely said of Garibaldi, 'He disdained the purple but kept the ermine.' Yet the Hungarian patriot was very different in talents and character from the Italian hero. With as large a heart as Garibaldi's, he had more brains; his enthusiasm was tempered with a lawyer's shrewdness; and, though he wanted firmness on some critical occasions, this seems to have been owing rather to the fact that he put too much confidence in certain unworthy individuals, than to ignorance of the methods by which men in general should be handled. He had most of the qualities which make up the practical statesman, and if he had cared for personal advancement he might have played a great part in Hungary to the end of his life. But, severely conscientious, he would never renounce for his own mere profit principles which he had inculcated upon others and for which others had bled although he was quite ready to admit that those principles might be relaxed by men who were less pledged to them than he was. That is why he spent his closing years in voluntary exile. He felt that his work was finished when Hungary became free, and, replying to deputations who came entreating that he would return to Pesth and place himself at the head of a political party, he always answered, 'Hungarians now want union, not parties.'

Louis Kossuth was born on the 16th of September, 1802, at Monok, in the county of Zemplin, a region of rich valleys and famous vineyards. His father, a small landowner of the noble class, was descended from an ancient Hungarian family of whose members no fewer than 17 were prosecuted for high treason by the Austrian Government between 1527 and 1715. 'My genealogical tree is like a gallows,' he once said, 'there is an ancestor hanging from every branch.' Louis's father was an advocate, whose landed property covered no more than a few acres of vines, and Louis himself was trained for the law. After learning the rudiments at a village school, he was sent to the Protestant College of Scharasehpatack and there took his degrees in law. At one time he contemplated becoming a Lutheran pastor, but it is said that he was diverted from clerical life by the jest of a professor, who said to him:– 'With a tongue like yours, you will always be taking up paradoxes; you will plead the Devil's cause just by way of novelty.' Kossuth took the reproach to heart, though it does not appear that he was more garrulous than the generality of his countrymen. Cardinal Michailovic has written of them, 'Incontinence of speech is the great fault of our Hungarians. In an assembly of a hundred members the smallest question brings out five-score harangues. When Hungarians meet to confer about cutting a country road, they begin by settling the affairs of the entire world, then go and dine and adjourn the road matter to another season.'

Upon getting his legal diploma, Kossuth was appointed steward to the Countess Szapary, and in that capacity had a seat in the Comitat Assembly, wherein nobles and officials met several times a year to discuss local affairs. It was the practice in those times – one that has not long been abolished – for the widows of magnates to be represented by their nominees, not only in the Comitat Assemblies, but at the Table of Deputies in the Hungarian Diet. These 'ladies' men' had right of speech but no votes, and they usually confined themselves to shouting *Haljuk, haljuk* ('Hear, hear') to the orations of their mistresses' noble kinsmen. But Kossuth would not treat his functions as a sinecure, nor would he even admit that he held *vom mandat impératif*, so that he soon fell out with the Countess, who was a very imperious dame. Like that Prince Esterhazy who, in answer to Lord Lansdowne's remark that he had 10,000 sheep, replied, 'And I, 10,000 shepherds,' the Countess Esterhazy owned retainers enough to form an army, and things looked very bad for young Kossuth when this lady, angered by his independence, accused him of falsifying her accounts. However, Kossuth cleared himself of the charge, and one of the Counts Hunyady, deeming that he had been unfairly treated, chose him to sit as his representative in the National Diet of Presburg. Kossuth was one of 300 similar delegates of absentee landlords. His position gave him a free residence in his principal's palace, and in many respects it was like that held formerly in England by the member of a rotten borough towards his patron. But one of its peculiarities was that a Deputy was required to furnish regular reports of the proceedings in Parliament to his principal; and Kossuth's reports were so very good, not only as summaries of business, but as descriptive sketches and comments, that Count Hunyady suggested that they should be published. A small lithographic press was purchased by subscription among the members of the Liberal Opposition, and hundreds of copies of the reports being thus struck off were circulated under the title of 'Parliamentary Gazette' among annual subscribers. All writers agreed that the effect of these gazettes was immense. Like Dr. Johnson in his reports for the

Gentleman's Magazine, Kossuth much improved the matter and style of the speeches which he edited; and the Austrian Government, which had always sought to prevent combined action on the part of the various Diets by forbidding the publication of their debates, took alarm at the Gazette and declared it illegal. The lithographic press had to be abandoned; but then a large staff of clerks was engaged to copy the reports in manuscripts and these were sent out to subscribers at six florins a month, just as the 'News Letters' were from London to the country in the seventeenth century. Again the Government endeavoured to stop these papers. They were being taken in by numerous clubs as well as by private persons, and Kossuth resolved to enlarge the scope of his enterprise by reporting the debates of some local Diet when the National Diet was not in session. He chose the Assembly of Pesth for this purpose, and the Government of Vienna issued an order for his arrest. The Chancellor of Hungary, Count Raviczky, refused to countersign the warrants; he was dismissed from office and his place given to Count F. Palffy, a zealous agent of Prince Metternich's, 'whereupon,' as Kossuth said in after years in relating his experiences before a British audience, 'the curious spectacle was witnessed of a whole company of Grenadiers marching about Pesth to try and catch one solitary man.' Kossuth fled to his residence among the hills of Ofen; but there he was captured, taken back to Pesth and put upon his trial for high treason along with several accomplices – that is, men who had done nothing worse than assist him in publishing Parliamentary reports.

One of these fellow Liberals was a wealthy and popular magnate, Count Nicholas Wesselenyi, whose daughter Kossuth was soon to marry. Having large estates to serve as bail for him, Wesselenyi was not shut up pending his trial; but he eventually, in 1839, received the same sentence as Kossuth that is, four years' imprisonment. The brilliant and high-minded count Stephen Szechenyi, who had begun to spend the whole of his income in relieving the condition of the Hungarian peasantry, founding schools, circulating works on national history, and Liberal newspapers, was condemned to a like penalty, while some 50 young men of the Liberal party, mostly advocates and students, were punished with lesser sentences. Kossuth was at first confined in the common gaol of Pesth, but his conviction caused such a ferment among the people that the authorities feared that a movement might be made to release him and he was accordingly transferred to the Castle of Ofen. The mass of the nation took up his cause, however, and the Government became involved in a serious conflict with the Diet. The elections of 1839 returned a majority of Deputies who had bound themselves to throw out every Government measure until Kossuth and his friends should be released. In vain did the Austrian party in the kingdom press upon Prince Metternich that he had better make a compromise; the autocratic Minister refused to yield, and the consequence was that the Deputies declined to vote the annual levy of troops and then proceeded to pass resolutions censuring the Septemvirate Tribunal which had condemned the patriots. A still more serious resolution was that which decreed by a majority of two that the Hungarian language should for the future be the only one used in the debates of the Diet. At this Metternich, seeing matters take an ominous turn, advised the Emperor to grant an amnesty, and Kossuth was released with his friends. He came out of prison amid frantic demonstrations of popular triumph, and a subscription that was started to present him with a testimonial produced a sum of 10,000fl. Soon after his liberation Kossuth was married to Mlle. Wesselenyi. This young lady, who was a person of great beauty and accomplishments, had conceived a romantic attachment for him on the strength of his reputation and before she had seen him. With her father's consent she sent the prisoner books, papers, and letters of encouragement during his incarceration, and in this way a correspondence sprang up. The fact that Kossuth was allowed to receive Mlle. Wesselenyi's missives and to answer them while in custody shows that his imprisonment was not a very rigorous one; and it is only fair to mention this because in after years it was generally believed in England that he had learnt our language in prison by studying an English Bible the only book allowed him. It seems that he did learn English out of the Bible, but he had plenty of other books as well. There is no comparison possible between his prison sufferings and those which Silvio Pellico and Baroncelli were enduring ten years later in the Spielberg. After his liberation, Kossuth, of course, saw Mlle. Wesselenyi, and an engagement was formed, but it was with the utmost difficulty that a dispensation could be obtained from Rome for a marriage between a Protestant and a Catholic. Popular as Kossuth was, no Catholic priest could be prevailed upon to solemnize the marriage, even after the dispensation had come, the clergy hoping, no doubt, that the Patriot might be induced to change his religion out of love for his bride if he found he could win her in no other way. But Kossuth did not change his religion, and his bride contented herself with a wedding in a Protestant chapel.

Up to the time of his prosecution Kossuth had not been regarded as a popular leader in Hungary. His influence was not on a level with Szechenyi's, nor with that of the calm, learned Francis Deák, the soundest lawyer and the most cogent speaker in the Diet. But persecution does wonders for a man, and when Kossuth had undergone 15 months' imprisonment for the Liberal cause, there was no name so dear as his to the people, because it was associated with a great and unexpected victory of popular agitation. It was Kossuth who had begun the strife out of which the conflict between the Diet and the Imperial Government arose. It was over his body that the Hungarian Deputies had fought with Austria and had actually forced the Imperial Government to yield. Kossuth at once made the most of his opportunities. In 1841, entering into financial partnership with a bookseller of Pesth, he founded the *Pesti Hirlap* (Pesth Journal) for the advocacy of Liberal opinions. The tone of this paper was very cautious, there was nothing in it to give the Government any pretext for saying that it was the organ of Hungarian Separatists, and Metternich took a sensible course, when, instead of trying to suppress the paper, he started a Conservative rival, the *Vilag*, under the editorship of Count Aurelius Dusseffy, a man of mordant wit and one of the ablest writers in the kingdom. Dusseffy, who was a popular character, collected a dashing staff, and the two papers attacked each other with great violence for about a twelvemonth; but, in 1842, the editor of the *Vilag* died – of his antagonist's pin-thrusts, as the wits of Pesth said – and then Kossuth remained master of the field. Upon this the Government set quietly to work to embroil him with his partner. Kossuth had been making money out the *Hirlap*, so that after a couple of years' editorship, he had been able to buy an estate of 30,000 florins value, near Gràn. But the proprietor of the *Hirlap* was a portly man with pushing wife and daughters, who wanted to get into Viennese society, and an invitation to a Court ball, with the promise of some more substantial Government favours, seems to have got the better of his Liberal principles. A dispute was started with Kossuth on a question of salary. The ponderous man was sarcastic and taunted his editor with drawing too much money. Kossuth, who was lean, choleric, and always terribly in earnest, raged away like a straw fire and ended by flinging his resignation into the bookseller's face, vowing that he would bring out a new paper and kill the *Hirlap*. But he forgot that before founding a newspaper he must get a licence from Government. The *Hirlap* happened to be the only independent journal in the kingdom, and it was tolerated because Metternich held that Liberalism ought to have at least one vent. When Kossuth applied for leave to start a new journal, the Minister had the audacity to propose that Kossuth should accept a State subvention and write on the Austrian side. It is not quite clear how such an offer came to be made; but as men seldom receive insulting proposals without having done something a little indiscreet it must be supposed that Metternich had drawn hasty inferences from some unsuccessful speculations in which Kossuth embarked at about this date.

It was a kindly failing in Kossuth that he was always disposed to think that others were as honest as himself. Though he could see clearly enough into a matter of business when be brought his mind to it, he would often let his common sense be overruled by the reflection that such and such an affair must be sound because so and so assured him that it was. He would sooner have lost a 1,000fl. note any day than put a friend out of conceit with a pet scheme, and once he was heard saying, with that kind of smile which Dick Steele must have worn, 'I can't refuse to show poor B. that I trust him; nobody else does.' Before leaving the *Hirlap*, Kossuth had entered into a project for creating a number of agricultural credit banks for small peasant proprietors; but he lost a good deal of money in this venture. Forsaking his editorship, he was deprived for a time of all occupation as a journalist and plunged deeper into speculations which always had some philanthropical object. One of these was a mutual relief association, which established branch lodges all over the kingdom and had tens of thousands of subscribers. It helped to strengthen his influence with the population, but cost him a great deal of money; and in fact his pecuniary affairs fell into such bad condition at last that he must have become bankrupt had not his wife opportunely inherited some property. One effect of Kossuth's economical undertakings was to give a much broader range to his political views. Studying the wants of the poor, he alienated himself more and more in spirit from the aims of Szechenyi and Deák, who were both ardent reformers, but not revolutionists or Socialists. Deák thought it would be a calamity for Hungary if it threw off the sovereignty of the Hapsburgs; Kossuth was already in 1846 contemplating revolution as a necessity. A somewhat hard religiousness brought him to contemn half-measures as products of moral cowardice and gave him an unbending demeanour also towards all politicians in whom he saw any reason to suspect insincerity. It was proposed to him that he should meet Metternich and have a friendly conference over Hungarian affairs. 'I could not pretend to be friendly,' said Kossuth, 'I should not believe a word he said, and it would be my duty to let him see this.'

Without being in any way a visionary, Kossuth had come to the conclusion that it was his duty to strive after 'the utmost that was possible.' That was his favourite formula but he stretched the limits of possibility very far. In 1847 be was elected to the Diet by the County of Pesth and he drew up a programme of reforms which at once caused a split in the Liberal party. The Magnates, who were most energetic in their championship of Magyar interests against Austria, were not prepared to accept Kossuth's agrarian schemes that is to surrender half their estates for the creation of a peasant proprietorship even though they were promised compensation on a scale to be assessed by elective Land Courts. However, in the Session of 1847, Kossuth took much higher rank as a practical politician than he had occupied before. He had formerly been a fluent and sharp debater; he now re-appeared as a solemn and often impassioned exponent of the people's grievances. There was less of the Magyar and more of the universal citizen in him. Outside the Diet he called himself a Republican; inside the Assembly he was careful to use no disloyal expressions, but his tone was that of a tribune who knows that he has a host behind him ready to march at the first move of his finger.

The time for action came abruptly in 1848. On the 24th of February the Parisians rose to overthrow Louis Philippe, and, after three days' fighting, proclaimed the Republic. On the 3rd of March Kossuth addressed a large open-air meeting at Presburg, where the Diet was sitting, and declared that 'the example of the French must not be thrown away upon the down-trodden subjects of Austria.' He incited the youth of Presburg to band themselves into a national guard, to elect officers, and to be ready to strike a blow for their liberties; at the same time he arranged with his friends that a Hungarian Ministry should be formed under the presidency of Count Louis Batthyany. Deák was to be Minister of Justice; Szechenyi, Home Minister; and he, Kossuth, Minister of Finance. The Table of Magnates demurred at this, but on the 13th of March an insurrection broke out in Vienna, causing the downfall of Metternich, and on the 15th Kossuth entered the city at the head of a Hungarian deputation which was received with a frantic enthusiasm. Viennese students drew Kossuth's carriage through the streets; Viennese National Guards, just enrolled, formed themselves into a guard of honour to protect him wherever he went; and there was loud talk of storming the Emperor Ferdinand's palace should Kossuth's appointment as Minister be refused. It was not refused, but Kossuth found that he could not force the Emperor to do all that he wanted. He had to be content with the appointment of Archduke Stephen to the Viceroyalty of Hungary and with the confirmation of Batthyany's Ministry; but it had been his wish to obtain for his country a charter of complete independence, and on his return to Presburg he applied himself to arm the nation against any possible attempt to withdraw the concessions that had been made. How he dragged on the Diet to vote all the measures which he proposed was a marvel to see. He was not the leader of the Ministry, half its members and more than half the Deputies in the Diet were afraid of his policy, and yet his voice seemed to have the magic power of forming majorities. In a short session all the reforms which he had advocated before coming into office were passed into law. The remains of feudalism were swept away. The peasants were declared free from all seignorial claims; in other words, the tenants in one-half the lands of Hungary were declared possessors of that land, rent free, the landlords receiving a promise of indemnities. The peasant and the burgher were admitted to all the rights of nobles, and a new electoral law was passed conferring the suffrage on every man who possessed property to the amount of 300fl. By way of raising funds to carry out these vast schemes, Kossuth decreed an immense issue of paper money, Prince Esterhazy, who was Minister of Foreign Affairs in the Batthyany Cabinet, guaranteeing the paper with his estates. Kossuth's bank-notes were little pink slips, having no ornament on them but only the amount for which they were issued and his signature. There was no difficulty at first about getting them circulated, for the whole nation was full of confidence, but later it became necessary to decree capital punishment against those who refused to take the pink paper, which had become discredited like the *assignats* of the French Revolution.

Indeed, the period of confidence lasted only a few months. Kossuth had reckoned without Joseph Jellachich, the Croatian leader. This extraordinary man – poet, minstrel, soldier, and patriot after a fashion – perceived in Austria's difficulties the chance of his own fortune. As a Croat he hated the Hungarians, and he harboured a particular personal antipathy towards Kossuth, who had once called him to his face 'a frivolous libertine.' While Kossuth was shaking off the yoke of Austria, Jellachich represented to the Croats that they had nothing to gain by Hungary's triumphs; for, if the control of the Imperial Government over the Magyars were removed, all the small Slavonic States would lie at the mercy of the Hungarians. The Croats, bristling at this idea, petitioned the Emperor that Jellachich might be appointed 'Ban,' or Governor; and Jellachich, having received this high office along with the rank of Field-Marshal and the command of all the troops in Croatia, refused to go to Pesth and have his authority confirmed by the Hungarian Diet. Kossuth protested and called upon the Vienna Government either to dismiss the Ban or to compel his submission. Meanwhile Jellachich had discovered that his cry, 'One Emperor and Austria undivided,' was not enough to keep the Slavonic States in union, unless the prospect were held out of converting Austria into a wholly Slavonic Empire. By force of harangues, cajoleries, promises, and bribes, he sustained his influence over the Southern States; but, while the people idolized him, many among the higher classes looked upon him as little better than a brigand adventurer, and he sometimes had to assert himself by rough means. Hearing that a meeting had been summoned at Agram to discuss an arrangement with Hungary, he walked boldly into it, disdaining the angry murmurs caused by the intrusion, whereupon a politician rose screaming that the assembly was not to be intimidated, even though Jellachich brought 10,000 bayonets with him. The Ban drew his sword and threw it on the floor, then knocked the speaker down with his fist, and roared that he had no need of weapons to keep order in the land. This little display of vigour evoked a burst of servile cheering, and one or two subsequent demonstrations of a similar kind, while they convinced the malcontents that their Ban was not a man to be trifled with, satisfied the Emperor that Jellachich was a safe instrument to use against Kossuth. But first a comedy had to be played, and at the instance of Batthyany Jellachich was dismissed, and even declared traitor. It has been said that he was profoundly affected and disgusted at this proclamation of outlawry, which he read in a newspaper at Linz after leaving Vienna, where the double-dealing Ferdinand had shaken him warmly by the hand and wept hysteric tears, calling him 'my good friend.' But there is no doubt that Jellachich was a party to the move, made to throw dust in the eyes of the Hungarian Ministry. Received with acclamations at Agram, notwithstanding his nominal deposition, he continued to govern as if he were still Ban, and soon returned to Vienna, breathing defiance against the Magyars. A mediation was offered by Archduke John on this occasion, but it was only a pretence. Batthyany and Jellachich met in the Archduke's palace for a conference, and in five minutes came to high words. 'We shall meet again on the Drave' (the river which separates Hungary from Croatia) cried Batthyany, shaking his fist. 'Oh, no,' laughed Jellachich, 'I will come and find you on the Danube.'

The insurrection of Croatia, Dalmatia, and Slavonia followed close upon this interview, and then Kossuth did a thing which ever afterwards he lamented with unaffected contrition. To make terms with Austria he threw over the Italian cause. One is only judging Kossuth by the high moral standard which he himself desired should be applied to all his acts in forbearing to offer any excuse for this treacherous proceeding, for such it was. An ordinary politician – 'one of those shift and shamble men,' as Carlyle called them – might have been forgiven for disentangling himself from fellowship with the Italians at a time when his own country needed his undivided services, but Kossuth had claimed the sympathies of Liberal Europe for the cause of Hungary as being that of all oppressed nationalities. He had called Venetians and Lombards brothers, had urged Daniel Manin by private letters to take up arms, and had promised various Italian emissaries that he would make his countrymen disown all participation with Austria in her rule over Lombardy. Instead of keeping his word, Kossuth now prevailed upon his colleagues to launch a proclamation which, solemnly abjuring Italian interests, caused an indignant shock throughout the Peninsula, surprised Europe, and did the patriot no good among his own friends. The Italian insurgents were crushed by Radetsky, and when the Moderate party in the Hungarian Diet became alarmed at the isolation of their country, the Moderate members of the Cabinet Batthyany, Messaros, and Deák resigned. This was just after the election of a new Diet, in which Kossuth's supporters had a majority. Hearing of Jellachich's advance towards the Drave, the Diet declared itself permanent, decreed the levy of four army corps and appointed Kossuth Governor with dictatorial powers. At this juncture Kossuth fell ill from overwork and anxiety; but, though parched with fever and so weak that he could not stand, he had himself carried to the rostrum of the Diet, and two friends supported him in their arms while he made a stirring speech which ended with these words:–

> 'Have no illusions. The Magyars are surrounded by enemies; they are alone in the world against the league of Sovereigns and races who encircle them. The Emperor of Russia is our foe; we find traces of his diplomacy and his gold everywhere, even in Servia. It is he who is arming the Croat revolt; and meanwhile the liberty-hating statesmen of Vienna are watching our troubles with sly looks, not daring to call us rebels yet, but waiting to do so and to load us with chains if we let ourselves be beaten. Say, Hungarians, will you be slaves or will you fight?'

The Magyars swore to fight, and they did. The first battle between their troops and Jellachich's took place at Valencze, and the day was one of frightful carnage on both sides. After 12 hours' fighting the issue was still undecided, when the

Hungarian General Moga at the head of his hussars made a series of heroic charges which broke the Croatian centre and forced Jellachich to retire. But this tough captain was not beaten. He concluded an eight days' truce, and fell back upon Raab, there to await reinforcements from Vienna – a course which brought matters between Kossuth and the Imperial Government to a crisis. Up to this date everything had been done by the Hungarians in the name of 'Ferdinand, King of Hungary;' Jellachich's defeat, however, rendered it imperative that Ferdinand and his *camarilla* of counsellors should either openly support the Magyars or throw off the mask. They threw off the mask, and five regiments in Vienna received marching orders to go and rejoin Jellachich. But the Viennese rose in the night to prevent these troops from leaving the city. For the third time within the year the Kaiserstadt was up in arms; the venerable General Latour was murdered by the Viennese rabble; Ferdinand fled to Schönbrunn, and the insurrectionary leaders called upon Kossuth for volunteers to help them in holding the capital. While ten Magyar battalions marching with Republican war cries answered this appeal, Jellachich, marching still faster with reorganized troops, appeared unexpectedly before the city gates. On that day he saved the Hapsburg Dynasty. Operating with Windischgraetz, who had come to besiege the insurgent capital, he directed all the tactics of the two days' siege (October 28–30, 1848), and, after capturing Vienna, went to meet the Hungarians at Schwechat. Once more the Republicans of Vienna tried a desperate rally, and on the 2nd of November there was fighting within and without the city; but while Windischgraetz massacred the insurgents Jellachich put the Hungarians to utter rout. They crossed the Leitha in disorder; and Kossuth, seeing that a war to the knife was now inevitable, withdrew with the Diet to Debreezin, where the seat of government was temporarily established.

Ferdinand abdicated on the 2nd of December, 1848, and was succeeded by his son, the present Emperor Francis Joseph. Kossuth has often been blamed for not trying to negotiate with the new Sovereign; but he really never had the chance of doing so. He declined to recognize Francis Joseph because he knew that no terms short of unconditional surrender would be accepted from him. The first act of the young Emperor was to send troops pouring into Hungary. Windischgraetz invaded the country with 50,000 men and 200 cannon; General Schlick occupied the Polish frontiers with 20,000 men; Nugent held the north of the Drave with 16,000. Against these and several smaller armies Kossuth could only bring 20,000 men into the field, but his genius rose equal to his difficulties, and he organized the defence of his country with an ability and a courage which have won for him an undying reputation. In 1849 Hungary surpassed itself, and the whole world thrilled to see this small nation fighting for its liberties and winning one victory after another against double and treble odds. In Generals Bem and Görgey Kossuth had two admirable lieutenants. The former, marching into Transylvania, defeated

Jellachich, and sent the news of his victory in the Caesar-like despatch, 'Bem Ban Böm' (Bem beat Ban). The latter, at the head of the dashing battalions of Honveds (national defenders), and with squadrons of that terrible light cavalry the Czikos who in addition to ordinary weapons carried three-tailed whips with leaden balls at the end of each tail scoured the Carpathians. Utterly demoralized by a series of defeats which culminated in the disaster of Tsaszeg, where they lost 9,000 men, seven flags, and 20 guns, the Austrians were gradually beaten back to the frontier, and the Imperial Government had at length to accept the assistance of Russia. At the same time Görgey, intoxicated by his successes, would not do as he was ordered by Kossuth, and the Dictator showed a lamentable weakness in dealing with him. Upon the re-capture of Pesth from Windischgraetz, Kossuth appointed Görgey Minister of War, hoping to control him in this way, but Görgey did not accept this arrangement. Resigning his portfolio to take active command, he besieged Komorn, contrary to the plan of Kossuth which was that he should fall back upon the Theiss and fortify himself there, and by this disobedience marred all the operations of Bem and Dembinski. On the 4th of July, 1849, Dembinski fairly thrashed an army of 15,000 men under Jellachich in the plains of Hagyes, but this victory came too late. A month previously the Russian Marshal Paskevitch had entered Hungary. The battle of Temesvar was fought; then came the capitulation of Villagos. Kossuth abdicated his power into the hands of Görgey, who, on the 11th of August, surrendered to the Russians at Arad with 40,000 men, throwing all the blame on Kossuth as he did so, and stigmatizing him as a 'Jesuit.' Early in September Marshal Paskevitch was able to write to the Tsar saying 'Hungary is pacified and lies at the feet of your Majesty.'

All lovers of freedom in every country, all admirers of valour, all men who had hearts to sympathize with the misfortunes of patriots mourned when the Hungarian cause was lost. Sinister reprisals followed upon the restoration of Austrian rule. The brave Louis Batthyany was shot; Szechenyi and many more, among whom was Count Andrassy, were sentenced to be hanged, and only escaped this fate by flight. Windischgraetz, Haynau, and Püchner went about holding Court-martials, shooting, hanging, and flogging; and meanwhile the Austrian Government was demanding the extradition of Kossuth, Bem, and Dembinski, who had taken refuge in Turkey with 4,000 of their followers. The strongest influence was brought to bear by the Russian Government on Sultan Abdul-Medjid in order that Kossuth might be delivered up; but the counter influence of the British Government prevailed. Kossuth and six of his companions were at first relegated to honourable confinement at Widdin, and then at Kutahia in Asia Minor, and for a time there was considerable anxiety in England lest Lord Palmerston's intercession for the prisoners should not be successful. It was owing to this strong public feeling aroused on Kossuth's behalf that General Haynau met with so brutal a reception when he came to England in August, 1850. Visiting Barclay and Perkins's Brewery, he was attacked by the labourers and draymen, who belaboured him with brooms and mud, shouting at him as an 'Austrian butcher.' The General had to be rescued by a strong body of police, and this incident leading to a stiff correspondence between the Austrian and British Governments made Prince Schwarzenberg, the Austrian Premier, more anxious than ever to wreak vengeance on Kossuth. However, on August 22, 1851, the ex-Dictator was released, and on September 1 sailed for England. He met with such a hearty reception at Genoa that President Louis Napoleon, who was just about to kill the French Republic, would not allow him to pass through France. Kossuth landed at Southampton on October 28, and two days later started for London. His progress was like a conqueror's triumph. On the 30th the Corporation of London presented him with an address, and he was cheered by immense crowds on his route from Eaton-square to Guild-hall. In his reply he said:– 'What I wish is that the public opinion of England may establish it as a ruling principle of the politics of Europe to acknowledge the right of every nation to dispose of its own internal concerns, and not to give a charter to the Tsar to dispose of the fate of nations.' Next day he was presented with an address from 'Republicans, Revolutionists, and Socialists, men, consequently, not attracted towards you by either the *éclat* of your title or the renown of your name.' On the 3rd of the following month a great metropolitan demonstration was made in his favour at Copenhagen-fields. It was estimated that about 25,000 people were present on the occasion. Great assemblies also welcomed him at Birmingham and Manchester, while addresses from almost every town of note in the kingdom were forwarded up to the 20th of November, when the popular exile sailed for the United States.

At this point the political life of Louis Kossuth properly ends. He returned to England after his visit to America, and lived for some years in this country, writing occasional pamphlets and corresponding with foreign newspapers. His frequent intercourse with Mazzini and Ledru-Rollin caused him to be suspected of being one among a revolutionary triumvirate who were planning the overthrow of all Monarchical Governments on the Continent, and on one occasion his lodgings in London were searched for arms. But though he declared that he was ready at the first favourable opportunity to stir up a new rebellion in Hungary, he was careful to add that 'his stores of arms were not in England.' While living as a refugee among us Kossuth forfeited much of the admiration and sympathy which he had won by his patriotic exploits. His name, always coupled with those of Mazzini and Ledru-Rollin, was too often to be found at the foot of demagogic manifestoes crying to foreign peoples to rise up; and Liberals came rather to resent the swaggering tone and turgid utterances of the triumvirate. It was not Kossuth's hand, however, that penned most of these manifestoes; and it may be noted that after his two turbulent allies were gone the Hungarian patriot was always heard preaching peace – not war, nor even civil war. For the last 30 years of his life he lived in Italy, enjoying easy circumstances. In 1867, after the Austro-Prussian war, when by Count Beust's advice the Emperor Francis Joseph consented to the establishment of the dual system and went to Pesth to be crowned King of Hungary, Kossuth gravely cautioned his country-men to beware of Austrian concessions. He had so often found them delusive that there was no faith left in him; yet he lived to see his confidence restored and to own that the concessions had been genuine. Elected to the Hungarian Diet in 1868, he refused to take his seat, saying that he would not play a part in a farce; but ten years later, when a deputation of Magyars sought him at Turin and offered to get him re-elected, he replied that he had no wish to be a firebrand. Still a Republican in theory, he had come to perceive that a Magyar Republic was hardly practicable for the present nor desirable, and, patriot to the end, he was content with the sight of his country's happiness not grudging her felicity because it had not been achieved by him or by means which he had once thought the best.

In the nineteenth-century Kossuth's international reputation as a patriot, a democrat and a defender of liberty was immense. He was especially admired by British liberals, particularly by those who were of Dissenting stock (Kossuth was a Hungarian Protestant, and the legend that he had learned English from the Bible while in prison added an extra sheen to his halo of righteousness). When he declined an invitation to speak at a Chartist dinner, however, Karl Marx sharply commented that Kossuth was '. . . all things to all men. In Marseilles he shouts "Vive la République!" In Southampton: "God Save the Queen!".' The strength of anti-Austrian feeling in Britain in the wake of the suppression of the Hungarian uprising of 1848 was evident, as the obituarist recalls, when the visit of the Austrian General, Haynau, provoked a riot in Southwark, and protests from Vienna obliged Lord Palmerston to cancel a planned meeting with Kossuth. Kossuth died, by this time merely a voluntary exile, in Turin. His body was taken back to Budapest, given an elaborate state funeral, with some half million people taking part, and buried in the Kerepesi cemetery. A particularly grand mausoleum was erected over his remains. Some of the nomenclature in the obituary needs to be explained: Kossuth was educated at the Calvinist College at Sárospatak; Ofen is modern Buda and Pesth is Pest (administratively united in 1873 as Budapest); the old seat of the Hungarian Diet, Presburg (Pozsony) is now Bratislava; Debreczin is Debrecen; Agram is Zagreb; Temesvár is Timişoara; and General Jellachich's name is now generally rendered as

Jellačić. Every village, town and city in modern Hungary has at least one street named after Kossuth.

* * *

ROBERT LOUIS STEVENSON

Novelist, poet and travel writer: 'Even when he brooded over the physical and metaphysical nightmares . . . the vagaries of his inspirations were invariably kept in check by exquisite taste and sound literary judgment.'

3 DECEMBER 1894

ROBERT LOUIS BALFOUR STEVENSON was born in Edinburgh on November 13, 1850, and was the son of Thomas Stevenson, Secretary to the Commissioners of Northern Lights, and the greatest practical authority on lighthouses of his generation. It was he who built the lighthouse at Skerryvore. Louis Stevenson, as he was familiarly called, was educated at private schools and the University of Edinburgh, and had been brought up for the law. We believe he served his apprenticeship to a Writer to the Signet and he was subsequently called to the Bar. But he never cared to tread the *salle des pas perdus* in the old Scottish Parliament House, and he wrote feelingly in his 'Picturesque Edinburgh' of that dreary purgatory of the gossiping unbriefed. The roving spirit and an hereditary tendency to literature were too strong for him. Nor can we conceive Mr. Stevenson submitting himself to the drudgery of legal routine, and bending his neck to the yoke of exacting Scottish observances. For he was always unconventional – in his costume, in the very cut of his hair, and, above all, in the brilliancy of his conversation and in his unrivalled talent as a raconteur. For example, the friends whom he fascinated have often heard him tell the story of 'the Bottle of Rousillon,' which appears as a chapter in 'The Wrecker,' and he never told it exactly in the same way, but always with new and more piquant embellishments. He went abroad for his health and it was borne in upon him to narrate his experiences. Whether he wrote of California or the Cevennes, the charm of the polished narrative was irresistible. Yet he never realized his veritable vocation, till he floated into fame, in 1883, after the cruise to his 'Treasure Island.' His first books had rather a *succès d'estime,* although they had commended

themselves to the appreciation of the most capable critics. It is very much to say of him that he subsequently made himself popular, without degenerating from that refined literary standard. It was no longer a question of settling to the practice of law in Edinburgh. He exchanged Scotland for the French Bohemia and became for a time a denizen of the Quartier Latin, while he was always the *bienvenu* in the artist colony at Barbizon. It seems strange, by the way, but the only reminiscences of those pleasant Fontainebleau visits are to be found in one of his latest novels, 'The Wrecker.' We need not catalogue his works in chronological order. His health had always been feeble. He gratefully dedicated the 'Child's Garden of Verses' to the good old lady who had lovingly nursed him into boyhood. Too soon again his strength showed signs of failing and it was delicacy of the chest which first sent him abroad. But he had always sufficient command of money, and latterly, at least, his malady and anxieties were alleviated by an ample and increasing income. English editors and publishers treated him handsomely; as for the Americans, their passion for him made them forget their usual sharp practice with unfortunate English authors; and their flattery took the agreeable form of substantial cheques. The descendant of sea-faring Norsemen was free to indulge his love for the sea, and when living on shore he could choose his places of residence at such sunny marine resorts as Bournemouth or Torquay. As for his native Edinburgh, much as he admired it, he wisely avoided what he has denounced as the vilest climate in the world. Finally, the man who paints himself in the 'New Arabian Nights' as the misanthrope of the Fiji Sandhills, had sought a home in the South Seas where he was destined to die. But to the last he never lost touch with his countrymen, nor interest in that new world where he was naturalized; and the magician of the realms of romance was still the hardheaded Scotchman, as has been proved by his exhaustive communications to us on the troubled politics of Samoa.

The death leaves a melancholy blank in the literary world. We regret Mr. Stevenson selfishly as well as sincerely, because in the crowd of successful and rising writers there is no one left who can even approximately fill his place. He had the instincts and susceptibilities of a born man of letters, and it is noteworthy that his earliest productions were not the least finished of his works. His most marked characteristics were distinctly his own, which is only another way of saying that he had rare and special genius. Though he had innumerable admirers in his own craft animated by laudable ambition, and stimulated by no dishonourable envy, no one has rivalled, or even approached, him in his special lines. To begin with, he had the charming and exquisitely graceful style which seems to have come naturally to him, and within certain wide though well-defined limits his versatility was as remarkable as his brilliancy. His tact and self-knowledge assured him against attempting anything where he was likely to fail. Yet no one could be less monotonous in the manner of his workmanship or the selection of his subjects. Few would have predicted that the vivacious author of the uneventful 'Inland Voyage' and the 'Travels with a Donkey,' would have cast irresistible spells on the devourers of sensational fiction as the author of 'Treasure Island' or 'Dr. Jekyll and Mr. Hyde.' Yet there is evidence of the same dramatic power in all these books; although in the former the dramatic element is toned down to the sober key in which the thoughtful travels are narrated. But whether Stevenson indulged in fond and picturesque recollections of the scenes and circumstances of his childhood and youth; whether he threw off his spirited, or pathetic verses or wrote fairy tales to please childish fancies; whether he gave free rein to a wonderfully vivid imagination in his wild romances of the Scottish Highlands and the South Seas or in almost grotesque extravaganzas of superstition and crime; even when he brooded over the physical and metaphysical nightmares which shaped themselves under the master's touch into terribly impressive possibilities, the vagaries of his inspirations were invariably kept in check by exquisite taste and sound literary judgment.

That his genius had a morbid tinge there is no denying, and, indeed, it is to that we are indebted for his most marvellous *tours d'esprit.* We fancy we can trace through the varied series of his writings the sad story of failing health, of broken nights, and the sowing of the seeds of pulmonary disease. He had his moods of inspired depression and pessimism, even while the vigorous intellectual powers were still unimpaired. 'The Suicide Club,' with its forbidding title, 'The Dynamiter,' and the 'Dr. Jekyll' may suffice to show that. But even in his middle life when memory revived early recollections, what can be fresher or more healthy? When he was still in the nursery or the schoolroom, we can already trace the evidences of precocious sentimentality, but had he been less of an invalid he might have lived a man of action, and we should never have owed a debt to one of the most delightful of writers. The 'Notes on Edinburgh,' with some of the tales in 'The New Arabian Nights' throw picturesque and pleasant light on the haunts and habits of his youth. Even as a youth he had learned to shudder at the fogs and winds and gray skies of his birthplace. Yet 'the romantic town' of 'Marmion' was a 'meet nurse' for such a poetic child. He revelled in the beauties of the scene and the wild romance of the associations, from the castle on its hill, down the High-street and gloomy Canongate to the Palace of Holyrood; from 'the Heart of Midlothian' to the Queensferry of 'The Antiquary.' In fact he was sitting at the feet of Scott, whom he worshipped. Like Scott he was the best of companions and the soul of good fellowship, as is shown in the dedication to one of his novelettes, when he fondly recalls the debates in the Speculative Society and the subsequent adjournments to some favourite convivial haunt. But there is far more of Sterne than Scott in the narratives of his early wanderings. He models himself on the author of 'The Sentimental Journey,' though in more masculine vein. The 'Inland Voyage' was the travel of a romancist who consciously made mountains of molehills and who succeeded in extending the hallucination to his readers. Always original, he struck sympathetically into a vein the riches of which had for long been left unworked; and we can almost fancy that the title of 'With a Donkey in the Cevennes' was ironically meant as an aggressive challenge to critical innocence. But the reviewers took the writer pleasantly and seriously, and he might well have been proud of the eulogies of hyper-critical connoisseurs.

The stories of his philosophical wanderings and ponderings, his poetry, his essays, and his 'familiar studies' might each have entitled him to a high place in literature, but it is as the popular novelist that he will be most widely remembered. Dramatic imagination comes to the aid of a realism which vividly reflects the scenes as his fancy paints them. We are haunted with the Highland outlaws and join in the revels of the pirates. Incident succeeds swiftly to incident, and each striking situation has its direct relation to the steady development of the ingenious plot. The interest never flags, and the curiosity is perpetually being stimulated. In the incidents there is almost invariably characteristic originality, and the situations, although often unexpected, are never unnatural. Most sensational writers devote themselves to developing the stage action and are either indifferent to the interpretation of character or incapable of it. Mr. Stevenson, on the contrary, is always suggesting studies in strange individualities, or human problems which excite the curiosity of the reader. He analyzes those individualities with subtle skill, or leaves them to analyze themselves in their conduct. Not unfrequently conflicting appreciations have left a difficult problem unsolved. For example, the most competent critics differ widely in their estimates of the meaning and artistic merit of the Master of Ballantrae. Are the inconsistencies in that commanding personality conceivable? Are the redeeming touches true to nature? We fancy that Mr. Stevenson has idealized a veritable personage, with his habitual tendency towards exaggeration and eccentricity of colour. So it is with that other most impressive personage, John Silver, the smooth-spoken tavern-keeper and cook of 'Treasure Island,' who for cold-blooded truculence and diabolical astuteness might have been the favourite *élève* of Satan himself. The greatest immortals in fiction, such as Scott or George Eliot, were in the habit of painting from people they had known, though they combined the results of their studies and observations. Stevenson, although always on his guard against absurdities, seems to carry romancing into his most powerful delineations. The practice is the more effective, from the sensational point of view, that elsewhere sobriety of drawing and colouring is more strictly observed. All the other leading characters in 'Treasure Island' are probable and natural enough, though several are as picturesque as the most rugged figures in any landscape by Salvator Rosa. The squire, the doctor, and the captain are all the manner of men we might expect, although each has an exceptional dash of the heroic and adventurous. As for the pirates in retreat and the mutinous crew, they give us a marvellously graphic idea of the savage and dissipated class with whose habits Stevenson had familiarized himself. The greed for gold, the unquenchable thirst for rum, the careless joviality which drowned conscience and remorse, the recklessness of the life which was always being risked, the strange oaths, the old rollicking sea-songs, and the Nemesis of the black shadows which would haunt the most thoughtless, are all terrible truth and terrible satire. Nor are the Scotch stories less graphic. 'Kidnapped' is as full of sensation as 'Treasure Island,' with greater variety of more probable incident. When Alan is run down in the Western Seas, when he is fighting for dear life in the deck-house, when the fugitives, exhausted by thirst, heat, and hunger, are being hunted through mountains and moorland by the soldiers, and when David is cast away on the reefs off Mull, there is as much of poetry as of prose in the epic. Few could paint scenery like Stevenson, and he is as much at home in the Cevennes or the South Seas as in Scotland. Cluny Macpherson's cage on Ben Alder is worthy of 'Waverley.' And there is sharper and deeper discrimination of character in 'Kidnapped' than in any of the other stories, except, perhaps, 'The Master of Ballantrae,' and of character in self-explanatory action. We know not whether to give the higher place to the chivalrous Alan with his petty Celtic vanity or to David; Balfour's miserly and wicked old uncle. And we may remark that both these books are masterpieces in boys' stories. For though the action of the juvenile heroes is the pivot on which everything turns, there is nothing in their exploits which shocks credibility. It was in 'The Black Arrow' that Stevenson came nearest to the limits of the ground on which he prudently hesitated to venture. For necessarily even his bright imagination almost ceased to be realistic in conjuring up the dim days of the 'Wars of the Roses,' and consequently he has failed in vividly presenting what he but faintly saw himself. The simple repetition of the expression 'shrew' shows how much he was at a loss in mediæval language.

One of his charms is that he is never prolix, and his tales in the 'Arabian Nights' are marvels of sensational condensation. Take, for example, 'The Pavilion on the Links,' in which the absconding banker is tracked to his doom by the gentlemanly *carbonari* he has been foolish enough to swindle. Scarcely less thrilling is 'A Lodging for the Night,' of which that most disreputable of all the Bohemian poets, Villon, is the hero. It would be difficult, to crowd more horror with more lucid indication of vilely depraved character into briefer space, and the sinister gibbets of Montfaucon are always looming in the background, pointing their morals as the signposts of the age. If we pass from the Paris of the 15th century to London of the 19th, we have the delightfully grim humour of 'The Dynamiter' with the subcurrent of pathetic tragedy. What can be more facetious than the case of the unfortunate gentleman who cannot safely get rid of the deadly machine which is bound to explode punctually at a certain hour? The handling of the horrible and grotesque culminated in the 'Dr. Jekyll and Mr. Hyde,' where the possible discoveries of the practical chemist are pressed into the service of the supernatural. We have spoken of the little volume as the expression of a nightmare, and indeed we happen to know that it was born of a dream. It has all the effect of having been dashed off in a prolonged trance of unhealthy inspiration, and for the touches which heighten the terrors of the unholy transformation we are indebted to a not very enviable phase of genius. Very different is the impression left on us by Mr. Stevenson's poems. It is delightful to see in the 'Garden of Verses' how happily the man can identify himself with the child; how he rises in estimation and reputation when he seems to stoop. The secret is that there is nothing of effort in the little book; that the many-sided man of the world could be a child when it pleased him, and that fancy lives freshly again in the past as it followed memory back to the nursery. Take this charmingly optimistic verse, absolutely chosen at random, and say if it is not inimitable of the sort down to the propounding of the dilemma –

The child that is not clean and neat,
With lots of toys and things to eat,
He is a naughty child, I'm sure,
Or else his dear papa is poor.

Or the fancy of that other child who could not get quit of his troublesome shadow, till he left the sluggard in bed one morning when he rose before dawn.

In the 'Ballads' from the South Seas, and we wish there were many more of them, we have all the border fire of an exiled Scott or Leyden. 'The Slaying of Támátea' is said closely to follow a tradition, and it is a wonderfully powerful picture of the wild manners of pagan Tahiti. The mother of the murdered man is an Antipodean Kriemhilde, who stirs up a sanguinary revenge like the transformed and unsexed heroine of the Niebelungen-lied. We are struck by the strange yet truthful blending of the sublime and the ludicrous, for mighty events spring from trivial causes. As for 'The Feast of Famine,' it is terribly and repulsively dramatic, and is perhaps the strongest example of what we have said as to Stevenson's turn to the morbid. Yet the banqueting of the famished cannibals with all the details of the revolting preliminaries, have a horrible attraction, and when Stevenson had once decided on the choice of his subject, he could not have treated it otherwise without giving himself away. To take the taste of that, cannibal feasting out of our mouths and the scent of the sodden human flesh out of our nostrils, we have only to turn to 'Ticonderoga,' a legend of the breezy West Highlands, with which the versatile poet follows up the lyric of the Marquesas.

It is enough merely to name Mr. Stevenson's latest books, which are fresh in the public memory. By far the most remarkable is the volume which, after appearing in *Atalanta* under the title of 'David Balfour,' was published in volume form, in 1892, with the name 'Catriona.' It has the double charm of continuing the fascinating history of David and of Alan Breck, and of being Mr. Stevenson's only love-story. Later came 'The Ebb-Tide,' a story of Tahiti, written, like 'The Wrecker,' in collaboration with Mr. Lloyd Osbourne, the author's stepson. Stevenson had met in America, some ten or twelve years ago, Mrs. Osbourne, a widow with two children, and had married her; and it was with her help that he wrote 'The Dynamiter.' Lastly, we may mention the elaborate and beautiful 'Edinburgh' edition of Mr.

Stevenson's collected works, which is now being issued under the superintendence of his intimate friend Mr. Sidney Colvin. By a sad coincidence the second volume of this edition appeared on the very day of the announcement of the author's death.

> Stevenson died of a cerebral hemorrhage at Valima, the house he had built himself on the Samoan island of Upolo, on 3 December 1894. He was 44. As this obituary emphasises, he was a restless and chronically sick man who found physical relief, satisfaction and inspiration in travel. It has struck some readers as incongruous that *The Strange Case of Dr Jekyll and Mr Hyde* was written in a resort as sedate as Bournemouth, but there Stevenson had briefly settled to indulge his love of the sea. The obituary does not mention his most taxing, but ultimately rewarding, journey. In France in 1876 he fell in love with a married American woman, Fanny Vandegrift Osbourne. When she returned to California, Stevenson resolved to follow her, travelling steerage to New York on board the *Devonian* and then taking the transcontinental railroad. At Monterey he collapsed and was nursed back to health by ranchers. He finally reached San Francisco in December 1879 and married the by-then divorced Fanny in May 1880. She was ten years his senior, and was to prove both a vivid companion and a devoted nurse.

CHRISTINA ROSSETTI

Poet: 'Grace and delicacy combined with a clear and pellucid style.'

29 DECEMBER 1894

WE REGRET TO record the death of Miss Christina Georgina Rossetti, the poet, who passed quietly away at her residence in Torrington-square on Saturday. The cause of death was cancer. Two years ago Miss Rossetti underwent an operation, and during the past five months she had been a great sufferer. Her nurse was the only person present when she died. The funeral will take place to-morrow. There will be a memorial service at Christ Church, Woburn-square, at 11 a.m., and the interment will take place at Highgate Cemetery later in the day.

Miss Rossetti was the youngest of a family all of whose members attained distinction in literature. Her father, Gabriele Rossetti, an Italian poet, critic, and man of letters, was born at Vasto, in the Abruzzi – then forming part of the kingdom of Naples – in 1783, and died in London in 1854. He had escaped to England after the constitutional struggle with Ferdinand in 1821. Settling down in London, he published various original works as well as critical dissertations on Dante, and he also taught the Italian language and literature. His wife (who died in 1886) was Frances Mary Lavinia Polidori, sister of Byron's travelling physician. The Rossettis had four children – namely, Maria Francesca, author of 'A Shadow of Dante,' &c, who was born in 1827 and died in 1876; Gabriel Charles Dante, usually known as Dante Gabriel, the famous poet and artist, who was born in 1828 and died in 1882; William Michael, the critical writer and editor of Shelley, who was born in 1829, and who still survives; and Christina Georgina, whose death we announce to-day.

Miss Rossetti was born in Charlotte-street, Portland-place, London, on December 5, 1830. She was educated at home, under her accomplished mother's tuition, and early became a member of the Church of England. In her opening years she furnished evidence of inherited genius; and it is stated that while still quite a child she wrote verses, 'remarkable not only for sweetness and purity of feeling, but also for genuine singing impulse and a keen sense of fitness in the means of expression.' Before she was 17 a little volume of her poetry, entitled 'Verses by Christina G. Rossetti, dedicated to her Mother,' was privately printed by her maternal-grandfather, Gaetano Polidori, who kept a printing press for his own convenience at his residence in London. In 1830, under the *nom de plume* of 'Ellen Alleyne,' she contributed to the *Germ*, the well-known but short-lived organ of the Pre-Raphaelites, Dante Rossetti, Holman Hunt, Thomas Woolner, and others. She also contributed fugitive poems to various other magazines. Her first published work in book form, 'Goblin Market and other Poems,' appeared in 1862, and it immediately established her reputation as one of the most promising poets of the day. It was followed in 1866 by 'The Prince's Progress and other Poems.' The poem which gave the title to this volume was, perhaps, the most important and ambitious of her lengthier efforts, but it lacked the spontaneity of her shorter pieces. Her next venture was in prose. It appeared in 1870, and was entitled 'Commonplace, and other Short Stories.' While not possessing the remarkable beauty and originality of her verse, this work still manifested real elevation and purity of thought and diction. 'Sing-Song, a Nursery Rhyme Book,' was published in 1872, and 'Speaking Likenesses' – couched in quasi-allegorical Prose – in 1874. Both these volumes were illustrated by Mr. Arthur Hughes, and were specially written for children. The devotional element had been conspicuous in Miss Rossetti's earliest poetical works, and it was further exemplified in 1874 by a work exclusively devotional, '*Annus Domini*; a Prayer for each day of the year, founded on a text of Holy Scripture.' A collected edition of her poems, which included besides a considerable number of new compositions, was brought out in 1875. Then came two religious works in prose – 'Seek and Find,' and a double series of 'Short Studies of the Benedicite' – issued in 1879. In 1881 appeared 'A Pageant and other Poems,' and the same year also witnessed the production of another prose work, 'Called to the Saints: the Minor Festivals Devotionally Studied.' In 1883 appeared 'Notes on the Commandments,' and two years later a work of a similar kind, but in alternate prose and verse, entitled, 'Time Flies: a Reading Diary.' A new edition of the 'Goblin Market, the Prince's Progress, and other Poems,' was published in 1884; and again in 1890 the majority of Miss Rossetti's poems were re-issued in a collected form. Several of her lyrics were set to music, and cantatas for two of her longer poems – 'Goblin Market' and 'Songs in a Cornfield' – were composed by Mr. Aguilar and Professor Macfarren.

For many years before her death Miss Rossetti led a very secluded life, partly due to her natural shrinking from the outer world and society, and partly to her enfeebled health. Her devotion to her aged mother – who survived her husband for the long period of 32 years – was touching and beautiful. The earnest religious convictions of the deceased poetess were ever translated into daily thought and action, and her life may well be described as saintly in character. It may here be mentioned that she sat for the face and figure of the Virgin in her brother's striking early Pre-Raphaelite picture, 'The Girlhood of Mary Virgin.' He afterwards painted several other portraits of his sister.

Miss Rossetti had much of the richness of style and beauty of imagery of her still more eminent brother, though she was not capable of his sustained flights. Some of her lyrics, such as the one beginning, 'Does the road wind up-hill all the way?' produce a very vivid and lasting impression. In all that she did she was the finished artist, while her poems were able to stimulate and to elevate as well as to delight. In the sphere of the religious emotions few writers have given the world thoughts so full of beauty and pathos. While Dante Rossetti excelled in masculine vigour and artistic excellence, Christina Rossetti's qualities were rather those of grace and delicacy combined with a clear and pellucid style and a singular tenderness and sensitiveness of feeling. Her death leaves a distinct gap in the poetic literature of the time.

As this obituary clearly suggests, Christina Rossetti was reclusive both by nature and by inclination. Her later years were marked not only by her devotion to her widowed mother but also by debilitating illness. She remained a singularly devout disciple of the principles of the Oxford Movement to which she, her sister Maria and her mother had been drawn in the 1840s. This loyalty to the Church of England was a decisive factor in her ending her engagement to the painter James Collinson after his reception into the Roman Catholic Church, and may also explain why she later declined to marry the translator Charles Cayley. She died on the morning of 29 December 1894 and was buried in the family plot at Highgate Cemetery on 5 January 1895. Her tombstone was later enigmatically inscribed with a quotation from Dante chosen by her brother, William Michael Rossetti: *Volsersi a me con salutevol cenno* ('They turned to me with signs of salutation').

T. H. HUXLEY

Naturalist and President of the Royal Society: 'a power of popular exposition almost unequalled'.

29 JUNE 1895

WE MUCH REGRET to announce the death of the Right Honourable Thomas Henry Huxley, which took place at his residence, Hodeslea, Staveley-road, Eastbourne, on Saturday. In the beginning of March Mr. Huxley had an attack of influenza. Bronchitis supervened, and lung and kidney complaints soon manifested themselves. There was also cardiac affection of long standing.

Against his many ailments Mr. Huxley struggled with wonderful vitality and cheerfulness. His mental acuteness was never impaired, and he took pleasure in both reading and writing up to the last week of his illness. In fact he read up to the day before his death. Through all his sufferings he preserved that amiable and kindly disposition which made him so beloved in his own household. Dr. Burney Yeo and Mr. H. D. Farnell, of Eastbourne, the Professor's regular medical adviser, and Dr. Huxley (his son) had a consultation as late as Friday, and it was found that, owing to exhaustion life was gradually ebbing away. There was a possibility, however, of his lasting some time; but on Saturday morning the patient became so much worse that all hope was abandoned, and he passed peacefully away in the afternoon at half-past 3 o'clock. Mrs. Huxley and one of her daughters were present at the last, and other members of the family arrived shortly after death.

The funeral has been fixed to take place at Finchley Cemetery on Thursday afternoon, at 3 o'clock.

Thomas Henry Huxley was born on May 4, 1825, at what was then the village of Ealing, in the semi-public school of which his father was one of the masters. This school he attended for a few years, but his educational progress was largely due to his own private efforts. At an early period he became familiar enough with German to plunge into the scientific literature of that language, and he seems to have got some help from a brother-in-law who was a medical man. In 1842 he entered the medical school attached to Charing-cross Hospital, where at that time Mr. Wharton Jones, distinguished alike as an oculist and physiologist, was lecturing on physiology. In 1845 he passed the first M.B. examination at the University of London, taking honours in Anatomy and Physiology. Even before this he had given evidence that his mind was occupied with something more than the technical

details of the medical profession, for, while yet a student at Charing-cross Hospital, he had sent a brief notice to the *Medical Times* and *Gazette* of that layer in the root-sheath of hair which has since borne the name of Huxley's Layer. After devoting himself for a short time to the practice of his profession among the poor of

London, he, in 1846, joined the medical service of the Royal Navy and was sent to Haslar Hospital. Here he did not remain long, but, like so many other men who have made their mark in biological science, set out on a voyage round the world.

Through the influence of the distinguished naturalist Sir John Richardson, who had accompanied Franklin in his early Arctic expeditions, young Huxley was given the post of assistant-surgeon on her Majesty's ship Rattlesnake, then about to proceed on a surveying voyage to the southern seas. The ship sailed from England in the winter of 1846 and did not return until November, 1850. She was commanded by Captain Owen Stanley, whose name is attached to a well-known range of mountains in British New Guinea, and during the greater part of the time the Rattlesnake was employed in surveying the eastern and northern coasts of Australia and the coasts of New Guinea. The seas lying between the great barrier reef and the coast of the mainland were of special interest to the naturalist. Huxley took ample advantage of his opportunities to study the fauna of the seas which he traversed, with the results known to all naturalists. The communications which he sent home during the voyage made his name well known to the scientific world even before his return. Several of these were published in the 'Philosophical Transactions' of the Royal Society, and it is interesting to note that the first which so appeared was presented to the society by the then Bishop of Norwich, and read June 21, 1849. It bears the title 'On the Anatomy and Affinities of the Medusae.' Huxley in vain endeavoured to obtain the publication by the Government of a part of the work done during his voyage, and it was not until 1859 that his great work, entitled 'Oceanic Hydrozon, a description of the Calycophoridae and Physophoridae observed during the voyage of her Majesty's ship Rattlesnake,' was given to the world.

The reputation which he had already attained at the early age of 26 is evident from the fact that in the year after his return, 1851, he was elected a Fellow of the Royal Society, and in 1852 was awarded one of the society's Royal medals. In 1853 he left the Naval Service, and the following year, on the removal of Edward Forbes from the Royal School of Mines to the chair of Natural History in Edinburgh, Huxley was appointed Professor of Natural History, including palæontology, in that institution, a post which he held until his retirement at the age of 60 – an age at which he used to declare every scientific man ought to commit the happy despatch. In the same year, 1854, he was appointed Fullerian Professor of Physiology to the Royal Institution and Examiner in Physiology and Comparative Anatomy to the University of London. Other posts and honours crowded thick upon him. From 1863 to 1869 he held the post of Hunterian Professor at the Royal College of Surgeons. In 1862 he was President of the Biological Section at the Cambridge meeting of the British Association, and eight years later held the Presidency of the Association at the Liverpool meeting. In 1869 and 1870 he was president of the Geological and Ethnological Societies. As might be expected, Professor Huxley held strong and well-defined views on the subject of education. He was a man who at all times had a keen sense of public duty, and it was this which induced him to seek election on the first London School Board in 1870. Ill-health compelled him to retire from that post in 1872, but during his period of service as chairman of the Education Committee he did much to mould the scheme of education adopted in the Board schools.

He was elected secretary of the Royal Society in 1873, and ten years later was called to the highest honorary position which an English scientific man can fill, the presidency of that society. During the absence of the late Professor Sir Wyville Thomson with the Challenger Expedition, Huxley, in 1875 and 1876, took his place as Professor of Natural History in the University of Edinburgh. From 1881 to 1885 he acted as Inspector of Salmon Fisheries. But this and all his other official posts he resigned in 1885, shortly after which he removed to Eastbourne.

During the 34 years that elapsed between his return from the Rattlesnake voyage and his retirement from his various official posts, Huxley's activity as an investigator, as a writer, as a lecturer, as a citizen of London and of England, and as a man of healthy social instincts was incessant. There is hardly a department in the wide field of zoology, in its most comprehensive sense, in which he has not done original work. Huxley's investigations have explained many difficult problems in the mechanism of men and animals. So far as the character of his work is concerned, he is to be compared rather with Owen than with Darwin; though not only was the quality of his work more solid and enduring, but in many ways his type of mind was essentially different from that of Owen, more liberal, more open, free from what may perhaps be called the pettiness which hampered Owen's scientific vision. Huxley's investigations, it may fairly be said, especially after the publication of the 'Origin of Species,' were to a large extent guided by the Darwinian theory, and the results may be regarded as among the most substantial confirmations and illustrations of the doctrine of evolution as propounded by Darwin. In order to illustrate the condition of Huxley's own mind and the stage which biological investigation had reached at the date of the 'Origin of Species,' we cannot do better than give an extract from the interesting chapter contributed by him to the 'Life of Darwin' on the 'Reception of the "Origin of Species"':–

> 'I think I must have read the "Vestiges" before I left England in 1846, but if I did the book made very little impression upon me, and I was not brought into serious contact with the "species" question until after 1850. At that time I had long done with the Pentateuchal cosmogony which had been impressed upon my childish understanding as Divine truth with all the authority of parents and instructors, and from which it had cost me many a struggle to get free. But my mind was unbiased in respect of any doctrine which presented itself if it

professed to be based on purely philosophical and scientific reasoning. I had not then and I have not now the smallest *a priori* objection to raise to the account of the creation of animals and plants given in "Paradise Lost," in which Milton so vividly embodies the natural sense of Genesis. Far be it from me to say that it is untrue because it is impossible. I confine myself to what must be regarded as a modest and reasonable request for some particle of evidence that the existing species of animals and plants did originate in that way as a condition of my belief in a statement which appears to me to be highly improbable.

And by way of being perfectly fair, I had exactly the same answer to give to the evolutionists of 1851–8. Within the ranks of the biologists of that time I met with nobody, except Dr. Grant, of University College, who had a word to say for evolution, and his advocacy was not calculated to advance the cause. Outside these ranks the only person known to me whose knowledge and capacity compelled respect, and who was at the same time a thoroughgoing evolutionist, was Mr. Herbert Spencer, whose acquaintance I made, I think, in 1852, and then entered into the bonds of a friendship which I am happy to think has known no interruption. Many and prolonged were the battles we fought on this topic till even my friend's rare dialectic skill and copiousness of apt illustration could not drive me from my agnostic position. I took my stand upon two grounds firstly, that up to that time the evidence in favour of transmutation was wholly insufficient; and, secondly, that no suggestion respecting the causes of the transmutation assumed which had been made was in any way adequate to explain the phenomena. Looking back at the state of knowledge at that time, I really do not see that any other conclusion was justifiable.

As I have already said, I imagine that most of those of my contemporaries who thought seriously about the matter were very much in my own state of mind – inclined to say to both Mosaists and Evolutionists "A plague on both your houses!" and disposed to turn aside from an interminable and apparently fruitless discussion to labour in the fertile fields of ascertainable fact. And I may therefore further suppose that the publication of the Darwin and Wallace papers in 1859, and still more that of the "Origin" in 1859, had the effect upon them of the flash of light, which to a man who has lost himself in a dark night suddenly reveals a road which, whether it takes him straight home or not, certainly goes his way. That which we were looking for and could not find was a hypothesis respecting the origin of known organic forms which assumed the operation of no causes but such as could be proved to be actually at work. We wanted, not to pin our faith to that or any other speculation, but to get hold of clear and definite conceptions which could be brought face to face with facts and have their validity tested. The "Origin" provided us with the working hypothesis we sought. Moreover, it did the immense service of freeing us for ever from the dilemma – refuse to accept the creation hypothesis, and what have you to propose that can be accepted by any cautious reasoner? In 1857 I had no answer ready, and I do not think that any one else had. A year later we reproached ourselves with dullness for being perplexed by such an inquiry. My reflection, when I first made myself master of the central idea of the "Origin" was "how extremely stupid not to have thought of that!" I suppose that Columbus' companions said much the same when he made the egg stand on end. The facts of variability, of the struggle for existence, of adaptation to conditions, were notorious enough, but none of us had suspected that the road to the heart of the species problem lay through them, until Darwin and Wallace dispelled the darkness, and the beacon-fire of the "Origin" guided the benighted.'

It was, then, in the searching rays of this new light that Huxley, like so many others during the last 35 years, carried on his many-sided work. Here, even if space permitted, it would be inappropriate to deal in detail with his many investigations in both vertebrate and invertebrate life. While his work in the latter field is of high importance, it was to the structure and physiology of vertebrate animals that he devoted most of his energy. In the year before the publication of the 'Origin' he chose as the subject of his Royal Society Croonian Lecture 'The Theory of the Vertebrate Skull,' in which, so high an authority as Professor Haeckel assures us, he first opened out the right track to a solution of a perplexing problem. Much of Huxley's technical work was published through the Royal Society, the Geological Survey, the Geological Society, and other media familiar to specialists, but never consulted even by the educated general public. To give a mere list of these many memoirs would serve no purpose. Such important subjects are dealt with as the Evolution of the Crocodilia, the Classification of Birds, the Dinosauria, Fossil Fishes, Glyptodon, the Affinity between Reptiles and Birds, Ceratodus, the Cranial and Dental Structure of the Canidae, Reproduction and Morphology of Aphis, the Development of Pyrosoma. These few from among the titles of many memoirs will suffice to show that Huxley's special researches deal with the history and structure of animals of many types, and that by themselves they would justify the verdict of Ernest Haeckel that Huxley was the first zoologist among his countrymen. In this connexion may be mentioned his 'Manual of the Invertebrata,' his 'Lessons in Elementary Physiology,' and other text books. 'When we consider the long series of distinguished memoirs with which,' to quote Haeckel, 'Professor Huxley has enriched zoological literature, we find that in each of the larger divisions of the animal kingdom we are indebted to him for important discoveries ... More important than any of the individual discoveries which are contained in Huxley's numerous less and greater researches on the most widely different animals, are the profound and truly philosophical conceptions which have guided him in his inquiries, have always enabled him to distinguish the essential from the unessential, and to value special empirical facts chiefly as a means of arriving at general ideas.'

Huxley had a power of popular exposition almost unequalled. He could make plain, even to an ordinary working-man audience, the bearings of the most recondite researches of the zoologist and botanist; witness his famous Norwich lecture 'On a Piece of Chalk,' and the memorable sermon which he gave on a Sunday evening a quarter of a century ago in the midst of shocked Edinburgh. But it is not only to the ordinary intelligent reader that his numerous lectures, addresses, and magazine articles appeal. It is to these in their collected form that the special inquirer must go to find the broad results of Huxley's arduous scientific investigations. It was his duty when first he assumed his post in the School of Mines to give a course of lectures every alternate year to working men; and it was through this channel that he first gave to the world his remarkable discussion on 'Man's Place in Nature.' This was one of the earliest and one of the most striking results of the publication of the Darwinian theory, for it was given to the world some ten years before the publication of Darwin's 'Descent of Man.' Even by those who maintain that influences have been at work in the development of man additional to those which have been common to him and the lower animals, it may be said that Huxley's conclusions as to the intimate relations between humanity and the higher apes have been generally accepted. It was in the same 'popular' form that Huxley gave to the world many other theories and disquisitions which have had much to do with moulding educated opinion during the last quarter of a century. Thus in his three addresses as President of the Geological Society on 'Geological Contemporaneity and Persistent Types of Life,' on 'Geological Reform,' and on 'Palaeontology and the Doctrine of Evolution,' he dealt in his characteristically clear and masterly manner with problems that still agitate evolutionists – the imperfection of the record, the duration of geological time, the succession of life on the face of the earth, and other matters of profound interest to geologists and biologists. In his papers on 'The Methods and Results of Ethnology' and on 'Some Fixed Points in British Ethnology' he introduced into the somewhat chaotic branch of investigation that deals with man a simplicity of treatment and a scientific method which have done much to raise it above a mere collection of unrelated facts. The lectures delivered in America in 1876 brought together the *data* as to the evolution of the horse with a cogency that forms one of the most telling arguments in favour of the Darwinian hypothesis.

In an equally 'popular' form Huxley dealt with matters of profound human interest and of the widest bearings. Much of what he has written, for example, on the relation of science to religion, and especially to Christianity, has appeared in the form of magazine articles. In these writings, as in his more purely scientific work, while he does not spare what he believes to be erroneous views and misinterpretation of facts, his candour and open mindedness are ever evident. He never hesitates to expose the sophistries, misconceptions, and unfair assumptions of his own side, even at the risk of weakening his own position. Take, for example, the short paper in the 'Lay Sermons,' on 'Emancipation – Black and White.' Among other things he deals with and advocates the 'emancipation' and higher education of women, but he does not for a moment allow it to be inferred that he believes in the equality of the sexes. In these days when 'sexuality' has become so rampant the whole paper is well worth reprinting if only to let the 'new woman' see what a man of Huxley's keenness of insight thought of her. We cannot forbear quoting one passage:–

> 'And the result? For our parts, though loth to prophesy, we believe it to be that of other emancipations. Women will find their place, and it will neither be that in which they have been held nor that to which some of them aspire. Nature's old Salique law will not be repealed and no change of dynasty will be effected. The big chests, the massive brains, the vigorous muscles and stout frames of the best men will carry the day whenever it is worth their while to contest the prizes of life with the best women. And the hardship of it is that the very improvement of the women will lessen their chances . . . The most Darwinian of theorists will not venture to propound the doctrine that the physical disabilities under which women have hitherto laboured in the struggle for existence with men are likely to be removed by even the most skilfully conducted process of educational selection . . . The duty of man is to see that not a grain is piled upon her load beyond what nature imposes, that injustice is not added to inequality.'

It was the robust sense which marks this passage that prevented Huxley from being carried beyond bounds in applying the doctrine of evolution either to scientific investigation or to practical life. The subject will also serve as a sample of the wide field of his interests. Both metaphysics and theology seem to have had a sort of fascination for him; in the former case shown by his admirable little book on Hume and his paper on Bishop Berkeley, and in the latter by his many divagations in magazine and review articles on subjects more or less connected with Christian doctrine and belief. However hardly in these essays he may have dealt with his opponent's position, he rarely, if ever, went beyond the bounds of courtesy, or exhibited the irascibility and intemperance of language of his friend Tyndall.

That he did sometimes allow his Darwinian enthusiasm to run away with him must be admitted even by his warmest admirers. In any notice of the career of Huxley it would be unpardonable to omit some mention of the famous *Bathybius* incident. The slimy mass which Huxley in 1868 conceived to be the elementary form of animal life and called after Haeckel *Bathlybius Haekeli,* and which was hailed by extreme Darwinists as a triumphant proof of the great theory turned out to be merely a calcareous precipitate. Huxley was honest enough to abandon his embryonic child, and naturally there was a great outcry among anti-Darwinists, an outcry wholly unreasonable. But the great biologist made very few mistakes of this kind, even in the hot period when he acted as the sworn champion of the newly launched 'Origin of Species.' It is interesting here to recall the fact that probably the first review of the 'Origin of Species' was written by Professor Huxley for *The Times*, under what circumstances will be found narrated in 'The Life of Charles Darwin.' One notable instance of his championship occurred at the Oxford meeting of the British Association in June, 1860. Bishop Wilberforce defended the then orthodox views and 'ridiculed Darwin badly and Huxley savagely.' He so far forgot himself as to ask Huxley whether he was related by his grandfather's or grandmother's side to an ape. One who was present states that 'Huxley replied to the scientific argument of his opponent with force and eloquence, and to the personal allusion with a self-restraint that gave dignity to his crushing rejoinder.' The exciting incident was a triumph for the new-born doctrine. A contrast to this stormy meeting was that of the same Association in Oxford 34 years later (August, 1894), when again the Darwinian theory was, if not exactly attacked, at least somewhat keenly criticized by one of the sanest of our politicians, who is also entitled to respect for his practical acquaintance with science, Lord Salisbury. Not less dignified were the words used by Professor Huxley on this occasion than those just referred to. His words may be regarded as a declaration of his scientific faith at the end of his long and busy career.

As evolution and the Darwinian attempt to explain it have been confounded, so Huxley's agnosticism has often been rashly identified with materialism, positivism, and even atheism. At the conclusion of his famous sermon on the Physical Basis of Life he repudiated the first with vehemence. He certainly did not believe that matter was the only thing in the universe. The positivism of Comte he almost despised; and nothing could be more unjust to a man of so absolutely sceptical a mind as Huxley than to charge him with anything so rashly positive as atheism. Agnostic is the only epithet that can adequately describe his attitude to what lies beyond the cognizance of our five senses. He is gone, but his work, as well as his works, remains. The latter may to a future generation become antiquated and unreadable, but the influence of the former upon the thought of the last 35 years has been deep and wide. It must be taken into account in any attempt to estimate the forces which have been at work to mould the intellectual, moral, and social life of the century. Whatever the verdict may be as to the character of Huxley's influence, it cannot but be admitted that he exercised his great powers with a seriousness of responsibility and with an unwavering loyalty to what he conceived to be the truth. What were the aims and motives of the man cannot be better expressed than in a passage which occurs in the brief autobiographical introduction to his collected essays:–

> The last thing that it would be proper for me to do would be to speak of the work of my life or to say at the end of the day whether I think I have earned my wages or not . . .
>
> But if I may speak of the objects I have had more or less definitely in view since I began the ascent of my hillock, they are briefly these:– To promote the increase of natural knowledge and to forward the application of scientific methods of investigation to all the problems of life to the best of my ability, in the conviction, which has grown with my growth and strengthened with my strength, that there is no alleviation for the sufferings of mankind except veracity of thought and of action, and the resolute facing of the world as it is when the garment of make-believe by which pious hands have hidden its uglier features is stripped off.

Honours were showered upon Huxley by learned societies and Universities both at home and abroad. On his retirement in 1885 he retained his connexion with the Royal School of Mines and the Normal School of Science as Dean and Honorary Professor of Biology, at the request of the Lord President. One of the last acts of the Marquis of Salisbury on leaving office in 1892 was to confer upon Professor Huxley the dignity of Privy Councillor. It was understood that he had been offered a baronetcy, which, as might have been expected, he declined.

One of Huxley's latest tasks was to superintend a complete edition of all his non-technical writings in nine volumes. It is by these, no doubt, he would wish to be judged by thinking men in the future. Reference has been made to Huxley's wonderful power of clear exposition. Apart from that, his skill in the use of our language entitles his writings to take a high rank as literature. He himself was familiar with the masterpieces of German, French, and Italian, as well as English, literature, and in this respect he stood in marked contrast to Darwin. Mr. Huxley leaves a widow and a numerous family.

It was Huxley who first coined the term 'agnostic', and this obituary judges well how the term can be broadly applied to his life and thought. He was Darwin's doughtiest, though not always most cautious, apologist and disciple, and it was Huxley who managed to trounce the rashly provocative Samuel Wilberforce, the Bishop of Oxford, in a public debate on the implications of Darwinian theory held at the Oxford Museum in 1860. When Wilberforce attempted to clinch his argument by asking from which side of his family did Huxley claim simian descent, Huxley won applause by responding, 'I would rather be the offspring of two apes than be a man and afraid to face the truth.'

FRIEDRICH ENGELS

German political philosopher:
'He has seen the grain sown by him burst upward.'

5 AUGUST 1895

FREDERICK ENGELS, the Socialist leader, whose death we briefly announced yesterday, was the son of a German manufacturer, and was born in 1820. At the age of 22 he was sent to Manchester in connection with his father's cotton business. He remained for two years, and then returned to Germany by way of Paris, where he met Karl Marx. From 1844 onwards he was actively engaged in the Socialist propaganda, and in 1847 he and Marx published the famous 'Communist Manifesto,' which was rapidly translated into most of the European languages. He returned to business at Manchester in 1850, and in 1864 he was made partner in the firm, but retired in 1869. He then proceeded to London, where he met Marx, and the two worked together, first on the *Deutsch-Französische Jahrbücher* and subsequently upon the *Neue Rheinische Zeitung*. Since the death of Marx he had been a kind of literary executor to his friend. Engels's own original works include 'The Condition of the Working Classes of England,' 'Origin of the Family,' and a work left unfinished, a portion of which has been published in England under the title of 'Socialism, Scientific and Utopian.' From the year 1870 Engels was corresponding secretary for the International for Belgium, Spain, and Italy. He has left a strong and durable impress upon the Socialist movement in Europe. Our Paris Correspondent telegraphs:– The death of Frederick Engels has called forth in the *Petite République* the following eulogy:– 'Engels, no one will deny, was, with Saint-Simon, Fourier, and Marx, one of the least disputable fathers of the Socialist doctrine. It was under his influence, owing to his pen, that it has assumed that character of rigour and scientific precision which we love in it . . . More fortunate than Marx, Engels almost touched the promised land towards which he had endeavoured to direct the steps of a distrusting proletariat. He has seen the grain sown by him burst upward, increase and bud with the first branches which will one day cover the world with their protecting shade. It is not as a conquered man doubting his work that he disappears, but as one who has triumphed.'

Engels died of throat cancer on 5 August 1895. He had come to England in 1842 to work for the Salford textile firm of Ermen and Engels, in which his father had shares. From this time in Manchester, and from his relationship with Mary Burns (a woman he declined to marry due to his disdain for the institution of marriage), Engels learned enough about working class life in an industrial city to write his important study, *The Condition of the Working Class in England*, published in German in 1845 but not translated into English until an American edition was published in 1885. A British edition, with a new preface by Engels, appeared in January 1892. Engels had returned to the Continent in 1844, but was obliged to resume his work in Manchester as a refugee in 1849. From the profits of his family firm he was able to support Karl Marx and his family, who were now resident in London. Engels himself moved to London in 1870 and took up residence at 122 Regent's Park Road, Primrose Hill. Engels's remains were cremated and his ashes scattered off Beachy Head.

* * *

LOUIS PASTEUR

Chemist and microbiologist: 'He surely deserves to be ranked among the greatest benefactors of humanity.'

28 SEPTEMBER 1895

SELDOM HAVE THE benefits conferred by science upon humanity been more direct and more patent than has been the case with the long series of researches conducted by Louis Pasteur. As has almost invariably been the case when science has conferred a lasting boon on humanity, this eminent chemist began his work with no thought of anything but his science; but, as so often has happened in the disinterested pursuit of knowledge, the results have been far-reaching and beneficent. The world at large has only recently heard of Pasteur in connexion with his famous 'cure' for one of the most terrible afflictions of mankind – hydrophobia. But this was only the culmination of a lifelong series of researches into the lowest forms of life. Pasteur's work was long ago well known to brewers, to agriculturists, to stock-rearers, to viticulturists and the followers of other industries, and by them he was universally recognized as a benefactor. To the chemist and biologist his name, it need hardly be said, was a household word.

Louis Pasteur was born nearly 73 years ago – in December 27, 1822 – at Dôle in the Jura, the son of a tanner, who had fought his country's battles with honour. Shortly after Louis's birth the family removed to Arbois, and here Louis was educated at the Communal College. Thence he went to the College of Besançon, and in 1843 was admitted to the Ecole Normale at Paris. Chemistry had become his favourite subject even at Besançon and under Dumas at Paris, as may be imagined his devotion was intensified. Pasteur worked hard both at chemistry and physics. He took his doctor's degree in 1847, and in the following year was appointed Professor of Physics at Strasburg University. In 1854 he removed to Lille, where he was appointed Dean of the Faculty of Science. Three years later he returned to Paris as Scientific Director of the Ecole Normale, and in 1867 he was appointed Professor of Chemistry at the Sorbonne. In recent years his Headquarters have been at the Pasteur Institute founded for him for the purpose of carrying out his invaluable bacteriological investigations.

Pasteur's earliest original researches, undertaken at the suggestion of M. Delafosse, who was specially interested in molecular physics, dealt with crystals. These were connected with an investigation of extreme delicacy into the differences which existed between the tartrate and the paratartrate of soda and ammonia. Into the technicalities of Pasteur's discoveries as to that nature and relations of these two isometric bodies, it would be out of place to enter here. A great anomaly was explained and a great problem solved. Moreover, the elaborate research, which occupied Pasteur six years, led him on to researches in other and more practical directions – researches which would scarcely have been possible if this initial problem had not been solved. So long ago as 1856 Pasteur's reputation had spread beyond France; in that year our Royal Society awarded him its Rumford medal for his researches on the Polarization of light, &c.

His next great scientific undertaking, with a practical end in view, was suggested by the chief industry at Lille, where, it has been seen, he was Dean of the Faculty of Science. The manufacture of alcohol from beetroot and corn was of the first importance to Lille. The methods followed seem to have been of a somewhat empirical character, and Pasteur saw that great improvements were possible, not only in this particular industry, but in the brewing of beer, of which, so far as the French market was concerned, Germany and Austria had the monopoly. This naturally led Pasteur to make an exhaustive investigation into the great and complicated subject of fermentation. The result was not simply important to the manufacture of spirits at Lille, but initiated the creation of what may be regarded as a new industry in France, the manufacture of beer on scientific principles. Certainly in this respect Pasteur was a great benefactor to his country, though as a matter of fact it is doubtful if beer of native manufacture has ever been so highly appreciated in France as that imported from the country of the enemy. But it was not only France that benefited by the results of Pasteur's researches, they have become the common property of brewers all the world over. In these investigations he was led from one stage to another, always bringing the microscope to the aid of his chemical methods, until he was convinced that all forms of fermentation were due to the action of minute living organisms. Only those who are familiar with the history of chemistry will recognize the magnitude of the innovation on accepted doctrines involved in Pasteur's theory. But the irresistible logic of facts convinced all impartial students of the essential truth of what is popularly known as the germ theory. It explained many obscurities in science, both in chemistry and biology, and its practical bearings soon became evident. Of course, others had been working in this direction before Pasteur – Appert, Caignard-Latour, Schwann, Heilmholtz – but it may with truth be said that it was Pasteur who put his finger on the real secret, who discovered nature's actual method of work in all those processes of which fermentation may be regarded as the typical example. To quote the words of Sir James Paget:–

> 'He proved the constant presence of living micro-organisms, not only in yeast, in which Caignard-Latour and Schwann, especially, had studied them, but in all the fermenting substances that he examined; he proved the certain and complete prevention of fermentation, putrefaction, and other similar processes in many substances, however naturally subject to them, by the exclusion of all micro-organisms and other germs, or by their destruction if present; and he proved the constant presence of various micro-organisms and their germs in the air, in the water, in the earth, in dust and dirt of every kind – their abundance "everywhere".'

The discovery of this vast hidden field of activity in nature has been fruitful in the most remarkable discoveries and the most beneficent applications. A whole world of obscure phenomena has been explained to science; diseases of various kinds have been traced to their birthplaces; much suffering has been spared to men and animals, and multitudes of lives have been saved. It was seen how these germ-diseases could be met and prevented, and Lister, carrying out Pasteur's discoveries into practice, devised the method, known by his name, and now all but universally applied in surgery. Pasteur carried his war against disease into the enemy's country, so to speak; he fought the battle against the foes of life and health with disease's own weapons. He found that every form of what may be called putrefactive diseases had its own particular bacillus, which could be separated from all others and cultivated. If allowed to work in their own way, and at their normal strength, the micro-organisms which produce contagious diseases work havoc upon living beings. But Pasteur found they could be attenuated and diluted, and when administered in their attenuated form by means of inoculation, the strength being gradually increased, the disease was contracted in a mild form, and all its deleterious consequences avoided. Of course, the fact that small-pox could be fought in this way is an old discovery; but it remained for Pasteur to discover the great principle which underlies such diseases, and to show how widely applicable was the preventive method which had been so effective in small-pox. To the agriculturists he did eminent service by showing how certain diseases in fowls and sheep could be met more than half way. His researches in splenic fever fully confirmed the discovery of Davaine. Koch's application of the principle to phthisis is well known. Less cautious and patient than Pasteur, he can hardly be said to have yet succeeded. Pasteur's greatest achievement in this direction, an achievement which drew upon him the attention and the blessings of all the world, was the discovery of an antidote to hydrophobia. Into the discussion of the absolute validity of this antidote we cannot enter; the evidence in its favour is so strong that in the opinion of impartial and competent judges Pasteur has been able to rob one of the most appalling afflictions of humanity of much of its terror.

It is not possible to recount in detail all the services rendered by Pasteur through the application of scientific discoveries, to industry and humanity. For a time (1865 onwards) he was diverted from his own special researches to cope, at the request of his master Dumas, with the disease which had been rendering havoc among silkworms, and affecting the silk industry of France to the extent of millions annually. He found that the minute 'corpuscle' found among the silkworms was really a disease germ, and by a careful series of experiments demonstrated that its havoc could be greatly diminished if not stopped by taking measures to prevent the propagation of diseased eggs. While carrying out this good work Pasteur spent several months every year for four years in a little house near Alais, where he watched every step in the life of silkworms bred by himself and others. Unfortunately, in 1868, he had a paralytic attack, from which he recovered, but which left him for life comparatively powerless on the left side. Again, the sad events connected with the Franco-German war interrupted his work, but for the past 20 years he has been constantly active in developing in many directions the great principle to which he may be said to have been the first to give precise and manageable form. 'It would be useless,' again to quote Sir James Paget, 'to imagine the probabilities of what will now follow from the researches that have already followed the discoveries of Pasteur.' He surely deserves to be ranked among the greatest benefactors of humanity.

On December 27th, 1892, Pasteur's 70th birthday was celebrated in the Sorbonne in a manner which, as *The Times* Correspondent stated at the time, affected all present. It was a great international gathering. England was represented by Sir James Lister, and the gold medal which was presented to the veteran investigator was subscribed for by representatives of science of various countries. On that occasion the most illustrious of Pasteur's English disciples said:–

> 'There is certainly not in the entire world a single person to whom medical science is more indebted than to you. Your researches on fermentation have thrown a flood of light which has illuminated the gloomy shadows of surgery and changed the treatment of wounds from a matter of doubtful and too often disastrous empiricism into a scientific art, certain and beneficent. Owing to you surgery has undergone a complete revolution. It has been stripped of its terrors, and its efficiency has been almost unlimitedly enlarged. But medicine owes as much to your profound and philosophic studies as surgery. You have raised the veil which had for centuries covered infectious diseases. You have discovered and proved their microbic nature; and, thanks to your initiation, and in many cases to your own special labour, there are already a host of these destructive diseases of which we now completely know the causes. This knowledge has already perfected in a surprising way the diagnosis of certain plagues of the human race and has marked out the course which must be followed in their prophylactic and curative treatment. Medicine and surgery are eager on this great occasion to offer you the profound homage of their admiration and their gratitude.'

If ever a man deserved a great international monument, it is surely this modest, unassuming, gentle, and humane French chemist, who has done more than most men to initiate the millennium. In his own science he ranks amongst the highest. The variety and multitude of his researches may be learned by a glance at the Royal Society List (where the titles of 137 papers are given), or into the pages of the *Comptes-Rendus* of the Academy of Sciences. Among his books are works on fermentation, on wine and its diseases, on the diseases of silkworms, and on beer. It need hardly be said that honours were showered upon Pasteur. He was a Grand Officer of the Legion of Honour. He was early elected to the Paris Academy of Sciences, and some 13 years ago to the Institute. Of our own Royal Society he was a medallist and a foreign member. He held the Albert Medal of the Society of Arts. The French Government long ago recognized his services by an annuity of 12,000f. The Pasteur Institute in Paris was built at a cost of £100,000, and since its completion both the French public and the French Government have contributed handsomely to the maintenance of an institution which, through the genius and disinterestedness of its chief, waged war not only against hydrophobia, but also against many other deadly foes of the human race and the domesticated animals.

Similar institutes have been founded in other countries; in London the British Institute of Preventive Medicine is conducted on the same lines as the Pasteur Institute under the able direction of Dr. Ruffer, and has more than justified its existence by the good work it has done in connexion with the anti-toxin treatment of diphtheria. It may with more truth be said of Pasteur than can be said of most eminent men that his death is a very great loss to humanity. His work will be taken up by others; let them follow his method and advice – 'N'avancez rien qui ne puisse être prouvé d'une façon simple et décisive.'

Such was Pasteur's international fame as the century's greatest scientific benefactor of humankind that the French government was anxious to commemorate him with a tomb in the Panthéon. This offer was declined by Pasteur's staunchly Catholic family. He is now interred in a purpose-built mausoleum in the Musée Pasteur in Paris. The museum itself is housed in the apartment in which Pasteur had lived from November 1888 to the time of his death in the Institut Pasteur. He had initiated a great international campaign for funds to found and develop the new research institute following the acclaimed introduction of his vaccine against rabies. Despite the first of his several debilitating strokes in 1868, Pasteur had remained an active researcher until well into his sixties.

LORD LEIGHTON

Painter and sculptor:
'He had no predecessors in English art, and leaves no one to succeed him.'

25 JANUARY 1896

WE ANNOUNCE WITH deep regret the death of Lord Leighton, President of the Royal Academy, which took place on Saturday afternoon at his residence, 2, Holland-park-road, Kensington.

Early last year Sir Frederic Leighton, as he was then, saw his friend Dr. Lauder Brunton, and subsequently Sir William Broadbent, in consultation with his usual medical attendant, Dr. Roberts, for some heart affection. He was with some difficulty dissuaded from presiding at the Academy dinner, and went abroad to Algeria. Since then, though frequently suffering attacks of pain, he continued to fulfil most of his numerous engagements. Last Monday he caught a slight cold, but seemed fairly to have recovered, when, on Thursday morning, severe symptoms set in suddenly, and Dr. Roberts and Dr. Lauder Brunton were in early attendance. On Thursday evening pain and heart distress became very severe, and Dr. Barton sat by his bedside all night. The pain and difficulty of breathing increasing, it was decided in the early hours of Friday morning to administer morphia, which greatly relieved him; and after some hours' quiet sleep he woke so much relieved that some hope of recovery was entertained. The pain was incessant all Friday, but was partially relieved by morphia, and even then hope was not abandoned. Dr. Barton again remained with him all Friday night, and undertook the nursing, but on Saturday morning a change for the worse set in, and the gravest fears were entertained. About noon it was evident that the end was fast approaching, the pain and distress becoming intense, and he passed away a few hours later, the last moments being free from pain, due to the merciful administration of chloroform. At his bedside were his two sisters, Mrs. Matthews and Mrs. Sutherland Orr, Dr. Barton, Mr. Prinsep, R. A., and his intimate friend, Mr. S. Pepys Cockerell. To them he uttered almost his last words, 'Love to the Academy and all its members.'

To the public at large Lord Leighton's death will be a painful shock. It was hoped that he had fully recovered from his illness of last spring – a hope that seemed confirmed by his recent visits to the Royal Academy on the occasion of the students' prize-giving on December 11 and at a private Academy dinner on the last day of the year, when he was able to announce that the Queen had honoured him with the offer of a peerage. It was understood a day or two later that he would take the title of Lord Leighton. He attended also a meeting of the council of the Academy as lately as the 9th of this month; and he has frequently within the last week or two appeared and chatted with friends at the Athenaeum Club, a favourite resort of his in the afternoon.

The news of Lord Leighton's death was telegraphed to the Queen by the officials of the Royal Academy, and her Majesty has telegraphed a message of condolence to Lord Leighton's sisters.

Messages of sympathy and condolence were left at Lord Leighton's home throughout yesterday. A telegram was sent by the Prince of Wales. The callers included Mr. F. A. Eaton, secretary to the Royal Academy, Sir Frederic Burton, Mr. Walter Ouless, R. A., Mr. Colin Hunter, A. R.A., and Mrs. Hunter, Mr. Philip Calderon, R. A., Colonel Edis, who succeeded the late Lord Leighton in the command of the 20th Middlesex (Artists') Rifle Volunteers, Mr. Sargent, A. R.A., Mr. Frampton, A. R.A., Mr. Harry Bates, A. R.A., and Mrs. Bates, Mr. and Mrs. C. E. Perugini, Sir Nathaniel Staples and Mr. R. Ponsonby Staples, Mr. George W. Joy, Mr. G. Henschel, Mr. W. E. Lockhart, R. S.A., Mr. John Leighton, Mr. and Mrs. Arthur Lucas, Mr. Seymour Lucas, A. R.A., and Mrs. Lucas, Mr. Alfred East, Mr. and Mrs. Arthur James Lewis, Lieutenant Stanley Clarke (20th Middlesex), Mr. Kiallmark, and Mr. Charlie W. Wyllie. It is true, in a sense, that art is of no particular country; but in the present case, while the whole world of art is the poorer for the loss of Lord Leighton, England especially has to mourn for one of her most distinguished men. No other artist of the Victorian age has done better work, has been better known in the world, or has filled a larger space in the eyes of the public. The Presidency of the Academy gave him a public position; but he was already eminent more than a quarter of a century ago, when Lord Beaconsfield, introducing a great artist into his novel 'Lothair,' portrayed most of Leighton's remarkable features, and to some extent characterized his genius. He had, indeed, very various gifts, and excelled in so many directions as almost to convey the impression that painting was less the business of his life than an incidental accomplishment. 'Paints, too,' was the epigrammatic remark of one of his brother artists; and Sir John Millais, presiding, in Leighton's absence, at last year's Academy dinner, spoke of him, with equal truth and compliment, as 'our admirable Leighton – painter, sculptor, orator, linguist, musician, soldier, and, above all, a dear good fellow.' As Sir John Millais's epithet suggests, he was a Crichton among painters, a follower not of one muse, but of many, a man whose insight into all forms of art raised him above the other artists of his time. The Academy, moreover, which admired him for these reasons, owes much to him for his fidelity to its interests, and for his great efficiency as its President. To say nothing of his ability as a man of business – and all artists are not businesslike – his whole nature fitted him for the presidency of a body of artists. He had courtesy, tact, and sympathy; a fine presence, and much personal distinction. His pictures spoke for themselves; but his biennial addresses to the students of the Academy, elaborate results of learning and observation, proved his critical knowledge of arts other than his own. Whenever it was necessary for him to appear in public, either as the representative of British art or as the spokesman of his fellow Academicians, he played his part with a happy mixture of dignity and vivacity. At the annual dinners of the Academy, his speeches, optimistic as they were, and somewhat florid, were never commonplace, but expressed even well-worn sentiments with verbal novelty. They were essentially the speeches of an artist – as, for instance, when he said of Linnell that 'on his canvas the drowsy reaper nods beneath the sheaf, the shepherd pipes and watches, the new-felled timber strews the ground or strains the wagon's aching wheel.' In this, as in many other passages that might be quoted, the artist does not for a moment forget art, but only exchanges one method of expression for another. Here is the true artistic instinct, many-sided and appreciative, and based on a general sense of beauty that might easily have made him a poet or an architect as well as a painter and sculptor.

But life, as the truism has it, is short, and Leighton's life, though full and energetic, was not even relatively long. He was born at Scarborough in December, 1830, the son of Mr. Frederick Septimus Leighton by a daughter of Mr. G. A. Nash. His grandfather, Sir James B. Leighton, was physician to the Empress of Russia and chief of the Medical Department of the Imperial Navy. His father also was a physician, but, in consequence of his wife's ill-health, relinquished his practice and lived and travelled on the Continent. Young Leighton's talent for drawing showed itself at a very early age, and was so far encouraged that when the family were in Paris, in 1839, he received a few lessons from the well-known George Lance. The next winter or two were spent in Rome, where the boy had drawing lessons from Filippo Meli. Then came visits to Dresden and Berlin, and more art teaching, and a longer stay for purposes of general education at Frankfurt-on-the-Main. It was at Florence, in the winter of 1846, that his father, yielding to young Leighton's wishes, allowed him to make art his profession. Hiram Powers, the American sculptor, was at the time in Florence, and was consulted by Mr. Leighton. 'Your son,' said he, 'may be as eminent as he pleases.' 'Shall I make him an artist?' asked the father. 'No, nature has done it for you;' and an artist, accordingly, the boy thenceforth became. The gifts of nature, however, were supplemented by a variety of good training at Paris, Frankfurt, and Brussels. At Brussels the young artist painted his first serious picture, 'Cimabue finding Giotto drawing in the fields.' At Frankfurt he spent several years under the tuition of E. Steinle, Professor of Historical Painting in the Academy. 'The Death of Brunellesco' is an early work belonging to this period. Three winters in Rome followed, in the course of which he painted his first great work, 'Cimabue and his Friends and Scholars at Florence accompanying his picture of the Madonna to the Church of Santa Maria Novella.' This was in the Royal

Academy of 1855, and was bought by the Queen. From that time Leighton never failed to secure admission to the exhibitions of the Academy, but began a long series of successes. 'The Triumph of Music,' 'The Fisherman and Siren,' and 'Romeo and Juliet' – all of them at the Royal Academy – were the work of the next four years, which were spent mostly at Paris. 'Capri-Sunrise' recalls a visit to that island in 1859. 'Paolo and Francesca' and 'The Star of Bethlehem' bring us to 1864, in which year he was made an Associate of the Academy. Soon afterwards he made a long tour in Spain, and on his return settled in London in Holland-park-road.

From this period date the majority of his important works – works that not only brought him success in the material sense of the word, but also proved to his countrymen that they had among them a great classical artist. The sensation, perhaps, was novel, for our great artists had usually been distinctly British and indigenous, and lost little or nothing of their nationality in their treatment of classical subjects. But here was an Englishman striking a true classical note, not lured into mere archaeology, but going on from strength to strength till at last his art seemed to culminate in the 'Daphnephoria.' In this great picture, which is comparable only to the 'Cimabue' of 20 years before, the artist shows a long and admirably grouped and animated procession of young men and maidens to the Temple of Apollo at Thebes. It has, like others of Leighton's works, a decorative background of dark pines and cedars, and in the multitude of its figures it contains not one that is not drawn with the utmost grace of line. The public, no doubt, felt the force of the maxim, *Omne ignotum pro magnifico*, and admired without appreciation; but that did not signify, for the work – it was nearly 20ft. long – was a private commission, and was painted for the country house of Mr. Stewart Hodgson. This was in 1876; but the preceding ten years had been rendered notable by such works as 'Venus Unrobing,' 'Daedalus and Icarus,' 'Electra,' 'Clytemnaestra,' and the 'Eastern Slinger.' 'Hercules wrestling with Death for the Body of Alcestis' was one of the pictures of the year in 1871, and one of the best ever painted by Leighton; it had the honour of being referred to by Browning in his poem 'Balaustion's Adventure.' But the 'Eastern Slinger' is, on the whole, the most truly classical, as it is certainly the most statuesque and the most virile. The slinger, it will be remembered, stands on a platform raised in the middle of a standing cornfield. He is all but nude, and is in the act of discharging his sling against a bird. In the distance, on another low platform, is a second man scaring birds in the same way, but the whole interest of the work centres in the drawing of the chief figure.

The personal event of these ten years was the election of the artist as a full Academician in 1868, an honour as certain as it was well deserved. In 1879 the death of Sir Francis Grant, the portrait painter, deprived the Academy of its President. The loss was great, for Sir F. Grant had the social as well as professional qualifications which it was desirable to find in his successor. No one was surprised when the vacant office was bestowed on Leighton. The singular efficiency with which he performed the various and onerous duties of the post has been already referred to. It is entertaining to recall – as Sir J. Millais did at last year's annual dinner – the words in which Thackeray many years ago prophesied, half in joke, young Leighton's coming eminence: 'Millais, my boy, I've met the most versatile young dog you ever heard of. His name's Leighton, and if you don't mind he'll run you hard for the presidentship some day.' The honour of knighthood in the same year was a matter of course, and a baronetcy followed in 1886, the peerage having only been bestowed on the first day of the present year.

It may be that the 'Daphnephoria' of 1876 remains an unsurpassed example of Leighton's pictures, but not a year has since passed without at least one memorable work from his easel. Among them will be specially remembered the large and imaginative 'Elijah raising the son of the Shunamite,' 'Elijah in the Wilderness,' also on a large scale; 'The Light of the Harem'; 'Phryne at Eleusis,' a single nude figure; 'Antigone'; 'Cymon and Iphigenia,' from Boccaccio; 'The Last Watch of Hero,' the finest, perhaps, of all his single figures; 'Captive Andromache,' a large and pathetic canvas; 'Greek Girls Playing at Ball'; 'The Bath of Psyche'; 'The Return of Persephone'; 'Perseus and Andromeda'; 'Hit'; 'Rizpah'; 'The Spirit of the Summit'; and, in the last Academy Exhibition, 'Lachrymae' and 'Flaming June.' These, of course, were all of them at the Academy. At the Grosvenor Gallery, besides some charming sketches of Damascus, the record of an Eastern tour, were a good many of his minor pictures, and some of his portraits, 'Mrs. Algernon Sartoris' for instance, and 'Miss Stewart Hodgson.' But his portraits, able as they were, were not numerous. We may mention chiefly his own portrait, a full face, painted by himself, for the collection at the Uffizzi; 'Professor G. Costa'; 'Sir B. Ryan'; 'Countess Brownlow'; 'Captain Burton,' 1876, an exceedingly fine head, almost in profile; and 'Lady Sibyl Primrose.'

These works – the few that we have named – to say nothing of the minor pictures that came from his studio and the mass of sketches and studies that remained in it, would surely be enough for a longer life than Leighton's. But so various was his activity that besides all this, besides his official and literary work in connexion with the Academy, he found or made time for sculpture, for fresco-painting, for travelling, for society, for public speeches, and for Volunteering. He was one of the earliest members of the Artists' Rifle Corps and subsequently its colonel; and he took a deep interest in its welfare and efficiency. As might be gathered from his active interest in the Volunteer movement, Leighton, though formed on Greek and Italian rather than English art, was an ardent patriot. He took a keen interest in the larger issues of politics; was a member of the original Liberal Unionist Association in 1886; and rejoiced, during the last days of his life, in the spirit shown by the country under menace from the East and the West, and in the determination universally shown to increase our defensive preparations. On so popular a man honours fell quite naturally. His genius was recognized in this country by the Presidency of the Academy and a baronetcy, which latter honour was merged for little more than three weeks in the only peerage that has ever rewarded an English painter. The Universities of Oxford, Cambridge, and Edinburgh gave him the honorary degrees of D. C. L. and LL. D. In France he was a Knight of the Legion of Honour, and, in 1878, President of the International Jury of Painting at the Paris Exhibition. As Lord Leighton died unmarried his baronetcy and peerage become extinct. The honours that were showered upon him only ratified the opinion formed of him by his friends in all classes, from the Royal to the Bohemian, to whom he was endeared by his many social qualities, his buoyant and cheerful spirit, his ready sympathy, his unfailing generosity – specially manifested to young and struggling artists and, we may perhaps add, his striking personal beauty, which yet had nothing effeminate or unmanly about it.

Anything like a complete estimate of Lord Leighton's work, and of its relation to contemporary art, would not be possible in an obituary notice, nor, perhaps, would it be appropriate. It is the artist whom we have lost, and not his works; and it seems, therefore, more proper to record the outlines of his career than to discuss his pictures. These may be left to the secure judgment of the future. But this much, at least, must be said of them, that for, a variety of reasons they gave him a position apart from his brother artists, and in some respects above them. He belonged to no English school of painting, was influenced little, if at all, by English art and English traditions, and, as far as we can see, has left behind him admirers only and not disciples. Much of his strength came from what may be called, not invidiously, the un-English qualities of his art. He drew his inspiration mainly from Greece and the Italian Renaissance, and thus learned the importance of dignity of form and line and consummate drawing. He had also a fine natural sense of colour, and was fond of such harmonies of white and gold and purple and red as appear, for example, in 'The Vestal,' 'Whispers,' and 'The Music Lesson.' But drawing was his delight, and not least the drawing of drapery, which he always accomplished in a most careful and learned manner, studying every figure first in the nude, and every fold of drapery separately. Many of his studies, in chalk on tinted paper, are charming proofs of his thoroughness and industry. And as with drapery, so with the nude human figure in all its attitudes; it was something more than the Paris life-school and anatomical studies at Rome that enabled him to render repose, activity, and violent exertion with the facility and truth of Greek art. His figures departed little from the classical ideal, and may sometimes have lost in interest what they gained by being 'faultily faultless'; but their beauty and the artist's mastery of drawing and colour are beyond dispute. And if, in consequence of the remoteness of his subjects, he rarely touched the heart, it must be admitted that in his handling of them he was frequently original and romantic. His great picture of 1892, 'And the Sea gave up the Dead which were in it,' is a sufficient proof of this, without further argument.

It should he remembered that Leighton was not alone a painter in oil colours. Water colour he seldom employed, and, unlike other artists, he hardly ever illustrated a book. 'Romola,' we believe, is the only instance; but he also worked in fresco, and added sculpture to his other achievements. His best known frescoes are the two large lunettes at the South Kensington Museum, representing respectively the Arts of War and of Peace. It is a pity that there is no attainable point of view from which they can be properly seen. Another of his frescoes is the altar-piece in Lyndhurst Church, which was painted almost entirely in the course of hasty Saturday afternoon visits to that village in 1866. The subject is the Wise and Foolish Virgins, decoratively treated, and full of fine grouping and drapery. More important, and more surprising, are Leighton's excursions into the art of sculpture. The kindred art is the usual phrase, though, in truth, the aims and the method of the sculptor are absolutely unlike those of the painter. The production, therefore, of two such works as the 'Athlete struggling with a Python,' 1876, and the 'Sluggard,' 1886, is a proof of remarkable versatility.

The contrast, too, is equally remarkable. The former, which is Leighton's representative in the Chantrey Gallery at South Kensington, is the very embodiment of intense muscular effort, and the uncertainty of the issue gives it a strange dramatic interest; in the latter work every joint and sinew is relaxed, and the whole figure is a type of nerveless and sensuous inertness.

Much more might be, and will be, written concerning the work of this great artist. We have attempted only to indicate its main features. It may be described summarily as idealistic, classical, and romantic, but not popular, except so far as all things of beauty have a limited popularity. He had no predecessors in English art, and leaves no one to succeed him. He was one of the very few men of whom it may be said, without exaggeration, that his place cannot be filled.

Yesterday afternoon Dr. Adler, the Chief Rabbi, took part in the ceremony of laying the foundation-stone of an extension of the Hammersmith and West Kensington Synagogue at Brook-green. The stone was laid by Mr. B. L. Cohen, M. P. The Chief Rabbi said that, while he was reluctant to introduce an element of sadness on an occasion of that kind, he was sure that being an assembly of Englishmen, they could not meet together that day without adverting to the great and irreparable loss which the nation had suffered in the death of Lord Leighton. It was his privilege to make his acquaintance, when he was Sir Frederic Leighton, some 12 or 13 years ago, when he sat next to him at the opening of Parliament on the last occasion when the Queen performed that ceremony in person. It was, Sir Frederic told him, the first occasion on which he had been present at that interesting ceremony. Since their acquaintance he had shown much kindness to their Jewish community, and only last year was a steward at the anniversary festival of the Jews' Hospital, and he expressed his regret that his many engagements, just before the opening of the Royal Academy, prevented his being present on that occasion. Weightier voices than his would bear tribute to one who was so great an artist, inspired by the loftiest ideals. The colours of his canvas, as the periods of his eloquent orations, were always glowing with the sunshine, beauty, and warmth of Italian skies. The country had of late suffered keen and great losses. Let them earnestly pray that the Almighty God would save and preserve them for a long period from losses so great and so keen as those which their country had had to deplore during the last few weeks.

As this singularly appreciative obituary notes, amongst Leighton's last words were, 'Love to the Academy and all its members.' At his funeral, cards bearing a version of these words were circulated amongst the crowds. He had been elected President of the Royal Academy of Arts on 13 November 1878 and, according to the *Magazine of Art* in 1885 he was 'with the exception of Sir Joshua Reynolds . . . the most skilful administrator and most enlightened President that the Academy has ever had'. It might seem strange, therefore, that the obituary lays so much stress on the 'un-English qualities' of Leighton's art, claiming that he was influenced 'little, if at all, by English art and English traditions'. It was almost certainly this Neoclassical and Italianate quality in his work that recommended him to George Eliot and to her publisher, George Smith, as the illustrator for her historical novel *Romola* (serialised in the *Cornhill Magazine* 1862–63). The obituarist also notes what he regards as the key works in Leighton's career, beginning with *Cimabue's Celebrated Madonna is Carried in Procession though the Streets of Florence* of 1854–55, a painting which had been purchased from the Royal Academy exhibition of 1855 by Queen Victoria on the advice of Prince Albert. He also considers the huge procession painting, *The Daphnephoria*, as Leighton's supreme achievement. The picture remained in private hands until 1913 when it was bought by Lord Leverhulme and presented to the Lady Lever Art Gallery at Port Sunlight. Beyond his achievement as a painter and sculptor, Leighton was also the designer of Elizabeth Barrett Browning's fine Renaissance style tomb at Florence. His own body was borne with great ceremony from the Royal Academy to be buried in St Paul's Cathedral on 3 February 1896. A wreath from Queen Victoria was placed on the coffin by John Everett Millais.

CLARA SCHUMANN

Musician: 'The most richly gifted of all female musicians.'

20 MAY 1896

WITH THE DEATH OF MME. SCHUMANN, which occurred at Frankfurt on the Main, on Wednesday, from paralysis, the musical world has lost, not only the ablest exponent of Robert Schumann's pianoforte music, but also perhaps the most richly gifted of all female musicians. Mme. Schumann, who had attained to a recognized position under her maiden name of Clara Wieck, was born at Leipzig, September 13, 1819, and, having studied the pianoforte under her father, the illustrious teacher, Friedrich Wieck, she made her first appearance in public just nine years later, and rapidly made her mark as a pianist of the first rank. Schumann's romantic attachment to her was the directly inspiring cause of many of his most beautiful and individual compositions. So little smoothly did the course of their love run that an action at law was one of the incidents of their story. Married on the eve of her birthday, September 12, 1840, she was not only a most devoted wife until the time of his tragic death in July, 1856, but a fellow-artist worthy in every way to help him in the interpretation of his best creations. From a period shortly before the composer's death until comparatively recently she devoted her life mainly to the work of obtaining wide recognition for his compositions. In England, where she appeared at a Philharmonic Concert for the first time but three months before Schumann's death, the task was a particularly heavy one; but in the course of years she was most amply rewarded, not so much by the heartfelt enthusiasm with which her later appearances were always greeted as by the high place ultimately accorded to Schumann's compositions in the musical world of London. Although these were peculiarly and in a special sense her own, yet she was not less remarkable as a player of the classics, and, indeed, as a distinguished critic has truly said, 'She was one of the greatest pianoforte players that the world has ever heard.' The sonatas of Beethoven received new meaning at her hands, and in works of lighter calibre, such as the harpsichord pieces of Scarlatti, her success was complete. In the expression of the deepest and most refined emotion, in dignity of style & breadth and variety of tone, she was without rival, and her compositions, though extending only to opus 23 or thereabouts, reach a very high degree of excellence and show real poetic insight. No doubt the excessive smallness of that list of her works is due to an artistic fastidiousness and a power of self-criticism which prevented her from publishing anything not entirely representative of the power that was in her. Gradually increasing deafness caused her latterly to shun the concert platform, but her work as a teacher was almost phenomenally successful. Among her English pupils Mr. Franklin Taylor (as a teacher), Miss Fanny Davies, Miss Adeline de Lara, and Mr. Leonard Borwick (as players) are the most distinguished, and the Hoch Conservatorium at Frankfort became famous mainly through the co-operation of Mme. Schumann and her daughters.

Robert Schumann finally married Clara Wieck in September 1840, after a three-year battle with, and a court case against, her father. Clara was already established as a consummate piano virtuoso (having given her first performance at the Leipzig Gewandhaus on 20 October 1828). Marriage proved an obstacle to Clara's developing career both as a concert pianist and as a composer (Robert insisted on silence when himself composing). There were also eight children, one of whom died in infancy. Robert's final mental collapse occurred in 1854 and he died in an asylum at Endenich in 1856 leaving Clara to care for the children. Clara had already fully resumed her concert tours, playing in England for the first time in 1856. She gave her last public performance in 1891. Though limited in number, her compositions, especially those dating from after 1853, have always had admirers, though Clara herself complained in her diary that 'a woman must not desire to compose – not one has been able to do it, and why should I expect to?' She died in Frankfurt am Main on 20 May 1896. Her four English pupils named at the end of the obituary all became professional pianists: Franklin Taylor (1843–1919) was also Professor of Piano at the Royal College of Music while Fanny Davies (1861–1934) and Leonard Borwick (1868–1925) pursued successful international careers; Adelina de Lara (1872–1961), who determinedly continued in the 'Schumann' tradition, wrote two piano concertos and spoke at the (Robert) Schumann centenary concert at the Wigmore Hall in London in 1956.

SIR JOHN EVERETT MILLAIS

Painter: 'No painter of any eminence has been a more general favourite, while preserving his art and refinement.'

13 AUGUST 1896

THE ROYAL ACADEMY has again lost its President. Lord Leighton died in January, and now, in late summer, it is our sad duty to record the death of his successor, Sir John Everett Millais, whose loss will be felt not only by his brother artists within and without the Royal Academy, but by many hundreds of others who admired and enjoyed the pictures that made him famous all over the world. He had been in ill health for a long time. Nearly two years ago the first indications of the disorder of the throat declared themselves, but down to about March last, though hoarseness was troublesome, Sir John Millais's general health was not affected. At that time, however, a change for the worse took place. Early in May he caught cold; the difficulty in breathing became much aggravated, and it was found necessary to perform tracheotomy. This gave considerable relief for a time, and the improvement was such that Sir John was able to leave his bed and see his friends, with whom he conversed by means of a slate. A few days ago the disease took an unfavourable turn, the distinguished patient became unconscious. The end, which was quite peaceful and without pain, came at half-past 5 last evening, Lady Millais, Mr. Everett Millais, and other members of the family being present in the room.

Though some critics may be found to deny that Millais was one of the two or three greatest English painters of this century, declaring that in each direction of his art others have excelled him, some in portraiture, some in landscape, and some in *genre*, he was undoubtedly one of the most popular and, from some points of view, one of the most interesting of our artists. When one hears of a popular painter, one inevitably recalls the cheap art for the people, religious it may be, or melodramatic, but always very cheap indeed, which serves to bring mediocrity into prominence. With Millais the case was different. His popularity, achieved early enough to turn the head of an inferior man, was due to nothing vulgar or pretentious, but solely to charming work and wholesome sentiment. His pictures appeal to us sometimes by the mere force of beauty and sometimes by their plain pathos and their noble humanity. 'The Huguenot,' for example, who refuses to accept from his lady the badge that is to save him at the expense of his honour, is popular just as Colonel Lovelace's famous lines have been popular for more than two centuries, and for precisely the same reason. 'The Highlander,' again whose order of release is brought to him by his young wife, is as pathetic and as popular a figure as can well be put upon canvas. 'The Black Brunswicker' and 'The Gambler's Wife' are in much the same vein of sentiment. 'Cinderella,' even in its sixpenny reproductions, has delighted children of all ages; a still more recent picture, unhappily lending itself to the purposes of advertisement, has been an isolated thing of beauty on all our hoardings. Certainly no painter of any eminence has been a more general favourite, while preserving his art and his refinement, than Sir John Millais.

Nor, probably, are there many painters whose artistic development is more instructive. It often happens that an artist does not develop at all – that is that his progress consists only in technical skill. In Millais's case, though the plenitude of technical ability came long ago, there came also change, development, and progress of a higher and an intellectual kind. Early genius, early enthusiasm for a particular school, and an almost radical change in mature manhood – this is briefly the history of Sir John Millais. Of his early genius he gave ample proof while he was yet only a small boy. His later works have been for many years among the principal attractions at the Academy and other exhibitions.

John Everett Millais, son of John William Millais and Mary, daughter of Richard Evermy, was born on June 8, 1829. His birthplace was Southampton, but he must be reckoned as a Jerseyman, seeing that his family were among the natives of that island. The earliest recorded fact concerning him is that in 1835, the family being then resident at Dinard, in Brittany, the child was in the habit of making vivacious sketches of the French artillery officers stationed there. It was evident that he had already found his vocation in life. Drawings and sketches were produced by the dozen, and seemed so promising that when he was only eight years old – terrible ordeal for so young a boy – some of his performances were submitted to Sir Martin Shea, President of the Royal Academy. Sir Martin told the boy's mother bluntly that it would be better to train him for a sweep than for an artist. But what successful man ever recommends his own profession? The result, however, of an inspection of the boy's work was that in the following year young Millais was sent, with the concurrence of the president, to Sass's Academy, where his earliest success brought him a silver medal from the Society of Arts. His second prize was gained two years afterwards, when he was a student at the Royal Academy, and only 11 years old. About this time he was sent to a private school in Caroline-street, Bedford-square, where he remained for two or three years. The master was an able teacher, but young Millais's ruling passion was too strong for his other studies; he preferred his pencil to his books, and drew incessantly; he was nominally a schoolboy, but in reality an art student. The art training of the period was in one respect not absolutely unlike that received by Clive Newcome and his friend Ridley. Historical pieces, such as would provoke a smile nowadays, were then much in vogue, and were the object of many a young painter's ambition. A good deal of well-painted drapery, and a number of figures, more or less skilfully grouped, and 'all studied from the hantique, Sir, the glorious hantique,' constituted as a rule these intelligent compositions. All the same, it was not given to every boy of 16 to exhibit his pictures in public, and Millais was only 16 when he painted his first Academy picture of 'Pizarro seizing the Inca of Peru.' The work, boyish as it was, was much praised, and was immediately succeeded by more history – 'Dunstan's Emistaries seizing Queen Elgiva,' and, in another year or so, by 'The Tribe of Benjamin seizing the Daughters of Shiloh.' Then, after 'The Widow's Mite,' came the picture of 'Isabella,' in 1849, which marks a turning point in Millais's artistic career. We may note in passing that this picture contains portraits of Mrs. Hodgkinson, the wife of Millais's half-brother; of Dante Rossetti; and of W. Bell Scott. This picture emerged from retirement not many years ago, and was purchased by the Corporation of Liverpool for their Art Gallery.

It was at this time that a remarkable, if not an enduring, movement began in English Art – a movement which proceeded on definite principles and had definite results. So much has been written from time to time of the Pre-Raphaelite Brotherhood that we need only remind our readers in a few words that Millais, at the age of 20, was one of its members, the others being the two Rossettis, Holman Hunt, Woolner, G. Collinson, and F. G. Stephens. Their journal, the *Germ*, was started in 1850, and preached above all things earnestness as the note of the new school. Their artistic creed enjoined the literal rendering of natural objects, no interference with nature, and no selection beyond the selection of the model. Details, even minute details, if these were present to the eye, were not to be generalized or omitted, but were to be rendered in a detailed manner. Roughly speaking, the extreme of Pre-Raphaelitism was diametrically opposite to the extreme of Impressionism. How far truth of fact is compatible with truth of impression is a problem for philosophers as well as for artists. We need not handle even the fringe of the question, but note only the fact that at this period of his life Millais, with the natural and laudable enthusiasm of youth, was a member of the straightest sect among his fellow-artists. It was under this influence that he painted, in 1850, 'Christ in the house of His Parents,' a famous work with all the most marked Pre-Raphaelite characteristics, which excited a furious controversy and was condemned by a 'literary' journal as 'a nameless atrocity.' Abuse, of course, is not criticism but the picture was undoubtedly strong meat for critics somewhat meagrely nurtured on the art of 50 years ago. To this period belong also 'Ferdinand lured by Ariel,' 'Mariana in the Moated Grange,' 'The Woodman's Daughter,' and a very large number of drawings for illustrated books. The two following years were years of great success and popularity. We need only mention 'The Huguenot,' 'Ophelia,' 'The Order of Release,' and 'The Proscribed Royalist' as the work of 1852 and 1853. These, but especially 'The Huguenot,' are as widely known as any pictures that have been painted in this century. We wonder in how many houses 'The Huguenot' and 'The Order of Release' hang side by side as companion engravings. 'The Huguenot' sold, we believe, for £150, to Mr. Miller, of Preston; it was not seen again in public till the Millais Exhibition at the Grosvenor. To this sum another £50 was afterwards added; a still better result, from the young artist's point of view, was that in 1853 he was elected an Associate of the Academy, and had an assured future before him. He had touched the public sympathies, and the greatest critic of the day, both in letters in our own columns and in his lectures, had publicly commended his work. But for 'Sir Isumbras at the Ford,' his Academy picture of 1857, which is a distinct relapse into Pre-Raphaelitism, and as such was brilliantly caricatured by Frederic Sandys, one would have thought that Millais was forsaking his earlier tenets, for the four pictures of 1852 and 1853 show little enough of the more pronounced mannerisms of the P. R. B. They are detailed, it is true, but not affected or overwrought. Perhaps there is room for the suggestion that Millais, daily becoming more and more conscious of his versatility, was not long a convinced Pre-Raphaelite, but only reverted in 'Sir Isumbras' to a style that seemed to suit a romantic subject. One thing alone is certain – that the real course of mental and artistic development is each man's own secret, even if it be not actually unknown to himself. The year before 'Sir Isumbras' Millais had proved his versatility by turning landscape painter and producing 'Autumn Leaves,' a picture of great beauty, which Mr. Ruskin described as 'by much the most poetical work the painter has yet conceived, and also, as far as I know, the first instance of a perfectly-painted twilight.' 'The Black Brunswicker' followed in 1861, and the painter of 'My First Sermon' was a full-blown Academician in 1863. It should be added that about this time, he made a great mark as an illustrator of books, working especially for *Good Words* and the newly-established *Cornhill Magazine.*

The most brilliant artist may consider himself exceptionally fortunate if he receives the highest honours of the Academy at the age of 34; and the Academy, which is usually in no feverish haste to recognize genius, was not less fortunate in its new member. Millais's genius had never suffered from disappointment; his whole life, indeed, had been a series of successes; the only question now was how he would bear the full tide of prosperity, which is not less trying than failure to a man of ability. A successful artist, rejoicing in his strength, and presumably free from urgent cares, would he grow and develop, or subside into a comfortable and lucrative groove of his own? Now, Millais was by no means a picture manufacturer, and was not content to turn out popular pieces of *genre*, one after another, as fast as each could be dismissed from the easel. Ambition, an absorbing love of art, and that versatility to which we have already referred, kept him from any such commonplace course. Gradually he drifted away from his earlier manner – 'Jephthah,' in 1867, perhaps marks a turning point in his career; and, if 'Hearts are

Trumps,' 'Yes or No?' and similar works lack something of the charm of 'The Huguenot,' the landscapes and admirable portraits of his later years, showing, as they do, the wide scope and range of his powers, are an ample compensation. Whether the landscapes would have been better still if he had confined himself to landscape work, or the portraits if he had resolved to paint only portraits, is, of course, another question. Apart from speculations of this kind, Millais's chief characteristic in the eyes of the public was his versatility and his success in several distinct branches of the painter's art. His landscapes certainly bear the impress of his own precept, that 'the painter ought to go on his knees before Nature as though he were worshipping in a temple.' His object was not to render bizarre effects, not to catch Nature in her violent moods, but to study beautiful scenes at the precise time when each is most beautiful. 'Chill October,' painted in 1871, the whole field of nature cold and dying after 'the usage of the year,' and 'Over the Hills and Far Away,' a Perthshire moor, the work of 1875, are probably his best and best-known landscapes. 'Chill October,' by the way, was shown at the Paris Exhibition of 1878 together with 'A Yeoman of the Guard' and 'The Gambler's Wife,' and is said to have elicited from Meissonier the remark that 'the English could paint.' Among Millais's other landscapes, mostly painted in Scotland, are 'The Fringe of the Moor,' 1875; 'The Sound of Many Waters,' 1877; 'St. Martin's Summer,' 1878 ; 'The Tower of Strength,' 1879; 'The Old Garden,' 1889; 'The Moon is Up, and yet it is not Night,' and 'Dew Drenched Furze,' 1890; 'Glen Birnam,' a snow scene, 1891; 'Halcyon Weather' and 'Blow, Blow, Thou Wintry Wind,' 1892.

On the whole, the 20 years that followed 1871 may be taken as the period of Millais's greatest work, for, besides these landscapes of somewhat unequal merit, he produced at this time such well-known pictures as 'Yes or No?' with its less successful sequel 'Yes'; the 'Princes in the Tower,' and 'A Yeoman of the Guard' remarkable if only for black velvet and dexterous scarlet respectively – 'Cinderella,' which an illustrated journal soon reproduced and sent to the ends of the world; 'Sweetest Eyes were ever Seen,' Cinderella's model, apparently, but a year older; and 'An Idyll of 1745,' in which two or three timid little Scotch lassies listen, after Culloden, to an English soldier-boy who is playing the fife for their amusement. All these or certainly most of them, have been rendered familiar enough by engravings to justify our earlier remarks as to Millais's popularity. If they pleased the public, so much the better for the public. Unpopularity is neither a criterion of art nor a moral obligation. But still greater works than these belong to Millais's last 20 years – that is, if portrait painting is the artist's greatest achievement. Whatever may be the truth as regards portrait painting in the abstract – and it has certainly been the work of great artists in all ages – it is a fact that the most remarkable of Millais's later works have been portraits. It says much for the singular flexibility of his genius that, though he had several accomplished rivals, and one or two superiors, he more than held his own with the long series of portraits that began about 20 years ago. A fashionable portrait painter necessarily has to paint a good many undistinguished people, and it is only the most consummate artist who can make a mere 'Portrait of a Man' interesting. Millais, perhaps, had not this supreme gift, but for his best-work very high excellence may be justly claimed. He was extremely fortunate in his subjects – Tennyson, Disraeli, Newman, Bright, Mr. Gladstone, and a host of minor celebrities were among them. We do not pretend to give anything like a complete list, but most of our readers will remember the Lord Shaftesbury, painted for the Bible Society in 1878; Mrs. Langtry, the 'Jersey Lily' of the same year; and Mr. Gladstone in 1879. In 1880 he contributed a portrait of himself, for a collection of similar portraits of artists at the Uffizi Gallery; Mr. Bright, Mr. Luther Holden, President of the Royal College of Surgeons, and Catherine Muriel Cowell Stepney, a child in black velvet, one of his best works, were at the Academy; and a portrait of Mrs. Louise Jopling at the Grosvenor Gallery. In 1881 he exhibited Lord Beaconsfield, at that time unfinished; Bishop Fraser, of Manchester; Sir John Ashley; Principal Caird; and Lord Wimborne, Cardinal Newman – engraved by T. O. Barlow – Sir Henry Thompson, and Princess Marie of Edinburgh appeared in the following year: and in 1888 Lord Salisbury, and his greatest portrait of all, Mr. J. C. Hook, R. A. A break in the series followed, other works mainly occupying the artist in the interval, until we come to the portrait of Mr. John Hare, in 1893. Then came a long attack of influenza and a blank year, but in 1895 we had two or three striking pictures, and in the exhibition of this year were the 'Lady Tweeddale', the 'Sir Richard Quain,' and others, to which we have referred in other articles.

We might easily follow out the chronicle of his works to much greater length; for in these days of widespread artistic appreciation the smallest works of so great an artist as Millais, their history and present home, are objects of profound interest to a number of people. It is, perhaps, enough to mention in this relation that the English public will soon come into possession of several of the painter's finest works, for the Tate Gallery will contain 'Ophelia,' 'The North-West Passage,' 'The Vale of Rest,' and three or four more. Owners of many pictures by him were the late Mr. W. Graham, the late Mr. Price of Queen Anne-street, and Mr. Matthews; it is said that Mr. C. Wertheimer has a whole room of the more decorative pictures, such as 'Cherry Ripe' and 'Christmas Eve.' To attempt to fix the artistic position of all these, or of the artist and his work as a whole, would be as premature as it would be difficult. Time alone can judge, for to time alone must be left the task of assigning to modern art its relative place by the side of the art of bygone centuries. At least, however, it may be said that our age has seen no English painter at once so varied and so powerful. He passed, in the course of 50 years of healthy, strenuous work, from the ideal represented by 'The Huguenot' to the ideal represented by

'Saint Theresa,' and at least every other year he produced what the best judgment of the day pronounced a masterpiece. What exquisite quality and finish in the early work – in the flowers of the 'Ophelia,' for example! What an understanding of childish beauty in 'My first Sermon' and in 'The Minuet'! What brilliancy of painting, what sympathy with the root-sentiments of our British nature in 'The Boyhood of Raleigh'! What grasp of character, and what power of pictorial effect, in such portraits as the 'Gladstone,' the 'Tennyson,' and the 'J. C. Hook'! What a power of rendering external nature as the eye of ordinary humanity perceives it in 'Chill October'! Immense range, unswerving fidelity, and an almost invariable distinction – these are the qualities in Millais's art which are admitted by all the world. They were brought home to the public mind with irresistible force at the Millais exhibition at the Grosvenor Gallery in 1886, and the work of subsequent years has not weakened the hold which the great artist then once for all obtained.

We need hardly remind our readers of the final honour paid to Millais by his election to the Presidency of the Academy in succession to Lord Leighton. As to his claims and qualifications, both social and professional, there could be no doubt. It was only a question whether his health would prove equal to new and onerous duties. And now that the end has come, all too soon for the Academy and his many friends, it can only be said that, when he was elected, there was reason to hope that those forebodings would not be realized. It should be added that he became a Knight of the Legion of Honour in 1878, a Trustee of the National Portrait Gallery in 1881, an Associate of the Académie des Beaux Arts in 1882, and a baronet in 1885. His handsome face and healthy frame suggested rather the country squire than the artist: and, indeed, he made no secret of the fact that he loved the moor and the salmon river, especially at Murthly where he spent so many autumns, even more than his brush. He married, in 1855, Euphemia Chalmers, daughter of Mr. George Gray, of Bowerswell, Perth, and is succeeded in the baronetcy by his son Everett, who was born in 1856, and married in 1886 a daughter of the late Mr. W. E. Hope-Vere. One of his daughters is the wife of the Right Hon. Charles Stuart-Wortley, M. P.

The Queen, having been apprised of the death of Sir John Millais, last evening telegraphed her condolence. The Prince of Wales, the Duke and Duchess of York, and Princess Louise have also telegraphed sympathetic messages. During yesterday there were many callers at Palace-gate, and numerous telegrams were received from America, Paris, and Berlin. A special executive meeting of the Royal Academy has been called with reference to the funeral, which will probably take place on Tuesday next.

In common with many contemporaries, the obituarist sees Millais's career as a painter as one of steady and explorative development. The highly gifted boy becomes the Pre-Raphaelite who in turn evolves into a modern genre painter, a landscapist and an admired portraitist. A different view began to emerge after Millais's death. In October 1896 the poet and critic Arthur Symons could comment on Millais's portraits that 'he painted them all with the same facility and the same lack of conviction; he painted whatever would bring him ready money and immediate fame.' For most of the subsequent century critics would continue to characterise him as a singularly brilliant young rebel who had sold out to slickness, easy popularity and, ultimately, to the social and artistic establishment. Earlier commentators were much kinder. The obituarist cites 'the greatest critic of the age', John Ruskin, as the young Millais's foremost champion, but he tactfully avoids mention of the scandal that had temporarily wrecked the painter's social ambitions. Ruskin had married Euphemia 'Effie' Chalmers Gray in 1848. There were strains in the marriage from the beginning. In the rainy summer of 1853 the Ruskins travelled to the Trossachs with Millais (who was engaged to paint Ruskin's portrait). By October, the portrait was still unfinished and it was evident that Millais and Effie were infatuated with one another. Ruskin's marriage was annulled in July 1854 on the grounds of non-consummation. Effie and Millais were married on 3 July 1855 and, as the scandal of the divorce receded and as Millais's success grew, it was she who encouraged him to move in higher social circles. The portrait was finally finished in December 1854. When the wounded but dignified Ruskin wrote to thank Millais, the painter replied, 'I scarcely see how you conceive it possible I can desire to continue on terms of intimacy with you.'

WILLIAM MORRIS

Craftsman, designer, poet and socialist: 'Only those who are willing to cry in the wilderness will prophesy the artistic millennium.'

3 OCTOBER 1896

THE DEATH OF MR. WILLIAM MORRIS, which, we regret to say, took place shortly after 11 o'clock on Saturday morning at Kelmscott House, Hammersmith, after a long illness, removes from the world a man whom we do not hesitate to call a great artist. A poet, and one of our half dozen best poets, even when Tennyson and Browning were alive; an artist whose influence is visible almost everywhere; a craftsman who devoted himself, in a commercial age, to the union of arts and crafts, it may be said of him, with little or no exaggeration, that he adorned all that he touched. And, if another famous epitaph may be allowed to suggest itself, we should say that, while his best work – a poem of his own, or a volume from the Kelmscott Press – is often present on our bookshelves, most of us find something in the nature of a monument to Mr. Morris in the better taste of our domestic surroundings. It is seldom, indeed, that an Englishman is an artist of this type. True, Mr. Morris was neither a painter nor a sculptor. He studied painting for a time, but preferred to give his energies to the more practical arts with which his name has been so long associated, and to the poems some of which, we do not doubt, will live long after him. No one who has witnessed the Arts and Crafts Exhibitions, which he helped to promote – and which are renewed this year in an exhibition opened for a private view on the day of his death – will deny that he possessed and effectively used a remarkable diversity of gilts. To these he added a strenuous and outspoken English nature, such as rarely combines with the typical artistic temperament.

Of Mr. Morris's poems, important as they are, we need not speak at any length. They have been before the world for a long time, and the world at once made up its mind that their author, if not a poet of the first rank, was an earnest and sweet singer, who did not fritter away his genius on fugitive pieces and newspaper lyrics, but had enough industry and ambition for large subjects. The 'Earthly Paradise,' a series of 24 romances told by travellers who take their way, not to Canterbury, but towards an imaginary Utopia in the West, is probably Mr. Morris's best known work. It had been preceded in 1868 by the 'Defence of Guenevere, and other poems,' and in 1867 by the 'Life and Death of Jason,' a great poem in more senses than one, in 17 books. The 'Earthly Paradise' was the work of the years 1868–70; or perhaps it would be more correct to say that those were the years in which its various parts were published. Then came 'Love is Enough; or, the Freeing of Pharamond – a Morality,' in 1873, and this was followed a few years later by translations in verse – and often in poetry – of the Æneid and the Odyssey, and 'Poems by the Way,' in 1892. Surely no poet can have worked harder, or, considering the extent of his work, with greater success. Nor should his prose romances be forgotten, 'A Dream of John Bull' (1888), 'News from Nowhere' (1891), and others. The latest of them 'The Well at the World's End,' was only issued just before his death. Besides these were 'The Story of Grettir the Strong' and 'The Story of the Volsungs and the Niblungs,' translations from the ancient Icelandic Sagas undertaken in collaboration with Mr. Eirikr Magnússon, and a translation, in 1895, of the famous Anglo-Saxon epic of Beowulf. Criticism, especially of well-known work, is out of place in an obituary notice. As regards these translations, we may adhere to what we said of them at the time – that their English is 'a marvel in these days of novel and newspaper.' But this is true also of all that Morris wrote or did. He never omitted to be thorough – never forgot that he was a craftsman as well as an artist. His English, indeed, was always singularly pure, and made up in simplicity what it may have lacked in vigour. If his verse, with its weak rhymes, is sometimes a little cloying, a little hyper-Lydian – though this is never the fault of his Virgil – his descriptions are often so vivid that one hardly knows where the real ends and the ideal begins. The following seven lines, taken nearly at random from the 'Earthly Paradise,' will serve as an example:–

Dusky and dim, though rich with gems and gold,
The house of Venus was; high in the dome
The burning sunlight you might now behold,
From nowhere else the light of day might come
To curse the Shame-faced Mother's lovely home;
A long way off the shrine the fresh sea-breeze,
Now just arising, brushed the myrtle-trees.

William Morris's birthplace was neither a library nor a studio. He was born in 1834, at Walthamstow, of that commercial class whose characteristics he so little admired in after life. His father, a substantial merchant, died in 1844, leaving, we believe, a considerable property. Young Morris was educated first at Forest School, Walthamstow, and then at the recently founded Marlborough College, whence he passed to Exeter College, Oxford. It was in the early days of the Pre-Raphaelites, to some of whom Oxford furnished a congenial home. Given the Pre-Raphaelite movement on the one hand, and a residence at Oxford on the other, it is easy to understand the forces that influenced an artistic undergraduate in those days. For a long time after 1856, the year of his degree he and his friends, Rossetti among them, left behind them a material memento of their Oxford life in the shape of the eight or ten frescoes of Arthurian subjects, since hopelessly ruined and at last removed, that used to decorate the debating-room of the Union. More lately, unless we are mistaken, some of Mr. Morris's handiwork has adorned the chapel of his old college, of which he was elected an honorary Fellow, with Sir E. Burne-Jones, in 1882. It was in 1863 that he established, with partners in the undertaking, the factory for the production of artistic glass, tiles, wall-paper, and the like, for which his name has long been famous; and it is in consequence of this unusual combination of manufacture and literature that he seemed to have a sort of dual existence in the eyes of the public. His poems were 'by Morris, the wall-paper maker,' his wall-papers 'by Morris, the poet.'

We have referred to his poems as his best work, and might justify the epithet on the ground that they are *aere perennius*, while the concrete productions of his factory must needs perish in process of time, or be debased by the imitations of inferior art. But we do not know that Morris himself would have taken this view of the fruits of his life. One cannot read his poems without feeling that their easy music, not hammered out, but flowing free, must have been a source of pleasure to the writer; yet his sense of beauty and his energy perhaps found a still keener gratification in the material things produced by his hand and under his direction. Enlarging on whatever Mr. Ruskin has said of the nobility of honest work, and utterly despising the notion that an artist should plan and design, but, save in the finest of fine art, not execute, Morris held not only that executive handicraft was within the province of an artist, but that all crafts demanded artistic treatment. This principle he preached and practised with a good deal of enthusiasm, we wish we could add with an equal degree of success. It was of 'us handicraftsmen' that he spoke to the Trades' Guilds; and it was as a 'common fellow' that he addressed a gathering of Birmingham artists and workmen. His cardinal principle was 'Art made by the people, and for the People, as a joy to the maker and the user.' 'I do not want art for a few any more than education for a few, or freedom for a few.' 'You,' he said, 'you whose hands make those things that should be works of art, you must be all artists, and good artists too, before the public at large can take real interest in such things; and when you have become so, I promise you that you shall lead the fashion; fashion shall follow your hands obediently enough.' That, he went on to say, is better than 'working helplessly among the crowd of those who are ridiculously called manufacturers, that is, handicraftsmen, though the more part of them never did a stroke of hand-work in their lives, and are nothing better than capitalists and salesmen.' It was the gospel of handiwork, its aims, methods, and rewards; taught, indeed, by a fellow-workman, but by one whom fortune permitted to exhort and to lead. There can be no doubt of the hopefulness with which Morris taught and followed his opinions. If they led him, as they have led other generous men before him, towards

Socialism, the world can afford to judge him indulgently, as not apprehending much danger from his rhetoric. We do not desire to enlarge on the unpractical extremes to which his industrial and political opinions tended; they are only the result of a warm heart and a mistaken enthusiasm; they indicate, not the strength of the man, but his weakness, and are as nothing compared with the lasting work of his better genius. It is to be feared that his ideals and aspirations for art will never approach realization. Here and there his example will continue to animate individuals; but no human power, even if the economic relations between consumers and producers, between users and makers, could change at his bidding, would give the mass of our workers a love or a knowledge of art. Our national nature, and the inevitable laws of economy, will not yield to persuasion, or promises, or dreams. Until they do so, only those who are willing to cry in the wilderness will prophesy the artistic millennium.

It must be allowed, however, that Morris's actual work was far more practical than his doctrine. The factory that he established more than 30 years ago in conjunction with such artists and kindred spirits as D. G. Rossetti, E. Burne-Jones, and Ford Madox Brown, was at first an experiment, but soon became a commercial success, and ultimately worked something like a domestic revolution. It may be suspected that fashion had as much share in the result as the latent aestheticism of the British public; and fashionable Mr. Morris's work certainly became, greatly to the improvement of our houses, and possibly of our taste also. To say that a thing, no matter what, was 'designed by Morris' was to pass a final verdict in its favour. Whether this improved state of things is permanent or not, and whether Mr. Morris's admirers and customers followed him with much conviction and intelligence, may be left as open questions. What is evident is that we are not at one with our fathers in matters of taste, and that our present ideas on such subjects have been mainly influenced by Mr. Morris and his school. Into the more serious issues that underlie his principles, and those of all real artists, it is not our business to enter. We record only work done, and only indicate the intention that inspired it; we say, in one word, that Morris's death has taken from us an original and singularly sincere artist, who worked hard to make the world a little more beautiful and a little more honest. His book on Socialism is nothing. It is always the expert in one subject who desires eminence in another. It is not the political visionary, but the delightful poet, the thorough craftsman, the subtle designer, the sumptuous printer, the many-sided man himself, whom we shall remember.

Punning on the name of Morris's most celebrated poem, some of his contemporaries jokingly referred to him as 'The Earthly Paradox'. He was a disconcerting man and he rejoiced in his ability to disconcert – it was not the simple matter of the poems being by 'Morris, the wallpaper maker' and the wallpapers being by 'Morris, the poet'. Morris famously saw no distinction between art and craft, and therefore no real distinction between the different arts. As a singularly alert disciple of Ruskin he began by adulating the craftsmen of the Middle Ages and ended by seeing the potential artist in the downtrodden industrial worker of the nineteenth century. He therefore preached a socialism which would be not only a means of liberating the artist but also of transforming society by purging it of the twin curses of capitalism and mechanisation. Morris died on 3 October 1896 at his house in Hammersmith where he had established his Kelmscott Press. Almost his last words were 'I want to get mumbo-jumbo out of the world.' Three days later his body was taken to Paddington Station, where a group of anarchists, including Russian Prince Kropotkin, laid wreaths on the coffin. It travelled by rail to Oxford and Lechlade and from thence, on a yellow-painted harvest cart, to the village of Kelmscott where Morris was buried in the churchyard.

JOHANNES BRAHMS

Composer: 'One and all of his works have in common the elements of absolute originality and distinction.'

3 APRIL 1897

We regret to announce that Herr Johannes Brahms, the illustrious composer, died in Vienna at 9 o'clock on Saturday morning from acute disease of the liver, from which he had been suffering for many months. The funeral ceremony will take place on Tuesday afternoon at the German Protestant Church; it is probable that the master's remains will be deposited in the municipal cemetery of Vienna, where the site for a tomb will be given by the town.

It is a far easier task to enumerate the outward events of Brahms's life than to attempt to assess his exact ultimate position among the great masters of music, though it is certain that his place is with the greatest of these. Reckoned by the ordinary standards of Court or official appointments, his career has been one of the least eventful that the history of art can show. The son of a double-bass player in the opera band at Hamburg, where he was born May 7, 1833, he was placed, while still a boy, under the care and tuition of Eduard Marxsen, of Altona, with the view of his becoming a pianoforte player. At the age of 20 he was engaged by a once famous violinist, Remenyi, as accompanist on a concert tour, in the course of which the current of his career was completely altered by a meeting with Joachim, whose friendship had the most important results on his life. Through the great violinist he was introduced to Schumann, who, on the strength of the compositions submitted to him – the earliest pianoforte sonatas and the first set of songs – declared the young man to be the composer for whose advent all Germany was as it were waiting. After his famous utterance on this subject, entitled 'Neue Bahnen,' the older master had but three years to live, but from that time until her death last year Brahms enjoyed the intimate friendship of Mme. Schumann, and treated her with almost filial love and reverence: by a curious coincidence, the chill from the effects of which the composer never quite recovered was brought on by an arduous journey undertaken in order that he might be present at Mme. Schumann's funeral. In 1854 Brahms was appointed choir-director and music-master to the Prince of Lippe-Detmold, a post he retained for a few years only; he had appeared occasionally at Hamburg as a pianist, and played his own concerto, op. 15, at the Gewandhaus at Leipzig in 1859. He went first in 1862 to Vienna still mainly as a pianist; in the following year he was appointed director of the Singakademie there, but gave this

up after a year, and travelled in Switzerland and other places until 1867, when he made his headquarters in Vienna. In 1872 he was conductor of the concerts of the 'Gesellschaft der Musikfreunde,' but resigned the appointment in favour of Herbeck in 1875, since which date he has held no official post of any kind.

It is seldom easy and never safe to predict either immortality or oblivion for a great man's work immediately after his death; but a few considerations concerning the work of Brahms as a whole may not be out of place. Although his life of nearly 64 years is more than the average length allotted to the great composers, his work contains not only no great revulsion of artistic convictions, but no very striking alteration of style from the beginning to the end of his career. The first song in the noble series of his lyrics, the passionate 'Liebestreu,' has many points in common with the sacred songs lately issued, and these again recall in many passages the beautiful solemnity of the 'Deutsches Requiem,' which marks almost the central point of his career as a composer. And a year or two ago the very first of his productions in concerted chamber music, the trio, op. 8, was revised by him, and here and there remodelled; the possibility of such a proceeding, and still more its complete success, is enough to prove that only very slight modifications of style and manner of expression had taken place between the earliest and latest periods. From this work in its first shape, to the two clarinet sonatas recently brought out, there stretches a succession of splendid chamber compositions, which, more than any other branch of his work, establish his position as the legitimate descendant of the great German masters, whose line appears to have ended with him. The two sextets, and the first of his three violin sonatas, won, by their flowing and melodious charm, many to the serious contemplation of his loftiest works who would otherwise have remained admirers only of his spirited Hungarian dances, or of the waltzes for vocal quartet which appeal to musical and unmusical people alike. His great orchestral works, the four symphonies, and the two overtures are remarkable far more for dignity of conception and the masterly thematic development than for the minor felicities of instrumentation which make for effect with the public at large; but such a work as the set of variations on a theme of Haydn is enough to prove his power of writing delicately as well as solidly for the band. In like manner his pianoforte works, or the bulk of them, appeal rather to the artist than to the virtuoso, although he provides abundantly for the latter's requirements in the stupendous variations on a caprice of Paganini. In the department of short choral works, of which his 'Schicksalslied' is, perhaps, the most famous example, he invented a new form, which has been used with good effect in England and elsewhere. It is not too much to say that one and all of his works have in common the elements of absolute originality and distinction, and that on each is stamped his own individuality; the peculiar beauty of his melodic invention is as much his own as his mastery of logical and powerful development of thematic material, often carried along lines entirely new in respect of form. This last characteristic, while it made the ultra-conservative critics of a past generation hesitate to accept his innovations, as they were then called, has procured for him the easy taunt of formalism from some of the newer critics of the present day, who have contrived to blind themselves to the beauty of his ideas and the grandeur of their treatment.

Brahms, who was not particularly enamoured of concert tours, never visited England. When he was proposed for an Honorary Degree by the University of Cambridge in May 1876 he declined the offer, and did so again when it was renewed in 1892. On the first occasion, however, his friend, the violinist, Joseph Joachim (who *had* accepted an Honorary

Degree) took with him the manuscript of Brahms's First Symphony and conducted the work in Cambridge on 7 March 1877. Cambridge may never have got its Academic Festival Overture (though the University of Breslau did in 1881) but London was to see the première of the 6 piano pieces *op.* 118 and the four piano pieces *op.* 119 in January 1894. Brahms died in Vienna on 3 April 1897 and was interred in the Central Cemetery.

* * *

CHARLES LUTWIDGE DODGSON (LEWIS CARROLL)

Humourist and mathematician: 'His chief title to fame will always rest on those jeux d'esprit *which have won him so secure a place in the affections of readers for whom mathematics are . . . the reverse of attractive.'*

14 JANUARY 1898

WE REGRET TO announce the death of the Rev. Charles Lutwidge Dodgson, better known as 'Lewis Carroll,' the delightful author of 'Alice in Wonderland,' and other books of an exquisitely whimsical humour. He died yesterday at The Chestnuts, Guildford, the residence of his sisters, in his 66th year. He was educated at Christ Church, Oxford, and distinguished himself in the Schools, taking a first class in Mathematical and a second in Classical Moderations, and a first in the Final Mathematical School, and a third in *Literae Humaniores.* He became a Senior Student of Christ Church in 1861 and in the same year mathematical lecturer, a post which he continued to fill for 20 years. In 1861 he was also ordained. He began his literary career in 1860 by the publication of 'A Syllabus of Plane Algebraical Geometry,' which was followed the next year by 'The Formulae of Plane Trigonometry.' 'A Guide to the Mathematical Student in Reading, Reviewing, and Writing Examples' made its appearance in 1864, and in 1865 'The Adventures of Alice in Wonderland' burst upon an astonished world. Few would have imagined that the quiet, reserved mathematician, a bachelor, who all his life was remarkable for his shyness and dislike of publicity, possessed the qualities necessary to produce a work which has stood the test of more than 30 years, and still captivates young and old alike by its quaint and original genius. This was the first, or one of the first, of those entertaining books, since become numerous, which afford almost equal enjoyment to boys and girls and to those children of a larger growth who, although years have rubbed off the bloom of their youthful illusions, yet preserve their love of innocent laughter and nonsense. 'Alice in Wonderland' was originally written to amuse one of Dean Liddell's daughters. The author was an intimate friend of the Dean and Mrs. Liddell, and took infinite pleasure in the society of their little girls. It was in order to beguile her hours of playtime that these diverting fancies were woven for one of the children. The success of the book was never in doubt, and the story is current, though we cannot vouch for its authenticity, that the Queen herself in reading it was so much delighted that she commanded the author to send his next work to Windsor. He did so, and her Majesty was almost as bewildered as Alice on finding that it consisted of 'An Elementary Treatise on Determinants'!

It is curious to notice how frequently 'Alice in Wonderland' is quoted in reference to public affairs, as well as to the ordinary matters of every day life. Hardly a week passes without the employment of its whimsicalities to point a moral or adorn a tale, and only yesterday a letter from a correspondent was published in *The Times* in which the Dreyfus-Esterhazy case was paralleled, with an aptness which was really surprising, from Lewis Carroll's immortal story. Some years ago Alice made her appearance on the London stage in a graceful dramatic version of the book, and delighted the children home for the Christmas holidays, for whose especial benefit ocular demonstration was given of her surprising experiences. In 1869 Lewis Carroll published 'Phantasmagoria and other Poems'; in 1870 'Songs from "Alice's Adventures in Wonderland,"' in 1871 'Through the Looking-Glass and What Alice Found There,' – a continuation which obtained almost the success of the original work – and in the same year 'Facts, Figures, and Fancies relating to the Elections to the Hebdomadal Council.' 'Euclid, Book V., Proved Algebraically,' made its appearance in 1874, to be followed two years later by another example of the author's versatility in 'The Hunting of the Snark, an Agony in Eight Fits.' His subsequent works include 'Doublets: a Word Puzzle,' 1871; 'Rhyme? and Reason?' 1883; 'A Tangled Tale,' 1885; 'Alice's Adventures Underground,' 1886; 'The Game of Logic,' 1887; 'Curiosa Mathematica, Part 1 – A New Theory of Parallels,' 1888; and 'Symbolic Logic,' 1896.

Although, as is abundantly evident from this list of his works, Lewis Carroll was a serious and hardworking mathematician, there can be no doubt that his chief title to fame will always rest on those *jeux d'esprit* which have won for him so secure a place in the affections of readers for whom mathematics are, as a rule, the reverse of attractive. In many a home and many a schoolroom there will be genuine sorrow today when it is announced that the author of 'Alice in Wonderland' and 'Through the Looking-Glass' has passed away.

> 'Lewis Carroll' was a talented mathematician, but his enterprise in that field is now almost certainly forgotten. His extraordinarily inventive *Alice* books, unlike most other Victorian children's books, continue to inspire, fascinate and enthral. They have been translated into most languages and have even been variously regarded as keys to the English sensibility and as the founding statements of European Surrealism. The obituarist dwells on the uneventful life of the 'quiet, reserved mathematician' and the shy bachelor and does not mention either Dodgson's only foreign trip – an extended overland visit to Russia in the summer of 1867 – or his pioneering work as a photographer. The 'infinite pleasure' Dodgson took in the society of little girls seems to have troubled the Liddell family and led to his alienation from his inspiration Alice Liddell. It also fascinates the far more scurrilous imaginations of latter-day commentators.

WILLIAM EWART GLADSTONE

Statesman: 'The first of our regular statesmen who, nurtured in the old régime, stepped forth as the spokesman of the new.'

19 MAY 1898

WILLIAM EWART GLADSTONE was born at Liverpool on the 29th of December, 1809. His father, created a baronet by Sir Robert Peel in 1846, was in 1809 Mr. John Gladstone, a Scotchman, partner in a great commercial house, of which he subsequently became the head, and already well known as a man of great energy and enterprise. He amassed a large fortune, and, the future of his children being secured, he was able to bring them up to whatever career seemed best suited to their characters. None can doubt that a wise choice was made when Eton, Oxford, and the House of Commons were selected for the fourth son. Mr. Gladstone's mother, a Miss Robertson, of Stornoway, is described as a lady of warm and sensitive disposition, and of a receptive and impressionable mind. On both sides, therefore, as he often subsequently pointed out, Mr. Gladstone was of Scottish descent. The paternal and maternal characters were blended in the statesman we have lost in almost equal degrees, and the combination is sufficient by itself to explain many passages of his public career which have provoked criticism and curiosity. And just as we may trace throughout his whole life these inherited elements of his nature in alternate or simultaneous operation, so, too, are we almost constantly reminded by it of the two very opposite worlds in which his youth was passed – Liverpool, the bustling centre of maritime and commercial industry, and Eton and Oxford, the homes of classic culture and medieval tradition.

Early life and development

Mr. Gladstone entered Eton in September, 1821, and remained there about six years. He carried off no prize, though his verses were frequently 'sent up.' While at school he was a constant contributor to the Eton Miscellany, and some of his fugitive pieces exhibit a maturity both of style and thought which is extremely striking. After leaving Eton he read for some time with a private tutor, Archdeacon Jones, and was admitted a student of Christ Church in the year 1828.

Those were stormy times both for England and the University. The passage of the Roman Catholic Relief Act had been a blow to political faith, from which perhaps it has hardly yet recovered. The Reform Bill which followed was described by Mr. Gladstone at the 'Union' as calculated 'to break up the very foundations of

An engraving (from an original painting) of a young Gladstone, at the time of his marriage

social order.' And it requires no great stretch of the imagination to picture to ourselves the young student sauntering along the stately avenues of Christ Church or Magdalen, fretting, like Newman, under the triumph of Liberalism, and framing to himself schemes for the salvation of society and the Church. We can imagine him during the heat of that momentous struggle, while carefully preparing for his final examination in the Schools, turning an eager eye at times from his cloistered studies to the tempest that was raging without and wondering perhaps whether his own voice would ever be heard above the storm. In October, 1831, the House of

Lords rejected the Reform Bill. Riots burst forth simultaneously in all quarters of the kingdom. Towns were sacked. The castles and manor houses of obnoxious aristocrats were burnt or plundered, and amid the din and havoc and bloodshed which almost became an insurrection, Mr. Gladstone, of Christ Church, was proclaimed to be a double first. A favourite of fortune from the first, a quiet Tory borough opened its arms to receive him as soon as he had quitted the shade of academic bowers, and after a brief tour on the Continent he took his seat for Newark in the Parliament of 1833.

Henceforth his life divides itself naturally into four parts – from 1833 to 1845, during which he was outwardly, at least, a Tory and High Churchman of the purest Anglican type; from 1845 to 1859, during which period no man could say for certain whether he was a Liberal or a Conservative; from 1859 down to 1885, during which he was at first the *spes altera*, and afterwards the honoured leader, of the whole Liberal party; and from the end of 1885 to his death, during which he broke away from the traditions of English statesmanship, parted with his most loyal followers, and erected the doctrines of Home Rule, flavoured with anarchy, into a cult.

In January, 1833, Mr. Gladstone is described as of robust appearance, with rather a full face, but decidedly handsome and engaging. He brought with him a high reputation, for an Oxford double first counted for much in 1833; while his known opinions at once caused him to be looked up to by the old High Church party in the House of Commons as the embodiment of all they held dear. He came into that assemblage, moreover, without any taint of those transactions about him which still clung to the Duke of Wellington and Sir Robert Peel, and made them objects of distrust and dislike among their own supporters. When Canning was being worried to death he had been writing elegiacs at Eton. When the Roman Catholic Relief Bill was sprung upon the Protestant majority he had been deep in Thucydides at Christ Church. He came up to Westminster in the full odour of orthodoxy, the representative of the new ideas and new feelings which had been breathed into men's minds by the 'Christian Year' and the Waverley Novels; the representative of the great Catholic and feudal revival which distinguished the first half of the present century; a scholar, a gentleman, and a young man of spotless private life. Here was evidently the future leader of the High Church Tories; here was the man they were on the look out for; and he continued to grow in favour with them till the time came for reducing their theories to practice, and then he discovered that he had been leaning on a broken reed.

In Sir Robert Peel's Administration of 1834–35 Mr. Gladstone was at first a Junior Lord of the Treasury and subsequently Under-Secretary to the Colonies. We are to presume that he saw nothing to object to in Sir Robert Peel's Ecclesiastical Commission and that it came under the head of those 'reforms of actual abuses' which he told his constituents at Newark were not inimical to Conservative principles, but the legitimate consequences of them. During the Parliamentary events of the next few years, Mr. Gladstone adhered strictly to the principles which he had professed from the beginning of his career – principles which were shortly to find their full literary and philosophical expression in his famous work on Church and State, published in the autumn of 1838, while the author was absent from England on a second Continental tour, undertaken for the benefit of his eyesight. It is curious that this effort, instead of being, as might have been expected, the formal inauguration of a policy which had long been floating in his mind, turned out to be in fact its knell. When the theory was thrown into distinct propositions, brought to the test of definition, and confronted with its practical results, the Tory party recognized its impracticability, and were, perhaps, also conscious that, after the events of 1828 and 1829, it was deficient in logic. During this sojourn in Italy at this period Mr. Gladstone made the ascent of Mount Etna and also witnessed one of its eruptions, which impressed him with a deep sense of Virgil's descriptive power and fidelity to nature. Returning home in the following year, he married, in July, 1839, Catherine, daughter of Mr. Stephen Glynne, of Hawarden Castle, in Flintshire. Shortly afterwards the Whig Ministry was dissolved, Sir Robert Peel returned to power, and Mr. Gladstone became Vice-President of the Board of Trade. As far as we can divine from his own account of the matter, some suspicion of the tenability of his own ground had began to creep into his mind before anything was said about the Maynooth grant. When, however, Sir Robert Peel opened his mind to him on the subject the film fell from his eyes at once. His long cherished theory was not to be carried out in England. If not absolutely, it was at least relatively, untrue. And frankly accepting this conclusion, which 30 years afterwards he explained and developed more fully, he retired from his position in the Ministry. He seems to have regarded this step in the light of a parting act of homage to the principles which he had so long and so earnestly professed, and as a recognition of the right of the public to some substantial and ample evidence of his sincerity. He represented his retirement from the Board of Trade as a very considerable sacrifice, and as a proof that he did not desert his old convictions in any spirit of levity or cynicism. It is, perhaps, to be wished that if Mr. Gladstone thought all this in 1844, he had not deferred saying it till 1868. However, he was now, in his own eyes, emancipated from the trammels of his former theory and free to act as he liked upon all ecclesiastical questions. 'With a great price purchased I this freedom,' he declares in his Chapter of Autobiography, and with this act of penance the first portion of his public life comes to its conclusion.

Evolution as a Peelite

When in the following year, 1845, Lord Stanley resigned upon the Corn Law question, Mr. Gladstone had no hesitation in accepting the vacant place in the Ministry; but on seeking re-election at Newark he found that he had forfeited the favour of his patron, the Duke of Newcastle, and he remained out of Parliament till the general election of 1847, when he was first returned for the University of Oxford. In the House of Commons he at once became a prominent member of that little knot of politicians who acquired for themselves the title of the Peelites, acknowledging no leader but Sir Robert Peel, who was now out of office, and holding a position between the Tories and the Liberals analogous to that once held by the followers of Mr. Canning and earlier still by the followers of Lord Grenville. During the Ministry of Lord John Russell, Mr. Gladstone distinguished himself on two memorable occasions. When Lord Palmerston's policy in the Pacifico case was challenged by Parliament, Mr. Gladstone delivered a most telling speech against the then Foreign Secretary – a speech so powerful and so damaging that Mr. Cockburn, the late Lord Chief Justice, who won his ermine on the other side, said that he supposed that Mr. Gladstone might now be regarded as Lord Derby's representative in that House *vice* Disraeli superseded. His criticism of the *Civis Romanus sum* doctrine was remarkably fine, and the style in which he repudiated the assumption that England had a mission to be the censor of vice and folly, of abuse and imperfection among the other countries of the world, stands in curious contrast to some of his later utterances. The second great speech to which we have referred was against the Ecclesiastical Titles Bill, in which will be found rhetorical passages of a very high order of merit. Of Mr. Gladstone it would probably be true to say that at this time he leaned rather to the Conservative than to the Liberal side of the Peelite party. He more than once spoke and voted in favour of resolutions proposed by Mr. Disraeli for the relief of the agricultural interest; and it was the common report in those days, sanctioned, indeed, by Mr. Gladstone himself at a later period, that he would not have been unwilling to serve under Lord Derby had any of the other followers of Sir Robert Peel been ready to accompany him. When Lord Russell resigned office, only to return again on Lord Derby's failure to form a Government, the leadership of the House of Commons was at the command of Mr. Gladstone had he chosen to join his old party. Events, however, took a different turn. On the Budget debate of 1852 Mr. Gladstone stood forth as the most acrimonious critic of Lord Derby's lieutenant, and is supposed to have done what has rarely been done by any single speech in the House of Commons – turned the division against the Ministry; and henceforth there was a jealousy between the two men, which interposed fresh obstacles to Mr. Gladstone's return to the fold, though for some years it was not considered absolutely hopeless. In the Government which followed, commonly known as the Coalition Government, the leading Peelites occupied important posts, and Mr. Gladstone became Chancellor of the Exchequer. And here, perhaps, one may be permitted to pause for a few moments to note the loss which the country had recently sustained in the death of Sir Robert Peel, who was killed by a fall from his horse in the previous year. Had he been alive, he, and not Lord Derby, would have been probably requested to succeed Lord Russell at the Treasury. He might perhaps have reunited under his command the whole Conservative party, and, being at that time only in his 63rd year, might have had a long career of power still before him. In that case what would have been the future of Mr. Gladstone, and what the future of Lord Beaconsfield?

That Mr. Gladstone, in common with the other Peelites, was no great admirer of the foreign policy of Lord Palmerston had been sufficiently proved by his speech in the Pacifico debate. Yet it must be owned that he himself in his letters on the Neapolitan prisons was in reality calling upon England to play much the same part which he had condemned in the case of that statesman. However this may be, there can be no doubt that these letters, which appeared at intervals in the years 1851 and 1852, and were the result of a visit to Naples in the winter of 1850–51, produced a profound sensation both in England and the Continent and contributed largely to the formation of that public opinion in this country which gave a moral support to the French war of 1859, led to the deposition of the Italian Bourbons, and paved the way for Italian unity.

During all the Cabinet deliberations which preceded the Crimean war, it appears from the correspondence of Lord Palmerston that the Peelite section of the Ministry acted as a check upon the more vigorous counsels of the Home Secretary, who seems to have thought from the first that a more decided attitude on the part of England might have prevented any outbreak of hostilities. It was not to be, however; and in March 1854, the forty years' rest which the land had enjoyed after the fall of Napoleon was broken by a declaration of war against Russia. During this period Mr. Gladstone seems to have been chiefly taken up with the business of his department, but in the year following he was destined to take up a position which bid fair at one time to bring him back to the Conservatives. When Lord Aberdeen resigned office in January, 1855, Lord Derby was requested by the Queen to form a new Administration. His party was very strong in the House of Commons, and on any great emergency could bring 300 votes into the field. Installed in power for the express purpose of bringing the war to a successful issue, it was calculated that they might have relied on a good deal of independent support, and that if this failed a dissolution would ensure them a majority. These were the views of Mr. Disraeli; but Lord Derby, on finding that neither Lord Palmerston, nor Mr. Gladstone, nor Mr. Sidney Herbert felt able to assist him, abandoned the attempt, and Lord Palmerston succeeded to the helm. Mr. Gladstone resumed the Exchequer; but on

Lord Palmerston consenting to a Committee of Inquiry into the conduct of the late Administration, which in Mr. Gladstone's eyes implied a censure on his former colleagues, he at once retired, carrying with him, if, indeed, they did not rather carry him, Mr. Sidney Herbert and Sir James Graham. Mr. Gladstone now remained out of office for rather more than four years, and during this period he again began to gravitate towards his former friends, the Conservatives. He joined with Mr. Disraeli in condemning the financial policy of Sir G. C. Lewis. He was a vehement opponent of the Divorce Bill, on which he engaged in a series of brilliant passages of arms with Sir Richard Bethell, afterwards his colleague as Lord Chancellor in the second Palmerston Administration. The use of the forms of the House to delay the progress of this measure offered, perhaps, the earliest example of the tactics perfected at a later day by Mr. Parnell's followers. Mr. Gladstone spoke warmly in condemnation of the Government in the memorable affair of the lorcha Arrow; and he concurred in the vote of censure which drove Lord Palmerston from office in 1858.

After the adverse vote on the China question Lord Palmerston had appealed to the country and obtained a great accession of strength, one result being the practical dissolution of the Peelites as a separate party. The consequence was that when, in 1858, Lord Derby consented for a second time to assume the conduct of the Government he found himself in a much worse position than he would have occupied three years before. But at the same time the very fact that the Peelite party as such had almost ceased to exist was one reason why the three or four eminent men who still represented it in Parliament should have agreed no longer to be bound by its mere shadow, and have declared themselves free to act independently of each other. Mr. Gladstone's ambiguous and hesitating movements were watched with interest by the British public during these eventful years. The approval of Mr. Disraeli's Budget in 1858; the mission to the Ionian Islands, which he accepted from the hands of Lord Derby; the support of the Ministerial Reform Bill in 1859; the vote against Lord Hartington's motion of want of confidence in the Government – all seemed to imply that Mr. Gladstone was paving his own way for a reunion with his former colleague, from whom at this period of his life he seemed severed by no difference of principle, while bound to him at the same time by a community of tastes and habits, the force of which no political conflicts had ever been allowed to weaken. It was with some surprise, therefore, that, on the resignation of Lord Derby, the public learnt that he had accepted office under Lord Palmerston. Mr. Gladstone's own explanation of it appeared in *The Times* of that date in the form of a letter to the Provost of Oriel on the occasion of his re-election for the University being opposed by the Marquis of Chandos. He acknowledged that he owed something to Lord Derby for the mission to the Ionian Islands, but declared that he had paid the debt by his support of the Reform Bill and his opposition to the vote of want of confidence.

A Liberal Minister

From these ambiguous passages in Mr. Gladstone's history, we pass on to what is still looked back upon by a few surviving Parliamentary veterans as the golden age of modern politics: Budgets which were as interesting as fairy tales, and as satisfactory in their results as they were interesting; abundant harvests; an ever-growing commerce; and a lull of all domestic strife such as had scarcely been experienced since the days of old, when Canning and Huskisson were serving under the judicious Liverpool. The year 1859, at the same time, marks another turning point in Mr. Gladstone's career, when he for the first time cut himself completely adrift from his former connexion and finally committed himself to the advanced Liberal cause. We say advanced, because Mr. Gladstone was regarded by this section of the Liberals as their own representative in the House of Commons, and because it is perfectly well known that between himself and his chief important differences of opinion existed to the last both on foreign and on financial questions. We need only remind our readers that the French Commercial Treaty was never much liked by the head of the Government which concluded it, and that in the year 1862 Mr. Gladstone made some financial speeches at Manchester which drew down on him a remonstrance from the Premier. The subject was the National Defences, and Mr. Gladstone had asserted that the country, under the influence of an unreasonable panic, had forced upon the Government a wholly unnecessary expenditure. Lord Palmerston denied either that the fears of the public were unreasonable or that the expenditure had been forced on the Government. In 1864, in a letter to Lord Russell on the subject of the Danish war, Lord Palmerston says:–

> 'As to Cabinets, if we had colleagues like those who sat in Pitt's Cabinet, such as Westmoreland and others, or such men as those who were with Peel like Goulburn and Hardinge, you and I might have our own way on most things; but when, as is now the case, able men fill every department, such men will have opinions and hold to them; but, unfortunately, they are often too busy with their own department to follow up foreign questions so as to be fully masters of them, and their conclusions are generally on the timid side of what might be best.'

And among the able men here referred to no doubt the ablest was Mr. Gladstone. During these years he was rapidly winning for himself his high financial reputation. The cheap breakfast table became a watchword among his humbler admirers, and served him well on several subsequent occasions. His views on the American Civil War were not, perhaps, quite so much to the popular taste, as all his sympathies lay with the gallant Southern aristocracy, in whose struggle for independence he may have seen something as deserving of admiration as in the Northern contest for supremacy. On the question of Church rates, 25 or 30 years ago, Mr. Gladstone seems to have vacillated. He spoke and voted against Sir John Trelawny's motion, as he did against Sir Morton Peto's Burials Bill and against Mr. Dodson's Clerical Subscription Bill, but always with an air of reservation, as if he was saying as little as he could and did not seem certain of his ground. In the Session of 1865, however, he was destined to let fall an *obiter dictum* on the subject of the Irish Church which had an important influence on events, and may have swayed Mr. Gladstone himself more perhaps than he was aware of at the time. He then said, in reply to Mr. Dillwyn, who on the 28th of March had moved a resolution to the effect that the state of the Irish Church was unsatisfactory and called for the early attention of the Government, that though he could not assent to this proposition, yet 'the Irish Church was the question of the future.' It is not surprising that these words should have produced a great sensation. On the majority of Mr. Gladstone's constituents they fell like a thunderbolt. Six years before they had complained of his definitely throwing in his lot with the Liberal party. But this was something far worse, and finally completed the alienation which his union with Lord Palmerston had begun. Nor did Mr. Gladstone much mend matters by the letter which he wrote in reply to Dr. Hannah, the Warden of Trinity College, Glenalmond, who had asked for some explanation of his words. The letter really amounted to this – that he had no explanation to give; the Irish Church was the 'question of the future,' though when that future might arrive was quite another matter, with which he was not called upon to deal. At this distance of time, and surveying the question quite calmly, we may be permitted, perhaps, to say that this answer could hardly be considered satisfactory by the English clergy, whom Mr. Gladstone himself had trained in such very different doctrines. He has himself left on record an admission that 'the great and glaring change' in his course of action on this question stood in need of justification. It will scarcely be thought now that the University of Oxford deserved all the reproaches which were showered on her for the rejection of so distinguished a representative, especially as he himself has acknowledged that his opinions on the Irish Church were not easily reconcilable with his duty to his constituents. However, at the general election of 1865 Mr. Gathorne Hardy, now Lord Cranbrook, was preferred to Mr. Gladstone, who, except on personal grounds, could scarcely have regretted the result. If he had been 'hampered' by his work on Church and State, he had also been hampered by his connexion with Oxford, and he was now entirely free to throw away the past for ever and deal as he chose with the future.

The first use which he made of his freedom was not perhaps prudent; but it did him no injury in the long run. After the death of Lord Palmerston he became leader of the House of Commons under Lord Russell, and immediately formed a close alliance with Mr. Bright for the purpose of carrying a Reform Bill. This step had the immediate effect of dividing the Liberal Party and producing the celebrated 'Cave.' But it proclaimed his sympathy with advanced Liberal opinions, and paved the way for his victory three years afterwards. The direct result was the defeat of the Government on a motion to substitue a rating for a rental franchise, and the return of the Conservatives to power for the third time. Mr. Gladstone for a time led the opposition to Mr. Disraeli's Reform Bill, but, finding that his party would not follow him, and being defeated by a majority of 21 on what he considered a test resolution, he announced his determination not to act as leader any longer. Though he did not carry out this intention literally, and indeed succeeded in obtaining material modifications in the Bill, he did cease as a matter of fact to take any very prominent part in the debates which followed. But in the Session of 1868 he again came to the front with his resolutions on the Irish Church, which he succeeded in carrying against the Government by large majorities. The Suspensory Bill was carried in the Lower House with the same rush, but, as was natural, in view of the pending general election, was thrown out in the Upper House.

First Administration

The appeal to the new constituencies was made in the following November, when Mr. Gladstone's triumph was complete. The Liberal Majority amounted to 120: and Mr. Gladstone, to whom Lord Russell had resigned the leadership of the party, at once became Prime Minister. This Administration will long be memorable in history, and it is certainly that portion of Mr. Gladstone's career which will look the brightest in the eyes of posterity. If that brightness is here and there chequered by a lurid shade, it is neither obscured nor deformed by it. Nor will history readily point to any other Administration in the annals of Parliamentary government, except perhaps the Government of Lord Grey, which for boldness and breadth of legislation and the intellectual power displayed by its leader will bear comparison with the five years of Liberal government from 1869 to 1874. If the Irish Policy of Mr. Gladstone be regarded as a whole, it involved a deeper and more far-reaching revolution than even the Reform Bill of 1832. The easy mastery of almost countless details, the luminous exposition of ramified and extensive changes, and the eloquent vindication of principles which distinguish all his principal speeches on the Church Act and the Land Act constitute them a treasure-house of Parliamentary oratory, unsurpassed, if not unequalled, in their kind by any others which have been preserved to us. It is noteworthy that on the Irish Land Act debates of 1870 Mr. Gladstone displayed no hostility of any kind towards the landed interest as a class. He almost went out of his way to pay the highest compliment to the English territorial aristocracy which has ever been clothed in words, and said more than once that if the Irish gentry, whom he fully acquitted as a whole of cruelty or unfair dealing, had been like the English no change would have been necessary, no improvement possible.

The legislative energy of which Mr. Gladstone's first Ministry possessed an extraordinary share was not perceptibly diminished by its expenditure on the Irish Church and Land Bills, but the forces of opposition quickly rallied, and hardly any other measures passed with equal ease. The Irish Peace Preservation Bill was an early admission that the policy of conciliation could not be exclusively relied upon. The Endowed Schools Bill was taken as a provocation by the Church, and the Elementary Education Bill aroused a still more dangerous spirit of discontent among the Nonconformists. The prerogative of the Crown was employed to carry out the abolition of purchase when the Army Regulation Bill seemed to be in danger. The Ballot Bill and the Licensing Bill were delayed by a vehement and obstinate resistance. Yet in addition to these measures the Government and the Liberal majority carried the Bankruptcy Bill, the University Tests Bill, the Habitual Criminals Bill, the Trades Union Bill, the Public Health Bill, the Mines Regulation bill, the Adulteration Bill, and the Judicature Bill – an aggregate of legislative work never before accomplished in an equal space of time. The collapse of the Irish University Bill was, perhaps, not wholly due to the demerits, palpable as they were, of the scheme, but also to the growing unpopularity of the Ministry, evinced by the results of by-elections and acknowledged by Mr. Gladstone himself. Apart from 'the harassed interests,' Mr. Gladstone had to reckon with the discontent of the public at many points in his external and domestic policy, the want of prevision displayed when the Franco-German war broke out, the reduction of armaments followed by panic-stricken expenditure, the cold shoulder given to the colonists, the surrender to Russia in the Black Sea, the attitude of submission on easy terms displayed in the Washington Treaty and the Geneva arbitration, the Army Warrant, the disasters in the Navy, Mr. Lowe's Match Tax, the Collier Promotion, and the Ewelme Rectory case. Mr. Disraeli hardly exaggerated the case when he said that the Government lived for months 'in a blaze of apology.' In passing the Education Act and the Licensing Act, and in carrying out the Abolition of Purchase, Mr. Gladstone, still more than in his Irish policy, had enormous difficulties to overcome, and powerful vested interests to appease. He succeeded in the first object, but not altogether in the second. The Army resented the abolition of purchase. The Church of England continued to resent the introduction of Board schools, the Dissenters sulked over the 25th clause, and the enmity of the licensed victuallers swelled the hostile array into irresistible proportions. On Mr. Disraeli's refusal to take office after the defeat of the University Bill, Mr. Gladstone was obliged to resume the reins of power, only, however, to find them torn from his hands a few months later, when, in January, 1874, he appealed to the country, notwithstanding the bait held out to it in the promised abolition of the income-tax.

It must not be forgotten that Mr. Gladstone's Government at the height of his successes at home was very unpopular on the Continent. On the outbreak of the Franco-German war he, though at the time Prime Minister, published an article in a review in which he read a sharp moral lecture to both belligerents. He rebuked France, then struggling with victorious Germany, for her levity and folly, which made her 'a calamity to herself' and 'a standing cause of unrest to Europe.' He was severe on Germany for 'the harsh, almost brutal, announcement' of her determination to annex Alsace and Lorraine, 'a proceeding which,' he said, 'could not be justified in the eyes of the world and of posterity by any mere assertion of power.' He contrasted the convulsions of Continental strife with the Olympian peace of 'Happy England,' protected against dangers and temptations by the 'streak of silver sea' that cuts her off from the mainland, a beatitude he seemed to have forgotten in later years when he was converted, in Opposition, to Sir Edward Watkin's Channel Tunnel project. The authorship of this curious production was from the first an open secret. It bred much bad blood and largely aided in creating that dislike and distrust of Mr. Gladstone, which was strongly felt in Germany and frankly expressed by Prince Bismarck, and which was for a long time a powerful factor in foreign policy.

Opposition and Eastern question

The history of Mr. Gladstone's career during the six years that followed his overthrow in 1874 can only be presented to the public in very blended hues. His first act in Parliament of any importance after the formation of the new Government was to oppose the Public Worship Regulation Bill for which he proposed to substitute six resolutions, declaratory of the inexpediency of interfering with diversities of practice in the Church. Mr. Disraeli at once invited the House of Commons to read the Bill a second time without delay, and to take the real debate on Mr. Gladstone's resolutions. After the second reading, however, the right hon. gentleman withdrew them all; but he continued to assail the ecclesiastical policy of the Government, both in their Scotch Patronage Bill and their Endowed Schools Bill. In the following year, however, he formally resigned the leadership of the Liberal party, and but for the events which shortly afterwards occurred in Eastern Europe might possibly never have resumed it. From 1876, however, to 1880 he threw himself on the foreign policy of the Government with a vehemence, or rather with a sustained ferocity, which produced a greater effect on public opinion than was perhaps apparent at the time. His denunciation of the 'Bulgarian atrocities' seriously shook the popularity of the Government, which was charged with conniving at them. And though, as soon as the war broke out between Russia and Turkey, and the people of this country clearly understood what the interests of this country demanded, a reaction began in favour of the Ministerial policy, yet with the Afghan and Zulu wars the original impression produced by Mr. Gladstone's rhetoric began to revive, and a feeling sprang up akin to that which took possession of the public mind some 50 years ago in regard to the policy of Lord Palmerston. Full justice has been done to that great statesman since his death, and the policy of Lord Beaconsfield is now better understood than it was in 1879 and 1880. But wars of this nature, Nullos habitura triumphos, are always dangerous weapons in the hands of a political adversary, and they lost none of their effect, assuredly, in the hands of Mr. Gladstone. On the head of these embarrassments came a falling revenue, deficient harvests, and commercial stagnation. And it shows the magic of Mr. Gladstone's oratory that he no doubt did succeed to some extent in persuading the working classes that his own return to power would improve the seasons and bring back prosperity at once. Down to the last moment, indeed, it continued to be extremely doubtful how deep was the impression he had made. Selected to stand against Lord Dalkeith for the representation of Mid Lothian, he spent a fortnight in addressing his future constituents, in which he travelled over the whole case against the Government, and brought out every point against them with merciless severity. Yet immediately afterwards at Liverpool, at Sheffield, and at Southwark came strong demonstrations of opinion in favour of the Conservatives. Relying upon these, Lord Beaconsfield dissolved Parliament at the end of March, 1880, with the result of restoring Mr. Gladstone to power with an overwhelming majority.

Second Administration

The second Administration of Mr. Gladstone originated in a misunderstanding, which was perhaps really at the bottom of its subsequent difficulties. A Whig or moderate Liberal Ministry, with a very temperate programme of reform, was looked upon as the necessary result of a Liberal victory at the polling booths, which, if won at all – a point which was considered very doubtful – would still, it was supposed, leave parties very evenly divided. Mr. Gladstone having come back like Achilles, to win the day for his friends, would take a graceful farewell of public life, and Lord Granville or Lord Hartington would be appointed the successor of Lord Beaconsfield. But the triumph of the Liberal party was like the battle of the Nile – not a victory but a conquest. The Conservative Government, apparently so strong, went down in a moment, as though the ground beneath its feet had been a quicksand. This result, however, was brought about by the votes of that moderate party, who, one for one reason and another for another, voted against the Government, in the expectation that it would be succeeded by a moderate Liberal Administration. The consequence was that when the new Ministry was formed with Mr. Gladstone at its head, and Mr. Chamberlain and Sir Charles Dilke in important offices, it did not correspond to the anticipations of many who had contributed to its establishment, and both inside and outside of the House many of its nominal adherents were disappointed and dissatisfied. This, however, was not Mr. Gladstone's fault. His fault lay in not fully recognizing the truth, and for want of doing so he exposed himself to several mortifications which it was quite within his power to have escaped. Among these may be reckoned the position of undignified neutrality to which he was reduced, by his own act, in connexion with the return of Mr. Bradlaugh for Northampton and the contest in which the House became involved through it with the electors of that borough. Throughout these transactions Mr. Gladstone allowed the lead of the majority to pass into the hands of Sir Stafford Northcote, who thus became the spokesman of the sense of the House of Commons, and the vindicator of its authority.

For the first three years of its existence Ireland was destined to be the stumbling-block of the new Administration. That Mr. Gladstone was in error in not renewing the Peace Preservation Act in 1880, in spite of the warnings and the actual information tendered him by the outgoing Government, was proved by what followed, and by the necessity for the Protection to Life and Property Bill, which was recognized in the following winter; nor will history say much more in favour of the Compensation for Disturbance Bill, which was the principal attempt at Irish legislation during his first Session. By the Act of 1870 non-payment of rent deprived the tenant of his right to claim damages for eviction. The Bill of 1880 was intended to nullify this provision by making it inoperative, wherever the tenant could plead bad crops, or the landlord's unwillingness to accept reasonable terms, which, of course, he could always do. The Bill was rejected by the House of Lords; but a dangerous spirit had been roused in the land, and during the following autumn began that 'reign of terror' which equalled, if it did not surpass, the blackest page of Ireland's history. In November of that year Mr. Gladstone made a speech at the Guildhall which all lovers of order received with pleasure. The Irish must learn, he said, that the resources of civilization were not yet exhausted; and when, in the following January, Parliament being called together a month earlier for the purpose, a Protection to Life and Property Bill, practically giving the Executive the power to imprison 'suspects' without trial, was introduced, men began to think that the Premier was about to strangle the serpent in good earnest. A few weeks later the Peace Preservation Act was renewed; and then, on the 7th of April, Mr. Gladstone, having declared that coercive and remedial measures must go hand in hand, produced his second Irish Land Bill. About this time his great rival and life-long antagonist – the words are Mr. Gladstone's own – was removed from the scene, and did not leave his peer. Lord Beaconsfield died on the 19th of April in the middle of the Easter Vacation, and it devolved on Mr. Gladstone to pay the customary tribute to his memory in the House of Commons. It was admitted on all hands that he performed this task to admiration, and his recognition of Lord Beaconsfield's triumphal return from Berlin *spoliis insignis opimis* and taller by a head than any of his contemporaries may rank among the masterpieces of elegiac rhetoric.

With the resumption of business, the second Irish Land Bill began to make progress and Mr. Gladstone displayed his usual energy and mastery of detail in dealing with it. It was felt, however, to be a somewhat dangerous, if not uncalled for, departure from the principles of the former one; it established fixity of tenure, fair rents, and free sale, all of which Mr. Gladstone had demonstrated in 1870 to be economically unsound and politically dangerous; and the dissatisfaction of his Whig supporters began now to appear. The Lords carried one important amendment in it, to the effect that the sum given for the tenant-right by the incoming tenant should form no title to a reduction, and the Bill passed, not, however, without a strong protest from Lord Salisbury. During the autumn the condition of Ireland grew worse and worse, and the League avowed a determination to nullify the Land Act, till eventually, in the month of October, Mr. Parnell was arrested and lodged in Kilmainham Gaol, when a manifesto was at once issued by the League declaring that no rent was to be paid till the 'suspects' were released.

The first business, however, proposed to the House in 1882 was the new Rules of Procedure, which Mr. Gladstone declared to be necessary in consequence of the new system of obstruction which had recently been developed. Events, however, caused the postponement of these resolutions for a time, and they were ultimately adjourned to an autumn sitting. Public opinion was still in a very heated state on the subject of Ireland; Mr. Gladstone had made a rather indiscreet allusion to 'separate Legislatures,' and the time taken up in protesting against the Committee of Inquiry into the working of the Land Act, adopted by the House of Lords, was not thought to have been very wisely spent. Meanwhile rumours got abroad with regard to a secret understanding between the Government and the Kilmainham prisoners, which made the friends of the Ministry look anxious. The release of Mr. Parnell, followed by the resignation of the Lord Lieutenant, Lord Cowper, and the Chief Secretary, Mr. Forster, was the prelude to an imperfect but sufficiently startling disclosure. It now became plain, in spite of ingenious verbal subtleties, that the Government had offered freedom to Mr. Parnell as the price of his putting down the outrages which the law was powerless to arrest. The organization which had created the reign of terror was to be employed to quell it, and as soon as this trafficking with treason became known, Mr. Forster declined all further responsibility for the government of Ireland. It is deeply to be regretted that Mr. Gladstone should have allowed himself to be betrayed into this unhappy error; and it was believed at the time, and is probably quite true, that had a leader of the calibre of Lord Beaconsfield existed on the other side, his Government would then and there have terminated. However, the storm blew over for the moment. Lord Spencer became Lord Lieutenant and Lord Frederick Cavendish Chief Secretary. But the momentary calm was ended by the most terrible tragedy of all which the roll of Irish crime had yet to show. On Saturday, May 6, the Chief Secretary and Mr. Burke, the Under-Secretary for Ireland, were murdered in the Phoenix Park, in broad daylight, by assassins armed with long knives, who drove away afterwards in a car and eluded all pursuit. A Crimes Bill was at once introduced creating a special procedure for the trial of offences that eluded the grasp of the ordinary law, and, true to his policy of combining severity with indulgence, Mr. Gladstone introduced at the same time an Arrears Bill, which, however, was naturally regarded by his enemies as one article of the Kilmainham Treaty. To the Crimes Bill the most determined opposition was offered by the Irish members, of whom on one occasion 16 were suspended in a batch. But it was, of course, carried through both Houses, and became law on the 12th of July.

Egypt and Reform

It was during the Session of 1882 that the Egyptian question first began to assume threatening proportions; and in consequence, as it was said, of dissensions in the Cabinet, was allowed to drift, till at last a British fleet found itself opposite the forts of Alexandria, and the rebel, Arabi, bold enough to appeal to force. His fortifications were shattered and the fortress taken by the British, but the town of Alexandria was destroyed; and for all this bloodshed and ruin there seemed to Mr. Bright so little justification that he retired from the Cabinet. The bombardment of Alexandria was followed by Lord Wolseley's expedition and the battle of Tel-el-Kebir on the 28th of August; and still Mr. Gladstone insisted on a speedy evacuation. However, after Arabi's trial and sentence to transportation, things remained tranquil for a time, and Mr. Gladstone was able to devote the month of November to the carriage of his new Rules of Procedure, the first attempt that had been made to effect a permanent alteration in the constitution of the House of Commons by placing an absolute control over freedom of debate in the hands of the Speaker, and the precedent for further changes in the same direction carried out at a later period by Mr. Gladstone's opponents.

With the Session of 1883 Mr. Gladstone found himself in a position to commence that course of legislative reform of which some years before he had published a comprehensive sketch. A Bill for securing purity of election, an Agricultural Holdings Bill, and a Bankruptcy Bill were passed into law this Session; while the Budget was accompanied by a National Debt Bill, of which great things were prematurely predicted. But the shadow of foreign affairs still hung over the Administration. Towards the close of the Session the Suez Canal became a source of much trouble and embarrassment. In an evil hour the Government had gone so far as to recognize M. de Lesseps's claim to a monopoly of the Isthmus communications; and the disclosure of the fact raised such a storm in England that Mr.

Gladstone, threatened with the censure of the House of Commons, was compelled to retrace his steps and withdraw from the position he had assumed. The attitude assumed by the Colonial Office towards the loyal Bechuanas in South Africa, who had assisted us during the Transvaal rebellion, and who now seemed likely to be abandoned to their fate, which simply meant serfdom under the Boers, drew a very powerful speech from Mr. Forster towards the close of the Session, and another at Bradford in December. And all these things contributed their share to that gradual labefaction, as Johnson would have called it, of Mr. Gladstone's Government, to which no man could shut his eyes at the time. But the personal weight of Mr. Gladstone, his great services, his undiminished popularity with a large section of the working classes, and his undeniable superiority in debate to every other living statesman, carried him through all his difficulties down to the beginning of the year 1884, and even then, could the Government only have known the things pertaining to its peace, and made up its mind to the only policy in Egypt which was consistent either with the welfare of that country or our own credit and honour, all might have yet gone well. Although the victory of Tel-el-Kebir had, it was fondly hoped, practically settled the Egyptian question, those best acquainted with the subject predicted that the withdrawal of our troops would lead to fresh troubles in the Sudan; nor was it long before these forebodings were justified. Ominous reports continued to reach this country of the progress of the Mahdi, but nothing serious had occurred when Mr. Gladstone, in the month of September, started, in company with Lord Tennyson, on a yachting tour. Mr. Gladstone visited many of the most interesting spots in the Western Orkneys, and was everywhere greeted with enthusiasm. He extended his voyage as far as Copenhagen, where he met the then Emperor and Empress of Russia and the King of the Hellenes. The Prime Minister returned home in excellent health and spirits. But the autumn and winter brought him renewed troubles, which clouded the last days of his Administration, and materially affected the progress of those great measures by which he had hoped to illustrate it.

The Session of 1884 opened under unfavourable auspices, for Mr. Gladstone was compelled by the force of public opinion and the hostile attitude of the House of Commons to bring in a Bill on the subject of cattle disease, of which no notice had been taken in the Queen's Speech, and which his Cabinet declared to be unnecessary. In attempting to expunge some amendments introduced into it in the House of Lords, he was defeated in the House of Commons by a majority of 24; while previously to this, on the 28th of March, he had been defeated on Mr. Pell's local taxation motion by a majority of 11. It was hoped, however, that the triumphs of the summer would eclipse the minor failures of the spring; and that with the lustre of three great reforms 'playing round his bayonets,' Mr. Gladstone would march on to a dissolution secure of victory. The Reform Bill was introduced by Mr.

Gladstone in a speech of great power and lucidity on the 28th of February, and was read a second time, after a debate of seven nights, on the 9th of April. The Government majority on this occasion was 130, but, as events proved, it was no fair test of the real opinion of the House. There were several objections to the measure which combined against it from the first many politicians of the most discordant views, though they did not think it necessary to oppose the second reading of the Bill. It was felt that all the reasons which had been pointed out with such fatal clearness by the late Lord Derby in 1866 against separating the scheme into two parts, and carrying a franchise Bill without the redistribution of seats being annexed to it, told with equal if not greater force in 1884. It was also urged that the extension of the Bill to Ireland in the then temper of the Irish people was a dangerous, if not desperate, experiment. The Government, however, were determined to go on as they had begun, and after two amendments embodying the objections we have mentioned had been successfully encountered, the House went into Committee. The progress of the Bill was unexpectedly rapid. It reached the Upper House towards the end of June. On the second reading Lord Cairns's amendment, declining to proceed with the measure till either the redistribution scheme had been produced or adequate security was given that it would come into operation simultaneously with the new franchise, was carried, but the Peers at the same time recorded their assent to the principles of representation contained in the Bill. Mr. Gladstone then announced the abandonment of almost all the legislation of the year, including the London Government Bill, the Merchant Shipping Bill, the Railway Regulation Bill, the Irish Land Purchase Bill, and many others, with a view to an early prorogation and an autumn Session. The interval was spent in an exchange of defiances, and Mr. Gladstone's language in Mid Lothian was menacing enough. But when Parliament met in October, the desire on both sides to bridge over the narrow point of difference prevailed. It was arranged that the redistribution scheme should be submitted to the Conservative leaders, and, when approved by them, that assurances should be exchanged between the parties for the passing of both Bills as nearly as possible at the same time. The Redistribution Bill, accordingly, was introduced early in December, and the Lords thereupon passed the Franchise Bill. After an adjournment over Christmas, the former measure went into Committee, but the compact, which was loyally observed both by Mr. Gladstone and Lord Salisbury, precluded any material changes.

The disquieting rumours which reached this country from the Sudan gradually grew worse and worse till they culminated in the report that an Egyptian army of 10,000 men, under Hicks Pasha, had been cut to pieces by the rebels. A subsequent disaster to Baker Pasha's native troops and the imminent danger of Suakin compelled the Government to intervene. Fresh troops were now despatched from England under General Graham, who, marching out from Suakin, attacked and defeated the rebels, who fought with the most determined bravery in two separate engagements. Meanwhile Mr. Gladstone, threatened with a Parliamentary crisis, had committed himself to a new course. General Gordon, commonly known as Chinese Gordon, who at the request of the English Government had undertaken a journey across the desert to Khartum with the view of effecting through his personal influence some pacific settlement, reached that town in safety, but was eventually surrounded by the enemy and, in spite of his appeals for succour, abandoned to his fate by the Government at whose instance he had rushed upon it. Public opinion was strongly moved by the desertion of Gordon and the 'indelible disgrace' he cast on those who refused him the means of redeeming the pledges he had given in the name of England. Ministers had a majority of 49 on Stafford Northcote's vote of censure in February, which sank to 28 on Sir M. Hicks Beach's vote of censure in May, and a further blow was only averted by the announcement that Lord Wolseley was to be sent with a powerful force to the relief of Khartum. It is needless to dwell on the fatal result of a long course of vacillation and delay. Lord Wolseley arrived just too late to save Gordon. Khartum was occupied and abandoned. When Parliament reassembled in February, 1885, another vote of censure was only repelled by a majority of 14. Mr. Gladstone was throughout puzzled by the interest taken in these subjects. 'Why,' he said in the House of Commons, 'one might suppose Egypt and the Sudan were in England!'

The Egyptian imbroglio and the fate of Gordon had probably the largest share in producing the reaction against Mr. Gladstone, which at this time had become indisputable, and which justified the Opposition in asserting that if Ministers had been defeated on any of the votes of censure, and had gone to the country on the old franchise, a Conservative majority as large as that of 1874 would have been certain. Other causes were working in the same direction. Mr. Gladstone's confident predictions of the success of his Irish policy had been confuted by events. There had been a succession of blunders in foreign and colonial policy, which had brought us into conflict with France over Egyptian finance, with Germany over the African settlements, with Australia about New Guinea and the New Hebrides, and with the Cape about Bechuanaland. The surrender to the Boers after Majuba Hill appeared to foreshadow a more humiliating capitulation to Russia in Central Asia; the Penjdeh affair drew from Mr. Gladstone an impressive Parliamentary harangue, in which he took his stand on the Anglo-Russian Covenant, and pledged the Government to meet 'the demands of justice and the calls of honour'; but the engagement was inadequately fulfilled, though a vote of credit for eleven millions was granted, which swelled the sum to be raised within the year to the then unprecedented total of £100,000,000. Mr. Childers, whose optional Conversion scheme had been rejected by the City, and whose proposed token half-sovereign had been withdrawn, saw all his plans confounded, while the sudden increase of expenditure at once annulled the merit of the economies in the Military and Naval Departments. It was also known that Ministers and Ministerialists were at variance among themselves on many points; the moderate section protested against projects of 'ransom,' the Radicals were unwilling to renew the Irish Crimes Bill, and the financial measures of the year gave rise, it was said, to sharp disputes in the Cabinet. In these circumstances it was scarcely a matter for surprise that the Ministry were defeated, through the abstention of a large body of Liberals, on Sir M. Hicks Beach's amendment to the Budget. Mr. Gladstone resigned, to the avowed satisfaction of many of his colleagues and Lord Salisbury was called to govern with a minority. But the interest had shifted from the Parliamentary scene to the coming election, at which Mr. Gladstone hoped that the support of the new voters would compensate him for the distrust of the old constituencies.

Mr. Gladstone's task was not an easy one. He had to keep together the divergent sections of his party, to prevent unauthorized cries from being prematurely raised, and to offer plausible reasons for his restoration to power. His 'authorized programme,' as set forth in his address to his constituents and in a new series of Mid Lothian speeches, was modest and unexciting; he declared for a further reform of Parliamentary procedure, a representative system of local government, a revision of local taxation, and those changes in the land laws that have lately been embodied in Lord Halsbury's Land Transfer Bill. He repudiated Disestablishment as an issue in the contest, and he protested that he would uphold the principles of property as stoutly as the national liberties. These themes did not lend themselves to impassioned treatment, especially as the Conservatives were committed to something very like the same policy. On the Irish question he made a notable declaration. He 'seriously and solemnly' affirmed that it 'would not be safe' to allow the Liberal party, however 'honourable, patriotic, and trustworthy,' to deal with the Parnellite demand for Home Rule if it were 'in a minority which might become a majority by the aid of the Irish vote.' It is true Mr. Gladstone was able afterwards to point to ambiguous expressions scattered among his writings and speeches which he treated as qualifying this position. But it was the position on which his whole party took its stand; it furnished a justification of the rancorous Parnellite address to the Irish electors on the eve of the election; it was reasserted by Sir William Harcourt when he called for an overwhelming majority to the only party that had the courage and the honesty to face those who threatened 'war with the boycotting pike.' None of Mr. Gladstone's colleagues had been made acquainted with his doubts, and, as he admitted, writing in the following autumn, 'the subject of Home Rule was twelve months ago almost as foreign to the British mind as the differential calculus.'

Conversion to Parnellism and Third Administration

The result of the election showed that Mr. Gladstone's following was exactly equal to the Conservatives and the Parnellites together. He had lost his hold on the boroughs, but he had gained largely in the newly-enfranchised counties in England, and he commanded a heavily preponderating vote in Wales and Scotland. But it was plain that the Liberals were not able to drive the Conservatives from office without the aid of the Parnellites, and that the Conservatives, even if provisionally supported by Mr. Parnell, could not maintain a stable Government. In this situation Mr. Gladstone took a momentous decision. One morning in December, 1885, there appeared in a provincial newspaper a sketch of his new Home Rule policy, which, though formally disavowed as 'inaccurate,' was substantially identical with the Bill afterwards introduced. The whole political world was thrown into turmoil. Some of Mr. Gladstone's colleagues hastened to 'find salvation' in a complete change of front; others, like Mr. Bright, were shocked by this abandonment of the attitude steadily held down to that day by the Liberal party, without public discussion, without consultation among the Liberal chiefs. But when the new Parliament met for business in January, 1886, the relations of parties rapidly became clear. In the debate on the address, Mr. Gladstone, though maintaining a certain reserve, as becoming 'an old Parliamentary hand,' was applauded by the Parnellites, and on Mr. Jesse Collings's amendment relating to small holdings, the whole Irish vote was thrown against the Government, who were defeated by a majority of 79. Mr. Gladstone was then called upon to form a Ministry for the third time. The conditions under which he approached the task were widely different from those he had to deal with in 1869 or in 1880. He had already parted company on various grounds with some of the leaders of Liberalism, Mr. Bright, Mr. Forster, Mr. Goschen, the Duke of Argyll, Lord Lansdowne, Mr. Courtney, and others, and though some of these would doubtless have joined him had he held to the position he had taken up before the General Election, his evident leaning to Home Rule decided their attitude. The earliest Ministerial appointment announced, that of Mr. John Morley, an avowed ally and admirer of Mr. Parnell, as Irish Secretary produced a further split in the Liberal camp. Lord Hartington and Sir Henry James refused to accept high office in a Cabinet of which the character was thus clearly foreshadowed, and, while refraining from open hostility till the Government plan was produced, they ranged themselves with the public men above mentioned, and with Lord Selborne, Lord Derby, Lord Northbrook, Lord Cowper, Mr. Rylands, and many others of Mr. Gladstone's former colleagues and followers, as a separate political group, soon popularly known by the name of Liberal Unionists, but called by their opponents dissentient Liberals. As, however, Mr. Gladstone still professed to be anxious for 'inquiry and information,' Mr. Chamberlain and Mr. Trevelyan entered the Cabinet provisionally, where they were associated with Lord Granville as Colonial Secretary, Lord Rosebery as Foreign Secretary, Sir William Harcourt as Chancellor of the Exchequer, Mr. Childers as Home Secretary, and other familiar personages in unfamiliar places.

The interval between the formation of Mr. Gladstone's Ministry and the introduction of his Home Rule and Land Purchase Bills was marked by a decisive hardening of educated and thoughtful public opinion against the Separatist policy. In addition to the leading politicians of the day, except those included in the Cabinet, the protest in favour of the Union was adhered to by the most eminent men in the ranks of the professions, by men of letters, men of science, and men of business, and even more strongly by Liberals than by Conservatives. A keen polemic out of doors in which the possibilities of Home Rule were closely examined preceded the Cabinet meetings in which the Bills were discussed, and which led to the withdrawal of Mr. Chamberlain and Mr. Trevelyan, immediately followed by that of Lord Morley, Mr. Heneage and Mr. Jesse Collings. The Home Rule Bill, which established a separate Parliament and separate Executive in Ireland and excluded the Irish members from the Imperial Parliament, was introduced by Mr. Gladstone in a speech exhibiting indeed his fluent and copious diction and his characteristic mastery of detail, but by no means equalling his more memorable performances of earlier days in force and clearness. No division was challenged on the first reading, but there was a long debate in which the Liberal Unionists declared themselves unreservedly against the measure, and at the Opera-house meeting, when Lord Cowper presided, and Lord Salisbury, Lord Hartington, Mr. Goschen, Mr. Plunket, and Mr. Rylands appeared on the same platform, the first step was taken towards founding the Unionist alliance. Mr. Gladstone saw the danger and strove to parry it in part by concessions and in part by coercion. He relied much on engaging the Irish landlords at least to neutrality by the terms offered in the Land Purchase Bill, which he brought in to discharge, as he said, a solemn national 'obligation of honour and of policy.' The bait was not taken. It was found that among the Radicals there was a wide-spread objection to the plan, and Mr. Gladstone shortly afterwards announced that his followers were at liberty to vote on this point as they pleased. He had already told the landlords, in a manifesto published during the Easter recess, that 'the sands were running in the hour-glass,' in spite of the solemn obligation aforesaid, and after his defeat he hastened to declare that the connexion between Home Rule and Land Purchase had been irrevocably severed. In the Easter manifesto he put forward by way of menace to those Liberals who declined to follow him the doctrine which had been the keystone of his policy both before and after the election, that the resistance to Home Rule was a movement of 'the classes' against 'the masses,' assuming that in such a conflict the former must be always in the wrong. As the critical strugagle on the second reading approached Mr. Gladstone made further overtures to the dissidents, especially promising to treat the retention of the Irish members at Westminster as an open question. A few yielded, but the main body stood firm. The debate on the second reading, which extended over 12 nights, and in which Mr. Gladstone intervened with more than his usual fire, turned mainly on the great, the inevitable issue – whether to give Ireland a separate Legislature and a separate Executive and yet to maintain the Imperial connexion was a practicable policy. In spite of the assurance that the Bill would be withdrawn, that it was really dead, and that a different measure would be brought in after the prorogation, the Unionists refused to vote for a dangerous principle, of undefined application, and the second reading was rejected by a majority of 30. Mr. Gladstone and his colleagues encouraged by Mr. Schnadhorst's assurances and by the certainty that they would have the Irish vote which had been thrown against them the year before, resolved upon an immediate dissolution. Parliament was dissolved on the 25th of June, and during the next three weeks a debate was carried on in the constituencies which was a prolongation of that lately closed in the House of Commons. Mr. Gladstone did not spare his personal efforts; he spoke at great length in Edinburgh, in Glasgow, in Liverpool, and in Manchester, and he carried on a brisk epistolary controversy with some of his critics. His tone was confident throughout, but it soon appeared that he had not got the nation on his side. In the new Parliament the Unionists, Liberal and Conservative, had a majority of 110 over the Gladstonians and Parnellites combined.

In Opposition as a Home Ruler

Mr. Gladstone's resignation and the return of Lord Salisbury to office were followed by a brief autumn Session, in which the principal feature was the united action of the Gladstonians and the Parnellites in endeavouring to reopen the land question. The Government, Mr. Gladstone predicted, 'could not give security for social order in Ireland,' and this prediction fell in with the assertions of the Irish Home Rulers that they would make the government of Ireland by the British Parliament an impossibility. In the pamphlet which Mr. Gladstone published after his defeat he strove to show that he had been really leaning to Home Rule for many years, and to minimize the weight of the decision just given by the constituencies, but, perhaps, the most important point was the suggestion that the sympathy shown by Wales and Scotland with Irish nationality must propagate a similar doctrine in those countries. During the recess Mr. Gladstone was politically torpid, though he entertained a large Irish deputation at Hawarden, but he turned a deaf ear to the appeals made to him to pronounce an opinion on Mr. Dillon's aggressive operations in Ireland, and on the morality of the Plan of Campaign. At this time he seems to have cherished the hope that the Liberal Unionists would withdraw their support from the Government as soon as the Executive was compelled to choose between succumbing to lawless dictation and applying to Parliament for new coercive powers. In the Session of 1887 this hope was shattered. The failure of the Round Table Conference, in which Mr. Gladstone took no active part though he watched its results closely, showed that even among the most Radical of the Unionists the objections to Home Rule were still unshaken. When Mr. Balfour's Crimes Bill was brought in, Mr. Gladstone met it at the very outset with the most determined opposition. He contested its right to precedence, and the enforcement of the closure to overcome the dilatory debates by which it was obstructed. He denied that a case had been made out for it; he assailed even the provisions borrowed from his own coercive legislation. In fact, he identified himself more and more with the ideas and the tactics of the Parnellites, and in proportion became acrimonious in his censures on the Liberal Unionists, who steadily supported the Government both on the Crimes Bill and on the proposal to refer the charges against Mr. Parnell to a Parliamentary Committee. When the Crimes Bill became law and the National League was proclaimed Mr. Gladstone moved a hostile address to the Crown. But it was out of doors that he exhibited in the most striking way the dominion which his Irish policy had obtained over his mind. To carry a Home Rule Bill had become with him a passion. To this he was willing to sacrifice traditions and principles, sympathies and antipathies, to take the Parnellites to his bosom, to quarrel with his oldest friends, and to modify, from week to week, the doctrines of what he continued to call the Liberal party in order to brigade sectional interests and subordinate agitations under the Separatist flag.

The extent to which Mr. Gladstone had moved from the position he held in 1885, or even in the following year, was not discovered fully by the public until his speeches on the occasion of the National Liberal Conference at Nottingham in October, 1887. There he not only attacked the whole administration of the law in Ireland, endorsing all the Parnellite charges in the spirit of his message 'Remember Mitchelstown,' but he opened a new budget of offers to those who would pledge themselves to vote the Home Rule ticket. Neither the 'one man one vote' demand nor disestablishment in Wales and Scotland had a place among the objects he had set before the electors when he asked the country to give him a majority in 1885, yet he plainly told those interested in such aims that the way to win was to give him a Home Rule majority. This dangerous fluidity of opinion, especially viewed in connexion with Mr. Gladstone's attacks on law and order, put an end speedily to the notion that the Liberal Unionists would again be induced to repose confidence in him and to trust him with the settlement of the Irish difficulty. Home Rule itself gradually sank into the background, and it was seen that the triumph of anarchy, the right of disorderly minorities to upset the law of the land, was even more than the recognition of Ireland as a separate nation the goal to which the Gladstonian party were being consciously or unconsciously hurried on. The Irish administration was again and again assailed, and with increasing acrimony as it became evident that Conservatives and Liberal Unionists were resolved to avoid disputes on side issues and to stand firmly together against an attack they conceived to be directed as much against the foundations of law as against the Union itself. The bitterness of feeling reached its height during the debates on the Special Commission Bill and did not abate during the autumn. Mr. Gladstone's activity increased as he discovered that there was no prospect of winning over the Liberal Unionists, against whom he directed henceforward his keenest shafts and whom he began to contrast unfavourably with the Tories themselves. His rhetorical powers were still great, and their effect was augmented by the almost superstitious worship of his personality among large masses of democratic voters. But the apparent levity of his changes, the inaccuracy of his statements, the readiness with which he accepted any accusations emanating from the Parnellites shocked men of sense and men of honour. It would be an ungrateful task to reproduce in detail the controversies, already half-forgotten, of that period. We may mention in passing that the shadow of the charge against Colonel Dopping, brought forward at Nottingham, and tardily withdrawn under pressure of a lawyer's letter, hung over all Mr. Gladstone's criticisms on the Mitchelstown incident, the Mandeville case, and the death of Kinsella, and that this impression was not removed by his comparison of the treatment of Irish political prisoners with the conduct of the Neapolitan Government, which a reference to his own writings showed to be absurd. At the National Liberal Conference at Birmingham in 1888 Mr. Gladstone followed up his speeches at Nottingham a year before, attacking the Government more fiercely, denouncing the Liberal Unionists more furiously, and still further enlarging the list of new articles of faith to which, in the interests of Home Rule, the Liberal party were to be committed. Already during the Crimes Bill debates he had surprised even his own friends by declaring in favour of the Channel Tunnel, and somewhat later he accepted the principle of the payment of members of the House of Commons. Among other concessions to the extreme section of his own party which he made after he had resigned the hope of converting the Liberal Unionists may be mentioned the enfranchisement of leaseholds and the taxation of ground-rents.

The political intimacy between Gladstonians and Parnellites was maintained in circumstances which afterwards acquired a peculiar interest. In 1889 Mr. Gladstone appeared for the first time on a platform with Mr. Parnell. While the report of the Special Commission was still pending, Mr. Gladstone, like the rest of his party, boldly declared that the charges and allegations had been one and all absolutely disproved, and, just about the time when the proceedings before the Commission closed, he received Mr. Parnell as his guest at Hawarden, and there discussed with him the form which Home Rule was to take in the event of the defeat of the Unionists at the General Election. When the Report appeared, a few months later, he distinctly refused to pay any attention to the findings adverse to the respondents, and fastened exclusively on the rejection of the Pigott letters. He brought forward in the House of Commons an amendment to Mr. W. H. Smith's resolution for the adoption of the Report, so violent in its language that it shocked many even of his own supporters.

The exigencies of those who could carry their support to an always open market naturally increased as they discovered their power. Mr. Gladstone was more and more closely pressed by the advocates of disestablishment in Wales and in Scotland, by the Scotch Federalist Home Rulers, by the semi-Socialist friends of labour, and other sectional fanatics. On many points he yielded, and adopted as articles of the Gladstonian faith projects which the Liberal party as a whole repudiated in 1885, and even in 1886. Other demands were met with ambiguous answers. After repeated refusals to treat the Eight Hours Bill as a serious political issue, he opened the door for concessions in his speeches during the Mid Lothian campaign of 1890. The most important question, however, which was thus juggled with was the modification of Home Rule that was understood to be accepted in principle by the Gladstonians. Long after he had discussed this with Mr. Parnell at Hawarden he declined to disclose the character of the changes contemplated in the defeated scheme of 1886, and treated the reasonable demands of Lord Hartington and others with contemptuous indifference.

The Parnellite split

Though Mr. Gladstone could still show on occasion, as in the Royal Grants debate in 1889, that his power as an orator had not departed from him, he had evidently become less capable of conducting long processes of careful reasoning, and his disregard for accuracy of statement introduced a new and painful element into public discussion. His Mid Lothian speeches in 1890 were far below the level of his former controversial achievements. The old legends of Mitchelstown, Killeagh, and Gweedore, supplemented by new stories imported from 'Mad Tipperary,' figured prominently in Mr. Gladstone's denunciation of the Unionist policy in Ireland just at the moment when Mr. Balfour's firm administration had gained the upper hand over the forces of disorder. His attack on the Liberal Unionists, too, reached the highest point of acrimony precisely at the time when the rupture in the Parnellite ranks was about to show from what danger and disgrace the country had been saved by the courageous refusal of Lord Hartington, Mr. Chamberlain, and their associates to follow their old leader in 1886. We need hardly dwell upon the part Mr. Gladstone took in the strange dispute that followed the decree of the Divorce Court in the case of 'O'Shea v. O'Shea and Parnell,' twelve months after the visit of the co-respondent to Hawarden Castle. For many days Mr. Gladstone was silent, while Mr. Labouchere and others among his followers protested against interference, and the whole body of the 'Irish Party' were white-washing their chief at the Leinster-hall. At length, after the Irish party had unanimously re-elected Mr. Parnell, and after the Nonconformist conscience had expressed its disgust at the transaction, Mr. Gladstone spoke out in a letter to Mr. Morley, in which he declared that Mr. Parnell's continuance in the leadership 'at the present moment' would be fatal to Home Rule and would reduce his own political influence 'almost to a nullity.' This letter, extorted from Mr. Gladstone, as Sir Charles Russell subsequently explained, by 'the rising, overwhelming tide of public opinion,' furnished Mr. Parnell's rivals and enemies with a pretext for revoking their recent pronouncement in his favour. Mr. Parnell retorted in a manifesto, in which he contested Mr. Gladstone's 'right of veto,' and published an account of the proposed modifications of Home Rule, as discussed during the Hawarden visit, which not only he but his opponents declared to be inconsistent with the Irish claims. Mr. Gladstone disputed Mr. Parnell's account of the business, but he did not produce his own 'written memoranda' of what passed at the interview. In his turn Mr. Parnell held up his former ally to Irish distrust as an 'unrivalled sophist,' who was constitutionally incapable of giving a straight answer to a straight question. This charge was by no means confuted by Mr. Gladstone's further negotiations with those who took Mr. Parnell's place.

The struggle between Parnellites and Anti-Parnellites continued, and did not cease when Mr. Parnell died suddenly in the autumn of 1891. The former insisted on Mr. Gladstone's giving explicit guarantees on the Irish Government question, which the latter were unable to secure in any public form, Mr. Parnell basing the demand avowedly on his conviction that not one Radical in three believed in Home Rule. The impatience of British Gladstonians to put the Irish question out of sight was received by Mr. Gladstone with sullen acquiescence. His most vigorous effort in Parliament was a speech in support of his own Religious Disabilities Removal Bill. But in the autumn his energies seemed to revive, stimulated by the approach of the General Election and some Unionist losses at by-elections. He plunged, as he had done more than once in previous years, into the speculations of political meteorology, working out at different times a Gladstonian majority variously estimated at from 56 to over 100. Diverging for an instant from politics, he delivered an interesting speech at the jubilee of Glenalmond, of which, as an outwork of Anglicanism in Presbyterian Scotland, he had, together with his early friend, Hope Scott, been a founder, while the first Warden, his old Oxford tutor, Charles Wordsworth, then Bishop of St. Andrews, was also present. At the Newcastle conference in October, a few days before Mr. Parnell's death, he boldly swallowed the whole of the 'multifarious programme' concocted by Mr. Schnadhorst and his associates as a great electioneering advertisement, including half-a-dozen policies he had previously evaded or abjured, and, as the party managers have lately declared, forced their hand by the sudden and unexpected completeness of his acceptance. He declined, however, to give a positive pledge on the Eight Hours Bill, as to which the miners themselves and his own colleagues were divided. Indiscreetly following Mr. Morley's lead, Mr. Gladstone called upon the Government to bring to an end the 'burdensome and embarrassing' occupation of Egypt, an indiscretion which Mr. Bryce took occasion soon afterwards to explain away.

But his heart was still set upon his Irish adventure. The most significant passage in his Newcastle speech was a threat against the House of Lords if in the next Parliament they ventured to oppose another Home Rule Bill. What that Home Rule Bill was to be no man could say, for, then and long after, even during his electioneering campaign in the following summer, Mr. Gladstone, with the joyful assent of nearly all his British followers, refused to disclose his plan. 'The secret,' as the late Lord Derby had previously remarked, 'was admirably kept, because there was no secret to keep.' The Anti-Parnellites, pacified by vague private assurances, resolved to cast in their lot with Mr. Gladstone, to exact no compromising public pledges, and to wait on events. The ultimate form of the Home Rule Bill remained in doubt till after the general election. Mr. Gladstone's attacks, in the closing Session of the Parliament of 1886, on the Uganda Survey Vote and Mr. Chaplin's Small Holdings Bill were spiritless, but he showed abundant rhetorical power in his vehement assault on the Irish Local Government Bill. Not less impassioned were his appeals to those Nonconformists of Great Britain to disregard the outcries of the Irish Protestants, and his denunciation of the Ulster Convention as a constructive conspiracy to defy the law, especially in an eloquent but eminently sophistical speech at the Farringdon-street Memorial-hall. Just before the dissolution the representatives of the 'advanced labour party' waited on Mr. Gladstone, who, by an ingenious adoption of the Socratic method, exposed the absurdity of their schemes, refusing to say 'even one encouraging word to them,' as he was bound 'in honour and character' to the Irish cause and was too old to take up any other question. During his campaign in Mid Lothian, at what he said in his address was the last general election he could be expected to face, Mr. Gladstone, pressed by a mining element in the constituency, wavered in his resistance to a compulsory shortening of hours. The reduction of his former majority of over 3,600 to barely the odd hundreds was a painful blow to the leader of the triumphant party, but a more practical check was given him in the disappointment of his hopes of obtaining such an unquestioned ascendancy in the House of Commons as he had started with in the Parliaments of 1869 and 1880.

Fourth Administration

Instead of a majority of 120, or 100, or 80, or even 60, Mr. Gladstone, at the general election of 1895, obtained only a majority of 42, which was further reduced by subsequent disasters. This left him in the position he had pronounced in 1885 to be intolerable – that of absolute dependence on the Irish vote, including the exigent and distrustul group of Parnellites. With these Mr. Gladstone could come to no terms, as Mr. Redmond showed in his first speech in the new Parliament; but the Anti-Parnellites were successfully 'squared,' Mr. Gladstone having an interview with Mr. McCarthy, Mr. Dillon, and others before he issued his address. His failure during the contest to fulfil his explicit promise of disclosing the outlines of his Home Rule scheme before the polling was an indication of a conspiracy of silence which was maintained for many months. The Anti-Parnellites, while professing confidence in Mr. Gladstone, were afraid to separate themselves from Mr. Redmond, and, for this and other reasons, a good deal of uneasiness, sometimes articulately expressed, prevailed during the autumn among the Gladstonians. Meanwhile, Mr. Gladstone was in no hurry. On the defeat of the Unionist Government in August, 1892, he became Premier for the fourth time, and formed his Cabinet. For the rest of the year he took little part in politics, refusing to be drawn on the Irish question. That question in the decisive debate on the Address he had described as 'the sole link that bound him to public life.' He had renewed his threats against the House of Lords in case they should oppose his will. But he saw the necessity for allowing the ground-swell of the general election to abate, and for conciliating discontented sections amongst his followers. His visit to Wales, including the delivery of a speech on Snowdon, for the time revived Welsh Radical enthusiasm, especially by a violent and groundless attack on the landlords of the Principality, the main allegations of which when challenged he was unable to substantiate. But generally his appearances had no political colour, as when he attended the Oriental Congress, lectured at Oxford on medieval Universities, and received the freedom of the city of Liverpool.

After a short visit to Biarritz, Mr. Gladstone entered upon the work of the last Session in which he was destined to take part, the portentous Session beginning on January 31, 1893, and closing on March 5, 1894, at the end of which his retirement from office was made known. His share in its proceedings may be practically summed up in the history of the second Home Rule Bill. To that subject he devoted all his remaining powers, astonishing, indeed, when exerted by a man in his 84th year, and husbanded by careful management, which, however, frequently threw upon Sir William Harcourt the burden of a task to which he was not equal. Mr. Gladstone's speech on the introduction of the Bill was much below the level of the oratorical efforts of his prime or even of 1886, and that on the second reading was, perhaps, still less worthy of the occasion. There were a few passages of impressive rhetoric, may instances of ingenuity in glossing over difficulties and in evading dilemmas, but, on the whole, these expositions of a great and far-reaching policy were wanting in the completeness and comprehensive character, the logical force and the moral consistency, that Parliament was entitled to look for. On the two points on which there had been the widest departure from the Bill of 1886, the retention of the Irish members at Westminster and the method of securing a financial contribution for Ireland for Imperial purposes, Mr. Gladstone so little sure of his ground that he was prepared – perhaps from the first – to alter them root and branch. The breakdown of the financial scheme in the Bill as introduced was a blow to Mr. Gladstone's credit in a sphere he regarded as his own, and the sense of his failure produced a considerable amount of irritability, which found vent not only in his conduct in the House of Commons, but in his cavalier treatment of two important deputations, from the business community of Belfast and from the City of London, which had approached him with a protest against the measure. The same imperious anger at the audacity of resistance to his will moved Mr. Gladstone to his despotic scheme of closuring the debate by compartments at the very moment when one of these radical changes had been recognized to be inevitable, and another, in spite of Ministerial evasions, was known to be impending. The moral authority of the Government, too, was weakened by the dwindling of their majority, which was 43 on the second reading and only 34 on the third reading, having sunk to under 25 on several occasions, and as low as 14 on one. Mr. Gladstone still spoke as if the passage of the Bill through the Lower House under these conditions gave him adequate authority to remodel the Constitution, but he must have soon convinced himself that the Lords were not to be overawed by his menaces, and that Home Rule must for the time be again placed in the background. In his speech on the third reading he intimated that there was to be an autumn Session devoted to British legislation in which he hardly professed to take any personal interest. This postponement excluded, for all practical purposes, the possibility of his resumption of the campaign, and to the perception of the fact as well as to the absence of the slightest sign of popular anger at the rejection of the Home Rule Bill by an enormous majority in the House of Lords may be attributed the doubtful and contingent character of his defiance of the Upper House in his Edinburgh speech. Still the blow to his hopes rankled all the more because it could neither be parried nor returned. In the business of the winter Session Mr. Gladstone took little part, but when the opportunity occurred he strove to fan the flame of strife between the two Houses. He failed to produce any effect in the case of the Employers' Liability Bill, and on the Parish Councils Bill he accepted the Lords' amendments in their final shape with a renewal of prospective menaces and the bequest of the feud to his successors. He had been previously crossed by the necessity for surrendering to a growing public opinion on the strengthening of the Navy, though he was supported by the same party majority of 34 which carried the Home Rule Bill in rejecting Lord George Hamilton's resolution as a vote of non-confidence. Yet while, on the whole, the events of this Session formed, perhaps, the least creditable chapter in Mr. Gladstone's political biography, it was not deficient in qualities that extorted admiration. Mr. Gladstone's rhetorical versatility, his firmness in the pursuit of his objects, his ingenuity as a tactician, his courage in confronting unexpected difficulties, combined to make it possible for him to keep the English, Scotch, and Welsh Radicals steady while he was amusing the Irish with the phantasm of Home Rule, and to keep the Irish to heel while the Employers' Liability Bill and the Parish Councils Bill were under discussion.

Resignation and life in retirement

But the end of this extraordinary career was approaching. The House of Commons was sitting on December 29, when Mr. Balfour was able to congratulate the Premier, in graceful and unexaggerated language, on having reached his 84th birthday. The Gladstonians had up to this time affected indignation at the merest hint that their leader's powers were impaired by age. Yet, it was obvious to ordinary observers that the conduct of Parliamentary business was suffering from Mr. Gladstone's infirmities, to which he drew attention himself from time to time. Still, when he went off to Biarritz in January, 1894, to return when the House of Commons reassembled, after a month's adjournment, to deal with the Lords' amendments, it was not generally suspected that he was unwilling to face another Session. A rumour, widely discredited at the time, but shown by the event to be well-founded, drew from him an ambiguous communication contradicting the statement, but pointing to the possibility of a resignation at any moment. Speculation on the subject had begun to flag on Mr. Gladstone's return to the House of Commons, when all doubt was removed by the announcement, confirmed by his own party organs, that his speech accepting the Lords' amendments to the Parish Councils Bill and, at the same time, declaring that the amending power of the Peers ought not to be allowed to continue was to be his last as Prime Minister. It seemed incredible that this somewhat feeble 'declaration of war against the Constitution,' as Mr. Balfour called it, should be Mr. Gladstone's farewell to the House of Commons. Even when within a few days his resignation was tendered to and accepted by the Queen, and Lord Rosebery was commissioned to reconstruct the Ministry, many persons persisted in believing that Mr. Gladstone would take an early opportunity of coming down to the House and of bidding adieu to the scene of so many of his triumphs in the dignified and solemn accents he knew so well how to use when he rose above the strife of party. The public, however, were not at first aware of the serious nature of the physical cause of his retirement. After much unnecessary mystery, it was authoritatively stated that it had become necessary to remove a cataract from his right eye, and though the operation was not performed till a couple of months after he ceased to be Prime Minister, he never appeared in the House during the remainder of that Parliament. In the summer he intimated to his committee in Mid Lothian, in a brief and almost bald letter, his resolution not to seek re-election. He subsequently occupied himself, while awaiting the complete recovery of his eyesight, in such literary amusements as a translation of some of the Odes of Horace. At a later date he took in hand an edition of the works of Bishop Butler, which was preceded by the publication of a series of 'studies' on the philosophy and theology of that great divine. He entered, also, with not a little zest into the controversy between the Anglican and the Roman Churches over the validity of the 'orders' in the former communion since the Reformation. Probably the most generally interesting production of Mr. Gladstone's closing years was the sympathetic appreciation and reminiscences – published a few months ago by the *Daily Telegraph* – of his old school-fellow at Eton, Arthur Hallam. It is to be regretted that he did not leave behind him many more such records of his intimacies with the long succession of eminent men to whom be stood in close relations both in public and private life. The biographies and journals published in recent years contain many interesting letters from his pen and some other side-lights on his character. This is especially true of the group of High Churchmen, chiefly representatives of the Oxford Movement, with whom he was closely connected between 1832 and 1852, and by whom he was latterly regarded as their Parliamentary spokesman – James Hope Scott, Henry Manning, the Wilberforce family, and others. Many of these followed Newman, with whom Mr. Gladstone appears to have never had any close friendship, into the Roman Catholic fold. But he was intimate with many eminent men of different types and different schools, as is shown in the memoirs of Charles Greville, of Monckton Milnes, of Cobden, of W. E. Forster, of Jowett, and of Sir M. Grant Duff, as well as in Tennyson's 'Life' and in the Autobiography and Letters of Henry Taylor.

But though Mr. Gladstone made it perfectly clear that he intended his resignation to be absolute and final, and though the suggestion that he should be recalled made last year by some of the politicians who call themselves the 'Liberal Forwards' met with no popular response, it was not in his nature for him to divest himself altogether of his interest in public affairs. He had not long given up his seat in Parliament when he was drawn into the controversy stirred up by the troubles in Armenia. His old antipathy to the Turks and their government revived in full force. On his 85th birthday he received a deputation of Armenians at Hawarden, whom he addressed in an impassioned speech, denouncing the Sultan's Government as a 'disgrace to civilization' and 'a curse to mankind.' In the following year he continued the campaign, but at first with some restraint and caution. He spoke at

Chester in August, 1895, at a meeting presided over by the Duke of Westminster, and expressed his wish to strengthen Lord Salisbury's hands, but a couple of months later he wrote with gathering violence, 'May God in His mercy send a speedy end to the governing Turk and all his doings: as I said when I could say, and even sometimes do, so I say in my political decrepitude or death.' In September, 1896, Mr. Gladstone addressed a great gathering in Liverpool in something like the same strain, not without some flashes of his ancient fire. But his policy, based upon a construction of the Cyprus Convention which was disavowed by his former colleagues, met with little acceptance. His letters on the changing aspects of the Eastern Question were chiefly remarkable for the contempt with which he spoke of the concert of Europe and of its success, at any rate, in preserving the peace of the world. In March, 1897, he wrote to the Duke of Westminster in this sense from Cannes, when every restraining influence was needed to keep the Greeks from rushing on their ruin. Occasionally Mr. Gladstone spoke or wrote on subjects disconnected with politics, and here he was at his best – a living witness, as in his speech at the opening of the Deo Bridge, to the vast changes which he has seen, since his childhood, in the social life of his country.

For several years it had been Mr. Gladstone's custom to spend a portion of the winter or early spring in a Southern climate, sometimes in Italy, sometimes at Biarritz, and most frequently somewhere on the Riviera. He generally came back, even in his later years, so much restored in health and refreshed in spirit that a deep feeling of disappointment was produced among his friends and the public when it was found that his visit to Cannes at the beginning of this year had not the usual success. Pains, supposed at first to be neuralgic, deprived Mr. Gladstone of the sleep which during his long life of strain and struggle he had almost always been able to command. His return to his native land and, after a short sojourn at Bournemouth, to his country home, with the hand of death visibly upon him, evoked general sympathy. It was soon acknowledged that there was no room for hope, that the pain was due to a malignant growth which surgery could not safely remove and of which medicine could not do much to mitigate the anguish. Universal admiration was felt for the fortitude and resignation with which the dying statesman bore this trial, and for the touching messages which he sent to his friends and his countrymen. Especially memorable was his solemn farewell, only a few days ago, to the University of Oxford: 'My most earnest prayers are hers to the uttermost and to the last!' The end came, at length, peacefully and almost without pain.

Public character and career

To form a just estimate of so many-sided a man as Mr. Gladstone will be no easy task even when contemporary events shall have ranged themselves in their final order and we see him in his true relation to them. We have seen that he entered political life after the Reform Act of 1832 even more of a High Churchman than of a High Tory. His book on Church and State was an attempt to vindicate the theory of the Church of England on *a priori* grounds, as it was the aim of the Oxford Revivalists to exhibit that theory in practice. This was Mr. Gladstone's contribution to the work, and what he did he did thoroughly. Yet no sooner had the book issued from the press, he tells us, than he became aware 'that there was no party, no section of a party, no individual person probably in the House of Commons who was prepared to act upon it. I found myself the last man on the sinking ship.' Henceforth it is clear that Mr. Gladstone's mind began to turn itself in a different direction, travelling by slow degrees and with long pauses to the position which it had finally reached in the year 1868. In that year he published his 'Chapter of Autobiography,' in which we read the outward and formal abandonment of the theory with which he had entered life. But we also learn from this essay that an inward and gradual departure from it had commenced in his own mind more than a score of years before; and that even in 1847, when a candidate for the University of Oxford, he had declined to give any pledges on the subject of the Irish Church. Another disclosure, equally startling and momentous, was that the collapse of the high doctrine taken up in his 'Church and State' left him without a logical basis for the defence of Established Churches, so that his adherence, so often eloquently set forth, to the Church of England after abandoning the Church of Ireland would seem to be rather the result of traditional attachment than of political or moral ideas. Nearly 20 years after this revelation he published in his 'History of an Idea' an explanation of the concealed process by which he had worked himself round from Unionism to Home Rule.

His career in politics, though dissimilar, of course, in detail, was analogous in principle to the transmigration of his mind in the region of ecclesiastical conceptions. Without attempting to reassert any political theory, as he had reasserted a religious theory, he gave in his adherence as a young man to the purest Toryism of the day. Sir Robert Peel saw the necessity for attempting a new point of departure; and so, of course, did the author of the 'Letters of Runnymede.' But Mr. Gladstone's mind at this time was occupied with other ideas, and he probably did not concern himself very anxiously with the difference between Toryism and Conservatism. He accepted the Tamworth manifesto and was not alarmed by the Ecclesiastical Commission. The dwindling majorities of the Liberal party; the assertion of his prerogative by William IV, with the general approval of the people; above all, the triumphal results of the elections in 1841, must all have contributed to blind men's eyes to the true situation of affairs. A generation passed away between his recognition of the ecclesiastical tendency and his recognition of the political tendency of the great events which followed the death of Mr. Canning. But when he did recognize them he adopted them with equal earnestness; and at once began to shape his policy with a view to the gradual consummation of them. In the earlier stages of this development he was held by many to be – perhaps he really was – the first real leader of the English Democracy – a leader actuated by no class hatreds or bigoted prejudices, who always spoke gratefully and tenderly of the past, who was no mere iconoclast or demagogue, but a statesman who in deliberately substituting one political theory for another believed himself to be acting only in accordance with those irresistible laws which determine the progress of nations and cannot be defied without destruction. Mr. Gladstone was the first man of this stamp whom England had produced. Sir Robert Peel and Lord John Russell may have had glimmerings of the truth, but they never fully grasped it, and were rather unconscious pioneers than actual leaders of the army. It is needless to say that men like Cobbett and Burdett represent a totally different order of ideas. Mr. Gladstone stood alone in England as the first of our regular statesmen who, nurtured in the old *régime*, stepped forth as the spokesman of the new. It is this one fact which seems to distinguish him more than any other from the many great contemporaries who surrounded him. He has done for Democracy what no other Liberal could have done for it. He raised it above the level of party and taught us to see in it something which all parties alike must recognize. Of the truth or falsehood, the policy or impolicy, of democratic principles this is not the place to speak. It is sufficient to say that Mr. Gladstone found them of mud and left them of marble. But that in politics as in religion he reached his conclusions very gradually may be seen from his speeches on Parliamentary reform, as well as from the fact that years ago, when he was turned 50 years of age, he had, he said, no reasons of his own for not joining a pure Conservative Administration.

It must be added that, in his latter years, the appreciation of Mr. Gladstone's character was gradually, but profoundly, changed. What has been said above would have been an adequate description of the view taken of him, a quarter of a century ago, by the great body of his countrymen, even including the majority of those who disapproved of his policy and distrusted the rapid changes in his attitude and conduct. But after he had failed to obtain a decisive renewal of his authority from the new electorate in 1885, he showed a levity and recklessness in his choice both of ends and means, a subjection to passion and caprice, a disregard for what Burke calls 'the great holdings of society,' which alarmed his followers as well as his opponents. It was not believed that he had become at heart a revolutionist, for he still showed that in many respects the natural tendency of his mind was conservative, but it was seen that to gain some object on which he had set his heart he was willing to arouse and to ally himself with revolutionary forces. His desperate efforts to break up the United Kingdom bred a deep and increasing distrust among the classes that represent property and intelligence, against whom, in consequence, he declared war. It is a legend that, early in his career, when his father was congratulated on the brilliant prospects that lay before his son, the shrewd man of business said, 'He has plenty of ability, but not enough stability.' The story, whether true or not, points to a weakness which grew with his growth and strengthened with his strength. It was not corrected by his training in the school of Peel. In the end, it became 'opportunism' in a perilous form. But, throughout all his opportunist developments, there were some principles which he never allowed himself to forget. Prominent among these was the monarchical principle, the sentiment of loyalty, which so many of those he was associated with in later years treated with scorn. Mr. Gladstone regarded himself as the servant of the people, but, at the same time, he never forgot that he was the servant of the Crown. He always recognized in the fullest degree the fact that when in office he was chosen by the Queen to carry on the government of the country, and that when out of office he was in a position, at any moment, to be so chosen. It would be difficult to find anywhere a more complete vindication of constitutional monarchy than might be compiled from his speeches and writings. They show, moreover, a strong personal devotion to the Queen. Her Majesty's regard for one who was so often her Minister is well known. On more than one occasion she was anxious that he should accept some distinguished mark of Royal favour; but he preferred to die, as he had lived, a simple commoner.

It may be that Mr. Gladstone's reputation as a financier will do more to perpetuate his memory than any other legacies of his genius. The principle of his fiscal system, adopted from Sir Robert Peel, was simple. The more you reduce taxation the more you stimulate consumption, so that while the people are benefited by the cheapness of commodities the revenue is secured by the greater quantity in demand. Mr. Gladstone was never weary of enforcing this, his favourite doctrine, or of moralizing it into a thousand similes. But if the reduction of taxation is followed by these beneficial results, the total remission has also the effect of contributing to the general prosperity and the development of trade, and thereby also helping to enlarge the revenue. It was a system, however, which he allowed might be pushed too far, or, at all events, might end in times of great distress in the rich being the only taxpayers. Experience has given us some reason to doubt whether he had foreseen or guarded against developments of his financial policy which were only shadowed forth during his lifetime. However this may be, Mr. Gladstone had the art of imparting to his financial statements a peculiar literary charm which makes some of them most agreeable reading, even to those who are ignorant of the subject-matter. 'Goldsmith,' said Dr. Johnson, 'is now writing a history of England, and he will make it as interesting as a fairy tale.' Considering the doctor's own ideas of history, this was a real compliment; and Mr. Gladstone did the same for his budget speeches. But he did more than Goldsmith, for, with all the grace and fancy of a literary artist, he sacrificed none of the more solid excellence appropriate to his subject. Some examples of this will probably occur to the minds of most of our readers. He has a Virgilian quotation ready for every fresh turn. When Spain suddenly bethinks herself of her obligations, and by the payment of so many millions extricates us from some financial difficulty, we have at once the Via prima salutis, Quod minimo reris, Graia pandetur ab urbe.

The conflicting objections raised against the French Commercial Treaty he likens to all the winds rushing together out of the cave of Aeolus. The remission of an indirect tax, followed by increased wealth, reminds him of the golden branch which Aeneas is bade to pluck on his way to the shades, Primo avulso, non deficit alter / Aureus; et simili frondescit virga metallo.

And we must all remember his famous comparison of direct and indirect taxation to the two equally lovely sisters, the one more frank and forward, the other more shy, retiring, and insidious, to both of whom the financier might pay his addresses at the same time without being guilty of immorality. What he intended to do in 1874 in order to get rid of the income-tax altogether was not at the time explained. But as the promise was coupled with the hint that it might be necessary to readjust existing taxes, the taxpayers were rather alarmed than comforted by the prospect.

Career as a man of letters and of taste

Mr. Gladstone's literary career would require a biography to itself. In scholarship, in history, in divinity, in literary criticism, and in constitutional and ecclesiastical controversies he has written far more than it comes within the scope of a notice like the present to describe or even to record. Besides the work on Church and State, he is the author of a variety of essays on the theological questions of the day, which, if not destined to retain a place in our standard literature, were read when they appeared with the deepest interest and provoked very earnest protestation. Ritualism and Vaticanism, to state these subjects in the shortest and most popular manner, occupied a great deal of his attention in the year 1874, and the conclusions which he formulated – namely, that the new Papal dogmas had substituted for the old *semper eadem* a policy of violence and change, and that no one now could become a convert to Rome 'without renouncing his moral and mental freedom, and placing his civil loyalty and duty at the mercy of another' – naturally drew down upon him the fire of all the most eminent champions of the Papacy in this country. Perhaps a later generation will rather be disposed to wonder that Mr. Gladstone should have thought the Vatican Decrees a theme worthy of his steel. To the vast majority of English people they sound rather like echoes from a previous state of existence than like the living voice of a practical power in the world. We have lost the ability even to conceive of such doctrines taking effect in this country, and to argue against them seriously and gravely as involving some real menace seems almost fantastic. Those, however, who have studied Mr. Gladstone's character and career will not, perhaps, feel equally astonished. With a certain feminine susceptibility to clerical and sacerdotal influences, it is only to be expected that we should find a proneness to exaggerate their weight and to be misled by their ambiguity.

Mr. Gladstone's various contributions to the periodical literature of the day were collected and republished in 1879 under the title of 'Gleanings of Past Years.' They fill seven small volumes, to which a supplementary volume was added early in the present year, and include many pieces of great and permanent interest. Among the political essays, such as the review of the Life of the Prince Consort and the articles on the County Franchise, we find some most valuable remarks on the working of Constitutional Monarchy and on the place of the Sovereign in the Government, together with observations on the history and results of Parliamentary reform, which afford matter for very deep reflection. Among the others we would specially mention 'The Place of Ancient Greece in the providential order of the world' – an essay marked by singular literary ability and a richer rhetoric than the late statesman usually affected. Last, but not least, we come to the Homeric studies. These are comprised in three principal publications – 'Studies on Homer and the Homeric Age,' in three volumes, published in 1858; 'Juventus Mundi,' which appeared in 1869; and 'Homeric Synchronism,' in 1876. Ingenious rather than profound, and showing that tendency to erect wide superstructures on somewhat limited foundations which is characteristic of men of strong imaginations, these works have been read with delight by thousands to whom the personality of Homer and the historic character of his great epic are a religion. They reflect some of Mr. Gladstone's most prominent moral and intellectual traits with great vividness, the play of his fancy, and his natural bent towards mysticism. His more purely literary criticism was not, perhaps, of the first order. The translation of the Odes of Horace to which we have already referred illustrated some of his weaknesses. He had not the lightness of touch that was needed to give a sympathetic rendering of the graceful *vers de société* of the Epicurean poet. He decidedly underrated Virgil, though he quoted him so often, and it was perhaps natural that he should do so, since his mind was cast rather in a Greek than in a Roman mould. He carried even into politics the sensitive temperament and the dialectic subtlety of the artist and the sophist. Both his successes and his failures in statesmanship were traceable to this source. The great Roman ideas of law, empire, and conquest were foreign to his nature. But his imagination was easily kindled by ideas of symmetry and completeness, by poetical traditions, or by highly wrought pictures of oppression and injustice. Just as Burke's imagination, a slave to the mysterious splendour of the Eastern world, led him greatly to exaggerate the wrongs of India, so did Mr. Gladstone's imagination, fascinated by a kindred spell, betray him into a similar exaggeration of the wrongs of Ireland, of the wrongs of Greece, of the wrongs of Armenia and Bulgaria. On these generous emotions indeed he may be said to have based his foreign policy. The result has been undoubtedly the amelioration of the lot of some oppressed races and the gain of their gratitude and sympathy for this country; but this has been accomplished more than once at the cost of permanent British interests, and has helped to create suspicion of our motives abroad.

The great instrument by which Mr. Gladstone has moved Parliament and the people has been his oratory. To his financial speeches we have referred already. Of his oratory in general it may be said that its most salient characteristic – the one we mean which, after listening to him for many years, remained uppermost in his hearers' minds – was its fluency. He avoided rhetoric in its highest flights and its most artistic form. He was not witty. He had not Mr. Bright's command of nervous English or simple directness and pathos. He had not the peculiar force which belonged to the speeches of Lord Derby. But he had what neither Lord Derby, the Prime Minister, nor his distinguished son, neither Lord Beaconsfield nor Lord Palmerston, nor any of their successors, ever had – the *torrens dicendi*, the power of sustaining an unbroken stream of limpid utterance for hours, and of interspersing it with metaphorical terms which served only to illustrate his meaning and attracted no attention for their own sake. With this, which we conceive to be a very high merit in an orator, Mr. Gladstone was endowed very largely. He had likewise during the greater part of his career what Aristotle calls the ἠθικὴ πιστις, or the art of persuading his hearers as he went along that he was thoroughly in earnest. No doubt this oratorical art can never be entirely dissociated from the moral character and general reputation of the speaker, as Aristotle says it ought to be, and Mr. Gladstone's general reputation for earnestness always reinforced the particular faculty in question. But still he possessed it in a very remarkable degree. His voice, at once sonorous and flexible without being too musical, his action, which, though rather mechanical, always seemed to be spontaneous, his flashing and commanding glance, and the expression of his countenance, which, though occasionally harsh or even peevish, was always serious and concentrated, combined to impress upon his hearers the belief that every word he uttered was the dictate of profound conviction. To whatever cause or combination of causes it was due there can be no doubt that Mr. Gladstone had won an ascendancy in the House of Commons which no English statesman – not even Sir Robert Peel – has enjoyed since the death of Pitt. He was emphatically – what his illustrious rival, Disraeli, aspired to be, and, indeed, was, though in a different way – 'a great Parliament man.' He was steeped in the traditions of the House of Commons. He shared the pride and the passions of that historic Assembly. No one could speak in the name of the House with more solemn and impressive dignity. At the same time, no one was a more accomplished master of Parliamentary tactics and Parliamentary management. It is true that again and again he wrecked the fortunes of his party, but what other leader could have dragged with him a large body of Englishmen through the bewildering transformation scenes of his later years?

The eager activity of Mr. Gladstone's mind, the keenness of his intellectual curiosity, and his love of disputation and disquisition made him one of the most interesting of talkers. He had the widest range of subjects apart from politics and theology, which had occupied him during the greater part of his life. On art, on archaeology, and even on science he loved to expatiate, always with fluency and eloquence, if not in all cases with the accuracy that satisfied the standard of experts. His wonderful memory and his un-paralleled experience furnished him with an abundant store of illustrations on every conceivable subject. He was during all his life an omnivorous reader, and was often as much absorbed in the last novel or biography as in the political controversies of the day. His tastes and his training kept him familiar to the end of his life with the Greek and Latin classics, but modern literature, too, had its charms for him. There are few indications that he read much German, but he was well acquainted with recent French books, and he had a thorough and scholarly knowledge of Italian – especially of Dante and his commentators. One of the most striking of his literary essays is that on 'Leopardi.' Mr. Gladstone's physical powers were only less remarkable than his intellectual. Throughout his life he was a man of extraordinary activity, equally fond of walking in the country and in town, and with sleep ever at his command; and his favourite relaxation was the energetic pursuit of woodmanship, which he was able to keep up till a very advanced age. Those who knew him best in private life could testify that the serious and even devout temperament which was most conspicuous to ordinary observers was intersected by a vein of geniality and playfulness all the more fascinating by the contrast. In his own home, among his friends and his dependants, among his books or in his woods, he showed to great advantage, and in an amiable and easy light. Indeed, he combined in an extraordinary degree the personal magnetism which charms intimates and colleagues with the popular gifts which attract and fascinate the common people. There has been no such popular idol in our time as he became in his later years, as the affectionate *sobriquets* of 'People's William' and 'Grand Old Man,' by which in succession he was universally known, unmistakably testify.

Mr Gladstone's Family

It is right to record briefly, and without intruding on the sanctity of private grief, how much Mr. Gladstone's career owed to his happy domestic surroundings, and especially to the sympathetic and watchful care of his wife. In 1889, when he had still some years of public life before him, their golden wedding was celebrated with the keenest sympathy on the part of many who differed widely from his recent politics. On the death without issue of Mrs. Gladstone's brother, Sir Stephen Glynne, a life interest in the Hawarden property passed to her husband, with a reversion to his eldest son. This son, Mr. William Henry Gladstone, sat in Parliament for some time and was a Lord of the Treasury from 1869 to 1874, but died at a comparatively early age in 1891. He was married to a daughter of the 12th Lord Blantyre and has left a boy who is heir to the Hawarden property. The second son, the Rev. Stephen Gladstone, has been rector of Hawarden since 1872, and married in 1885 a daughter of Mr. O. B. Wilson, surgeon, of Liverpool; the third is Mr. Henry Gladstone, who is married to a daughter of Lord Rendel; and the youngest is Mr. Herbert Gladstone, M. P. for West Leeds, who has held various subordinate posts in different Governments and was First Commissioner of Works under Lord Rosebery. Of Mr. Gladstone's daughters, one is Mrs. Wickham, wife of the Dean of Lincoln (formerly Headmaster of Wellington College); another is Mrs. Drew, wife of the Rev. Harry Drew, vicar of Buckley, whose little daughter Dorothy has been so great a favourite with her grandfather in his declining years; while Miss Helen Gladstone was till recently a vice-principal of Newnham College and well-known for her work in connexion with women's education. In close touch with his children throughout all his life, Mr. Gladstone has known the truest blessings and joys of family relationship. He could truly have repeated the saying of Edmund Burke that when once he crossed the threshold of his home all the troubles he encountered outside it would vanish. Mr. Gladstone had, of course, various residences in London during the course of his long career, but those with which his memory will be principally associated are the official residence in Downing-street and the house he occupied in Carlton-house terrace. Of late years he has had no permanent house in London, but Hawarden Castle has been his home, and his position as a resident within the borders of Wales added to the enthusiasm of Welsh Radicals for his policy and his personality.

The length and critical substance of this biography is testimony to the considerable esteem in which Gladstone was held by his contemporaries. He was, by the time of his death, the admired political hero of the liberal middle class and, thanks to his longevity and moral authority, something of a legendary figure among the influential body of religious Nonconformists of all classes. That he was a familiar figure in households the length and breadth of Britain is testified to by the manufacture of no fewer than six separate busts and statuettes of the great man in the popular Parian china. Disraeli had only managed five and Palmerston four. Nevertheless, as this obituary subtly suggests, the 'Grand Old Man' (GOM) of the Liberal Party was, to many of his parliamentary enemies, the 'Murderer of Gordon' and the culpable divider of his cabinet and his party over his Irish policies. Despite the reference to his 'strong personal devotion to the Queen' there is no suggestion that the devotion was not reciprocated on the Queen's part. When he finally resigned as Prime Minister in March 1894 she behaved graciously to him but declined to ask, as was then customary, whom he would recommend as his successor.

SIR EDWARD BURNE-JONES

Painter: 'He was as original as his art.'

17 JUNE 1898

We deeply regret to learn that English art has suffered another great loss in the death of Sir Edward Burne-Jones, which occurred at an early hour yesterday morning at his house, the Grange, West Kensington. He had been ailing for some time, repeated attacks of influenza having sorely tried his constitution, but he was able to work and to see his friends until seized by a heart attack – which carried him off after a few hours of suffering. This loss, following so soon upon the deaths of Lord Leighton and Sir John Millais, removes the third of the four most conspicuous figures in the English art of our day, and now only Mr. Watts survives – the eldest of the four – to carry on the great tradition. Nor is it only in the world of art that Sir Edward Burne-Jones's death will be felt, for no man had warmer friends or was more sincerely loved by those who were intimate with him. His character was as individual as his painting; there was nobody like him; in his view of life, in his quaintly delightful geniality of manner, in his humour, he was original as in his art.

Edward Burne-Jones, who like his friend William Morris was (in whole or in part) of Welsh descent, was born in Birmingham in 1833, and was educated at the King's School. He passed in due course to Exeter College, Oxford, and it is said that his intention was to become a clergyman; but falling in with Morris and other young men who were strongly under the influence of the Pre-Raphaelite movement, then in its youth and vigour, he determined to take to art as a profession, and came to London in 1856 without taking a degree. He fell under the influence of Rossetti, whose views of the scope and objects of painting agreed with his own, and whose vivid imagination and eloquent tongue completely captivated the younger man. He was never Rossetti's pupil, but habitually watched him at work, and learned from him a number of lessons which he put into practice in his earliest pictures and drawings, such as the 'Christ and the Knight' and other semi-mystical works which we saw with so much interest when the whole oeuvre of the painter was collected at the New Gallery three or four winters ago. For ten or 12 years, however, his painting was known but to few, except when he chanced to exhibit a drawing or two at the Old Water-Colour Society's rooms. His name came to be whispered abroad; one or two of his designs for stained glass, carried out by Morris, were seen, passionately admired, and fiercely criticized; but not until the opening of the Grosvenor Gallery in 1877 was his art revealed to the public of London. Here in the following years were shown those five works of his middle period the 'Days of Creation,' 'The Golden Stair,' 'The Annunciation,' the 'Pygmalion' series, and 'King Cophetua,' with many more and his works may be said to have struck the note of the Grosvenor exhibitions, as they did afterwards of their successors, the exhibitions at the New Gallery. Finally, on the death of the principal purchaser of the artist's works, Mr. William Graham, his collection was sold at Christie's in 1886, and the 'Chant d'Amour' realized over 3,000 guineas. Till then no important picture of his had been submitted to auction, and there was naturally some anxiety among his admirers as to whether the opinion of wealthy buyers would agree with their own. From that time there was no doubt whatever as to the eagerness felt by great collectors to possess a fine Burne-Jones, and only the other day the beautiful 'Mirror of Venus' when sold with the Ruston collection, realized no less than 5,000 guineas.

This test is of little value where the qualities of an artist are purely popular, as in many instances that one might name; but it is of interest where an artist paints types of his own, not understood and perhaps positively hated by the many, and gradually conquers his way by the possession of the higher gifts alone. To force the recognition of those gifts upon the great public and upon those who purvey for them is a triumph; and that triumph Sir Edward achieved. Many people still dislike his work; many very competent critics find his whole view of art unfruitful, his subjects mere 'psychological puzzles,' and his types of men and women far removed from reality; but there can be no question at all of the effect that his work has made, and still makes, not only in England, but even in France and America. The French feel that their own Puvis de Chavannes has so many points in common with him that to admire the one means to admire the other, and accordingly they were prepared to find, and found, in the 'King Cophetua,' when it was shown in Paris in 1889, a number of the highest elements of art. In drawing, which was for many years the weak point of the artist, he had made great way before that picture was painted, thanks to those innumerable studies and designs in pencil and chalk of which large selections have been sometimes exhibited of late years. In colour he was at that moment at his best, unless we are to give the palm to the earlier picture, 'Chant d'Amour.' Nor was there any tortured symbolism; the story was simply told, and the painting, though not after the French pattern, was such as no artist could fail to admire. So the Burne-Jones cult began to have its votaries in Paris, and the artist's name is still highly regarded there. England, it may be said that the moment of his highest popularity was when the four pictures forming the 'Briar Rose' series were exhibited at Messrs. Agnew's. Thousands of the most cultivated people in London hastened to see, and passionately to admire, the painter's masterpiece – Celtic imagination translating into colour and form the Celtic legend.

Sir Edward was for a short time an A. R. A. but he was never at home in the

Academy. He exhibited only one picture, 'The Depths of the Sea' or 'The Siren,' and resigned his associateship, from a simple feeling of ennui, in 1893. He was created a baronet in 1894; an 'elevation' which surprised, amused, and somewhat shocked his friends. He married in 1860 one of the daughters of the Rev. G. B. Macdonald; one sister of Lady Burne-Jones is the mother of Mr. Rudyard Kipling, and another is the wife of Sir Edward Poynter, P. R. A. The title goes to the artist's only son Philip; the only daughter is married, to Mr. J. W. Mackail, the well-known scholar. We are informed that the remains of the late Sir E. Burne-Jones will be cremated on Monday next at 1.30 o'clock.

The opening of the Grosvenor Gallery in Bond Street in May 1877 suggested the extent to which Burne-Jones's often idiosyncratic paintings had affinities with the French Symbolist *avant-garde.* At the 1877 exhibition his paintings hung beside Gustave Moreau's *L'Apparition.* Twelve years later when *King Cophetua and the Beggar Maid* was shown at the Paris Exposition Universelle, the painter Puvis de Chavannes was so impressed by it that he attempted to secure it a medal. Puvis was later to invite Burne-Jones to collaborate with the Salon du Champ de Mars and works were subsequently sent in 1892, 1893, 1895 and 1896. Although the roots of Burne-Jones's style lie in the art of the early Renaissance, his impact on twentieth-century art in Paris, and especially on Picasso's 'Blue' period, was to be both surprising and fulfilling. This obituarist expresses particular admiration for the *Briar Rose* series, based on the story of the Sleeping Beauty. The paintings were shown at Agnew's in 1890 and attracted vast crowds both there and later at Toynbee Hall in Whitechapel. They were purchased for £5,000 and were installed by their owner, Lord Farringdon, in a room at Buscot Park in Berkshire in frames designed by the artist himself.

OTTO VON BISMARCK

First Chancellor of Germany:
'One of the rare men who leave indelible marks on the world's history.'

30 JUNE 1898

THE DEATH OF PRINCE BISMARCK removes the greatest personality in Europe. Though it would have been better for his fame had he immediately followed his old master to the grave, yet the heavy clouds which have overhung the sunset of his life cannot diminish the splendour of his zenith. He was one of the rare men who leave indelible marks on the world's history. He would, perhaps, have resented the Pagan idea of being a 'man of destiny,' for he was pious in his fashion, and might have grown into a Puritan but for the exuberance of his animal spirits. That he, however, regarded himself as the chosen instrument of Providence to accomplish a grand patriotic work he has, we believe, confessed in the moments of frank expansion that were common with him. He was a Prussian to the backbone, and a splendid type of his strongly-marked nationality. Displaying in a high degree all its good and many of its evil qualities, he added to them that indescribable something which we call genius. Resolute, masterful, and daring to the verge even of rashness, he combined with the indomitable strength of will of a stubborn Northern race a good deal of the flexibility and cunning which we usually associate with the suppleness of Southern races. With all his love of power, with the jealousy and vindictiveness that have left some grievous blots on his reputation, his ambitions were in a great measure legitimate and his aims undeniably patriotic. He loved his country with his whole heart and his whole mind and his whole soul, though his was undoubtedly a fierce and jealous love which could never tolerate the thought that others might love as well, if differently. None ever destroyed more ruthlessly, but when he destroyed it was always with a view to replace what was effete with solid and durable materials and to prepare the way for his own magnificent schemes of construction. As with all great intellects, his conceptions grew and broadened out with the greatness of his opportunities. The creation of a new German Empire under the hegemony of Prussia was certainly not an idea which sprang ready made from his fertile brain; indeed it was too closely associated with the liberal dreamings of German democrats to commend itself at the outset to his rigid Prussian conservatism. It was only after he had gradually redressed the balance of power in the old Germanic Confederation in favour of Prussia, so as to secure for her complete equality with Austria, that his ambition expanded and contemplated a new

order of things, in which, to the exclusion of Austria, Prussia should enjoy the undisputed hegemony of the German States, and it was only at a further stage that he reluctantly recognized the necessity of merging the individuality of Prussia in a great German Empire in order to give a definite and enduring sanction to her supremacy. But when he had once recognized that necessity he threw his whole energy into the work, carrying it out with a masterful hand at home, whilst firmly intrenching it against foreign attack. So far as his own prescience could do it, he assured its permanent stability; but there are limitations to mortal genius, however great, and the human race, in its onward march to an unknown goal, every day develops new forces which ignore finality.

With all his faith in himself and the future, we know that the Chancellor had his moments of depression, and he must have often been beset with doubts and fears. He knew that, like every mortal, he was toiling against time, but it was not death alone – the death of himself or others – that he had to dread. He was but a Minister, and only master on sufferance. He was the Minister of a semi-autocratic King and of a semi-constitutional country. He had to reckon at once with the Royal favour and with formidable political combinations. The champion of the Crown and of Divine right, he set himself first to stem and then to direct the tide of Teutonic democracy without perhaps ever fully realizing its nature or strength. He might be disgraced, sacrificed, or overthrown, and even if the enforced retirement were only temporary, the lost time might be irretrievable and the threads of his fine-spun policy might be snapped or hopelessly entangled. For at least twenty years of his life, from his appointment as Prussian Minister to the Germanic Confederation at Frankfurt until the memorable day at Versailles when the King of Prussia became German Emperor, he was constantly playing a hazardous, although a deliberately-calculated, game. He courted the burden of an immense responsibility. On each successive card that came from his hand he staked not only personal credit and ascendancy, but the interests of his Sovereign and the fortunes of his country. Had Benedek or Bazaine led their armies to Berlin and both Vienna and Paris were sanguine as to those contingencies Prussia would have again lost caste among European Powers, and the Sovereign to whom Bismarck was, in his own fashion, loyally devoted might have bitterly reproached his audacious adviser. His constancy achieved his work and crowned it; his fixity of purpose and far-sighted shrewdness never neglected a single detail of the means by which the comprehensive purpose was to be accomplished. He used, and, as some said, he abused, his personal ascendancy over the Sovereign. That he might perfect his formidable military machinery he provoked unpopularity by laying heavy burdens upon Prussia, by exacting what seemed in those days to be an unendurable blood-tax, and by setting the popular Chamber at defiance when it refused him the indispensable money votes. He knew well that he was risking impeachment and disgrace. But the Providence in which he believed befriended him, and the wise counsels of the somewhat unscrupulous Pomeranian Achitophel were never turned to foolishness by stress of adverse combinations. Bismarck enjoyed a marvellous run of good luck. Hardly another man who was merely a statesman and not an absolute Monarch or master of armies ever exercised such uninterrupted influence or had leisure to accomplish so much.

His career was altogether a romance, and perhaps the beginnings of it were more extraordinary than the later adventures, which remodelled political Europe and readjusted the balance of power. In his *jeunesse orageuse*, or even in his calmer middle age, who could have predicted the future awaiting him? It was nothing that as a young man he should have sown his wild oats, but even when he had turned his attention to the graver business of life he seemed to have all the failings and prejudices which prevent a politician from making his way. He loved the country, and was devoted to field sports as he detested city life and the drudgery of official routine. He was the typical *Junker*, the man of prejudices and prepossessions, and his mind, which even then held doggedly to fixed ideas, was essentially opposed to concessions or compromises. With an affectation of frankness that was blunt almost to brutality, no one could have dreamed that he had the makings of a diplomatist. With a self-independence and a sturdy pride of caste, violently and sometimes insolently aggressive, he seemed the last man likely to turn into a courtier, or to be the trusted counsellor of a Sovereign claiming obedience by Divine right. He was no orator to win the ear of Parliament; he had nothing in him of the flexible hypocrisy that can stoop to flatter the mob it despises, and seldom has a statesman ventured to display so much cynical contempt for the parties which he in turn used and spurned. Yet it is curious to observe how, in establishing his supremacy over his countrymen, from the Monarch on the throne down to electors of the lowest grades, his character asserted and developed itself with no radical changes. Some of his apparent defects in reality helped him, and the secret of his successes lay in the consciousness of his strength. He spoke his mind with freedom in the Royal closet as in the Chambers; he had always straightforward reasons ready to back his proposals, and the reasons were almost invariably justified by results. Natural confidence gradually grew into a belief in his infallibility, and when a man is implicitly believed in and blindly followed his power increases in something like geometrical progression. When it suited his purpose he introduced unaccustomed candour into the antiquated forms of diplomacy, so that he puzzled and baffled the formal practitioners of the old school and secured some of the most remarkable triumphs on record. Reading between the lines of letters, speeches, and biographical notices; the brawling, beer-swilling, duel-fighting student of Göttingen becomes the Chancellor of Germany and the arbiter of Europe with no conspicuous change and by an easily-conceivable transition. His conduct was thoroughly consistent throughout, though with the growing consciousness of responsibility the consistency was tempered by expediency.

Birth and Childhood

Descended from an ancient family of provincial nobility, which had for centuries held lands in the Alt Mark of Brandenburg as vassals of the House of Hohenzollern, Otto Eduard Leopold von Bismarck was born on the 1st of April, 1815, in the hereditary manor of Schönhausen, close to the village of the same name, amidst the pine woods and sandy plains between the Elbe and the Havel. Some of his ancestors had served with distinction both in the army and in diplomacy, and one of them had come to London as Minister of the Brandenburg Elector. But his own father, though a pleasant and kindly country gentleman, seems to have been neither very energetic nor very intellectual, and Otto von Bismarck's talents and gifts, so far as he inherited them from his parents, came more directly from his mother a highly educated and deeply religious lady, Luise Wilhelmine von Menken, the daughter of a Privy Councillor who had figured conspicuously in the public service under three successive Sovereigns. As a child of six he was sent to a private school in Berlin; as a boy of 12 he quitted it for the Friedrich Wilhelm Gymnasium there. The winters were spent at home with his parents; in the summers, with his brothers, he was left in charge of an old family servant. His mother, with her mind already set upon his succeeding in a diplomatic career, for which she is said to have quickly detected his peculiar aptitude, took care that he should be well grounded in modern languages. To that he owed his familiarity with French, and the more than fair acquaintance with English displayed in the Motley Correspondence, while later on he acquired a useful colloquial knowledge of Russian in the intervals of his duties as Minister at St. Petersburg. In his early education and intellectually he owed much to his mother; but, physically, he was equally indebted to his father. Strange as it may seem, young Bismarck was rather a mild-mannered and retiring boy, and might possibly, under exclusively feminine influences, have turned into a book-worm. But, as he spent his holidays in Pomerania, and in his father's company, his healthy animal instincts asserted themselves. At school he is said to have been a model pupil; he performed tasks which were severe enough with no visible effort. He seldom infringed the rules, and was rarely called up for punishment. But when he left Berlin and his schoolbooks behind him in holiday-time he soon brushed away the scholastic cobwebs. At that time it was a three-day journey by stage-coach from the capital to Kniephof, over execrable roads, with night-halts in indifferent inns. In mid-winter the journey might be indefinitely prolonged. With the prospect of the pleasures awaiting him, the boy delighted in roughing it, as is shown by his juvenile letters. At home at Kniephof, he was mounted on his pony, following his active father afield, clearing the fences as they came, and scrambling through the swamps and the ditches. A letter written many years afterwards describes the habits of the house and the tastes of the elder Bismarck:–

'I have lived here with father; reading, smoking, walking, helping him to eat lampreys, and joining in a farce called foxhunting. We go out in the pouring rain or at six degrees of frost, surround an old bush in a sportsmanlike way, silent as the grave, whilst the wind blows through the cover, where we are all fully convinced even, perhaps, my father that the only game consists of a few old women gathering fagots.'

For Bismarck had always plenty of natural humour and the pen of a very ready writer. If he had neither the polish nor the delicate *verve* of a Madame de Sévigné, he had his own graphic powers of description with a gift of shrewdly caustic observation, and he knew how to ring the changes between humour, satire, and even seductive pathos.

His 'Jeunesse Orageuse'

As a student at Göttingen, where the old fashioned house in which he resided is still shown, and later on in Berlin, he adapted himself more easily to the roystering life of his fellow-undergraduates than to the more serious side of University routine. 'Mad Bismarck' was ever ready to drink beer with the best of them, and to send or accept a challenge for a duel in which his combative nature found relief from the tedium of college lectures. In spite of all his pranks, however, he managed to pass his examinations with credit, and, in June, 1835, in his twenty-first year, was sworn in as examiner in the Berlin Tribunals. Shortly afterwards a meeting occurred of which neither the personages immediately concerned nor the spectators could anticipate the consequences. He was presented at a Court ball to the future German Emperor, then Prince William. As it chanced, another member of the legal profession, as tall and as powerfully built as Bismarck, was presented to the Prince at the same time. It is recorded that the soldier Prince was pleased to say facetiously, 'Well, Justice selects her young advocates according to the regulation standard of the Guards.'

But another anecdote of the same period shows that even for the modest duties of an 'Auscultator,' young Bismarck scarcely possessed an adequate sense of judicial gravity and decorum. He was taking down the evidence of a citizen of Berlin whose manner was not to his liking. 'Sir, if you do not behave more decently I'll have you kicked out.' The sitting magistrate interposed with the remark that the kicking out was the business of the Bench. Bismarck calmed down, the business went on, but very soon he was again on his legs. 'Sir, behave yourself better, or the magistrate shall kick you out.' He was probably more at home in the quarters of the *Garde Jäger*, the regiment which he entered in 1838 to perform his military service, or among the hard-riding and hard-drinking squires of Pomerania and of the Alt Mark, whom he loved to astonish by his wild pranks and dare-devil recklessness quite as much as by the shrewdness with which he managed the paternal estates. Summoned home in 1839 to look after the property which his father had desperately neglected, he threw himself with characteristic energy into all the pursuits of a landed gentleman, and exhibited first on the family estates in Pomerania and then at Schönhausen, which fell to his share on his father's death in 1845, the remarkable administrative ability which he was able later on in his life, thanks to the generosity of a grateful country, to display on a much grander scale in the development of his princely estates at Varzin and Friedrichsruh. He was then only a sadly embarrassed country gentleman, but he reclaimed, embanked, manured, and drained with the same foresight and discrimination with which he subsequently, as a great territorial magnate, administered his forests and his paper mills and his distilleries. But when things had begun to mend visibly under his management, when his subordinates came to understand their duties and move smoothly forward in the grooves of routine, Bismarck's energetic intellect began to prey upon itself, and for a time it seemed probable that he might bring himself to shipwreck. He sought relief from *ennui* in violent exercises and wild dissipation; riding from house to house and from carouse to carouse, he galloped about the woodlands in the dark, like the wild horseman of the ballad: he tested his strength of brain by deep draughts of champagne and porter, and the echoes in Kniephof were awakened by light catches and pistol practice at unholy hours.

Marriage

His strength of will and sound sense might have saved him in any event in the struggle between the powers of good and evil. But in a happy hour he made the acquaintance of the religious and accomplished Fräulein von Putkammer. He seems to have fallen in love at first sight; he loved with all the strength of his impetuous nature; and the passion was fanned into a violent flame by the very natural opposition it encountered. To the pious Putkammers 'Mad Bismarck' was no welcome suitor, and the young lady, although she was fascinated, was, nevertheless, inclined to fear him. But when he presented his ultimatum she confessed her affection, and her parents, who doted on their only daughter, felt themselves forced to give way. The betrothal took place, and to his sister and confidante Bismarck triumphantly announced it in the court bulletin – 'all right.' He was married in the summer of 1847, and the young couple went to Switzerland and the South for their wedding trip. As it happened, the King of Prussia, Frederick William IV, was then at Venice. Bismarck was bidden to the Royal dinner-table; the Sovereign appears to have taken a fancy to his free-spoken subject; they had a long conversation on German politics; and the impression then made may probably explain the otherwise almost unaccountable suddenness of Bismarck's appointment a few years later to the responsible and difficult post of Prussian Minister at Frankfurt.

Early political life

Even in his wildest days his mind had been perpetually turning upon politics, and he often puzzled and bored his boon companions by starting at the midnight supper-table political monologues of interminable length. In the same year in which he was married his Pomeranian neighbours sent him up to Berlin as their representative in the United Diet, and his first speech was exactly what might have been expected from a youthfully enthusiastic champion of the most unbending form of Prussian Conservatism. It was towards Prussia and her King that all that was liberal and national in Germany at that time looked for relief from the narrow and intolerant *régime* identified with the ascendency of Austria under Prince Metternich. When Bismarck entered the House a Liberal member was speaking and reminding his audience amongst thunders of applause that the object of the great War of Liberation in 1813–14 had been not only to sweep away the foreign invader but to establish a national system of government on the basis of a free Constitution. With characteristic boldness Bismarck at once flung himself into the fray, and, in a maiden speech constantly interrupted by hostile clamour, set repeatedly at defiance the sentiments of a large and angry majority. He traversed in a tone even more aggressive than his actual language the preceding speaker's statement, for it was, he declared, patriotism and not the paltry spirit of faction that had animated the nation in 1813. For a moment he was shouted down, and whilst the storm raged he pulled out a newspaper and pretended to be reading until order was restored. But he was soon on his legs again, pouring out his scornful wrath upon those who would degrade 'the national struggle for independence into a domestic squabble over political catchwords.' The result of this and other speeches, in which he vindicated with uncompromising fervour the prerogatives of the Prussian Crown – 'a Crown which,' he asserted, 'the Sovereigns of Prussia wear not by the will of the people, but by the grace of God, a positively unconditional Crown' – was to identify him at once with the party of extreme reaction. As one of its most fanatical champions he provoked the bitter animosity of the Liberal and Radical newspapers, and the violence with which he replied, both in the Chamber and in the columns of the *Kreuz Zeitung*, of which he was one of the chief founders, merely added fuel to the fire.

The events of 1848 and the capitulation of the King before the Berlin mob were a cruel blow to his monarchical pride, but his political sagacity recognized the necessity of yielding to accomplished facts. In the earnestness of his grief he became almost pathetically eloquent. He mourned the past 'because it was buried beyond resurrection, since the Crown itself had scattered ashes on the coffin,' but he could not bring himself to tread in the new paths. There would be no salvation, he declared, until the great cities, which were so many hotbeds of revolution, were levelled to the ground, and turning his back upon Berlin, where the red, yellow, and black tricolour of German democracy waved triumphant in the place of the black and white standard of Prussia, he retired for a time to the country to brood over the wickedness of a world that was out of joint. But in 1849 he was back again in the capital as a member of the Lower House of the Prussian Diet, elected under the new Constitution. Still his heart was hardened against the great patriotic and national aspirations which underlay the revolutionary movement in all parts of Germany, and he rejected with Prussian scorn the idea that a Hohenzollern might accept the Imperial Crown of Germany from the hands of the Frankfurt Parliament as an adequate compensation for the curtailment of his prerogatives as King of Prussia. The constitutional conditions attached to the offer were in themselves an insult. It was for Prussia to impose, and not to accept Constitutions. Speaking already with the authority of a leader, he declared against those projects of union that would sacrifice and subordinate Prussia. The popular schemes for national regeneration he contemptuously denounced as dreams and delusions. In fact, they ran directly counter to his principles and most cherished plans. They tampered with the allegiance of the nation to the dynasty, with the devotion of the disciplined soldiery to the officers from the *noblesse* who had hitherto led them to victory. Indeed, no Churchman of the dark ages ever believed more devoutly in the divine virtue of consecrating oil, and, though a fervent patriot according to his lights, he was always much more of a Prussian than a German. At that period the very word German had a democratic flavour at which his *Junker's* gorge rose in revolt. It was by the strength of her own right arm, not by the tricks of Parliamentary charlatans, that Prussia must be saved. He scoffed at the comparisons between England and Prussia which were freely used as arguments by the Progressive party. The British Crown was only an ornament at the apex of the State edifice, the Prussian Crown was its foundation stone. Like most Prussian Conservatives of that period he worshipped at the shrine of Russian autocracy and deemed no sacrifice of national pride too great to secure to the Prussian Crown the all saving benefit of 'our Emperor's' (Nicolas') good will. He would doubtless gladly have disposed in the same way of all his opponents and political passion seemed for a time to have entirely obscured his judgment. Thus we find him in the following year actually applauding the Olmütz agreement, which is now universally admitted to have marked the lowest depth of degradation to which Prussia had sunk since Jena, and, indeed, in some respects a lower one even than that, for it involved a moral rather than a physical abdication. But in the interests of a policy of blind reaction the future maker of Germany was for the nonce willing to abdicate into the hands of Austria and Russia the right to prescribe the lines upon which the internal government of Prussia and of the other States of Germany should in future be conducted. Just as a few years before his abilities had seemed on the eve of running to seed in the dangerous *désoeuvrement* of a narrow provincial life, so they appeared at this juncture to be threatened with the sterility of a bigoted Prussian Conservatism.

Bismarck as a Diplomatist

As the responsibilities of marriage had saved him on the former occasion, so now again he was to be saved by the responsibilities of active public service. His monarchical stanchness and fearlessness had gained for him the confidence of the King and of his Prime Minister, Herr von Manteuffel, and the world, which knew him only as an impulsive, rash, and habitually overbearing freelance, was astounded, in 1851, to learn that he had been suddenly appointed Prussian Minister to the Germanic Confederation represented by the Frankfurt Diet, at that time probably the most important and difficult post in the diplomatic service of his country. It is only fair to add that Bismarck was himself equally astounded, but, with his usual decision, he at once accepted the appointment whilst admitting that it was a venturesome experiment. But the good seed had at last fallen on to fertile ground. In the stimulating atmosphere of Frankfurt, which, in spite of all the pettinesses of daily diplomatic intrigue, was the centre of German political life, Bismarck's statesmanlike instincts soon threw off the narrow parochialism of Junker prejudices. He saw Prussia no longer from the inside, but from the outside, and it was a bitter disillusion to him to find that she looked less like a planet ruling in a firmament of her own than like a satellite of Austria, gravitating with the rest of the German States in her rival's orbit. As he himself said in after years, he had been brought up 'in feelings of admiration, nay, of almost religious reverence, for the policy of Austria,' and it was mainly in order to bring Prussia's policy more thoroughly into line with that of Austria that he had been sent to Frankfurt. Yet he had not been at Frankfurt three months before he had come to the irrevocable conclusion that the one constant feature of Austrian policy was its jealousy of Prussia, and that for every minor German State the Royal avenue to Austria's favour was hostility to Prussia. 'Every one here,' he writes, 'is either Prussian or Austrian, although one would have thought that, with the *entente cordiale* which exists between Berlin and Vienna, it should have been impossible for any one to be other than either for Prussia and Austria, or against both.' He analyzes the situation dispassionately, but mercilessly, without the slightest indulgence for his own prejudices or for those of his masters in Berlin. He still retains for a time some of his old contempt for the sentimental idea of 'a German policy.' 'Each Government understands under "a German policy" something different. Indeed, one may say that each one describes under that name the policy which it would like to see adopted by the others.' But he is quick to perceive that Prussia, being exclusively a German State, has a much better claim to be the authoritative exponent of a

German policy than Austria, a State which is as much Italian and Danubian as German. A few months more and Austria is already, in his eyes, the enemy with whom Prussia is bound sooner or later to enter upon a life-and-death struggle. He has weighed the whole system upon which the existing confederation of the German States is based, and found it wanting. It must be 'ended, not amended,' in order to make room for a new system, in which there will be no place for Austria. In the meantime Prussia's policy must aim at increasing her own *clientèle* in the German Diet in order to neutralize every attempt made by Austria to use her influence over the Germanic Confederation for the furtherance of her non-German interests.

For this purpose Bismarck becomes for the nonce the apostle of German particularism. On the plea of giving greater weight to the Germanic Confederation in the councils of Europe, Austria wishes to make the decisions of the majority of the Diet binding upon the minority. Bismarck fights tooth and nail against this proposal, and upholds the rights of each individual State to shape its own policy within the limits of its general obligations towards its confederated allies. He sees in those obligations as they stand a source of weakness for Prussia, 'the remedy for which will have to be sought one day *ferro et igne*,' and he will not consent to anything which may tend to increase or perpetuate that weakness. The majority of the Diet is Austrian, and he cannot hope to win it over bodily to the side of Prussia, but he may and does detach individual States from the Austrian allegiance, and draws them nearer to Prussia by economic and political ties. For eight years he never wearies in the task. Through the Press, through diplomatic channels, in repeated conferences with the minor German statesmen and Sovereigns, whose acquaintance and good will he neglects no opportunity of personally cultivating, he labours ceaselessly to maintain the political system of Germany in its existing state of flux, lest it should consolidate into a shape more difficult for Prussia to mould successfully to her own ends. Complicated, however, as is the game which he is playing on the crowded chessboard of German politics, he knows that his own victory cannot be decisive unless Prussia plays up on the wider field of European politics. If Austria is to be checkmated in Germany she must be checkmated in Europe generally. The influence which he exercises over the policy of Prussia during the Crimean War is entirely directed towards that one purpose, and it is a decisive influence. In the Eastern question and, later on, in the Italian question, the point upon which he never tires of insisting from Frankfurt is that the resources of Prussia and of the German States must not be squandered in the defence of Austria's non-German interests. Nor is that in itself enough. Prussia must take advantage of her rival's difficulties in order to provide herself with future allies. He strikes the keynote of his future policy throughout his long career when he writes – 'Prussia must never let Russia's friendship wax cold. Her alliance is the cheapest amongst all Continental alliances, for the eyes of Russia are turned only towards the East.' He braves the prejudices of his ultra-conservative friends in Berlin, who refuse to see in Napoleon III, anything else than 'the child of the Revolution,' and does not hesitate to pay a visit to Paris, which they call 'Babylon,' in order to form his own estimate of 'the man of December.' 'Do not,' he writes, 'be alarmed for my political health. I have something of the duck's nature about me, and I can shake the water out of my feathers. Moreover, there is a long way from my skin to my heart.' He takes Napoleon's measure at a glance, and henceforth the Emperor of the French is only an instrument upon which he plays with unerring skill until, having no further use for it, he crushes it under his iron heel.

There is, perhaps, no period in Bismarck's life so instructive and fascinating as those eight years which he spent in Frankfurt for the letters which he wrote from the seat of the German Diet to his powerful friend and patron, General von Gerlach, the King's aide-de-camp and confidential adviser, enable one to follow closely, and almost from day to day, the rapid and constant development of his massive intellect amidst new and congenial surroundings. They were years of self-education, in which was sown the seed of all his future achievements; but the process was so rapid that within the first twelvemonth after his appointment we have the extraordinary spectacle of this young, untrained diplomatist, still under 40 years of age, not only educating himself in the school of active politics, but educating his Royal and Ministerial masters at Berlin. It is he who, before long, lays down from Frankfurt the lines upon which the policy of the Prussian Government ought to be shaped, not with regard merely to German questions, but to European questions generally. He writes to the Prime Minister, Herr von Manteuffel, that 'our answer' to such and such a diplomatic move should be so and so, and the Prime Minister yields to the inexorable logic of the youthful envoy, or, should he not yield, Bismarck, regardless of that official discipline which 20 years later he was to enforce in similar circumstances with such pitiless severity against Count Arnim, does not scruple to go behind his chief straight to the King and urge his own views with such cogency that the King overrules the Prime Minister in his favour. Presently they are not content at Berlin to have merely his written advice on all the important questions of the day. He must come and discuss them personally with the King and the Ministers. Every year he travels more and more frequently to and fro between Frankfurt and Berlin, and in one year alone more than 20 times, in order to give them the benefit of his clear, incisive judgment, of his fearlessness and energy. Yet he has put away in the meantime many of the prejudices and preconceptions which had first ingratiated him with the ruling powers in Berlin. He has abated none of his loyalty to the Monarchical principle, none of his zeal for the Prussian Crown, but he has conceived for them new ideals which overshadow his former beliefs. Beside such vital questions as those of Prussia's position in Germany and in

Europe, the constitutional questions which fired his youthful enthusiasm have paled into relative insignificance. He realizes that the destinies of the Prussian Crown will be determined not within the walls of the Berlin Chambers, but outside the frontiers of Prussia, in the council rooms of European statesmanship, and in last resort upon the battlefield. Let Prussia arm and be strong against the coming struggle, let the voice of her Sovereign make itself heard and respected abroad, and the Prussian Crown need fear no *diminutio capitis* at home. Even the words 'Parliament' and 'Democracy' lose their original terrors, and when he has made up his mind that Prussia has little to hope for from the Princes of Germany, he begins to cast about for the support of the middle classes 'whose aspirations might be easily enlisted in our favour by very moderate concessions.'

The familiar letters written to his wife at that time are full of curious self-revelations; of regrets for the follies of a wasted youth; of the strong expression of his innate piety:–

> 'I went the day before yesterday to Wiesbaden to ——, and with a mixture of sadness and wisdom we went to see the scene of former follies. Would it might please God to fill this vessel with his clear and strong wine, in which formerly the champagne of 21 years of youth foamed uselessly and left nothing but loathing behind! . . . I cannot understand how a man who considers his own nature and yet knows nothing of God, and will know nothing, can endure his existence for contempt and weariness.'

Nor does he mean those regrets to be barren, for he abounds in wise resolves for the future. He plunges into the Rhine off Bingen for a moonlight swim, meditates as he is drawing his powerful strokes, and comes back to read in his small Testament and discourse with his companion Lynar on Christianity. Those letters also reveal his love for nature, as they are enlivened by picturesque sketches of the common people. So whether he is travelling in Russia, Austria, or Spain, he always delights in descriptions of the scenery, whether seen in summer or winter, in sunshine or in storm. It is interesting to compare the sentimental side of his nature, the old-fashioned German *Schwärmerei*, displayed in these letters with the merciless iconoclasm of the political letter-writer who brutally tramples under foot the dreamy *Ideal-politik* of his fellow-countrymen, and in his bold, massive hand writes over the time-honoured platitudes of the past the grim motto, 'Might before right.'

For the moment, however, he was making the pace too hot for people in Berlin. Frederick William IV had been for some time incapacitated from discharging the duties of his kingly office, and these were formally transferred in 1858 to Prince William as Regent (afterwards William I). A more liberal Ministry was appointed and welcomed by popular opinion as the inauguration of a 'new era,' and Herr von Schleinitz at the Foreign Office had his own ideas about Prussian policy, for which, by the way, Bismarck thereafter never ceased to bear him a relentless grudge. Transferred to St. Petersburg in 1859, he considered himself to have been at least temporarily 'shelved,' but, whilst improving the opportunity to establish friendly relations at Court and in official circles, he was by no means prepared to surrender without a further struggle the influence he had so long exercised in Berlin. He is still working out the menacing but inevitable solution of the German question, and he writes an elaborate memorandum upon it for the Prince Regent's perusal. It is suggested to him by the Italian complications, as well as by proceedings in the Diet. 'We have always found ourselves face to face with the same compact majority, with the same demands for concessions.' The invariable deduction is that an intolerable situation must be put an end to. And his Machiavellian idea is that Prussia should secure moral sympathy by inducing Austria to violate the principles of the confederation by straining legal forms. As to that, having regard to the domineering attitude of Austria, he says there need be no great difficulty, and he urges more than ever the strengthening of Prussia's military power, with a view to immediate eventualities. His resolutions are taken; he is clear as to his ends and the means of attaining them; neither scruples nor fears weigh against his patriotism; and when the opportunity shall come he is ready to act.

Premier of Prussia

A change from St. Petersburg to Paris in 1862 was not unwelcome, but he was only destined to remain in Paris for a few summer months. During that short period nothing note-worthy occurred, so far as his diplomatic duties were concerned; but it was in France that he received a communication of momentous import to himself and to Europe. Bismarck had one devoted friend in the Prussian Cabinet, the Minister of War, General von Roon, who for some time past had been indefatigable in promoting his interests with the King. Roon was engaged in preparing the great scheme of army reorganization which was to convert the Prussian army into the finest fighting machine in Europe, but the scheme was unpopular, the tide of democratic opposition in the Prussian Chamber was rising rapidly, and King William, of whose mind the humiliating memories of 1848 were still painfully vivid, was visibly losing heart. When Bismarck was at Frankfurt he had been brought into frequent and intimate contact with his future Sovereign, who was then residing in a sort of honourable exile at Coblenz, and the young Envoy had gradually conquered his esteem and confidence. In 1862 King William doubtless felt that Bismarck was the 'strong man' he was looking for to stem the torrent, but he hesitated to send for him, knowing full well what a storm of popular indignation his appointment to the Prussian Premiership would provoke. Roon took it upon himself to precipitate the solution which the King both wished and dreaded. On the 18th of September he telegraphed to Bismarck, who was travelling in the south of France, the code-words already agreed upon between them, 'The pear is ripe,' and on the 20th the latter arrived in Berlin. On the same day, when the King, who was on the point of abdicating, poured out his troubles to his War Minister, Roon once more pressed him to send for Bismarck. 'But he will not come now even if I send for him, and he is so far away one cannot talk things over with him.' 'Your Majesty,' Roon replied, 'he is here, and he will willingly obey your Majesty's call.' A few days later the *Gazette* announced Bismarck's appointment to the highest office of the State, which he was destined to hold for nearly eight and twenty memorable years, first as Prussian Premier and Foreign Minister and then as Chancellor of the North German Confederation and afterwards of the German Empire.

All the odds seemed, nevertheless, against the new Minister when he undertook to uphold the privileges of the Throne against the Liberal Chamber. The Progressists, who had carried the Moderate Liberals with them, were already assured of victory. The Moderate Liberals, although possibly open to a compromise, felt as bitterly as the Radicals towards the Premier, who was still known to them chiefly as the fiery champion of reaction. There were few Conservatives in the Lower House, and Conservative writers in the Press were still more rare. Even many of the Monarchists distrusted him, for there was still a powerful Austrian party amongst the aristocracy of Berlin. The King himself was subject to frequent fits of depression, and on one occasion, at least, it was only by a vigorous appeal to his honour as a soldier and a Hohenzollern that Bismarck succeeded in averting a fresh threat of abdication. His own proud spirit never faltered, and he defied with equal boldness both the open opposition of an enormous numerical majority in the Chamber, and the more subtle antagonism of powerful Court influences. He repeatedly remarked that a death on the scaffold might be as honourable as a death on the battlefield. The first Parliamentary engagement was fought over that perpetual matter of dispute, the right of the national representatives to control the national expenditure. To Bismarck, with his far-reaching plans, the question was vital. Their failure would be assured beforehand if he had not practical *carte blanche* for placing the army in a state of perfect efficiency. And he spoke out plainly to the Chamber and the world, with the phrase which has since given him his *sobriquet.* Prussia must prepare for the opportunity which should rectify her indefensible frontiers. The questions of the day could never, he declared, be settled by speeches and majorities, but by 'blood and iron.' With his back to the wall, he answered for the 'budgetless Government,' and accepted responsibility in reliance upon a future indemnity. That was one of the turning points in recent Prussian history; for had the Parliamentary majority had its way, Prussia would have been paralysed for prompt action. It is noteworthy, if only in contrast to his later tactics, that through all the hardly-contested fight the Premier kept the King scrupulously in the background, and he seldom showed his courage more conspicuously than when he stretched constitutional prerogative against himself and courted the fullest personal responsibility in place of sheltering himself behind the immunities of the Throne.

The war with Austria

These domestic and Parliamentary difficulties were doubly irritating, as he had come to the fixed determination to try conclusions with Austria as soon as an opportunity presented itself. With that purpose in view he had lost no time in establishing a solid claim upon the goodwill of Russia. No sooner had the insurrection of 1863 broken out in the Polish provinces of Russia than he caused the Tsar to be informed that 'Prussia was prepared to stand shoulder to shoulder with him against the common enemy,' and a secret convention for eventual military co-operation was speedily signed. At the same time Bismarck was equally determined not to precipitate events, and when Alexander II proposed that Russia and Prussia should forthwith declare war against Austria and France, he courteously rejected the offer, in spite of the obvious temptation to seek relief from internal complications in a European war. It was his policy to choose his own time for creating his opportunities. He already saw his opening in the question of the Duchies of Schleswig and Holstein. At the outset, in 1864, he announced in a Cabinet Council, to the astonishment even of his most stalwart colleagues, that its only satisfactory solution could and must be the annexation of the Duchies to Prussia, but he was careful to hold no such language in his diplomatic capacity. His first business was to force the hands of Austria, and place her in a false position by inducing her to join with Prussia in the Schleswig-Holstein campaign. The actual fruits of the campaign he could afford to wait for. They would be swept later on into his store room with the rest. The Treaty of Gastein, providing for the administration of the duchies by the two German Powers, simply marked time until he could deal with the hesitations of Italy and the equivocal attitude of Napoleon III, which, for the time being, rendered a more radical treatment of the German question underlying the Danish question inexpedient or premature. King William's final refusal to join in the Congress of Princes convoked by Austria at Frankfurt in the autumn of 1863, for the purpose of considering a comprehensive scheme of reform in the constitution of the Germanic Confederation – a refusal which Bismarck wrung out of his Sovereign 'by the sweat of his brow' – had practically closed the door against any compromise between the conflicting claims of Austria and Prussia. Bismarck's policy of 'ending, not amending,' the old order of things henceforth held the field. For the so-called 'scheme of reform' which he finally put forward in the spring of 1866, a few months before the outbreak of hostilities, was only an audacious attempt to anticipate the results of a victorious war without having to undergo the risks and sacrifices of a campaign. The substitution for the old Germanic Confederation of a South and North German Confederation to the complete exclusion of Austria was a revolution in which neither the Austrian Court nor its German allies could be expected to acquiesce except under the pressure of military disaster. Nor did Bismarck expect them to do so. But his arrangements were now complete. He had had his famous interview with Napoleon III at Biarritz in the preceding autumn, he had secured the active cooperation of King Victor Emmanuel in the event of war, the dual administration of the duchies under the Treaty of Gastein teemed with excellent pretexts for a rupture, and the tone which Austria adopted was all that he could himself have desired to pique the pride and arouse the patriotism of the Prussian people. Even the bitterness of party passion was at the crucial moment disarmed by Bismarck's narrow escape from the bullet of an assassin. The King, breaking through all formal etiquette, drove from his own dinner-table to congratulate the Minister. Political opponents attended the levées improvised at his residence. The populace of Berlin, gathering beneath his balcony, cheered him to the echo as he made a spirited address. He himself accepted his escape as a sign from heaven, and girded himself with renewed resolution for his great work.

In his book on 'Our Chancellor,' Busch reports a curious revelation as he remembers to have heard it from the Chancellor's own lips. It shows that Bismarck already regarded the encounter with Austria as a mere affair of outposts before the more momentous struggle with France. A fortnight previous to the outbreak of hostilities he had sent the brother of Von Gablenz to Vienna to propose that Austria and Prussia should make a common change of front, unite their forces, precipitate themselves upon France, reconquer Alsace, and make the old Imperial city of Strasburg a federal bulwark as it had been before. There may have been worldly wisdom in the proposal from a German standpoint, but it outraged international law and comity; for the only pretext for attacking France which Bismarck could suggest was that Strasburg had been stolen a couple of centuries before. The proposal was, of course, rejected, and it is almost impossible to suppose that it was seriously meant, for, even if the Emperor Francis Joseph could have foreseen the issue of the forthcoming campaign, he was certainly not the man to have saved even his Empire at the expense of his honour.

But nobody in Austria was prepared for the rapidity with which Prussia struck the blows which followed, or rather accompanied, the final declaration of war. They were in strange contrast with the dilatory proceedings of the cumbrous Confederation. Bismarck left Berlin with the King for the seat of war on June 23, and only ten days later, looking on at the stubborn fight of Sadowa, he was the first to see the decisive advance of the Crown Prince, who had been as eagerly expected as Blücher at Waterloo. 'Those are not plough-furrows,' he declared, 'they are the lines of a marching army.' But having gained the great victory by Germans over Germans, he declined to inflict any gratuitous humiliation upon the vanquished foe. He persuaded the King to forgo the military satisfaction of entering Vienna at the head of a triumphant army, and he steadily resisted those who urged the exaction of extortionate conditions of peace. Towards those minor States whose territories he required to round off the frontiers of the Prussian Monarchy he showed, indeed, no mercy. Hanover, Hesse-Cassel, Nassau, Frankfurt, and, of course, Schleswig-Holstein were definitely annexed to Prussia. But, as he already foresaw that he would some day want the friendship of Austria, he insisted that she should be spared, and on her account also Saxony. Equally essential to his grand programme was the moral, rather than the material, conquest of the South German States, and the military treaties which he imposed upon them were carefully kept secret until popular opinion was ripe for their publication. His statesmanlike moderation was doubtless to some extent prompted by the growing restlessness of France, whose scarcely-veiled demands for territorial compensation were couched in language of almost threatening insistence. But he wished to choose his own moment for picking a quarrel with her, or, better still, for inducing her to pick a quarrel with him. So for the time being he was ready enough to lull her into temporary quietude by vague and not over-scrupulous assurances. On the 7th of August, we are told on reliable authority, he was asked by a French Envoy returning to Paris, 'M. le Ministre, do I take back war or peace?' The answer given with affected animation was, 'Friendship, a lasting friendship with France.' But the words are said to have been accompanied by a smile which suggested unpleasant reflections. And a Prussian Privy Councillor communicated next day to the Frenchman what may possibly have been meant as a friendly warning, 'Before a fortnight we shall have war upon the Rhine, should France "insist on her territorial demands."'

North German Organization

The Prussian troops had come back in triumph from the Danube. The new Prussian Diet, elected on the day of Sadowa, had closed 'the period of conflict' by passing a Bill of Indemnity, and in the spring of 1867 there was the meeting of the first North German Parliament. The Reichstag represented the 22 States situated to the north of the Main. Among many conflicting interests and factions, the new party of the National Liberals was supposed to hold the balance. It was led by Von Bennigsen, a Hanoverian country gentleman, and by Lasker, a shrewd Jewish lawyer, from Posen. The National Liberals, like the Progressists, were earnest for internal reforms; nevertheless, they were so far in accord with Bismarck that they consented to subordinate those objects to the completion of German unity. Bismarck, who now held the office of Chancellor of the North German Confederation, was compelled to reckon with the forces of popular opinion, but on one point he stood firm. He would have *carte blanche* for a definite time as to keeping up the strength of the army during peace. Yet even on that point he assented to a compromise, and accepted a vote for five years in place of ten. He was resolved that Germany should be ready in any event, and soon afterwards his prescience was justified when the Luxemburg question was raised by France, nearly precipitating the war of 1870. He had undoubtedly encouraged Napoleon to hope for the cession of the Duchy, though he probably foresaw that the Fatherland would refuse to ratify the bargain. By one of those singularly dexterous coincidences, of which he possessed the secret, it was at this juncture that the military treaties with the South German States were published. When the notion of the cession was broached in Berlin there was a violent explosion of patriotic feeling, which Bismarck did nothing to suppress. Did he hope to force the French Emperor's hand and compel him to declare war at a disadvantage? It seems not unlikely, considering his whole course of action; for Prussia and her allies were fairly ready to fight, while France, politically isolated and hampered with the Mexican business, was far from being prepared for the invasion of a country 'bristling with fortresses.' Napoleon III drew back, and the London Conference settled the terms of a compromise which both parties accepted. King William paid a visit to the French Court during the Paris Exhibition of 1867, and Bismarck, who accompanied his sovereign, was not only the object of marked attention, but Napoleon III even paid him the extraordinary compliment of consulting him with reference to the more liberal measures of policy which he was then contemplating at home. The two men were not to meet again until the French Emperor came to surrender his sword into the hands of the King of Prussia at Sedan. Bismarck had gained time for completing his work of organization, and he prosecuted it with his habitual prudence and sagacity. Baden, threatened from Strasburg in the event of a French invasion, had applied for admission to the Confederation. Bismarck entreated the Grand Duke to wait, preferring to have an unattached friend in the South. Using one of the homely similes in which he delighted, he said that to separate the Grand Duchy from the adjacent Southern States would be like skimming the cream from a basin of milk, which was sure to sour the rest. It was more difficult to deal with the ex-King of Hanover. King William, who had some scruples of conscience with regard to his deposed fellow-Sovereign, was anxious to treat him liberally in pecuniary matters and to grant him an indemnity of 16 millions of thalers. The Federal Council grudged the grant, and only sanctioned it on the Premier's threat of resignation. Bismarck himself had somewhat reluctantly assented. But he was by no means sorry when King George refused to compromise his freedom of action on any conditions, and the rejected millions were devoted to the 'Reptile fund,' which for many years continued to subsidize the obsequious organs of his Government. But the journalists he had in his pay served his will in his struggle with Parliament, when, revolting against the 'one-man power,' it strove to shake off his dictatorship. They stirred national feeling in favour of the Chancellor, who declined to be embarrassed by responsible colleagues.

The war with France

Bismarck was now ready for the war with France, which he felt to be inevitable, and, indeed, indispensable, if the unification of Germany was to be completed. Had the struggle been delayed Parliamentary dissensions might have slackened the federal bonds, the South German States might have been seduced from their mostly half-hearted allegiance to the new order of things, the military machinery itself might have got out of gear. Nor was the external situation reassuring. Austria, still unresigned and hostile, was gradually recovering, and, in spite of the fighting alliance between Italy and Prussia in 1866, Victor Emmanuel still considered himself bound to Napoleon by the prior claims of Magenta and Solferino. The longer the struggle was postponed the greater was the danger of a coalition against Prussia. Bismarck's affectation of candour had hitherto thrown dust in the eyes of Benedetti, although the French diplomatist by no means lacked shrewdness; and he had carefully locked up in his secret drawers certain compromising proposals for a readjustment of the balance of European power at the expense of Belgium, which, if produced at the psychological moment, were, he knew, bound to alienate from France the sympathies of other Powers, and especially of England. All that he wanted, therefore, was a *casus belli* which should put the French technically in the wrong. With this object in view he had been for some time past secretly nursing the candidature of Prince Leopold of Hohenzollern to the Spanish throne, never indeed openly supporting it, but, on the other hand, never allowing it altogether to drop. The train had been carefully laid, but there is some reason to believe that it was fired sooner than he himself had intended. Emile Ollivier had declared in the French Chamber that the political atmosphere was absolutely serene, King William was taking the waters at Ems and Bismarck was resting at Varzin, when the explosion took place with startling suddenness. The announcement that the Spanish Government had on July 3 officially put forward the candidature of the Hohenzollern Prince provoked in Paris a wild outburst of warlike indignation. Partly from weak subserviency to the popular outcry, partly from ignorance of the real situation in Germany, the French Government fell headlong into the trap. Angry speeches from the French tribune, peremptory instructions to the French Ambassador, who had been told to repair forthwith to Ems and place himself in communication with the King, roused the national spirit in Germany, and at last exhausted even King William's forbearance. That, personally, the King did everything in his power to avert war there can be no manner of doubt. He would not allow that he had any direct authority over Prince Leopold, who belonged to another and very distantly connected branch of the house of Hohenzollern, but he was willing to exercise his influence in order to secure the Prince's spontaneous withdrawal, and he exercised it successfully. The French had practically won a far greater diplomatic triumph than their intemperate action deserved, but even that was not enough for them. They wanted not only to defeat Prussia but to humiliate her. Benedetti was told to insist upon a formal pledge that the King would never allow Prince Leopold's candidature to be revived. To this outrageous demand the King very properly demurred, and, when Benedetti again presented himself he was informed in courteous terms that the King had nothing to add to his former declarations. Bismarck, who was on his way from Varzin to join his master at Ems, received a telegram in Berlin announcing this momentous incident, and at once saw his opportunity. The forbearance which the King had hitherto displayed was not at all to his liking, for, the French in their folly having dealt all the trump cards into his hand, he was determined to make them play the game out to the bitter end. He dined that night with Roon and Moltke, and, as he has himself related the story, he began by obtaining from them a definite assurance that their military preparations were complete, and then, taking the King's telegram, he proceeded to 'edit' it and sent it out for communication to the Prussian representatives abroad and for publication in the Press in such a shape as to remove any further chance of a compromise. The attitude of France was unquestionably one of deliberate provocation, but in the light of his own subsequent revelations it is impossible to acquit Bismarck of a decisive share, both in originally preparing and in finally precipitating the conflict. He sounded a war-blast which resounded through the Fatherland, and a single day of intense enthusiasm accomplished what years of patient diplomacy had failed to do. The mobs of Berlin, like the mobs of Paris, were cheering their Monarch and shouting 'To the Rhine.' The whole of Germany had consolidated itself at the signal; the South was as eager for battle as the North, and, pride being swallowed up in patriotism, it not only invited, but demanded, the leadership of Prussia. King William hurried back from Ems to the capital, and Bismarck made a speech, amid the unanimous cheers of the Reichstag, in which he declared that, thanks to the overbearing action of France, Prussia had to choose between war and humiliation. A few days later he dealt a final blow at the French Emperor's political reputation by producing from the secret archives of the Foreign Office the original draft of Benedetti's proposals for the annexation of Belgium to France as a compensation for the aggrandisement of Prussia. He had for four years kept it carefully in his possession, and now the moment had come to use it. It was published in *The Times*. The effect was instantaneous. No one stopped to inquire how much encouragement Bismarck himself had given to Benedetti. So astounding a revelation of French duplicity completely won over public opinion, in England at least, to the German side.

Bismarck in France

Though diplomatists, like Carteret in Marlborough's wars, have followed the marches of armies, it is seldom that a statesman directing the Government has actually taken the field. Bismarck, who held military rank and wore a military uniform, met his Sovereign at Mainz, and accompanied him by easy stages to Versailles. Then was seen the strange spectacle of an ambulant Foreign Office billeted in the chateaux, villages, and towns where the march of each day happened to terminate, flashing telegrams and despatching couriers in all directions, till it finally established itself in the ancient residence of the Bourbon kings. But the progress of the great Chancellor was no mere promenade in the rear of the combatants. Searching about at Mars-la-Tour, he had found his eldest son, Count Herbert, lying in a farmhouse among a number of wounded comrades, and had learnt with great pride the gallantry with which his second son, Count William, at the risk of his own life, had rescued a trooper of his regiment. Bismarck himself was under heavy fire at Gravelotte, and throughout the earlier part of the campaign he had his full share of hardships as well as of work. The rapid succession of German victories had, however, relieved Bismarck of his chief anxiety, for they paralyzed the friends of France both in Vienna and in Florence, and he felt that he could henceforth rely upon the neutrality of the other great Powers. As it chanced, on the very day when Thiers came to Versailles to ask for a truce Russia broke loose from the stipulations of the Treaty of Paris. We hold it as certain that German consent had been given in consideration of Germany having freedom of action towards France; although, as Bismarck declared to Mr. Odo Russell that Gortchakoff's circular had taken him by surprise, we must assume that he had not been consulted as to the precise moment of the declaration. The result of the Conference in London was a foregone conclusion.

The German Empire

But more momentous negotiations engaged the Chancellor's attention – those for an Imperial union of North and South Germany. The grandest of his aims was achieved at last, with a completeness, an unanimity, and an enthusiasm he could hardly have dreamed of. Whatever share the Crown Prince had in these events, to suppose that Bismarck could have hesitated or held back is as inconsistent with demonstrated facts as with his character and the whole tenour of his policy. The German Empire was proclaimed in the palace of the great King who had seized Strasburg by stealth; in the palace sacred to the military triumphs of that greater instrument of destiny who had paved the way for present events by shattering the Holy Roman Empire.

As for the peace negotiations with Thiers, they were protracted and exquisitely painful for the French patriot. Bismarck, who had felt only contemptuous pity for Jules Favre, respected Thiers and showed him genuine sympathy. 'He pleased me much,' said the Chancellor, 'for he has a fine intellect, good manners, and can tell his story well. I feel for him, for he is in a bad position, but all that cannot help him.' Yet apparently, with regard to Belfort at least, Thiers's fervent pleadings were not all in vain. It was a purely French city, it had never belonged to Germany like Strasburg and Metz, and it had made a successful and heroic defence during the war. Bismarck could afford to be magnanimous, and to leave it in French possession, even though, according to military authorities, it would have been a valuable complement to the new line of German defences. Even as to Alsace, and still more as to Lorraine, Bismarck affected to demand their annexation to Germany mainly in deference to the advice of the strategists and to the pressure of public opinion, though the latter at least had been largely manufactured by the semi-official Press, which he had continued to feed from his headquarters throughout the war just as he had always done from the Wilhelmstrasse. On the other hand it is certain that the money ransom would have been greatly increased had he foreseen the facility with which it was raised and the rapidity with which French prosperity was to retrieve itself. In fact, a few years later, in tardy repentance, he threatened a renewal of the war – an attitude which called forth the remonstrances of Lord Derby and the personal interposition of the Tsar. Bismarck had seen the astounding resources of French wealth and of French patriotism enable the country to give something like *carte blanche* for the expansion of its military forces and for the construction of an artificial military frontier, which for the greatest part of its length is said to be practically impregnable.

Foreign relations of the Empire

Yet he had good reason to be proud of the results embodied in the treaty of Frankfurt, which established the position of the New Empire in Europe. So far as the French were concerned, though he could not hope to disarm their resentment, as soon as the treaty was signed he showed himself willing to soothe them by important concessions. He recognized the honourable conduct of Thiers; he finally came to his help in putting down the Commune, after having for a time played with its leaders, and he met the wishes of M. Pouyer-Quertier, who had been despatched to Berlin on a special mission, by consenting to accept financial instead of military guarantees for the payment of the second milliard. He had won much more than he expected by the war, and now the gains were to be secured and consolidated. The danger of a coalition against Germany, averted at the outset of the French campaign by the terrific rapidity of her victories, was still present to his mind, and to avert it permanently by diplomatic combinations was the main task to which he henceforward devoted his statesmanship. Thus originated the scheme of a closely-knit

Drei-Kaiser-bund. Immediately after the war Bismarck approached Austria under cover of a proposal to form an international league against the forces of revolution, but, under Count Beust's guidance, she was not prepared to do more than recognize accomplished facts. The Emperor Francis Joseph, however, gradually realized the danger of isolation in view of the intimate relations which existed between the Courts of Berlin and St. Petersburg, and when Bismarck renewed his overtures he sensibly resolved to make the best of the situation. That France would always be a danger to Germany so soon as she became strong enough to threaten again Bismarck never doubted, and though no friend to republics, he on the whole approved of a republican *régime* for her. The Republic separated her from alliances that might be possible on a monarchical restoration. Hence arose the difference of opinion with Count Arnim, his Ambassador in Paris, whose personal and political sympathies were all with the Bourbons, and who imagined that, with his powerful backing at Court, he could go behind his chief just as Bismarck in the Frankfurt days had reached the King's ear behind Manteuffel's back. No doubt he had friends in the highest places, but he found, as others have found since, that Court favour and influential connexions were no protection against the calculated wrath of the Chancellor. When the indispensable Minister threatened resignation, combinations dissolved, Princes and potentates were forced to bend, Court favourites had to hand over their badges of office, and ambassadors had to pack up their trunks and go.

For reasons which can be easily surmised Bismarck stood aloof from the Russo-Turkish War, though he had done not a little to encourage the warlike policy of Russia. He watched events carefully, but would not interfere. As he said in his memorable speech, so often quoted, Bulgaria was not worth the bones of a single Pomeranian Grenadier. It was his business to see how the clashing interests of Germany's allies were to be reconciled. He felt his difficulties culminate when the moment came for him to preside over the Berlin Congress, where he was in close and hourly communication with the representatives of the allied Empires. His conduct was alternately governed by his determination to retain the friendship of Russia, and by his knowledge of the necessities of Austria. With the Plenipotentiaries of the Great Powers paying him court and waiting their turns of audience in his ante-chamber, Bismarck modestly professed to play the part of 'the honest broker.' Courteous to all, he protested somewhat too much to impose upon shrewd and suspicious diplomatists. He displayed a great admiration for Lord Beaconsfield, and, in return, induced him to concede certain points, reminding him that Russia had made unexpected concessions. The secret Salisbury-Shuvaloff agreement having been signed, Lord Beaconsfield was willing to give way; Austria had to be content with the occupation of Bosnia and Herzegovina, and assuredly the Russian representatives had no reason to complain. Yet they did complain, and, although Bismarck had risked offending other friends, his concessions to Russia failed to satisfy her, and the Treaty of Berlin, revising that of San Stefano, was the beginning of the end of the Drei Kaiser Bund. Russian discontent threw Germany back upon Austria. Having assured the success of his mission beforehand in confidential interviews with Count Andrassy at Gastein, in the autumn of 1879, Bismarck went to Vienna. He was welcomed by the Emperor as an honoured guest, and the formal etiquette of the Hapsburg Court for once was suspended in his favour. They stipulated for a defensive alliance, to come into force under certain circumstances. Of course it was aimed at Russia, and Austria had everything to gain. The assent of the Emperor William was more difficult to obtain, and nothing, perhaps, more conclusively shows the ascendancy Bismarck had obtained over his Sovereign. Not that the Monarch submitted to the Minister unconditionally, and it is suspected that it was against the Chancellor's wish that the Emperor chose that moment for an interview with the Tsar, to whom he tendered explanations – or apologies. Yet Bismarck himself probably never wavered even then in his determination sooner or later to bribe or browbeat Russia back into the old relations of friendship with Germany.

In the meantime, however, his efforts were mainly directed to completing the isolation of France. It was his occult diplomacy that sedulously fomented the differences between Italy and the French Republic, and at the same time incited a threatening campaign in the Austrian Press against the *Italia Irredenta*. Frightened by the latter, and stirred to passionate jealousy by the French occupation of Tunis, Italy was driven into the arms of Germany, who arranged matters for her at Vienna, and in 1883 the fact that Italy had joined the Austro-German alliance was officially announced in the Italian Senate. The accession of Italy forwarded Bismarck's policy in two ways. It strengthened the position of Austria in the event of war with Russia by securing her southern frontier from attack, and it equally weakened that of France by compelling her to watch the Alps as well as the Vosges. The Chancellor's policy in the Egyptian question was governed by similar considerations. He was quick to foresee in it the germs of a permanent estrangement between England and France.

The only danger he still had to guard against was that of an understanding between Russia and France, and, in spite of all his endeavours to ingratiate himself again with Russia during the Bulgarian difficulties, he felt that she was still drifting away from him. The three Emperors had continued to meet annually with all the outward appearances of friendship for some years after the Drei-Kaiser-Bund had died a natural death. But after 1885 the conflict of interests between Austria and Russia in the Balkan Peninsula grew too acute for even such an exchange of outward civilities between the two Sovereigns, and 'the honest broker's' position became proportionately difficult. The renewal of the Triple Alliance in March,

1887, had given fresh umbrage at St. Petersburg, and Bismarck himself at last gave the world to understand that he could no longer run with the hare and hunt with the hound. Few of his great political speeches are more memorable than that which he delivered in the Imperial Diet on February 6, 1888. It created universal sensation, for it could only be interpreted as a solemn declaration *urbi et orbi* that the ancient friendship of Germany and Russia was at an end. With more even than his usual affectation of frankness, he discussed the external relations of the German Empire, and, after laying special stress upon the value of the Austrian alliance, he went on to declare that though Germany was still anxious to maintain peace with her other neighbours, and especially with Russia, she could run after no one. 'Russian public opinion has shown the door to an old and powerful and reliable friend.' Germany, he added, in a splendid peroration, could be easily – perhaps, too easily – influenced by friendship and good will, but never by threats. 'We Germans fear God, but none else in the world.' No one who listened to that speech could have believed that the statesman who uttered it had at that time in his pocket a secret treaty which he had himself concluded a few months previously with Russia. Except at Berlin and St. Petersburg, its existence was undreamt of, until nearly 10 years later Bismarck suddenly revealed it in the *Hamburger Nachrichten.* Its precise stipulations are still unknown, but it seems to have effectually guaranteed the neutrality of Russia and Germany respectively in the event of a war other than one of absolutely unprovoked aggression against any third Power. How even so elastic a conscience as that of Bismarck was able to reconcile his treaty obligations towards Austria with the 're-insurance' thus effected at St. Petersburg it is difficult to explain, and he himself must have felt the difficulty to be at the time insuperable, for he never ventured to enlighten the Austrian Government on the subject. Fortunately for Germany the secret treaty itself was long since dead and buried when the revelations of the *Hamburger Nachrichten* compelled another Chancellor of the Empire to tender posthumous explanations which were accepted on the principle of 'least said soonest mended.' The historian, however, will note with less surprise, perhaps, than Bismarck's contemporaries the profound duplicity with which the last of his diplomatic achievements and the greatest of his responsible utterances on international policy are mutually marked.

Colonial Policy

The political consolidation of Germany gave a tremendous impulse to her commerce. The stream of French gold pouring into her coffers after the war had, it is true, given rise in the first place to excessive and disastrous speculation. But, after a temporary reaction, German enterprise rapidly developed and expanded in every direction and on sounder lines. The new Empire was not only the most formidable of European Powers, but it was gradually becoming a great industrial State for whose surplus production new markets were indispensable. It therefore not unnaturally began to direct its ambition towards the creation of colonies beyond the seas, and the Chancellor ultimately encouraged its aspirations. Perhaps he hoped to direct into channels which he might still control the tide of German emigration which continued to flow annually into the United States and other distant countries where it was lost to the Fatherland. Perhaps, also, he might have displayed less energy in the matter had it not been for the cooling of his relations with England, and for the contempt which the flaccid Government of Mr. Gladstone had not unnaturally provoked. Mr. Gladstone and Lord Granville had persistently and almost obsequiously pressed for Prince Bismarck's advice in their Egyptian policy, and when the advice was reluctantly given, they had hesitated or declined to follow it. Be that as it may, it is certain that Bismarck had modified his own views on German colonization. Formerly he had set his face against it, declaring that colonies to Germany would be like the silks and sables of the ostentatious Polish nobles, who had no shirts to their backs. But in 1884 he was actively interesting himself in promoting German annexations in South Africa, although they clashed with claims which England advanced to regions lying 'within the sphere of her influence.' We do not say that he had not strict right and the sanctions of international law upon his side; but his attitude towards England was unfriendly and his proceedings were more than brusque. Declaring that he would not see German interests sacrificed, even to his sincere desire for a good understanding with England, he declared a Protectorate over the Angra Pequeña Settlement, and compelled the reluctant assent of our Cabinet. He followed that up by the annexation of Togoland and of the Cameroons, against the feelings of the native chiefs, and again the English Government yielded. He then turned his attention to the Fiji Islands and New Guinea, but at last, in deference to the protest of our colonies in the South Seas, the British Government made a firm stand, which had its immediate effect on the overbearing Chancellor. It declared that, much as England valued German friendship, it declined to admit that the friendship of any country was necessary to enable her to maintain her position. So the Chancellor, as was always his habit, when pushing secondary objects so far as they could safely be pushed, drew quietly back and modified his pretensions. Since then Germany has acquired large possessions in East Africa, but the Chancellor henceforward showed more consideration for the susceptibilities of the European neighbours whose interests were affected.

Internal Policy

Though one may condemn the methods he sometimes employed, Bismarck's foreign policy possessed in a supreme degree what he himself called 'the saving virtue of success,' and, up to the unification of Germany in 1870, the same must be granted to his internal policy. But after the constitution of the Empire, his treatment of domestic affairs exhibited chiefly the defects of his qualities. It is one thing to create out of a nation a powerful political organism, and another to quicken and co-ordinate the moral forces by whose operation it must live and move and have its being. No one who has studied the internal situation in Germany can contend that Bismarck, after his twenty years' tenure of power, left her in any way better equipped for the task of self-government, or even trained any school of officials competent to carry on his own system of government. He himself probably never believed in moral forces. At any rate, though he was by no means blind to the imperfections of the Constitution which he had himself framed, he looked for no remedy outside his own genius. His motto at home as well as abroad was *Divide ut imperes*, not so much perhaps from sheer love of power as because he believed himself to be alone *imperii capax*. In the same way as on the European chessboard he played off one Cabinet against another, so in the domain of internal politics he played off one set of men against another, entertaining for all the same supreme contempt. In order to overcome the resistance of dynastic and aristocratic particularism as well as of the philistine *bourgeoisie* he had endowed the Empire with institutions in some respects of a most democratic type, but the old *Junker* in him never realized the true nature of the forces which he had set in motion. He recognized the existence of democracy, but only as he recognized the existence of steam-power – that is, as a motive power which was to drive the engine whilst he sat on the safety-valve and controlled it. He never courted popularity, but when it came to him he welcomed it because it served to grease the wheels and make the machinery of government work smoothly. Political parties were to him mere voting machines with which it was his misfortune not to be able to dispense, but so long as they gave him a majority he did not care much what was their precise colour or complexion. One day they were National Liberals, another day they were Conservatives. He had coquetted with the Socialists during the Prussian conflict and on the eve of his fall he was ready to coquet with the Ultramontanes. So long as people voted as he wished he labelled them *Reichsfreundlich*, otherwise they were *Reichsfiendlich*. In the same way with his Ministers from the moment when they took office they belonged to him personally. All their other ties were *ipso facto* severed. Even from those whom he successively termed by courtesy, 'My august master,' he expected almost the same submissiveness to his imperious will. So thoroughly had he identified with himself the Germany he had created that his self centred patriotism could not conceive loyalty or disloyalty except in relation to his own personality. When it served his purpose he was equally ready to invoke the prerogative of the Crown or the pressure of public opinion, but the former could only be exercised at his instigation, the latter only be manufactured under his orders. The discipline of the German army was never more rigid than that of the German Press under Bismarck.

Its war-chest was constantly replenished from the Guelph funds. Its general staff, as well as its pay department, was installed under the Chancellor's own roof, and at a given signal from his office its territorial forces could be mobilized throughout the Empire. Yet in spite of the almost absolute power, unparalleled prestige and unlimited resources which Bismarck enjoyed and used unsparingly for two whole decades after the creation of the Empire, all his dexterity ended in the gradual clogging of the governmental machinery, in the disintegration of the so-called 'national' parties, in the revival of racial and sectarian differences aggravated by the newly imported strife of class and material interests, and, amidst the general demoralization of public life, in the consolidation of the two great parties against whom he had successively waged war to the knife, the Ultramontanes and the Socialists, who are now the dominant factors in at least the Parliamentary life of Imperial Germany.

The Culturkampf

Returning in triumph from the war in France, Bismarck plunged headlong into a campaign at home to the full as bitter and destined to end not in victory but in disaster. The population of Prussia contained a very large Roman Catholic minority, and that of the new Empire with Bavaria and the other South-German States was altogether more than one-third Roman Catholic. But the Roman Catholic Germans had fought shoulder to shoulder with their Protestant fellow-countrymen on the battlefields of France, and though the Vatican could hardly be expected to welcome with much enthusiasm the creation of a great Protestant Empire in the heart of Europe, it was certainly not in a position to revive the medieval feuds between Pope and Emperor. The Ultramontane party in the new Imperial Diet was, however, imprudent enough to provoke Bismarck's displeasure by selecting for its leader Dr. Windthorst, an ex-Minister of the deposed King of Hanover, and by openly demanding German intervention in favour of the Temporal Power The Chancellor believed the moment to be opportune for securing once and for all the supremacy of the State in the new Empire. The dogma of Papal Infallibility proclaimed by the Vatican Council of 1870, notwithstanding the opposition of the German episcopate, had caused serious dissensions amongst the laity, and though most of the Bishops had ultimately yielded a reluctant assent, their example was by no means universally followed. By giving, wherever he could, State countenance to the Old Catholic movement, Bismarck hoped to stiffen the resistance of the Roman Catholic laity to the authority of Rome, and ultimately to provoke a schism, which, even if it failed to detach the whole Roman Catholic population from its allegiance to the Papal See, would be serious enough to cripple the power of the Roman Catholic hierarchy as a political force in the new Empire. The fight broke out over the maintenance by the State of Old Catholics as religious teachers in Roman Catholic schools. But the Chancellor, deceived, perhaps, by the eminence of some of its leaders, had overrated the importance of the Old Catholic rebellion against Rome. It had distinguished officers like Rheinkens and Döllinger, but no rank and file. The allies upon whom Bismarck had relied vanished from the field before the battle had been half fought. The all-powerful Chancellor of a victorious Empire was, however, in no mood to draw back. Cheered to the echo by the National Liberal party, then in the heyday of its popular power, he vowed before Parliament that he would 'never go to Canossa.' We need not dwell on the details of the protracted struggle. The State enforced its rights with the utmost rigour; archbishops and bishops pushed the prerogative they asserted to extremes. They were suspended, fined, and even sent to prison. In January, 1872, Dr. Falk had been appointed Minister of Public Worship, and the appointment was significant of subsequent measures. The new Minister was there to carry out the anti-Papal policy of the Chancellor. Measure succeeded to measure, and all in the same sense. The inspection of schools was transferred from the Church to the State, the inspectors being brought under departmental control and rendered liable to dismissal for the abuse of their functions. The Jesuits were declared ineligible for all priestly and scholastic charges. The famous 'Falk Laws' were passed in May of 1873 – a radical revision of the spiritual constitution of the country. They were subsequently supplemented by others still more severe; recalcitrant clergymen forfeited their civil rights, and might be condemned to expulsion from the Fatherland. The Chancellor's passions were thoroughly roused, and his wrath found vent in a speech in the Reichstag, when he had narrowly escaped another attempt at assassination. He contemptuously declared that Kullmann was no lunatic, but a champion of the Clerical cause. 'Yes, gentlemen, you may thrust the man away if you will, but for himself he clings fast to your coat-tails.' The charge was unfounded, but it served its purpose. The strife was becoming terribly envenomed. Then followed 'the bread-basket law,' which suspended State payments to the Church till the clergy should give unconditional submission. Next came the Cloister Law, which expelled all religious orders and transferred the administration of ecclesiastical property.

The Chancellor had given proof of his habitual determination, and no doubt his blood had got heated with the unexpected resistance he encountered. The severity of his successive enactments had been making more martyrs than converts. He could punish churchmen who declined to submit, but he could not touch the congregations, except when the laws were infringed, and then there were riots over the arrests and battles in the sacred buildings. Thoughtful Protestants began to deplore the scandalous effect of such scenes upon the religious feeling of the country, and sober-minded patriots pointed out the incalculable mischief which was being done to the cause of national unity. Bismarck himself at last had to sacrifice his pride, for he had by this time used up the National Liberal party as an instrument for controlling Parliament, and he could not gain over the Conservatives except by closing what they regarded as a mutually destructive conflict between Altar and Throne. The death of Pius IX in 1878 and the accession of a new Pontiff seemed to offer an opportunity for a dignified retreat. But Leo XIII promised at first more than he was in a position to perform, and though Bismarck hoped to be let down easily the negotiations dragged. Falk was invited to resign, and then he was brought back again, the resignation indicating concession, the return implying a menace. But in 1880 the Discretionary Powers Bill relieved the strain by mitigating the harshness with which the Falk Laws had hitherto been enforced. It was a practical pledge of readiness for a compromise. Subsequently Van Schlözer was sent to the Vatican as being a *persona grata*. The Crown Prince, during a stay at Rome, had an interview with the Pope, which went off pleasantly. Bismarck astutely invoked the arbitration of Leo in the dispute with Spain as to the Caroline Islands, and as he became more yielding the tension of the situation relaxed. The actual terms of settlement agreed upon have never yet become known. Henceforward the Chancellor in his dealings with the Catholics went as far as possible on the principle of *quieta non movere*. But he could not undo the harm already done, for he had permanently estranged one of the great conservative forces in the country, and, instead of breaking up the Ultramontane party in the Imperial Diet, the Culturkampf had welded it into a formidable phalanx, whose numbers, discipline and independence have remained unbroken to the present day.

The Anti-Prussian Parties

In the first outbreak of patriotic enthusiasm the Constitution of the new Empire had been voted almost by acclamation; but there remained difficulties still to be overcome, and others soon began to crop up. Poles, Guelphs, and Danes were in Bismarck's eyes so many *Reichsfeinde* whose hostility he neither hoped nor cared to disarm, but whose power he was determined to crush. He gave an earnest of the temper in which he meant to deal with them in the scornful answer with which he brushed aside in the first Reichstag a resolution of the Polish group in favour of Polish autonomy and the exclusion of the Polish provinces from the new Empire. The Hanoverian malcontents met with as little mercy at his hands, and nothing would ever induce him to relax the implacable harshness he had displayed from the outset towards the ex-reigning family and their adherents. Only in his treatment of the stiff-necked populations of Alsace-Lorraine did he depart from his usual practice and attempt, if somewhat clumsily, to disguise the iron hand under a velvet glove. In spite of many drastic regulations for discouraging too close an intercourse between the new provinces and their French neighbours, the system he enforced was not improperly described by him as 'an amicable despotism.' He hoped to win over the new subjects of the Empire by according them greater civil indulgences than they had formerly enjoyed. On the expiration of the dictatorship 15 Deputies had taken their seats in the Reichstag. So far the results were not satisfactory, for all the Deputies were returned for their French sympathies. Bismarck, however, made the best of things; he said that if the provinces were not reconciled it was well at least that their complaints should not be stifled. He even went some way towards meeting their wishes, advising the Emperor by a revocable ordinance to grant them a measure of autonomy. A Provincial Council with consultative powers was assembled at Strassburg, and he was so far satisfied with its proceedings that its powers were afterwards extended. Next Marshal Manteuffel was appointed as Statthalter, with instructions to be as lenient in administration as was compatible with the security of the Empire. But Manteuffel's rule turned out to be weak rather than lenient, and it was not till Prince Hohenlohe succeeded him at Strassburg that the fruits of 'twenty years of firm government' began to ripen. There have been at least occasional indications that the task which Bismarck set himself may not after all be foredoomed to such everlasting failure as he himself in moments of discouragement was apt to fear.

The growth of Social Democracy

Another difficulty, and one that was perpetually recurring, was to persuade Germany to accept and endure the burdens required by the national defence. It is true that taxation had been lightened for a time by the exaction of the French ransom. The milliards had been devoted to fortifying the frontiers, to the construction of strategical railways, to the formation of a fleet, to replenishing the State coffers, and to laying up a central war-reserve fund against contingencies. Nevertheless, the blood-tax pressed heavily on the population, and while peace seemed assured it was hard to induce the popular representatives to vote all that was demanded by the Chancellor and declared indispensable by the military authorities. The difference was one of principle. The Government demanded the power of fixing the peace establishment of the army indefinitely, whilst the representatives of the taxpayers were not prepared to surrender the control of the purse. Finally there was a compromise; and in fact after the war Bismarck had to deal with Parliament chiefly by compromises and threats of resignation. Only at intervals did he have his own way. When all seemed to be going smoothly the House stood out for economy or reductions; when there were ominous forebodings of trouble the House became suddenly amenable, which lends a certain probability to the suspicion that when the Chancellor was in difficulties he deliberately disturbed the political atmosphere as a means of attaining his ends. A war scare was naturally the most appropriate weapon for overcoming resistance to military expenditure. Resignation was the argument he held in reserve for other difficulties, and, although these repeated resignations came to have rather the air of comedy, the threat never failed to relieve his political worries and break up the opposition that irritated and baffled him. Now it was the Emperor who prayed or commanded him to keep his place; now it was the nation that, with a clamour of protest, put irresistible pressure on their representatives.

Thus he was able to use the familiar weapon to effective purpose when he determined to try conclusions with another and, perhaps, more formidable enemy than the Ultramontanes. The Ultramontanes claimed to be good Germans, though they might be Catholics first; but the Social Democrats called themselves cosmopolitans, and criticized the institutions of the Fatherland with irreverent freedom. For nearly a quarter of a century the Socialists had been steadily gaining ground, not so much, perhaps, from any general acceptance of their economic doctrines as from widespread discontent with the excessive militarism and bureaucratic despotism of Imperial Germany. When Bismarck was fighting the *bourgeoisie* in Prussia before the war of 1866 he was quite ready to encourage for his own purposes the revolt of the masses, at least against the middle classes, and, as his subsequent policy showed, he had some sympathy with Lassalle, the first and the most brilliant apostle of the new ideas. Lassalle advocated State-help for the poor and the helpless, and Bismarck had recognized, long before he broached his proposals for a compulsory national assurance fund, that the State in common prudence should recognize its responsibilities to the wretched. He had spoken in that sense, not, we may be sure, as a soft-hearted philanthropist, but as an eminently practical statesman. But under Lassalle's successors Socialism had become ultra democratic and international and, in theory at least, even revolutionary. Bebel, in his place in the Reichstag, had glorified the Commune of Paris, or, at any rate, the principles which it was supposed to represent. The Socialist members, whose numbers were steadily increasing, formed a fiercely irreconcilable group, whose defiant voices re-echoed thence as from a sounding-board throughout the country. Bismarck, undeterred by the failure of similar methods in the Culturkampf, was already bent upon crushing Social Democracy by repressive legislation when Hödel, as an avowed Socialist, made an abortive attempt on the old Emperor's life. The Chancellor hurried from his retirement in the country to Berlin in the belief that at last he had found his opportunity. He was sadly disappointed to discover that the Parliament was less sympathetic than he had hoped. They refused, because an assassin had failed in his purpose, to give back any portion of their newly-won rights and liberties. Next, Nobiling partially succeeded where Hödel had failed, and Bismarck determined on a final appeal to the country. The new Reichstag consented to pass strongly repressive measures. The meetings and publications of the Socialists were suppressed, the suspected were practically proscribed and placed at the mercy of the police.

But although the measures could hardly have been more severe, their success was at the most only temporary. Socialism, driven under ground, only struck deeper roots. In vain Prince Bismarck strove to exorcise the evil spirits of Social Democracy in the name of State Socialism. His legislation in favour of the working classes met with no acknowledgment amongst those it was intended to appease, whilst it alarmed and irritated the possessing classes, upon whose support he had chiefly relied. The elections of 1890, when the Socialist vote was found to have leapt up from 600,000 to nearly 1½ million and its representation from 11 to 35 members, showed that the period of Socialist repression had in reality been the period of Socialist expansion. Nor was this the only writing on the wall. Bismarck had taken up and flung aside in turn the different Parliamentary parties in whom he could hope to find the makings of a Parliamentary majority. As we have already stated, he never looked upon them in any other light than as instruments for carrying his own measures through the Reichstag. At last he had used them all up and for the first time he found himself on the eve of facing a hostile majority fresh from the polls elected for the express purpose of defying him. He was saved from actually confronting so novel a position by what appeared at the time to most onlookers as a bolt from the blue.

But before dealing with the circumstances of his fall we must touch, only briefly, important as they are, on some of the measures which Bismarck carried simultaneously with his social and political campaigns. Partly from economical, partly from strategical reasons, he made Prussia adopt at an enormous cost a general system of State railways. The cost was undoubtedly very heavy, but the relief to commerce and the convenience to the public, as well as brilliant financial results, at first augured well for the success of this bold experiment. Subsequent experience has, however, told a different tale. He reformed and unified the debased and antiquated currency of the country: he revised and developed the whole fiscal and financial system, although as a reactionary and in the interests of protection; and he promoted in the Imperial Bank of Germany, independently of the facilities which it affords to trade, a great banking institution, worthy of the credit of the State.

Dismissal from Office

On the accession of the present Emperor, Bismarck's position seemed more assured than ever. Death had removed the Sovereign whose advent to the throne he had formerly looked forward to with jealous apprehension. There had been many differences between the Crown Prince Frederick and the domineering Minister, who suspected him of having contracted liberal tendencies through his English connexion. Occasionally things must have come very near to a quarrel, for Bismarck did not scruple to make mischief between the old Emperor and his son, and once even went to the length of taxing the latter with betraying German State secrets to the Court of St. James's. Moreover, Bismarck, who was outspoken, blunt, and even coarse of speech, is said by a single offensive phrase to have outraged the feelings of two exalted ladies beyond all hope of forgiveness. But when the Emperor Frederick came to the throne his days were already measured, and Bismarck could afford to wait. The Battenberg incident, nevertheless, showed what sort of weapons he was prepared to use against his Sovereign in order to impose his will. Fortunately, the sagacity and firmness of Queen Victoria, who had a long interview with Bismarck during her visit to Berlin, made a deep impression upon him and removed the danger of a deplorable conflict between the doomed Emperor and his all-powerful Chancellor. Whatever Bismarck's own feelings may have been, his *entourage* at any rate did not conceal the satisfaction with which they welcomed the end of that brief and tragic reign. William II, whom Bismarck himself had for his own purposes introduced to a knowledge of State affairs, had repeatedly gone out of his way to testify publicly his devotion to 'our great, our only Chancellor,' and the latter never seems to have reckoned with the transformation which is apt to take place when an heir-apparent actually enters upon his inheritance. At any rate he continued to spend the greater part of the year at Friedrichsruh or Varzin, where he was too far away to keep touch with the rapid development of his vivacious young master's character. Thus he left the field open to his enemies, and he had more enemies than he imagined, for he stood in too many people's way. There were some who urged that he had demoralized the public service by constituting himself a bureaucratic autocrat, and that no official, however able or however loyal, could hope to thrive who did not resign himself soul and conscience into the Chancellor's hands. Others declared that he was no longer physically able to deal with the vast mass of public business which he refused to delegate to other hands, or which he would commit only to his son, who had unfortunately inherited a greater share of the paternal faults than of the paternal qualities. Some, again, insinuated that he was treating his Sovereign as a *quantité négligeable* and taking the same advantage of William II's youth as he had formerly taken of William I's old age.

There was undoubtedly considerable truth in these allegations; at all events, the whisperers had their Emperor's ear. Bismarck had grown accustomed, during the declining years of the old Emperor's life, to wield such absolute and uncontrolled power that he resented his young Sovereign's keen interest in public affairs as an intrusion on his own domains. On one occasion at least, in an important matter of foreign policy, the Chancellor declined to inform his Sovereign of the steps he intended to take until they could no longer be undone, and there is reason to believe that he even withheld from the Emperor until just before his fall the real nature of the engagements he had secretly contracted with Russia. There was, moreover, essential and growing incompatibility, though Bismarck was slow to notice it, in their equally masterful tempers, and the will of the veteran Minister clashed with that of the youthful Monarch. As Bismarck said afterwards, it did not answer to harness an old draughthorse with a young one; and it was impossible that they could have pulled well together. The first serious breach was, we believe, brought about at Munich in the autumn of 1888. The Emperor, in the bustle of Court receptions, chanced to discover among documents sent to him from Friedrichsruh for formal signature one which was of the highest importance, and which touched both him and Bismarck personally. It gave authority for the prosecution of Herr Geffcken, who had published in the *Rundschau* the private diary of the Crown Prince. The Emperor resented and never forgot what he considered a gross attempt at deception.

The end, however, did not come till 1890, when the whole civilized world was startled on March 18 by the announcement that the all powerful Chancellor had placed his resignation in the hands of the Emperor. It was known that Bismarck had entertained strong objections to the policy set forth in the Imperial Rescripts of February 4 foreshadowing further social legislation, and they had been issued without his countersignature, but he had been willing to preside over the international conference on the labour question, and it was assumed that, whatever divergence of views might have existed, it had passed away. Even now little has transpired as to the scenes which preceded the event, but they are known to have been of a most painful character. By a strange nemesis one of the incidents which contributed to the catastrophe arose out of a visit paid to Bismarck by his old foe, Dr. Windthorst, the veteran leader of the Roman Catholic party in the Imperial Diet. The Chancellor, seeing himself reduced to unprecedented Parliamentary straits by the recent general election, had been driven to contemplate the possibility of reopening relations with the Ultramontanes, who held the balance in the new Reichstag. The Emperor asked Bismarck for explanations, which he refused to give. Windthorst's visit had been a private one, and the Emperor's authority, he replied, did not extend to his Chancellor's drawing-room. Another and more serious difference occurred in connexion with Bismarck's insistence upon a rigid observance of the Cabinet Order of 1852, directing Ministers to report to the Crown solely through the medium of the President of the Prussian Council of Ministers. The Emperor resented this as an interference with his right to consult his official advisers when and as he pleased. But it may be stated with confidence that the final and irreparable breach was caused by questions of foreign policy. Bismarck held in his hands all the tangled threads of European diplomacy, and he felt he could safely dare his youthful and inexperienced master to disentangle them without his assistance. How tangled they were the revelations of his own organ with regard to the secret treaty with Russia have since shown. But William II was not the man to be overawed by either open or veiled threats. As Bismarck afterwards bitterly remarked, '*Er lässt sich nicht imponiren.*' We should like also to think that the young Emperor was too honest to acquiesce in the sophistical subtleties by which Bismarck tried to reconcile his Russian 'reinsurance' treaty with the loyal fulfilment of his avowed obligations towards the Emperor Francis Joseph. Bismarck's studied indiscretions leave no doubt as to the correlation of cause and effect in this instance, for he has invariably and persistently denounced the severance of the underground wire he had laid to St. Petersburg as the immediate consequence of his fall. A curious detail we believe to have been hitherto unpublished is that the last words exchanged between the Chancellor and Emperor were spoken in English. After a long and somewhat heated discussion Bismarck rose and said in English. 'Then I am in your way, Sir?' The Emperor answered 'Yes'; and from that moment the old Chancellor knew that he also was doomed to learn and to teach the lesson that no man is indispensable. He returned to his palace only to prepare for finally vacating it, and slowly and reluctantly set forth in a lengthy State paper, of which the contents are only given to the world to-day, the reasons for his resignation, together with an elaborate defence of his policy.

Bismarck in Retirement

Everything that the Emperor could do publicly to lessen the mortification of that hour was done with an unstinting hand. A grateful country had already conferred upon Bismarck such splendid rewards, both material and honorific, that even the title of Duke of Lauenburg and the rank of General of Cavalry in the army, accompanied by an autograph letter couched in such terms as a Sovereign rarely uses towards a subject, however eminent, could hardly add lustre to so great a name, and unfortunately Bismarck himself was not in the mood to submit patiently to the honours of 'a first-class funeral.' In his case, if ever, dignified silence would have been golden; but there was a certain coarseness of fibre in his composition which irresistibly bade him seek relief for his wrath in violent language. He was not the man to turn the cheek to the smiter, and, if he behaved indiscreetly, and, as some say, even disloyally, we must remember all that is to be said in excuse. The charge of deliberate disloyalty we fain would not admit, although, if Bismarck is to be judged by the standard he himself laid down in the Arnim and Geffcken prosecutions, it cannot be denied that he more than once laid himself open to even graver charges of treasonable indiscretion. He was passionately attached to the policy he had pursued with triumphant success abroad, whilst he refused to recognize that his retirement had in reality saved him from confronting the threatened bankruptcy of his domestic policy. He knew there was no likelihood of his being recalled to the Imperial counsels. He was advancing in years and events were developing. He believed before all things, as we know, in keeping upon terms with Russia, and he watched with increasing anxiety the growth of the new intimacy between the Northern Empire and the French Republic. The Triple Alliance was all very well; England, with her naval strength, would have been better worth considering had she been less insular and had her Cabinets always followed a consistent policy. But the Germany which had annexed Alsace and Lorraine ought in common prudence to have friends at her back if she was to face with a stout heart the ever-present prospect of a war of revenge. Moreover, he had always been a good hater, and if in the days of his prosperity, when he might have afforded to be magnanimous, he had never spared his adversaries, even when they lay prostrate at his feet, he was not likely to show much consideration for those who had benefited by his fall. With his inborn inclinations to jealousy was mingled a certain contempt for successors who were, in his opinion, fitted to obey, but scarcely to command. Caprivi was an accomplished soldier, with broad and liberal views uncommon amongst men of his profession in Prussia; he was a polished and lucid speaker, well read in many languages and many branches of knowledge, and a man of most amiable manners. But he once confessed, and probably with greater sincerity than marked similar phrases which Bismarck himself was wont to use, that he took his orders from his Sovereign as from a superior officer. We may add that, though Bismarck's married daughter counselled differently, there were other members of the household at Friedrichsruh who felt with the added keenness of their own disappointed expectations the fancied wrongs of the revered *Hausvater*, and were by no means inclined to let his resentment sleep. He would speak out *à tort et à travers* to deputations he cordially welcomed over the beer-flagon. He became frank and confidential as he always used to be, in clouds of tobacco-smoke. He still used the Press he was wont to corrupt with the sequestrated funds of the ex-King of Hanover, and he had found a complacent organ in the neighbouring *Hamburger Nachrichten*. His indiscretions were doubtless not intended merely to embarrass his successors, but also to enlighten and direct public opinion, although he can hardly have weighed their general consequences.

It is needless to recall the painful controversies to which the incidents of his last journey to Vienna, on the occasion of his eldest son's wedding, gave rise in 1892, or the bitter newspaper feuds which raged between his supporters in the Press and the semi-official organs, which served the Government of the day with the same often injudicious zeal he had himself formally inspired. It is pleasanter to remember that in the following year the Emperor seized the opportunity offered by Bismarck's serious illness at Kissingen to pave the way, by a graceful message of sympathy, for a renewal of personal relations, and that when a few months later the old Chancellor paid a visit to the Royal Palace at Berlin, which the Emperor hastened to return at Friedrichsruh, public opinion greeted with unusual unanimity the removal of an estrangement which, whatever might have been the provocation offered, savoured of ingratitude on the one side and of disloyal resentment on the other. Nothing, however, could ever reconcile Bismarck to loss of power, and though Prince Hohenlohe, when he succeeded Caprivi, left no stone unturned to propitiate the old Chancellor, his hostility was never permanently disarmed. But even under such dire provocation as the revelation in the *Hamburger Nachrichten* of the secret treaty with Russia, the Emperor wisely abstained henceforth from widening the breach which he had failed to heal. Even those who are able to separate their estimate of the man from that of the statesman must regret for the sake of his own reputation that Bismarck so long survived his great coadjutors in the creation of modern Germany. Nevertheless, as his eulogists were wont to say when King William had been crowned Emperor at Versailles, Bismarck, with all his faults, has remained for most of his fellow-countrymen more of a demi-god than an ordinary mortal; nor can we doubt that, whatever the final verdict of history may be, the gratitude of future generations of Germans will do ample justice to his memory.

This is a full, perceptive and generally sympathetic account of Bismarck's long and highly influential career, though one written with a distinctly British bias. *The Times* appears to be particularly taken with the revelation that Bismarck's last words as Chancellor were addressed to the Emperor Wilhelm II in English. The obituary is also frank about the Chancellor's concerns about the accession of the Emperor Friedrich III and his English wife, Victoria, Queen Victoria's eldest daughter – as Crown Princess, Victoria had been in regular, and very frank, correspondence about German affairs with her mother. The somewhat obscure 'Battenburg incident' to which the obituarist refers had divided the German Imperial family and therefore, typically, invited Bismarck's interference. Prince Alexander of Battenburg's secret engagement to Friedrich and Victoria's second daughter, Viktoria, was denounced by Bismarck as a British ploy to embroil Germany with Russia – Alexander, formerly the ruler of Bulgaria, had incurred the distrust of the Tsarist government and had been arrested at pistol point by Russian officers and forced to abdicate. The matchmaking Queen Victoria approved of the match, but her grandson, Wilhelm, snobbishly took the view that Alexander was insufficiently well-born for his sister. After a tense meeting between the Queen and Bismarck in Berlin, it was agreed that Prince Alexander should break off the engagement (he later married an opera singer). Friedrich succeeded to the German throne in 1888 but died of throat cancer after a mere ninety-nine days. Bismarck's fears of the new Empress's pro-British political interference were thus removed, but, as the obituary makes plain, he was to lose his influence over her son, the new Emperor, within two years.

HELEN FAUCIT

Actress: 'She could endow comparatively poor characters with at least temporary vitality.'

31 OCTOBER 1898

WE RECORD WITH regret the death of Lady Martin (Helen Faucit), wife of Sir Theodore Martin, which took place yesterday at Bryntysilio, in the Vale of Llangollen, after a long and painful illness. Lady Martin had for several years been an acute sufferer from neuralgic pains. She and Sir Theodore arrived in Wales from 31, Onslow-square, their town house, three months ago, and for the last six weeks she had been confined to her room. The Queen sent daily messages of inquiry, and Sir Theodore yesterday received a telegram of sympathy from her Majesty, together with messages of condolence from representatives of the political, literary, scientific, artistic, and dramatic worlds.

Except on a few rare occasions, as when Sir H. Irving induced her to appear at the Lyceum in a performance for his benefit of *King Renés Daughter*, Lady Martin had not been seen on the stage since the beginning of 1861, and to most of the playgoing public of the present day she was accordingly unknown. But for a long period she was the most popular of English actresses, the cynosure of all eyes. Besides identifying herself with Shakespeare's gentler heroines, such as Rosalind and Imogen, she could endow comparatively poor characters with at least temporary vitality. Indeed, it is not too much to say that if she had died half a century ago, in the heyday of her fame, the news would have been received with almost universal sorrow.

A daughter of Mrs. Faucit, herself an actress of high repute in the days of the Kembles, Lady Martin was born in London about 1816. Like a sister, Harriet Faucit, afterwards Mrs. Bland, she soon showed a taste for the stage, and her mother, while bestowing considerable pains on her education, made no attempt to discourage her. At the age of 16 she had the temerity to come forward at the Richmond Theatre, then in the hands of Edmund Kean, as Juliet, Mariana, and Mrs. Haller. No doubt these youthful essays left much to be desired, but it is indicative of the progress she had already made that a sober-minded critic found one of them to be distinguished by 'freshness, ease, grace, and propriety of action and demeanour.' Macready and Farren, both old friends of Mrs. Faucit, heard of the promise the girl had shown, and each did something to familiarize her with the mysteries of her art. In 1836, after three years' preliminary study, she appeared before London playgoers, at Covent

Garden Theatre, as Julia in *The Hunchback*. Her success was instant and decisive. One spectator declared that he 'never witnessed a better first performance, or one in which approbation was more constantly and enthusiastically expressed.' In two other plays, *Venice Preserved* and *Separation* – the latter being one of the proofs furnished by Joanna Baillie that she was ill advised in restricting herself to the portrayal of a single passion – Miss Faucit contrived to deepen the impression she had created in Knowles's masterpiece, to which her acting gave a new lease of life. Covent Garden Theatre was at this time under the management of Osbaldiston, but in the following year he was constrained by circumstances a little beyond his control to surrender it to Macready, and the first place in the company formed by the latter was allotted to the young actress who had done so much to justify his good opinion.

Miss Faucit now entered upon the most important period of her life. At first, it is certain, she found herself at a signal disadvantage. Macready, though not a Garrick, a Kemble, or an Edmund Kean, was great enough to throw his fellow-players into the shade, and it was inevitable that the least experienced of his recruits should suffer for a time from his predominance. Before long, however, Miss Faucit acquired a popularity hardly, if at all, inferior to his own. It was beyond question that she largely added to the attractiveness of his Shakespearean revivals, and many of the new plays he brought out owed their success almost exclusively to her acting. Especially is this true of *The Lady of Lyons* and *Money*; her Pauline Deschappelles and Clara Douglas, as some may still remember, were long the talk of London. Even when the part assigned to her was comparatively slight, as in *Richelieu*, her performance stood out in clear and striking relief. But her gifts, uncommon as they were, could not avert failure, partial or absolute, from other pieces accepted by her manager, such as Lytton's *Duchesse de la Vallière* and *Sea Captain*, Mr. Browning's *Strafford* and *A Blot on the 'Scutcheon*, Gerald Griffin's *Gisippus*, Sheridan Knowles's *Brian Boroihme* and *Woman's Wit*, Talfourd's *Glencoe*, Serle's *Master Clarke*, Troughton's *Nina Sforza*, and Westland Marston's *Patrician's Daughter* (the last of these, by the way, had a prologue from the pen of Dickens).

It was not upon the same stage that she went through all this work: in 1840 the company migrated to the Haymarket, and in 1842 to Drury Lane. Three years afterwards, at the Salle Ventadour, Paris, they gave a series of Shakespearian performances, varied by *Virginius* (the piece in which Macready's fame originated) and *Werner*. By this time, notwithstanding a reaction in favour of the moribund classical school – a reaction not long previously manifested in Ponsard's *Lucrèce* and Emile Augier's *Ligue* – the movement identified with the name of Victor Hugo had acquired sufficient strength in France to invest the creations of the great English dramatist with a new interest, and the players' trip was more remunerative than they had anticipated. But for Miss Faucit, perhaps, the result would have been less gratifying. It was principally to see her that the Parisians besieged the doors of the house so long given up to Italian opera. Macready, jealous though he was of his supremacy in the theatrical world, showed no disposition to withhold from her the credit she deserved. For instance, speaking in his diary of a representation of *Macbeth*, he notes that the audience 'applauded her sleep-walking scene more than anything else in the whole play.' It should be added that the company represented *Hamlet* at the Tuileries before Louis Philippe, who testified his appreciation of Miss Faucit's Ophelia by presenting her with a costly bracelet. In the same year the actress went over to Dublin, where, possibly in consequence of having seen Rachel as some of the heroines, legendary or historical, of antiquity, she appeared in one of the greatest of Greek tragedies. 'Suddenly,' writes De Quincey, 'oh heavens, what a revelation of beauty! – forth stepped, walking in brightness, the most faultless of Grecian marbles, Miss Helen Faucit as Antigone. What perfection of Athenian sculpture, what an unveiling of the ideal statuesque! Is it Hebe? Is it Aurora? Is it a goddess that moves before us?' The Royal Irish Academy, in common with play-goers of all classes, went into similar raptures over the essay. By this learned body she was presented with a brooch of Irish gold, four inches in diameter, and having in the centre a representation of Antigone at the funeral urn of Polynices. 'With the writings of the Grecian dramatists,' ran the accompanying address, 'we have long been familiar. But their power and their beauty have come down to us through books alone. "Mute and motionless" that drama has heretofore stood before us. You, madam, have given it voice and gesture and life.' Miss Faucit also came forward as Iphigenia in Aulis, but therewith abandoned the new path into which she had struck. Returning to London, she added the heroine of *As You Like It* to her repertory, and in this character achieved, perhaps, her most distinctive and lasting triumph.

In the year 1851 we come to what, from the professional point or view, may be regarded as the beginning of the end. Her grace and spirit as Rosalind had completely subjugated the heart of a young Scotch lawyer of literary tastes but then pushing his fortunes in London as a Parliamentary agent. He penned very tender verse to this 'beauteous Rosalinda,' together with more than one essay designed to show that as an actress she had never had, and was never likely to have, an equal. He wrote in the *Dublin University Magazine*:–

> 'Miss Faucit is one of those rare creatures "with wits and graces eminently adorned" whom we have felt it to be a privilege to have seen, and, whom having seen, we can afford to resign all regret at not having known her great predecessors. Her genius is of a class that renders comparison impertinent. She is original in her greatness, and herself supplies the standard by which alone she can be fitly judged. She is not to be criticized, but studied, as we study the masterpieces or some great sculptor or poet. And she is the greatest poetess of our time, in the power, the variety, the beauty of the images which she places

before us, of the sentiments which she awakens, of the memories to endure with life itself implanted in us by her "so potent art." Words, however powerful, produce no such impression, do not so permeate and steal into the very depths of our being, as the unwritten poetry of this lady's acting. Her impersonations are nature itself but they are nature as it appears to the poet's eye – nature in its finest and most beautiful aspect. Where the author has furnished but a barren outline she pours into it the strength and radiance of her own spirit, and a noble picture glows before us.'

In this same year that this eulogy was written (1851) Helen Faucit became the wife of Mr. Theodore Martin. If we are not mistaken, her marriage, combined with the retirement of Macready, diminished her enthusiasm for the stage. From this time she appeared less and less before the public, though always assured of a hearty reception at their hands. Her last original character was that of Iolanthe in *King Renés Daughter*, an adaptation by her husband of Henrik Herz's play. Mrs. Charles Kean and Mrs. Stirling had anticipated her in this task, but any reputation which the Swedish dramatist's work may have gained in England was due almost exclusively to her skilful impersonation of the blind Princess. In 1864–65, at Drury Lane Theatre, under the management of Messrs. Falconer and Chatterton, she appeared in a revival of *Macbeth*, with an old and esteemed comrade, Mr. Phelps, as the Thane who waded through slaughter to a throne. 'The younger generation,' her husband wrote in *Fraser*, 'have seen for the first time what true acting is, and may form an idea of its value in developing and sending home to the hearts of the audience the conceptions of the dramatist's brain.' Therewith her connexion with the theatre was informally brought to an end. Now and then, however, the first representative of Pauline Deschappelles and Clara Douglas would come from her retirement – in 1874 she played Beatrice at the Haymarket Theatre in aid of the General Theatrical Fund; two years later, at the instance of Sir H. Irving, who found in her a generous and discriminating admirer, she gave one performance at the Lyceum, as already mentioned, of the heroine *in King Renés Daughter*. And that was her last appearance on the London stage.

Miss Faucit's style of acting may be described in a few words. In her youth there was a reaction in favour of the histrionic school which Edmund Kean had temporarily overthrown – that is to say, in favour of the precise, the formal, and the statuesque. No one contributed to this change more largely than Macready; and it was from Macready that Miss Faucit derived some of her earliest ideas on the subject of theatrical effect. Doubtless as a consequence of his tuition, her work was generally characterized by artificiality both in tone and in movement. But though her acting may have been somewhat lacking in spontaneity, it was undoubtedly full of charm, and her popularity was great and deserved. Her conception of the parts she played gave evidence of intelligent sympathy and careful study. She rarely failed to illustrate the meaning of her author. Her attitudes, notably in reading Macbeth's letter to his wife and in approaching the cave in Cymbeline, were such as a great sculptor might have wished to copy. 'Her expression of love,' wrote one of her comrades at Covent Garden Theatre in *The Lady of Lyons* period, Vandenhoff, 'is intensely fascinating – the most beautifully confiding, trustful, self-abandoning in its tone that I have ever witnessed in any actress.'

In her private life Lady Martin was very retiring, but she was a singularly beautiful and attractive character. She was especially sympathetic with young authors, artists, and actors, to many of whom she extended much practical help. In her social life she entertained many of the greatest literary, artistic, and scientific men of her time, including Browning, Tennyson, Sir Walter Scott, Thackeray, Dickens, Froude, Carlyle, Lord Leighton, Sir John Millais, Sir Henry Irving, and many others. At Llangollen she took great interest in the public library of which she, in conjunction with Sir Theodore Martin and Robert Browning, was the founder. She gave a valuable edition of Shakespeare in ten large volumes, Sir Theodore gave 500 volumes from his private library, and Robert Browning contributed his own works complete, together with those of his wife, of Thackeray, Miss Thackeray, and the Brontes. During recent years Lady Martin gave public readings from Shakespeare in the Llangollen Town-hall on behalf of the public library and a cottage hospital. Her last appearance on the stage was at Glasgow, when £500 was realized by her performance of *The Merchant of Venice* for the sufferers in connexion with the Glasgow Bank failure in 1878.

A book written by Lady Martin 'On some of the Female Characters of Shakspere' has passed through several editions.

By the time of her death, Helen Faucit was, as this obituary implies, an actress whose highly acclaimed performances in the 1840s were distant memories. She had realised a common, but often empty, thespian's dream of success in her chosen profession followed by a highly respectable marriage and a comfortable retirement. The obituary lists Faucit's many performances in now neglected dramas by Sheridan Knowles, Bulwer Lytton, Robert Browning and Gerald Griffin but rightly recalls her Shakespearian roles, particularly those she had undertaken in William Macready's famous productions. The obituarist's unkind comment that her acting style had been 'characterized by artificiality both in tone and movement' is supported by the critic Henry Morley who noted that, when she played Imogen, she made 'every gesture an embodiment of thought' and that her voice failed her 'whenever she has a violent emotion to express, and passion sounds often like petulence'.

HENRY TATE

Businessman and philanthropist:
'A thank-offering for a prosperous business career.'

5 DECEMBER 1899

WE REGRET TO announce the death of Sir Henry Tate, Bart., which occurred yesterday morning at his house, Park-hill, Streatham-common. He had been ailing for a long time, but it was only on Monday, November 27, the day of the opening of the new rooms in the gallery at Millbank – the completion of the great building which British art owes to his munificence – that he took to his bed. He was in his 81st year.

An inscription in the vestibule of the Tate Gallery records, in words not wanting in simple dignity, that the building was given to the nation by Sir Henry Tate 'as a thank-offering for a prosperous business career of sixty years.' Of that business career there is little else to say; it was long, and it was very prosperous. Henry Tate, a son of the Rev. William Tate, of Chorley, Lancashire, was born in 1819. Beginning life in Liverpool, he came to London some 25 years ago, and very soon took a leading position in the Mincing-lane market, rapidly developing his already large business till it assumed gigantic proportions and until 'Tate's cube sugar' became known all over the world. It is not, however, by the way he made his money as by the use to which he put it that he will be remembered. He early began an active course of public utility in two directions – first, by helping the institutions of his native city, and, secondly, by encouraging British art and artists. It is interesting to note – and the fact is characteristic of the commercial class both in England and America, and of its desire to stimulate education – that Henry Tate gave no less than £2,000 to the newly- founded University College, Liverpool. He gave a still larger sum to various Liverpool hospitals, dividing his benefactions between the Royal infirmary, the Hahnemann Hospital, and the Training Home for Nurses. His bounty was also extended to South London, and the Brixton Free Library (which he built) is only one of several good works on which he spent large sums of money. In the other direction – that of the encouragement of British art – he was at first merely known, as so many others have been, as a liberal purchaser from the Academy and other exhibitions. Gradually the idea grew in his mind to form a thoroughly representative collection of the works of the leading artists of the day. To his large house at Streatham he added a spacious private gallery, where, in course of time, nearly a hundred pictures took their place, including four or five of the principal works of

Millais, 'The Vale of Rest' and 'The North-West Passage' taking the lead. Just before the opening of the Academy exhibition in every year Henry Tate gave a great dinner at Park-hill to the leading artists and to others interested in art; and this became an institution only second in importance, in the mind of the painters at all events, to the Academy Banquet itself.

As time went on, the question arose, What should ultimately be done with the pictures? Mr. Tate had always meant to leave them in some form to the public; and, as they were outgrowing their home, he finally decided to offer the whole collection to the National Gallery. But difficulties arose, first and foremost being that of want of space in Trafalgar-square. The Trustees could not possibly accept more than a selection; they had no room for more, nor, as must inevitably be the case with a collection of modern works, were some of the pictures quite up to the standard which that choicest of all galleries is bound to maintain. So Henry Tate was thrown back on his alternative idea, of building a gallery himself. At first, anonymously, he approached Mr. Goschen, then Chancellor of the Exchequer, through Mr. Humphrey Ward, offering to give his pictures to the nation and to build a gallery at the cost of £80,000 if the Government would grant a site. Mr. Goschen gladly accepted, but the matter did not prove so simple as had been hoped. The City Corporation was approached with reference to the then vacant land on the Embankment at Blackfriars, but, though Mr. Goschen offered to rent the land in perpetuity, and to give the Corporation a share in the management of the galleries, the offer was declined, and the City lost the chance of possessing a fine art gallery on an unrivalled site. Negotiations for a site at South Kensington broke down for the very good reason that the land in question had been promised to the men of science for their future college and museum. For a time there seemed to be a considerable danger that the whole plan would be abandoned. To the credit of Sir William Harcourt – who became Chancellor of the Exchequer on the change of Government in 1892 – must be placed the final settlement of the scheme. He offered Mr. Tate the Millbank site, vacant through the demolition of the old prison, and at the same time he proposed to place the whole control the new foundation in the hands of the Trustees of the National Gallery. Mr. Tate accepted, and the result is the gallery which everybody now knows so well, officially described as the National Gallery of British Art, but always spoken of under the name of its founder. This building, planned and carried out by Mr. Sidney R. J. Smith as architect, was formally opened by the Prince of Wales in July, 1897, and the additional rooms were, as we have already stated, only thrown open a week ago. The building, as is well known, contains not only the Tate Collection, but the pictures purchased under the Chantrey Bequest to the Royal Academy, and nearly all the English pictures from the National Gallery which have been painted within the last 80 years. In sculpture it is, as yet, weak, but the new sculpture hall stands there, ready to be filled. It may be added that the total cost has far exceeded Henry Tate's original offer of £80,000. We should not much exceed the truth if we put it at double that sum. Mr. Tate was made a Trustee of the National Gallery a few years ago, and was created a baronet in 1898. He was twice married, first, in 1841, to a daughter of Mr. John Wignall, of Aughton, in Lancashire, and secondly, in 1885, to a daughter of Mr. Charles Hislop, of Brixton-hill. He leaves several sons and daughters, and is succeeded in the baronetcy by Mr. William Henry Tate, who was born in 1842. Mr. W. H. Tate married, in 1863, Miss Caroline Glasgow of Old Trafford, Manchester.

> Sir Henry Tate, created a baronet in 1898, is here chiefly commemorated not for the commercialisation of the sugar cube, or for his benefactions to his native Liverpool, but for the endowment of the London art gallery that still bears his name. His 'National Gallery for British Art' was 'National' partly because the Corporation of the City of London, in one of its periodic fits of parsimony, had declined to offer it a site on the Embankment and partly because the Gallery was first established as an annexe to the National Gallery in Trafalgar Square. His Gallery was also given charge of art created since the early nineteenth century. Despite the fact that one of the National Gallery's trustees dismissed Tate's collection of paintings as 'representatives of a bad period of English art', there has always been a movement of pictures between the two galleries and a formal separation was not achieved until 1954.

JOHN RUSKIN

Art critic: 'The man who . . . woke up the English people to a knowledge of what art really meant.'

20 JANUARY 1900

THE FOLLOWING STATEMENT as to Mr. Ruskin's last hours has been sent to us for publication:–

The end came with startling suddenness. On the morning of Thursday, the 18th, Mr. Ruskin was remarkably well; but when Mrs. Arthur Severn went to him as usual after tea, in order to read to him the war news and 'In the Golden Days,' by Edna Lyall, his throat seemed irritable. His cousin was alarmed, for several of her servants were ill with influenza; but the Professor was inclined to laugh it off, although he said he did not feel well, and admitted, when questioned, that he felt pain 'all over.' Helped by his faithful body servant Baxter, he was put to bed, and he listened while Mrs. Severn sang a much-liked song, 'Summer Slumber.' It was now 6.30, and Mr. Ruskin declared that he felt quite comfortable. Nevertheless, Dr. Parsons was immediately summoned. He found the temperature to be 102, and pronounced the illness to be influenza, which might be very grave if the patient's strength were not kept up.

That evening the Professor enjoyed a dinner consisting of sole and pheasant and champagne, and on Friday he seemed to be much better. On Saturday morning there was a change so marked that the doctor was alarmed, and from that time Mr. Ruskin sank into an unconscious state, and the breathing lessened in strength, until, at 3.30, it faded away in a peaceful sleep. He was holding the hand of Mrs. Severn, and Dr. Parsons and Baxter stood by, now and then feathering the lips with brandy and spraying the head with eau de Cologne.

And so he passed away, amid silence and desolation. Then, a little later, when the first shock was over, Mrs. Severn's daughter prevailed upon her to look from his little turret window at the sunset, as Ruskin was wont to look for it from day to day. The brilliant, gorgeous light illumined the hills with splendour; and the spectators felt as if Heaven's gate itself had been flung open to receive the teacher into everlasting peace.

The remains of Mr. Ruskin will lie in state in Coniston Church from noon to-morrow until two p. m. on Thursday, the day of the funeral. The interment will take place at 3 o'clock.

A meeting of the Royal Institute of British Architects was held last evening at

Ruskin (left) with painter William Holman Hunt in Ruskin's garden at Coniston

the rooms, Conduit-street, W., for the purpose of hearing a paper on 'The John Rylands Library at Manchester' by Mr. Basil Champneys. The chair was taken by Mr. J. M. Brydon, vice-president, who, in opening the proceedings, said it was his sorrowful duty to announce the death of an honorary Fellow of the institute of worldwide renown. John Ruskin had been a power in this country for over half a century. In their own particular art probably no man in his time influenced architecture as he did. He was responsible to a great extent for that wave of Venetian Gothic which passed over the country, and of which notable examples were to be found in Oxford and London. Ruskin was the man who, probably more than any one else, woke up the English people to a knowledge of what art really meant – that art was the life of the people of the country; that art, in the true sense of the word, was an ennobling faculty to raise men and make them think of higher and nobler things. The idea of truth was held in a very hazy fashion, and probably the idea of sacrifice for art's sake had never occurred to the great proportion of the English people until Ruskin told them what it really meant. They were, he thought, too near to Ruskin to estimate his true position in English life, in English literature, and in art criticism, though he would venture upon the personal opinion that he was probably the greatest art critic they ever had among them. He hoped that it would be possible for the Literature Committee of the institute to arrange that a paper might be written for a meeting in the near future on the great influence of Ruskin in relation to architecture in this country. In accordance with their custom he had to move that a letter of condolence should be sent to the late Mr. Ruskin's relatives in the loss they had sustained. The resolution was at once agreed to.

This is more of an editorial notice than it is an obituary; nevertheless it pays due tribute to the greatest writer on art of the nineteenth century and to a critic who alerted society at large to the philosophical and social problems attendant upon industrialisation and urbanisation. It quotes the tribute paid to Ruskin at the Royal Institute of British Architects (RIBA) by the architect John Brydon (1840–1901) who was working on neo-Baroque government buildings in Whitehall. Ruskin's last years had been spent at his home at Brantwood in the Lake District; there the 'silence and desolation' were Ruskin's own, not those of the landscape. He had been lovingly tended to the end by his cousin, Joan Severn, the daughter-in-law of Keats's faithful companion, Joseph Severn.

SIR ARTHUR SULLIVAN

Composer: 'A synonym for music in England.'

22 NOVEMBER 1900

IT IS WITH great regret that we announce the sudden and premature death of Sir Arthur Sullivan, the eminent musical composer, which took place yesterday morning at his residence, Queen's-mansions, Victoria-street, Westminster. His health had been ailing ever since his visit to Switzerland, from which country he returned about the middle of September. While in Switzerland Sir Arthur Sullivan caught a severe chill and he came back to London feeling very unwell, but for a time there were no serious developments. He suffered at first from a loss of voice, but was able to go about as usual. Then his chest and lungs became affected and a fortnight ago he was obliged to take to his bed. Mr. Buckston Browne, his medical adviser, was in constant attendance, and under his treatment Sir Arthur Sullivan was believed to be making satisfactory progress towards recovery. On Wednesday night he was not so well, but even then there appeared to be no reason for anticipating any serious result. Yesterday morning, however, quite suddenly and altogether unexpectedly, alarming symptoms were observed by the nurse in attendance upon him. A messenger was at once despatched to Mr. Buckston Browne, but before that gentleman could arrive the end came at 9 o'clock. The only relative present in the house at the time was a nephew, and even he had no warning of the imminence of death and was absent from his uncle's chamber. The immediate cause of death is said to have been failure of the heart's action. Sir Arthur was aware that he was suffering from heart trouble.

It has been decided to embalm the body, and, pending this, the date of the funeral cannot be fixed, but it will probably be Tuesday. The Rev. Edgar Sheppard, Sub-Dean of her Majesty's Chapels Royal, a personal friend of the composer, will officiate at the funeral, and the choir of the Chapel Royal, St. James's Palace, will render the musical portions of the service. Numerous telegrams of condolence, chiefly from private and professional friends, have been sent to Queen's-mansions, and there have been several personal callers.

The death of Sir Arthur Sullivan, in his 69th year, may be said without hyperbole to have plunged the whole of the Empire in gloom; for many years he has ranked with the most distinguished personages, rather than with ordinary musicians. Never in the history of the art has a position such as his been held by a composer; and it was earned simply and solely by his own achievement, unaided by interest or side influences of any kind. For all the English-speaking races, with the exception of a very small and possibly unimportant class, Sullivan's name stood as a synonym for music in England. Perhaps it is not strange that, this being so, the small class referred to was principally if not entirely composed of musicians of earnest aims and highly cultivated tastes. These regarded Sullivan as a 'lost leader'; one who, dowered with natural gifts of an almost unexampled kind, had preferred the applause of the patrons of comic opera to the less noisy appreciation of genuine musicians. It is true that this opinion was to some extent modified in recent years. When *The Golden Legend* was brought out the lovers of music were amazed to find that the wonderful early promise of the man who wrote *The Tempest* music was not, as they feared, unfulfilled, for here was a work of picturesque and imaginative quality, poetical in conception, artistic in design, and consummate in workmanship. Yet he had not relinquished the more popular methods by which he had so long held the public ear, and the later Savoy operas were certainly not on a higher level than their predecessors in that successful series. In some ways his most representative work was the serious opera concerning which public expectation was brought up to so high a pitch nine years ago. If *Ivanhoe* represents Sullivan at his best, as it undoubtedly does in its most dramatic scenes, it is not without examples of his less happy vein; and the story of its production illustrates as completely as possible the position in public estimation held by the composer. For no other composer that the world has seen would a manager have even dreamt of mounting a serious opera or a long run; yet the performances of *Ivanhoe* stretched to so large a number that the enterprise of Mr. D'Oyly Carte was almost justified. Not altogether, for within the first weeks of its appearance the truth, which had been patent to all observant persons from the beginning, forced itself at last upon public notice, that in the present day, and indeed as long as lovers of music form a minority in the population, no serious opera can command the amount of attention which even an ordinarily successful comic opera is sure to attain.

It is interesting to see how up to a certain turning point in his career, Sullivan lived the life of an ordinary musician. Born on May 13, 1842 the son of a bandmaster at Kneller Hall, the school of military musical instruction, Arthur Seymour entered the Chapel Royal at twelve years of age, and remained there until 1857. While still holding this office, he obtained the Mendelssohn scholarship, then quite recently established, and studied at the Royal Academy of Music under Goss and Sterndale Bennett. In 1858 he went to Leipzig, remaining at the Conservatorium till the end of 1861. In the following year his music to *The Tempest* was brought out, and it was perceived by all musicians of discernment that the young composer had a great future before him. The cantata *Kenilworth*, produced at the Birmingham Festival of 1864, was his next work of importance; it is now remembered chiefly by the lovely duet, 'How sweet the moonlight.' His opera *The Sapphire Necklace*, written to a very poor libretto by H. F. Chorley, was never produced, and the overture alone remains in its original form. Time brought its revenges, for very few composers have owed as much to their librettists as Sullivan did to the writer with whom he was so long and successfully allied. The 'In Memoriam' overture, played at the Norwich Festival of 1866, commemorated the death of the composer's father. Other works of minor importance belong to this early period, among which was a symphony in E, played at the Crystal Palace, the Philharmonic, the Leipzig Gewandhaus, and other concerts. A good many of the songs which at first drew the attention of the larger public to his talents date from the same time; among, them is the beautiful 'Orpheus with his Lute.'

In 1867 was produced (at first in private), that famous adaptation of Maddison Morton's farce under the title of *Coz and Box*, a work which its author never surpassed in freshness or wealth of musical drollery. Up to that time, in England, music of a light or comic order had never been remarkable for elegance of design or piquant melody, such as Sullivan displayed in this and the operettas by which it was followed, *The Contrabandista* (1867), *Thespis* (1871), and *The Zoo* (1870). Of these, *Thespis* alone was written by Mr Gilbert, who from the date of *Trial by Jury* (1875), worked with the composer in a whole series of light operas which have achieved an extraordinary popularity. The uninterrupted series were ten in number, and they made the name of the Savoy Theatre – which was built for them – famous throughout the world. Out of the ten (*The Sorcerer, H. M. S. Pinafore, The Pirates of Penzance, Patience, Iolanthe, Princess Ida, The Mikado, Ruddigore, The Yeomen of the Guard*, and *The Gondoliers*) only some two or three failed of complete success, while in almost all are to be found songs or phrases that have become national possessions. As a matter of course it is impossible to say how far the extraordinary success of the undertaking was due to the composer, or how much credit should be given to the witty librettist; still, there can be no doubt that if associated with dull or unattractive music even Mr. Gilbert's funniest ideas would have failed of their object. It is beyond controversy, too, that not only the admirable way in which the works were produced, but their entire freedom from all trace of objectionable allusion or suggestion, had much to do with their effect on the public at large. The first of several experiments in connexion with other librettists was *Haddon Hall* (Sydney Grundy) (1892); a welcome return to Mr. Gilbert was made in the following year, when *Utopia, Limited*, seemed to have revived the fortunes of the theatre. Near the end of 1894, *The Chieftain*, a rearrangement of *The Contrabandista* (by F. C. Burnand), was produced. Yet another example of the famous combination was forthcoming in *The Grand Duke* (1890), but this, the last of the series in which Sir Arthur Sullivan collaborated with Mr. Gilbert, was not one of the great successes of the house, and another experiment was tried in *The Beauty Stone* (1898), in which the librettists, Messrs. Comyns Carr and A. W. Pinero, were apparently compelled by the traditions of the theatre to make their serious story more or less comic, and so achieved something very like a failure. Far different was *The Rose of Persia* (Captain Basil Hood), produced in November, 1899, a work which can only be pronounced one of the best of the whole series; it did not attract the public for very long, but in any estimate of the composer's work it must be given a place beside *The Mikado.* Grace, spontaneity, originality, humour, all these qualities are present more conspicuously than in any of the series, if we except *The Sorcerer.* The frequent necessity for filling up gaps in the Savoy productions, when the new opera was not ready by the time the old one had ceased to draw large audiences, led to the occasional substitution of some other name for Sir Arthur Sullivan's as composer, and on one occasion a classic of the comic stage, Offenbach's *Grande Duchesse,* was revived, although in so exceedingly prudish a spirit that all its point was gone. More recently a regular set of revivals of the older operas has taken place, in chronological order, *Patience* being brought out again only the other day, and proving little, if at all, the worse for wear.

Sir Arthur Sullivan was appointed to succeed Costa as conductor of the Leeds Festival in 1880, and directed the subsequent festivals until two years ago, when he announced his intention of giving up the work after the festival of 1898.

Of the three oratorios, properly so called, which preceded *The Golden Legend,* the earliest, *The Prodigal Son,* written for Worcester, 1869, is perhaps the best. In the others, *The Light of the World* (Birmingham, 1873) and *The Martyr of Antioch* (Leeds, 1883), a want of spontaneity was felt in all the more serious portions of the music, and the influence of the comic operas was not entirely thrown off in some of the less earnest parts. The comparative failure of these of course enhanced the success of *The Golden Legend,* (Leeds, 1886), which still enjoys a popularity accorded to no other English work of the kind.

It remains to speak of a few works which are now comparatively seldom heard. The brilliant 'Overtura di Ballo,' first played at Birmingham in 1870, is fairly often found in concert programmes, but the cantata, *On Shore and Sea,* written for the International Exhibition of 1871, and the 'Festival Te Deum' composed in celebration of the recovery of the Prince of Wales in 1872, possibly from their 'occasional' character, are almost forgotten. Besides the *Tempest* music, incidental music was written for several other Shakespearian plays – *The Merchant of Venice* (1871), *The Merry Wives of Windsor* (1874), *Henry VIII* (1878), and *Macbeth* (1888). The last was a conspicuous feature of the revival of the play at the Lyceum Theatre, and the dance tunes from Henry VIII are often heard.

In connexion with the festivities in commemoration of her Majesty's Diamond Jubilee, Sir Arthur Sullivan wrote an elaborate ballet for the Alhambra Theatre, 'Victoria and Merrie England,' and at that time it seemed as if the attention of our best composers would be turned to the ballet as affording a new opportunity for their powers; but the piece failed to please for very long, and the prospect of getting good music in the ballet has faded for the present. It was at the same house that Sir Arthur's setting of Kipling's 'Absent-Minded Beggar' was brought out.

During the early days of the comic operas, the composer's popularity was drawn, to a large extent, from certain songs which became fashionable, and were, of course, each in its turn, sung to death. Such effusions as 'Will he come?' 'O ma charmante,' 'Looking Back,' 'Sweet-hearts,' and the rest, among which 'The Lost Chord' enjoys still an unenviable supremacy, have done more to advance the estimation of the writer among the general public than the beautiful 'Orpheus with his lute' of the earlier times did to endear him to musicians. It is strange that the dainty set of songs to words by Tennyson, published under the title of 'The Window, or Loves of the Wrens,' never reached the highest degree of popularity. A couple of settings of Tennyson's famous lyrics, 'Tears, Idle Tears' and 'O Swallow, Swallow,' were lately sung for the first time by Mr. Kennerley Rumford, and admired by a large number of hearers; these seem to have been the last compositions of Sullivan's yet made public, although rumours have been for some time current that an Irish opera, written for the Savoy, is nearly ready. The many hymn-tunes and anthems composed by Sullivan point to his early career as a church organist in London, which only ceased in 1871; in the early days of the Royal Aquarium he organized the musical performances there for two seasons, 1878 and 1879, he conducted the Promenade Concerts, and from 1875 to 1877 the Glasgow Festivals. From 1876 to 1881 he was principal of the National Training School of Music, the predecessor of the Royal College; he received the honorary degrees of Mus. D. at Cambridge in 1876, and at Oxford in 1879, and in 1883 the honour of knighthood.

It is, of course, impossible to give a decided opinion as to what proportion of Sullivan's music will be added to the great and lasting heritage of music; even if the Savoy operas should fail of a permanent place in the history of the art, their influence will be felt on other productions of the same order for many a year to come; there is no reasonable doubt, however, that *The Golden Legend*, as a whole, and many scenes from *Ivanhoe*, to say nothing of the orchestral works, the early vocal compositions, and much of the incidental music to plays, will perpetuate the name of Sir Arthur Sullivan, though they will not perhaps explain to posterity the position which he held for so long among his contemporaries.

The Savoy Theatre was closed last night out of respect to the memory of Sir Arthur Sullivan.

The news was received with universal regret in Bristol, which city Sir Arthur Sullivan had promised to visit next week to take part in the inaugural ceremonies of the new Colston-hall and conduct a performance of his *Golden Legend* at a festival concert to be given in the hall. He was feeling unwell when he responded to the invitation, but he said he would attend if his health permitted him to do so.

The obituarist appears well aware of the problem some people had with Sullivan's music in hindsight, though his scruples are accredited to 'a very small and possibly unimportant class'. This 'earnest' class of persons has tended to view Sullivan as one who 'dowered with natural gifts . . . preferred the applause of the patrons of comic opera'. That the best of Sullivan's music for the Savoy Operas is still as familiar to British and American ears as it was at the time of his death suggests how substantial the numbers of 'patrons of comic opera' have proved to be. His association with W. S. Gilbert began in 1875, and the partnership brought both fame and financial success (*The Mikado* of 1885 ran for 672 consecutive performances; *The Gondoliers* of 1889 for 554). Sullivan was knighted in 1883 and, as a celebrity, had his portait painted by Millais in 1888 (he bequeathed it in his will to the National Portrait Gallery). His serious 'Romantic' English opera, *Ivanhoe*, opened at D'Oyly Carte's Royal English Opera House in January 1891 and ran for some 150 performances, though the expense of the production ruined the theatre's finances (it became the Palace Music Hall and is now the Palace Theatre). *Ivanhoe* was revised for a Liverpool production in 1895 and was performed in Berlin in the same year. A production at Covent Garden in 1910 proved to be the last for over sixty years. Sullivan died on 22 November 1900 and was buried in St Paul's Cathedral.

OSCAR WILDE

Dramatist: 'A paradoxical humour and a perverted outlook on life.'

30 NOVEMBER 1900

A REUTER TELEGRAM from Paris states that Oscar Wilde died there yesterday afternoon from meningitis. The melancholy end to a career which once promised so well is stated to have come in an obscure hotel of the Latin Quarter. Here the once brilliant man of letters was living, exiled from his country and from the society of his countrymen. The verdict that a jury passed upon his conduct at the Old Bailey in May, 1895, destroyed for ever his reputation, and condemned him to ignoble obscurity for the remainder of his days. When he had served his sentence of two years' imprisonment, he was broken in health as well as bankrupt in fame and fortune. Death has soon ended what must have been a life of wretchedness and unavailing regret. Wilde was the son of the late Sir William Wilde, an eminent Irish surgeon. His mother was a graceful writer, both in prose and verse. He had a brilliant career at Oxford, where he took a first-class both in classical moderations and in *Lit. Hum.*, and also won the Newdigate Prize for English verse for a poem on Ravenna. Even before he left the University in 1878 Wilde had become known as one of the most affected of the professors of the aesthetic craze and for several years it was as the typical aesthete that he kept himself before the notice of the public. At the same time he was a man of far greater originality and power of mind than many of the apostles of aestheticism. As his Oxford career showed, he had undoubted talents in many directions, talents which might have been brought to fruition had it not been for his craving after notoriety. He was known as a poet of graceful diction; as an essayist of wit and distinction; later on as a playwright of skill and subtle humour. A novel of his, 'The Picture of Dorian Gray,' attracted much attention, and his sayings passed from mouth to mouth as those of one of the professed wits of the age. When he became a dramatist his plays had all the characteristics of his conversation. His first piece, *Lady Windermere's Fan*, was produced in 1892. *A Woman of no Importance* followed in 1893. *An Ideal Husband* and *The Importance of Being Earnest* were both running at the time of their author's disappearance from English life. All these pieces had the same qualities – a paradoxical humour and a perverted outlook on life being the most prominent. They were packed with witty sayings, and the author's cleverness gave him at once a position in the dramatic world. The revelations of the criminal trial in 1895 naturally made them impossible for some years. Recently, however, one of them was revived, though not at a West-end theatre. After his release in 1897, Wilde published 'The Ballad of Reading Gaol,' a poem of considerable but unequal power. He also appeared in print as a critic of our prison system, against the results of which he entered a passionate protest. For the last three years he has lived abroad. It is stated on the authority of the *Dublin Evening Mail* that he was recently received into the Roman Catholic Church. Mrs. Oscar Wilde died not long ago, leaving two children.

When the Marquess of Queensbury provocatively left his card at Oscar Wilde's club on 18 February 1895, the dramatist had two plays, *The Importance of Being Earnest* and *An Ideal Husband*, running simultaneously in the West End. As damning evidence emerged during the subsequent trial in April, Wilde's name was removed from hoardings outside the theatres; then, with audiences falling away, the plays themselves were withdrawn. He was convicted of gross indecency on 25 May and, having served his harsh sentence, released from Reading Gaol on 18 May 1897. On Twyford Station on his way to London he extravagantly opened his arms to a bush in bud and proclaimed, 'Oh beautiful world! Oh beautiful world!' The prison warder accompanying him warned of the new need for anonymity with the words, 'Now, Mr Wilde, you mustn't give yourself away like that. You're the only man in England who would talk like that in a railway station.' Wilde, in exile in Italy and France, was more cautious thereafter. The terseness of this obituary suggests the degree of ignominy still linked to his name at the time of his death. He was buried on 2 December in a cheap grave at Bagneux. His remains were removed to the Père Lachaise cemetery in Paris in 1909, where the sculptor Jacob Epstein's fine monument to him was placed.

DR BARNARDO

Philanthropist: 'He professed always to legislate for the future.'

19 SEPTEMBER 1905

WE REGRET TO announce the death of Mr. Thomas John Barnardo, F.R.C.S. Edin., the founder and director of 'The National Incorporated Association for the Reclamation of Destitute Waif Children,' more familiarly known as Dr. Barnardo's Homes. His death took place at his home, St. Leonards-lodge, Surbiton, at 6 o'clock on Tuesday evening, of *angina pectoris*. Dr. Barnardo had been in a precarious state of health for some time, and while at Nauheim, where he had gone for his health, he had two severe attacks of *angina*, and at his earnest request was brought home. As soon as his condition would permit, this was done by easy stages, and he arrived last Thursday evening. After his return he had several more severe attacks, during which his sufferings were very intense. He so far rallied from these attacks as to give great hopes; but, when apparently his condition was improving, he suddenly passed away.

Dr. Barnardo was the ninth son of the late Mr. John M. Barnardo, a gentleman of Spanish origin, but born in Germany; and it is remarkable that his famous son, who was born and brought up in Ireland, should have come to be so intrepid a benefactor of poor English children. It is perhaps still more remarkable that one who was by race a Spaniard and by birth-place an Irishman should have been withal a keen Protestant; but young Barnardo grew up among Protestants, and in early life came to have strong religious convictions. He was born in 1845, and was educated privately, and entered as a student at the London Hospital, proceeding in due course to Edinburgh and Paris. His idea was to qualify for medical mission work in China; but as a medical student he found philanthropic interests in the East-end, some work that he undertook during a cholera epidemic opening his eyes to the needs of the neighbourhood. He procured a room in which he began to teach the rough, ragged boys of the district. Dr. Barnardo owed much of his success to his powers of vivid description; and in his book, 'My First Arab; or, How I began my Life-work,' he told the story of the way in which he realized how many London children were absolutely homeless and always 'slept out.' What he now began to do came to the ears of Lord Shaftesbury and others, who went down East under his guidance to satisfy themselves about the facts. The result was that instead of going to China, Barnardo was urged to give himself to this work, and the Homes were started in a small way in 1866. It need not be added that the headquarters of the

undertaking have in process of time developed into the small town whose address is Stepney-causeway. It would take too long to describe all the various uses to which the buildings are put; and, indeed, the plentiful supply of literature which he put out in explanation of the work makes it unnecessary. His principle was never to refuse any deserving case, and when this was once accepted he was committed to making suitable provision for the immense variety of cases that he was liable to receive. So he had a home for destitute boys, all-night refuges for homeless boys and girls, an infirmary, a crêche, a labour house for destitute youths, an industrial home for girls, a home for deaf and dumb girls, a shoe-black brigade home, and children's free lodging-houses. Nor did London content him. He had institutions of various sorts – to name a few – at Stockton-on-Tees, Birkdale, Middlesbrough, Bradford, Exeter, Brighton, and Jersey. It is some time since he could say that 55,000 children had passed in and out of his Homes, of whom the great majority had done well in after life.

For it is in this respect that the credit of his work stands or falls. He professed always to legislate for the future. For many years he had organized the emigration of his young hopefuls to Canada, where he had emigration depôts in Ontario for girls, and in Toronto and in Winnipeg for boys, while he took a farm of some thousands of acres in Manitoba, where he set the elder boys to work. He went on the principle that Canada was large enough to receive all that he could send, and that it was at once good for Canada and good for the children that they should go. His output in this particular was from 1,000 to 1,500 yearly; and he believed and stated that only two per cent failed to give satisfactory proof of the care that had been bestowed upon them. At home, two characteristic developments of his energy deserve notice. One is the Girls' Village Homes at Barkingside, near Ilford, the first cottage being built at the expense of one who was a stranger to Dr. Barnardo and had merely seen an appeal of his for help. The one cottage has multiplied into nearly 60. The village has a church, a day school, a school of cookery, and a residence for his workers, the gift of some admirer of his activity. The village has frequently been visited by Poor Law officials and by foreign philanthropists, and the girls are trained for domestic service and other occupations. In 1901 he was enabled, by the generosity of Mr. E. H. Watts and his family, to take over the premises of the Norfolk County School, at North Elmham, near Norwich, as a training school for the Navy and the mercantile marine, to which likely lads are drafted from his other homes.

It need not be said that Dr.Barnardo's religious convictions continued to play a large part in the daily life of his various institutions. He remained throughout of the type that for want of a better word is called undenominational. But the growing importance of the Church of England Waifs and Strays Society showed him that nothing was to be gained by displaying any hostility to the Church of England. He continued to maintain at the 'Edinburgh Castle,' Limehouse, where there is a hall holding 3,000 people, his mission work among adults, without connecting that work, with any definite system of religious teaching; but at the Ilford Girls' Homes the congregation was ministered to by a Church of England chaplain, who was in some way recognized by the Bishop of the diocese. Even here the Doctor held himself free to invite Nonconformists or laymen to occupy the pulpit, so that the dread of some of his Nonconformist supporters that Dr. Barnardo was going over with all his great following to the Church of England had no foundation in fact. He was most in his element at the great gatherings at the Albert Hall, when the various objects of his care, especially the most pitiable, were brought out on exhibition with the benevolent Doctor as showman. Considering that he had long suffered from a serious affection of the heart requiring occasional treatment at Nauheim, his activity and his excitable energy were really marvellous; and it will indeed be difficult for his successor, if he is to have one, to maintain the multifarious work of the incorporated homes now that their founder has gone.

With all his ill-health, he died as he would have wished – in harness. Only in

July we published an appeal, to which a large number of influential names were attached, with a view to a national contribution to the Homes in celebration of the Doctor's 60th birthday. The fact that the signatories included the Bishop of London and Sir John Kennaway, Mr. Samuel Smith and the Bishop of Stepney, Lord Roberts and Mr. Stead, is a sufficient indication of the various minds and interests to which the work appealed, while at the subsequent meeting at the Mansion-house Dr. Barnardo was able to read out a message from Queen Alexandra wishing him God-speed in his work. At that meeting mention was made of proposals to get grants for the Homes from the great City Guilds and even from the County Council, so that the 'Founder' leaves his beloved work at a critical stage, when it can perhaps hardly continue as a merely philanthropic venture, but must be acknowledged as the national concern that it really is.

Dr. Barnardo married in 1873 the only daughter of Mr. William Elmslie, of 'Lloyds' and Richmond.

Together with the labours of 'General' William Booth, founder of the Salvation Army, Barnardo's career marks the final great charitable and evangelical enterprises of Victorian Dissenters. Barnardo started a Ragged School at Hope Place in Stepney in November 1867, a venture which grew into the home he established for destitute boys on Stepney Causeway in 1870. After the death of a boy he had been forced to turn away due to lack of room, he adopted the slogan 'The Ever Open Door'. His charitable work was to extend beyond London and to caring for both boys and girls. By the time of his death he had managed to assist some 250,000 children.

SIR HENRY IRVING

Actor: 'His greatness lay in his brain, not in his feelings.'

13 OCTOBER 1905

WE REGRET TO announce that Sir Henry Irving died suddenly at Bradford last night. He had an attack of syncope on returning from the theatre, where he had appeared as 'Becket,' and expired in his hotel. His death was entirely unexpected, for he had shown no sign of illness and appeared in his usual health when, only two days ago, he was entertained at luncheon by the Mayor of Bradford, and was presented with an address from his admirers in that town.

Henry Irving, whose original name was John Henry Brodribb, was born at Keinton, near Glastonbury, Somerset, on February 6, 1838. His parents, who were of Cornish extraction, came to London during his boyhood, and sent him to Dr. Pinches's school in George-yard, Lombard-street, where Creswick saw him play Adrastus in a school performance of Talfourd's *Ion.* At the age of 14 he was given a place in the counting-house of Thacker and Co., the East India merchants, of Newgate-street, and he remained there four years, reading a good deal in his spare moments and studying elocution under Henry Thomas in the City elocution class at Sussex-hall, Leadenhall-street. In 1856 he gave up his employment in business and joined the stock company at the Theatre Royal, Sunderland, his first part being that of Gaston, Duke of Orleans, in *Richelieu.* For the next nine years he worked hard in various stock companies in the provinces, principally at Edinburgh and Manchester, playing a great number of different parts in pieces ranging from tragedy to pantomime. In 1859 he made a brief appearance at the Old Surrey Theatre, but returned to the provinces till 1866, when Dion Boncicault offered him the part of Rawdon Scudamore in *Hunted Down,* at the St. James's Theatre. His success there both as actor and as stage-manager was sufficient to keep him in London. From the St. James's he passed to the old Queen's Theatre in Long-acre, where, in *Katherine and Petruchio,* the burlesqued version of *The Taming of the Shrew,* which was then in fashion, he first acted with Miss Ellen Terry, and increased his reputation in a number of parts, among them Bill Sikes and Falkland. After leaving the Queen's he was out of employment for six months, until his close friend, and in those days his constant benefactor, Mr. J. L. Toole, secured him an engagement at the Gaiety. Here he made a hit as Richard Chevenix in Byron's *Uncle Dick's Darling,* in 1869, and in the following year at the Vaudeville as Digby Grant in Albery's *Two Roses.* In 1871 he joined the Bateman management at the Lyceum. The theatre had long been unlucky, and, admirable as it was, Irving's Jingle in Albery's version of 'The Pickwick Papers' did nothing to restore its fortunes. The management, almost in despair, allowed him to force upon them *The Bells*, an adaptation by Leopold Lewis of Erckmann-Chatrian's *Le Juif Polonais*. It was a desperate measure. The town of that day had no taste for tragedy, for anything, indeed, but farce and opera bouffe of the vulgarest order; the Lyceum Theatre was unpopular and the leading actor in the piece all but unknown. The audience on the first night was scanty, but by the next, morning Henry Irving was famous. There is no need to describe here a performance so well known to playgoers of all generations but the very youngest; it is enough to say that it restored the fortunes of the theatre and marked a turning-point in the history of the English drama. Later in the long run of the play the lavish programme of the times included a performance of *Jeremy Diddler*, in which Irving gave further proof of his powers as a comedian, and *The Bells* was succeeded by W. G. Wills's *Charles I*. The two emotions which this unemotional actor could command were terror and pathos. *The Bells* had illustrated the former, *Charles I* was well chosen to exhibit the latter. It may be questioned whether in his youth, Mr. Irving's *Charles I* can have been quite so majestic a figure as it was in later years, but its success was great. Then, as later, the figure that the audience saw had stepped straight from Vandyck's canvas, and gathered up around it all the romantic, pitiful, and tender associations that float about the name of *Charles I*. Its dignity, its stately melancholy, its tenderness, and its rare bursts of righteous indignation made it one of the most moving parts he ever acted, and entirely concealed the falseness of a one-sided and shallow play. *Charles I* was followed by *Eugene Aram*, which repeated the triumph of *The Bells*, and *Eugene Aram* by *Richelieu*. Here for the first time Mr. Irving definitely pitted himself against Macready, and the school which still looked upon Macready as the last word in great acting. The new methods challenged the old, and the new were championed, not only by the young and ardent Clement Scott, who was then the mouthpiece of the dramatic revival, but by sound and sober critics like John Oxenford, who described Mr. Irving's Richelieu in *The Times* as 'tragic acting in the grandest style.' On October 31, 1874, Mr. Irving made a bid for the highest honours by appearing as Hamlet. In spite of the good work he had done, one is tempted to say, and perhaps without much exaggeration, that that evening was as important in the history of the drama as the first night of *Hernani*. Had Mr. Irving failed, the revival of the stage as a serious factor in the intellectual and social life of the nation might have been put back, though bound to come in time, for many years. There were still people of intelligence – so low had all serious interest in the drama fallen – who were found to ask, 'And who is Henry Irving?' For ten years at least people had been content to let Hamlet sleep under the shadow of great names, Charles Kean, Macready, or Fechter. The moment was critical. For the first two acts the audience received the new Hamlet in complete silence. They could not understand what he was at. He made no 'points,' he never ranted, he was not ludicrous or idiotic or extravagantly dressed; he was nothing that Hamlets traditionally should be, but only a prince and a gentleman, with an engaging tinge of melancholy and a quiet, almost familiar, demeanour. When he came to his parting with Ophelia the house 'rose at him' for now they understood. Mr. Irving's Hamlet was not a thing of lightning flashes, but a consistent and reasoned whole; a prince and a gentleman who failed to do the great things demanded of him, not so much from weakness of will as from excess of tenderness. His reading of the character was hotly contested. A war of pamphlets was waged between the supporters of this or that among the Hamlets of the past and the new Hamlet, and, generally, between the champions of tradition and of the young actor who had dispensed so completely with the conventions and thought out an entirely independent reading of his own. That war was renewed over all the Shakespearian productions that followed, more hotly than ever, perhaps, over his Macbeth. It seems a little surprising now, in a generation which accepts Macbeth as a poet, 'a man of letters *manqué*,' that such fierce storms should have been raised by the view that he was a moral coward. It is possible that Mr. Irving's lack of 'weight' injured his representation of the character, as it certainly ruined his first performance of Othello in 1876, and again, though to a less extent, in 1881, when he and the American actor, Booth, played Othello and Iago alternately. To continue the story of his Shakespearian productions, in 1877 he revived *King Richard III;* in 1879 *The Merchant of Venice*; in 1882 *Romeo and Juliet* and *Much Ado About Nothing*; in 1884 *Twelfth Night*; in 1892 *King Henry VIII* and *King Lear*; in 1896 *Cymbeline*; and in 1901 *Coriolanus*. In no single case was his own performance universally accepted as even good. Long after the days had passed when he was a bone of contention between coteries, there were still large numbers of people to whom his acting did not appeal. Some found his marked mannerisms insuperable obstacles to enjoyment or sympathy; some, and these possibly the least thoughtful portion of the audience, objected to an actor who, whatever he did or did not, always insisted upon having his own reading of every part and every play, a determined innovator who went back invariably to his author and himself for guidance. But, whether people liked him or not, they all crowded to see him and discussed him eagerly afterwards. He appealed to their minds; he interested rather than excited them; and he gave them the opportunity of seeing, what possibly had never been seen in England before, a play of Shakespeare's presented, not as series of opportunities for a 'star' actor, but as a single and artistic whole. In the words used by Lord Lytton on the 100th night of *Romeo and Juliet*, 'he threw the whole force of his mind creatively into every detail of a great play, giving to the vital spirit of it an adequately complete, appropriate, and yet original embodiment.' But this is to anticipate a little. We can do no more than mention the production, under the Bateman management, of Tennyson's *Queen Mary, The Lyons Mail,* which introduced his astonishing performance of the two characters of Lesurques and Dubose, *Louis XI,* which is too well known to need comment, and *The Flying Dutchman,* an unsuccessful play in which his performance of the part of Vanderdecken was yet held by some to be almost his finest achievement.

In 1878 Mr. Irving became manager of the Lyceum. One of his first steps was to engage Miss Ellen Terry as his leading lady, and not the least of his triumphs was the making of a tragic actress out of a born comedian. Miss Terry remained in his company until the end of his American tour of 1901–2, and played Portia in the last performance on the stage of the Lyceum Theatre in July, 1902. The names of actor and actress are inseparably connected in the mind, and each owed to the other a great part of the success and fame that rewarded them. It was thus, too, that, Mr. Irving first had the opportunity of bringing the arts of the scene-painter, the musician, the designer, and others to reinforce the work of his own mind. It is noteworthy that in his original performance of *Hamlet* the scenery was scanty and shabby, much of it having been used in the preceding plays. Henceforth, there was to be no scantiness nor shabbiness. Recollections of the splendour of Charles Kean's productions were eclipsed by the artistic beauty of Mr. Irving's; and in spite of all the criticisms that were passed on the amount of attention lavished on accessories, it cannot justly be claimed that the mounting was allowed to supersede the acting, so long as the Lyceum was the scene of the Irving productions. Those productions were not very many in point of number. Without reckoning the Shakespeare plays already mentioned, the chief of them were as follows:– 1879, *The Lady of Lyons, Daisy's Escape,* by A. W. Pinero, and *The Iron Chest,* by George Colman; 1880, *The Corsican Brothers*; 1881, *The Cup,* by Tennyson, and *The Two Roses*; 1885, *Olivia,* originally produced by Mr. Hare at the Court Theatre, and W. G. Wills's *Faust*; 1887, Byron's *Werner* (at a special *matinée* in aid of a testimonial to Westland Marston); 1889, *The Dead Heart,* rewritten from Walter Phillips's drama by Walter Herries Pollock; 1890, *Ravenswood,* adapted by Hermann Merivale from 'The Bride of Lammermoor'; 1893, Tennyson's *Becket*; 1895, *King Arthur,* by J. Comyns Carr, *A Story of Waterloo,* by A. Conan Doyle, and *Don Quixote,* a condensation of a play written by W. G. Wills on the favourite hero of Sir Henry Irving's boyhood; 1896, *Madame Sans-Gêne,* by Sardou; 1898, *Peter the Great,* by Lawrence Irving, Sir Henry's second son, and *The Medicine Man,* by Robert Hichens and H. D. Trail; and 1899, *Robespierre,* by Sardou. In 1899 Sir Henry nominally gave up management, and in 1902, after a revival of *Faust* and a final performance of *The Merchant of Venice,* his tenancy of the Lyceum Theatre expired, and his only subsequent production in London was Sardou's *Dante* in 1903, a vast spectacular drama, staged at Drury Lane and irresistibly suggestive of pantomime, which did neither author nor actor any credit. Sir Henry Irving was always an indefatigable worker, and the intervals between his seasons in London were filled with provincial tours and long visits to America and Canada, where his popularity and success were enormous.

Whether Sir Henry Irving was or was not a great actor was a question hotly discussed in his lifetime, and one which his lamented death will doubtless revive. There is only one possible answer. A great actor he was, but his greatness sprang from a different source than that of any other actor that can be mentioned. The success of his famous predecessors lay in the power to affect the emotions of their audience through the strength of their own emotions. They watched for opportunities of emotion, and tore the heartstrings of their hearers, without much regard for the cohesion or the general humanity of the characters they represented. Sir Henry Irving was not an emotional actor, or one who touched the emotions. His greatness lay in his brain, not in his feelings; his appeal was to the brain, and not to the feelings. His first care was to read the part and the play, to find out what the author intended, and to build up for himself a conception (and it must be admitted that he preferred a totally new conception, wherever possible) of the character he was to represent. He played not for moments, but for general effects; he was willing to be tedious through half a play rather than sacrifice the unity of his intellectual apprehension. The novelty of idea was an unfailing source of interest, and another was his magnetic personality. His tall figure, his beautiful, intense, ascetic face, threw a spell over his audience – a spell not so much of sympathy as of interest. But a strong personality necessarily implies limitations. Sir Henry Irving's mannerisms, his peculiar pronunciation, his halting gait, the intonations of his never very powerful or melodious voice, the often excessive slowness that grew upon him with the years, were welcome to some as the result and expression of his personality; others they inspired with a feeling that might be described as a desire to laugh if they dared. His personality, again, while, in Charles I, Hamlet, Richard III, Mathias, Becket, and a number of other parts, it gave him extraordinary and impressive power, made him ill-suited to play such characters as Romeo, Claude Melnotte, or even Benedick, the last of whom in his hands became too sardonic and too little merry a person for the gay and witty bachelor. Wherever there was room for his brain to work he was at home; anything approaching the commonplace, the full-blooded, or the sentimental left his peculiar gifts unemployed.

But there was always occupation for those gifts in the play, if not in the part, and they were unsparingly exercised on every new production. His friends used to say that for weeks before a first night at the Lyceum it was impossible to get Sir Henry to answer the commonest question without a reference to his new play. His mind was absorbed in it, its period, its atmosphere, its characters, its clothes. The result aimed at, and almost invariably achieved, was just that unity of impression that was a new thing. He regarded a play as a single whole; as a whole, no doubt, of which he himself should be the central point; but still neither merely as a field for the exhibition of his own powers nor as an excuse for beautiful scenery and dresses. Himself and his painters, designers, and musicians were all to be subsidiary to the author's intentions; and a Lyceum production could be counted on to reveal not only ingenuity of invention nor artistic beauty, but propriety and proportion. It was to that end that he swept into his service the revival of interest in art that was contemporary with the revival of interest in the stage. Like most exceptional men, he was partly a product and partly a creator of the progress achieved in his day. He came into prominence at a time when comedy was already beginning to be regenerated, socially, morally, and artistically, by Mr. and Mrs. Bancroft at the Haymarket. Tragedy was waiting for her champion, and found it in Mr. Irving. It will be seen from the list of his productions that he did little for the original work of contemporary English playwrights. His services to the stage came from another source, that of his own brain. By the unsparing use of his intellect he succeeded in recalling to the theatre the intelligent public which had deserted it for ten years, in making play-going fashionable among all classes, and in accustoming the thousands of new and old playgoers, whom he attracted, to look to the theatre for more than empty amusement. To scholars he appealed by his reverent and often acute treatment of the text of Shakespeare, to people of taste by the beauty of his productions, to people of fashion by having become the fashion, and to all classes by the force of his personality. His career was a career of almost unbroken triumph, not only for himself, but for the English stage.

It was in recognition of these services that in 1895 Queen Victoria conferred on him the first knighthood that was ever won by an actor; and among other honours he held the degrees of D. Litt. Dublin, Litt. D. Cambridge, and LL. D. Glasgow. Of the many lectures he was asked to deliver, we may mention those at Edinburgh in 1881 and 1891, at Harvard in 1885, and at Oxford, by the invitation of Dr. Jowett, then Vice-Chancellor, in 1886. These lectures have since been printed, and the Irving edition of Shakespeare, in which he was interested, is widely known. Sir Henry Irving was married and leaves two sons; Mr. H. B. Irving, the actor, and Mr. Lawrence Irving, who is also on the stage.

Irving died virtually penniless but in harness as an actor. He played Shylock at the Theatre Royal at Bradford on Monday 9 October, Becket on the Tuesday, Louis XI (in the play of that name by Casimir Delavigne) on the Wednesday and Mathias in *The Bells* on the Thursday. These were the parts for which he had been long celebrated. He had created a sensation in *The Bells* in London in 1878 and had followed it with a three-month run in *Louis XI*. It was Irving who had premiered Tennyson's drama, *Becket*, in February 1893. He played Thomas Becket in Bradford again on Friday 13th, and then died in the Midland Hotel, having collapsed in a cab immediately after the performance. Despite his well-known mannerisms, Irving was the most esteemed actor of his day, one whose intellect and flair as a producer were applauded by a new generation of discriminating theatregoers. Irving took over the management of the Lyceum Theatre in London in 1878, with Ellen Terry as his leading lady. He resigned as manager in 1899 and appeared there for the last time (as Shylock) on 19 July 1902. The Lyceum's great days were over. Stripped of its original fittings, it was reopened as a music hall two years later. Irving was cremated and his ashes buried in Poets' Corner in Westminster Abbey.

* * *

JOSEPHINE BUTLER

Social reformer: 'I love my country. It is because of my great love for her . . . that I will not cease to denounce the crimes committed in her name so long as I have life and breath.'

30 DECEMBER 1906

WE REGRET TO announce the death of Mrs. Josephine Butler, which occurred on Sunday night at Wooler, in Northumberland.

A correspondent writes:– 'Josephine Grey was a Northumbrian, the daughter of John Grey, of Dilston, where she was born on April 13, 1828. In 1851 she met George Butler, then a tutor at Durham University, who his intimate Froude described as "the most variously gifted man in body and mind that I ever knew"; and the marriage took place at Dilston early in 1852. The first five years of her married life were spent at Oxford, where she proved a most capable and sympathetic helpmate to her husband, drawing maps for his lectures, or puzzling out old Chaucers in the Bodleian. It was here in Oxford that her indignation was first aroused against "certain accepted theories in society" – as "that a moral lapse in a woman was immensely worse than in a man," and that the social evil was to be passed over in silence. "There echoed in my heart," she says, "the terrible prophetic words of the painter-poet Blake:– "The harlot's curse, from street to street, / Shall weave old England's winding-sheet."

'It was here too that the Butlers, who were absolutely at one on the moral question, took from Newgate into their service a young betrayed mother who had been sentenced for the murder of her infant; "the first of the world of unhappy women" who were thus welcomed. In 1857 came a double trial; her father's heavy losses by a bank failure, and her own ill-health, which made removal from Oxford imperative. Her husband now accepted the vice-principalship of Cheltenham College. At Cheltenham her health greatly improved, but a still greater trial was in store – the death of her only daughter by falling over a banister. From 1866 till 1882 her husband was principal of Liverpool College; and in that great city she was, as she says, "possessed with an irresistible desire to go forth and find some pain keener than my own." The result of her visits to the hospital and oakum-picking sheds of the Liverpool workhouse, and to the quays, drew down upon her "an avalanche of miserable but grateful womanhood." Into the garrets of their house the Butlers "crowded as many as possible of the most friendless girls who were anxious to make a fresh start." In time the pair of good Samaritans established a House of Rest for such cases – which long afterwards became a municipal institution – and also an industrial home for healthy and active but friendless girls.

'It was in 1869 that a group of medical men, who had been strenuously opposing the introduction into England of "the principle of regulation by the State of the social evil," became convinced that some far stronger force than scientific argument was needed to ensure a success; and that women, "insulted by the Napoleonic system," must find champions among their own sex. Appeals for Mrs. Butler's help poured in, and the call seemed clear to her mind; but at first she shrank back. A woman of extreme delicacy and refinement of mind, with a horror not only of contact with vice, but of publicity and agitation, she was only driven to action by passionate love of purity and justice, and boundless love of her unhappy sister-women. She entered the arena in the spirit of a martyr going to the lions. "The toils and conflicts of the years that followed," she says, "were light in comparison with the anguish of that first plunge." Her husband, forseeing what it meant for her and for himself, loving peace and hating strife, his happiness (like hers) centring in domestic life, nevertheless recognized "the call of God to conflict." Mr. Butler – Canon Butler, as he became of Winchester – took an active and by no means perfunctory part in the movement; and on one occasion, at the Church Congress of 1872 in Nottingham, when he began to read a paper on "The Duty of the Church of England in Moral Questions," he was shouted down; but he was necessarily fettered by his work at Liverpool, and one of the many trials with which they paid for their devotion to public duty was the frequent separation of husband and wife. Together or apart, as Mrs. Butler says, they had to endure "the cold looks of friends, the scorn of persons in office and high life, the silence of some from whom one hoped for encouragement, the calumnies of the Press, and occasionally the violence of hired mobs." But, she adds, "the working classes were always with us"; and the forces of organized religion by degrees ranged themselves largely, and in many cases enthusiastically, on the same side. One of her earliest helpers in the movement was Mrs. Butler's cousin, the Rev. Charles Birrell, a gifted Baptist minister at Liverpool – Mr. Augustine Birrell's father. Among the distinguished women who supported the movement were Florence Nightingale, Harriet Martineau, and Mary Carpenter. The agitation spread to the Continent; international congresses were held, and a central office for the propaganda was established in Switzerland. In France Mgr. Dupanloup and M. Yves Guyot were among those who welcomed the Butlers' aid. In England a Royal Commission was appointed in 1871, but reported against the object of the agitation, though Mr. Cowper-Temple and Mr. Applegarth dissented from the view of their fellow Commissioners. The first debate and division on the subject in the House of Commons took place in 1873, when the attack on the Contagious Diseases Acts was repelled by 265 to 128 votes. Ten years more of persistent agitation led to a practical victory; the enforcement of the obnoxious laws was suspended in consequence of a vote of the House of Commons. In 1886 the House resolved, *nemine contradicente*, that the Acts ought to be repealed – an amendment, declaring that repeal should be accompanied with the provision of hospital accommodation for women voluntarily seeking admission, having been defeated by 245 to 131. The repeal actually came in April of the same year.

'Canon Butler died in 1890, and it is from Mrs. Butler's published "Recollections" of him that I have drawn the quotations in this article. Mrs. Butler also wrote a life of Catharine of Siena; a biography of Oberlin; and a sketch of her sister, Mme. Meuricoffre; besides such controversial books and pamphlets as "Government by Police" and "Personal Reminiscences of a Great Crusade." She did not consider the crusade ended with the legislation of 1888; and in 1898, in a prefatory note to a pamphlet attacking the continuance in India of the system abolished in England, she wrote:– "I love my country. It is because of my great love for her . . . that I will not cease to denounce the crimes committed in her name so long as I have life and breath." Mrs. Butler's father had been an active worker with Clarkson for the abolition of the slave trade; and she herself, published in 1900 a book, "Native Races and the War," controverting the pro-Boer views of many of her friends.

'Mrs. Butler is described by one of her fellow-workers as "an almost ideal woman; a devoted wife, exquisitely human and feminine, with no touch in her of the 'woman of the platform,' though with a great gift of pleading speech; with a powerful mind, and a soul purged through fire." '

Josephine Butler

As the author of a *Life of St Catherine of Siena* (1898), Butler was well versed in the history of determined and crusading women. She was also alert to the importance of women's higher education. It is, however, as the defender of working women and of prostitutes in particular that she is remembered. The Contagious Diseases Act, passed by Parliament in 1866, was designed to restrict the spread of sexually transmitted diseases in garrison towns, and empowered the military authorities to give compulsory medical inspections to prostitutes. Women found to be infected were detained in a hospital. Despite medical opposition, amendments to the Act between 1869 and 1871 extended its provisions to the civilian population. It is easy to see why Butler's profound commitment to the Ladies' National Association for Repeal of the Contagious Diseases Act so disturbed the more priggish and censorious of her husband, George Butler's, clerical colleagues.

LORD KELVIN

Scientist and inventor:
'He may be said to have taken all physical science to be his province.'

17 DECEMBER 1907

WE DEEPLY REGRET TO announce the death of the most distinguished British man of science, Lord Kelvin, which took place last night, at his Scottish residence, Netherhall, Largs. Lord Kelvin had not been well for over three weeks. He caught a chill on November 23, and his condition became serious some days ago.

Memoir

William Thomson, Baron Kelvin of Largs, was born in Belfast on June 24, 1824. The second son of James Thomson, a remarkable man who, though he started with very slender advantages of education, died in 1849 Professor of Mathematics in the University of Glasgow, he began to attend the classes at Glasgow at the age of 11, and in the year he attained his majority graduated from Peterhouse, Cambridge, as Second Wrangler and first Smith's Prizeman. His success immediately earned him a Fellowship at his college, and in the following year, after spending a short time in Regnault's Laboratory in Paris, he returned to succeed Dr. Meikleham in the Chair of Natural Philosophy at Glasgow. It is not often that a father and son simultaneously hold professorships at an important University; but even that does not exhaust the academic record of the Thomson family. Lord Kelvin's elder brother James was Professor of Engineering in the University from 1873 to 1889, so that three professors at Glasgow were provided by two generations of the descendants of a small farmer in the north of Ireland. The rest of Lord Kelvin's life is chiefly a record of strenuous and successful scientific work which obtained early recognition. The Royal Society made him one of their number in 1851, and, after conferring on him successively a Royal and a Copley medal, accorded him in 1890 the highest honour at their disposal by choosing him to be their president. At the British Association, of which he acted as president at Edinburgh in 1871, he was an assiduous attendant. Much of his work was first published as communications or reports to that body, and it was only at its last meeting that he delivered a long address on the constitution of matters and the electronic theory. Honorary degrees he received in abundance, among them being D. C. L. from Oxford and LL. D. from Cambridge, Dublin, and Edinburgh, together with many foreign academical distinctions. In 1896 he was knighted for the part he took in the laying of the Atlantic cable, and when, in 1892, Lord Salisbury created him a peer he borrowed his title from the stream that flows below the University in which his scientific life had been spent. He received the Order of Merit on its institution in 1902 – he was already a member of the Prussian Order 'Pour le Mérite' – and in the same year became a Privy Councillor. But perhaps the crowning occasion of his life was the celebration of his jubilee as professor at Glasgow in 1896, when a unique gathering assembled to do him honour, and congratulations from scientific men in all quarters of the globe testified to the universal admiration with which his genius was regarded. Three years later, after 53 years' service, he resigned his Glasgow professorship. But his retirement by no means meant the cessation of active work. While still maintaining his connexion with the University, of which in 1904 he was unanimously chosen Chancellor in succession to the Earl of Stair, he continued to contribute to the proceedings of various scientific societies, and much of his time was devoted to the rewriting and revision of his Baltimore lectures on molecular dynamics and the wave theory of light. These lectures were delivered at Johns Hopkins University in 1884, and the printing of them, begun in 1885, was only brought to a conclusion in 1904. He chose the wave-theory as his subject with the deliberate intention of accentuating its failures, but in his preface to the volume published in 1904 he was able to express his satisfaction that it contained a dynamical explanation of every one of the difficulties which had been encountered in the lectures 20 years before. Lord Kelvin was also a director of several manufacturing companies, and his name formed part of the style of the Glasgow firm which manufactures his compass and measuring instruments. He was president of the institution of Electrical Engineers for the present year, though he did not live to deliver his inaugural address.

Within the limits of a short article it is impossible to give a full account of Lord Kelvin's achievements in the realms of scientific thought and discovery. Generally recognized at the time of his death as the foremost living physicist, he was not less remarkable for the profundity of his researches than for the range and variety of his attainments. Not confining himself to a single more or less specialized department of learning, he may be said to have taken all physical science to be his province; for there were few branches of physical inquiry that he did not touch, and all that he touched he adorned. Perhaps this many sidedness of his intellectual interests may be connected with the deep conviction he cherished of the unity of all Science, and his impatience of conclusions which, drawn from a limited field of study, were in opposition to the well-ascertained facts of wider generalizations. On one occasion, when accused of being 'hard on the geologists,' he repudiated the suggestion with the remark that he did not believe in one science for the mathematician, another for the chemist, another for the physicist, and another for the geologist. All science, he said, is one science, and any part of science that places itself outside the pale of the other sciences ceases for the time being to be a science. Some idea may be obtained of the amount of his scientific work from the fact that, according to the Royal Society's Catalogue of Scientific Papers, down to the year 1883 he had published 262 memoirs under his name, not including papers published jointly with other men; while his republished mathematical papers – not yet completed – already fill three substantial volumes. Nor must his contributions to the increase of natural knowledge – to use one of his favourite expressions – be reckoned merely by the sum of the results at which he was personally able to arrive. Hundreds of men are proud to recognize him as their master, and in all parts of the world scientific workers may be found who have not only profited by his advice and been stimulated by his enthusiasm, but owe to him in many cases the very subjects of research upon which they are engaged – either as his direct suggestions or as problems opened out by his prior investigations.

Atomic Theory

To solve the puzzle of the ultimate constitution of matter may be regarded as the goal of the pure physicist's ambition. The problem afforded Lord Kelvin a congenial field of speculation, and he succeeded in propounding an hypothesis as to the nature of atoms which, according to Clerk Maxwell, satisfied more of the conditions than any hitherto imagined. Starting from a number of mathematical theorems established by Helmholtz respecting the motion of a perfect, incompressible fluid, he suggested that the universe may be filled with such a primitive fluid of which in itself we can know nothing, but of which portions become apparent to our perceptions as matter when converted by a particular mode of motion into vortex-rings. These vortex-rings (of which a fair imitation is given by smoke-rings in air) are the atoms or molecules that compose all material substances. They are indivisible not because of their hardness and solidity, but because they are permanent both in volume and in strength. The fluid being frictionless, those portions of it that have once been set in rotation continue in that state for ever unless stopped by a creative act of the same order that first gave them motion, while the infinite changes of form of which the vortices are capable are sufficient to account for the differences between atoms of different kinds. On this hypothesis many properties of matter can be successfully accounted for. For example, in a lecture delivered before the Royal Institution in 1881, and again in greater detail before the British Association a few years later, Lord Kelvin brought forward instances of elasticity as exemplified in an elastic solid being developed by mere motion, and felt justified in looking forward to a time when the elasticity of every ultimate atom of matter should be explained as a mode of motion. On the other hand, the hypothesis can do little with such properties as gravitation and mass – a fatal defect, for, as its author said, the kinetic theory of matter is a dream, and can be nothing else until we can explain chemical affinity, electricity, magnetism, gravitation, and the inertia of masses. It should be remembered, however, in pointing to its deficiencies, that it is still very young, and, moreover, that, while pure mathematical analysis is the only means by which it can be more fully worked out, the mathematics involved present difficulties of the most formidable character. Lord Kelvin's work on the atomic theory, though perhaps his most striking contribution to mathematical physics, is only a small part of the whole. Light, electricity, and magnetism, to mention a few wide departments, all engaged his attention, to what extent may be judged from the fact that his papers on electrostatics and magnetism alone up to 1872 filled a volume of 600 pages. For the most part, however, the results are of so abstruse and technical a character that they can only be comprehended by a highly-trained mathematical intelligence. To the ordinary man it is more interesting to note Lord Kelvin's own appreciation of his long researches into the ultimate nature of things. Speaking at his jubilee at Glasgow in 1896, he said:–

> 'One word characterizes the most strenuous of the efforts for the advancement of science that I have made perseveringly for 55 years that word is failure. I know no more of electric and magnetic force, or of the relation between ether, electricity, and ponderable matter, or of chemical affinity, than I know and tried to teach my class-students in my first session as Professor.'

Thermodynamics

Some of the earliest and not least important of Lord Kelvin's work was in connexion with the theory of heat: indeed he is to be looked upon as one of the founders of the modern science of thermodynamics. In 1824 Sadi Carnot published his book on the motive power of heat, setting forth the conditions under which heat is available in a heat-engine for the production of mechanical work, but it attracted little or no attention until Lord Kelvin about the middle of the century drew the notice of the scientific world to its value and importance. Although there is reason to believe that Carnot before his death realized that heat is a mode of motion, still his book was written in accordance with the old theory that it is a separate entity, and what Lord Kelvin did was to modify and restate Carnot's propositions in the light of the dynamical theory which had by that time been placed on a firm experimental basis by Joule's recent determination of the mechanical equivalent of heat. Lord Kelvin and Joule first saw each other at the Oxford meeting of the British Association in 1847, and apparently neither knew anything of the other before that date. But the acquaintanceship was fertile in results. One of the first was the presentation of a number of papers to the Royal Society of Edinburgh putting thermodynamics on a firm scientific basis. Another was an important series of joint experimental investigations on the thermal effects of fluids in motion. One of the discoveries thus made is of special interest owing to its subsequent application. It was found that when a compressed gas, at a temperature not too much above its critical point, is allowed to pass through a narrow orifice it undergoes a slight degree of cooling. The apparatus by which Dewar was able to liquefy hydrogen depends on the application of this phenomenon, which is generally known as the Thomson and Joule effect.

A direct and immediate result of Lord Kelvin's study of Carnot's work was his definition of the 'Absolute scale of temperature' – that is, a scale which, unlike the graduations of an ordinary thermometer that are based on the observed alterations in volume produced in a particular material by heat or cold, is independent of the physical properties of any specific substance. A second addition to science soon followed in the principle of the dissipation of energy, enunciated in 1852. This principle declares that of the energy taken in by a heat-engine in the form of heat only a portion is converted into mechanical work: the rest is dissipated or degraded and thus, though not annihilated, is wasted in the sense that it ceases to be available for the production of mechanical effect. Such a process is continually going on in the world, and as all energy can be transformed into heat, it follows that there is a universal tendency to the dissipation of mechanical energy. A further general inference is that this earth, as now constituted, has been within a finite time, and within a finite time will again become unfit for human habitation.

Age of the Earth

Lord Kelvin soon applied the theory of heat in a more definite manner to the elucidation of cosmical problems. Turning it against those geologists who, opposing all paroxysmal hypotheses, held that practically unlimited time must be assumed for the explanation of geological phenomena, he pointed out that they were asking what physical science could not for several reasons allow them to have. In a paper communicated to the Royal Society of Edinburgh in 1862 he declared that for 18 years it had been pressed on his mind that much current geological speculation was at variance with essential principles of thermodynamics, and proceeded to show from considerations founded on the conduction of heat that the earth must within a limited time have been too hot for the existence of life. For the purposes of the geologists who demand most time the Leibnitz theory, which supposes the earth to have been at one time an incandescent mass of molten rock without attempting to explain how it got into this condition, is, he pointed out, the most favourable, yet it implies a finite limit. Taking the average rate of increase of underground temperature at one degree Fahrenheit for every 50 feet of descent, he calculated that the date of consolidation was not less than 220 million years ago and could not possibly be placed further back than 400 million years, while if the temperature of melting rock were put at the reasonable figure of 7,000° F., Leibnitz's *consistentier status* must have emerged less than 100 million years ago. Six years later, in an address on 'Geological Time' which provoked a lively controversy with Huxley, he brought some other physical considerations to bear on the question. Since the tides exercise a retarding influence on the rotation of the earth, it must in the past have been revolving more quickly than it does now, and calculations of its deceleration indicate that within the periods of time required by some geologists it must have been going at such a speed that it could not have solidified into its present shape. But Lord Kelvin did not think the amount of centrifugal force existing 100 million years ago incompatible with its present form. Again he pointed out that the sun cannot be regarded as a permanent and eternal factor in the universe. Continuously dissipating a prodigious amount of energy and not receiving any equivalent supply from external sources, it must be steadily losing energy, and it was impossible on any reasonable estimate founded on known properties of matter to suppose it had illuminated the earth for 500 million years, though it was conceivable that it had for 100 million. From these three lines of argument Lord Kelvin concluded that some 100 million years was the extreme limit that could be allowed for geological history showing continuity of life. Doubtless owing in some measure to the considerations thus urged upon them, the geologists became more moderate in their demands. But, as they reduced their requirements, a corresponding reduction seemed to appear in what their antagonist was willing to concede, and when he discussed the question some 30 years later, the date of solidification, as inferred from the thermal properties of rocks and from an increased knowledge of underground temperatures, had fallen to 'more than 20 and less than 40 million years ago, and probably much nearer 20 than 40.' It is only fair, however, to say that his arguments have not been universally endorsed even among physicists; and it has been urged that there are other assumptions – in regard, for instance, to the conductivity of the earth's interior – not less admissible than those adopted by him, which lead to results much more favourable to the geological and biological demand for more time. Radium, too, has been invoked to explain the maintenance of the sun's heat.

Inventions

Great as were Lord Kelvin's achievements in the domains of scientific speculation, his services to applied science were even greater. His mathematical powers were undoubtedly high, but as a pure mathematical thinker he was surpassed by several of his contemporaries, for his strength lay rather in the faculty which he possessed in an extraordinarily developed degree of applying mathematics to the solution of practical problems, and further in the mechanical ingenuity and resource which enabled him to design and construct apparatus successfully embodying results given by abstract theory. It is related of a celebrated mathematician that, though his mind could move with ease in realms of abstruse thought whose very existence is undreamed of in the philosophy of the ordinary intellect, he was hopelessly bewildered by the architectural plan of a common dwelling house. Lord Kelvin's mind was of a very different, probably rarer, order. It was nothing if not practical. There cannot, he once remarked, be a greater mistake than that of looking superciliously upon the practical applications which are the life and soul of science. That mistake was one of which he himself at least was never guilty, and his scientific inquiries were accordingly pursued with a keen eye for practical applications. A prolific and successful inventor, he had nothing in common with that frequent class of patentees who are brimming over with ideas, all crude, most worthless, and only in occasional instances capable of being worked up into something valuable by men combining the requisite mechanical skill with an adequate knowledge of scientific first principles. Invention with him was not a mere blind groping in the dark, but a reasoned process leading to a definitely conceived end. Of the scores of patents he took out few have not been found of practical and commercial value. Of course all the instruments that he designed did not spring perfect from his hands, but that his first models were workable machines which time and experience improved into the beautiful appliances that are now admired and used all over the world is sufficient proof of his great inventive ability.

Ocean telegraphy

It was in connexion with submarine telegraphy that some of his most valuable inventions were produced in this department, indeed, his work was of capital importance and of itself sufficient to establish his title to lasting fame. Though so distinguished a man as the late Sir George Airy declared that not only was it a mechanical impossibility to lay a cable across the Atlantic, but that, even if the feat were accomplished, no electric signalling could be carried on, Lord Kelvin was a firm believer in the practicability of transoceanic telegraphy and did not hesitate to show by acts the faith that was in him. He became a director of the Atlantic Telegraph Company, which hazarded large sums in the enterprise of making and laying a cable, and he took an active and personal part in the operations which culminated in the successful laying of the shortlived cable of 1853. As to the transmission of electric impulses, he shoved how little doubt he had on that point by publishing a paper in which he gave a mathematical theory expressing the rapidity of transmission and proved that the speed at which signals pass through a long submarine cable decreases in proportion to the square of its length. But, more than that, he described the most advantageous conditions of working, and designed instruments that enabled those conditions to be realized, thus rendering submarine telegraphy commercially practicable. Mr. Whitehouse, the electrician who was put in charge of the first completed cable, held the opinion – and he did not stand alone – that for signalling through the cable currents of very high potential were required. He therefore employed big induction coils five feet long and poured the current obtained from these into the cable. As is well known, it broke down completely after it had been in use for a very short time, and there is little reason to doubt that the reason of its untimely end was the inability of its insulation to stand the potentials to which it was exposed. Lord Kelvin, who believed that but for this treatment the cable would have worked satisfactorily, declared that feeble currents ought to be employed together with very sensitive receiving instruments, and, characteristically, was ready, not only with a theoretical prescription, but with the working instrument, his mirror galvanometer, that enabled it to be carried into effect. In this the magnet, delicately suspended by a fine fibre, carries a tiny mirror that, by reflecting a beam of light, makes visible and magnifies its movements. Mirror and magnet in some cases weighing only a grain or so, instrumental retardation is reduced to a *minimum* and extreme sensitiveness secured. Thus indications are obtained of the very beginning of the wave into which an electric impulse is flattened in passing through a long cable, and the instrument does not wait before responding until the impulse has risen to its full value – indeed, the increase of the current is stopped, by 'curb sending' also suggested by Lord Kelvin, as soon as it has become strong enough to give its signal. How great was the advance marked by the introduction of this arrangement may be gathered from the fact that the best instruments in existence at the time could scarcely receive two words a minute, whereas in its earliest form it could deal with ten or 12, and subsequently its capacity was increased to 20. Lord Kelvin made another immense improvement in receiving apparatus when, in 1867, he invented the siphon-recorder, which is not only more speedy than the mirror instrument, but has the additional advantage of giving a permanent record of the message in ink.

Measurement

Some of his finest work is to be found in his electric measuring instruments, a subject in which his knowledge and authority were unrivalled. More especially was this the case in regard to electrostatic measurements – perhaps the most difficult of all. When the need for accurate instruments in his studies on atmospheric electricity caused him to take up the matter, the electrometers in existence were little more than electroscopes – capable of indicating a difference of electric potential, but not of measuring it; but in his quadrant, portable, and absolute electrometers his skill and ingenuity put at the disposal of electricians three beautiful instruments of exact research. Nor were his services to the cause of measurement confined to the invention of apparatus. Measurement he regarded as the beginning of science and as the origin of many of the grandest discoveries. Hence he was always ready to do anything by which it could be facilitated, whether in matters of daily life or abstruse scientific inquiry. Thus on the one hand the metric system found in him a strong supporter, and he rarely missed a chance of bestowing a word or two of half-humorous disparagement upon the unhappy English inch or 'that most meaningless of modern measures, the British statute mile.' On the other, he was a strenuous advocate of the absolute system of measurement, which he used in his own electrical investigations so far back as 1851, and he was largely instrumental in obtaining in 1861 the appointment of a committee of the British Association on electrical standards which fairly launched the absolute system for general use.

Navigational Apparatus

The sailor has to thank Lord Kelvin, who was himself a keen amateur yachtsman, for several valuable inventions in connexion with the art of navigation. The most important of these were directed to the improvement of the mariner's compass. One of the first *desiderata* in a ship's compass is steadiness at sea, but until he took the matter in hand scarcely any scientific attempt had been made to achieve that end. In fact no one seems to have reached a clear conception of what was wanted, and the ruling idea was that the unsteadiness due to the motion of the vessel was to be remedied by introducing the sluggishness that follows from friction on the bearing-point. He saw that a steady compass was to be obtained on the same principle as a steady ship. Just as a vessel rolls most violently when its vibrational period is the same as that of the waves it encounters, so a compass oscillates most wildly then its period coincides with that of the ship upon which it is carried. The remedy in both cases is to make the periods as different as possible. Again, to secure accurate indications the frictional error must be reduced as much as possible. This was managed by making the compass-card very light. Another innovation consisted in employing needles of small magnetic moment; in other words, their magnetic force is small. Formerly it was argued that the more highly magnetized the needles the more powerful their attraction to the Pole, and the better the compass. But Lord Kelvin saw that a large magnetic moment tended to unsteadiness at sea and also rendered difficult the correction of the quadrantal error; hence his needles are not strongly magnetized, directive force being gained by delicacy of adjustment. Moreover they are short, to admit of the compass errors in iron ships being rectified without the use of inconveniently large magnets and masses of iron. As a result of all these improvements, none of which, it has been said, could have been made by any one but a mathematician, he constructed a compass with a period of vibration much longer than that of an old-pattern compass of the same size, having a card some 17 times lighter, and admitting of a complete correction of the quadrantal error by Airy's method. He also invented improved methods of suspension to prevent disturbance by shock or vibration, and lastly devised a procedure for correcting the compass error without sights of heavenly bodies or compass marks on shore. His instrument is now widely adopted on well-found ships of the merchant marine; and in the Navy is the service compass for all vessels except boats, torpedo-boats, and torpedo-boat destroyers.

Another appliance that has proved of great value to sailors is his sounding-machine, which consists essentially of many fathoms of galvanized pianoforte wire wound on a drum provided with a suitable brake. For deep-sea surveying it presents many advantages of speediness and convenience over older machines for the same purpose, and by its aid soundings can be taken, every quarter of an hour if desired, with ease and accuracy in any depth up to 100 fathoms from ships going at any ordinary speed, without stopping or rounding-to. It may thus enable a navigator to discover his position when the weather renders land, lights, sun and stars alike invisible. For finding a ship's place at sea Lord Kelvin was also fond of urging the extended employment of Sumner's method, and in 1876 he published a series of tables to facilitate its practice. Mention too must be made of his work in connexion with the calculation of the tides. He constructed three machines designed conjointly to effect the prediction of the tides for any port. The first was a tide gauge which automatically registers the rise and fall on a strip of paper in the form of a curve. The object of the second machine, the harmonic tide analyser (an application of an invention made by his elder brother James), is to analyse out from this curve the several elementary constituents that make up the whole tidal rise and fall, and thus substitute for methodological, though laborious, arithmetical calculations the mechanical motion of a couple of cranks. As to the third machine, the tide predictor, though Lord Kelvin was probably the first to suggest the possibility of such an instrument, yet the plan upon which it was constructed was not entirely of his origination. When supplied with the tidal constituents for any port as obtained by the harmonic analysis of tide-gauge records and connected with some source of power, it traces a curve that indicates not only the times and heights of high water, but the depth of water at any and every instant. It can be worked at such a speed as to run off the curve for a year in a few hours.

Publications and Personal Characteristics

In conjunction with Professor Tait, of Edinburgh, Lord Kelvin wrote a 'Treatise on Natural Philosophy' which long ago became a standard text-book. Unfortunately 'Thomson and Tait,' as it is often familiarly called – 'T and T' was the authors' own abbreviation – is not finished, and only covers a comparatively small part of the ground which would have been included had not the authors abandoned their original intention of treating in succession the various branches of mathematical and experimental physics. Lord Kelvin was also the author of the articles on 'Heat' and 'Elasticity' in the Encyclopaedia Britannica and of numerous scientific papers and more or less popular addresses. A selection of the latter has been published under the title 'Popular Lectures and Addresses.' As a lecturer he was rather prone to let his subject run away with him. When this happened, limits of time became of small account, and his audience, understanding but little of what he was saying, were fain to content themselves with admiring the restless vivacity of his manner (which was rather emphasized than otherwise by the slight lameness from which he suffered) and the keen zest with which he revelled in the intricacies of the matter in hand. Similarly, the intelligence and patience of his Glasgow classes were not always equal to the mental strain entailed by his expositions, and, though they were thoroughly proud of him and his attainments, their orderliness was not of the strictest kind, and they were not above varying the proceedings with an occasional practical joke. Probably his best work as a teacher of youth consisted in the experimental and practical training which his pupils underwent in the physical laboratory, and the initiation into the methods of original research received by the more promising students. To the modest inquirer in genuine search of information his vast stores of learning experience were always available, though shallow pretenders to knowledge were liable to find themselves disconcerted by a few simple questions, put in an innocent, childlike manner, but going right to the root of the matter. But he was quick to express his approval of a piece of good work, or his delight at a new result or well-planned experiment; and no one could come in contact with him without feeling the charm of his kindly, lovable nature, and falling under the spell of the enthusiasm and untiring energy with which he devoted himself to the advancement of knowledge. Lord Kelvin was twice married; first, to Margaret, daughter of Mr. Walter Crum, of Thornliebank; and, secondly to Frances Anna, daughter of Mr. Charles R. Blundy, of Madeira. There was no issue of either marriage.

Kelvin was famous for pronouncing both that 'all science is one science' and that 'failure' was the one word that characterised his work. His first statement summed up the breadth and purport of his research; the second was a self-deprecating jest. His was an extraordinary achievement, even by the demanding standards of international scientific advance in the nineteenth century. The obituary dwells on the theoretic advances he made in the fields of electromagnetism, light and telegraphy, and on the practical application of his research in the laying of the trans-Atlantic cable. A devout Christian, Kelvin believed that his theory of heat-death and his calculations of the age of the earth exposed flaws in Charles Darwin's idea of evolution. To some Victorians, however, the implications of his ideas about the finite habitability of the earth seemed to offer a doom-laden vision of an icy end to all things rather than a fiery one.

FLORENCE NIGHTINGALE

Reformer of hospital nursing: 'One of the heroines of British history.'

13 AUGUST 1910

WE DEEPLY REGRET to state that Miss Florence Nightingale, O. M., the organizer of the Crimean War Nursing Service, died at her residence, 10, South-street, Park-lane, on Saturday afternoon. She had been unwell about a week ago, but had recovered her usual cheerfulness on Friday. On Saturday morning, however, she became seriously ill and she gradually sank until death occurred about 2 o'clock. The cause of death was heart failure. Two members of her family were present at the time.

Miss Nightingale, who had for some time been an invalid and had been under the constant care of Sir Thomas Barlow, was in her 91st year. She celebrated her 90th birthday on May 12 last, and one of the first acts of the present King since coming to the throne – King Edward had died on May 6 – was to send her a telegram of congratulation. The message was worded as follows:–

'On the occasion of your 90th birthday I offer you my heartfelt congratulation, and trust that you are in good health. – GEORGE R. & I.'

The funeral will take place in the course of the next few days, and will be of the quietest possible character in accordance with the strongly expressed wish of Miss Nightingale.

Memoir

In Miss Florence Nightingale there has passed away one of the heroines of British history. The news of her death will be received to-day with feelings of profound regret throughout not merely the land of her birth, but in all lands where her name has been spoken among men.

Florence Nightingale was born May 12, 1820, at Florence, from which city she took her name. She was the younger of the two daughters and co-heiresses of Mr. William Shore Nightingale, of Embley Park, Hampshire, and Lea Hall, Derbyshire, a descendant of the old Derbyshire family of Shore, and himself the possessor of large estates and considerable wealth. Her mother was a daughter of William Smith, the friend of Wilberforce and his supporter in the House of Commons in the abolitionist and other movements. From Lea Hall the family removed, about 1826, to Lea Hurst, a house about a mile distant, and the one with which the name of Florence Nightingale has been more especially associated. Florence, who even in her young days was a child of extremely strong sympathies, quick apprehension,

and excellent judgment, was carefully trained, acquiring, among other accomplishments, under the direction of her father, a knowledge of the classics, mathematics, and also of modern languages. But while applying herself to the culture of her mind she was, at the same time, the consoler and benefactress of all the villagers to whom her help or her kindly words might be of service, displaying even thus early in life that bent of her mind and disposition which afterwards spread her fame throughout the world.

Seeking for wider experience than her position as a squire's daughter in a small Derbyshire village could give her, she visited all the hospitals in London, Dublin, and Edinburgh, many country hospitals, and some of the naval and military hospitals in England; all the hospitals in Paris, studying with the Soeurs de Charité; the Institute of Protestant Deaconesses at Kaiserswerth, on the Rhine, where she was twice in training as a nurse; the hospitals at Berlin, and many others in Germany; while she also visited Lyons, Rome, Alexandria, Constantinople, and Brussels. On her return to Derbyshire, where she hoped to have the rest of which she stood in need after her travels, she was appealed to, in 1850, on behalf of the Home for Sick Governesses, 90, Harley-street, London, which was languishing from lack, not only of proper support, but also of proper management. She responded to the appeal by herself taking over the entire control of the institution, and devoting alike time, energy, and fortune to re-establishing it (with the help of Lady Canning, the original founder) on a sound basis. She also took an active interest in the ragged schools and other similar institutions in London. Altogether something like ten years had been spent by her in preparing, unconsciously, for the great events of her life, and these came with the Russian war.

The Crimean War

On September 20, 1854, the battle of Alma was fought, and it is not too much to say that the accounts published in the columns of *The Times* from our Correspondent, the late Dr. (afterwards Sir William Howard) Russell as to the condition of the sick and wounded sent a feeling of horror throughout the length and breadth of the land. There is no necessity to dwell here in detail on the harrowing stories he related. Suffice it to say that he showed how the commonest accessories of a hospital were wanting; how the sick appeared to be tended by the sick, and the dying by the dying; how, indeed, the manner in which the sick and wounded were being treated was 'worthy only of the savages of Dahomey'; and how, while our own medical system was 'shamefully bad,' that of the French was exceedingly good, and was, too, rendered still more efficient because of the sisters of charity who had followed the French troops in incredible numbers.

On October 12, 1854, a leading article appeared in *The Times* in which it was pointed out that while 'we are sitting by our firesides devouring the morning paper in luxurious solitude . . . these poor fellows are going through innumerable hardships'; and the article went on to suggest that the British public should subscribe to send them 'a few creature comforts.' On the following day we published an extremely sympathetic letter from Sir Robert Peel, starting a fund with a cheque for £200, and so generally and so liberally was his example followed that £781 was received by us within two days, £7,000 within seven days, and £11,614 by the end of the month, when the fund was closed. But, in the meantime, the terrible cry from the East had met with a response which was of even more effectual service to the suffering soldiers than the thousands of pounds thus promptly and generously contributed. On October 15, Miss Nightingale wrote to Mr. Sidney (afterwards Lord) Herbert, Secretary at War, offering to go to Scutari, and, as it happened, her own letter was crossed by one to herself from Mr. Sidney Herbert. Medical stores, he said, had been sent out by the ton weight, but the deficiency of female nurses was undoubted. Lady Maria Forrester had proposed to go with or to send out trained nurses, 'but there is,' Mr. Herbert went on to say, 'only one person in England that I know of who would be capable of organizing and superintending such a scheme . . . A number of sentimental and enthusiastic ladies turned loose in the hospital at Scutari would probably, after a few days, be *mises à la porte* by those whose business they would interrupt and whose authority they would dispute . . . My question simply is, Would you listen to the request to go out and supervise the whole thing?' Miss Nightingale, as we have seen, had already answered this question, and preparations could thus be set on foot without a moment's delay. But, as showing how little she was known to fame at that time, we may mention as a curious fact that in *The Times* of October 19, 1854, there appeared the announcement – 'We are authorized to state that Mrs. (*sic*) Nightingale' had undertaken to organize a staff of female nurses, who would proceed with her to Scutari at the cost of the Government. Not, indeed, until several days had elapsed does it seem to have been realized that 'Mrs.' Nightingale was really 'Miss' Nightingale, and even then the *Examiner* found it necessary to publish an article, headed 'Who is Miss Nightingale?' setting forth who she really was, and bearing eloquent testimony to her accomplishments, her experience, and the nobility of her character.

Within a week Miss Nightingale had selected from hundreds of offers, received from all parts of the country, a staff of 38 nurses, including 14 Anglican sisters, ten Roman Catholic sisters of mercy, and three nurses selected by Lady Maria Forrester. It may be interesting to recall that among the ladies forming the gallant little band was Miss Erskine, eldest daughter of the Dowager Lady Erskine, of Pwll-y-crochan, North Wales. Miss Nightingale and her nurses left London on October 21, passing through Boulogne on October 23 on their way to Marseilles; and a letter which appeared in *The Times* some days afterwards, written by a correspondent who had been staying at Boulogne, related how the arrival of the party there caused so much enthusiasm that the sturdy fisherwomen seized their bags and carried them to the hotel, refusing to accept the slightest gratuity; how the landlord of the hotel gave them dinner, and told them to order what they liked, adding that they would not be allowed to pay for anything; and how waiters and chambermaids were equally firm in refusing any acknowledgment for the attentions they pressed upon them.

Arrival at The Front

From Marseilles the party proceeded to Constantinople, where they arrived on November 4, the eve of the battle of Inkerman. They found there were two hospitals at Scutari, of which one, the Barrack Hospital, already contained 1,500 sick and wounded, and the other, the General Hospital, 800, making a total of 2,300; but on the 5th of November there arrived 800 more who had been wounded in the course of that day's fighting, so that there were close on 3,000 sufferers claiming the immediate attention of Miss Nightingale and her companions. In the best of circumstances the task which the nurses thus found before them would have been enormous; but the circumstances themselves were as bad as the imagination can conceive, if indeed, imagination, unaided by fact, could call up so appalling a picture. Neglect, mismanagement, and disease had 'united to render the scene one of unparalleled hideousness.' The wounded, lying on beds placed on the pavement itself, were bereft of all comforts; there was a scarcity alike of food and medical aid; fever and cholera were rampant, and even those who were only comparatively slightly wounded, and should have recovered with proper treatment, were dying from sheer exhaustion brought about by lack of the nourishment they required.

Miss Nightingale, as 'Lady-in-Chief,' at once set to work to restore something like order out of the chaos that prevailed. Within ten days of her arrival she had had an impromptu kitchen fitted up, capable of supplying 800 men every day with well-cooked food, and a house near to the Barrack Hospital was converted into a laundry, which was also sorely needed. In all this work she was most cordially supported by Mr. MacDonald, the almoner of *The Times* Fund, the resources of which were, of course, freely placed at her disposal. But in other directions Miss Nightingale had serious difficulties to encounter. The official routine which had sat as a curse over the whole condition of things continued as active, or, rather, as inefficient, as ever. Miss Nightingale was at first scarcely tolerated by those who should have co-operated with her. She had, at times, the greatest possible difficulties in obtaining sufficient Government stores for the sick and wounded; for though, as Mr. Sidney Herbert had written, medical stores had been sent out by the ton weight, they were mostly rotting at Varna instead of having been forwarded to Scutari. On one occasion, when she was especially in need of some that had arrived, but were not to be given out until they had been officially 'inspected,' she took upon herself to have the doors opened by force and to remove what her patients needed. But her zeal, her devotion, and her perseverance would yield to no rebuff and to no difficulty. She went steadily and unweariedly about her work with a judgment, a self-sacrifice, a courage, a tender sympathy; and withal a quiet and unostentatious demeanour that won the hearts of all who were not prevented by official prejudices from appreciating the nobility of her work and character. One poor fellow wrote home:– 'She would speak to one and nod and smile to a many more; but she could not do it to all, you know. We lay there by hundreds; but we could kiss her shadow as it fell, and lay our heads on the pillow again, content.' Mr. MacDonald, too, wrote in February, 1855:–

> 'Wherever there is disease in its most dangerous form and the hand of the despoiler distressingly nigh, there is that incomparable woman sure to be seen. Her benignant presence is an influence for good comfort, even amid the struggles of expiring nature. She is a ministering angel without any exaggeration in these hospitals, and as her slender form glides quietly along each corridor, every poor fellow's face softens with gratitude at the sight of her. When all the medical officers have retired for the night and silence and darkness have settled down upon those miles of prostrate sick, she may be observed alone, with a little lamp in her hand, making her solitary rounds. The popular instinct was not mistaken which, when she set out from England on her mission of mercy, hailed her as a heroine. I trust she may not earn her title to a still higher though sadder appellation. No one who has observed her fragile figure and delicate health can avoid misgivings lest those should fail. With the heart of a true woman, and the manners of a lady, accomplished and refined beyond most of her sex, she combines a surprising calmness of judgment and promptitude and decision of character.'

It was also written of her:–

'She has frequently been known to stand 20 hours on the arrival of fresh detachments of sick apportioning quarters, distributing stores, directing the labours of her corps, assisting at the painful operations where her presence might soothe or support, and spending hours over men dying of cholera or fever. Indeed, the more awful to every sense any particular case might be the more certainly might be seen her light form bending over him, administering to his case by every means in her power, and seldom quitting his side till death released him.'

Criticism at home

Meanwhile the reports which Miss Nightingale made both to Lord Raglan, the Commander-in-Chief, and to the War Minister at home were of invaluable service in enabling them to put their finger on the weak spots of the administration. On the other hand, it is painful to recall the fact that while, in all these various ways, Miss Nightingale was doing such admirable work in the East, sectarian prejudices at home had led to unscrupulous attacks being made alike on her religious views and on her motives in going out. 'It is melancholy to think,' as Mrs. Herbert wrote to a lady correspondent, 'that in Christian England no one can undertake anything without these most uncharitable and sectarian attacks. . . . Miss Nightingale is a member of the Established Church of England, and what is called rather Low Church; but ever since she went to Scutari her religious opinions and character have been assailed on all points. It is a cruel return to make towards one to whom all England owes so much.' Happily a check was put to this campaign of slander and uncharitableness by a letter written by Queen Victoria from Windsor Castle, dated December 6, 1854, to Mr. Sidney Herbert, asking that accounts received from Miss Nightingale as to the condition of the wounded should be forwarded to her, and saying:–

> 'I wish Miss Nightingale and the ladies would tell these poor noble wounded and sick men that no one takes a warmer interest, or feels more for their sufferings, or admires their courage and heroism more, than their Queen. Day and night she thinks of her beloved troops. So does the Prince. Beg Mrs. Herbert to communicate these my words to those ladies, as I know that our sympathy is much valued by these noble fellows.'

The eminently tactful indication conveyed in this letter of her Majesty's complete confidence in Florence Nightingale did much not only towards silencing the ungenerous critics at home, but also towards strengthening the position of the Lady-in-Chief in meeting the difficulties due to excessive officialism in the East.

Growth of the work

In January, 1855, Miss Nightingale's totally inadequate staff was increased by the arrival of Miss Stanley with 50 more nurses; and how greatly they were needed is shown by the fact that there were then 5,000 sick and wounded in the various hospitals on the Bosporus and the Dardanelles, 1,000 more being on their way down. By February there was a great increase of fever, which in the course of three or four weeks swept away seven surgeons, while eight more were ill, twenty-one wards in the Barrack Hospital being in charge of a single medical attendant. Two of the nurses also died from fever. Miss Nightingale told subsequently how for the first seven months of her stay in the Crimea the mortality was at the rate of 60 per cent per annum from disease alone, a rate in excess, she added, of that which prevailed among the population of London during the Great Plague. By May, however, the position of affairs had so far improved at Scutari, thanks mainly to the untiring energies and devotion of Miss Nightingale, that she was able to proceed to Balaclava to inspect the hospitals there. Her work at Balaclava was interrupted by an attack of Crimea fever, and she was afterwards urged to return home; but she would go no further than Scutari, remaining there until her health had been re-established. Thereupon she again left for the Crimea, where she established a staff of nurses at some new camp hospitals put up on the heights above Balaclava, and took over the superintendence of the nursing department, herself living in a hut not far away. She also interested herself in organizing reading and recreation huts for the army of occupation, securing books and periodicals from sympathizers at home. Among the donors were Queen Victoria and the Duchess of Kent. Another institution she set up was a café at Inkerman, as a counterattraction to the ordinary canteens. Then she started classes, supported the lectures and schoolrooms which had been established by officers or chaplains, and encouraged the men to write home to their families. Already at Scutari she had opened a money-order office of her own, through which the soldiers could send home their pay. She then set an example which the Government followed by establishing official money-order offices at Scutari, Balaclava, Constantinople, and elsewhere. Some £70,000 passed through these offices in the first six months of 1856.

The end of the War

Florence Nightingale remained in the Crimea until the final evacuation in July, 1856, her last act before leaving being the erection of a memorial to the fallen soldiers on a mountain peak above Balaclava. The memorial consisted of a marble cross 20ft. high, bearing the inscription, in English and Russian – LORD HAVE MERCY UPON US, / GOSPODI POMILORI NASS.

Calling at Scutari on her way home, Miss Nightingale left that place in a French vessel for Marseilles, declining the offer made by the British Government of a passage in a man-of-war, and reached Lea Hurst on August 8, 1858, having succeeded in avoiding any demonstration on the way.

Before returning to England Florence Nightingale had received from Queen Victoria an autograph letter with a beautiful jewel, designed by Prince Albert; the Sultan had sent her a diamond bracelet; and a fund for a national commemoration of her services had been started, the income from the proceeds, £45,400, being eventually devoted partly to the setting up at St. Thomas's Hospital of a training school for hospital and infirmary nurses and partly to the maintenance and instruction at King's College Hospital of midwifery nurses. For herself she would have neither public testimonial nor public welcome. She was honoured by an invitation to visit the Queen and Prince Consort at Balmoral in September, and addresses and gifts from working men and others were sent or presented privately to her. But though her fame was on every one's lips, and her name has ever since been a household word among the peoples of the world, her life from the time of her return home was little better than that of a recluse and confirmed invalid. Her health, never robust, broke down under the strain of her arduous labours, and she spent most of her time on a couch, while in the closing years of her life she was entirely confined to bed.

Later Reforms

But, though her physical powers failed her, there was no falling off either in her mental strength or in her intense devotion to the cause of humanity. She was still the 'Lady-in-Chief' in the organization of the various phases of nursing which, thanks to the example she had set and the new spirit with which she had imbued the civilized world, now began to establish themselves; she was the general adviser on nursing organization not only of our own but of foreign Governments, and was consulted by British Ministers and generals at the outbreak of each one of our wars, great or small; she expanded important schemes of sanitary and other reforms, though compelled to leave others to carry them out, while at all times her experience and practical advice were at the command of those who needed them.

Almost the entire range of nursing seems to have been embraced by that revolution therein which Florence Nightingale was the chief means of bringing about. Following up the personal services she had already rendered in the East in regard to Army nursing, she prepared, at the request of the War Office, an exhaustive and confidential report on the world of the Army Medical Department in the Crimea as the precursor to complete reorganization at home; she was the means of inspiring more humane and more efficient treatment to the wounded both in the American Civil War and the Franco-German War; and it was the stirring record of her deeds that led to the founding of the Red Cross Society, now established in every civilized land. By the Indian Government also she was almost ceaselessly consulted on questions affecting the health of the Indian Army. On the outbreak of the Indian Mutiny she even offered to go out and organize a nursing staff for the troops in India. The state of her health did not warrant the acceptance of this offer: but no one can doubt that, if campaigns are fought under more humane conditions today as regards the care of wounded soldiers, the result is very largely due to the example and also to the counsels of Florence Nightingale.

But advance no less striking is to be found in other branches of the nursing art as well. In regard to general hospitals, the pronounced success of the nursing school established at St. Thomas's as the outcome of the Nightingale Fund led to the opening of similar schools elsewhere, so that today hospital nursing in general occupies a far higher position in the land than it has ever done before, while this, in turn, advanced the whole range of private nursing in the country. Then, again, the system of district nursing, which is now in operation in almost every large centre of population, has had an enormous influence alike in bringing skilled nurses within the reach of sufferers outside the hospitals, and of still further raising the *status* of nursing as a profession. 'Missionary nurses,' Florence Nightingale once wrote, 'are the end and aim of all our work. Hospitals are, after all, but an intermediate stage of civilization. While devoting my life to hospital work, to this conclusion have I always come – viz., that hospitals were not, the best place for the sick poor except for severe surgical cases.'

District Nurses

District nursing was really set on foot in this country by the late Mr. William Rathbone, who, in compliance with, the dying request of his first wife, started a single nurse in Liverpool in 1859 as an experiment. The demand for district nurses soon became so great that more were clearly necessary, and Miss Nightingale was consulted as to what should be done. She replied that all the nurses then in training at St. Thomas's were wanted for hospital work, and so recommended that a training school for nurses should be started in Liverpool. The suggestion was adopted, and in November, 1861, on being consulted about the plans, she wrote to the chairman of the training school committee:–

> 'God bless you and be with you in the effort, for it is one which meets one of our greatest national wants. Nearly every nation is before England in this matter – viz., in providing for nursing the sick at home; and one of the chief uses of a hospital (though almost entirely neglected up to the present time) is this – to train nurses for nursing the sick at home.'

By about 1863 there was a trained nurse at work among the poor in each of the 18 districts into which Liverpool had been divided for the purposes of the scheme. The example of Liverpool was speedily followed by Manchester, where a district nursing association was formed in 1864; the East London Nursing Society was established in 1868, and the Metropolitan and National Association followed in 1874. In the organization of the last-mentioned society Florence Nightingale took the deepest interest, sending to *The Times* a long letter, in which she expressed her gratification at the idea of the nurses having a central home, set forth in considerable detail the nature and importance of the duties the district nurses were called upon to perform and appealed strongly – and successfully – for donations towards the cost of a home. After these pioneer societies had been successfully started many others followed; but the greatest development of all was afforded by Queen Victoria's Jubilee Institute for Nurses, the operations of which have been of the highest importance in spreading the movement throughout the United Kingdom. When, in December, 1898, a meeting was held at Grosvenor House for the purpose of organizing a Commemoration Fund in support of the Institute, a letter from Florence Nightingale was read, in which she expressed the heartiest sympathy with the proposal. Great and most beneficent changes, again, have followed the substitution in workhouse infirmaries of trained nurses for the pauper women to whose tender mercies the care of the sick in those institutions was formerly left. It was a 'Nightingale probationer,' the late Agnes Jones, and 12 of her fellow-nurses from the Nightingale School at St. Thomas's who were the pioneers of this reform at the Brownlow-hill Infirmary, Liverpool; and it was undoubtedly the spirit and the teaching of Florence Nightingale that inspired them in a task which, difficult enough under the conditions then existing, was to create a precedent for Poor Law authorities all the land over.

Midwifery was another branch of the nursing art which Florence Nightingale sought to reform. She published in 1871 'Introductory Notes on Lying-in Hospital'; and, in 1881, writing on this subject to the late Miss Louisa M. Hubbard, who was then projecting the formation of the Matrons' Aid Society, afterwards the Midwives' Institute, she said, referring to these 'Introductory Notes':–

> 'The main object of the "Notes" was (after dealing with the sanitary question) to point out the utter absence of any means of training in any existing institutions in Great Britain. Since the "Notes" were written next to nothing has been done to remedy this defect . . . The prospectus is most excellent . . . I wish you success from the bottom of my heart if, as I cannot doubt, your wisdom and energy work out a scheme by which to supply the deadly want of training among women practising midwifery in England. (It is a farce and a mockery to call them midwives or even midwifery nurses, and no certificate now given makes them so.) France, Germany, and even Russia would consider it woman slaughter to "practise" as we do.'

No less keen was her interest in rural hygiene. The need of observing the laws of health should, she thought, be directly impressed on the minds of the people, and to this end she organized a health crusade in Buckinghamshire in 1892, employing – with the aid of the County Council Technical Instruction Committee – three trained and competent women missioners, who were to give public addresses on health questions, following up these by visiting cottagers in their own homes and giving them practical advice.

Writings

Further evidence of Florence Nightingale's activity and beneficent efforts is afforded by the series of books, pamphlets, and papers that came from her pen. In 1858 appeared her 'Notes on Matters affecting the Health, Efficiency, and Hospital Administration of the British Army,' a volume of 560 pages, in which, 'so far as the state of my health,' she writes 'has permitted me,' she makes an exhaustive review of the defects that led to the 'disaster' at Scutari, and discusses in the most thorough and lucid manner the various points calling for consideration in regard to the management and efficiency of army hospitals. The value of this work, still great, was simply incalculable at the time it was first issued. In October, 1858, Miss Nightingale contributed two papers to the Liverpool meeting of the National Association for the Promotion of Social Science on 'The Health of Hospitals' and 'Hospital Construction.' In 1860 she published 'Notes on Nursing.' So popular has this work become by reason of its thoroughly practical hints, given in the clearest possible language, that some 10,000 copies of it are said to have been sold. For the Edinburgh Meeting of the National Association for the Promotion of Social Science held in 1863, Miss Nightingale contributed a paper on 'How People may Live and not Die in India'; and she followed up the same subject, when the association met at Norwich, in 1878, with a paper on 'Life or Death in India,' this paper being subsequently reprinted with an appendix on 'Life or Death by Irrigation,' in which considerations arising out of the Bengal famine are discussed more especially from the point of view of the paramount necessity of combining drainage with irrigation.

Closing years

In these various ways one sees how Florence Nightingale, though a bedridden invalid and well advanced in years, was still ever ready, as she had been throughout life, to devote her energies to promoting the practical well-being of her fellow-creatures. What with writing papers, pamphlets, and letters, receiving reports concerning the many movements in which she was interested, and dealing with communications from Governments, authorities, and others all the world over, she was, even in the closing years of her life, essentially a hard-working woman. How great, indeed, were the demands made upon her time is well shown by a letter addressed by her on October 21, 1895, to the Rev. T. G. Clarke, curate of St. Philip's Birmingham, and local secretary of the Balaclava Anniversary Commemoration. In the course of this letter she said:– 'I could not resist your appeal, though it is an effort to me, who know not what it is to have a leisure hour, to write a few words' and she added:– 'I generally resist all temptations to write, except on ever-pressing business. I am often speaking to your Balaclava veterans in my heart, but I am much overworked.'

Yet, among all these manifold claims upon her attention, she never forgot that unpretending 'Home' in Harley-street, W., over which she was still presiding when she went out to the Crimea. In *The Times* of November 12, 1901, she appealed for further support for this institution, declaring that it was

> 'Doing good work – work after my own heart, and I trust, God's work. There is [she continued] no other institution exactly like this. In it our governesses (who

are primarily eligible), to wives and daughters of the clergy, of our naval, military, and other professional men, receive every possible care, comfort and first-rate advice at the most moderate cost . . . Every one connected with this home and haven for the suffering is doing their utmost for it and it is always full. It is conducted on the same lines as from its beginning, by a committee of ladies of which Mrs. Walter is the president, and she will be glad to receive contributions at 90, Harley-street, W. I ask and pray my friends who still remember me not to let this truly sacred work languish and die for want of a little more money.'

On the occasion of her 84th birthday, in May, 1904, Miss Nightingale (who had already received the Red Cross from Queen Victoria) had conferred upon her by King Edward the dignity of a Lady of Grace of the Order of St. John of Jerusalem. October 21, 1904, was the jubilee of the memorable expedition on which she set forth in 1854; to few great reformers had the mercy been vouchsafed of seeing within their own lifetime results so striking and so beneficial as those that had followed the noble efforts of 'The Lady with the Lamp'; and the congratulations she received on the occasion of her Jubilee were but a sample of that universal veneration she had won.

Further recognition of the value of her life's labours came to Miss Nightingale with the announcement in the *London Gazette* of November 29, 1907, that the King had been graciously pleased to confer upon her the Order of Merit, she being the only woman upon whom this exceptionally distinguished mark of Royal favour has been conferred. On March 16, 1908, Miss Nightingale received the honorary freedom of the City of London, an honour which had been conferred upon only one woman before – namely, the late Baroness Burdett-Coutts. Owing to her advanced age, Miss Nightingale was unable to be present at the Guildhall to receive this mark of distinction, and her place was taken by a relative. At her own request the money which would have been spent on a gold casket was devoted to charity, the sum of 100 guineas being given instead to the Hospital for Invalid Gentlewomen; and the casket presented to Miss Nightingale was of oak.

The death of Florence Nightingale was yet another occasion when *The Times* was right to congratulate itself on having excited public debate. As the obituarist notes, it was William Howard Russell's critical dispatches to the newspaper during the first stages of the Crimean War, and the editorial response to those dispatches, that stirred Nightingale into action. Once the nature of her mission in both peace and war became clear to her, she never wavered from it, even though it required breaking through barriers of male prejudice and a consistent lobbying of recalcitrant government ministers. The obituarist also remarks on the religious-based opposition Nightingale encountered at home. Roman Catholic orders of nuns had been re-established in England at the time of the French Revolution, but Anglican sisterhoods, inspired by the teachings of the Oxford Movement, were very new. There was a great deal of (often scurrilous) opposition to these sisterhoods. Nightingale took ten Roman Catholic and fourteen Anglican nuns with her to Scutari and thereby began to challenge public opinion. In a larger sense, she also changed British attitudes to women in social service.

* * *

COUNT LEO TOLSTOY

Novelist: 'Both artist and prophet . . . among the most influential writers of his time'

9 NOVEMBER 1910

Petersburg. Nov. 17, 1.51 A. M. (from our own correspondent)

NEWS OF COUNT TOLSTOY'S death reached St. Petersburg only a few minutes before the despatch of this telegram. No details are yet known here. Conflicting rumours prevailed the whole of yesterday. It seems that the journey in the crowded train from the monastery, during which Count Tolstoy was compelled by lack of room to stand on a platform exposed to bitter cold and rain, was the direct cause of the inflammation of the lungs which unhappily proved fatal.

Memoir

The death of Count Leo Tolstoy removes one who was both artist and prophet, and who, in both these capacities, must be ranked among the most influential writers of his time. It has taken place in circumstances as characteristic of the man and his genius as any previous episode in his wonderful career. At the very end of his days his spirit rebelled once more against the tyranny of accepted things, and he sallied forth upon the final pilgrimage in search of calm and solitude which we have chronicled in the last few days. There are many persons, whether writers themselves or readers, to whom the artistic qualities of a book count for everything, who

Leo Tolstoy (left) with his brother before leaving for the Caucasus in 1851

prefer Tolstoy the artist, and who regard the spiritual and social doctrines of his later works as so much surplusage; but to multitudes of readers in Russia, and to many throughout Europe and America whose soul is disquieted within them in regard to the moral condition of mankind, Tolstoy is regarded first and foremost as a prophet; as the teacher of a new creed, or the reviver of a very old one; and it is as such that they will deeply mourn his death.

Count Leo Nicolaevitch Tolstoy was born at Yasnaya Poliana, the country home of his parents, on August 28, 1828. This place, the name of which means 'Clear Streak,' is in the Government of Tula, and, if we except a few years of his youth, it was Tolstoy's home for almost the whole of his life. His mother, Princess Marie Volkonsky, died when he was an infant, and soon afterwards the family went to live in Moscow, but the children returned to Yasnaya Poliana when the father died, a few years later. It is said that the character of the father more or less agrees with that of Nicholas Rostoff in 'War and Peace,' the admirable head of a family, whose simple, unworldly habits stand out in contrast to those of the gay worldlings of Petersburg society. At the country home where he spent his boyhood, Tolstoy received those first and indelible impressions of peasant life which afterwards took shape in his stories; but at sixteen he entered the University of Kazan, and remained there for some years. In 1851 he entered the army, and began that service in the Caucasus which afterwards formed the groundwork of his early tales, especially 'The Cossacks.' In 1853–55 came the war against Turkey and her allies, and Tolstoy accompanied his regiment to the Crimea, and went through the terrible experience of the siege of Sevastopol which he afterwards described in three of his most powerful sketches. Although the Tolstoy of those days was but the germ of what he afterwards became, the experience of Sevastopol had a profound effect upon both sides of his character; for, on the one hand, his impressions of actual events became the more vivid in proportion to their greatness and terror, and on the other it was then that he first began to feel that loathing of war which was the foundation of the doctrine of his late writings, the doctrine of non-resistance. An often-quoted passage from these early sketches of Sevastopol, that describing the death of Prascouchin, proves the first point; assuredly never before did any writer realize so completely and paint with such vivid truth of detail the feelings and thoughts of a man struck down in battle. Naturally, the book in which these masterly pages occur made a deep impression in Russia; and intelligent readers saw at once that – though the word perhaps had not then been invented – he was a realist of the first order, an artist who cared nothing for literary conventions, but who, with unerring insight and with a power of psychological analysis of which the world had given few examples, went straight to the heart of his subject and laid bare its inmost truth.

'War and Peace'

Several of the other early works of Tolstoy showed a similar power exercised upon a wholly different milieu. If Sevastopol had given him the experience to which we owe the Sevastopol sketches, and afterwards, to a certain extent, 'War and Peace,' it is to his life in his own country-house that we owe the whole series of peasant stories of which 'Poliekoushka' was perhaps the most famous. The story is of a tipsy, thievish serf who had tried to reform himself, was entrusted by his mistress with the mission of going to the town to fetch some money, lost the money by accident, and, sooner than face her disappointment and the scorn of his neighbours, hanged himself in his miserable cottage. Here, again, the tragedy of humble life was expressed with the most penetrating power, and in this and other stories, while Russian readers found much food for meditation on the state of their country foreign critics recognized the work of a new genius. Consequently when, during the two or three years which followed Tolstoy's marriage in 1862, there appeared the different instalments of 'War and Peace' the world was not taken by surprise, and translations into French and German – the English did not appear till many years later – soon made Tolstoy's name a household word in Western Europe. It is quite unnecessary to give any lengthened account of a book that is so well known, at all events to every one to whom the name of Tolstoy means anything at all. Let it suffice to say that this vast and crowded canvas serves, better than anything written by him before or since, to exhibit the author in his double aspect of artist and prophet. On the one hand we obtain from workmanship which may at first seem ragged, and from a composition that appears confused such an impression of Russian life as a whole, as it may have been at the epoch of Napoleon, as we can derive from no other book in the world. Viewed closer, the workmanship is seen to be precise and accurate; the characters, complex as they are, stand out clear and true, all different from one another, and each, from the beginning to the end, consistent with itself. Who has not fretted with impatience at that picture of hollow, insincere Petersburg society as he would fret at the reality of it? Who has not followed the campaign of Borodino with a new sense that here is no conventional war, but the real thing with all its blunders, its confusion, its helplessness, its silent heroism? Who has not shed a tear over the deathbed of Prince André? and who to this day is not in love with Natacha? But it is, of course, in the character of Pierre, honest, dreamy, self-devoted Pierre, ill-matched at first with the 'superb animal' Hélène, and finally rewarded with the love of Natacha, that the author has put most of himself. Pierre, who may be almost said to reappear in 'Anna Karenin' in the character of Levin, represents all that is most essential in the personality of Tolstoy – above all, his idea that if the corruption of the age is to be cured it must be by a return to nature and a simple life. In the case of both Pierre and Levin, the revelation comes from a peasant. It is Karataeff, arrested with Pierre by the French at Moscow on a false charge of incendiarism, who convinces him of the truth and beauty of what may be called the central doctrine of Tolstoy the prophet – the doctrine of non-resistance to injury. So it is Theodore the peasant who teaches Levin the way 'to live for the soul and keep God in remembrance.' And in each case the moral is that success may be best achieved through what the world calls failure.

'Anna Karenin'

'Anna Karenin' was first published in 1875–76 as a *feuilleton* in Katkoff's paper, the *Russki Vestnik*, or *Russian Messenger*. It aroused universal interest throughout Russia, but one day, just as the novel was drawing to its close, its readers were disgusted to find that the paper appeared without it. The reason was a characteristic dispute between Tolstoy and his editor, for, just at that moment when Russian feeling was becoming wildly excited against Turkey, and volunteers were being called for to help Servia, Tolstoy made one of his characters express a wish that in every war a battalion of journalists should be placed in the first rank with Cossacks to flog them on. The passage and his refusal to suppress it were alike characteristic, for this apostle of non-resistance could himself resist. But 'Anna Karenin' contained very much besides doctrines of moral or social regeneration; it made an instant mark as a story, and even those who had found 'War and Peace' too confused and voluminous soon fell under the spell of Anna and Vronsky, Levin and Katia. The contrast between these two couples is more obvious than any contrast in 'War and Peace.' Levin and Katia are in the right way of life. Anna has taken a wrong turning from the first. She does not love her husband, and therefore there is room in her heart for the love of Vronsky; but this love, when she yields to it, only puts her in a more impossible position. It cannot settle down in the tranquil domestic love enjoyed by Levin and Katia. It remains a fierce passion growing always more jealous and morbid, until at last it makes life intolerable for her. It is the tragedy of a noble creature wasted; and however strong Tolstoy's desire may be to point a moral, he does not let it interfere with his artistic conscience. He is still the triumphant artist; and we can draw our own morals from his art, feeling sure that there is no perversion of reality in that. Whether we are content with the morals which he draws is a wholly different question, and does not affect the real value of the work. Perhaps if it were not for the extraordinary art of his stories, Tolstoy's social and philosophical doctrines would have got little attention from the world.

We listen to what Pierre and Levin have to say; we give a respectful hearing to their new gospel, not so much from a persuasion of its truth as because those who profess it are so extraordinarily real. The art of the writer is such that, while we are under the spell of it, he can make us believe what he will.

Tolstoy's teaching

For nearly twenty years after 'Anna Karenin' Tolstoy abandoned the writing of stories and betook himself to cultivating his estate, taking an active and reforming part in the practical affairs of his district, and writing pamphlets. Religious and philosophical ideas took a stronger and stronger hold upon him, and found constant expression in a whole series of small books or articles, from 'My Religion' to 'What is Art?' More and more these have been adopted as the profession of faith of a set of idealists in Europe and America, and, to speak of England alone, cheap translations of them have found a large and growing sale. If we may adopt the classification made by one of the most fervent of the English Tolstoyans, Mr. G. H. Perris, in his 'Life and Teaching of Count Tolstoy,' we may say that the teaching of these pamphlets amounts to a new Pentalogue, covering the whole of human life. First comes the Law of Reason – 'avoid dogma, mysticism, the binding of the will by ceremonial observances, oaths, or other inventions of authority in the spheres of religion and politics.' Next, the Law of Peace – 'avoid violence, and all organizations depending on violence' (the army, police, &c.). Third, the Law of Labour – 'avoid exploitation, luxury, &c.' (this easily passing into a general prohibition of private property). Fourth, the Law of Purity – 'avoid anything tending to physical degradation.' Fifth, the Law of Sacrifice – 'avoid devotion to self'; in which last commandment we may truly say that all the others are summed up. More generally it may be said that the constant aim of Tolstoy in these later writings was to bring back the doctrines of the Founder of Christianity, as they are expressed in the Sermon on the Mount, so that they shall once more play an effective and a dominant part in the social life of mankind. To urge this as Tolstoy urged it is as much as to say that the official religion of Russia is not the Christian religion – that the Orthodox Church is a blind leader of the blind. In the case of any other writer or speaker the answer of the Russian Church and Government would have been prompt and unmistakable, but Tolstoy was a privileged person, and to strike at him might be dangerous. So the Church hesitated long, and it was not till 1901 that he was formally excommunicated by decree of the Holy Synod. It does not seem, however, that any very serious consequences followed from this solemn pronouncement, though it provoked some rioting amongst the students in St. Petersburg and made a considerable stir all over Europe and America. Count Tolstoy's reply was to address a comprehensive and eloquent appeal to the Tsar in favour of far-reaching administrative reforms and the removal of restrictions on educational and religious liberty.

It will be within the memory of our readers that he continued to issue letters, pamphlets, and manifestoes through the critical times of the Japanese war, and the still more critical years that followed upon it. Many of these appeared, in an English form, in these columns, and that widely-extended and zealous body. Tolstoy's disciples in other lands, circulated them in America and in various languages, over the continent of Europe. The Russian authorities, however, were consistent in following out the principle that, whatever happened, the temptation to make a martyr of Leo Tolstoy must be resisted at all costs.

His conception of art

Tolstoy's doctrine of art was all of a piece with his other doctrines. He held that art, like religion and morality, had become over-sophisticated, that true art, like true morality, could be immediately understood by the simplest minds, and that, in so far as it was not intelligible to them, it ceased to be art. But he seems to have made a mistake in supposing that simple people have necessarily an unsophisticated taste in matters of art, or, indeed, an unsophisticated judgment in matters of morality. This is the old mistake of Rousseau, the theory of the noble savage changed to the theory of the noble peasant. Tolstoy came very close to the aesthetic ideas of William Morris. Both held that unwholesome social conditions had produced an unhealthily complicated art, but Morris knew too much about art to suppose that mere absence of education could make any one a good judge of it, however much miseducation might prevent judgment. There was something puritanic in Tolstoy's whole attitude towards art. He distrusted its pure emotional delight and wished to make it the handmaid of morality. But it would be too great a task now and here to examine the soundness of his general position, or to ask what would be the effect upon human society as a whole of a general attempt to 'return to nature' in the sense that Tolstoy would have it. Nor are we concerned to ask whether the theories of penal legislation laid down in that wonderfully powerful late work of his, 'Resurrection,' are capable of application to any modern State. It is enough if we admit that they are put forward with the same artistic power, the same observation of truth and nature, and the same transparent sincerity which Tolstoy showed from the beginning. Eccentric as he had become of late years, all that he wrote was worth reading, and when he threw his ideas into the form of fiction, as in 'The Kreutzer Sonata' and 'Resurrection,' even his latest work was singularly impressive. Though his name continued to be venerated, his influence, in his own country at all events, diminished rather than increased during the last years of his life. By making the world a present of his copyrights he secured an enormous circulation for his propagandist leaflets; but Russia, in the throes of an abortive revolution, sat at the feet of more energetic counsellors. Gorki, trying to arouse the Slav from pessimism to action, preached to more attentive hearers than Tolstoy, whose exhortations to the downtrodden to resist evil only by passive disobedience did not seem either to Cadets or Social Democrats to meet the needs of the time. Passive resistance, it appeared to them, was only another way of saying 'nitchevo,' and not a hopeful means of throwing off the yoke of the oppressor. Yet Russia may some day come to feel that he was her greatest man, and it may be that time will prove his ideas were indeed prophetic, and that, however unsuited to the imperfect conditions of his own age and country, they may be a guide, even in practice, to a future and better society. The prophet has no honour in his own country, just because he is a prophet and sees the world as it will be, not as it is. In his novels Tolstoy speaks to us. In his latter works, perhaps, he speaks to posterity.

In the days immediately preceding his death at the railway station at Astapovo, *The Times*'s correspondent in St Petersburg had been sending dispatches to London recounting the novelist's extraordinary flight from his wife. 'Never surely,' he had commented, 'was there a man of genius so bewildering to his contemporaries'. The fact that this flight was news of international import indicates something of the reverence felt in the West for Tolstoy the novelist, and even more so, for Tolstoy the tormented philosopher. Here the obituarist deals appreciatively with the fiction, but seems unsure of the future implications of the Tolstoyan lifestyle. He readily recognises that, for two of the new political parties that had emerged in Russia after the 1905 Revolution, the Cadets and the Social Democrats, Tolstoy's ideas did not meet 'the needs of the time'. Tolstoy had visited London in 1861. He later told his English disciple, Aylmer Maude, that he had heard Lord Palmerston speak for three hours in the House of Commons and had attended a lecture on education given by Charles Dickens 'in a large hall'. Despite his vast admiration for Dickens, either his memory or his limited English must have failed him. Dickens never lectured on education, but it is likely that Tolstoy was present at the public reading of 'The Story of Little Dombey', which Dickens gave at the St. James's Hall on 22 March 1861.

W. S. GILBERT

Dramatist and comic poet: 'He was a fairy down to the waist, but his legs were mortal – and too often he wrote his prose with his legs.'

29 MAY 1911

WE RECORD WITH much regret that Sir Wiliam Schwenck Gilbert, the poet and dramatic author, died suddenly yesterday afternoon of a heart affection while bathing at his home at Harrow Weald.

He was in London in the morning, and returned home about 4 o'clock, accompanied by two lady friends. On arrival at his residence, Grimsdyke, he said he should take his customary bath in an ornamental lake in the grounds. He subsequently dived into the water, and as it was some time before he reappeared on the surface his friends, who were on the bank, became alarmed. Going closer they saw that he was in some difficulty. One of the ladies tried to give him some assistance, while the other rushed off for help. By this time Sir William sank again. Ultimately some menservants arrived, and succeeded in recovering the body. It was examined by a doctor, who pronounced life to be extinct. It is believed that death was caused by syncope, brought about by undue exertion in diving into the water. The lake is about 6ft. deep.

Memoir

Sir William Gilbert was born at 17, Southampton-street, Strand, on November 18, 1836. On his mother's side he was Scotch; his father was descended from one of the Devon Gilberts, who married a sister of Sir Walter Raleigh. While he was still an infant his parents left London to travel in Germany and Italy; he returned so beautiful a child that Sir David Wilkie, seeing him coming out of church, insisted on painting his portrait. At the age of seven he went to school at Boulogne; from ten to 13 he was a pupil at the Western Grammar School, Brompton, and from 13 to 16 at the Great Ealing School, where he took prizes in English, Greek, and Latin verse, spent much time in drawing, though without lessons, and wrote a number of plays for performance by his schoolfellows, painting his own scenery and taking a part himself. The woodcuts in the original sixpenny quarto edition of the 'Bab Ballads' prove him a delightful, if entirely self-taught, artist; and no one who had the good fortune to see his rare appearances on the stage in the cause of charity will need to be reminded how clever an actor he was.

At 16 he entered the University of London, and, having taken his B. A. degree at 19, began to read for the Royal Artillery. Meanwhile, however, the Crimean War had come to an end; no more officers were wanted, and the next examination was deferred to a date at which Gilbert would have been over age. Thereafter his military career was limited to the Militia. He became a captain in the Royal Aberdeenshire Highlanders (now the 3rd Batt. Gordon Highlanders) in 1868, and retired with the honorary rank of major in 1883.

The army being closed to him he turned to the Bar, and became a student in the Inner Temple; from 1857 to 1862 he held a clerkship in the Privy Council Office, and in 1864 was called to the Bar and began to practise on the Northern Circuit; might be found, in fact, working mildly at the Bar, after a touch at two or three professions. At one of those professions he did more than touch; he was writing plays all the time. Before he was 24 he had written 15 dramatic pieces, most of them farces and burlesques. Not one was accepted.

The 'Bab Ballads'

At this time he was living in Clement's Inn, in rooms which have since been destroyed, reading a great deal, especially Dickens and Thackeray, and writing for the *Cornhill Magazine, London Society*, and, most important of all, the comic paper *Fun*, then edited by H. J. Byron. It was the columns of this journal that first enshrined, or buried, the immortal 'Bab Ballads,' which contained the germs of all his later work.

Early Plays

In 1866 came his first chance of having a play produced. Tom Robertson had promised Miss Herbert a Christmas piece for the St. James's Theatre. Being too busy to write it, he engaged Gilbert to supply his place. The result was *Dulcamara*, written in ten days, rehearsed in a week, and played for 120 nights. Then followed rapidly a number of amusing and successful but unimportant burlesques; and it is said that for 24 years – from the production of *The Vivandière* (with J. L. Toole in the east) at the Queen's Theatre, Long-acre, to the end of the run of *The Gondoliers* at the Savoy – Gilbert's name was never out of the London play-bills. From 1868 to 1870 he acted as dramatic critic of the *Observer* and the *Illustrated Times*.

The year 1870 may be taken as marking the commencement of Gilbert's second period. Hitherto he had been known as a writer of burlesques and extravaganzas; he now began to make a name as a writer of 'serious' plays. *The Palace of Truth*, adapted from a story by Mme. de Genlis, was produced by Buckstone at the Haymarket Theatre in November, 1870, and ran for 270 nights. It is the first of the series which contained such plays as *The Wicked World, Pygmalion and Galatea*, and *Broken Hearts*. They are written in blank verse; the root idea of each is fantastic – some piece of magic, like the spell over the Palace of Truth which obliges every one to speak precisely what he thinks while he fancies that he is uttering the usual conventional lie; or some direct intervention of supernatural power; in *Pygmalion and Galatea* the gods', in very many of Gilbert's plays, the fairies'.

The satire in these plays bites sharper than that of the Savoy operas; the author was younger and less inclined to be merciful; he sneers where later he laughed. At the same time, the satirist who spared the feelings of his fellow-men so little had an exceedingly tender heart where life, and especially animal life, was concerned. Galatea's outcry at the murder of the fawn and the satire on Luicippo who murdered it may be taken as a faithful expression of the views of Gilbert, who forbade all taking of life in sport on his property at Grim's Dyke, Harrow Weald.

But, brilliant cynic as he shows himself in these earlier plays, he is not heartless. He contrives to be what we should now call sentimental without an approach to mawkishness, except, perhaps, in one instance, the character of Vavix in *Broken Hearts.* It is hard, now, not to feel annoyed with a young person who knows she is to die young without any specific reason to show for her conviction. But, at the same time, *Broken Hearts* is just the play that contains the finest imaginative poetry Gilbert ever wrote.

These 'serious,' romantic, fantastic, satiric plays were all produced within the five years from 1870–1875 – *The Palace of Truth, Pygmalion and Galatea,* and *The Wicked World* by Buckstone at the Haymarket, *Broken Hearts* by Hare at the old Court Theatre. Gilbert was then 35–39. Contemporary with them, and a little later, came *Charity,* a social play (produced by Buckstone at the Haymarket), which was even more in advance of the times than the others, and was condemned as immoral; the still popular *Sweethearts,* produced by Miss Marie Wilton (Lady Bancroft) at the Prince of Wales's; *Dan'l Druce,* a romantic play partly founded on 'Silas Marner' (played by Mr. Hermann Vezin at the Haymarket), and a couple of excellent farces, *Engaged* and *Tom Cobb, or Fortune's Toy.* All these are in prose, and with the mention of them we may close Gilbert's second period.

'Gilbert and Sullivan'

Before entering on the third we must go back a step. It must have been somewhere about 1869 or 1870 (for he had just finished *The Palace of Truth*) that Gilbert first met Sullivan. The meeting (every detail of it is worth chronicling) took place in the old Gallery Of Illustration in Regent-street, then occupied by the German Reeds. Gilbert knew no note of music, but he had been getting up a few points for his own use. The first remark he addressed to the musician was a plea for guidance on a highly technical question concerning 'the simple tetrachord of Mercury, that knew no diatonic intervals, and the elaborate dis-diapason' and the rest of it, which had all been found in the 'Encyclopaedia Britannica' and transferred to Act I of *The Palace of Truth.*

Sullivan wisely promised to look the matter up – and never replied. Fortunately, he was not frightened away; the acquaintance was continued, and five or six years later came the first blossom on an immortal tree, *Thespis, or The Gods grown Old,* which was produced at the Gaiety in 1875, with Mr. Toole in the cast. *Thespis* was never printed, and is all but completely forgotten. Its successor, *Trial by Jury* (Royalty Theatre, 1876), is one of the most characteristic things we possess. Its lightning access, the extraordinary freedom and finery of its versification, the choice of our legal procedure as a mark for the author's satire, and the exquisite absurdity of the whole treatment make it only describable by the word that has enriched our language for the purpose. 'Gilbertian.'

In 1877 Mr. D'Oyly Carte produced *The Sorcerer* at the Opera Comique; some six months later came *H. M.S. Pinafore* at the same theatre, and its two years' run established the fortunes of the most extraordinary combination of talent that English opera, that any opera, serious or comic, has ever seen. The most extraordinary combination; there have been greater writers, though possibly none more individual, than Gilbert, and greater musicians than Sir Arthur Sullivan; there has never been regular collaboration between a poet and musician who could play so unerringly into each other's hands. The 'lyrics,' unlike those of our later librettists, were always written first, and the music fitted to them afterwards, usually without advice or interference from the author; but it may be questioned whether any composer but Sir Arthur Sullivan could have fitted it so well. He had a fertility, an ease, and a melody which matched those of Gilbert. He had, too, a musical humour of his own that could reinforce Gilbert's poetical humour, could actually increase its effect, without ever straining or superseding it, and a musical pathos, if the phrase may be allowed, which exactly hit the tone of the rare but beautiful elegiac or love songs. If 'Oh, foolish fay,' or the Judge's song from *Trial by Jury,* or 'Is life a boon?' or 'He loves, if in the bygone years' give exquisite pleasure in themselves, they give still more when heard or remembered to the music from which it is now almost impossible to dissociate them.

The 'Savoy Operas'

The names of the 'Savoy operas' as they are called (though it was not till 1882, during the run of *Patience,* that the Savoy Theatre was opened) are too familiar and their subjects too well known to need recapitulation here. They followed each other without interval until *The Gondoliers* of 1889, and were revived for a brief space with *Utopia Limited;* or *The Flowers of Progress* (Gilbert's sub-titles are usually delicious) and *The Grand Duke.*

Some are better than others; they are all unlike anything else that ever was written. They contain the fine flower of Gilbertianism. Nearly all the ideas they handle may be found in the 'Bab Ballads,' lightly sketched with extraordinary *fougue*, as the painters have it, a riotous freedom of absurdity; in the operas the absurdity is tamed, polished, and reasoned out, while the fertility of invention and the suppleness and freedom of versification remain unimpaired. It is a mad world, and at the same time an absolutely sane world. The most fearful catastrophes happen, and are reversed as easily as they occurred; the characters all move in a palace of truth, revealing themselves to the core, and no one is the least surprised. You find a tradesman dealing in spells with a horoscope at three and six that he can guarantee; a shepherd who is a fairy down to the waist, but whose legs are mortal; a king who turns company promoter, and a smug slave of duty bound apprentice to a pirate. Everything is seen upside down, and yet everything is severely logical. Mad world as it is, it moves by exact rule, from premise to conclusion; but the author has settled the premisses. No better vehicle for satire could be imagined. It enabled the author to keep up the appearance, so to speak, of a bland innocence. It was not this world he was writing of, he might claim, but one of his own invention; and thus he remained free to put his finger unerringly on weak spots in women, Parliament, the law, the Army, the aesthetic fashion of the day, anything and everything he chose. His satire in these operas is, on the whole, very kindly; it is the satire of a gentleman – winged and barbed, but never thrown unfairly or with ill-nature. Perhaps, after all, the *differentia* of Gilbert's method, both in his plays and operas, is the relating of his whimsicalities to life.

A True Poet

With regard to the literary quality of his work, he may be compared to his own Strephon; he was a fairy down to the waist, but his legs were mortal – and too often he wrote his prose with his legs. There is humour in it, but it is apt to be crushed under a load of long words and involved sentences. Now and then it was characteristically whimsical but of the most part it was built on traditional and turgid lines. In his verse he was all fairy. It has been well said that for lyrical facility he can only be compared with Shelley. He was absolutely at home in song-writing, and only then. It is as well to claim for him definitely and at once the title of poet, which could only be denied him from want of reflection or from an idea that poetry and fun are incompatible. If his poetry is nearly all humorous, it is none the less exquisitely musical, easy, and perfect in form. With no more than the usual classical attainments of a gentleman, he not only did in his patter-songs what no one had done since Aristophanes and his *parodoi*, but he attained to a classical perfection of form that few English poets have ever equalled. The nicest refinements of metre seemed to come natural to him; the late Canon Ainger was fond of quoting as examples of metrical mastery the lines –

I took and bound that promising boy
Apprentice to a pirate.

It is not often given to a poet to combine such a spring of humorous ideas with such skill in humorous expression. Like his predecessors in point of time, Reece, Farnie, or Byron, he could make puns with the best, if he wanted to; but his own merely verbal wit is on a far higher scale. In the 'Bab Ballads' or the Savoy operas the actual juxtaposition and play of the words would rouse laughter of themselves; when used to express such humorous ideas as Gilbert's they are irresistible.

It is difficult to estimate at its proper worth the service he did to our comic drama. He was the first of his day to restore it its literary self-respect. The characteristics of the burlesque and *opera-bouffe* of Gilbert's youth were worthless doggerel, senseless puns, and the tasteless misuse and often degradation of poetic themes. For these Gilbert substituted gentlemanly, if rather heavy-footed, prose, exquisite verse, true wit, and original invention. It has been well said that where others had burlesqued poetry he poetized burlesque.

It may be added that he was a master of another art, that of stage-management. He himself credited Tom Robertson with the invention of the art, but its development was greatly advanced by his own care. Every play was rehearsed in his study by means of a model stage and figures, and every group and movement settled in the author's mind before the rehearsals, which he always conducted in person, were begun. He had a clever company (now, alas! dispersed to less classic fields) to work for him; but most of the finish and unity of those delightful performances was due to his own forethought and his very stern and right determination that nothing should be said or done, even on the 300th night, except precisely as he had written or planned it.

His latest years were not productive of much drama, though within the last few weeks there was seen on the variety stage a very un-Gilbertian little sketch of criminal life. In dealing with such a subject, as in his treatment of the law in earlier plays and operas, Sir W. S. Gilbert was writing of what he knew. He was a J. P. and D. L. for Middlesex, and took his magisterial duties seriously, devoting to them much time and trouble. In 1907 he was knighted. In 1867 he married Lucy Agnes, daughter of the late Captain Thomas Metcalf Blois Turner, Bombay Engineers, and Lady Gilbert survives him. A well-known figure in clubland, he was a member of the Garrick, Beefsteak, Junior Carlton, and Royal Automobile Clubs.

Gilbert is a great librettist, by turns witty, sharp, ebullient, whimsical, satirical and occasionally lyrical, but always splendidly apt for Sir Arthur Sullivan's musical settings. That Gilbert was to prove less mutually inspirational to his other collaborators, and that he was a playwright who seems strangely clumsy without Sullivan's complementary musical wit, has been proved by the passage of time. Gilbert was knighted in August 1907. He had married Lucy Agnes Turner ('Kitty') in 1867, and as Lady Gilbert she lived on at Grim's Dyke until her death in 1936. Gilbert was not alone in the lake in his garden; nor, it seems, were his two young female companions merely looking on from the lakeside when he suffered his fatal heart attack. He was giving them swimming lessons when one lost her footing and called for his help.

* * *

OCTAVIA HILL

Housing reformer: 'One of the most practical and most energetic of women philanthropists of her day.'

13 AUGUST 1912

Housing and Social Reform

WIDESPREAD REGRET WILL be felt at the announcement of the death, on Tuesday, at her house in Marylebone-road, of Miss Octavia Hill, who deserves to be remembered as one of the most practical and most energetic of women philanthropists of her day.

Born about 1838, she was the daughter of Mr. James Hill, and a granddaughter of Dr. Southwood Smith, an earnest promoter of sanitary science. Quite early in life she showed leanings in the same direction, and when still young she was one of the band of workers who laboured among the London poor under the leadership of Frederick Denison Maurice. The experiences she thus gained convinced her that people are greatly influenced in their habits and ways of thought by their domestic surroundings, and that sanitary science should be followed up in the case of the poor for the purpose of improving not only their dwellings, but the people themselves. In this way, she thought, the work of bringing about their social and spiritual elevation was to be advanced by enabling people to live in conditions of cleanliness, comfort, and decency, and she argued that an important educational reform could be effected by developing in their minds an actual taste in these directions. But she found it hopeless to think of all this as long as tenants were left to the tender mercies of a low-class type of landlord or landlady, whose only idea was to make as much money out of them as possible; and Miss Hill conceived the then novel idea of herself obtaining possession of some squalid house property, of collecting her own weekly rents, and of exercising what influence she could in securing the transformation alike of dwellings and of tenants. She laid her proposals before Mr, Ruskin, who not only entered heartily into the scheme, but himself advanced altogether £3,000 for the carrying out of what was avowedly an experiment. It is true that the experiment proved a financial success, the £3,000 being duly returned, but it was none the less creditable to Mr. Ruskin that he should have risked so large a sum when, as Miss Hill herself confessed, 'not many men would have trusted that the undertaking would succeed.'

Housing Experiments

Having secured the necessary means, Miss Hill began operations by purchasing, for £750, the unexpired term of the lease of three houses near to her own home in Marylebone. They were well-built houses, but in a deplorable condition of dirt and neglect. As her own rent-collector, Miss Hill entirely did away with a middleman; but in the interests of the people themselves she was extremely strict in enforcing punctual payment of rent. On the other hand, she encouraged the tenants to keep the houses in the cleanly condition to which she had them put, and she set aside a certain amount per year for repairs for each house, the surplus, after breakages and other damage had been made good, being expended in such improvements as the tenants themselves desired. Any suggestion of charity, however, was absolutely discarded. The scheme was organized on a business footing, and it was worked so well that, though tenants got two rooms for the amount they had previously paid for one, Miss Hill secured, in a year and a half, 5 per cent. interest on the capital, and had repaid out of the rents £48 of the money she had borrowed from Mr. Ruskin.

The next purchase was one of six houses, which were also in a most squalid condition, but crowded with inmates. The houses faced a bit of desolate ground occupied by dilapidated cowsheds and manure heaps. The needful repairs and cleaning were carried out, the waste land was turned into a playground, where Mr. Ruskin had some trees planted (in addition to creepers against the houses), and Miss Hill, with a strong idea of the moral effects of the playground, arranged with lady friends to go there and teach the children games. For the boys she started a drum and fife band, and for the parents she built at the back of her own house a large room where she could meet them from time to time for the purposes of talk or entertainment. Her weekly call for the rent was, however, the great hold which she kept over her tenants, though her treatment of them was the very reverse of that of merely a sympathetic and easy-going philanthropist. 'The main tone of action,' she wrote, 'must be severe. There is much of rebuke and repression needed, although a deep and silent undercurrent of sympathy may flow beneath. If the rent is not ready notice to quit must be served. The money is then almost always paid, when the notice is, of course, withdrawn. Besides this inexorable demand for rent (never to be relaxed without entailing cumulative evil on the defaulter, and setting a bad example, too readily to be followed by others) there must be a perpetual crusade carried on against small evils.' Happily, too, this crusade was completely successful. Not only did the tenants acquire the habit of being punctual in their payments, but they learned the blessings of cleanliness and of an abundance of air, light, and water, while the lady-crusader herself, strict as she was in all these things, became the family counsellor for each household and the peacemaker in the settlement of neighbours' quarrels.

Towards the end of 1869 six ten-roomed houses in a court in Marylebone were bought by the Countess of Ducie, and five more by another lady, and placed under the care of Miss Hill. The inhabitants of the houses were mainly costermongers and small hawkers who were supposed to have sunk to the lowest depths of degradation, and the houses themselves were in an indescribable condition of filthiness and neglect. Even so brave-hearted a woman as Miss Hill might have hesitated to go to these dwellings at night to collect the rents, for the people could only be seen at the end of their day's toil. But she did not shrink from her task. She had a few improvements done at once – though, for the most part, these were done only gradually, as the people became more capable of valuing them. Then she paid the elder girls to scrub regularly and preserve as models of cleanliness the stairs and passages for which the landlady was responsible, with the result that the girls acquired cleanly habits, and the lesson taught by the stairs soon spread to the rooms. In the same way the tenants, when out of work, were employed to do repairs to the premises, so that 'little by little the houses were renovated, the grates reset, the holes in the floor were repaired, the cracking, dirty plaster replaced by a clean smooth surface, the heaps of rubbish removed,' and a general progress made towards order. There was, too, a corresponding moral improvement in the people, and though the new landlady never unduly interfered, never entered a room unless invited, and never offered any gift of money or necessaries of life, she came to be regarded as the best friend of the tenants, and not only 'got hold of their hearts,' but was often able to help them at some important crisis or other in their lives.

Development of her work

Altogether Miss Hill secured a distinct success in the working out of the principle on which she had started. As time went on many more blocks of dwellings came under her management in different parts of London in addition to those mentioned, and a number of ladies assisted her in her self-imposed labours. In 1887 a very practical step in this direction was made by the formation of the Women's University Settlement in Blackfriars-road, whose members have co-operated with Miss Hill in working some dozen or more courts or streets of cottages in Southwark. In addition to this a number of blocks erected by the Ecclesiastical Commissioners were put at once under Miss Hill's care. Recognizing, however, the comparatively limited scope of such efforts as her own – inasmuch as they depended so much on individual workers – and the necessity for providing increased accommodation for the working classes generally, Miss Hill gave an active support to the Artizans' Dwellings Act of 1874, and in 1884 she was one of the witnesses examined by the Special Commission which inquired into the question of the housing of the poor. Of late years this question, in its wider development as the housing of the artisan classes, has assumed proportions far greater than either Miss Octavia Hill or Mr. Ruskin could have contemplated when they started joint operations as social reformers, and the action taken alike by private companies, wealthy philanthropists, and the London County Council in the provision of improved dwellings for the working classes seems to put entirely in the shade Miss Hill's modest efforts. On the other hand, she was undoubtedly one of the first if not actually the first, to start the general movement, and on this movement her example and her writings have had a most powerful effect, notwithstanding the fact that it has been continued along broader, more comprehensive, and much more costly lines than were within the limits of her own resources. In 1905 she was appointed a member of the Royal Commission on the Poor Laws and signed the Majority Report in 1909.

Miss Hill also took part in the foundation and development of the Charity Organization Society, whose principles are so well in accord with her life-long contention that an ill-advised almsgiving merely undermines the providence of the poor. She also became an active supporter of the Commons Preservation Society as the result of an effort of her own – though an unsuccessful one – to save from the builder certain fields in the Finchley-road, which she was anxious to preserve as an open space for the enjoyment of the poorer residents of Swiss Cottage. At the instance of Miss Hill a second society, known as the Kyrle Society, was formed for the purpose of brightening in every practical way the homes of the poor, while from the Kyrle Society there was developed Lord Meath's Metropolitan Gardens Association, which has done, and is still doing, invaluable work in the protection, provision, and improvement of open spaces. Still another organization with which Miss Hill had been actively connected from the first was the National Trust for Places of Historical Interest.

Octavia Hill came from earnest stock (Thomas Southwood Smith was an influential sanitary reformer) and grew up influenced by the Christian

Socialist values of the Reverend F. D. Maurice. It was said that she even slept with Christian Socialist pamphlets under her pillow. When she looked for financial sponsorship for her housing schemes in 1864 she turned to the most eloquent critic of the dreariness of Victorian urban life, John Ruskin. She had encountered Ruskin as a seventeen year old in 1855 and sought his advice on becoming an artist, but art was forgotten when her housing schemes began. Her ruthlessly practical methods of tenant management were not always as benign as the obituarist suggests, and she encountered persistent hostility from those she aspired to help. Ruskin, angry with her slighting of his own St. George's Guild and impatient with what he saw as her sanctimoniousness, sharply criticised her in the February 1878 issue of his *Fors Clavigera.* Nevertheless, it was the passion for the English landscape inspired by Ruskin that moved her to become a co-founder of the National Trust in 1895.

* * *

W. G. GRACE

Sportsman: 'A masterful personality . . . which . . .
made an impression which could never be forgotten.'

23 OCTOBER 1915

The Greatest of Cricketers
(By Sir Arthur Conan Doyle)

THE WORLD WILL be the poorer to many of us for the passing of the greatest of cricketers. To those who knew him he was more than a great cricketer. He had many of the characteristics of a great man. There was a masterful personality and a large direct simplicity and frankness which, combined with his huge frame, swarthy features, bushy beard, and somewhat lumbering carriage, made an impression which could never be forgotten.

In spite of his giant West-of-England build; there was, as it seemed to me, something of the gipsy in his colouring, his vitality, and his quick, dark eyes with their wary expression. The bright yellow and red cap which he loved to wear added to this Zingari effect. His older brother, the Coroner, small, wizened, dark, and wiry, had even more of this gipsy appearance. I speak, of course, only of the effect produced, for I have no reason to think that such blood was in his veins, though, following Borrow, I am ready to believe that there is no better in Europe. There was a fine, open-air breeziness of manner about the man which made his company a delight and added a zest to the game. He was, of course, a highly educated surgeon, but he had rather the fashion of talk which one would associate with a jovial farmer. His voice was high-pitched, considering the huge chest from which it came, and it preserved something of the Western burr.

Deceptive Slowness

His style and methods were peculiar to himself. In his youth, when he was tall, slim, and agile, he must have been as ideal in his form as in his results. But as this generation knew him he had run to great size and a certain awkwardness of build. As he came towards the wicket, walking heavily with shoulders rounded, his great girth outlined by his coloured sash, one would have imagined that his day was past. He seemed slow, stiff, and heavy at first. When he had made 50 in his quiet methodical fashion he was somewhat younger and fresher. At the end of a century he had not turned a hair, and was watching the ball with as clear an eye as in the first over. It was his advice to play every ball as if it were the first – and he lived up to it. Everything that he did was firm, definite, and well within his strength.

I have had the privilege of fielding at point more than once while he made his hundred, and have in my mind a clear impression of his methods. He stood very clear of his wicket, bending his huge shoulders and presenting a very broad face of the bat towards the bowler. Then, as he saw the latter advance, he would slowly raise himself to his height, and draw back the blade of his bat, while his left toe would go upwards until only the heel of that foot remained upon the ground. He gauged the pitch of the ball in an instant, and if it were doubtful played back rather than forward. Often he smothered a really dangerous length ball by a curious half-cock stroke to which he was partial. He took no risks, and in playing forward trailed the bottom of his bat along the grass as it advanced so as to guard against the shooter – a relic, no doubt, of his early days in the sixties, when shooters were seen more often than on modern grounds.

Command of the Off Ball

The great strength of his batting was upon the off side. I should not suppose that there was ever a batsman who was so good at controlling that most uncontrollable of all balls, the good-length ball outside the off stump. He would not disregard it, as is the modern habit. Stepping across the wicket while bending his great shoulders, he watched it closely as it rose, and patted it with an easy tap through the slips. In vain, with a fast bumpy bowler pounding them down, did three quivering fieldsmen crouch in the slips, their hands outstretched and eager for the coming catch. Never with the edge of the bat but always with the true centre would he turn the ball groundwards, so that it flashed down and then fizzed off between the grasping hands, flying with its own momentum to the boundary. With incredible accuracy he would place it according to the fields, curving it off squarely if third man were not in his place or tapping it almost straight down upon the ground if short slip were standing wide of the wicket.

In no shot was he so supremely excellent, and like all great things it seemed simplicity itself as he did it. Only when one saw other great batsmen fail did one realize how accurate was the timing and the wrist-work of the old man. When he was well on towards his 60th year I have seen him standing up to Lockwood when man after man was helpless at the other wicket, tapping these terrific expresses away through the slips with the easy sureness with which one would bounce a tennis ball with a racket. The fastest bowler in England sent one like a cannon-shot through his beard with only a comic shake of the head and a good-humoured growl in reply.

A Bowler Full of Guile

Of his bowling I have very clear recollections. He was an innovator among bowlers, for he really invented the leg-theory a generation before it was rediscovered and practised by Vine, Armstrong, and others. Grace's traps at leg were proverbial in the seventies. His manner was peculiar. He would lumber up to the wicket, and toss up the ball in a take-it-or-leave-it style, as if he cared little whether it pitched between the wickets or in the next parish. As a matter of fact this careless attitude covered a very remarkable accuracy. His command of length was absolute, and he had just enough leg spin to beat the bat if you played forward to the pitch of the ball. He was full of guile, and the bad ball which was worth four to you was sent, as likely as not, to unsettle you and lead you on.

Those who know him will never look at the classic sward of Lord's without an occasional vision of the great cricketer. He was, and will remain, the very impersonation of cricket, redolent of fresh air, of good humour, of conflict without malice, of chivalrous strife, of keenness for victory by fair means, and utter detestation of all that was foul. Few men have done more for the generation in which he lived, and his influence was none the less because it was a spontaneous and utterly unconscious one.

The Funeral

The funeral of Dr. Grace took place yesterday at Elmers End Cemetery, Beckenham. The mourners included Mrs. W. G. Grace, Captain C. B. Grace, R. E. (son), Mrs. Dann (sister), and Mr. C. L. Townsend (Gloucester Cricket Club), and others present were:–

Lord Hawke and Mr. John Shuter (M.C.C.), Lord Harris, the Jam Sahib of Nawanagar, Captain P. F. Warner, Mr. F. G. F. Ford, and Mr. G. McGregor (Middlesex), Captain H. D. G. Leveson-Gower (Surrey), Mr. B. W. Bainbridge (Warwickshire), Mr. J. R. Mason, Mr. O. J. Burnup, Mr. R. N. R. Blaker and Mr. W. M. Bradley (Kent), Mr. C. E. Green, Mr. A. P. Lucas and Mr. O. R. Borradale (Essex), Lieutenant A. C. MacLaren (Lancashire), Mr. J. A. Bush and Mr. R. E. Bush (Gloucestershire), Mr. Frank Townsend and Mr. R. Fenton Miles (members of the Gloucestershire Eleven in 1871), Sir George Riddel, Mr. C. I. Thornton, Mr. P. J. de Paravicini, Mr E. H. D. Sewell, Mr H. D. Sewell, Mr. H. J. Hill, Sir A. Priestley, M. P. Captain G. J. V. Welgall, Mr. R. J. Cooper-Murray (Sydney N. S.W.), Mr. C. Wreford-Brown, Mr. A. T. Kemble, Mr. S. A. P. Kitcat, Mr. G. Brann, and Mr. Alec Hearne.

The warmth of this obituary notice may help to explain why Grace's name, his 'huge frame' and his 'bushy beard' remain so readily recognisable nearly a century after his death. The celebrated obituarist properly concentrates solely on Grace's forty-four years as a cricketer, scarcely alluding to his professional life as a general practitioner or to the fact that he was also a prime mover in the foundation of the English Bowling Association in 1903. As a gentleman amateur, Grace was obliged to employ two locums to tend to his Bristol medical practice during the cricketing season. His greatness lay in his genius as a player, and he is probably the first sporting personality to have made a lasting impact on national life.

ELIZABETH GARRETT ANDERSON

Physician: 'The cause both of justice and humanity.'

17 DECEMBER 1917

The First English Woman Doctor

WE REGRET TO announce that Mrs. Elizabeth Garrett Anderson, M. D., died at Alde House, Aldeburgh, Suffolk, yesterday. She was 81 years of age.

Mrs. Garrett Anderson was one of the pioneers of that phase of the movement for the 'emancipation' of women which aimed at throwing open to them the profession of medicine, and was herself the first woman to secure a medical diploma in this country. The world has, by this time, become familiar with the idea of women doctors, alike as private practitioners and as the holders of public appointments, and the war has made them as necessary at home as they have been for years in India, where the Countess of Dufferin's Fund has conferred an incalculable boon on native women. Yet when Miss Elizabeth Garrett and a few others endeavoured to devote their lives to this work, and sought to obtain the necessary qualifications for so doing, they had to endure for many years an amount not only of prejudice but of direct and sometimes violent hostility, which would have broken down the courage of persons of less determined spirit and less convinced than they were that their cause was the cause both of justice and of humanity.

Elizabeth Garrett, known after her marriage as Mrs. Garrett Anderson, was the daughter of Mr. Newson Garrett, of Aldeburgh, Suffolk, and was born in London in 1830. Her attention was attracted to medicine by Miss Elizabeth Blackwell, an Englishwoman who had emigrated with her parents to the United States, and, after many fruitless attempts to enter various medical schools there was permitted to graduate M. D. of the University of Geneva, U. S. A. in 1849. Ten years afterwards, on the strength of this foreign qualification, and of her having prescribed for friends during a visit to England, she was put on the British Medical Register; so that, while, as already stated, Miss Garrett was the first woman to secure an English diploma, Miss Blackwell had precedence of her as regards registration. Miss Garrett made Miss Blackwell's acquaintance in 1858, and resolved to follow in her friend's footsteps, but to get an English qualification instead of a foreign one. She began her medical studies in earnest in 1860. There were, however, two great difficulties before her. In the first place, there was no school where she could be received, and in the next place, there was no examining body willing to admit her to its examinations. At Middlesex Hospital the male students presented a memorial against the admission of women, and though she made repeated attempts elsewhere, she met for some years with effectual repulse in every direction. In these attempts she had the cordial support of her father, to whose sympathy and courage she afterwards attributed the success she secured.

The Society of Apothecaries

After a time the Society of Apothecaries was advised by its counsel, Mr. (afterwards Lord) Hannen, that as the purpose of its charter was to enable it to sell drugs, and as there was no legal ground for refusing to allow a woman to sell drugs, the society could not refuse to admit a woman to the examination imposed on candidates for its licence. Thereupon the society authorized Miss Garrett to get her education privately from teachers of recognized medical schools, and finally gave her, in 1885, the desired qualification of L. S. A. In 1860 she opened a dispensary near Lisson-grove, Marylebone, for the benefit of poor women and children, and for some years she was the only medical officer there. The Society of Apothecaries had adopted a new rule which refused recognition of certificates granted for private studies – there was no medical school in England that would admit women, and the struggle carried on by the late Miss Jex Blake and others at Edinburgh University had been in vain. But medical degrees were to be had abroad; Miss Garrett herself passed the examinations, and took the M. D. of Paris in 1870; and, others taking similar steps, she secured assistants at her dispensary, which was subsequently converted into a small hospital, and after various changes developed into the 'New Hospital for Women' in the Euston-road. It was during the period of these early struggles that a woman pamphleteer, writing in opposition to 'women's rights' in general, said of Miss Garrett:–

'Miss Garrett possesses a superior mind as well as superior attainments, and her character appears to correspond to her intellectual qualities. She has great calmness of demeanour, a large amount of firmness, usually a good deal of fairness and coolness in argument, a pleasant countenance, a decided but perfectly feminine manner, and attire at once apart from prevalent extravagance and affected eccentricity.'

In November, 1870, Miss Garrett became a candidate at the London School Board election, and was returned at the head of the poll for Marylebone with no fewer than 47,858 votes. In 1871 she married Mr. J. G. S. Anderson, of the Orient line of steamships to Australia, but she lost none of her zeal for the profession she had adopted, and continued it as actively as before, devoting herself especially to the diseases of women and children. In October, 1874, Miss Jex Blake returned from Edinburgh vanquished in her attempts to secure admission to the medical schools in that city, the male students having carried their opposition so far as to mob her and her friends. Mrs. Garrett Anderson thereupon joined with Miss Jex Blake and other ladies in establishing the London School of Medicine for Women. But the General Medical Council of England stipulated that only a general hospital having 150 beds could be recognized as adequate for the purposes of teaching, and the hospital, which Mrs. Garrett Anderson was carrying on had then only 26 beds. The larger hospitals were appealed to, but in vain, until at last, in 1877 an alliance was formed between the Women's School and the Royal Free Hospital, Gray's-Inn-road, which met all requirements in respect to teaching.

An Act of Parliament

In the meantime there had been proceedings in the Law Courts and attempts at legislation in the House of Commons in the interests of the would-be women doctors and at last, thanks to an more enlightened public opinion and to the abundant proofs of the excellent work which Mrs. Garrett Anderson and her sister practitioners were doing, a bill introduced in the House of Commons in 1876 by Mr. Russell Gurney was passed 'enabling' the British examining bodies to extend their examinations to women as well as men. The King and Queen's College of Physicians in Ireland was the first to take advantage of this enactment, and a number of other bodies afterwards adopted the same course. But in 1878 the feeling in the medical profession against women doctors was still strong, and Mrs. Garrett Anderson remained the only female member of the British Medical Association until 1892, when the Nottingham meeting, on the proposal of Dr. S. H. Galton, carried by a large majority the repeal of a rule which he described as 'a blot on the association's fair fame, a stain left from the high tide of prejudice.' Mrs. Garrett Anderson, who was present at this meeting, had thus the satisfaction of seeing the victorious end of the campaign on which she had started in 1860.

For 23 years Mrs. Garrett Anderson was Lecturer on Medicine at the London School of Medicine for Women, and for 10 years its Dean. For 24 years she was Senior Physician of the New Hospital for Women. In 1896–97 she was President of the East Anglian branch of the British Medical Association, and in 1908 she was elected Mayor of Aldeburgh, where she had her home, being the first woman made a Mayor in England. Her interest in sanitation and housing here made itself felt to good practical effect. In the following year she was re-elected. Of such a woman as Dr. Garrett Anderson it need scarcely be said that she believed that women ought to have Parliamentary votes and that she worked to that end in the years preceding the war. Recently her powers were failing; but she was fond of going to London stations to bid God-speed to soldiers starting for the front. Mrs. Garrett Anderson's sister is Dr. Millicent Garrett Fawcett, to whose husband the blind Postmaster-General she acted as medical adviser. Her son, Sir Alan Garrett Anderson, last August succeeded Sir Eric Geddes as Controller of the Navy; and the first list of appointments to the new Order of the British Empire, which we published last

August, contained not only his name among the Knight Commanders, but that of his sister, Dr. Garrett Anderson, among the Commanders, as 'organizer of the first hospital run by women at the front.' Dr. Garrett Anderson is now head of the military hospital in Endell-street.

The entrance of women into the medical profession was one of those events that would certainly, in any case, have been brought about sooner or later, but it was none the less to the credit of Mrs. Garrett Anderson that she recognized the desirability and the justice of this step at a time when few other persons did, and that she herself fought so valiantly against prejudices so strong and interests so powerful as those confronting her in that 'fiery ordeal' from which it was her happy lot to emerge not only successful but still a 'womanly woman.'

The funeral will be at Aldeburgh on Friday, at 2.10 p. m., and there will be a memorial service at Christ Church, Endell-street (Military Hospital) on Saturday, at 11 a. m.

> This obituary, written at the height of the First World War, fully acknowledges not simply the progress made by professional women since the mid-nineteenth century, but also their important contribution to the life of a nation drained of male doctors by the demands of the military struggle. Garrett Anderson's determined struggle to open medical training to women and, later, for due recognition by her male peers is fully catalogued here, though, as the obituarist notes, the only real fruit of her ambition to see women fully involved in the political process was her election as Mayor of Aldeburgh in 1908. The 'New Hospital for Women' moved to its final site in Euston Road in 1888. Its name was changed to the 'Elizabeth Garrett Anderson Hospital' after her death, but it gradually lost its distinctive identity in the Health Service changes in the 1970s.

SARAH BERNHARDT

Actress: 'The French Queen of Tragedy.'

26 MARCH 1923

WE REGRET TO announce that Mme. Sarah Bernhardt died at 8 o'clock last evening at her Paris residence.

Paris, March 26
(from our own correspondent)
Mme. Sarah Bernhardt's condition changed for the worse this morning. Her strength had diminished, and she was unable to take either food or medicine. Drs. Provost and Marot were in close attendance during the day, and M. Maurice Bernhardt, M. Louis Verneuil, and Mme. Verneuil (her granddaughter) remained constantly at the bedside. Mme. Simone, the great actress, was among the morning visitors.

For the greater part of the day Mme. Bernhardt was in a state of coma. In her more lucid intervals she complained in a feeble voice of her prolonged suffering, and asked that a priest should be sent for. Later in the morning a priest arrived, and the Last Sacrament was administered.

Afterwards Mme. Bernhardt relapsed into a state of coma and never recovered consciousness. She died in the arms of her son Maurice. Other persons present by the deathbed were Drs. Provost and Marot and Mme. Bernhardt's grandson, M. Grosse. Among the last callers at the house were M. Maurice Rostand and his mother, Mme. Edmond Rostand, and M. Arthur Meyer.

Immediately after Mme. Bernhardt passed away those present, to whom the great actress had recently talked of the arrangements she desired to be made after death, brought in masses of roses and lilac and dressed the chamber with them.

The news of Mme. Bernhardt's death aroused an immense and sympathetic interest in Paris. She had given an impression of such invincible vitality that even in these last days people have been unwilling to believe that she would die, and the end, now that it has come, takes people aback. Memories of her performances, of her personality, of her vicissitudes, form the sole subject of conversation everywhere tonight.

It is stated that the Théâtre Sarah Bernhardt will be closed until after the funeral. The date of the funeral has not yet been settled.

A Great Creative Artist
Sixty years on the stage

No temperament more histrionic than Mme. Bernhardt's has, perhaps, ever existed. To read her memoirs or her biographies is to live in a whirl of passions and adventures – floods of tears, tornadoes of rage, deathly sickness and incomparable health and energy, deeds of reckless bravado, caprices indescribable and enormous. Her determination and independence of character were always strong; and when they, with her energy, became concentrated on her principal art they established a supremacy which would have been unmistakable even without the aid of her eccentricities. The marvellous voice of gold, that wide range of beautiful movement, queenly, sinuous, terrible, alluring, that intensity of passion and that bewitching sweetness have brought men and women of all degrees – from professional critics to ranchers, from anarchists to kings, from men of pleasure to Puritan ladies – in homage to her feet.

In spite of their common training, her theory of her art was the opposite of Coquelin's. She was all for the 'artist,' the creator, as opposed to the 'comedian,' the exponent of science and rule. She loved 'the limelight,' and time was when she kept it pretty constantly upon her off the stage, whether in her wonderful house (or museum) in the Boulevard Péreire in Paris, on tour over the habitable globe, or in her holiday home at Belle-Ile-en-mer, near Morbihan, in Brittany. But all the fierce battles which raged about her life and conduct never obscured the fact of her greatness, by temperament and by accomplishment alike.

Early Years

Sarah Bernhardt was born at No. 265, Rue Saint Honoré, Paris, on October 23, 1845. She was the eleventh of a family of fourteen children. Her mother was a Dutch Jewess, but Sarah was baptized at the age of 12 and sent to school at the Augustinian Convent at Grandchamp, Versailles. At the age of 16, on the advice of her mother's friend, the Duc de Morny, she was put to the stage as a profession. She had no inclination to it, but won a couple of second prizes at the Conservatoire. She never won a first prize. When she made her *début* at the Français in *Iphigénie*, her fellow-student Coquelin *ainé* being in the cast, the only genuine emotion that she felt was fear, and the audience laughed at her long, thin arms. Less than a year had passed when the gawky young Jewess gave a taste of her elemental fury. Mme. Nathalie, a well-known old actress, was rough with Mlle. Bernhardt's younger sister. Sarah flew at her and boxed her ears. An apology was demanded by the Comédie Française – and refused. Very soon afterwards Mme. Nathalie found means to render Mlle. Bernhardt's life at the theatre intolerable. She gave in her resignation and left the Français – for the first time. For the next two or three years her career was chequered. She played in burlesque at the Porte Saint-Martin (the scene of some of her later triumphs), and at the Gymnase in vaudeville. In 1864, disgusted with a poor part at the latter house, she ran away, with characteristic impulsiveness, for a totally unauthorized holiday in Spain.

In 1867 brighter days dawned. She joined the company at the Odéon. Here, as Zacharie in *Athalie*, Mlle. Bernhardt made her first success; here, too, she won great favour in M. Coppée's *Le Passant*; and here she boxed the ears of Taillade because he asked her, in a play, to kiss the hem of his robe. In 1860, shortly after the production of George Sand's *L'Autre*, the Franco-Prussian War brought about the closing of the theatre. Mlle. Bernhardt was patriotic to the core. Few things made the Dutch-French Jewess more angry than to be taken for a German Jewess; some years later she reduced to confusion the German Minister at Copenhagen and all the other guests present at a public banquet by remarking aloud, as he proposed the toast of 'France,' 'I presume, Baron, that you mean the whole of France?' During the war her patriotism found vent in equipping and managing a hospital for wounded soldiers in the Odéon, one of the first patients being M. Porel, later the husband of Mme. Réjane and manager of the Vaudeville.

The 'Sarah' Legend

When the war and the Commune were over the Odéon became a theatre again, and Mlle. Bernhardt improved her position. She owed a great deal to the consistency with which Sarcey championed her in the *Temps*, while other critics were complaining of her thin voice and still thinner figure, her monotony and her languor. In 1872 there came a turning-point in her career. Victor Hugo had returned to Paris, and in the production of his *Ruy Blas* at the Odéon Mlle. Sarah made so great a success as the Queen that Perrin, the manager of the Français, was practically compelled by the newspapers and by public opinion to re-engage her for the national theatre.

Her membership lasted for eight years, and little by little – certainly not all at once – she forged her way to eminence. Her enemies on the Press were active, and even Sarcey seemed for a while to turn against her. But she worked with her characteristic energy and did her best to overcome her disabilities. In December, 1874, she played Phèdre for the first time. During the first act nervousness drove her into a fault which she had, apparently, picked up from her mother – that of speaking nasally through clenched teeth. As the performance went on she warmed to her work, and played so well that her audience raised no protest when she made nonsense of a line which, of course, they knew, with the rest of the play, by heart. Sarcey declared her superior to Rachel, and thenceforward she was one of the lions of Paris. The exhibition of two specimens of her sculpture in the Salon of the following year made her still more notorious.

This was the period when the Sarah legend began to grow – the legend of the coffin in which she slept (a white satin-lined coffin with the softest of mattresses and the richest of perfumes, and love-letters, bouquets, and so forth stitched into the lining); the legend of wild animals kept for pleasure and decapitated or tortured from curiosity; the legend of retirement to a convent after one of her frequent attacks of apparently grave, but very momentary, illness – legends which at least suffice to show that Mlle. Sarah was one of the most talked-of persons in Paris. Meanwhile she went on working hard at the Français, and found in Zola a sturdy and generous champion, who did his best to dissipate the clouds of gossip which gathered round her exploits in ballooning, animal training, and the rest of it.

Breach with The Français

In 1879 came the well-remembered visit of the members of the Comédie Française – Got, Coquelin, Delaunay, Mounet-Sully, and others – to London and the Gaiety Theatre. Their repertory included *Phèdre, L'Etrangère, Le Sphinx, Hernani, Andromaque, Zaïre,* and other great pieces, and Mlle. Bernhardt was a very important person in the troupe. Even during her absence Paris was full of gossip about her: she was exhibiting her works of art in London; and hanging about at the gallery to show herself off; she was going about in man's clothes, and so forth; and Mlle. Sarah felt herself compelled to write to the French Press to state that she was not going about in man's clothes because she had left her suits at home.

Meanwhile, in spite of several little *contretemps,* she was being loudly acclaimed by the English Press and public. But the engagement in London was not over before her friends and foes were provided with a real scandal to quarrel over. Mlle. Bernhardt was due, on a certain Saturday, to play in *L'Etrangère* in the afternoon and in *Hernani* in the evening. She sent a message that she was too tired to appear. But she had not been too tired to give, the evening before, a performance at a private house; and the right to give these private performances was a bone of contention between her and the Français. There was an uproar. When the news reached Paris, Paris was furious. The company had been insulted. But Mlle. Sarah was too valuable to be lost. When she hurled her resignation at the head of Got, the Français replied by making her a *sociétaire,* with a full share in the profits.

After all, the breach was only healed for a time, and a short time. Less than a year later she failed notably in a revival of Augier's *L'Aventurière.* She complained of insufficient rehearsal, resigned on the spot, and was off to Havre before they could stop her. So, for the second time, she left the Comédie Française, and this time never to return. An interviewer flew north to Sainte-Adresse and found Mlle. Sarah wielding brush and chisel and determined never to return to the stage.

Triumphal World-Tours

A month later she was acting in London with her sister Jeanne and others, playing in *Adrienne Lecouvreur* and *Froufrou*. Then the news reached her that the Courts had fined her 100,000f. and deprived her of her share in the reserve fund; and she realized that great measures must be taken. And so began that long series of tours – royal progresses, triumphal processions, theatrical hurricanes sweeping over the habitable globe – which lasted till not so long ago. Her first tour was in 1880; it embraced Sweden, Norway, and Denmark, and was followed by a run through the south of France and Switzerland. That autumn she whirled herself, her company, her servants, agents, animals, and her 28 trunks full of dresses across the Atlantic for her first tour in America. Here, amid incredible adventures, she added an alligator to her menagerie (but it died in the flower of its youth – of champagne), a very large sum to her fortune, and thousands to her admirers. When she landed at Havre in May, 1881, she was welcomed by a crowd reckoned at 50,000 persons. There followed almost immediately a tour which embraced practically the whole of Europe except the hated Germany (although on one occasion in her career she did act in Berlin). While St. Petersburg paid £20 for a box to see her, Kieff insulted her and Odessa stoned her in the streets for a Jewess; at Genoa she all but died one night, and started next morning for Basel; in London, on April 4, she committed 'the only eccentricity she had not yet perpetrated' by getting married at the Greek Consulate to a member of her company, M. Damala, and whisking him off the same morning to Marseilles, en route for Spain. Almost before Paris had got over the shock the pair had separated.

In 1886 came one of her greatest undertakings, the tour which began in London and ran through South America, the United States, and Canada for 13 months. Adulation reached its limits. Jules Lemaître has described how 'already rich men, wearing black whiskers, and covered with jewels, like idols, used to wait outside the stage door and lay their handkerchiefs on the ground so that dust should not soil the feet of Phèdre or Théodora.' The Argentines gave Mme. Bernhardt an estate of 13,000 acres; and Mme. Bernhardt gave a lady in her company a horse-whipping, which brought them both before the law. The profits of the whole tour were one million dollars, and her own share amounted to £60,000.

She rarely failed once a year to visit London, a place which she grew to love, and one in which her admirers were as hearty, if not so fiery, as the whiskered gentlemen of Buenos Aires. In 1882 London first saw her in *Fédora*; in 1888 she played *Françillon* at the Lyceum; in 1889 she brought us *La Tosca*. In 1891 she started on another immense tour through the Americas and Australia (the trunks now numbered 80), which lasted for 17 months; and in 1900 came yet another American tour, her company then including Coquelin *aîné*.

Sardou's Plays

Meanwhile, when Paris had been sufficiently punished, she consented to forgive it. In the winter of 1882 she took a regular engagement at the Vaudeville in M. Sardou's new play of *Fédora*. Nearly every year from 1883 to 1893 she spent her winters at the Porte Saint-Martin, and it was here that she produced some of her greatest modern successes, many of them written by M. Sardou. In 1884 came *Théodora*, in 1887 *La Tosca*, in 1890 *Jeanne d'Arc* and *Cléopâtre*; and here too she appeared as Lady Macbeth in Richepin's version, and as Ophelia in a subsequently discarded version of Hamlet. Year by year she fortified her position of eminence. In 1893 she bought the Théâtre de la Renaissance, her temple of dramatic art, and opened it with M. Jules Lemaître's *Les Rois*; it was here that she was joined for a short time by Coquelin in 1895, and here she produced in the same year M. Rostand's *La Princesse Lointaine*, and in 1897 his great religious drama, *La Samaritaine*, Musset's *Lorenzaccio*, and d'Annunzio's *La Ville Morte*. In 1896 Paris indulged itself in a great festival in her honour, with banquets, speeches, performances, and a sonnet from M. Rostand.

In 1899 she moved to a larger theatre, now the Théâtre Sarah Bernhardt; and here she produced the version of *Hamlet* by MM. Morand and Schwob in which she gave Paris, and, later, London, the chance of seeing her as Hamlet himself – a weak and violent prince, whose character she thought 'perfectly simple.' What is there to add? There is *Magda*, which she played in a French version in London in the eighteen-nineties, giving an opportunity for hot little disputes between the worshippers of Bernhardt and Duse; there is *L'Aiglon*; there are one or two huge spectacular dramas, and the performance of that repertory in which her *Phèdre* has won its way to recognition as the masterpiece. And there is the fact that years after she had passed her prime, Mme. Bernhardt became an idol of the English music-hall public. Her annual visit to play snippets at the Coliseum was an 'event of the vaudeville year'; and in 1921 the great Mme. Sarah, now 75 years old, was acting in *Daniel* by Louis Verneuil at the Princes Theatre. An address from the actresses of England was presented to her as 'the greatest artist of our time.'

The Loss of a Limb

During the year 1914 an old injury condemned her to lie for eight months on her back with her right leg in plaster of paris. By February, 1915, the indomitable woman could endure it no longer, and demanded an operation. 'Operation,' in this case, meant nothing less than amputation, and amputated the leg was. It is no exaggeration to say that the event turned the thoughts of many aside from the Great War. Crowned heads sent telegrams of inquiry and condolence; and Mme. Bernhardt, then a woman of 70, was no sooner safely relieved of the offending limb than she began to make plans for future tours and the adaptation of old plays to the new needs.

By the autumn she was back in her own theatre in Paris, playing M. Morand's dramatic war poem, *Les Cathédrales*; and when she brought the piece to the London Coliseum in December London found that, though she must sit in a chair throughout the performance, her power, her fury of energy, and her incomparable charm were undiminished. So it went on throughout the war. She went to the United States in 1916, when she played Shylock in *The Merchant of Venice* (her caprices were indeed violent), and again the following year. She even played Phèdre, though she could no longer move about the stage. She believed that French drama was to be ennobled by the great trials of the French nation; and to the last she was full of plans. In the autumn of 1921 she achieved a fresh triumph in Maurice Rostand's drama, *La Gloire*, and last summer she produced *Régine Armand*, a play written for her by M. Verneuil. In November she toured in Italy, and in December was taken ill in Paris while rehearsing a new play by Sacha Guitry.

Sarah Bernhardt's extraordinary, and extraordinarily long, theatrical career first flourished back in the 1870s. In the 1880s she recorded an extract from Racine's *Phèdre* for Thomas Edison, and by the time of her death she had also appeared in eleven silent movies, the last of which, *La Voyante*, had to be completed in 1923 with a stand-in replacing its dead star. For fifty years she rejoiced in an international reputation and a flamboyant lifestyle. Even the amputation of her right leg in 1915 did not dampen the enthusiasm of her adoring audiences (though P. T. Barnum's offer of $10,000 to display the leg, without its former owner, was refused). Apart from her celebrated roles in the French classical repertoire, plus her famous performance as Hamlet in 1899, Bernhardt was best known for her association with the plays of Sardou and, above all, for *Fédora* and *La Tosca*. Her appearance in Sardou's *La Sorcière* in 1903, however, occasioned George Bernard Shaw's unkind comment on her having displayed 'the whole Bernhardtian range of sensational effects . . . hardly more of a fine art than lion-taming'. She is buried in the Père Lachaise cemetery at Paris.

INDEX